INSIDERS' GUIDE® TO

BOULDER

AND ROCKY MOUNTAIN NATIONAL PARK

HELP US KEEP THIS GUIDE UP TO DATE

We would love to hear from you concerning your experiences with this guide and how you feel it could be improved and kept up to date. Please send your comments and suggestions to:

editorial@GlobePequot.com

Thanks for your input, and happy travels!

INSIDERS' GUIDE® SERIES

INSIDERS' GUIDE® TO

BOULDER

AND ROCKY MOUNTAIN NATIONAL PARK

NINTH EDITION

ANN ALEXANDER LEGGETT

INSIDERS' GUIDE®

GUILFORD, CONNECTICUT
AN IMPRINT OF GLOBE PEQUOT PRESS

All the information in this guidebook is subject to change. We recommend that you call ahead to obtain current information before traveling.

To buy books in quantity for corporate use
or incentives, call **(800) 962–0973**
or e-mail **premiums@GlobePequot.com**.

INSIDERS' GUIDE®

Text design: Sheryl Kober
Maps: XNR Productions, Inc. © Morris Book Publishing, LLC

ISSN 1532-592X
ISBN 978-0-7627-5027-6

Printed in the United States of America

10 9 8 7 6 5 4 3 2 1

CONTENTS

Directory of Maps

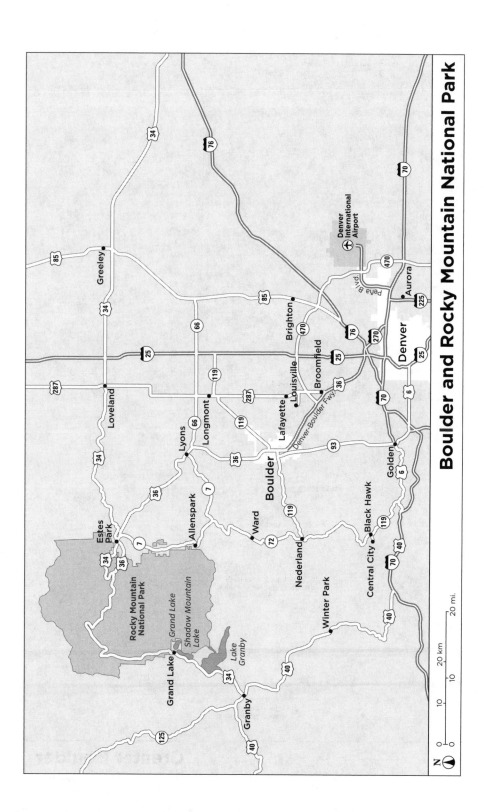

Boulder and Rocky Mountain National Park

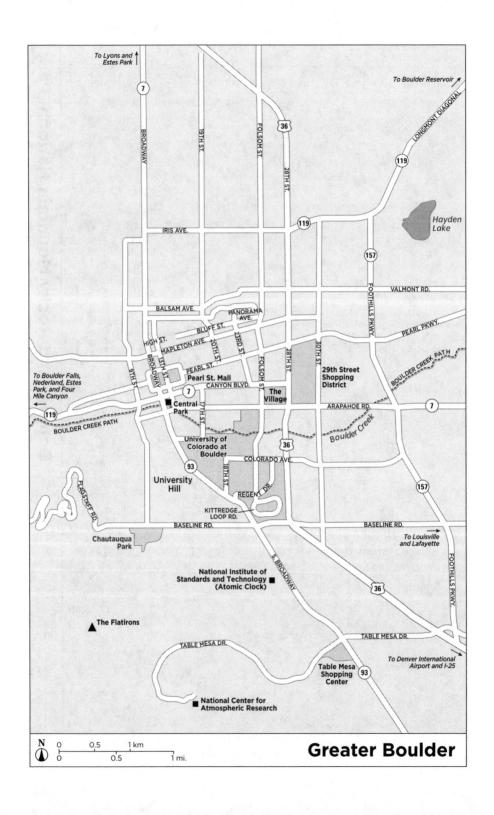

Greater Boulder

PREFACE

It's infamous, it's notorious, it's beautiful, and it's certainly unique. Welcome to Boulder. Nestled at the foot of the Flatirons—the great upthrust slabs of red rock that line the city's western border—Boulder is a vibrant city in the midst of breathtaking natural beauty. Surrounded by gently rolling plains, glittering threads of creeks and streams that attract and sustain a remarkable wealth of wildlife, and the great Rocky Mountains to the west, Boulder is, well, Boulder.

Why visit Boulder? It's not exactly a tourist spot, nor a mountain resort—though it's close to many of Colorado's most popular ones. It takes about an hour or so to drive to Rocky Mountain National Park, the Indian Peaks Wilderness, and many of the ski areas, including Winter Park, Breckenridge, and Keystone. A couple of hours more takes you to Vail, Aspen, and Steamboat Springs. Just up Boulder Canyon, Eldora Mountain Resort, a smaller ski area, is less than an hour away. Visit because Boulder has all the attractions of a big city—art and culture, fine educational institutions, an interesting populace, many excellent restaurants, and points of attraction—but without the hassle of the big city.

Most visitors to Boulder come to see family and friends—not your typical tourists on a vacation adventure—though adventure possibilities abound in the area. The University of Colorado attracts families for graduation, holidays, and ski vacations, with many of the graduates staying in the area. After its early days as a mining supply town—there was no gold discovered right in Boulder, but nearby in the mountains—Boulder's identity became firmly established as a university town in the late 1800s and continues to be so, with the university comprising about one quarter of the city's population. With its various scientific institutes, including the National Oceanic and Atmospheric Administration, the National Institute of Standards and Technology, and the National Center for Atmospheric Research, Boulder attracts an international population of scientists and engineers.

But Boulder is also an attraction unto itself. It's a national model for municipally owned open space and controlled growth. It's an inspiration for cities that want to preserve and revitalize their historic hearts, while nurturing commerce, the arts, and entertainment. It's an outdoor recreation mecca for regular folks and professional athletes alike. Anyone who enjoys hiking, backpacking, bicycling, rock climbing, mountaineering, running, and skiing will love Boulder. The annual Bolder Boulder 10k footrace is one of the nation's largest.

Many of us moved to Boulder because it's such a great place to live. It has Colorado's sunny dry climate, is close to the mountains, and is a manageable size. We enjoy the health-promoting attitude, good schools, recreational opportunities, and wholesome atmosphere for raising families and living the good life. Athletes from all over the world live and train in Boulder for many of the same reasons, plus the high elevation gives them a competitive edge.

Boulder also hosts many annual events and festivals, such as the Colorado Dance Festival, Colorado Shakespeare Festival, and Colorado Music Festival, welcoming a whole entourage of performing artists and audiences each summer.

So read on and explore all of Boulder's fine offerings.

ACKNOWLEDGMENTS

This city constantly evolves, yet it remains the same. I know that may sound contradictory, but it's true. And it also happens to be one of the reasons I love it. The famous Flatirons stand as sentinels over one of the most beautiful places imaginable; to see them dusted with snow on a winter's morning still takes my breath away. They, like the surrounding foothills and other familiar landmarks and institutions, are the constants that frame the artsy, cosmopolitan, diverse, controversial, and crazy city that is Boulder. In writing this newest edition of *Insiders' Guide to Boulder,* I was constantly reminded of just how much this place has to offer, and how much it has become a part of my life for the last 30 years.

The help of the following people made my job easier and enjoyable, and for that I thank them wholeheartedly. My thanks to Pam Gonacha, friend extraordinaire, for her technical assistance with this book and in all areas of my life; to all of the people with the various organizations and businesses who provided information to make the guide a comprehensive resource, especially Kim Farin at the Boulder Convention & Visitors Bureau and Jennifer Pinsonneault at the Boulder Chamber of Commerce; to Kathryn Howes Barth for her love of history; to all the previous authors—going all the way back to Shelly Schlender, Claire Walter, Reed Glenn, Linda Cornett, and Roz Brown—who provided the excellent backbone text that makes this guide a success; and to my family and friends for putting up with all my craziness.

HOW TO USE THIS BOOK

Most people, even those who have never been to Colorado, believe they have a pretty clear image of the state. Chances are it involves a skier flying down a mountainside with a fan of lighter-than-air powder rooster-tailing behind. And many are surprised when they land at Denver International Airport that the ski slopes aren't just outside the jetway.

The fact is there's a whole lot more going on here, geographically, socially, economically, and recreationally. Oh, the skiing is here, and it's great. But Colorado is also a place of flat-as-a-pancake plains—upthrust tables that bear a geologic history of inundation and drought, rich alluvial plains that nourish fields of potatoes and onions, tomatoes and corn, and orchards heavy with apples and peaches. The Rockies draw a handy north-south line through the state, dividing Colorado into the Eastern Slope and Western Slope. Although the line is blurring somewhat, a shorthand description puts the state's agriculture primarily on the West and its population and growing high-tech industry along the Front Range on the East.

Boulder lies tight against the Front Range at an elevation just over a mile above sea level. Boulder is not an easy place to describe, but it is characterized by the arts, education, scientific research, and technological innovation that goes on here. It also has a well-deserved reputation for recreation and fitness, with kayaking, running, hiking, bicycling, hang gliding, fishing, in-line skating, and street skiing just the beginning of the list of popular activities. Boulder is considered part of the Denver metro area and is linked to Denver by the increasingly crowded U.S. Highway 36, but Boulder residents have spent upwards of $140 million buying a ring of undeveloped land (a "greenbelt") to ensure that the city maintains a unique identity. And boy, does it. The generally liberal attitudes fostered by the presence of the flagship campus of the University of Colorado have won Boulder the nickname "The People's Republic of Boulder" from others in this politically conservative state.

This book is designed as a guide for visitors or newcomers to the unique, independent enclave that is Boulder. Chapters reflect logical areas of interest, from how to get around the place to where to eat, sleep, shop, listen to music, take a hike, worship, or find a good dentist. There are specialized chapters for children and for the elderly, for house hunters and for sports fans. All the chapters are independent and can be read in any order. They are cross-referenced where appropriate, so if you find only a sentence in one chapter about something that sounds intriguing, it's likely there's an expanded paragraph elsewhere.

Insiders' Tips (look for the **i**) in each chapter will have you behaving like a native in no time. Close-ups provide a little more information about the places and people that the locals love to talk about. There are also chapters devoted to the glories of Rocky Mountain National Park to the north and the city of Estes Park, which flanks the park.

We update the guide regularly, so let us know what you like and don't like or if we've missed something that you feel should be included. Write us at the *Insiders' Guide® to Boulder*, Globe Pequot Press, P.O. Box 480, Guilford, CT 06437, or visit our Web site at www.InsidersGuide.com.

AREA OVERVIEW

Boulder . . . there's simply no other place like it. When first–time visitors gaze down upon Boulder from the scenic overlook on U.S. Highway 36, they know they've arrived someplace special. Snuggled serenely against the pine-covered foothills, punctuated dramatically with the red Flatirons and backed by the white snow-covered peaks of the Continental Divide, Boulder is truly a sight to behold.

In 1858, early settler Capt. Thomas Aikins peered at the Boulder Valley through his field glasses and remarked, "The mountains look right for gold, and the valleys look rich for grazing." Aikins and his party did find gold in the hills above Boulder, and many have driven the highway over the hill and found their Shangri-la in one form or another.

A mere 29 miles from Denver, Boulder is sometimes considered part of the greater Denver Metropolitan Area for statistical purposes. But Boulder considers itself a world apart—and indeed it is.

This green haven at the foot of the Rocky Mountains is a unique enclave of science, education, research, outdoor enthusiasm, elite athletic training, health food, bicycling, recycling, the arts, and New Age culture—a kind of Berkeley of the Rockies, sometimes jokingly dubbed "The People's Republic of Boulder."

Boulder is home to Celestial Seasonings tea company, the Naropa Institute (started by Tibetan Buddhists), the Boulder School of Massage Therapy, the Rolf Institute (international headquarters), Ball Aerospace, the National Center for Atmospheric Research, the National Oceanic and Atmospheric Administration, the National Institute of Standards and Technology (home of the atomic clock, by which all U.S. time is set), and one of the four campuses of the University of Colorado (referred to throughout this book as CU-Boulder). The university's student and staff population makes up more than one-third of Boulder's total population of 102,569. The median age in Boulder is 30; Boulder County's median age is 35.7. The *Denver Post* once described Boulder as "the little town nestled between the mountains and reality."

BOULDER PEOPLE: A CONFLUENCE OF CULTURES

Boulder is full of old and new refugees from congested East and West Coast cities and Chicago—many of them professionals—seeking a better life. And they find it here, along with compatible company and culture in what many longtime residents feel is near-utopia: low crime, high mountains, plentiful blue skies and sunshine, glacial-melt drinking water, good schools, a lively arts scene, an enlightened city government, and a wholesome, healthy outlook. In fact, parents often urge their college-age offspring away from Boulder for an eye-opening dip into "the real world." Escapees from the Midwest find the cultural milieu they were missing—and mountains! Boulder natives do exist, but they're rare creatures.

Though Boulder has a predominantly white, upper-middle-class population, there's a cosmopolitan element provided by the staff and students from foreign countries at the many scientific institutions and the university.

Unfortunately, plentiful well-paying jobs and affordable housing are not among Boulder's amenities. Many local engineers and scientists came to work at IBM or one of the national centers. But most people who live in Boulder have deliberately chosen to do so for the mountains and general ambience, not necessarily for the job opportunities—and they pay the price in underemployment and a daunting real estate market. Compared to prices in California or Washington, D.C., Boulder's average single-family home price of $550,500 might seem affordable. But for those operating within the local economy, surviving in Boulder can be a real challenge. Students vie for all the low-paying jobs and affordable housing, and many CU-Boulder graduates, originally from other states, like it so much that they stay here.

Traditionally, many people, both young and old, have worked for next to nothing just to live in Boulder. But as rents and housing costs continually escalate, it becomes more difficult. Rock-climbing bums, writers, certified massage therapists (there are hundreds), teachers, psychotherapists, and scientists are some of the colorful—often unemployed—clients lingering in local coffeehouses. Some of these same folks may deliver your pizza, drive your cab, or sell you skis at a local mountain sports shop. Boulder County unemployment is 4.6 percent, but underemployment is much higher.

Boulderites participate in a number of humanitarian and volunteer efforts, including local government, environmental activism, and a strong Sister Cities program. Among Boulder's sister cities are Jalapa, Nicaragua; Lhasa, Tibet; Yamagata, Japan; and Dushanbe, Tajikistan. The Sister Cities programs include cultural exchange as well as humanitarian aid shipments; environmental projects; and exchange of students, doctors, and technicians. Boulder families and other organizations host foreign students and sponsor Bosnian refugees. In past years many Vietnamese refugees were also brought to Boulder, and they have since succeeded professionally here. Habitat for Humanity has a local contingent, and there's a controversial local program to help the trade-embargoed, economically stressed Cubans.

Despite the natural beauty outside their back door, Boulderites do love to travel. Go to a remote island in Fiji, and don't be surprised to bump into someone from Boulder.

BOULDER COUNTY ETHNIC DEMOGRAPHICS

Source: 2007 American Community Survey, US Census Bureau

Caucasian	93.4%
Hispanic	7.0%
Asian	4.5%
African American	1.4%
Native American	1.1%

OPEN SPACE, LIMITED GROWTH, AND ENLIGHTENED DEVELOPMENT

Unlike sprawling Greater Denver and other Colorado communities mushrooming to infinity, Boulder is a sort of fixed island surrounded by the protective reefs of open space. In 1967, Boulder became the first city in the United States to tax itself for funds to be used specifically for the acquisition, management, and maintenance of open space—and it's an ongoing program. But even earlier, at the turn of the 19th century, Boulder's city government and citizens established a mountain park system by purchasing portions of the city's dramatic mountain backdrop, often called the greenbelt, to protect it from development. (See our History chapter for details.)

Today, Boulder's citizens enjoy more than 44,000 acres of open space in and around the city, 7,000 acres of adjacent city-owned moun-

i The Atomic Clock—the NIST-7—has an accuracy of plus or minus one second in one million years. NIST-7, housed at the National Institute of Standards and Technology, is the official timekeeper of the United States. To set your watch by the most correct time on earth—NIST-7's coordinated universal time—call (303) 499-7111. For Boulder Mountain Standard Time, subtract seven hours, because the time you hear is the local time in Greenwich, England. Be patient through the series of beeps and pauses.

tain parks, and about 60,000 acres of county open space, some of which is under agricultural lease and is not open to the public. Residents of Greater Denver and nearby communities frequent Boulder's 78 miles of trail-laced open space, too. The city of Boulder itself encompasses 27.8 square miles.

In 1977, Boulder instituted a limited-growth ordinance called the Danish Plan, the brainchild of then-city councilman (now county commissioner) Paul Danish, restricting new building to 2 percent annual growth. In 1985 it was replaced with another growth moratorium, which is still in effect.

There's no getting around the fact that this makes Boulder a more desirable, yet more expensive, place to live. Because of limited growth, affordable housing is one of the biggest problems in this small city where the student population occupies most of the lower-priced dwellings. Many people find less-expensive housing in the nearby smaller cities of Louisville and Lafayette, currently bursting at the seams with new development. (See the Neighborhoods and Real Estate chapters for more information.)

Because so much natural habitat has been preserved, thousands of deer share the environs with residents. Deer grazing in neighborhood yards is a common sight. Though undeniably picturesque, the deer wreak havoc on local gardens. Gardeners have been distressed to find their tomatoes trampled, peas pilfered, and tulips nipped off at the bud. Smart gardeners plant a wildlife garden and build a tall fence around the human garden. Mountain lions and bears occasionally wander into town, too. In one case, a concerned citizen fetched his futon to provide a soft landing pad for a treed bear, tranquilized by wildlife officials. Another young bear led police on a chase right down the Pearl Street pedestrian mall. Skunks, raccoons, and coyotes are regulars in areas near open space. A city-sponsored backyard wildlife program promotes landscaping that will attract and accommodate songbirds, butterflies, and bats.

OUTDOOR-SPORTS CAPITAL

Look in any Boulder garage and you're likely to find several bicycles (mountain, touring, and racing), several pairs of skis (downhill and cross-country), snowshoes, perhaps a sailboard and/or kayak, crampons (climbing spikes), an ice axe and mountaineering gear, rock-climbing ropes and harnesses, backpacks, in-line skates, a fly-fishing rod, and a plethora of running shoes. It's no coincidence that *Outdoor Explorer* magazine listed Boulder among the 25 "best places to raise an outdoor-loving family" in 2000.

Residents also engage in more traditional pursuits, such as tennis and golf. Boulder's population of couch potatoes is probably one of the nation's smallest. In 2006 *Bicycling Magazine* named Boulder the best city for cycling. That same year, Forbes.com dubbed the city the best for singles. In 2007 *BusinessWeek* voted Boulder one of the top 10 cities for artists. And these are just a sprinkling of Boulder's honors. The city has won more tributes and accolades than any other city in America for just about everything, from its weather to its recreation to its overall quality of life.

Why Boulder? The mountains seem to attract outdoors-oriented people. Perhaps Boulderites felt obliged to lead the way when citizen Frank Shorter became the first American ever to win an Olympic medal in the marathon—gold in 1972 in Munich, silver in 1976 in Montreal. "When Frank won the gold, everybody in America started running," says Neill Woelk, a veteran sports reporter at Boulder's *Daily Camera* newspaper. Another famous Boulder runner, Arturo Barrios, held the world record for 10 kilometers until 1993.

Boulder is also known nationwide for its huge bicycling population and local celebrities. Boulder cyclist Connie Carpenter won Olympic gold in 1984 for the road race, and her husband, Davis Phinney, was the first American ever to win a Tour de France stage. Alexi Grewal won an Olympic gold medal in 1984 for the road race. With more than 90 miles of bike lanes and off-street bike paths, citizens can cycle almost everywhere, sometimes faster than by car—and without the parking hassle.

Elite athletes from all over the world, including mountaineers Pete Athans and Jon Krakauer, move to Boulder specifically to train in its health-promoting atmosphere and high altitude. Dozens of outdoor recreation publications, including *Rock and Ice, Trail Runner,* and *Ski* magazines, and *Velo News,* are based here, as are hundreds of outdoor recreation–oriented businesses.

The University of Colorado's football team, the Golden Buffaloes, was the 1990 co-national champion. Under the guidance of a new coach named in 2005, the "Buffs" have set their sights on reclaiming the national title. The women's basketball team is also tops. CU-Boulder's alpine and Nordic ski teams train at nearby Eldora Mountain Resort, only 21 miles away.

For mere mortals there are health clubs galore, the most popular being the great outdoors. Boulder boasts 100 miles of hiking trails in the mountain parks, literally outside our back doors. One of the world's largest 10-kilometer footraces, the annual Bolder Boulder through the city's streets, attracts more than 45,000 runners. The Flatirons, numerous rock formations, and nearby Eldorado Canyon make Boulder a rock-climbing mecca. Read the Sports chapter for a full description.

HEART AND SOUL

Boulder's Pearl Street Mall forms the heart and center of the city. Historic buildings, housing shops, galleries, offices, and sidewalk cafes line this photogenic, four-block, open-air walkway—formerly part of Pearl Street. Sadly, since the mall was completed in 1977, constant "upscaling" and rising rents have driven out many of the older businesses, replacing them with a musical-chairs array of new establishments. But Boulder's downtown mall still lures as many locals as visitors, especially on summer evenings when string quartets, bagpipers, Peruvian bands, and all manner of performers stake out spots by storefronts. One musician hauls in his piano on a wheeled

platform. Jugglers, fire and sword swallowers, tightrope walkers, and even a Rastafarian contortionist complete the circus-like scene. Lively entertainment, people-watching, and the piney aroma of the summer breeze make mall strolling a warm-weather favorite.

The Boulder Creek Path, just two short blocks from the Pearl Street Mall, meanders along Boulder Creek as a peaceful but sometimes perilous thoroughfare for bicyclists, in-line skaters, joggers, and strollers. Seven-and-a-half miles of scenic path follow the creek as it tumbles down from Boulder Canyon and out onto the plains. Bicycling is so highly regarded in Boulder that sometimes the city plows the snow off the bike path before it plows the streets.

During spring runoff and early summer, kayakers and kids of all ages take tumultuous rides down the creek in boats and inner tubes. Also along the path, adjacent to Central Park, the Boulder County Farmers' Market operates on Saturdays and Wednesdays from spring through fall, offering local, organically grown vegetables, fruits, and flowers as well as crafts and baked goods.

No Boulder summer is complete without a concert and meal at Chautauqua. Chautauqua Park, with its historic dining hall and barn-like concert hall, houses some of the best music and meals anywhere, including the Colorado Music Festival with artists from around the country. Elsewhere in town, summertime offerings include the Colorado Dance Festival, Colorado Shakespeare Festival, Colorado Lyric Opera, and the Boulder Creek Festival, just to name a few.

INDUSTRY AND ECONOMICS

To dispel any notion of Boulder as a bedroom community to Denver, consider this: 78 percent of Boulder County's population works in the county, 45 percent of the city of Boulder's population works in the city, and 45 percent of the city's workforce commutes in from surrounding communities. Boulder industry focuses on education, scientific research, and technology at such places as the University of Colorado at Boulder, the National Oceanic and Atmospheric Administration, the National Center for Atmospheric Research, and various other government and university scientific institutes.

Celestial Seasonings, the largest U.S. herbal tea manufacturer, makes its home here on Sleepytime Drive. The company revolutionized the tea industry, and founder Mo Siegel literally picked his way to an herbal tea fortune—he started out gathering herbs in Boulder's foothills. He is renowned as the hippie who became a millionaire. A bicycling aficionado, Siegel also brought international bicycle competition to Boulder for more than a decade with the Red Zinger Bicycle Classic race. Started in the mid-1970s, it eventually became the now-extinct Coors Classic.

The University of Colorado and IBM Corp. are among the top employers in Boulder County. Other top employers are the Boulder Valley School District (4,296 employees) and Ball Aerospace (3,000 employees).

BOULDER NOTABLES

The University of Colorado has in the past housed such scholars as Robert Bakker, a world-renowned paleontologist who transformed the study of dinosaurs with his now widely accepted theory that they were warm-blooded and more closely related to birds than reptiles. Movie mogul Steven Spielberg consulted Bakker during the filming of Jurassic Park. CU-Boulder is currently home to Patricia Nelson Limerick, renowned teacher and historian of the American West and a leader among the "new Western historians." Limerick's groundbreaking work on the roles played by women, Native Americans, and other ethnic groups in settling the West won her the 1995 MacArthur Fellowship, a "genius grant" of $275,000 over a five-year period with no strings attached.

Also at CU-Boulder is Nobel laureate Thomas Cech, who received that prize for his work proving that the genetic messenger RNA can also function as an enzyme, leading to the speculation that RNA could have played a key role in the origin of life. Nationally recognized as a leader in the field of educational testing, professor of education Robert Linn received the university's highest honor, a distinguished professorship, in 1996. He is an advisor to key professional and governmental committees as an expert in evaluating test reliability and validity; test comparison, bias, and ethics; and the strength and weakness of the mathematical models that define testing.

CU physics professor Carl Wieman was one of two people who created the coldest temperature in 1995. The other scientist was Eric Cornell, a staff physicist with the National Institute of Standards and Technology in Boulder. They led the scientific team that created the long-sought Bose-Einstein condensation—a state that occurs when individual atoms meld into a "superatom" at a few billionths of a degree above absolute zero. In recognition of their achievements, the pair was awarded the 2001 Nobel Prize in physics.

CU law professor Charles Wilkinson is a nationally renowned attorney and expert in natural resources management. He has won awards from the National Wildlife Federation and served as special counsel to the Department of the Interior in connection with the creation of the Grand Staircase–Escalante National Monument in Utah. The author of many books, he is also an expert in Western land and water issues and Native American law and rights.

CU is fourth among U.S. universities in the number of astronauts it has produced (excluding the military academies), exceeded only by MIT, Purdue, and Stanford.

Atmospheric scientist Walter Orr Roberts, who died in 1990, founded the National Center for Atmospheric Research (NCAR—pronounced "en-car") in Boulder, and his work in solar physics established Boulder as an atmospheric science center, attracting such other scientific facilities as the National Bureau of Standards and Technology (now known as NIST) and Ball Aerospace. He helped found CU-Boulder's Joint Institute for Laboratory Astrophysics and Department of Astrophysical, Planetary and Atmospheric Sciences. Roberts also helped bring Boulder's greatest architectural gem into being: the stunning mesa-top NCAR laboratory, designed by architect I. M. Pei, who also designed the National Gallery

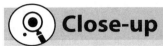

Close-up

Boulder Trivia

- Bicycling is so highly regarded in Boulder that sometimes the city plows the Boulder Creek bike path before they plow the streets!
- The exterior of a Boulder house was used as the characters' home in the well-known *Mork & Mindy* television show. It is now a private residence.
- A *Colorado Daily* poll found that 7 out of 10 Boulderites own bicycles. Another guidebook states that Boulder's bicycle count is approximately 93,000—almost equal to the total population!
- The Chautauqua Auditorium is an all-wood structure built in 1898. In the evening, when the Colorado Music Festival musicians are playing, you can often hear the rafters-dwelling owls hooting along with the music.
- The Flatiron Mountains got their name by pioneer women who said they looked like flat, metal irons used to iron their clothes.
- Scott Carpenter, a NASA astronaut, grew up in Boulder. He named his space capsule, *Aurora 7*, after his home on Aurora Avenue and Seventh Street.
- The University of Colorado at Boulder's buildings are built with red sandstone quarried in nearby Lyons.
- With Coors, Anheuser-Busch, and local microbreweries, this area has become the largest beer-producing triangle in the world.
- Robert Redford was a janitor at The Sink restaurant before moving on to become famous.
- Boulder's going to the dogs! Recent visitor counts to Boulder Mountain Parks found a ratio of 1 dog to every 5 visitors.
- Every year, Boulder Mountain Parks' core area receives 1.8 million visits. If that many people made a human chain, it would stretch from Boulder, Colorado, to New York City.
- The Hotel Boulderado was named by combining Boulder and Colorado so no visitor would ever forget where they had stayed.

of Art in Washington, D.C., and the pyramid-shaped entrance to the Louvre in Paris. NCAR is also known for being the futuristic setting of Woody Allen's 1970s comedy film *Sleeper*.

CLIMATE

It's no wonder that weather and climate are two big topics of study at local scientific institutes: Boulder's climate is marked by unusual extremes. Foot-deep snow and below-zero temperatures can suddenly transform to breezy 60-degree T-shirt weather by Boulder's capricious Chinook "snow-eater" winds. These warm, dry winds blast down from the eastern slope of the mountains and melt the snow with blinding speed. Boulder's winds have also been known to blow in gusts exceeding 120 mph, removing roofs and toppling telephone poles.

Because of these strong winds, Native Americans chose not to make permanent settlements in the area and mainly visited for summer hunting. The dreaded high winds, Boulder's biggest weather affliction, can come at any time but are the worst in winter and can continue for days. It can be so windy that schools won't let young children leave the building without an adult. Safeway supermarkets sometimes post a note on the door asking that shopping carts be returned to the store so errant, wind-blown carts don't damage cars in the parking lot. The winds can make people irritable, and there are tales of pioneer women wandering off onto the prairie or committing suicide, driven insane by the gales. Similar winds (in Europe called the *foehn* or *mistral*) are common throughout the world near high mountain ranges.

Sometimes it seems like Boulder has only two seasons: summer and winter. The tulips do bloom in spring, and the leaves change in fall for a brief but spectacular show. But these two fickle seasons are often accompanied by a foot of snow, burying the crocuses and lilacs or blackening fall's golden aspen leaves. Halloween is often one of the most miserable nights of the year, with the poor trick-or-treaters braving the freezing rain or snow. Then again, Thanksgiving and Christmas can sometimes have outdoor cafe weather. It rarely rains in Boulder except for summer afternoon thunderstorms and the August monsoon—a week or two of rainy weather.

Boulder's high elevation, 5,430 feet, keeps temperatures cool at night even on the hottest summer days. Mountain breezes and low humidity help, too. Tornadoes generally stay well to the east, though hailstorms occasionally shred summer flowers and vegetables.

The record low temperature in the Boulder area is –33 degrees (1930) and the record high is 104 degrees (1954). Boulder has an average of 33 days above 90 degrees and 133 days below freezing. January, the coldest month, averages 21 degrees; July, the warmest, averages 88. Average precipitation is 17.13 inches. The most snow in a season was 158.70 inches; the least, 17.40 inches. Though it may snow or blow, low humidity and a higher-than-California average of sunny days make Boulder's climate one of the most pleasant in the nation.

AREA GEOGRAPHY

The foothills of the Rocky Mountains divide Boulder County from north to south. Eastern Boulder County lies on the western edge of the Great Plains, with rolling terrain, small ridges, and the Davidson Mesa, which runs northeast from south of Boulder to Louisville. Western Boulder County rises from the foothills to the Continental Divide, to a breathless summit of 14,255 feet atop Longs Peak in Rocky Mountain National Park in the extreme northwestern part of the county.

BOULDER ENVIRONS

Roughly 20 towns dot the mountains and plains of Boulder County, ranging from rustic, high-country settlements like Eldora and Raymond, with only a handful of year-round residents, to sizable burgs like Longmont, the second-largest city in Boulder County after Boulder. A former sugar beet and canning capital, Longmont—northeast of Boulder—is now home to Longmont Foods, a turkey-breeding and meat-processing company.

Nothing could be farther from Longmont in both locale and flavor than lofty, funky Ward, former mining boom-and-bust town, now a home for old and young hippies and other escapees from the system. After Longmont, the small plains cities of Broomfield, Lafayette, and Louisville are the most populous.

The small towns of Lyons (north of Boulder) and Eldorado Springs (south of Boulder) lie at the mouths of spectacular canyons. Eldorado Springs is also the site of a state park and mineral springs and is a famous rock-climbing area. Hygiene and Allenspark are unincorporated small settlements of a few hundred residents each. Jamestown was once a mining boomtown with a population of 10,000; now it has fewer than 300 residents. Its picturesque mercantile cafe is a popular bicycling stop.

Spectacularly sited at the top of Boulder Canyon on Barker Reservoir, Nederland is Boulder County's largest mountain town and an odd mix of eccentric mountain folk, young families, old hippies, environmental activists, self-sufficient rugged individualists, and a small contingent of out-of-staters who fall in love with it during the summer move-in and beat a fast trail out after their first winter.

Of course a lot more can be said about each Boulder County town and its unique character and history. See the chapters on Boulder Real Estate and Neighborhoods and Nearby Communities for more information.

NIWOT'S CURSE?

Though Boulder has been utopia for many residents for many years, the city (like the rest of the planet) is currently experiencing an uncomfortable population expansion. Since the late 1970s, the population has increased by about 45 percent, or 30,000 people. Three million people—75 percent of Colorado's population—live in a 60-mile-wide swath along the Front Range, from Fort Collins to Colorado Springs. By 2020, that number is projected to reach four million. "Too many people and too many cars" is the complaint of residents who remember traffic-free streets and the ability to get anywhere in town in ten minutes. Gone are those days, and in their place are frustrating waits in traffic jams, rude drivers, a dearth of parking spaces, and long lines at supermarkets, restaurants, and movies.

i Boulder's backdrop and trademark, the Flatirons, are Pennsylvanian red sandstone and conglomerate that were deposited as alluvial fans and aprons along the edges of the ancestral Rockies. They were dragged upward at their current angle by the rebirth of the Rockies about 65 million years ago. The Third Flatiron (third from the north) is one of Colorado's and the nation's premier, classic rock climbs. It towers 1,400 feet high, a couple hundred feet higher than the Empire State Building, and has been climbed by people without using their hands, on roller skates, naked, and in eight minutes (all separate climbers).

City of Boulder and Boulder County Demographics

Estimated Population (2007)	City of Boulder	Boulder County
Total Population	102,569	302,525
Households	43,687	119,884
Average household size	2.35	2.52
Source: Denver Regional Council of Governments		
Ethnicity	**City of Boulder**	**Boulder County**
Caucasian	93.4%	90.2%
Hispanic	7.0%	13.1%
Asian	4.5%	4.5%
African American	1.4%	0.8%
Native American	1.1%	1.2%
Source: 2007 American Community Survey, US Census Bureau		
Other	**City of Boulder**	**Boulder County**
Median Age (2007)	30 years	35.7 years
Median Household Income (2007)	$52,759	$63,257
Median Rent (2007)	$888	$901
Median Sales Price - Single Family (8/07)	$550,500	

Median Sales Price - Attached (8/07)	$240,000
Average annual rainfall (2007)	17.13 inches
Average annual snowfall (2007)	85.5 inches
Mean temperature (2007)	52

Source: 2007 American Community Survey, NOAA (Weather data)

Marital Status (2007)	City of Boulder	Boulder County
Married	30.6%	47.2%
Single, never married	60.4%	40.6%
Divorced	7.1%	10.5%

Source: 2007 American Community Survey, US Census Bureau

Educational Attainment (25 years+)	City of Boulder	Boulder County
Didn't finish high school	4.0%	7.2%
Graduated high school	10.2%	15.8%
Some college or associate degree	17.7%	22.4%
Bachelor's or graduate degree	68.1%	54.6%

Source: 2007 American Community Survey, US Census Bureau

Other

Library Circulation - Boulder Library (2008)	1,183,717
University of Colorado enrollment (Fall 2008)	29,709
Boulder Valley Public Schools enrollment (2007-2008)	28,490

Scholastic Aptitude Test (SAT) scores for Boulder Valley students, 2008:

Verbal, 580 in Boulder Valley, 502 nationally

Mathematics, 594 in Boulder Valley, 515 nationally

American College Test (ACT) scores for Boulder County students, 2008:

22.2 in Boulder Valley, 19.4 average

Source: City of Boulder, University of Colorado, Boulder Valley School District

Top 10 employers:	City of Boulder	# Employees
	University of Colorado	7,050
	Boulder Valley School District	4,296*
	IBM	4,000
	Ball Aerospace	3,000
	Boulder Community Hospital	2,380
	Boulder County	1,684*
	UCAR (University Corporation for Atmospheric Research)	1,350
	Covidien	1,300

	City of Boulder	1,238
	Emerson Process Micro Motion	598

Source: Boulder County Business Report Book of Lists 2008

* Employees in Boulder County

Top 10 employers:	**Boulder County**	**# Employees**
	University of Colorado	7,050
	Boulder Valley School District	4,296
	IBM	4,000
	St Vrain School District	3,392
	Ball Aerospace	3,000
	Boulder Community Hospital	2,380
	Boulder County	1,684
	Seagate	1,500
	UCAR (University Corporation for Atmospheric Research)	1,339
	Exempla Good Samaritan Medical Center	1,310

Source: Boulder County Business Report Book of Lists 2008

Number of Employees by Industry (2007)	**City of Boulder**	**Boulder County**
Accommodation and food services	8,522	14,608
Administrative and waste services	3,306	6,557
Agriculture, forestry, fish and hunting	55	348
Arts, entertainment, and recreation	1,552	2,532
Construction	1,820	5,638
Educational services	12,577	17,896
Finance and insurance	3,432	4,956
Health care and social assistance	7,601	16,649
Information	7,124	9,174
Management of companies & enterprises	824	1,615
Manufacturing	8,845	17,843
Mining	74	892
Other services	2,713	4,277
Professional, scientific, technical services	12,933	22,811
Public Administration	6,456	7,301
Real estate and rental and leasing	1,516	2,481
Retail trade	7,966	16,564
Transportation and warehousing	660	2,159

Utilities	184	308
Wholesale trade	2,837	5,372
Total	90,997	159,981
Unemployment Rate (September 2008)	4.6%	

Source: Colorado Department of Labor and Employment; CU Business Research Division

Reported Crimes (2007)	City of Boulder
Aggravated assault	154
Arson	40
Burglary	404
Larceny theft	1,910
Motor vehicle theft	96
Murder	1
Rape	37
Robbery	27
Total	2,669

Source: City of Boulder

GETTING HERE, GETTING AROUND

Boulder is about 25 miles northwest of Denver, via I-25 and U.S. Highway 36, better known locally as "The Turnpike" because it was once a toll road. Most visitors arrive here by car or by plane into Denver International Airport, about an hour's drive south and east.

In the city, the car is the favorite mode of transportation. But more than most cities, Boulder offers and encourages use of alternative modes of transportation to the car and has a city agency, the Transportation Planning Group (TPG, also known as GO Boulder), to promote, set, and achieve such goals. The 2000 census survey found that Boulder residents carpool and walk to work at a much higher rate than their Denver neighbors. Among 14 comparable cities, Boulder ranks No. 1 in people who walk to work, work at home, and drive with more than one person in the car. It ranks second among those who bike. (The TPG of Boulder says Davis, California, probably ranks first, with Boulder right on its heels.) Alternative modes of transportation can become one of your favorite things about Boulder.

GETTING TO BOULDER

By Air

DENVER INTERNATIONAL AIRPORT (DIA)
8400 Peña Boulevard
(303) 342-2200, (800) 247-2336
www.flydenver.com

Opened in 1995, Denver International Airport is the biggest in the nation and one of the biggest in the world. Twenty-three carriers service the airport: United Airlines dominates, with some 60 percent of the flights out of DIA, but American, American West, Continental, Delta, Frontier, Northwest, TWA, and US Airways also serve the airport. Others include Air Canada, Alaska Airlines, British Airways, Lufthansa, Mexicana, and Sky West.

DIA is posh, with polished granite floors, $7.5 million worth of artwork, and an expansive main lobby roofed with 34 translucent, Teflon-coated fiberglass tent canopies designed to invoke snow-covered peaks and cast light like stylized, billowy clouds. Those canopies were canted in different directions for structural efficiency in the wind and heavy weather. Despite its monumental 5-million-square-foot interior, walks are short. The ticket counters are a short way from passenger drop-offs on both sides of the main terminal. Common carriers (i.e., buses and vans) use a separate level, off-limits to private cars. There are three concourses. You have the option of walking to Concourse A via an air bridge over a taxiway, but a swift subway whisks you to all concourses. Stand near the front windows if you want to see the little propellers along the walls whirl as the train passes.

DIA has excellent shops, including some not usually found in airports: Images of Nature, a national wildlife photographer's store; Hudson Booksellers, a well-stocked bookstore; and a Body Shop are among the stores in the airport. You can also find a travel agency and a massage therapist at DIA. An interfaith airport chapel opened in 1996. Restaurant offerings include McDonald's, Einstein Bros. Bagels, the Cantina Grill Express, specialty pizza, croissant, and coffee shops (including Seattle's Best Coffee), and Schlotzskys, just to name a few. The popular Denver Chophouse & Brewery has a restaurant planned for Concourse A at the end of 2008. Most of these establishments are open daily from 7 a.m. until 10 p.m.

If you need information on Denver International Airport's ground transportation, call (303) 342-4059; for parking information, call (303) 342-7275; for luggage storage and lost and found, call (303) 342-4062.

Driving time between DIA and Boulder takes about 45 minutes. The quick and easy route is the Northwest Parkway (a toll road), which opened in 2003.

Airport Shuttles

There is currently only one van service that offers scheduled airport shuttle service to and from Boulder. Super Shuttle Boulder (303- 227-0000) picks up at Boulder's major hotels, CU-Boulder, and your own front door. The service departs the Rodeway Inn & Suites/Boulder Broker Inn hourly between 4 a.m. and 10 p.m. (if you order door-to-door, they'll schedule your pick-up to coincide with a departure from the Broker) and from the airport at 10 minutes past each hour between 8:10 a.m. and 11:10 p.m. Call them for rates.

Bus Service

The Regional Transportation District, also known as RTD (303-299-6000, www.rtd-denver.com), also operates hourly buses between DIA and Boulder. The bus trip takes about 90 minutes, with intermediate stops including the Louisville-Superior and Table Mesa Park-n-Ride lots. The fare is $11 one-way.

RTD also offers a family plan that allows up to three children age 15 and younger to ride to or from DIA free with an adult.

Taxis and Limos

Boulder Yellow Cab (303-777-7777, www .yellowtrans.com) charges around $70 for an airport trip for one to five people and also picks up in Lafayette and Louisville. If you are feeling flush, you can call an on-demand limo service. Boulder Trip Service (303-938-1234, www.bouldertrip .com) provides transportation in Lincoln Town cars, and four-wheel-drive Chevrolet Suburbans, each equipped with television, beverage service, and ski and luggage racks. It operates as an on-demand airport charter, particularly for business travelers and groups. By-the-hour rates range between $85 and $110 for trips between Boulder, Denver, Louisville, or Lafayette and DIA. Prices are higher to Centennial Airport south of Denver and from Eldorado Springs, Gold Hill, Gold Lake, Lake Valley, Longmont, Pine Brook Hills, Walker Ranch, and Ward. Boulder Trip Service also will take you to or pick you up from Colorado Springs, general-aviation airports, and mountain towns. Other limo services include Foothills Limousine (720-394-3779, www.foothillslimo.com) and Boulder Limousine Service (303-332-3992, boulderlimousineservice.com).

Car Routes

With the Northwest Parkway (also known as E-470), which is a toll road, travel to DIA is a snap. Sometimes it seems you're virtually the only one on the road. You can pick up the parkway by exiting US 36 at the Interlocken Loop/Storage Tek Drive exit, near the Flatiron Crossing Mall. The old tried-and-true options work, too, but expect traffic along these routes.

- **Option A (38.5 miles):** Take US 36 to Sheridan Boulevard. Exit at 104th Avenue/Church Ranch Boulevard and follow 104th Avenue east all the way to Tower Road. Until you get well east of I-25, which is still rural, tremendous growth is happening along this route, which has about two dozen traffic lights. At Tower Road, along the airport's western edge, turn right and take it south to Peña Boulevard; turn left and go east into the airport.

- **Option B (45 miles):** Take US 36 to Denver. Go south briefly on I-25, then take I-76 for about a mile to I-270, heading southeast. It merges into I-70 east. Exit at Peña Boulevard and go east into the airport.

- **Option C (45 miles):** Take Arapahoe Road (Highway 7) east to U.S. Highway 85. Take US 85 south to Henderson Road. Go east on Henderson Road to Tower Road. Take Tower Road south to Peña Boulevard and go east into the airport.

General-Aviation Airports

If you have a private plane, you can fly into one of the region's smaller general-aviation airports. Some i For an easy-to-carry free pocket map of Boulder streets and pedestrian/bicycle paths, stop by the Transportation Department, on the second floor of the Park Central Building at 1739 Broadway.

also have air taxi services that can fly you quickly to a town not on a regular commercial air route.

BOULDER MUNICIPAL AIRPORT
3300 Airport Road, Boulder
(303) 440-7065
www.ci.boulder.co.us/airport
Like most airports in Colorado, Boulder's airport is uncontrolled, meaning it has no control tower. Private propeller planes and a few smaller turbojets land here. There is a comfortable lobby where a selection of videos about flying are for sale.

Despite being open to the public and visiting aircraft, there are no commercial airlines operating from the facility. There are, however, 234 aircraft based at the site and various businesses operating there, such as flight training schools, aircraft maintenance facilities, charter operations, aircraft sales, and various flight clubs. There are three flight schools at the airport, Journeys Aviation Boulder (303-449-4210), Specialty Flight Training (303-530-0550) and Mile High Gliding (303-527-1122). There are hangar and tie-down rentals available as well, and a parachuting outfit (1-800-498-JUMP). To reach the airport, take Valmont Road east to Airport Road.

ERIE MUNICIPAL AIRPORT
395 Airport Drive, Erie
(303) 604-0043
www.ci.erie.co.us/PW/airport.html
Located in east Boulder County, this airport has a runway big enough for small jets, but most of its air traffic is single- and twin-engine propeller planes. A full range of flight instruction is available. Experimental and unique home-built airplanes occupy many hangars. And the jet-set—that is, the propeller-set—has settled nearby. More than a dozen houses adjacent to

the airport sport private hangars with taxi lanes connecting to the runway.

VANCE BRAND MUNICIPAL AIRPORT
10383 North 85th Street, Longmont
(303) 651-8431
www.ci.longmont.co.us/airport
This landing field provides full services for business and pleasure aircraft. There is a small lobby with snacks available and pilot supplies. They do not have a courtesy car but can arrange for a local rental-car company to transport guests to their destination. To reach Vance Brand, take the Diagonal Highway or US 36 northeast of Boulder to Airport Road and go north 1.5 miles. Air West Flight Center Inc. (303-776-6266, www.airwestinc.net) is a flight school based at Vance Brand Airport. They teach flying lessons ranging from private pilot to instructor.

Another flight school based at Vance Brand Airport is Twin Peaks Aviation (303-776-8467). Lessons and scenic rides are available.

ROCKY MOUNTAIN METROPOLITAN AIRPORT
11755 Airport Way, Broomfield
(303) 271-4850
www.co.jefferson.co.us/airport
Located just outside Boulder County, this airfield is nonetheless used by many Boulderites. No scheduled commercial passenger flights leave this airport, but it has plenty of general aviation in addition to flight schools, avionics, repair and maintenance shops, charter services and conference facilities. In addition, there are two restaurants open to the public in its modern 25,000 sq. ft. terminal building.

By Car
To drive to Boulder from Denver, take I-25 north to US 36 west, better known as "The Turnpike." The last hill is Davidson Mesa, where you'll get a spectacular view of town and find a visitor center kiosk.

If you ask for directions and someone says "Foothills," clarify whether they mean Foothills Highway (US 36), which starts as 28th Street and leads to Estes Park, or Foothills Parkway (Highway 157), which links US 36 with Highway 119 and leads to Longmont.

If you are driving to Boulder from the ski areas on I-70, you have two options. The first is to take the Morrison/Golden exit (exit 259) to U.S. Highway 40. Go north toward U.S. Highway 6, turn left onto US 6, and then head north on Highway 93 to Boulder. The second, and to us preferable, option is the Central City/Golden exit (exit 244) off I-70. Follow US 6 east for about 15 miles through beautiful Clear Creek Canyon. At the second traffic light, just on the outskirts of Golden, turn left (north) onto Highway 93, which becomes Broadway in Boulder.

GETTING AROUND BOULDER

The No. 1 rule of thumb to help newcomers orient themselves in Boulder is: The mountains are to the west. Most of the north/ south streets are numbered, starting with Third Street on the west side of town then going beyond 75th Street as you head east. Broadway is a major north-south thoroughfare on a slight diagonal, and Folsom Street is a significant north-south street from North Boulder to the University of Colorado campus. Other important roads are US 36, which becomes 28th Street through Boulder, and Foothills Parkway, a divided roadway on the eastern edge of town, but with some traffic lights at major intersections, which connects US 36 and the Longmont Diagonal (Highway 119). It is a way to bypass Boulder, though we wonder why anyone would wish to bypass our wonderful city.

Baseline Road is a significant east-west route, not just to Boulderites, but also to cartographers, for it marks the 40th parallel on maps of the Earth. If you made a beeline down this road, after a few hundred miles you'd hit the boundary between Kansas and Nebraska. The major east-west cross-streets are Table Mesa Road/South Boulder Road and Baseline Road in the southern part of the city; Arapahoe Avenue in central Boulder (and, to an extent, Canyon Boulevard, a short but important major street); and the Alpine Street/Valmont

Road routing and Iris Avenue in the northern part of the city.

North Boulder's alphabetical "tree streets"—Alpine, Balsam, Cedar, and so on—are easy to find and remember. Making your way through cul-de-sac-filled subdivisions, however, requires good directions. Broadway and 28th Street converge in North Boulder, again becoming US 36 toward Lyons.

You'll find basic orientation maps in the front of this book, and more detailed street maps in the front of local phone books. A variety of easier-to-tote maps is available from the city's Transportation Planning Group (303-441-3266), on the second floor of the Park Central Building, 1739 Broadway, including free pocket-size maps for streets and bus and bicycle routes. And remember, it never hurts to ask for directions.

By Car

If you just arrived from a congested metropolitan area on either coast, Boulder might not seem to have much traffic, but if you've been in town a while, you would notice the change over the past few years. More than 200,000 cars flow through the city daily, and people drive a cumulative 2.2 million miles in this little valley every day. That's loads of cars, especially at a higher altitude more prone to air pollution. It's also unsettling to people who don't like the way roads and parking lots eat up land and create canyons clogged with vehicles and the accompanying din and exhaust fumes.

Boulder has given itself a mandate to reduce the car and traffic problem while enhancing its residents' ability to get around. In a classic example of Boulder's foresight and compulsive worrying about quality-of-life issues before they become crises, the city developed its first Transportation Master Plan in 1989, when, believe it or not, the city was still suffering under a regional recession and few people were worrying about too many commuters, too many jobs, or too many homes. The Transportation Planning Group tracks traffic patterns, keeps statistics, creates charts, and most important, tries to use these figures to solve the congestion conundrum. Periodic studies confirm that what most people like about downtown Boulder is its atmosphere and pedestrian orientation, and what most people don't like about Boulder is the parking dilemma. The latest version of the Transportation Master Plan, designed to take Boulder through the year 2020, includes a whopping $1 billion worth of projects (including more than $250 million for improved bus service and $30 million for better bike paths), proving that Boulder takes its traffic and growth issues seriously and is willing to back them up with big bucks.

Individuals do their bit, too. There's a sprinkling of electric cars on Boulder's streets. Many serve on the city's Transportation Advisory Board which studies the issues in depth and makes informed proposals to the city. Planners strive for small-scale neighborhood centers so people don't have to drive as far to reach necessary services. And many people take public transportation whenever possible or get around town on bicycles or on foot as often as they can. A few even put their commitment into action by living carless.

FasTracks, an integrated transit improvement program, will vastly improve transportation options in Boulder and surrounding cities in the Denver metro region. FasTracks is RTD's 12-year comprehensive plan to build and operate high-speed rail lines and expand and improve bus service and Park-n-Rides throughout the region. FasTracks will include 122 miles of new light rail and commuter rail, 18 miles of bus rapid transit service, 57 new transit stations and 21,213 additional parking spaces at transit Park-n-Rides, and enhanced bus service and FastConnects throughout the region. The US 36 corridor portion of the project will bring 18 miles of bus rapid transit service between downtown Denver and Boulder along US 36 and a rail line from Denver through Boulder to Longmont. The final design of these improvements will begin in 2010.

Plans and dreams aside, the majority of Boulder residents still depend on their cars, even if they secretly wish there were a better way. Don't feel guilty if your car's packed with visiting sightse-ers or your kids' soccer teammates; you're being a carpool! But if you're all alone, at least try to consolidate your errands so you drive less often.

Boulder has many designated bike lanes, but where there are none, bicyclists may occupy a lane of traffic, just like cars. Pedestrians at crosswalks have the right-of-way, which means you are supposed to stop when you see someone waiting to cross the street.

Car Rentals

The overwhelming majority of fly-in visitors to Boulder rent cars at Denver International Airport or from agencies near the old Stapleton Airport and drive to Boulder, but rental cars are also available in town. Locals whose cars are undergoing major repairs, business travelers in the area for several days but only requiring a car for part of the time, CU-Boulder students (you must be age 25 or older to rent), and visiting academicians are among those who might wish to rent a car in Boulder for the short time they really need one.

Boulder has several rental car companies. Choices include such national firms as Hertz (303-443-9122, www.hertz.com); Avis (303-499-1136, www.avis.com); Enterprise Rent-A-Car (303-449-9466, www.enterprise.com); and Budget (303-444-9054, www.budget.com). Smaller regional and local companies abound, too.

Rush Hour

Most cities get only two rush periods. Boulder has three. Morning rush spans 7 to 9 a.m. Also, because many of the new commercial and business parks are lacking in restaurants, workers often drive somewhere for lunch, creating a noon mini-rush that starts around 11 a.m. and lasts until 2 p.m. Traffic really swells between 4 and 7 p.m. A fourth rush sometimes revolves around CU-Boulder home football games, which jam streets around campus. If you hate traffic, make your car trips outside these most popular times or (hint-hint) consider other ways of getting around (see this chapter's subsequent "Alternative Modes of Transportation" section).

Weather Hazards

Boulder's normally benign climate often lulls us into thinking that the driving, like the living, is easy. But meteorological aberrations can be hazardous. Summer hailstorms can pock windshields, impair visibility, and temporarily cause slippery road surfaces. Snowstorms often start with drizzling rain that freezes before the snow falls, and that snow can undergo several days of melt-to-slush, freeze-to-ice cycles before melting and evaporating completely. Hilly streets and intersections are generally sanded rather than treated with chemicals. Highways and arterials are plowed, but snow on most residential streets is left to be melted by the sun. Good snow tires are a must for Colorado winters.

If you drive a camper or sport utility vehicle or are moving your belongings into town in a rental truck, you'll want to pay attention to high-wind warnings. Highway 93 between Boulder and Golden is especially vulnerable to wicked crosswinds and is occasionally closed because of them. Mountain driving can be pleasurable or terrifying, depending on the individual driver's skill and confidence. Shifting into a lower gear helps save wear and tear on the engine while ascending and on the brakes while going downhill.

Accidents

As elsewhere, serious accidents demand a 911 call to dispatch emergency police, ambulance, and even fire units. The Boulder Police accident investigation unit deals with non-injury-producing accidents. For information, call the department's general information line, (303) 441-4444, or visit www.ci.boulder.co.us/police. Vehicle insurance is mandatory in the state of Colorado, with current minimum required coverage of $25,000 for bodily injury, $50,000 per accident, and $15,000 property damage. Motorists who leave the scene of an accident without exchanging license, registration, and insurance information may have their driver's licenses suspended. (There are other offenses that can result in loss of license, too, including driving while intoxicated, reckless driving, and possession of certain firearms.)

i No matter what form of transportation you use, this city of Boulder Web site can help you reach your destination: www.gettingthere.com.

Emergency Services

You only need to use the American Automobile Association (AAA) emergency road service once to make your membership pay off. AAA Colorado (303-442-0383; www.aaa.com) provides a variety of services, including changing a flat tire, refueling an empty gas tank, pulling vehicles out of snow drifts or mud, and towing a broken-down vehicle to a repair center. Because of the distances involved, anyone who drives in the mountains is probably wise to sign up for AAA. The association also offers towing services from as far as 250 miles from home. In addition to road services, AAA maintains a walk-in center at 1933 28th Street, upstairs from Blockbuster Video. The center features a travel agency, traveler's check sales, discount luggage, book sales, and routing assistance. Many of the services are available for nonmembers as well as members. In addition, AAA sells insurance and provides a locator service for good deals on new cars, bail bonds (not than any *Insider* would ever need one!), and other services.

Parking

If Boulder accommodated every single driver who wanted a quick trip to a perfect parking space, we would need so many roads and parking spaces that little room would remain for buildings, sidewalks, trees, or flowers. On the other hand, for retail businesses and restaurants to remain viable, there must be reasonably convenient customer parking. Periodic studies confirm that what most people like about downtown Boulder is its atmosphere and pedestrian orientation; what most people don't like about Boulder is the parking dilemma. Four downtown blocks of Pearl Street are pedestrian-only, so obviously there's no parking there, and pay-and-park spaces limit parking on adjacent commercial streets. A new parking program was initiated in 1997 on adjacent neighborhood streets to discourage daylong parkers. Two- to three-hour nonresident parking is permitted.

Boulder maintains several staffed parking garages and metered surface lots, which are in great demand. If you get a downtown job, you can get on a waiting list for reserved, long-term parking by checking with the city's Parking Services; call (303) 413-7300 or visit www.bouldercolorado.gov.

In addition to downtown, another problematic parking area is The Hill, the area around the university. There are metered spaces on retail and commercial streets, but long-term parking is also restricted here. Your best bet is to park in the large CU visitor lot on Euclid Avenue, just east of the University Memorial Center (UMC). All other lots on the campus are permit-only parking. CU has its own Parking Services for students, faculty, and staff; call (303) 492-7384 or visit www.ucbparking.edu.

Alternative Modes of Transportation

For information about alternative modes of transportation, including pedestrian, bicycle, and carpool options, call the Transportation Planning Group, a city agency that offers multiple transportation options. It offers easy-to-read maps of bus routes, bike paths, and open-space trails. The pocket-size maps are free, and the larger full-scale ones are a few dollars. Call the TPG at (303) 441-3266, or stop by its offices on the second floor of the Park Central Building, 1739 Broadway, 2 blocks south of the Pearl Street Mall.

If you need a car only for an occasional errand or trip to the mountains, call Boulder's Car Share (303-271-3510, www.carshare.org). Car Share has cars, titled and licensed, that are shared, free of charge, by local residents.

To encourage bus use, participating businesses and the Boulder Downtown Management Commission (303-441-4000, www.gettingthere.com) provide ECO-Passes so their employees can ride the bus for free.

So far more than 41,000 residents have ECO-Passes. One of the great perks of the program is the guaranteed ride, which uses taxis to take people directly to their door at night. In addition, many Boulder neighborhoods have Neighborhood ECO-Passes, and new neighborhoods join the program yearly.

> ℹ️ Among fourteen comparable cities, Boulder ranks No. 1 in people who walk to work and people who work at home.

Boulder's Pathways

Boulder has been ranked among America's most walkable cities by *USA Today* and by *Walking* magazine. It's also a wonderful city for runners, bikers, in-line skaters, and wheelchair users. The most pleasing "roads" are the pedestrian and bicycle paths. They follow streams. They go by parks where you can hear birds sing, and they pass pretty homes with kids playing or adults gardening. Many people along the way smile. The major non-motorized-vehicle thoroughfare is the Boulder Creek Path (see the Attractions and Parks and Recreation Centers chapters), which is primarily an east-west route.

Walking some of these pathways to your destination often is faster than driving. Try it with a friend. Eat at some lovely spot on the Pearl Street Mall, then plan to meet on the CU-Boulder campus. You start walking while your friend gets the car. As you head up Broadway, look for a little sidewalk adjacent to Broadway, just up the hill from Arapahoe Avenue. You'll probably have time to stop at Andrews Arboretum located on this sidewalk on the east side of Broadway between Grandview and Marine Streets, an area once occupied by train tracks. The arboretum is open every day free of charge. You can continue on this pleasant pathway to the university and enjoy the sights on your stroll. You'll get lung-filling exercise and might even have time to read a chapter in your book before your friend gets the car, drives up to the university, parks, and finally joins you.

The Transportation Planning Group (TPG) has several programs designed to increase walking by improving pedestrian facilities. Many neighborhood sidewalks are being replaced for safety reasons and intersections have been made more pedestrian friendly.

Bicycling

Boulder is one of America's best cycling cities. At this writing, the city boasts more than 100 miles of off-street bike paths, bike lanes on city streets, and bike routes. That includes underpasses that allow university students safe biking to outlying dormitories and apartments, and a climbing lane exclusively for bicyclists on Table Mesa Drive. Savvy locals know that errands-by-bike sometimes go faster than errands-by-car. The whole idea of the bicycle as transportation is promoted heavily by the TPG, especially during the annual Boulder Walk and Bike Week in late June.

Designed to increase the awareness of Boulder's transportation options, especially walking and biking, Boulder's Walk and Bike Week is coordinated each June by the city's GO Boulder office. It was first hosted by the city of Boulder in 1977 as "Bike to Work Day." As its local popularity and sponsorship interest grew, so did the event. In 1982, it expanded to Walk and Bike Week. Since 2003, Boulder has coordinated with the Colorado Department of Transportation (CDOT) and Denver Regional Council of Governments (DRCOG) to include Walk and Bike Week in the celebration of Colorado Bike Month and in the Denver metro region's Bike to Work Day. In 2008, a record 7,500 people pledged to commute by bicycle on Bike to Work Day.

Every day of Walk and Bike Week brings something new, and participants can enjoy such events as $10 bike tune-ups, a vintage bike swap, a silent auction, a bike rodeo, bike relays, a cruiser ride, a walk and bike rally, and a happy hour for all participants, just to name a few. In 2008, there were 35 breakfast stations sponsored by local businesses providing complimentary breakfasts to hungry riders on Bike to Work Day. Walk and Bike Bingo is a very popular citywide event designed to encourage the community to integrate walking and biking into its daily routine. Participants pick up a Walk and Bike Week bingo card from participating businesses or print it online at www.goboulder.net. Participants walk or bike to any of the 25 participating business destinations around town and receive a stamp on their card. Those with five stamps, or Bingo, earn the chance to win prizes that include bikes, gift certificates, and much more.

In 1990, transit ridership was about 5,000 riders daily for all local and regional routes in and out of Boulder. In 2007, ridership was at a daily average of 31,062. Give one of Boulder's great buses a try for local trips around town.

Buses and Taxis

The Regional Transportation District, also known as RTD, is the greater Denver metropolitan area's public transportation agency. RTD recorded-information lines are (303) 299-6000, (800) 366-7433, and (303) 299-6089 (TDD).

RTD buses are promoted as "The Ride." The main bus station in Boulder, currently the hub of RTD's hub-and-spoke system, is at 14th and Walnut Streets. Rides within Boulder cost $1.75 (exact change only), 85 cents for seniors age 65 and older (off-peak hours); a 10-ride ticket book costs $15.75. Various monthly passes are also available at the bus station and at King Soopers and Safeway grocery markets. Boulder students can buy reduced-rate bus passes. Seniors are also eligible for discount passes.

RTD buses on Boulder city routes operate every half-hour. The schedules and prices vary for intercity service to Broomfield, Denver, Golden, Lafayette, Longmont, Louisville, Nederland, and Westminster. RTD also offers rush-hour express buses to the Denver Tech Center, hourly express buses to Denver International Airport, and special buses to the Eldora ski area via Nederland. Buses for Colorado Rockies and Denver Broncos games depart from the main Boulder terminal and various Park-n-Ride lots.

Many buses are equipped with wheelchair ramps, and many allow some bicycles on board. Call one of the RTD numbers for details on these amenities or for information on how to reach your destination by bus. Tell the RTD operator where you need to be, when, and from where you're starting. Schedules are available on buses and downtown at the main Boulder terminal.

You can get just about anywhere with Boulder's Community Bus Network. The Hop (303-441-3266, www.ci.boulder.co.us/goboulder) is a fantastic idea for unclogging traffic without greatly inconveniencing people. It uses midsize buses operating frequently instead of infrequent runs by often-empty behemoths. The Hop's circuit has 40 stops, including Crossroads Mall, the University Hill shopping area near CU-Boulder, and the Pearl Street Mall. Buses drive both clockwise and counterclockwise on the circuit. The Hop runs every 10 minutes Monday through Friday, 7 a.m. to 7 p.m., and every 15 minutes Thursday and Friday, 7 to 10 p.m., Saturday, 9 a.m. to 10 p.m., and Sunday, 10 a.m. to 6 p.m. Night Hop runs a CU–Pearl Street Mall loop Thursday through Saturday from midnight to 3 a.m., free to CU students with ID and ECO-Pass holders. The fare is $1.50, 75 cents for seniors during off-peak hours, or free for folks with a CU ID or any RTD pass. Some merchants also give out Hop tokens to their customers, good for a complimentary ride.

The Hop has been so successful, the RTD Board of Directors has introduced smaller, brightly colored buses in other metropolitan areas. A similar service called The Skip debuted in August 1997. The 22-passenger buses operate every 10 minutes, running north-south on Broadway. The Jump shuttle recently began service on Arapahoe Avenue between Boulder and Erie. The Leap serves Pearl Street commuters, while The Bound, with its Superman-inspired graphics, travels a route along Boulder's 30th Street. Another shuttle, The Stampede, serves the university area, and the DASH connects Boulder to Lafayette and Louisville. The Bolt provides service between Boulder and Longmont.

One of the best ride services around is RTD's Call and Ride, www.rtd-denver.com/SpecialRides/call-n-Ride/index.html. Small green wheelchair-

i **RTD runs special buses to Rockies and Broncos games and many other big events. For information, call (303) 299-6000 or (800) 366-7433; (303) 299-6089 (TDD).**

accessible buses will pick you up at your front door and deliver you to where you need to go, whether it's to a medical appointment, to grocery shopping, or to a movie. Simply give them a call with one hour's notice. Trips can be scheduled up to two weeks in advance. The contact numbers vary by neighborhoods served, so it's best to go online for the phone number for the buses that serve your neighborhood. Rates are $1.75 for adults, and 85 cents for seniors, students, and disabled riders.

There are several options for getting to the ski resorts from Denver International Airport; go to the DIA Web site (http://flydenver.com), and click on the ground transportation link. A variety of the airport shuttle services, most of which must be booked in advance, offer varying price options depending on how many people occupy the shuttle. Options from Boulder are limited. Coloradans generally drive their own vehicles and most visitors rent vehicles. Certain shuttle services will come to Boulder.

Need a taxi to a destination other than a ski resort? Boulder Yellow Cab (303-777-7777, www.yellowtrans.com) can pick up in Lafayette and Louisville as well as Boulder. Boulder Freedom Cabs (303-444-4444, www.freedomcabs.com) is another local taxi service. There are no taxi stands for either company, so call for service. Town and Country Taxi (303-776-0496) serves Longmont.

For people with disabilities, life would be even more challenging without wheelchair-lift-equipped, door-to-door, on-demand transportation service. More than 2,000 people use Boulder's Special Transit (303-447-9636, www.specialtransit.org), which offers low-cost rides to people with disabilities. Call well in advance for reservations and prices.

HISTORY

On a high, hot, and arid Boulder summer day, it may be comforting to remember that a mere 70 million years ago, this was beachfront property. For hundreds of millions of years, inland seas rose and receded in central Colorado, pushed around by the emerging Rocky Mountains. When the mountains became the unquestioned victor, the ocean drained away east and west, leaving the western edge of an endless high prairie pressing against an abrupt wall of mountain where the region's history is written in rock.

For far longer than humans have recorded, plants and animals lived, fed, were fed upon, reproduced, and adapted to the complex ecosystem of the high plains, the mountains, and the wetlands. In the areas where they've been left to it, the cycles continue.

The increasingly frantic scribbling of human settlement on that big canvas may now seem to dominate the landscape, but the mountains and the prairies remember where they came from.

FIRST HUMANS

The first humans passed through Colorado about 10,000 years ago, on foot and armed with stone-tipped spears. They are believed to have descended from Asians who migrated over the Bering Land Bridge 10,000 years earlier. University of Denver scientists found the first signs of human activity in North America near the New Mexico–Colorado border. The Ice Age Folsom man, named for the nearby New Mexican town, was unearthed in 1924. Such early "Westerners" hunted mastodons, woolly mammoths, and giant sloths.

Colorado's first-known settlements were those of the Anasazi in southwestern Colorado's Four Corners area around a.d. 550. The Anasazi are known for their basketry and distinctive pottery, but most of all for Mesa Verde, the spectacular cliff-side dwellings they built and inhabited around a.d. 1150. It's not known why the Anasazi abandoned their cliff dwellings around 1300 and disappeared, but researchers suspect they overfarmed the thin prairie soil and a great drought forced the tribe to migrate to literally greener pastures in the Rio Grande Valley to the south. Today's Acoma, Sandia, Taos, Zuni, and other Pueblo peoples are believed to be descendants of the Anasazi.

During the 16th and 17th centuries, Colorado was home to several tribes descended from the Shoshone and Algonquins. The Utes were Shoshonean mountain-dwellers. Plains tribes included the Cheyenne, Comanche, Arapaho, and Kiowa. Other tribes in the area were the Pawnee, Sioux, Navajo, Blackfoot, and Crow.

American Indians throughout the Southwest visited Colorado for such things as clay for their pottery, fossil seashells for their medicine men's magic, and turquoise for adornment. Bands of Cheyenne and Arapaho traveled to the Boulder Valley regularly to collect flint for arrowheads and colorful clays for war paint.

By the mid-19th century, the Comanche and Kiowa had been driven out of the Boulder Valley by the Cheyenne and Arapaho, who came originally from the Minnesota–Great Lakes area, where they, in turn, had been driven west by the Sioux. The Arapaho wintered here because the game was plentiful and the winters mild. They also enjoyed and venerated the warm thermal waters at Eldorado Springs. The Utes, the oldest continuous residents of Colorado, still lived in the mountains above the Boulder Valley and ranged west to the Salt Lake Basin, lending their name to the state of Utah.

FIRST EUROPEANS AND PIONEERS

Gold brought the first European explorers to the area. Perhaps the first to venture into Colorado was Francisco Vásquez de Coronado, who arrived in New Mexico in 1541 searching for the mythical Seven Gold Cities of Cibola.

During the 17th and 18th centuries, both the French and Spanish alternately claimed the territory that included all present states on the Mississippi River plus Montana, Wyoming, the Dakotas, and part of Colorado. For a while the territory was called Louisiana after King Louis XIV of France; it became New Spain when the Spanish defeated the French in the French and Indian War in 1762. In 1800 Napoleon gave the Spanish an Italian kingdom for the territory, reclaiming it again for France.

American adventurer James Purcell of Kentucky explored the area in the early 1800s, before it became U.S. territory, and found gold along the Platte River. Then, in 1803, President Thomas Jefferson paid $15 million to France for some 830,000 square miles of the region in the famous Louisiana Purchase, doubling the size of the United States. At the time, Jefferson was maligned for squandering money on questionable, unexplored land.

U.S. Army Lt. Zebulon Pike and Maj. Stephen Long were commissioned to explore the territory, and later, John Fremont came looking for a route across the Rockies. One of Fremont's men, William Gilpin—later to become the first governor of the Colorado Territory—reported that gold could probably be found in the area, stirring some initial interest in what was then considered "the Great American Desert . . . totally unfit for cultivation and, of course, uninhabitable by a people depending upon agriculture for their subsistence," according to Long.

A wave of loners—fur traders, trappers, and mountain men—followed the explorers, establishing trading posts in the Arkansas and South Platte Valleys, including Bent's Fort, one of the most important trading posts in the West.

Mexico, hoping to win friends and maintain its claims in the territory, ceded land to wealthy settlers in the 1840s but abandoned its claims after the Mexican-American war.

In 1836 Texas, enjoying brief status as an independent republic, also claimed a strip of Colorado extending northward to the 42nd parallel. The federal government bought out the Texas claim in 1850, but Texans have been recapturing the territory ski condo by ski condo ever since.

Colorado's first permanent non-Native settlement was established in 1851. Determined farmers began irrigating the arid plains under the increasingly concerned watch of area Natives, who realized that the influx of newcomers was not abating.

THE GOLD RUSH

The next gush of settlers came in 1858, after gold was discovered in the sands of the South Platte River near present-day Denver. Prospectors worked their way north, panning Cherry Creek (Denver), Clear Creek (Golden), Boulder Creek, and others. As these lower "placer deposits" of gold were eventually mined out, prospectors and miners followed the creeks up into the mountains, sometimes finding the "mother lode" in such places as Central City and Black Hawk, then went even higher to Breckenridge, Gold Hill (above Boulder), Empire, Aspen, Leadville, and Cripple Creek. Along with gold, they would also find silver, iron, tungsten, molybdenum, and on the plains, oil and coal. Among the most notable beneficiaries of the mountains' largesse were the unsinkable *Titanic* passenger Molly Brown and "Baby Doe" Tabor, who became a wealthy socialite, thanks to her mine above Leadville. (Unfortunately she later froze to death there, penniless and alone.)

The arrival of the miners encouraged a rash of organization in the region. On the present site of Denver, towns named Montana City, St. Charles, Auraria, and Denver City were founded. The first stagecoach carried mail to Cherry Creek settlements in 1859. The region's first newspaper, the *Rocky Mountain News,* published its first edition on April 23, 1859. Bypassing Congressional approval, settlers organized the Jefferson Territory to govern the gold camps

FIRST BOULDER SETTLEMENT

In 1858, Capt. Thomas Aikins, a Missouri farmer, led a gold-prospecting group of farmers and merchants to the area. From Fort St. Vrain to the northeast, he peered through his telescope and saw "bands of Indian Ponies and bands of deer and antelope grazing close up to the high foothills; . . . and could see that [it] was the loveliest of all the valleys . . . a landscape exceedingly beautiful, those mountains are so high and steep . . ." (There's some debate about what Aikins actually viewed through his telescope; the Boulder Valley cannot be seen from Fort St. Vrain because of the topography. There's also "first settler" John Rothrock, about whom less is known.)

In October or November, Aikins and party camped near the mouth of Boulder Canyon beneath the jagged vertical red rocks—an area now designated as Settlers Park. According to Aikins, before they had bedded down for the night, Chief Niwot of the Arapaho paid a visit, encouraging the company to move along and commenting prophetically, "Go away; you come to kill our game, to burn our wood, and to destroy our grass." But the miners fed and flattered the tall, handsome Niwot (whose name means Left Hand), and he eventually agreed to coexist in peace.

Boulderites love to tell newcomers the story of another of the chief's comments, which became known as Niwot's Curse. Popular legend has it that Niwot warned the white settlers that they would never be able to leave the Boulder Valley. The number of students who make their lives in Boulder after graduation, the profession-

als who return after retirement, and the vacationers who come back year after year seem to prove the legend true. What Niwot actually said, however, was, "Boulder Valley is so beautiful that people will want to stay and their staying will be the undoing of the beauty"—a prediction that Boulder policymakers and citizens have been working hard to disprove.

In January 1859, the Aikins party found gold in a small creek bed between Sunshine and Four Mile canyons. Word got out and within a month there were 2,000 men and 17 women in the Boulder area.

TOWN DEVELOPMENT

Winter closed in, making mining difficult and causing many miners to leave. In February, Aikins called a meeting to form a "Town Company." Later that month, A.A. Brookfield became the first president of the Boulder City Town Company, and 56 shareholders divided 1,280 acres along Boulder Creek into 4,044 lots. Each shareholder received 18 lots; a few lots were given for free to those who promised to provide such services as sawmills. The remaining lots were for sale at $1,000 each. Other homesteading lands at the time cost $1.25 an acre, so the Boulder lots weren't hot sellers, and further settlement was quite slow. Other camps and settlements in the area grew much faster.

Boulder, named after the area's plentiful rocks, began as a raw frontier settlement of tents and crude log cabins along the creek. Roofs and doors were made of split pine, and the floors were dirt.

True to its later identity as a seat of education, Boulder built the territory's first schoolhouse in 1860, at the southwest corner of Walnut and 15th Streets. The first Boulder Post Office was established that same year. Originally part of the Nebraska and Kansas Territories, Boulder became part of Colorado when Congress established the Colorado Territory in 1861. South of present-day Baseline Road—the 40th parallel—was the Kansas Territory; north was the Nebraska Territory.

i **Why does Boulder, which is nowhere near the ocean, have a Marine Street? It was named for Marinus Smith, one of Boulder's first citizens and a local farmer.**

In 1867, Boulder became the county seat, and the town was incorporated in 1871. Unlike the region's boom-and-bust mining towns, Boulder's economy remained stable because the city functioned mainly as a supply and transportation center for the miners and prospectors—and, later, as a hub for plains farmers. Boulder's population from 1860 to 1870 remained at about 350.

Boulder's first newspaper, the *Boulder Valley News,* began publication in April 1867. Telegraph service was established in 1874. The town's first hospital was built in 1873 and the first bank a year later.

LAND GRABS AND THE SAND CREEK MASSACRE

The technicalities of stealing the land from the Native Americans were set forth in the Pre-emption Law of 1841, which stated that a person had prior right to purchase a piece of land if he occupied it and improved it. The Kansas-Nebraska Act of 1853, which referred to preemption of "the public lands to which the Indian title had been at the time of such settlement extinguished," further assisted settlers in laying claim to the area. In 1866 Congress validated various settlers' claims to these lands.

Land "ownership" and "improvement" were not understood in the American Indian culture as they were by Europeans. If anything, the American Indians believed the land owned them and didn't need any "improving." The result was a classic clash of cultures, East versus West—living in harmony with nature versus controlling it. In the 1850s and 1860s, the clash became more and more violent. Natives attacked caravans of supplies, sending the cost of food soaring. Forts were built around the state to shelter settlers and house troops brought in to fight the Indians.

In the summer of 1864, reports of Natives attacking some wagon trains and express wagons led to the creation of the "100 Day Volunteers," a group commissioned under Capt. David Nichols, along with other citizens. Friends of Chief Left Hand (Niwot) in Boulder refused to take part in this brigade, which found and attacked peaceful American Indian families camped, in accordance with treaties, at Sand Creek in eastern Colorado. Thinking the attack was a mistake, the besieged Indians raised the American flag, but were ruthlessly massacred nonetheless. Women and children were scalped, and gentle Chief Niwot, who met with the first settlers, was killed.

BOLD MINERS, BLIZZARDS, BOOM, AND BUST

The original gold deposit that fueled Boulder's early economy was depleted after about a year. Next, silver from mines in Caribou, west of Boulder and almost twice as high, stimulated Boulder's growth.

Four miles from the Continental Divide at 10,500 feet, life was cold and tough at Caribou, but in the early 1870s the lure of silver had drawn nearly 500 residents, who built houses two stories high so they could find them in the 25-foot-high snow drifts that followed winter storms. The second story also allowed citizens to come and go through their bedroom windows in the deep snow. A rope ran from the mine to the town's center so miners could feel their way home in blizzards. When asked about Caribou's winters, one miner remarked that he did not know how long winter lasted, because he had been there only three years. Perhaps mercifully, Caribou was eventually destroyed by fire, diphtheria, scarlet fever, and the mining bust over the next few decades.

Mines popped up all over the area: Sunshine, Salina, and Magnolia—today the names of a local canyon, town site, and road. Many booming mountain mining towns, such as Ward, soon went bust when the gold ran out. A smelter built at Black Hawk in 1868 renewed interest in deeper mining in the area, because ores containing gold could be processed. A few years later, a gold-silver ore was found at Gold Hill, and during 1892, the peak year, more than $1 million in gold and silver was produced.

In 1900, ferberite, an ore of tungsten, was identified in Nederland, starting a new rush to the area. (Nederland, meaning "low lands," was named by the Dutchmen who bought the higher Caribou mine.) By 1918, Boulder County had become the main producer of tungsten in the United States, with a total production of 24,000 tons of tungsten trioxide worth $23 million. By 1910, $20 million in silver had come from Caribou, but it finally ran out. "Caribou, like the reindeer it was named after, pawed its food—silver—from beneath the frozen snow. The lifeblood of its silver veins pinched out, and the town stumbled to a stop, and died," wrote historian John Buchanan.

TRAINS AND TRANSPORT

Trains were the lifeblood of the mining industry and early settlement of the area. Railroad service connected Boulder with the bigger world in 1873, connecting the town to Denver and Golden and the mining camps to the west. A depot was built near Boulder Creek at 14th and Water Streets (now named Canyon Boulevard). One of the old trains now sits near the site, in Central Park, and the depot has been preserved in a commercial area at 30th and Pearl Streets, although the narrow-gauge tracks are long gone.

By 1883 Union Pacific Railroad had 14 miles of narrow-gauge track to Four Mile, Salina, Wallstreet, Sunset, and later, Ward. By 1904 the line went all the way to Eldora and was known as The Switzerland Trail. It became a popular tourist attraction that provided an additional source of revenue to the railroads. But the route had financial problems by 1909, and then-owners Colorado and Northwestern folded. The line continued to be operated by the reorganized Denver, Boulder and Northwestern Railroad, which spent the next 10 years debating whether to close The Switzerland Trail line. In 1919 a cloudburst washed out 2,500 feet of track, and the line was never rebuilt.

COLORADO'S FIRST SCHOOL AND THE UNIVERSITY

Boulder citizens lobbied fiercely to have the city chosen for the territorial (later, state) university. The same Capt. Nichols involved in the Sand Creek Massacre served as a horseback mediator, making an overnight ride from the capital in Denver to secure a pledge of local funds from Boulder businessmen and then back again in time to secure the university for Boulder. (In honor of that ride, a University of Colorado dormitory was named for Nichols. In the 1980s, in recognition of his involvement in the massacre, the dormitory was renamed Cheyenne-Arapaho Hall.)

Boulder's citizens donated 44.9 acres of land and money to match the $15,000 appropriated by the state legislature for construction of the university on a barren, windswept hill south of town.

Construction began in 1876, the same year Colorado became a state. Completed in 1877, Old Main, the university's first building, housed the entire university—a few classrooms along with living quarters for the president and janitor, and their families. With much ceremony the university opened its doors in September 1877 to 44 students, a president, and one instructor. The students lived with families in town and hiked daily up the hill to class.

When Mary Rippon of Detroit was invited to be CU's third faculty member, Ann Sewell, wife of first CU president Joseph A. Sewell, predicted that Rippon "would not stay two days in this lonely place." Rippon decided to come West and give it a try after reading about Colorado's wildflowers in the *Atlantic Monthly* and hearing that banker Charles Buckingham had donated $2,000 for a university library. She was a French and German professor for 57 years—the first woman in the United States to teach at a state university. She also helped open Boulder's first public library. CU's lovely outdoor theater, site of the Colorado Shakespeare Festival (see the Festivals and Annual Events chapter), is named for her.

To beautify CU's barren, windswept campus, Ann Sewell ordered 50 wagonloads of soil for landscaping purposes. The dirt promptly blew away with the first high wind, but she ordered another 50 wagonloads, and by 1881 the univer-

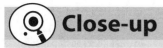 Close-up

The Industrial Mine Camp House

A few miles south of Boulder in Original Town Superior there is a recent addition to the rich historic fabric of the area. The Industrial Mine Camp House has come home, so to speak, and now the little structure is a museum and interpretive center for the town's coal mining history.

In 1943, as the demand for coal was declining, this house was moved away from Superior to the southwest corner of 144th and Zuni in Broomfield. It remained there until 2006 when it was donated back to the Town of Superior and moved to its new location, less than one mile from its original site.

To say it was meticulously rehabilitated is an understatement. Many design elements were missing from the structure that had to be replaced or fabricated based on historical specifications. For example, all walls were replastered using historic techniques, windows were replaced with replica glass, and exterior paint colors were matched to a historic 1930s photograph. Beaded board wainscoting was discovered on the west wall of the kitchen, so new wainscoting was milled and installed in the rest of the kitchen area to match. The scope of the work was extensive. The end result is charming.

Located in Asti Park, near the intersection of US 36 and McCaslin Blvd. in the Town of Superior, this small, four-room, 24-foot-square wood-frame building now brings the history of the area to life.

Around 1907 approximately 23 houses were built for the coal miners and their families. But between 1911 and 1914 during the notorious and violent "Long Strike," striking miners and their families were evicted from their homes and replaced by strikebreakers and their families. The strikers were "protected" from the local residents by a high wire fence, but in fact the miners, often recent immigrants from Europe who did not understand that they had come to America to be strikebreakers, were not able to leave the fenced area. After that strike and others in the 1920s, miners and their families moved back into the houses until the mine closed permanently in 1945.

The Industrial Mine Camp House originally was located south of Coal Creek in the Industrial Mine Camp. These days the only evidence of this mine, which produced the highest-grade coal in the Northern Colorado Coal Field, is the remaining foundations of the buildings. The site of the Industrial Mine is now located on Boulder County Open Space, and is visible from the Marshall Superior Coalton Trail network.

There are so many stories to be told of the difficult times and hard lives of coal mining families. If only the walls of the Industrial Mine House could speak! In a way, now they do.

—Contributed by Kathryn Howes Barth, AIA/Preservation Architect

sity had two acres of lawn with trees and flowers. The rest of the barren town took heart from Mrs. Sewell's persistence, and soon the grassland was dotted with young trees.

The first private school in Boulder, Mount St. Gertrude Academy, was opened in 1892 west of the university. Nuns and students reported falling asleep in the isolated building to the sound of coyotes howling.

SALOONS, RED LIGHTS, RELIGION, AND LAW

Meanwhile, Boulder began to take on the features of a permanent settlement. By 1872, various churches had been built: Presbyterian, Baptist, and Methodist-Episcopalian. Some citizens became concerned that the town's young men spent too much time in saloons and opened a reading room, where the men could come and peruse the newspapers while inspecting the genteel young ladies occasionally invited in as an inducement.

By the 1870s, Boulder residents had acquired money and real estate and needed a government and laws to protect their assets. In 1871, Capt. Aikins' son, Lafayette, was appointed town marshal and paid a salary of $72 a year. The only previous law enforcement was the mining district's "club rules," whereby a wrongdoer would have the hair shaved off half his face and head (opposite sides) and be expelled from town.

A stately county courthouse was built in 1883 at Pearl Street between 13th and 14th Streets. It burned to the ground in 1932, a fire that also destroyed many county records. The current courthouse was built on the same site in 1934. Liquor licenses costing $100 per saloon were established to raise some revenue for the fledgling town. Loose dogs were a big issue; in 1871 a dog-control program was initiated, along with a formal tree-planting program.

By 1875, local Republican, Democratic, and Prohibition parties had formed. Well-educated and feisty, Boulder's women started lobbying for the right to vote that year. In 1893 Colorado became the second state after Wyoming (then a territory) to grant women voting rights, although the motivation was more a desire to pack the polls over issues of advantage to Colorado than a recognition of women's equality.

Less-liberated women (or, perhaps, more—depending upon one's perspective) occupied a red-light district, which stretched from the north side of Boulder Creek at Canyon Boulevard (formerly Water Street) to the present-day library. Pearl Street, Boulder's original main street for commerce, was reportedly named for a well-respected madam. Prostitution and gambling were declared illegal in 1873, but the law was reversed in 1878. Some houses of "ill repute" closed down temporarily and others not at all, and the so-called "brides of the multitude" continued their business.

The increasing number of buildings and the fear of fire—a great danger with the high winds—finally brought about the construction of a waterworks in 1874 and the first hook-and-ladder company in 1875. Bucket brigades were the first means of firefighting. The first volunteer firemen were the cream of Boulder society and popular at firemen's balls, parades, and firefighting tournaments. So important and highly regarded were the firemen, the election of the firemen's officers drew more attention than city elections.

By the late 1870s, increased mining activity was bringing in more crime, and Boulder needed a jail. Prisoners had been kept everywhere from the basement of the fire department to the sheriff's hotel room.

Water also became an issue by the late 1870s, as the population increased and Boulder Creek became polluted with mine tailings. People who didn't have wells had to use the creek water. A reservoir had been built in 1874 at the base of Boulder Canyon, but it too had become increasingly polluted. In 1884 horses were found dead in the creek, and the reservoir was shut down. To avoid the mine-tailing runoff, a new reservoir was built at the mouth of Sunshine Canyon. The Boulder City Improvement Society formed in 1881. By 1882, Boulder's population had reached 3,000.

i History buff? Spend an afternoon at Boulder's Carnegie Branch Library for Local History, 1125 Pine Street. It's well worth the trip!

COAL, OIL, NEWSPAPERS, AND AN INTERNATIONAL POPULATION

In the late 1860s, there were 77 buildings in town. Local businesses included sawmills, a brickyard, several blacksmiths and general stores, stables, and liveries. Downtown Boulder had a wobbly boardwalk that rose and fell to a different height in front of each different shop—ripping ladies' skirts and gouging shoppers with loose nails.

The business of mining was expanding to other minerals. Coal was discovered east of Boulder on David Kerr's farm. Coal prospector Louis Nawatny bought nearby land, registered a town plat in 1878 and named it Louisville after himself. Two years later, 500 people had settled there. In 1887 a coal mine was dug in Lafayette (named for Lafayette Miller), and by 1892 there were five mines and 200 homes. Polish, Italian, Greek, and French immigrants joined the Welsh, Scotch, and English miners who had been here since the 1860s. By the 1920s the coal industry would be Boulder County's largest employer, with 1,000 men.

Oil was discovered in 1901 near Boulder, and for a while Boulder had its own oil stock exchange and a specialized newspaper, *Oil News*. Wells sprang up all over east of Boulder, and it was predicted that the oil field would stretch to Wyoming. By March 1902 there were 92 oil companies operating near today's Longmont Diagonal. Natural gas was also discovered along with the oil, but it was considered a nuisance. Ultimately, 183 holes were drilled in Boulder County, but only 81 were functioning. Of these, 76 produced oil; 5 produced gas.

The weekly *Camera* newspaper, so named because it printed photographs on its front page, became the *Daily Camera* in 1891 and still publishes today (see the Media chapter).

THE 100-YEAR FLOOD

Just when Boulder was getting its feet on the ground and becoming an established city with various amenities, disaster struck. The winter of 1894 was long, cold, and snowy. The heavy snowpack still plastered the Front Range at the end of May. Easterly winds brought a warm spring rain that lasted for 60 hours and melted the snow too quickly. The creeks began to rise in the early morning hours of May 31, soon unleashing an awesome display of nature's power.

"One seething mass of black water, bowlders [sic] and crushed buildings. Nearly every tree has been torn out by the roots and the road bed is entirely destroyed," read the *Daily Camera*, describing the scene at Left Hand Creek near Glendale.

Boulder was experiencing a 100-year flood—so called because there is only a 1 percent chance of such a devastating disaster occurring in any year.

All the mountain roads, bridges, rooming houses, and even mines broke apart on Four Mile Creek, Boulder Creek, Jim Creek, Left Hand Creek, and the St. Vrain. Buildings washed away at Sunset, Jamestown, Crisman, and Ballarat. Jamestown's church floated downstream with its bell ringing. The two-year-old boomtown of Copper Rock was washed off the map. The raging waters destroyed the road at Estes Park and a section of Lyons.

The flood roared down Boulder Creek into town, first wiping out the railroad bridge at Fourth Street, then the bridges on 6th, 9th, 12th, and 17th Streets—each piling up on the other in a maelstrom of boulders, buildings, railroad tracks, and trees. Witnesses recalled the terrifying sound of the rock- and wreckage-filled water. "From the Boulder Hotel to University Hill was one vast lake with here and there a small patch of an island," read the *Camera*. After the waters calmed, one resident caught a 7-inch trout on Water Street (now Canyon Boulevard).

For five days, Boulder was cut off from the outside world, and residents on one side of the creek couldn't get to the other side. CU commencement was postponed, and the first mail arrived after five days with news of flooding all over the Front Range. Afterward, miners were out of work because of flooded mines. Amazingly, no one was killed in the flood, and no crimes were committed except the ransacking of someone's trunk. Boulder cleaned up and rebuilt.

More than a hundred years later, the city has embarked on a campaign to gradually buy buildings in the Boulder Creek floodplain and clear a path for the inevitable next major flood. Pedestrian bridges across the creek are designed to break away and swing to the side so they don't become dams for flood debris. Canyon highways are marked with signs telling motorists to abandon their cars and climb to higher ground in case of flood. In the spring and summer, alarms are tested weekly, reminding residents of the continuing possibility of flood.

TUBERCULARS, TOURISTS, AND TROLLEYS

As the 19th century came to an end, Boulder was beginning to draw visitors and newcomers other than miners. From its earliest days, Boulder, like other places in the Southwest, attracted people with tuberculosis who hoped the pure air, dry climate, and vigorous life would restore their health. One such transplant was gunman Doc Holliday, who eventually succumbed to his illness in Glenwood Springs on Colorado's Western Slope. Many eminent CU professors were recovered tuberculars.

In 1895 Seventh-Day Adventists built a sanitarium (later to become Boulder Memorial Hospital and now the Mapleton Rehab and Sports Medicine Center) for tuberculars on Boulder's west side.

Along with the tuberculars came a group of Texas professors in 1897 looking for an airy summer camp and retreat to escape the Texas heat. Boulder, by then accessible to visitors by railroad, was known as a community with a prosperous economy, a comprehensive educational system, and well-maintained residential neighborhoods. The Texans chose Boulder as a site for their proposed Chautauqua; the creation of these family summer camps, which emphasized culture, nature, recreation, and sometimes religion, was part of a respected national movement at the time. They were named after Lake Chautauqua, New York, site of the first such camp. The city bought its first park land and named it Texado Park for the Texans; it is now called Chautauqua Park. The dining hall and auditorium were completed for the grand opening of Colorado Chautauqua on July 4, 1898, and the first Chautauquans camped in tents, later replaced by cottages. A 1903 brochure described the camp as "not a casino," offering "retirement without loneliness," and "quiet without ennui."

Well-known Boulder photographer Joseph Bevier Sturtevant ("Rocky Mountain Joe")—who

i A 100-year flood is a disastrous flood with only a 1 percent chance of occurring in any one year.

produced many memorable photographs of the city's early years—was the official Chautauqua photographer. Chautauqua had a full and varied program, from music and art to political and ethical discussion groups and well-known speakers and performers such as William Jennings Bryan and John Philip Sousa. Operas, magic shows, displays of military tactics, lace-making demonstrations, baby shows, food booths, fish hatchery exhibits, photo contests, children's races, and gypsy camps were but a few of the offerings. Physical health and exercise were emphasized from the start, and the Chautauqua Climbers Club made annual hikes to local landmarks and the higher mountains. Boulder druggist Eben Fine, one of Chautauqua's regular climbers, literally stumbled upon the discovery of Arapaho Glacier in 1900 when he nearly fell into one of its crevasses.

The Switzerland Trail railroad was a popular excursion for Chautauquans, who would ride into the mountains for a picnic and snowball fight. The more adventurous rented handcars and pumped their own way up for a day's outing.

Transportation to and from Chautauqua was difficult, so for the camp's second season in 1899, the city inaugurated its first electric streetcar, which for a nickel "sped" visitors from downtown to the Chautauqua gate at 15 miles per hour. A few years later a line to the sanitarium was put in, and others followed.

The railroad brought more tourists to Eldorado Springs, south of Boulder, where a popular resort developed around the area's thermal springs. It attracted such rich or famous—or soon to be—visitors as young Dwight and Mamie Eisenhower (who honeymooned there), budding musician Glenn Miller (a CU student), actress Mary Pickford and her husband, actor Douglas Fairbanks Sr. (a Jamestown native), writer Damon Runyon, fighter Jack Dempsey, and gossip columnist Walter Winchell. From 1907 to 1948, Ivy

Baldwin performed his famous high-wire walk 600 feet across the canyon on a steel cable averaging 582 feet high. He made his last trip at age 82.

MORE PARKS AND CITY PLANNING

Chautauqua began Boulder's golden age of land and park acquisition. The day after the camp opened, the city bought the eastern slope of Flagstaff Mountain from the U.S. Government. Shortly after, the city purchased another 1,800 acres of Flagstaff Mountain west to Four Mile Creek and from Sunshine Canyon south to South Boulder Creek.

The Boulder Women's Club planted trees in town, and in 1907 a parks board became an official city department. Next, the city slowly acquired the land along Boulder Creek from the Colorado and Southern Railway. At the time, the parks board wanted a park along Boulder Creek stretching from the mouth of Boulder Canyon to the eastern edge of town. Central Park land was acquired in 1906, and steadily the town purchased more lots and parcels from the railroad. Citizens gave gifts of land. Dr. and Mrs. William J. Baird donated 160 acres of their Gregory Canyon holdings in 1911. Hanna Barker and other citizens gave parcels of land. Boulder bought Arapaho Glacier after a battle with U.S. Park Service, which wanted to add it to Rocky Mountain National Park.

A CITY VISION

In 1908, the Boulder City Improvement Association hired Frederick Law Olmsted Jr., who was Harvard-educated in the new field of landscape architecture. Olmsted's father had designed New York City's Central Park. The city asked Olmsted how he thought the city could be improved "to help make it increasingly convenient, agreeable and generally satisfactory as a place in which to live and work?"

Olmsted said Boulder should not arrange itself for the benefit of the tourists, "who hastily pass through . . . and often conducting themselves so as to interfere seriously with the com-

fort and welfare . . . of the permanent residents." Olmsted was suspicious of developers, saying they were usually from out of town. He said that dirty industry only denigrates a community, and to keep it out of Boulder.

On parks, he said, "As with the food we eat and the air we breathe, so the sights habitually before our eyes play an immense part of determining whether we feel cheerful, efficient and fit for life, or the contrary." He was concerned with the "mental and nervous condition of the people." Order was the goal, but "We aim at Order and hope for Beauty," he said.

He envisioned Boulder as a city of homes surrounded by small farms and gardens and advised preserving that feeling of "coziness and quiet attractiveness." He recommended underground wiring and making the Boulder Creek floodplain into a park—"the cheapest way of handling the flood problem." He said the sign of civilized society was the effectiveness of "police" powers to ensure good land use, and he recommended the city manager form of government. Boulderites liked what Olmsted said and, to a large extent, followed his advice.

SLOW GROWTH, SOBERING LEGISLATION, WAR, AND DEPRESSION

Apparently taking Olmsted's advice to heart, Boulder became notable for its lack of industry except for the necessities: sawmills, lumberyards, blacksmith shops, brickyards, flour mills, a brewing company, and a foundry. Before World War I, Boulder's biggest industry was Western Cutlery and Manufacturing Company. The CU student population had grown to 6,000, and small businesses began opening in the area around the university known as "The Hill."

By 1905, the economy was faltering, and Boulder counted heavily on tourism for city-sustaining income. What was needed, civic leaders decided, was a first-class hotel. Local business owners contributed to a fund to fill that need, and on December 30, 1908, the Hotel Boulderado invited Boulder to its grand opening. The hotel still welcomes a steady stream of visitors to downtown Boulder.

By 1908, Boulder's population was 10,000, including enough teetotalers to outlaw liquor 13 years before national Prohibition. Boulder remained "dry" from 1907 until 1967. During that period "liquor islands," where people could purchase packaged goods, grew up outside the city limits. (Not until 1969 did it become legal to serve liquor in a public establishment; the Catacombs Bar in the Hotel Boulderado was the first to do so.)

After World War I came the Great Depression. During the 1930s the Civilian Conservation Corps built and improved trails, made fire lanes in mountain parks, pulled out diseased trees, and rebuilt Flagstaff Road up Flagstaff Mountain, overlooking Boulder. They built the Sunrise Amphitheater on Flagstaff, a lodge on Green Mountain, and a rock garden at Chautauqua. The Works Progress Administration built the Mary Rippon Outdoor Theater at the university, a golf course at Flatirons Country Club, and other buildings around town.

SMALL-TOWN AMERICA AND THE FABULOUS '50S

To try to raise Depression-weary spirits, the Boulder Pow Wow was begun on August 1, 1934, to celebrate Colorado's statehood day with a rodeo and various contests, including pie-eating and greased-pole climbing. Ladies had rolling pin and slipper-throwing contests and needle-threading relays. Men tested their strength and skills at hay-pitching, hog-calling, and hard-rock drilling.

In 1937, Boulder High was dedicated, and its "modern" nude sculptures entitled *Strength* and *Wisdom* caused a brief but heated controversy. The stunted, muscular figures were called everything from "powerful and effective" to "wads of chewing gum," but were finally accepted as harmless and have since been nicknamed Minnie and Jake.

By 1945 Boulder was beginning to wake up after the Depression and war. During World War II, 4,077 Boulderites went to war and 77 were killed. The CU campus became a training center for young officers, and their pre-dawn fitness runs were cheered on by coeds from the dormitory windows.

In 1946, the city installed 340 parking meters downtown, and a group of young CU graduates founded Arapahoe Chemicals (bought by Syntex in 1965). Chicago-based *Esquire* magazine moved its subscription operations to Boulder in 1949, the first "Eastern" business to relocate here. In 1950 the National Bureau of Standards (NBS) chose Boulder as its main base after considering 26 cities. Boulder's citizens voted to buy 217 acres of land for the bureau and gave it to the United States. Fifteen years later, NBS was a major employer. Initially at an isolated site south of town, NBS was soon surrounded by small ranch houses in a regular suburbia.

The Boulder-Denver Turnpike (U.S. Highway 36) opened in 1952 and was the first toll road in the nation to pay for itself—13 years ahead of schedule in 1967.

CU's enrollment increased after World War II as returning military personnel took advantage of the GI Bill. In 1947, someone named "Joe" autographed the northernmost Flatiron formation and began a series of Flatiron-painting pranks, usually by university students who painted a giant "C" or "CU" on the First and Third Flatirons. (Look closely at the Third Flatiron and you can still see a faint, slightly orange CU.)

In 1948, an 850-foot ski tow ran up the Chautauqua meadow, but it operated only for a few seasons due to poor snow.

Industry continued migrating to the area. The Atomic Energy Commission chose an area south of Boulder to install its secret weapons plant, Rocky Flats, in 1951—despite many misgivings of area residents. In 1955, "Tommy" Thompson of Thompson Engineering Co.—builder of the short-lived Chautauqua ski lift—began building respirators for polio victims. Soon after, Automation Industries moved to town. That same year, Beech Aircraft bought 1,500 acres north of Boulder and started its Aerospace Division there.

The chamber of commerce bought 18 acres east of town for Boulder Industrial Park, and

Ball Brothers Research Corp. became the major tenant starting in 1957. The Muncie, Indiana, canning-jar company expanded into aerospace technology in Boulder and helped design the Hubble telescope.

With all the new enterprise, Boulder's population shot up in the 1950s, and water became a concern. The population in 1950 was 19,999; by 1960 it was 66,870. In 1959 the Blue Line was established as the first project of the newly formed PLAN-Boulder, an early group of environmentally concerned citizens who wanted to preserve Boulder's unique natural assets. An imaginary boundary line was drawn along the mountain backdrop at an average of 5,750 feet, above which no city water service would be supplied.

THE EARLY 1960S

In 1940, a young solar physicist named Walter Orr Roberts began manning the Harvard-run High Altitude Observatory in Climax, Colorado (near Leadville). Twenty years later, Roberts was offered the directorship of a new National Center for Atmospheric Research (NCAR), and he recommended Boulder as the site. The state donated 530 acres of mesa land south of town for the new laboratory, which was designed by noted architect I. M. Pei. Though controversial at the time, an exception was made to the new Blue Line ruling to give NCAR water. NCAR was to become a jewel in Boulder's crown, and a setting for Woody Allen's futuristic comedy, *Sleeper*.

The U.S. Department of Commerce established its Environmental Sciences Service Administration (ESSA) in Boulder in 1966. ESSA became part of the National Oceanic and Atmospheric Administration (NOAA) in 1970.

Shopping centers began springing up around town during this period, and the Crossroads Shopping Center opened in 1963 outside the city limits, funded by Texas money.

Boulder's water supplies were increased in 1964, which spurred a controlled-growth plan along several "spokes" radiating outward from the city: one east on Arapahoe, one northeast

along the Diagonal Highway, and one south. In 1969, there were controversial referendums concerning fluoridation of water, a bond issue for a new library, and an amendment that would allow the sale of liquor-by-the-drink. All three passed. Though citizens rejected a $500,000 parks bond that same year, two years later they passed a $1 million bond to build the north and south recreation centers.

Historically, both liberals and conservatives have agreed on greenbelt acquisition, supporting the continued purchase of land in the mountains and plains to "belt" the city with undeveloped land. To stop the building of a luxury hotel atop Enchanted Mesa, citizens approved the purchase of 155 acres of that land for $105,000.

In 1967, Boulder citizens made history by becoming the first in the country to vote to tax themselves for open-space purchases. The initial 0.6-cent sales tax has provided for purchases totaling $140 million, and the 30,000 acres of open space have been merged with the 7,000 acres of mountain parks land to provide a true greenbelt around the city.

THE TURBULENT LATE '60S AND EARLY '70S

The late '60s brought the hippies, the "transient problem," and general turmoil to Boulder. The first gentle flower children camped out in Central Park, which had to be closed because it became a health hazard. Later came the more militant anarchists, whose bombs exploded in the Hall of Justice Building, United Bank, and Flatirons Elementary School. The Board of Education's auditorium was firebombed. Fortunately, no one was killed in these incidents. Riots in 1971 on University Hill left stores looted and windows broken. Police teargassed the mob and arrested 40 people. In 1972, 3,000 anti-war demonstrators barricaded the Boulder Turnpike at the Baseline interchange to protest President Nixon's blockade of North Vietnam and the mining of Haiphong Harbor. Also during this time, politically active Mexican-Americans were seeking to assert their identity and demand equal treatment, recognition, and respect. In 1974, six activists in the Chicano movement were killed in two separate bomb explosions in cars, one at Chautauqua Park and the other in front of a business on 28th Street. The explosions were believed by police to be accidental and meant for some other target.

More quietly, the first gay human rights ordinance law was passed by City Council in 1973, but when it had its second reading some citizens objected vociferously. Mayor Penfield Tate and Councilman Tim Fuller, the most outspoken supporters, received death threats, and Tate, a dignified heterosexual black man, was dubbed "The African Queen" by detractors. Fuller was recalled from office and Tate barely kept his seat. The ordinance was overturned by voters. (Boulder voters later approved a gay rights ordinance and were overwhelmingly opposed to the state constitutional amendment that would have prevented protection for gays.)

During this period new County Clerk and Recorder Clela Rorex attained notoriety after issuing licenses for several same-sex marriages. To express his opinion, one citizen appeared with his horse, Dolly, saying, "If a boy can marry a boy, and a girl can marry a girl, why can't a lonesome old cowboy get hitched to his favorite saddle mare?" He was refused because the horse was under age. Ultimately, same-sex marriage licenses were declared illegal in 1975 by the state attorney general.

PLAN-Boulder County helped write part of Boulder's first Comprehensive Plan in 1970. In 1971 a height-limit ordinance was passed so that, in the wave of new construction, residents could keep their mountain views. New buildings could not exceed a height of 55 feet—the height of most mature trees. Voters that year also chose a growth-control study plan to prevent the kind of rapid growth that had occurred in the 1950s.

THE "NEW WAVE" PLUS GROWTH AND LIMITATIONS IN THE '70S AND '80S

The late '70s saw calmer times but also a huge influx of newcomers, particularly from the North-

east, as many young adults tired of life in the drab, polluted, often politically corrupt and overcrowded big cities. Most were well educated and hopeful of finding jobs in one of Boulder's clean industries. Many had visited the area during vacations and were delighted (or requested) to be transferred here by IBM or Ball Aerospace. Many were single parents starting new lives and seeking gold of another sort: good schools and neighborhoods for their children and a happy life.

By word of mouth and the "underground" communications network, Boulder had also become known nationwide to neo-Buddhists, bicyclists, runners, the urban disenchanted, spiritual seekers, health food converts, and just about every New Age religion as a great place to live. And it's no wonder. Boulderite Frank Shorter became the first American ever to win Olympic gold and silver in the marathon (1972 and 1976); Celestial Seasonings founder Mo Siegel began the international Red Zinger Bicycle Classic through Boulder streets and surrounding country roads; Tibetan Buddhist leader Chögyam Trungpa Rinpoche founded the Naropa Institute in 1974; and the Boulder School of Massage Therapy opened its doors in 1976.

Meanwhile, fearful of urban sprawl and uncontrolled shopping center construction, PLAN-Boulder County campaigned in the late '70s for preservation of open space throughout the county. In 1976, almost $2 million was spent to complete Boulder's downtown pedestrian mall on Pearl Street to draw people back into the city's center. In 1977, the Danish Plan—originated by City Councilman Paul Danish—was approved to limit residential growth to 2 percent annually. To discourage the building of a megamall in Louisville (which Danish described as an "environmental pig"), City Council approved a controversial expansion of Crossroads Shopping Center (within the Boulder city limits and now redeveloped and called 29th Street) in 1979.

When a California-based computer software company, System Development Corporation, announced its plans in 1980 to locate on a plateau at the city's southern entrance, on county land

Close-up

Good Books on Colorado

GEOLOGY
Prairie Peak and Plateau by John and Halka Chronic
Roadside Geology of Colorado by Halka Chronic

HISTORY AND GOOD READING
A Colorado History by Carl Ubbelohde, Maxine Benson, and Duane A. Smith
A Lady's Life in the Rocky Mountains by Isabella Bird
A Look at Boulder: From Settlement to City by Phyllis Smith
Stampede to Timberline by Muriel Sibell Wolle (stories and legends of Colorado's gold camps)

OTHER REFERENCE WORKS
The Coloradans by Robert Athern
The Colorado Guide by Bruce Caughey and Dean Winstanley
Colorado Handbook by Stephen Metzger
Colorado: Off the Beaten Path by Eric Lindberg
Glory Colorado! by William Davis (University of Colorado history, 1853–1963)
Our Own Generation by Ron James (CU-Boulder history, 1963–1976)

designated as open space by the Boulder Valley Comprehensive Plan, city officials nixed it and ultimately decided to buy the land to put the issue on hold until Boulder residents could vote on it. SDC packed up its plans and left Boulder County.

During the 1980s some of Boulder County's plentiful high-tech industries began to falter. Louisville-based Storage Technology Corporation laid off 1,300 people in October 1984, the largest single-day cutback in county history. By the end of the year, it had trimmed another 1,290 employees and filed for reorganization under federal bankruptcy law. The ripple effect was felt throughout the county's economy.

The late 1980s brought changes affecting Boulder's runners and readers. The Boulder Creek Path, which runs from Eben Fine Park at the mouth of Boulder Canyon east to 55th Street, was completed in 1987 and remains one of the most popular walking, biking, and in-line skating avenues in town. After bitter debate in 1988,

Boulder voters approved expansion of Boulder's public library at its current site, a beautiful setting next to Boulder Creek and in the path of a major flood.

An actual natural disaster—the largest fire in the county—burned 2,300 acres and destroyed 44 homes in July 1989 on Sugarloaf Mountain. The fire was believed to have been caused by careless campers, but the cause was never definitely identified.

In 1989, federal agents raided Rocky Flats nuclear weapons plant (8 miles south of Boulder) and brought health and safety questions about the plant to local and national attention, much to the satisfaction of activists who targeted the plant with anti-nuclear demonstrations for many years.

SHUTDOWNS, THE 1990S

By 1991, in the warm glow of glasnost and following several massive demonstrations, the beginning of the end had come for Rocky Flats. The U.S. Energy Secretary eliminated 1,000 jobs in non-radioactive work at the plant and revealed plans to move the whole operation to Kansas City. Many of the plant's employees accepted the government's offer to retrain them at local colleges for new careers.

Later, Rocky Flats operators pleaded guilty to 10 environmental crimes after more than two years' investigation by a grand jury, and the nuclear plant's official work was ended in mid-1992. The building and site are still being decontaminated, and officials are still trying to figure out what to do with it all. In mid-December 1993, a Denver district judge ruled the controversial Amendment 2 unconstitutional, and in 1996 the U.S. Supreme Court did the same.

Also around this time, neighbors of the National Institute of Standards and Technology (NIST, formerly the Bureau of Standards) were upset with the government facility's plans to expand on 205 acres they had come to think of as permanent open space. After intensive wrangling, the building was built, but in somewhat modified form to reduce its impact on the view of the mountain backdrop.

In February 1993, the Boulder City Council stunned developers by imposing a building moratorium; the council decided it needed time to develop the Integrated Planning Project to determine "what's best for what's left" of developable land in Boulder. County commissioners also initiated a moratorium on mountain building. In September of that year the City Council put a hold on developing large parcels—the so-called last 10 percent of developable land—and firmly established a population-growth cap of 2 percent a year by imposing a limit on the number of building permits issued.

In the same spirit, in 1993, Boulder County voters passed a .25 percent sales and use tax to buy open space, which could amount to as much as $90 million in the next 16 years. The county's first purchase with the funds was the 5,000-acre Heil Ranch in the Foothills between Left Hand Canyon and Lyons.

Several corporations moved into town in the 1990s. Schwinn Cycling and Fitness arrived in Boulder hoping "to update its stodgy image with a Boulder address and new attitude," according to the *Daily Camera*. Warren Miller Entertainment, a California ski- and sports-movie maker, also put down roots in Boulder—the company already shoots most of its ski footage in Colorado. Two new subsidiaries of IBM set up shop. Centrobe, formerly Neodata, the world's largest magazine subscription fulfillment service (located in Boulder since 1963), moved its corporate headquarters from Dallas to Louisville (Boulder County) in 1993.

Stock in Celestial Seasonings, another local company, sold like hotcakes when 2.1 million shares went on the block in July 1994. Local investors complained that large investors snapped up all the shares before locals had a chance.

In 1995, scientists at the University of Colorado and National Institute of Standards and Technology created a form of matter never before seen but predicted by Albert Einstein more than 70 years ago. Called a superatom, the matter was created by cooling rubidium atoms to within a fraction of a degree above absolute zero, where theoretically all atomic motion ceases. The scientists created the coldest temperature on earth—and possibly the universe—for the experiment. Practical applications are not yet clear.

Later that year, Boulder voters made national headlines and created a local uproar by expanding the city's smoking ordinance to ban smoking in all indoor public places except dwellings, sites of private social functions, and tobacco stores. Some bars and restaurants have built fully enclosed, separately ventilated rooms for smokers. The Boulder Dinner Theatre had to get special dispensation so an actor could light up on stage, as called for in a play.

In the late 1990s Boulder's mostly reliable economy began to falter. The Crossroads Mall, a huge source of sales tax revenues, had seen better days. The Front Range was welcoming new malls, in particular Flatiron Crossing, featuring Nordstrom, Pottery Barn, and Crate and Barrel, plus dozens of high-end clothing shops. Boulder shoppers remained loyal for a short time, avoiding the drive to Bloomfield, but soon the temptation was too much and shoppers fled along with the Crossroads merchants. But 2006 brought new economic life to the city with the opening of the 29th Street Shopping District where Crossroads once stood. Shoppers spend their dollars locally now in a variety of stores such as Apple, Origins, and Borders, with Macy's and Home Depot acting as anchors. Many new restaurants also grace 29th Street, giving Boulderites many more dining options than ever before. The local economy is slowly but surely making a comeback.

Before the true impact hit, however, the downtown mall got a facelift, three new large-scale business buildings were approved, and a new hotel, only the second downtown, broke ground. A yearlong road improvement project was started on Broadway, and north Boulder was given the nod for hundreds of new affordable homes. Boulder Community Hospital began building an east campus facility, and the North Boulder Recreation Center was given a badly needed overhaul. Local developers added not only hundreds of new urban housing units around town, but provided a face-lift for many locations on Pearl Street, just east of the mall. The housing market dropped only slightly, and the influx of new residents continued. True, Boulder has suffered for a lack of spending money, but less so than many cities in Colorado or other parts of the country.

BOULD-LY INTO THE FUTURE

Its destiny dictated by geology—gold, silver, and other minerals—Boulder still attracts contemporary settlers because of its spectacular mountain setting. Though settled by miners, farmers, and fortune seekers, Boulder somehow identified the importance of education, environmental preservation, and quality of life from its earliest days. Holding onto these values, the city has nurtured a major university, internationally known research centers, clean industries, and an interesting assortment of citizens who have come from around the country and the world. Boulder has seen many changes from its rustic and humble beginnings, but then again, the more things change, the more they remain the same.

Boulder leaders today continue to deal with the same issues as the town's founders: dog control, water, the price of land and housing, and what to do with all those newcomers "looking for gold."

Coyotes still howl, soaring raptors still dive onto plump prairie dogs, streams still gush dangerously with spring snowmelt and subside to drowsy trickles in the heat of summer through carefully preserved open land. Beneath a growing sea of houses and highways, the prairie still stretches to the horizon and beneath the shush of racing skis, the mountains remember where they came from.

RESTAURANTS

oulder has earned a nationwide reputation for fine dining. In fact, many of the "best restaurants of Denver" lists include a fair number of Boulder restaurants. Good spots abound
in the Pearl Street Mall area, but stupendous possibilities also exist in other shopping areas,
the mountains, and plains. This chapter is organized by type of restaurant rather than by geo-
graphic region, since they're all within an easy drive of Boulder.

You could enjoy a different Boulder eatery every day and not repeat for weeks. Boulder has
a stunning variety, from rollicking party places to quiet and intimate restaurants perfect for
conversation or romance. Basic food, served fast, suits some people, especially families. Others
prefer meals custom-prepared, and some folks like to linger over a gourmet meal.

In addition to your taste buds, you need to consider your budget. Our price-code key uses
dollar signs to give the range for the likely cost of dinner for two, not including cocktails, beer
or wine, appetizer, dessert, tax, and tip. Please remember that these symbols provide only a
general guide.

If you live in Boulder you've become accustomed to smoke-free dining. If you're new or
visiting, Boulder's rigid no-smoking regulations might come as a shock. With our 300+ days of
sunshine a year, you'll find it easy to light up outside. But be prepared to have someone tell you
that it's bad for you…in a caring way, of course.

Wheelchair accessibility is common, but it makes sense to call ahead. And if a restaurant
sounds elegant, eclectic, or spicy, you can bet your booster chairs that your kids will get a
fidget attack unless the place also caters to children—or unless your children are used to finer
dining than the usual pizza and burger joints that parents often choose in the name of family
dining. Many places have special children's menus and entertainment tricks for the kids, so
ask about them.

Unless otherwise noted, these restaurants take Visa and MasterCard. Some also take American Express, Diner's Club, and Discover.

For more on takeout or informal food service, or lively nightspots, check our Shopping and
Nightlife chapters. Our Estes Park chapter includes details on dining and might provide you
with an excuse to explore this mountain town.

Price-Code Key

$..................less than $25
$$ .... $26 to $50
$$$ .... $51 to $75
$$$$ .... $76 and more

AMERICAN/ TRADITIONAL/ CASUAL

BJ'S RESTAURANT AND BREWERY $$
1125 Pearl Street, Boulder
(303) 402-9294
www.bjsbrewhouse.com
Enjoy a wide-ranging menu of pizza, giant stuffed
potatoes, garden fresh specialty salads, and AWE-

SOME burgers. For those of you who are connoisseurs of beer, the brewery strives to provide consistently good beer in a variety of ale and lager styles. BJ's is the recipient of many medals for its brewed beers.

THE BOULDER BROKER INN $$$
555 30th Street, Boulder
(303) 449-1752
www.boulderbrokerinn.com

The Victorian atmosphere, with dark wood and stained glass, is a perfect complement to entrees such as beef Wellington, Rocky Mountain trout, Alaskan king crab legs, and New York steak. A Broker trademark is the complimentary, bottomless bowl of peel-and-eat gulf shrimp served with a tangy sauce. Consistently voted "the best Sunday Brunch" in Boulder in area surveys, the Broker Inn features a different theme each Sunday. Reservations are recommended. There is nightly dancing at Bentley's. The inn is open for breakfast, lunch, and dinner daily.

BOULDER CHOPHOUSE AND TAVERN $$$
921 Walnut Street, Boulder
(303) 443-1188
www.chophouse.com

Located in the heart of downtown Boulder, the ChopHouse offers a wonderful array of delicious entrees ranging from filet mignon and porterhouse steaks to sesame salmon and herb-crusted rack of lamb. You absolutely must try their mashed potatoes! Daily menu items include vegetarian, fresh fish, and grilled choices. Open daily at 4 p.m.

BOULDER CORK $$
3295 30th Street, Boulder
(303) 443-9505
www.bouldercork.com

The Boulder Cork has provided excellent service and quality food for more than 30 years. The diverse menu features an enticing offering of steaks, fish, poultry, and pastas. *Wine Spectator* has recognized the Boulder Cork's wine list as one of the best in the nation, and it has received the

award for excellence for eight consecutive years. The strong presentation of all the meals makes it as popular for a business lunch as for a special dinner. You also can stop for a sip and a light bite at the bar; choices include angel-hair pasta, fresh steamed artichokes, fresh fish, and salads. The Cork is open seven days a week for dinner and weekdays for lunch.

CHAUTAUQUA DINING HALL $$
900 Baseline Road, Boulder
(303) 440-3776
www.chautauquadininghall.com

This historic 1898 dining hall has been serving summer visitors for more than 100 years in beautiful Chautauqua Park. Since 1997 the restaurant has featured the Rocky Mountain cooking of acclaimed chef Bradford Heap. The interior dining room was beautifully renovated in 1999. The vistas from the wraparound porch are breathtaking, and the overall experience has earned this gem "Best Outside Dining" awards. Fresh soups, salads made with organic Boulder County greens, lamb, griddle-seared ahi tuna, pan-roasted venison, fresh vegetables from local organic farmers, and dry-aged New York steak are just a few of the offerings. A children's menu and award-winning fresh fruit pies make this a memorable family dining experience. The Dining Hall's days and hours change with the seasons, so call ahead.

CORNER BAR $$
2115 13th Street, in the Hotel Boulderado
Boulder
(303) 442-4560
www.boulderado.com/dining

This is the ideal location for a quick lunch, a lively happy hour, a late-night meal, or a perfectly poured martini. One block off the Pearl Street Mall, the Corner Bar is less formal than Q's (also in the Hotel Boulderado), but features the same award-winning menu from chef-owner John Platt. Fresh salads, superb sandwiches, house-made pastas, and unique appetizers are served. Enjoy the intimate Corner Bar atmosphere, or savor the award-winning wine list, exceptional cuisine, and premium cigars under the stars on the heated patio. Open for lunch Monday through Friday, and dinner daily.

FOOLISH CRAIG'S CAFE $
1611 Pearl Street, Boulder
(303) 247-9383
www.foolishcraigs.com
Just 1 block east of the Pearl Street Mall, this eatery specializes in crepes and omelets. The "Amazing Homer" is a crepe wrapped around onions, Feta cheese, Greek spices, olives, artichokes, mushrooms, tomatoes, spinach, and sour cream. The caramelized three-onion soup is too good to miss. Everything is homemade, and the menu items are served throughout the day. Open for breakfast, lunch, and dinner daily.

i Boulder's grocery stores–including Ideal Market and Whole Foods–have dynamite delis for lunch-on-the-go.

THE FOUNDRY $$
1109 Walnut Street, Boulder
(303) 447-1803
www.foundryboulder.com
For many years the Foundry has been the best pool hall in Boulder, with a dozen billiard tables, a smoking lounge, and a bar that features live music on the weekend. With one of the finest views of the Flatirons from its rooftop deck, it was probably only a matter of time before patrons insisted on a full menu. Try the baked Brie or hummus for an appetizer, or for an entree there's the chicken Caesar wrap and assorted paninis. Open daily for lunch and dinner.

GOLD HILL INN $$$
Gold Hill
(303) 443-6461
www.goldhillinn.com
This family-owned restaurant has served six-course dinners in an old-style log inn since 1962. The menu depends on what chef Chris Finn deems good and fresh. One June day, the

offerings included hot and sour duck soup, a cold banana bisque, a salmon soufflé appetizer, venison with blackberry sauce, and a choice of chocolate torte or apricot-strawberry pie.

The inn opens in May, when the mountain snow flurries abate, and it closes at the end of December. During summertime, it's open for dinner all week except Tuesday. Reservations are recommended. It's a 20-minute drive into the mountains from Boulder, straight up Sunshine Canyon, and about an hour from Estes Park. No credit cards.

HUCKLEBERRY INN $$
700 Main Street, Louisville
(303) 666-8503
www.thehuckleberry.com
Located in Old Town Louisville, the Huckleberry is a combination of a restaurant, bakery, and tearoom. Enjoy the American classic food you love with a modern twist. Visit the Huckleberry for afternoon tea and enjoy tasty scones, small sandwiches, and other delectable treats. Open seven days a week for breakfast, lunch, and dinner. Reservations are required for afternoon tea.

ISLANDS FINE BURGERS AND DRINKS $
29th Street Mall, Boulder
(303) 449-0333
www.islandsrestaurants.com
This fun restaurant specializes in gourmet hamburgers with free fries, and specialty drinks with a tropical theme. It's located on the west side of 29th Street. Open Sunday through Thursday 11 a.m. until 9:30 p.m. and Friday and Saturday from 11 a.m. until 10:30 p.m.

JILL'S $$
St. Julien Hotel & Spa
900 Walnut Street, Boulder
(720) 406-9696
www.jillsdining.com
Opened in the spring of 2005, Jill's is a modern bistro located in Boulder's new St. Julien Hotel. Award-winning chef Jason Rogers runs the kitchen and delights patrons with his creations. The restaurant decor is warm with rich wood

tones and large glass panels studded with the leaves of Colorado. Jill's offers a metro American menu with Mediterranean influences. Dishes are prepared daily with fresh organically grown products, and there's a selection of more than 50 wines by the glass. Jill's serves breakfast, lunch, and dinner and manages to maintain a quality that attracts food-savvy locals as well as the most discriminating business and vacationing traveler.

JW'S STEAKHOUSE $$
2660 Canyon Boulevard, Boulder
(303) 440-8877
www.bouldermarriott.com
The restaurant at the Boulder Marriott in central Boulder has made steak the centerpiece of its menu. The roasted prime rib of beef is a 10- or 16-ounce cut and can be served with a Madeira-laced herb butter sauce. Or try the grilled chicken breast with roasted potatoes and papaya relish. An appetizer could be a meal by itself, with escargot, grilled shrimp in garlic butter, and crispy onion straws on the menu. Dessert can be accompanied by one of several espresso drinks, and a full bar and extensive wine list are available. Breakfast, lunch, and dinner are served daily.

MURPHY'S GRILL $
28th Street and Iris Avenue
Willow Springs Shopping Center, Boulder
(303) 449-4473
This has been a favorite neighborhood restaurant since 1985. The decor resembles an Irish pub, with dark wooden tables and old-fashioned golf club accents. The varied menu includes an assortment of Mexican dishes, burgers, sandwiches, and salads. Beef brisket is a featured specialty item. The walls are covered with nearly every "Murphy's Law" you've ever heard. Murphy's has a full bar and wine list and is open daily for lunch and dinner.

MUSTARD'S LAST STAND $
1719 Broadway, Boulder
(303) 444-5841
Chicago-style hot dogs, German bratwurst, hamburgers, and thick homestyle fries are served in this Boulder institution, and the place provides a funky view of Broadway. Okay, they've bowed to popular demand and added veggie dogs and tempeh burgers, but you don't have to eat them if you don't want to. The "best hot dogs" winner in all the local publications, Mustard's is open for lunch and dinner daily. You can also find a second Mustard's in Denver. No credit cards.

OMNI INTERLOCKEN RESORT/MERITAGE
RESTAURANT AND WINE BAR $$$
500 Interlocken Boulevard, Broomfield
(303) 464-3330
www.omni-interlocken-resort.visit denver.com
This is the place for innovative, unpretentious cuisine. Begin with an appetizer such as roasted portobello mushrooms, bacon-wrapped prawns, or jumbo lump-crab cakes. Move on to the entree, which could be peppercorn-seared salmon, mint-and-mushroom-crusted rack of lamb, or ruby-red trout. Their extensive wine selection rounds out your meal. Breakfast, lunch, and dinner are served daily.

PIONEER INN $
15 First Street, Nederland
(303) 258-7733
Built during Nederland's historical mining days, this landmark offers hearty American fare. Funky and fun, the rustic inn is known for traditional, filling breakfasts, Mexican-accented favorites, great charcoal-grilled burgers, homemade green chili, and varieties of beer. When you come to the Pioneer, you get to hang out at the big bar with gritty local mountaineers as well as skiers and hikers who stop in to be part of the fun. It's open daily for breakfast, lunch, and dinner. The bar is open until 2 a.m. every night (see the Nightlife chapter for more information).

RED ROBIN AMERICA'S GOURMET
BURGER AND SPIRITS $
2580 Arapahoe Avenue, Boulder
(303) 442-0320
www.redrobin.com
Enter one of Boulder's major family and teen hangouts. It's a place with high energy, fueled by

a variety of burgers, sandwiches, and fries. Features include their trademark "smiling" chicken. There's a bar up front and a video game room off to the side. It's open for lunch and dinner daily.

THE SINK $

1165 13th Street, Boulder
(303) 444-7465
www.thesink.com
This college hangout has been gathering character since the 1930s. But without that college grunge, it just wouldn't be authentic. "Ugly Crust Pizzas" with various toppings; a huge selection of munchies, including nachos and pizza bread sticks; Sink-Burgers; and soups and salads fill the menu. There's live music, great beer, happy-hour specials, and an unsurpassed youthful exuberance. After all, many of the patrons have only recently reached legal drinking age. Organized graffiti serves as decor. Robert Redford was the janitor here before he scuttled art at CU-Boulder and went on to make a few major motion pictures. The Sink is open for lunch and dinner daily.

SOBO AMERICAN BISTRO $$

657 South Broadway, Boulder
(303) 494-7626
www.soboamericanbistro.com
South Boulder is finally becoming a place for great restaurants. Sobo pairs excellent food with

---

i Restaurant Runners delivers restaurant meals to your door for just $4 more than the total meal price (the delivery person also appreciates a tip). Many of Boulder's best restaurants subscribe to this service, ranging from sushi palaces to hot dog joints, including many Boulder favorites, such as Old Chicago, Cafe Gondolier, Japango, Hungry Toad, Mustard's Last Stand, RedFish, Sunflower, and Rudi's. Meals arrive from 20 minutes to an hour after you call. Call (303) 402-0556 to order or to have a menu delivered. You may also place your online order at www.restaurant-runners.com.

---

a diverse selection of wines, beers and spirits. Seasonally evolving menus ensure a memorable evening for all guests.

TURLEY'S $$

2805 Pearl Street, Boulder
(303) 442-2800
www.turleysboulder.com
This friendly and unpretentious restaurant is the keeper of the flame, preserving a particular kind of Boulder eating place. Paul Turley has operated three restaurants in Boulder, all of which were immediate hits. Entrees here include lots of vegetables, served with a choice of quinoa or brown rice, plus grilled tuna, a chicken-and-black-bean burrito, scrambled tofu, and other Boulderish offerings that eschew red meat or anything resembling gravy. Turley's offers comfort food, too, including chicken potpie and buffalo meat loaf served with knockout mashed potatoes. All entrees come with a choice of soup or salad and a roll or the muffin of the day. There's a good selection of microbrews and wines as well as full bar service, and the restaurant does fine with smoothies and desserts as well. Turley's is open for breakfast, lunch, and dinner daily.

CONTEMPORARY CUISINE

ALICE'S RESTAURANT $$$

3371 Gold Lake Road, Ward
(303) 459-3544
www.goldlake.com/dining
This is a romantic, honeymoon kind of place about 35 minutes up the mountain and over a country road. The 100-plus-year-old lodge is charming and rustic, yet it is big enough to hold a private party for 350 people for special occasions such as wedding receptions. Generally, it's a more intimate crowd, with about half the people staying at the Gold Lake Mountain Resort and the other half coming up from Boulder.

The cuisine is innovative American with Pacific Rim overtones, such as Thai crab cakes with lemongrass. Fare includes gourmet vegetarian dishes, seafood, wild game, and juicy steaks. The wines are reasonably priced, and the meal is well worth the trip. You can have a cocktail before dinner at Karel's Bar or retire there for an after-dinner drink, but the best treat is to retire to your own quaint cabin for the night instead of driving back to town. Alice's is open for lunch and dinner daily during summer, with somewhat shortened winter hours. Reservations are highly recommended.

DOLAN'S RESTAURANT $-$$
2319 Arapahoe Avenue, Boulder
(303) 444-8758
www.dolansrestaurant.com
Boulder businesspeople voted Dolan's the best lunch restaurant, with the prime rib special featuring mashed potatoes a sure bet for closing the deal. There's a cozy wood-paneled bar, perfect for watching sporting events in the afternoon and yet elegant enough for appetizers or dinner in the evening. There's also a separate dining room. Both the bar and restaurant serve seafood and steaks, soup, and salads. The ahi tuna quesadilla with sliced blackened rare tuna, cilantro, Monterey Jack cheese, and pickled ginger is a huge hit. Live Maine lobster is the special every Wednesday and Sunday. Lunch and dinner are served Monday through Friday; dinner only on Saturday and Sunday.

14TH STREET BAR AND GRILL $$
1400 Pearl Street, Boulder
(303) 444-5854
www.14thstreetbarandgrill.com
This bustling, sunny restaurant serves gourmet pizza baked in a wood-burning oven, along with fine salads and rotisserie chicken. Salmon might be accompanied by a cantaloupe salsa during the summer. The turkey sandwich is like a Thanksgiving meal. The vanilla-bean cheesecake is only one example of the knockout desserts. Everything is consistently good, fresh, and innovatively prepared. The patio seating lets you be part of the mall scene. It's open for lunch and dinner daily.

GATEWAY CAFÉ $$
432 Main Street, Lyons
(303) 823-5144
www.gatewaycafe.com
There's no better place to stop on the way to Estes Park and the Rocky Mountain National Park than the Gateway. There's seafood, game, and vegetarian entrees, often with an Asian or European slant. The menu changes nightly, but the awards keep coming from *Bon Appetit* and the Food Network, plus local food writers who rave about the pies. Open for dinner, Wednesday through Sunday.

JAX FISH HOUSE $$
928 Pearl Street, Boulder
(303) 444-1811
www.jaxfishhouseboulder.com
The winner of several awards, Jax is the place people want to be when they're hungry for fresh seafood. Or is it the martinis? Local newspaper readers say Jax makes the best martini in town. Chef Hosea Rosenberg's restaurant resides on trendy Pearl Street, just west of the Pearl Street Mall. The raw oysters and clams are exceptional. You can doodle on your crisp butcher-paper "tablecloth" while you wait for your spicy gumbo, clam chowder, soft-shelled crab linguine, steamed mussels, and vegetarian specials. Save room for the key lime pie. Jax is open daily for appetizers and dinner only.

THE KITCHEN $$-$$$
1039 Pearl Street, Boulder
(303) 544-5973
www.thekitchencafe.com
Recipient of many accolades *from Wine Spectator* and the *Zagat's Survey* 2006, The Kitchen came to Boulder and took the town by surprise. There is an emphasis on managing the source of all ingredients and buying local and organic whenever possible. The menu changes daily to reflect the best seasonal ingredients available. The Kitchen is committed to offering fresh, eclectic dishes. Try the veal chop with apple potato gratin, seared greens, and truffle butter, or the house-

made gnocchi with hazel dell mushrooms, truffle cream, and fennel salad. The lunch features salads, sandwiches, and entrees made with chicken, beef, fish, or vegetables. In November 2005, The Kitchen opened the "Upstairs"—a casual, urban wine lounge. The Upstairs has a 4,500-bottle wine cellar with 25 wines offered by the glass. The Upstairs Kitchen holds a wood-burning oven, serving casual, fun-to-share foods, from wood-roasted flatbreads with prosciutto and burrata cheese to wood-roasted mussels with chili and chorizo. The Kitchen is open for breakfast, lunch, and dinner daily and on Saturday and Sunday for brunch and dinner. The Upstairs is open Tuesday through Saturday from 4 p.m. to midnight.

Q'S RESTAURANT $$-$$$
In the Hotel Boulderado,
2115 13th Street, Boulder
(303) 442-4880
www.qsboulder.com

Q's was a 2003 Mobile Award winner, and receives a four-star rating in the *Zagat Survey*. Q's is regarded as one of Colorado's finest restaurants. Chef-owner John Platt offers changing monthly menus that might include grilled asparagus with arugula, lobster-stuffed gold potato, roasted pheasant breast, chile-crusted Colorado trout, or adobe-grilled pork loin with peach salsa, all presented like a 3-D food sculpture. Organically grown green salads accompany all dinners. A fabulous dessert menu and wine list are standard procedure at the hotel. Breakfast, lunch, and dinner are served daily.

ZOLO GRILL $
2525 Arapahoe Avenue, Boulder
(303) 449-0444
www.zologrill.com

Zolo Grill is regularly named the "Best Southwestern Restaurant" in Boulder, and regulars rave over the duck tacos and chicken enchiladas. Since opening in 1994, Zolo has become known not only for its food but for its decor, which is eclectic electric, from the copper wires crossing the ceiling to the huge abstract murals on the walls, all with a hip Santa Fe underpinning. The food is spicy and visually exciting. Start with a Zolorita, the house margarita, and finish with a dessert from a list that includes incredible grilled banana cream pie. Zolo is open for lunch and dinner Monday through Saturday and for brunch and dinner on Sunday.

ASIAN

AI SUSHI AND STEAK $
29th Street Mall, Boulder
(303)440-9600
www.aisushi.com

A full-service, sit down Japanese restaurant/sushi bar with restaurants in Denver and now at 29th Street located on the southwest corner of 29th Street & Canyon Blvd. Every Monday night is family night! Come in with your family and kids six years of age and under receive a free kid's plate! Also open for lunch!

BIMBAMBOO $
1710 Pearl Street, Boulder
(303) 442-4575
www.bimbamboo.com

Conveniently located on Pearl Street, Bimbamboo is a modern Asian restaurant inspired by the unique and bold flavors of Vietnam, Thailand, Korea, and East India. Their signature recipes are prepared with great care and enthusiasm and they offer a comfortable, modern dining space with both traditional and communal seating options.

DUSHANBE TEAHOUSE $$
1770 13th Street, Boulder
(303) 442-4993
www.boulderteahouse.com

If you can take your eyes off the decor, you will find a variety of distinctive entrees as well as unique bakery and dessert items here. Mapo tofu (a spicy Chinese dish), eggplant, wild mushroom pasta, Thai curry noodles, salads, and soups are just a few of the menu items. And don't forget the huge variety of tea.

The Tea House was a gift from Boulder's sister city of Dushanbe in 1986, but money to erect the elaborate structure was not approved until

1997. The Tea House was an instant hit, in part because it's on the Boulder Creek Path, next door to the Museum of Contemporary Art, across from Central Park, and adjacent to the Farmers' Market. Artisans from Tajikistan spent most of 1997 living in Boulder to complete the intricate assembly. It is the only authentic Persian teahouse in the Western hemisphere. The creekside patio is a great place to people-watch. The Tea House is open daily for breakfast, lunch, and dinner.

CHEZ THUY $$
2655 28th Street, Boulder
(303) 442-1700
www.chezthuy.com

This pretty restaurant, with deep green, brocade booths and a big, carved dragon-and-peacock motif mural, dishes up elegant Vietnamese food so well it regularly makes one of the "best" lists. Specialties include quail stuffed with seafood served with vegetables and noodles, pork sautéed in a clay hot pot, curried chicken, and vegetarian specials, all cooked by owner/chef Thuy Twee. The portions are generous, and you can dine in or take out. It's open daily for lunch and dinner.

GOLDEN LOTUS $
1964 28th Street, Boulder
(303) 442-6868
www.ufeedme.com/goldenlotus

A casually elegant restaurant featuring authentic Chinese fare, including Szechwan, Cantonese, and Mandarin dishes, the Golden Lotus uses the freshest ingredients and no MSG. Enjoy the dim sum daily at lunch and Chinese "small bites" on the weekends. This is a large restaurant with plenty of parking just outside the door. It's open daily for lunch and dinner.

HAPA SUSHI GRILL & SAKE BAR $–$$
117 Pearl Street, Boulder
(303) 473-4730

1220 Pennsylvania Avenue, Boulder
(303) 447-9883
www.hapasushi.com

No one was happy when Boulder's New York Deli, made famous as the setting for the *Mork & Mindy* television show, closed for good. Hapa, however, made everyone, or at least those who love sushi, very happy when it moved into the same space. The decor is more tricked-out than traditional, and the menu is the same, featuring the Statue of Liberty roll, the Philadelphia roll, and the Cheeto roll. There is a wide variety of sashimi and nigiri that you can enjoy either inside or on the patio while watching the colorful cast on the Pearl Street Mall. Hapa is open for lunch and dinner daily.

> **i** For large parties or for special places, dinner reservations are recommended. Reservations matter more in the summer, especially during weekends or events such as CU-Boulder graduation in May. In winter, Valentine's Day and other special evenings book up fast. That doesn't mean you generally need reservations weeks in advance. Even at the finest places, a call just before you leave can mean a table waiting for you when you arrive.

JAPANGO $$
1136 Pearl Street, Boulder
(303) 938-0330
www.usmenuguide.com/japango.html

Enjoy excellent sushi and Japanese cuisine in contemporary-styled Asian surroundings. All the action at this happening restaurant takes place at the sushi bar. Choose from more than 100 sushi and sashimi selections, each one prepared right in front of you. Entrees feature a number of Pacific Rim seafood offerings as well as the more traditional chicken, beef, and vegetable tempura. Open for lunch and dinner Sunday through Thursday and dinner only Friday and Saturday.

LEE YUAN CHINESE CUISINE $
4800 Baseline Road, Boulder
(303) 494-4210

Boulder has a tremendous selection of good, small, family-owned restaurants. Lee Yuan is one of them. Two decades ago, this was Lee Yuan Burger Hut, serving both burgers and carry-out Chinese food. Now the restaurant, in the Meadows shopping center, is a morning-glory-decorated, sit-down establishment that is popular for its less-than-$5 lunch specials as well as its dinner selections. It's very friendly to families. Wine and beer are available. It's open for lunch weekdays and for dinner daily.

MOONGATE ASIAN BISTRO $
1628 Pearl Street, Boulder
(720) 406-8888
This great little Asian bistro offers a mix of Thai, Vietnamese, Chinese and Japanese cuisines. Open every day except Sunday.

ORCHID PAVILION CHINESE
RESTAURANT & LOUNGE $$
1050 Walnut Street, Boulder
(303) 449-4353
www.orchidpavilion.com
Voted "Best Chinese Restaurant" in the *Daily Camera*'s reader's poll for more than a decade, the Orchid Pavilion is staffed by New York–style Chinatown chefs, who cook sesame chicken in huge chunks, crispy whole fish, champagne beef, and eggplant in garlic sauce. There are also gourmet seafood dishes and Szechwan vegetables. MSG is never used—you don't even need to ask. The soothing, peach-colored interior includes a huge, genuine Chinese silk screen and fine reproductions of Tang Dynasty horses. Children are welcome. The restaurant's early-bird specials take the most popular menu items and add a choice of soup, chicken wings, egg roll, or fried wonton, as well as a choice of steamed or fried rice for one price. Orchid Pavilion is open for lunch and dinner daily.

PANASIA FUSION $
1175 Walnut Street, Boulder
(303) 447-0101
This section of Walnut Street has been transformed in recent years to include a brewery, an upscale pool hall, a Mexican restaurant, and now

Asian fare. East meets West at this restaurant featuring Pacific Rim cuisine made with authentic recipes. Favorites include the Korean-style baby back ribs, garlic and soya beef tenderloin, a salad with spicy tempura prawns, and a warm spinach salad with lime vinaigrette and scallion goat cheese. A bonus is the brewed premium loose-leaf tea, served in cast-iron pots. Open for lunch and dinner Monday through Friday and for dinner only on the weekend.

SAWADDEE THAI $
1630 30th Street, Suite B, Boulder
(303) 447-3321
Sawaddee is a regular on the "Best of Boulder" list. Garlic pepper shrimp and Thai iced tea, made with spices and sweetened milk, will tempt you. Lemongrass and curried vegetables add their distinctive flavors to many dishes. The food is mildly spicy, but you can ask for it to be hotter or not spicy at all. The chefs will add more vegetables when requested, which is one reason the spot earns high points from Boulder's many health enthusiasts. Sawaddee is open for dinner daily and for lunch daily except Sunday and Monday.

SIAMESE PLATE & SUMIDA'S SUSHI BAR $$
1575 Folsom Street, Boulder
(303) 447-9718
www.siameseplateonthego.com
Recognized by the Thai government for its delicious Thai cuisine, the Siamese Plate gives diners a choice of Western seating or benches with bright cushions. Try the spicy green curry with vegetables and coconut milk, the green-lipped mussels with spicy garlic sauce, or the exceptional red curry with chicken, and get an appetizer from Sumida's Sushi Bar one level below. Sumida's also offers happy-hour sushi specials and two-for-one sake midday on weekdays, in the early evening, and all evening on Sunday and Monday. If you sit down at Sumida's, you can also order from the Thai menu. Both the Plate and the Sushi Bar are open for lunch Monday through Saturday and for dinner daily. Multiple locations in Boulder.

SUSHI TORA $$

2014 10th Street, Boulder
(303) 444-2280

This is Boulder's most authentic Japanese sushi restaurant, from the low cloth curtains you walk through to enter during good weather to the excellent raw fish, beautifully presented. This quiet restaurant offers tempura, soups, and appetizers, too. It's open weekdays for lunch and daily for dinner.

SUSHI ZANMAI $$

1221 Spruce Street, Boulder
(303) 440-0733

There is nothing quiet or low-key about this brassy sushi bar and Japanese restaurant. The sushi is first-rate; the owner, chef Nao-San, is a shameless extrovert; and the restaurant is rarely without a line out the door. This popular Japanese restaurant was voted by *Daily Camera* readers as the best place for karaoke singing in the metro area. One part of the bustling restaurant features the sushi bar and wood-top tables. At the bar, you can watch the flamboyant Japanese chefs prepare miniature boatloads of artistic sushi. Another part of the restaurant features tatami rooms and grill tables where the chef performs cooking magic.

Sing-along karaoke starting at 10 p.m. on Saturdays make this noisy place even noisier—and that much more enjoyable. Lunch and happy-hour specials bring down the cost of good Japanese food and great Japanese-accented fun. This restaurant is open for lunch weekdays and dinner nightly.

TRA LING'S ORIENTAL CAFE $$

1305 Broadway, Boulder
(303) 449-0400

Boulder newspaper readers who don't vote for Orchid Pavilion as the area's best Chinese restaurant instead vote for Tra Ling's. The place is nothing special but the food is. The sweet and sour pork is a favorite, as is the Kung Pao Chicken. The egg rolls are always excellent, and you can never order enough wontons. It's convenient to the Pearl Street Mall, but with free and reliable delivery why not stay home? Tra Ling's is open daily for lunch and dinner.

BARBECUE

DADDY BRUCE'S BAR-B-QUE AND CATERING $

2000 Arapahoe Avenue, Boulder
(303) 449-8890

This place is usually packed with folks, so it's fun to carry-out after sniffing the maple-stoked stove, where ribs get slathered with sauce that's tangy—not sweet. Not exactly health food, but, oh, what a decadent treat. The beef sandwiches are popular with a side of potato salad. Eat a slab of pork ribs and you'll sweat for two hours . . . with a smile on your face. This place is run by Bruce Randolph Jr., an associate minister of Boulder's Second Baptist Church and son of the late and greatly missed Denver philanthropist "Daddy" Bruce Randolph. Daddy Bruce's is open for lunch every day except Sunday. No credit cards.

KT'S BARBECUE $

7464 Arapahoe Road, Boulder
(303) 786-7608
2675 13th Street, Boulder
(303) 442-3717

Hickory-smoked barbecue (fat trimmed) gets served with sweet-to-spicy sauces rated like ski runs—easy way down, more difficult, and double diamond for experts only. KT's is open for lunch and dinner Monday through Saturday.

THE RIB HOUSE $-$$

1920 South Coffman Street, Longmont
Located in New Town Prospect
(303) 485-6988
http://64.187.101.6

Merry Ann and Tracy Webb brought authentic Kansas City/Colorado Barbeque to Longmont on July 5, 2001. The Rib House serves several hickory-smoked meats, such as pork, brisket, chicken, turkey, smoked ham, and sausage. If you can't decide, try the sampler! Sides are equally as appetizing. Choose from spicy BBQ pit beans, red-skinned mashed potatoes, and cheesy corn bake. Open seven days a week for lunch and dinner. Take-out is available as well.

BREAKFAST AND LUNCH

ANNIE'S CAFE $
20 Lakeview Drive, Nederland
(303) 258-3600
Perched atop the Nederland Shopping Center, Annie's is a popular local hangout that serves eggs, pancakes, omelets, sandwiches, salads, and homemade soups. It is open for breakfast and lunch daily.

THE BUFF $
1725 28th Street, Boulder
(303) 442-9150
www.thebuffrestaurant.com
It might be the slogan "Eat In the Buff" or the unique breakfast items, but either way, *Daily Camera* readers have voted this restaurant the "Best Breakfast in Boulder." Frittatas, panini sandwiches, muffalettas, and breakfast chimichangas are offered along with traditional breakfast items. There's a full espresso bar, or you can sip a mimosa or Bloody Mary with a Denver omelet. A children's menu makes this a great weekend stop for families. A pleasant atmosphere and fast service are the norm. The Buff is open for breakfast and lunch daily.

DOT'S DINER $
2716 North 28th Street, Boulder
(303) 449-1323

1333 Broadway, Boulder
(303) 447-9184
Dot's was a fixture at 8th and Pearl for 20 years, but a developer's offer in 1998 was just too good to refuse. The restaurant has moved to north Broadway, with a second location on busy 28th Street. The ambience doesn't match the old gas station, but the menu is still much the same. It has some of the best buttermilk biscuits in town, along with huevos rancheros and cinnamon rolls.

Dot's is open for breakfast and lunch daily. No credit cards.

EGGCREDIBLE CAFÉ $
5397 South Boulder Road, Boulder
Days Inn Hotel
(303) 301-0005
www.eggcredible.com
This breakfast cafe features Colorado food with a European influence. Specialties include pierogies (Polish-style dumplings with hearty fillings) and whipped-cream-topped Belgian waffles. Burritos and omelets are also part of the breakfast menu. Open daily for breakfast and lunch.

LE PEEP $
2525 Arapahoe Avenue, Boulder
Village Shopping Center
(303) 444-5119
www.lepeep.com
There simply may not be a better breakfast than this. Le Peep offers an excellent selection of breakfast foods and lunch items. Enjoy a Strawberry Fields smoothie while feasting on Belgian waffles. Lunch includes paninis, sandwiches, salads, and burgers. Open daily until 2:30 p.m.

MARIE'S CAFE $
2660 Broadway, Boulder
(303) 447-0320
Marie's is open through lunch (a hearty Middle European one at that), but it is at breakfast that this cafe really shines. Pancakes, eggs, and huge pastries abound. None of the regulars, who include medical professionals from the nearby Boulder Community Hospital and assorted medical groups and support services, seem shy about

---

i Enjoy breakfast or lunch while shopping at Boulder's Farmers' Market on Saturdays and Wednesdays, mid-April to November. Located on 13th Street in front of the Dushanbe Tea House, the market features a variety of food vendors. Check them out at www.boulderfarmers.org.

slathering on the butter or piling on the jam. Maybe they know where to get help if they need it! The atmosphere is luncheonette-basic, with bright lights for perusing the morning paper, and suitably efficient service. Marie's is open daily for breakfast and lunch. No credit cards.

CAFES/COFFEEHOUSES

Boulder has become a coffee town. Great java is everywhere, and even food and gourmet stores serve eye-opening, high-caffeine espressos right next to the fresh vegetable juices. There's even an espresso bar in the Boulder Public Library. Boulder's coffee craze is most apparent in its abundance of coffeehouses and cafes. Most of these places sell only coffee. You can get a regular coffee for around a dollar at most of these places, while something like a latte can range from $3 to around $4.

ACOUSTIC COFFEEHOUSE $
95 East First Street, Nederland
(303) 258-3209
This quaint coffeehouse is located in a redbrick house with a summer patio and decorated rocking chairs on the porch. Inside are tables printed with chessboards where customers can play, a sitting area with a tattered Victorian couch, and an old wooden ironing board holding the milk and sugar. Used books and new magazines are for sale, and the artwork is both original and daring. In addition to coffee you can buy herb tea, fresh scones, and specials such as mango-apple pie and Italian potato-vegetable soup. Locals come here for poetry readings, too. The cafe is open 7 a.m. to 5 p.m. on Monday, Thursday, and Friday; 7 a.m. to 2 p.m. Wednesday; 8 a.m. to 5 p.m. on Saturday; and 8 a.m. to 6 p.m on Sunday.

THE BOOKEND CAFE $
1115 Pearl Street, Boulder
(303) 440-6699
This hip cafe is connected to the Boulder Bookstore. It's a see-and-be-seen place for the cellular-phone set, especially those who want a little

lunch with their coffee. The scones, spelt muffins, and coffee cake start the day off sweetly, and there's a good selection of salads and other light fare for lunch and supper on a daily basis.

THE BREWING MARKET $
2525 Arapahoe Avenue, Boulder
(303) 444-4858

1918 13th Street, Boulder
(303) 443-2098

2610 Baseline Rd., Boulder
(303) 499-1345
The first shop has been around for about 20 years, but only in recent years has an in-house master roasted the beans. The Brewing Market atmospheres are simple, but they open daily at 6 a.m., and the crowds line up because they love the coffee and the excellent chai—black tea, sweetened milk, and spices. Don't be misled by the Arapahoe Avenue address; the Arapahoe Brewing Market is actually a half-block off Arapahoe, next to McGuckin's on the southwest corner facing Folsom.

BUCHANAN'S $
1301 Pennsylvania Avenue, Boulder
(303) 440-0222
On the path between student apartments and CU, this conveniently located shop serves all types of coffee specialties and various pastries from local bakeries. Students in a hurry can even have copies made in Buchanan's copy center downstairs while they wait for the milk to foam. Buchanan's is open daily and stays open late at night; there's outdoor seating, weather permitting.

ESPRESSO ROMA $
1101 13th Street, Boulder
(303) 442-5011
www.espressoroma.com
This is The Hill's version of *Cheers*—with caffeine. Students hang here for hours in between classes, savoring the extensive espresso beverage offerings plus bagels, cake, cookies, biscotti, and pastries. Espresso Roma is open daily.

JAVASTOP $
301 Main Street, Longmont
(303) 772-1731

Longmont's answer to Boulder's burgeoning coffeehouse business, this elegant spot is located in the Old Imperial Hotel. It has a wide assortment of coffees and serves fresh pastries daily. Lunch, including soup, sandwiches and salads, is also served. Javastop closes at 4 p.m. on weekdays, at 2 p.m. Saturdays, and at 1 p.m. Sundays.

PEABERRY COFFEE, LTD. $
2721 Arapahoe Avenue, Boulder
(303) 449-4111
www.peaberrycoffe.com

Peaberry's owners are from Boulder, but they started their stores in Denver, then expanded to Boulder when it became clear Boulderites love gourmet coffee, too. Especially known for their own coffee concoction, Polar Bears, they serve fresh baked goods, bagels, scones, desserts, and more daily.

PEET'S COFFEE AND TEA $
1695 29th Street, Boulder
(303) 544-1234
www.peets.com

One of the finest purveyors of coffee and tea has finally moved to Boulder. Enjoy specialty, artisan-crafted coffees and teas. Peet's fresh, deep-roasted coffees are brewed to exacting standards and made for you by skilled baristas. All espresso drinks are crafted by hand. Peet's uses freshly pulled espresso shots poured within 10 seconds, and they never re-steam milk. Open daily until 9 p.m.

STARBUCKS $
3033 Arapahoe Avenue, Boulder
(303) 440-5090

1402 Broadway, Boulder
(303) 442-9199

1427 Pearl Street, Boulder
(303) 245-9368

2770 Pearl Street, Boulder
(303) 449-1881
www.Starbucks.com

The Seattle purveyor that launched the coffee craze has four Boulder locations. They are clean-cut stores, for Boulder that is, and serve a full range of coffees plus pastries and bagels. For the coffee lover in your life, Starbucks is sure to please with great gift items.

TRIDENT BOOKSELLERS AND CAFE $
940 Pearl Street, Boulder
(303) 443-3133
www.tridentcafe.com

Regularly voted the best by *Daily Camera* readers, Trident attracts endangered bohemians who love to converse over coffee. It's Boulder's answer to Greenwich Village, or as close as you can get in these parts. A full range of coffees and pastries and lots of interesting conversation at the next table are the draws here. The attached bookstore helps promote the sought-after intellectual feeling.

VIC'S $
2680 Broadway, Boulder
(303) 440-8209

3305 30th Street, Boulder
(303) 440-2918

801 Main Street, Louisville
(303) 666-1402

Everybody who's anybody knows Vic doesn't exist. But North Boulder baby boomers who frequent Vic's all know the owner, Mike, and he never forgets a name. Vic's serves coffee and pastries, with Ella Fitzgerald on the CD player. Vic's is a local favorite.

CARIBBEAN

AJI $$
1601 Pearl Street, Boulder
(303) 442-3464
www.ajirestaurant.com

Latin America comes alive at Aji. Feast on a fresh ceviche bar and enjoy an extensive list of exotic cocktails and an excellent selection of South American wines. Creative main dishes include plantain and peanut-crusted yellow fin tuna served with aji amarillo and red-pepper salsa with a side of banana rice and steamed banana leaf–wrapped pompano, served in a coconut and lime broth with a side of Roman beans. For dessert, try the chocolate empanadas! Open Sunday through Thursday 11 a.m. to 10 p.m. and Friday and Saturday 11 a.m. to midnight.

CENTRO LATIN KITCHEN & REFRESHMENT PALACE $$
950 Pearl Street, Boulder
(303) 442-7771
www.bigredf.com

If you crave Latin food, this is the place for you. Their menu boasts of "soulfully" delicious foods such as Mexican long noodle spicy chicken salad, and roasted pork adobo with baked yams. For dinner they offer small plates, not so small plates, and big plates so there is something for everyone. The flavors are exotic and rich. Try something you've never had before. But don't leave without sampling a mango spritzer, or two.

i If you've been out of New York too long and need a bagel fix, you'll find the best bagels at Moe's. *Daily Camera* readers and *Denver Post* critics all agree the homegrown/corporate bagel biz seems to have mastered the bagel for taste and consistency: not too sweet, not too salty, not too chewy. There are three Boulder outlets and several Moe's locations in Denver, too.

CENTRAL AND EASTERN EUROPEAN

ANDREA'S HOMESTEAD CAFE $$
216 East Main Street, Lyons
(303) 823-5000
www.andreashomesteadcafe.com

Since 1977, German favorites have been offered by Bavarian native Andrea Liermann. Even if you can't spell them, you know the sauerbraten, spatzle, rouladen, and Matjesfilet are authentic. There are also steaks, seafood, pasta, and vegetarian dishes. Homemade desserts include cinnamon rolls, apple strudel, and walnut torte. On weekends accordion and bell musicians play, and dancers perform the "Lederhosen Slapptanz." Andrea's is open for breakfast, lunch, and dinner daily Thursday through Monday. Call for summer schedule.

BLACK BEAR INN $$$
42 East Main Street, Lyons
(303) 823-6812
www.blackbearinn.com

Classic European cuisine with a French touch appears on the menu, which changes seasonally. Wiener schnitzel is especially popular. In the wintertime, patrons with a sweet tooth prefer the chocolate taco. In the summer, they go for homemade ice cream. Black Bear is open Wednesday through Saturday for dinner and Sunday from noon to 3 p.m.

BLACK FOREST RESTAURANT $$$
24 Big Springs Drive, Nederland
(303) 279-2333
www.blackforest.com

Dine with beautiful views of the Continental Divide, Rollins Pass, and Eldora ski area. Located 17 miles from Boulder on Highway 119 (Canyon Boulevard), this German-American restaurant offers casual and fine dining. The menu includes a range of wild game and fowl, such as duck, elk, and goose, along with traditional German favorites like Wiener schnitzel and sauerbraten. Finish the meal with homemade German apple strudel and ice cream or the Kirschwasser on pineapple. Open daily for lunch and dinner.

PRAHA RESTAURANT AND BAR $$$
7521 Ute Highway (Highway 66)
Longmont
(303) 702-1180
www.praharestaurant.com

Bohemian plates and hand-stenciled walls give this pre-1900 schoolhouse an elegant, homey ambience. Entrees include roast duck or pork, Czech-style, served with dumplings and sweet-and-sour cabbage. Reservations are recommended. Praha is open for dinner daily except Tuesday.

CONTINENTAL

FAWN BROOK INN $$$$
Highway 7 Business, Allenspark
(303) 747-2556
This tiny mountain hamlet isn't where you'd expect fine continental dining, but it's been served here since 1978 by Chef Hermann Groicher and his wife, Mieke, who hail from Austria and Holland, respectively. Secret ingredients include the crisp mountain air and beautiful flower garden, but even if the surroundings weren't so inviting, the Fawn Brook's exquisite homemade fare, from beef vegetable soup through dessert, would be memorable. All that attention to homey mountain detail just makes it better. Venison served with wild berries and mushrooms, and roast duckling are favorite meals.

Hours vary by the season. During summer, it's open Tuesday through Sunday for dinner. During fall and winter, it's open weekends, depending on the weather. Reservations are recommended. Call ahead for directions. It's about 45 minutes from Boulder and a half-hour from Estes Park.

FLAGSTAFF HOUSE $$$$
1138 Flagstaff Road, Boulder
(303) 442-4640
www.flagstaffhouse.com
When the Emperor and Empress of Japan came to America in 1994, they dined at only one restaurant on their entire national itinerary: Boulder's Flagstaff House. Chef Mark Monette offered their entourage pan-smoked salmon salad with caviar, tossed with local greens in wasabi vinaigrette, along with lobster consommé with spring vegetables and black truffles. Entrees were Boulder trout from the Cline Trout Farm and rack of Colorado lamb with Provencale vegetables, goat cheese, and Japanese eggplant chips. Desserts included Golden Egg Surprise, a cocoa sorbet

wrapped with 24-karat gold leaf to make it look like a gold egg.

When legendary French chef Paul Bocuse set up a cooking event with great American chefs from both coasts, he chose the Flagstaff House. *Zagat* calls it one of Colorado's top 20 restaurants and it makes every "best" list that covers the Rocky Mountain dining scene. You get the idea?

The Flagstaff House, perched high on Flagstaff Mountain, has the most romantic, panoramic view of Boulder around. The Monette family has owned it for more than 30 years, and chef Mark Monette has trained at the Taillevent in Paris, the Trogois Brothers in Roanne, La Poularde in southern France, and also in Singapore, Tokyo, Thailand, and Hong Kong. His rich blend of culinary knowledge has brought the restaurant increasing fame. More than 40 entrees grace the menu, which changes daily but always includes a commendable selection of meat, seafood, and game. The food is extraordinarily well prepared and artfully presented, and service is excellent, too. The wine list is nationally renowned, and the sommeliers are knowledgeable and helpful. The tasting menu with paired wines is a fine way to tap into the best and freshest ingredients that have inspired the chef's creativity that very evening.

The Flagstaff House is by and large an expense-account restaurant, where a full-course dinner for two will easily run into the three figures, but it is definitely worth a once-in-a-blue-moon, all-out grand dinner. Wise locals drive up at sunset or after the lights start twinkling in the valley below and order just appetizers and wine or dessert and wine or coffee—not as grand as a full-course meal but easier on the pocketbook. It's open daily for dinner. Reservations are highly recommended, although drop-ins often can be accommodated.

THE GREENBRIAR INN $$$
8735 North Foothills Highway, Boulder
(303) 440-7979
www.greenbriarinn.com
Picture an English earl strolling home with his spaniel to his grand estate, and you're close to the

ambience of this country inn. It has stained glass, dark wood decor, and the vote from one Denver newspaper as the most romantic restaurant in the area. The executive chef presents lordly traditional fare, great for special occasions. Menu items include tiger shrimp and bay scallop cerviche, beef Wellington, pan-seared duck, and Colorado rack of lamb. Follow with seven-layer Valrhona chocolate cake or Meyer lemon chiffon cake.

The Greenbriar is in the country but only 6.5 miles north of Boulder and about 45 minutes from Estes Park. It's open for dinner Tuesday through Sunday and for Sunday brunch. Reservations are recommended.

JOHN'S RESTAURANT $$$
2328 Pearl Street, Boulder
(303) 444-5232
www.johnsrestaurantboulder.com

John's is a charmingly small, award-winning restaurant that opened in 1975. It serves classic and contemporary dishes that blend French, Italian, Spanish, and American cuisines with skill and finesse. Dishes inspired by influences of the American Southwest, Louisiana, the Caribbean, and Asia may also appear on the menu. John's has a reputation for consistency, quality, and an eye for detail, and dishes are well-grounded in recognizable culinary traditions. Chef-owner Corey Buck (who bought the place from founder John Bizzarro in 2003) starts with the classic cuisine of southern Europe, then adds his own creative signature spin to each dish. For starters, apple Stilton pecan salad and ricotta-and-spinach gnocchi verde set the stage for the continually changing main-course offerings. Menu mainstays include filet mignon with Stilton ale sauce and surrounded by grilled Bermuda onions; chile-crusted pork tenderloin with cranberry-orange sauce; and a variety of fresh seafood dishes—chowder and several succulent plates featuring plump gulf shrimp are always available. The menu also includes vegetarian items. John's is known for its creative desserts (all made in-house) and offers a well-selected wine list, microbrews, and classic cocktails.

RED LION INN $$$
38470 Boulder Canyon Road, Boulder
(303) 442-9368

This Old World inn is just 4 miles up Boulder Canyon. The rambling country inn is popular for family gatherings, business dinners, banquets, and weddings. A specialty is wild game, such as venison or pheasant. Much of the menu is devoted to American cuisine, but there are such decidedly Austro-German influences as red cabbage and spaetzle noodles, a good accompaniment with entrees; meals are followed by a tasty dessert tray. The restaurant offers early-bird specials. It's open for dinner daily.

THYME ON THE CREEK $$–$$$
1345 28th Street, in the Harvest House
Boulder
(303) 998-3835
www.milleniumhotels.com

Most recently the Fancy Moose, this sun-filled restaurant at the Harvest House Hotel has changed its name and changed its menu. Still offering a New York strip, braised lamb, and a smoked rack of pork, with sweet potato fries, there's more emphasis on seafood, including salmon and lobster with fresh vegetables. Lunch is a smaller version of the dinner menu plus sandwiches and burgers, and there's a breakfast buffet. Enjoy your meal inside, or dine on the heated outdoor terrace by the waterfall. Breakfast, lunch, and dinner are served daily.

CREOLE

LUCILE'S CREOLE CAFE $
2124 14th Street, Boulder
(303) 665-2065

518 Kimbark Street, Longmont
(303) 774-9814

Sashay up the porch steps of a side-street Victorian house, open the door, and you're in Cajun country. It's just that easy. Faded calico napkins, tables in every nook, and a casual, bustling atmosphere provide a perfect setting in which to enjoy the red beans and grits. Try eggs sardou or a lunch of crawfish etouffé. Rice pudding porridge with currants and raspberry sauce is comfort food, Lucile-style. It's open for breakfast and lunch daily.

REDFISH FISHHOUSE & BREWERY $$
2027 13th Street, Boulder
(303) 440-5858
www.redfishbrewhouse.com

Voted the "Best New Restaurant" by *Daily Camera* readers when it opened in 1997, RedFish features Louisiana Creole–influenced cuisine with a menu that changes frequently. Appetizers include seafood gumbo, crawfish Caesar, fresh oysters on the half shell, spiced shrimp, and oysters Rockefeller. If there's time for dinner, fresh seafood and house-aged steaks head the list. Desserts include "Chocolate Love" and Louisiana bread pudding with bourbon sauce. The brewmaster offers handcrafted beers, including Wild Magnolia Pale Ale, Angry Monk Belgian-Style Ale, and Gaston's Swollen Delta Big Easy. Live music Thursday through Saturday is the draw for many. Open daily for dinner.

FRENCH

BRASSERIE TEN TEN $$$
1011 Walnut Street, Boulder
(303) 998-1010
www.brasserietenten.com

Located in the heart of downtown Boulder, this bistro-style restaurant features French-inspired cuisine from all the regions of France. Entrees include pepper-crusted ahi, petite whipped potatoes, and pistou emulsion and chicken simmered in a red wine sauce. For those of you with a sweet tooth, try the triple chocolate frozen mousse bomb or the beignet (French donuts) for dessert. Come in on Sunday for brunch and sample Belgian waffles, eggs Benedict, and croissants. The restaurant features a wine list focusing on French wines and offers French-press coffee. Open for lunch Monday through Friday, dinner daily, and brunch on weekends.

MATEO $$–$$$
1837 Pearl Street, Boulder
(303) 443-7766
www.mateorestaurant.com

Boulder may not be known for its French restaurants, but Mateo fills the void with romantic ambience and entrees such as bouillabaisse and sides such as sensational frites and the perfect marinated olives. Skip dinner and go for the dessert, petit pot au chocolat. Open for lunch and dinner Monday through Friday and dinner on Saturday.

INDIAN

BOMBAY BISTRO $$
1800 Broadway, Boulder
One Boulder Plaza
(303) 444-4721
www.thebombaybistro.com

Bombay Bistro combines traditional Indian spices with a modern flair. The restaurant provides customers with the best-tasting and exotic flavors in their continental-style Indian-fusion cuisine. Start your dining experience with delicious vegetable somosas or one of the chef's creations—coconut-crusted sea bass or fork-tender boneless beef short ribs. The bistro is open daily for lunch and dinner.

HIMALAYAS RESTAURANT $
2010 14th Street, Boulder
(303) 442-3230
www.himalayasrestaurant.com

Authentic Indian, Nepalese, and Tibetan food such as tandoori breads and thali, a vegetarian sampler, are available here. You can order the chicken and lamb curries milder or hotter. Don't miss the live Indian music on Sundays. The restaurant is open for lunch and dinner. Reservations are recommended on weekends.

ROYAL PEACOCK $$
5290 Arapahoe Avenue, Boulder
(303) 447-1409
Each year, the owners, who are Bombay natives,

add yet another peacock decoration to their beautiful restaurant. Hot curried Indian dishes are served, along with vegetarian choices in rich cream sauces, good basmati rice (order lots for anyone who prefers mild food), and yogurt/cucumber salads. The chai (tea with spices and sweetened milk) is delicious. Service is impeccably polite. The staff loves kids, although the leisurely pace here can make the meal a bit long for the youngest tykes. Royal Peacock is open for lunch weekdays and for dinner daily.

SHERPA'S $
825 Walnut Street, Boulder
(303) 440-7151
www.sherpaascent.com/restaurant.htm
With all the rock climbers in Boulder, what could be more appropriate than a restaurant and bar named Sherpa's? Just off the Pearl Street Mall, beyond serving fabulous Himalayan dishes, Sherpa's offers an atmosphere that includes climbing memorabilia and a library of adventure and travel books. Named one of the "Best New Restaurants" in 2003 by the *Daily Camera* and the *Colorado Daily*, the menu features a variety of Indian curries, all made fresh to order. Sherpa's is rockin' daily for lunch and dinner.

THE TAJ $$
2360 Baseline Road, Boulder
(303) 494-5216
The sights, sounds, smells, and tastes of this Indian restaurant are so genuinely Indian that it seems strange to see the Basemar shopping center's acres of asphalt just outside the windows. This large space is divided into a rambling procession of dining areas brought to intimate scale by the personal service and excellent food. Note that we said "personal," not "speedy" or "efficient," for The Taj is a place for dining and lingering. Everything is custom-prepared at dinner. The opulent, inexpensive lunch buffet provides a sampling if you're in a hurry. There is a full bar. The Taj is open for lunch and dinner.

TANDOORI GRILL $$
619 South Broadway, Boulder
(303) 543-7339
Featuring a daily lunch buffet, the Tandoori offers East Indian cuisine in the Table Mesa Plaza in south Boulder. It's a casual dining experience that offers a large menu, including chicken masala, grilled chicken in creamy tomato gravy, and bengen bartha, a roasted eggplant dish cooked with onions, tomatoes, herbs, and spices. The Bindi Masala, a combination of fresh okra, fresh tomatoes, and garlic, is a favorite. Desserts include mango custard and pistachio ice cream. The Tandoori is open for lunch and dinner daily.

IRISH

CONOR O'NEILL'S IRISH PUB AND GRILL $$
1922 13th Street, Boulder
(303) 449-1922
www.conoroneills.com
If you're only going to have one Irish restaurant, let it be as close to authentic as possible. This one is, right down to the wood paneling, bar, and antiques all shipped directly from the isle known for its traditional pubs and hearty beer. Speaking of that, you'll find a large selection of draft imported beers and a wide variety of Irish and Scotch whiskeys. Entrees include traditional fish and chips served with coleslaw and malt vinegar; shepherd's pie with lean ground beef, lamb, leeks, carrots, peas, and onions simmered in Bass Ale and topped with roasted garlic mashed potatoes; and steak-and-cheddar boxty. Along with daily beer specials, there is also live music. The restaurant is open daily for lunch and dinner.

ITALIAN

ALBA $$
2480 Canyon Blvd., Boulder
(303) 938-8800
albaboulder.com
Alba is the successor to the critically acclaimed Full Moon Grill, which owner Rick Stein opened in 1992. The Full Moon became one of Boulder's

best-loved restaurants, renowned for its delicious food, friendly and attentive service, and its acclaimed wine list. Over his thirty years of traveling to Italy, Rick Stein became especially enchanted with the Piemonte region and its beautiful towns and rolling hills. He was inspired by the many unpretentious ristorantes, osterias, and trattorias throughout the region. He particularly liked the city of Alba and its warm and generous people. In 2006, he decided to open a restaurant that would reflect Piemonte's wonderful food and wine in a relaxed, congenial setting.

BÁCARO RISTORANTE $$$
921 Pearl Street, Boulder
(303) 444-4888
www.bacaro.com
Located on the west end of Pearl Street, Bácaro has a simple decor and more complicated Northern Italian cuisine. A house antipasto specialty is carpaccio, thinly sliced raw meat drizzled with olive oil and lemon juice. Fresh homemade pastas include spinach and ricotta cheese ravioli, angelhair pasta with fresh tomato sauce, and black and white tagliolini with mixed seafood in a lightly spiced tomato sauce. Entree highlights include veal scalloppine topped with prosciutto and sage, served with creamy baked potatoes. The desserts are as extravagant as the pastas, and the wine list is comprehensive. The service is also excellent. Open Monday through Friday for lunch and dinner.

BLUE PARROT $
640 Main Street, Louisville
(303) 666-0677
Long before "ethnic" food became trendy, this family-run restaurant was providing locals with informal, inexpensive Italian food. The restaurant opened in 1919, when Louisville's coal mines brought many Italian families into the area. For decades, a special evening in Boulder often would end with a trip to the Blue Parrot for a homestyle Italian meal. Today, the noodles are still homemade, including the gnocchi, made with mashed potatoes.

The atmosphere here has stayed unpretentious, so it's a good choice for casual family dining,

especially for finicky young eaters who prefer bland to zesty. You can even buy Blue Parrot pasta sauce at grocery stores these days. Blue Parrot is open for breakfast, lunch, and dinner daily.

CAFÉ GONDOLIER $
1600 Pearl Street, Boulder
(303) 443-5015
www.cafegondolier.com
Owned by the same family for more than 40 years, this Boulder restaurant has moved to 17th and Pearl Streets but still offers fresh, homemade, and affordable Italian cuisine in a casual atmosphere. A variety of Italian breads, soups, and antipasti are served as appetizers. Eggplant parmigiana, lightly breaded and fried eggplant, spaghetti, fettuccine Alfredo, and fettuccine pesto are just a few of the entrees. Desserts include homemade lemon cheesecake and tiramisu. The special on Tuesday and Wednesday is all-you-can-eat spaghetti for $4.69. Open for lunch and dinner Monday through Friday and for dinner only on Saturday and Sunday.

CARELLI'S OF BOULDER RISTORANTE
ITALIANO $$
645 30th Street, Boulder
(303) 938-9300
www.carellis.com
Another Boulder favorite, Carelli's meals are prepared with the finest imported and domestic ingredients and all-natural chicken and beef. Specialties include pesto di penne, shrimp scampi, chicken picatta, and steak pizziola. Carelli's has a cozy fireplace for winter dining and a garden patio in the summer. The restaurant is open for lunch and dinner weekdays, dinner only on Saturday; it's closed Sunday.

DA GABI CUCINA $$–$$$
3970 North Broadway, Boulder
(303) 786-9004
www.dagabicucina.com
This unique Italian eatery in north Boulder has an intimate atmosphere with food to match the romantic surroundings, making it hard to believe

it's located in a strip mall next to a grocery store. There is a chicken breast in artichoke heart cream sauce, or black ravioli stuffed with salmon that shouldn't be difficult to complement from the extensive wine list. The service is excellent, and will make you wish this restaurant was open all the time rather than just for dinner nightly.

D'NAPOLI RISTORANTE $–$$
835 Walnut Street, Boulder
(303) 444-8434

Filling Italian fare, mostly of the traditional Southern Italian variety, is served in this amiable, casual restaurant. Spaghetti, ziti, and fettuccine, the most popular pasta shapes, dominate the menu and are available with an assortment of sauces. Perennial favorites include eggplant parmigiana, lasagna with or without meat, and shrimp fra diavolo. Some seafood, some poultry, and some meat dishes are served, and there's pizza, too. D'Napoli is open for dinner from 4 to 10 p.m. nightly.

FRASCA $$–$$$
1738 Pearl Street, Boulder
(303) 442-6966
www.frascafoodandwine.com

Frasca's menu is a tribute to the food of Friuli-Venezia Giulia, Italy. The menu is never the same as it changes seasonally to make the most of current harvests and the freshest produce, herbs, and spices. It favors products from the best local farmers and purveyors and reflects Friulian sensibilities about ingredients and proportion according to weather, climate, and calendar. The entrees feature beef, fish, and poultry and are inspired by the sophisticated flavors and international influences of the area that are at once quintessentially Italian yet unique to this extraordinary region. Frasca supports local farmers and provides the finest naturally raised meats and organically grown produce. Experience the traditional dessert of the region—artisan cheeses with sumac-marinated grapes, or indulge in the house-made chocolates. Frasca is open for dinner Monday through Saturday. Call for reservations.

L $$–$$$
1710 29th Street, Boulder
(303) 442-1300
www.laudisio.com

Laudisio's, one of Boulder's landmark eateries, moved from its former home of 20 years to the brand-new 29th Street Shopping Center in the fall of 2006. With the move, came a change in name—the old Laudisio is now "L." L is a large, airy space with an outdoor area enclosed by grape-leaf metalwork, leading to a brick, tile, and wood interior that showcases a 4,000-bottle wine cellar, wood oven, and rotisserie. The restaurant's rotisserie will allow the chefs to design specials around local products such as Colorado leg of lamb, organic chicken, and Coleman beef. L makes its bread, egg pastas, sauces, and soups daily. Entrees are made to order specifically to your tastes. The dinner menu includes such spectacular dishes as wild mushroom pate, chicken milanase, braised calamari, and veal rustico. L meets the needs of all diners. Visit the cafe for a cappuccino and panini for lunch, have an intimate dinner in the evening, or enjoy a glass of wine after the movies. L is open daily for lunch and dinner.

LOUIE'S ITALIAN RESTAURANT $$
138 East Main Street, Lyons
(303) 823-8856

This family-friendly restaurant is located in downtown Lyons. Louie's specializes in fresh pizza and homemade pasta dishes and bread. The lunch menu features calzones, pizza, salads, and sandwiches. The dinner menu is the same, with some traditional meat and chicken dishes, seafood, and the homemade bread and rolls. Louie's offers a fine selection of wines and domestic and imported beers. Open for lunch and dinner Wednesday through Monday.

MILLSITE INN $
44365 Peak to Peak Highway, Ward
(303) 459-3308

They make the dough for their calzones and pizzas fresh here, with a good sauce and anything in them. There are homemade pies and good desserts as well. Friends give high ratings to the chicken marsala and other full dinners. The food tends toward Italian-American with a few Mexican dishes, and pizza and burgers thrown in. Add to that a comfortably rustic, log-cabin atmosphere. The locals hang out here, meaning residents of the nearby funky town called Ward, along with skiers, and hikers. The guys in the bar have an amiable grubbiness to them and usually pay close attention to the TV broadcasting a game. The Millsite Inn is open for lunch and dinner daily, with the bar open until 2 a.m. when someone's still thirsty.

NEAPOLITAN'S $$
1 West First Street, Nederland
(303) 258-7313
There's a variety of Italian food here just 20 minutes west of Boulder in a cozy family-style restaurant. The stuffed shells are delicious, as are the tasty pastas covered in cream or marinara sauces and combination plates. Homemade garlic rolls are always a nice accompaniment. Neo's serves an outstanding white pizza in addition to the traditional red—both are available with a variety of toppings. Reservations are taken, and carryout is available. Neapolitan's is open for dinner daily and additionally for lunch Saturday and Sunday.

PASTA JAY'S $$
1001 Pearl Street, Boulder
(303) 444-5800
It's no surprise why Pasta Jay's has a huge following. The food is amazing. The menu is constructed on a solid foundation of the most popular Italian dishes: manicotti, spaghetti, and various tubular pastas with several flavorful sauces, and pizza, too. Fans love Pasta Jay's mixed salad, drenched in a flavorful dressing, and warm herb and garlic bread. A good selection of robust domestic and imported wines is available. Pasta Jay's serves lunch and dinner daily. Be prepared to wait, it's a very popular place.

RADDA TRATTORIA $–$$
1265 Alpine Ave., Boulder
(303) 442-6100
www.raddatrattoria.com
New to the restaurant scene, Radda Trattoria is a popular North Boulder neighborhood restaurant inspired by the cuisine and culture of Tuscany, Italy. Radda is the second creation of chef Matthew Jansen, after the much-lauded Mateo Restaurant Provencal that opened in 2001. The spirit, beauty and hospitality of Tuscany are transported to the very neighborhood that Matthew grew up in. Open for breakfast, lunch, and dinner daily.

SALVAGGIO'S ITALIAN DELI $
2609 Pearl Street, Boulder
(303) 938-1981
Looking for the best sandwich in town? Boulder newspaper readers say you'll find it here. Try the hot prime rib or pastrami; both are served on freshly baked rolls. Salvaggio's serves special Italian sausages and Boar's Head–brand meats— among the highest-quality domestic cold cuts you can buy. Prime-rib sandwiches are slow-roasted in the rotisserie oven, and when it comes to popularity, they blow everything else away, hands down. The Cajun roast beef and mortadella ham are knockouts. Roasted red bell peppers and fresh mozzarella can be added, too. The sandwich bread is homemade. Order your meal to go, or eat it on the premises. The deli is open for lunch and dinner daily. No credit cards.

TRATTORIA ON PEARL $$–$$$
1430 Pearl Street, Boulder
(303) 544-0008
www.trattoriaonpearl.com
Tucked into the east end of Boulder's Pearl Street Mall is Trattoria on Pearl. Chef Daniel has taken seafood cuisine to a new level. Each day a new menu of specials is printed that features the great catches he has scouted out from vendors who fly in their fresh ingredients from around the world. This charming cafe also has a menu that includes saltimbocca prepared with veal, pork, or chicken and marinated duck breast over roasted

potatoes, apples, and mushrooms in a honey-burgundy glaze. Pasta choices include penne alla vodka, asparagus and cherry tomatoes sautéed in a light vodka tomato cream with your choice of chicken, salmon, or shrimp. Pizza is also included in the menu. The Trattoria has a 300-plus-bottle wine list that will complement any meal. Open daily for lunch and dinner.

MEDITERRANEAN/AFRICAN

4580 $$
4580 Broadway #D-1, Boulder
(303) 448-1500
www.restaurant4580.com
This neighborhood restaurant located on Uptown Broadway features food emphasizing flavors of the Mediterranean including Portugal, Greece, and Spain and a beautifully paired wine list. Reservations are recommended.

MATAAM FEZ MOROCCAN RESTAURANT $$
2226 Pearl Street, Boulder
(303) 440-4167
This richly decorated, exotic restaurant is as much about entertainment as fine dining. While sitting on plump pillows under tented ceilings and listening to Moroccan drums, you will eat with your fingers, but you won't be eating what we think of as finger food. Dine sumptuously on five-course meals such as couscous with vegetables, lamb with artichokes, and delicious Moroccan tea and pastries. There is a selection of meat and vegetarian dishes. But best of all, belly dancers entertain Thursday through Sunday. Belly dancing originated to encourage women through childbirth—hence the focus on strong abdominal movements. This is not Las Vegas belly dancing, which is why children are welcome. This restaurant serves dinner daily.

THE MEDITERRANEAN $–$$
1002 Walnut Street, Boulder
(303) 444-5335
www.themedboulder.com
From the bright-red trim to the beautiful iron

gate and the avant-garde wood-burning brick oven, this place is stylish and lively. It has been voted "Best Mediterranean Restaurant in the Denver Area" by *Westword* magazine, and "Best Appetizers" by *Daily Camera* readers. It's what you want it to be: a romantic spot, a congenial gathering place with a good bar and summer patio, or a family spot—kids get kind treatment here.

Spanish tapas, which are small plates of interesting appetizers, include croquetas de gambase y pollo (shrimp and chicken) and lovely mini pizzas. These are served at the bar or at the table. Light dishes include well-prepared calzones and perfectly dressed salads. Spaghettini di Mare is especially popular. The chefs know how to cook chicken and fish without leaving the heat on a moment too long. Spanish friends say the saffron-gold paella is pretty close to authentic. The Mediterranean is open for dinner daily and for lunch Monday through Saturday.

RAS KASSA'S ETHIOPIAN RESTAURANT $
2111 30th Street, Boulder
(303) 447-2919
www.raskassas.com
A Boulder favorite since 1988, Ras Kassa's moved into the city from Eldorado Springs. Meat and vegetarian dishes are served with a big slab of injera, a crepe-like Ethiopian sourdough bread, which you use to scoop up the rest of the food. Use the bread like a spoon to capture every drop of the hot, red sauces or the milder ginger and garlic sauces. Entrees include chicken or lamb, sweet potato stew, and butternut squash. You can eat in the Ethiopian-decorated interior, with authentic basket-woven tables, or enjoy the creekside patio. It's open for lunch Monday through Friday and dinner daily.

MEXICAN

AJUUA $$
Table Mesa Shopping Center
627 South Broadway, Suite A, Boulder
(303) 494-9204

Cottonwood Square
7960 Niwot Road, Suite 11d, Niwot
(303) 652-3995

Main Street at Flatlrons
535 Zang Street, Suite C-D, Broomfield
(720) 887-3799
www.ajuua.com

Voted "Best Mexican Restaurant" by a number of local newspapers and magazines. Ajuua! (a-huu-a) is an ultimate expression of cheerful celebration, and Ajuua was the name chosen for this restaurant because it reflects a friendly, celebratory environment. The owners, the Garcia family, offer traditional Mexican fare with some distinctly different selections, such as Azteca soup (grilled chicken breast in a broth topped with tortilla strips, avocado, and cheese) and Discada (a sautéed mixture of steak, bacon, chorizo sausage, ground beef, pico de gallo, and spices). Ajuua is open Monday through Saturday for lunch and dinner and Sunday for breakfast, lunch, and dinner.

CASA ALVAREZ $
3161 Walnut Street, Boulder
(303) 546-0630

502 South Public Road, Lafayette
(303) 604-4396
www.casaalvarezboulder.com

No sooner did Casa Alvarez open in a corner of the Walnut Garden shopping center than people started raving about its chili—and the honors started pouring in, including winning the Boulder Chile Olé Contest. The red and green chili are each just about the best of their type around, but the restaurant has a way with other Mexican specialties, too. When it's mild out, the patio is a pleasant place to enjoy your meal. Casa Alvarez makes good margaritas and sells them two-for-one during happy hour, from 4 to 6 p.m. every evening. There are also beer and drink specials. Takeout is available, too. They are open for lunch and dinner daily.

CILANTRO MARY $
450 Main Street, Lyons
(303) 823-5014
www.cilantromarys.com

When you tire of Boulder's choices for Mexican food, head north to the colorful and rustic Cilantro Mary for a slight twist on the traditional theme. If your partner likes plates full of enchiladas covered in cheese while you prefer eclectic fresh salads chock-full of unusual ingredients, you're in the right place. Traditional and non-traditional, try the slow-cooked pork topped with salsa verde and crema Mexicana, served with guacamole and red cabbage slaw. The restaurant offers specialty margaritas, and for dessert, double vanilla flan served with fresh whipped cream and fresh fruit. It's open for lunch and dinner every day except Wednesday and Sunday.

EFRAIN'S $
101 East Cleveland Street, Lafayette
(303) 666-7544

1630 East 63rd Street, Boulder
(303) 440-4045

451 South Pratt Parkway, Longmont
(720) 494-0777

Efrain's in Lafayette is in an old miner's house, where the dining area is relaxed and homey. All three locations offer great tamales, authentic enchiladas, and sizzling tostadas making them some of Boulder County's favorite Mexican restaurants. Be sure to try the costillas, which are Mexican ribs cooked in chile verde … considered to be the house specialty! Efrain's is open for lunch and dinner. Each restaurant has different hours so call in advance.

ILLEGAL PETE'S $
1320 College Avenue, Boulder
(303) 444-3055

1447 Pearl Street, Boulder
(303) 440-3955
www.illegalpetes.com

A Boulder favorite, Illegal Pete's is famous for its sizable burritos. You might not be able to eat the whole thing! You have your choice of fish, beef, chicken, or vegetarian burritos smothered with your choice of salsa, sour cream, or cheese. Other menu items include tacos, quesadillas, and taquitos. The environment is casual and is popular with the college crowd. Open daily for lunch and dinner.

JUANITA'S MEXICAN FOOD $
1043 Pearl Street, Boulder
(303) 449-5273
www.juanitas-boulder.com
Consistently voted "Best Mexican Dining" by *Daily Camera* readers, Juanita's is one of Boulder's favorite Mexican restaurants. This place is noisy and usually packed, so don't expect a quiet, intimate meal. The front half is slightly more formal. The back half is good for families, if you're not too distracted by loud music, pool playing, or a TV screen in every corner; kids love to sit in the back where wooden booths make it easier to color the children's menu. Enjoy the traditional Mexican food, which is always hot; fast service; icy cold margaritas; and a huge selection of beer. Lunch and dinner are served daily.

RIO GRANDE MEXICAN RESTAURANT $
1101 Walnut Street, Boulder
(303) 444-3690
www.riograndemexican.com
The Rio Grande is a popular margarita dispensary and Mexican restaurant. Juanita's may win the best Mexican restaurant contest, but the Rio Grande always wins top votes for the best margarita. Colorful Tex-Mex burritos, enchiladas, and fajitas with loads of cheese, black beans, and Spanish rice are featured. The restaurant also offers tortilla chips and pico de gallo, a spicy vegetable relish. The restaurant is open for lunch and dinner daily.

TAHONA TEQUILA BISTRO $$–$$$
1035 Pearl Street, Boulder
(303) 938-9600
www.tahonaboulder.com
Tahona Tequila Bistro brings to Boulder the excit-ing flavors of the Yucatan Peninsula in a colorful and energy-charged setting. The menu focuses on fresh, local ingredients with a modern twist on traditional dishes from the coastal regions of Mexico. The tequila bar, with more than 80 artisan tequilas, will offer freshly squeezed lime margaritas, tequila cocktails, and wines selected to complement your food. For dinner, choose the roast pork guisado—chunky pork stew with pineapple, peppers, plantains, and chayote squash topped with a Tahona hot sauce—or fried whole tilapia—prepared in the traditional style with sauce Vera Cruz, including olives, tomatoes, and almonds with red rice and warm tortillas. Top your meal off with pineapple-mango upside-down cake! Tahona is open for dinner every evening. Reservations are recommended.

TERRACE MAYA $$
4929 North Broadway, Boulder
(303) 443-9336
You have to travel to the very northern edge of Boulder to find Terrace Maya, but the authentic Mexican fare and festive cantina atmosphere make it worth the trip. Appetizers include chili con queso, bowls of pork or veggie green chili, nachos, jalapeño poppers, and chicken wings. The menu features traditional enchiladas, bean burritos, flautas, fajitas, and chimichangas, too. If you're more adventuresome, try Especial Mexican Barbecue, Mexican rib-eye steak, or house favorites such as Acapulco shrimp or pescado Veracruz. A full bar pours delicious mango margaritas, Mexican cervezas, and microbrews. There's a large outdoor patio with live music every Saturday night. Open daily for lunch and dinner.

NATURAL

LEAF VEGETARIAN RESTAURANT $–$$
2010 16th Street, Boulder
(303) 442-1485
www.leafvegetarianrestauruant.com
Leaf Vegetarian Restaurant is dedicated to creating a superb vegetarian dining experience in a tranquil, sophisticated environment. Leaf uses the finest organic, seasonal ingredients in providing a

vegetarian global cuisine and health-conscious dining option for herbivores and omnivores alike. Leaf also provides a full bar highlighted by an enviro-friendly wine list, Boulder's own organic Vodka 14 martinis, fresh juices and smoothies, and specialty loose teas and coffees. The dinner menu includes a wide choice of salads, pasta, and exciting vegetable dishes. The restaurant claims to offer the only strictly vegetarian brunch in Boulder. Stop by for vegan happy hour and dinner seven days a week. Open for lunch daily and brunch Saturday and Sunday.

ORGANIC ORBIT $

1200 Yarmouth Avenue, Boulder
(303) 443-8348
www.organicorbit.com

Voted best new restaurant of 2008 by *Boulder Weekly*, Organic Orbit takes the Birkenstocks out of organic food, and the stuffiness out of fine dining, all with a mission of reconnecting with nature through food. The restaurant was developed with the overriding vision of moving the planet in the direction of an organic lifestyle. Key to that concept is the importance to returning to sustainable agricultural practices that both reduce the damage caused by conventional farming and improve the nutritional value of our food. The restaurant features great-tasting organic food and delivers an authentic dining experience in a chic and intimate atmosphere.

RUDI'S RESTAURANT $$

4720 Table Mesa Drive, Boulder
(303) 494-5858
www.rudismenu.com

This is a natural-food restaurant that looks and feels like a "normal" place, not like a granola-and-tofu dispensary. It offers fine dining based on a variety of influences from all over the world but with natural and organic ingredients. Samosas, a type of Indian snack food made with mildly spiced vegetables, are a fine starter. Thai vegetable curry and crab-stuffed trout are typical entrees and are served with homemade soup or salad and brown or basmati rice. The tenderloin filet is organically

grown. If you come for brunch, try the gingerbread pancakes with whipped cream. Homemade desserts include coffee toffee and Key lime pie. Vegans and people on special diets can get made-to-order food here. Rudi's is open for lunch and dinner daily and for dinner on the weekend.

SUNFLOWER NATURAL FINE DINING $$$

1701 Pearl Street, Boulder
(303) 440-0220

Natural food fans can enjoy contemporary fine dining in two spacious dining rooms. The menu features fresh natural ingredients, including organic produce, free-range poultry, fresh seafood, and vegetarian and vegan items. Pesto-stuffed portobello mushrooms and pepper-seared ahi tuna salad can serve as starters. Entrees include sesame-crusted seared Atlantic salmon on Thai rice noodles with miso-sake glaze and ginger broth, and tempeh-mushroom scalloppine with mashed organic Yukon gold potatoes and steamed organic vegetable medley. Seasonal desserts include Key lime cheesecake and tempura bananas. There are fresh salads and sandwiches for lunch, or choose one of several daily specials. Try an organic coffee drink or fresh-squeezed juice. Sidewalk patio dining or delivery service is available. Sunflower is open for lunch Monday through Saturday, dinner nightly, and brunch on Sunday.

PIZZA

ABO'S $

2761 Iris Avenue, Boulder
(303) 443-1921

1110 13th Street, Boulder
(303) 443-3199

637 South Broadway, Boulder
(303) 494-1274

Abo's has been a Boulder institution since 1977. Stop in for a slice or call ahead for a whole pie. Because of its great two-for-one plus free drinks special, this pizzeria has a huge following with the college crowd. Abo's is open daily for lunch and dinner.

LEFTY'S PIZZERIA $
641 Main Street, Niwot
(303) 652-3100

The favorite pizzas at this down-home local pizza parlor are the California veggie (artichokes, broccoli, sun-dried tomatoes, spinach, mozzarella, garlic, and olive oil) and Craig's Cardiac Arrest (pepperoni, ham, sausage, and bacon). But you can also get a pie with pineapple, jalapeños, and/ or black olives. Best of all, the pizzeria delivers in Niwot and the surrounding 80 square miles, ranging from Longmont to north Lafayette. A percentage of all proceeds goes to Niwot's youth team sports. This little pizza parlor is open for lunch and dinner daily. No credit cards.

NICK-N-WILLY'S TAKE-N-BAKE PIZZA $
801 Pearl Street, Boulder
(303) 444-9898

4800 Baseline Road, Boulder
(303) 499-9898
www.nicknwillyspizza.com

Hands down, *Daily Camera* readers favor Nick-N-Willy's pizza to anything else around. You can buy pizza by the slice and eat it in the store, or call ahead and, 20 minutes later, pick up a whole pizza to take home and bake in your oven. It all started when a friend of Keith McQuillen and Terry Jones opened a great pizza store in California. Keith and Terry found the take-and-bake pizza so delicious, they brought the idea to Boulder. Over the years, different pizzas and toppings have been added, and Nick-N-Willy's has expanded into a dozen different Colorado locations. The Aegean vegetarian pizza is one of the most popular, with olive oil, Feta, mozzarella, garlic, spinach, sun-dried tomatoes, and oregano. There's a big cooler with soft drinks and pre-made salads if you need something to complement your pie. Nick-N-Willy's is open daily for lunch and dinner.

PROTO'S PIZZERIA NAPOLETANA $$
4670 Broadway, Boulder
(720) 565-1050

600 South Airport Road, Building B
Longmont
(303) 485-5000

489 North Highway 287, Lafayette
(303) 661-3030
www.protospizza.com

Proto's first opened in 1999 when Pam Proto finally decided that in order to get true Neapolitan pizza in Colorado she would have to do it herself, and she has succeeded. The pizzeria has received critical acclaim from the *Daily Camera*, the *Rocky Mountain News,* and *Bon Appetit* magazine, among others. The choice of napoletana-style pizza is extensive—17 at last count and that doesn't include create-your-own pizza. Sample the Atomica Pie (mozzarella, tomato sauce, garlic, and oregano sprinkled with crushed red pepper and black olives and topped with Italian sausage) or perhaps the Pontiff Pie (olive oil, garlic, fresh spinach, sun-dried tomatoes, and mozzarella and Haystack Mountain Feta cheese). All the ingredients are fresh. Proto's offers wine by the glass and a wide selection of beer and cocktails. Open most days for both lunch and dinner.

PUBS AND BREWPUBS

BOULDER BEER $
2880 Wilderness Place, Boulder
(303) 444-8448
www.boulderbeer.com

Eight different fresh ales are made on the premises. Three are gold-medal winners, pronounced the best beer in the country at the Great American Beer Festival. Sandwiches and salad go with the fresh beer, and if you arrive around 2 p.m., you can tour the establishment, see the whole beer-making process, and sample the current brews. Open for lunch and dinner daily except Sundays.

THE HUNGRY TOAD $$
2543 Broadway, Boulder
(303) 442-5012
www.thehungrytoad.com

This is Boulder's original English pub. Four English beers are on tap, and eight are available by the bottle. Fish and chips, shepherd's pie, salads, and burgers are popular. The food's not arty, my lad, but it's hearty, and accompanied by comfortable chatter and a pint at your elbow. The pub is open for lunch and dinner daily.

MOUNTAIN SUN PUB AND BREWERY $
1535 Pearl Street, Boulder
(303) 546-0886
www.mountainsunpub.com

SOUTHERN SUN PUB AND BREWERY $
627 South Broadway, Boulder
(303) 543-0886

Mountain Sun on Pearl and Southern Sun in south Boulder are Boulder's "New Age" brew pubs, with seven made-on-the-premises fresh brews that burst onto the microbrew scene by winning awards. The food at both locations is a winner, too. Most of it is vegetarian, including meatless salads, chili, soup, garden burgers, burritos, and pizzas, so you might call them health-food brewpubs. Both ountain Sun and Southern Sun are open for lunch and dinner daily. No credit cards.

OLD CHICAGO $
1102 Pearl Street, Boulder
(303) 443-5031
www.oldchicago.com

It's hard to decide whether to describe this spot on the west end of the Pearl Street Mall as a pub that serves popular Chicago-style pizzas or a pizzeria with a whopping beer selection. More than 110 beers are available from the bar, and the deep-dish pizza is buttery crusted and delicious; whole-wheat crust is also available. The main part of the restaurant truly has a pub feel, while the seating in the back is more spacious. There's also a small patio in the rear. Old Chicago's stout mud pie has layers of coffee and chocolate ice cream, flavored with Australian Sheaf Stout beer.

It's open for lunch and dinner until midnight on weekdays and until 1 a.m. on weekends; unlike many brewpubs, the kitchen stays open until Old Chicago closes.

WALNUT BREWERY $$
1123 Walnut Street, Boulder
(303) 447-1345
www.walnutbrewery.com

This was Boulder's first true brewpub, and it's still the best. The brewing process is on display here, and you can watch while you drink and dine. The brewmaster concocts six original and seasonal ales, including Buffalo Gold, brewed in small batches to provide a malty, floral happiness . . . we mean, hoppiness. The Walnut Brewery pioneered the practice of donating leftovers from the brewing process to feed happy livestock and to enrich soil in flower beds on the downtown mall. Sometimes, walking the mall is a truly heady experience. Salads, tenderloin, seafood, pastas, and vegetarian entrees help draw the crowds to this distinctive, tall-ceilinged, lively space. The brewery is open for lunch and dinner daily.

WEST END TAVERN $
926 Pearl Street, Boulder
(303) 444-3535
http://thewestendtavern.com

This is more a bar than a pub, for it is really basic and ungentrified—just the way fans like it. It serves good basic salads, soups, and plenty of burgers, along with 20 different beers and concoctions from the full bar. There's live music or comedy five nights a week—sometimes seven. The rooftop, with the view of the Flatirons, is the most popular summer spot at this friendly neighborhood tavern. Open for lunch and dinner daily, the West End closes at 2 a.m.

NIGHTLIFE

Boulder isn't particularly known for its wild nightlife, though there's plenty to do and plenty of places to go after dark. The college crowd has its hangouts, as do the single professionals and families. Most residents and visitors looking for a night out go to a restaurant, concert, or movie—or to one of the many spots listed below.

Because our state is so beautiful and the weather so fine, Boulderites and Coloradans thrive on the out-of-doors. Therefore, many cafes and concert halls are alfresco. On warm evenings from spring through fall, one of the most popular activities, unrivaled in entertainment value (not to mention free), is strolling on the Pearl Street Mall. During summer weekends the pedestrian mall is transformed into a six-ring circus on every block with jugglers, musicians, magicians, bagpipers, and a dreadlocked man in tights who folds himself into an impossibly small box. Though the mall entertainment is free, performers usually have a donation "hat" and appreciate financial support (they have to pay for permits to perform on the mall).

Another uniquely Boulder form of entertainment is *etown,* a locally produced weekly public radio show that focuses on the environment and is recorded live with audience participation at the historic Boulder Theater. It's our own homegrown, eco-version of Garrison Keillor's *A Prairie Home Companion. Etown* is aired weekly by National Public Radio on various stations across the country and has featured such celebrities as James Taylor, Dan Fogelberg, Dave Barry, Emmylou Harris, Rickie Lee Jones, and The Persuasions. Tickets are quite inexpensive, and it's fun to play a part in a nationally broadcast radio show. Audience members also get to enjoy the beauty of the restored art deco former movie theater.

Those in search of the really bright lights and big names will usually have to travel to the magnificent Red Rocks amphitheater near Golden, or to Denver's park-like Coor's Amphitheatre, its Paramount and Ogden Theatres, the Grizzly Rose, or other venues larger than what Boulder has to offer. Some top Denver hot spots regularly frequented by Boulderites are listed among the Boulder nightspots; for a complete Denver listing, see the *Insiders' Guide® to Denver.*

Don't forget that the legal drinking age in Colorado is 21, and that drinking and driving don't mix. Don't jeopardize your life—and ours—by getting behind the wheel after you've been drinking. Boulder police have a very low tolerance for alcohol-related offenses. Make sure your group includes a designated driver.

Note that most Boulder bars don't have a cover charge. Those that do usually only charge for admission a couple of nights a week, when there's live music or a special event such as dance lessons.

BENTLEY'S NIGHTCLUB
The Boulder Broker Inn,
555 30th Street, Boulder
(303) 444-3330
www.boulderbrokerinn.com
In disco days, Bentley's Nightclub at the Broker (see our Accommodations chapter) vibrated to the dance-dance-dance beat of Donna Summer and the brothers Gibb, an experience complete with lighted dance floor and a DJ with a diamond stud. Today, it remains a favorite spot for less frenetic dancing and meeting interesting people. It

attracts an older, more professional baby-boomer crowd (versus college kids). Dancing is popular Wednesday through Saturday, with salsa Thursday and swing Saturday. The bar menu is available every night until 11 p.m., and the bar closes an hour or two later.

BOULDER THEATER
2032 14th Street, Boulder
(303) 786-7030 (Boulder Theater Box Office, noon to 6 p.m. weekdays, noon to 5 p.m. weekends)
www.bouldertheater.com
An art deco gem (along with the county courthouse across the street, one of only two in Boulder), the former movie theater has evolved into a lively venue for everything from classical performances by the Colorado Music Festival to world music from Kitaro to concerts by former John Coltrane jazz pianist McCoy Tyner. Lately, the theater has returned to its roots with classic and art movies.

The theater is best known, though, as the home of the nationally broadcast radio program *etown*. "Live from the historic Boulder Theater in the foothills of the Rocky Mountains, it's *etown*," begins the radio show, which focuses on entertainment and environmental issues—a sometimes difficult twosome. *Etown* celebrated its 15th year in 2006. The show is taped live to be run by National Public Radio and commercial stations. The audience is part of the show, clapping and cheering on cue, sometimes for several takes. It's interesting to see how a radio show works. The show recognizes individuals from around the country, nominated for their grassroots work for better communities and environment, with the E-chievement Awards.

Etown records several shows a year. It features musicians, environmentalists, politicians, authors, and others, including Rickie Lee Jones, Taj Mahal, Sweet Honey in the Rock, Paul Winter, Joan Baez, cowboy poet Baxter Black, Earth Day founder Denis Hayes, Bruce Cockburn, Arlo Guthrie, and Leftover Salmon. Run on a shoestring budget and volunteer efforts, *etown* is the brainchild of Boul-

der husband-and-wife co-producers Nick and Helen Forster. Nick was formerly principal bassist, guitarist, and vocalist for the bluegrass group Hot Rize (which still plays reunion concerts), and Helen, an actress and singer, has provided harmony for performers from Michelle Shocked and John Gorka to Rosanne Cash.

Drinks and snacks are available, so the audience can sip their favorite beverage while they watch the show. Part of the theater has cafe tables and chairs. Tickets are available at the Boulder Theater Box Office, or from the theater Web site at www.bouldertheater.com. Visit the Web site at www.etown.org for more information. Come early for dinner on the Downtown Mall and grab a handy parking space before the crowd arrives.

THE CATACOMBS
Hotel Boulderado
2115 13th Street, Boulder
(303) 443-0486
www.boulderado.com
The appropriately named Catacombs was the first bar in Boulder to legally serve liquor in 1969. It has had several incarnations, including one as an inexpensive Italian restaurant and another as an expensive continental restaurant, but has now resumed its original identity as an easygoing local bar catering to a mixed-age crowd (average age 35). There's live music Wednesday through Saturday nights. Happy hour is daily from 4:30 to 9 p.m., and snacks and appetizers are served until midnight. Pool tables are scattered through the underground warren of stone-walled rooms. A smoking section is available—a rarity in Boulder, where bars and restaurants may have smoking sections only if they are completely shielded from nonsmoking patrons.

CENTRO LATIN KITCHEN & REFRESHMENT PALACE
950 Pearl Street, Boulder
(303) 442-7771
www.bigredf.com
Formerly called Rhumba, Centro is now the place

to go for Latin food and amazing cocktails. The outdoor patio/bar still rocks and draws a big crowd, and the indoor ambiance is still the same. Colorful and bright, with food and drinks to match, Centro is a favorite with locals. Try the pisco sours and the hibiscus fruit punch with your daylong roasted chicken dish served with hot rice salad and sweet mole. Happy hour brings $2 tacos and $1.50 Modelo Especial cans, Monday through Saturday 3:30 to 5:30 p.m.

COMEDY WORKS
1226 15th Street, Denver
(303) 595-3637
www.comedyworks.com

5345 Landmark Place, Greenwood Village
(720) 274-6800
"See tomorrow's stars today" is the slogan of this intimate downtown Denver club where Roseanne Barr got her start. Comedy Works, which celebrated its 20th anniversary in 2003, regularly runs headliner shows. Tuesday is improv and new-talent night; Wednesday through Sunday are for established performers. Reservations are recommended (only ages 21 and older are admitted). Cocktails and a limited food menu are available during the show.

CONOR O'NEILL'S IRISH PUB AND GRILL
1922 13th Street, Boulder
(303) 449-1922
www.conoroneills.com
Since 1978, The James Pub & Grille was the closest thing to a real Irish pub in Boulder—red potatoes were a popular dish and live music filled the bar with the trill of traditional folk tunes. Now the restaurant and bar is a step closer to Tipperary in its new incarnation as Conor O'Neill's Irish Pub and Grill, with an interior created in Ireland and brought to Boulder piece by piece for assembly. The bar has returned to its entertainment roots, too, with live music Tuesday through Sunday and an open mike on Tuesdays. The pub is open 11:30 a.m. to 2 a.m. daily and serves lunch and dinner, including Irish stew and shepherd's pie,

teas, and 20-ounce English pints of beer from England and Ireland.

COORS AMPHITHEATRE
6350 Greenwood Plaza Boulevard
Englewood
(303) 220-7000 (mid-May through October)
About an hour's drive from Boulder, Coors Amphitheatre, southeast of Denver, offers summer performances by all types of top nationally known groups, including rock, classical, and oldies (a recent season included Snoop Dog and REO Speedwagon). Enjoy these outdoor events either from reserved seats or with a picnic on the lawn. The usual types of food and drinks are sold in the amphitheater, but the venue is strict about allowing no outside food or drink—no coolers, picnic baskets, or thermoses. Also outlawed: cameras, tape recorders, lawn chairs, knives, and firearms. You may bring small backpacks and blankets, umbrellas, and binoculars. No exit is allowed once you enter the concert area; if you forget your ID for alcoholic beverages, you can't go out to your car and get it. Concert season is mid-May through October. For tickets call the box office at (303) 770-2222 during the concert season or Ticketmaster at (303) 830-8497.

CORNER BAR
Hotel Boulderado,
2115 13th Street, Boulder
(303) 442-4560
www.boulderado.com
An extensive list of wines by the glass, a variety of martinis, and eight microbrews on tap (five made in Colorado) are available in this historic bar decorated in dark wood. Upstairs from the Catacombs (see previous page), the Corner Bar has a casually elegant atmosphere. In the summer, the bar spills onto a charming sidewalk cafe along Spruce Street, 1 block off the Downtown Mall. Food, from macho nachos to elegant rock shrimp and crab cakes, is served until midnight.

FLAGSTAFF HOUSE
Flagstaff Road (west end of Baseline Road, partway up the mountain), Boulder
(303) 442-4640
www.flagstaffhouse.com
Even those who can't afford dinner at the Flagstaff House—one of Boulder's most elegant and expensive restaurants, perched 6,000 feet up Flagstaff Mountain (see the Restaurants chapter)—can still enjoy the great view and wonderful, outdoor terraced bar for the price of a drink. Overhead heating units are installed for comfort on cool evenings. If you're lucky, you might catch a fantastic summer lightning show out on the plains. For a really romantic drink with someone special, choose this beautiful spot. Flagstaff is open daily from 5 to 10 p.m.

THE FOUNDRY
1109 Walnut Street, Boulder
(303) 447-1803
www.foundryboulder.com
A full bar with wine, cognacs, beer, mixed drinks, and cigars, along with 11 full-size Brunswick pool tables, makes this upscale spot a favorite. It's a great place to meet people and mingle in a comfortable, spacious yet intimate atmosphere. There's free live music Friday and Saturday, with a blues and jazz band starting around 9:30 or 10 p.m. and playing until closing at 2 a.m. Happy hours are 11 a.m. to 7 p.m. daily and drinks are served until 1:30 a.m. An interesting group gathers at the Foundry—people of all types. Lunch and dinner are served.

FOX THEATRE AND CAFE
1135 13th Street, Boulder
(303) 447-0095, (303) 443-3399 (box office)
www.foxtheatre.com
The Fox has become one of the top clubs for live music in North America, with acts like Fat Mama, Disco Inferno, Hootie and the Blowfish, and Run-D.M.C. Another converted movie house, this cafe/concert hall on University Hill holds more than 600 people and has three full bars and nightly live music by local, national, and international performers. People of all ages attend the shows

(those older than 21 get a bracelet to indicate they can order alcoholic drinks). The lobby sushi bar, Hapa on the Hill Sushi Grill, serves up raw fish and sake from noon 'til the music ends. Call the box office for ticket prices.

THE GRIZZLY ROSE SALOON & DANCE EMPORIUM
5450 North Valley Highway (I-25), Denver
(303) 295-2353,
(303) 295-1330 (for concert information)
www.grizzlyrose.com
Voted the nation's No. 1 country music dance hall by the Country Music Association, Grizzly Rose has a 5,000-square-foot dance floor and gets such top names as Merle Haggard and Wynonna. There are free introductory dance lessons Wednesdays at 7 p.m., with various contests and specials other nights. Call (303) 42-DANCE for contest information. Thursdays are ladies' nights from 8 p.m. to midnight with free wine, well and draft drinks, and no cover charge for women (men pay $5 cover). Concert tickets are available through Ticketmaster (303-830-8497), or at the door; advanced ticketing is necessary for national acts. The Grizzly Rose is open from 11 a.m. (serving lunch) to 1:30 a.m. Tuesday through Friday, from 5 p.m. until 1:30 a.m. Saturday and Sunday.

JAX FISH HOUSE
928 Pearl Street, Boulder
(303) 444-1811
www.bigredf.com
A local favorite, Jax is known for its fresh seafood, but savvy Boulderites have latched onto it as a place for a before- or after-dinner drink and plate of raw oysters or shrimp. The full, fishy menu is served in the bar. Jax opens at 4 p.m. daily, closing

ℹ Some of Boulder's best nightlife is along the Pearl Street Mall on warm evenings from spring through fall. String quartets, bagpipers, magicians, and other street performers keep the crowd entertained for hours. And it's free (donations are suggested for the performers).

at 9 p.m. Sunday, 10 p.m. Monday through Thursday, and 11 p.m. Friday and Saturday. Happy hour is from 4 to 6 p.m. daily, with East Coast oysters for 50 cents.

JOHNNY'S CIGAR BAR
One Boulder Plaza,
1801 13th Street, Boulder
(303) 449-0884
www.johnnyscigars.com
If you are a cigar-lover, this is the place for you. This exclusive cigar bar offers the finest cigars in five humidors and a separate smoking room with fresh air ventilation. Add a deluxe martini and wine list, Colorado microbrews, gourmet small plates, and live jazz and blues, and you have the perfect evening. Enjoy their overstuffed leather chairs, the handcrafted cherry bar, and the HD plasma-screen TVs. Johnny's hours are seasonal, but they are generally open Monday through Friday 5 p.m. until 11 p.m., Thursday through Saturday 5 p.m. until 1 a.m, and Sunday from 10:30 a.m. during football season.

LAZY DOG SPORTS BAR AND GRILL
1346 Pearl Street, Boulder
(303) 440-3355
www.thelazydog.com
Broncos, Av's, Nuggets, Rockies, Buffs; no matter what your team, the game will be on at the Lazy Dog. Spend the afternoon on the rooftop deck that overlooks the Pearl Street Mall enjoying a varied menu that's a step up from the usual bar-style food. With everything from salmon steaks to tasty crab cakes to fantastic burgers and drinks of all kinds, you'll find something to please your palate. The Lazy Dog is open from 11 a.m. to midnight Monday through Saturday. Depending on game schedules, the restaurant may open earlier or stay open later. Join them for happy hour any Monday through Friday from 3 to 6 p.m.

NISSI'S
2675 North Park Drive, Lafayette
(303) 665-2757 (after 4 p.m. only)
www.nissis.com
Everyone is talking about the newest music venue to arrive in East Boulder County. The award-winning Nissi's in Lafayette serves up some great live music acts and delicious food. Local, national and emerging musicians consider Nissi's to be the place to play. In addition to good music, their gourmet menu revolves around tapas—which are served family style—and is accented with an array of fine wines and popular beers. Come have a glass of wine and listen to Hazel Miller belt out some blues! Hours are Tuesday through Saturday 5 p.m. until 9:30 or 10 p.m. Happy hour is from 5 to 6 p.m. Dinner is served from 6:30 until 9:30 p.m. Featured entertainment is from 7:30 until 9:30 or 10 on weekends.

OLD CHICAGO
11th and Pearl Streets, Boulder
(303) 443-5031
Known far and wide for its World Beer Tour and Hall of Foam, Old Chicago has more than 110 international and microbrewery beers, with 24 on tap. It's also known for its deep-dish, Chicago-style pizza, its pleasant patio, and "the big cookie," a delicious, deep-dish, fresh-baked chocolate-chip cookie served hot. Old Chicago opens daily at 11 a.m. and closes at 2 a.m.; last call is 1:15 a.m.

OSKAR BLUES GRILL AND BREW
303 Main Street, Lyons
(303) 823-6855
www.oskarblues.com
This beer-blessed home opened in 1997 and became a brewpub in 1999. Today it plays host to some of the nation's best beers, live blues, and Cajun-inspired food. What consistently brings folks back to this venue is great beer, food, exceptional bands, and that Dixie-meets-Rockies hospitality. The restaurant is open Monday through Saturday 11 a.m. until 10 p.m. The bar is open Sunday through Thursday 11 a.m. until midnight, and Friday and Saturday 11 a.m. until 2 a.m.

PARAMOUNT THEATRE
1631 Glenarm Place, Denver
(303) 892-7016 (tickets/information)
www.paramountdenver.com

Built in the 1930s by Temple Hoyne Buell, a renowned Colorado architect, this beautiful art deco theater opened as a vaudeville house and was later a movie theater. It still houses one of only two Mighty Wurlitzer organs in the country (the other is in New York's Radio City Music Hall). The theater averages 10 to 12 shows a month, including comedy, pop music, children's programming, ballet, noted speakers, and rock concerts. During rock concerts the front row of the 1,870 seats is sacrificed to make room for fans who just have to bounce to the beat, dance, mosh, etc. The box office is open 10 a.m. to 9 p.m. the day of events only. Tickets may be purchased through Ticketmaster outlets or charged by phone at (303) 830-8497.

PIONEER INN
15 East First Street, Nederland
(303) 258-7733

For some entertainment with great mountain atmosphere, stop at the rustic "P.I.," where you can dance to live music Friday and Saturday nights. Thursday is "open mike" night and on Wednesday nights you can enjoy either Irish music or bluegrass. The Pioneer also serves great burgers and Mexican food. They have a pool table, foosball table, and other games. The bar closes at 1:30 a.m. and the kitchen closes at 9 p.m.

THE PUB AND CELLAR
1108 Pearl Street, Boulder
(303) 939-9900

This cozy bar offers one of the few smoking areas in the city. The pub opens daily at noon (11 a.m. Saturday and Sunday during football season) and stays open 'til 2 a.m. The Cellar, right on the Downtown Mall next to Old Chicago, is the only place in Boulder where you can get a late-night snack, according to those who have tried elsewhere to no avail. The Cellar really serves food until 1:30 a.m. nightly. Pool tables, upstairs and down, keep patrons busy. A dart room attracts pick-up games.

RED ROCKS AMPHITHEATER
Off I-70 West (north of Denver)
Morrison
(303) 640-7334,
(303) 830-8497 (ticket information)
www.redrocksonline.com

This spectacular natural-rock amphitheater is the venue for many top performers (one summer lineup included Dave Matthews, John Mellencamp, and Blues Traveler). Red Rocks information and tickets are available through Ticketmaster (303-830-8497). Or check the Web site for more concert information.

REDFISH FISHHOUSE & BREWERY
2027 13th Street, Boulder
(303) 440-5858
www.redfishbrewhouse.com

You'll feel like you are back in the Big Easy at RedFish, a quirky Boulder venue that serves up fantastic New Orleans–style fare and soulful music. The bar features comedy nights on Sundays, $3 mojitos on Wednesdays, $1 pints on Thursdays from 9 to 11 p.m., and small musical acts that bring down the house sprinkled in throughout the week. The bar opens every day at 4 p.m.

RIO GRANDE MEXICAN RESTAURANT
1101 Walnut Street, Boulder
(303) 444-3690
www.riograndemexican.com

The Rio is a restaurant, no question about that, but mention it to anyone in town and their first reaction will be, "Oh, yeah, margaritas." Double-shot margaritas in birdbath-size glasses have been winning the Rio awards since 1986. The place opens daily at 11 a.m. for lunch and at 5 p.m. for dinner. The Rio won't sell you more than three margaritas, but if even that number proves overwhelming, the restaurant will cheerfully call you a cab to help you get home safely.

THE SINK
1165 13th Street, Boulder
(303) 444-7465

For a venerable institution (it opened in 1949),

The Sink on University Hill is a funky piece of work, with exposed pipes, concrete floors, walls splashed with bright cartoons referring to Boulder institutions and events, and ceilings and bathroom stalls covered with the graffiti greetings of several generations of CU students. In addition to a traditional hungry-student menu of burgers and pizza, The Sink offers beer and potent mixed drinks (limit two) and historical significance—Robert Redford used to sweep floors there when he was a CU student. Food is served from 11 a.m. until 9:45 p.m. and the bar stays open until 2 a.m. Choose from a selection of 18 beers on tap.

SUNDOWN SALOON
1136 Pearl Street, Boulder
(303) 449-4987
A little off the beaten path in atmosphere but right on the Pearl Street Mall, the Sundown is for those who want a bit of a different scene. It's a bit more blue collar overall but has an unlikely mix of patrons. College students might find themselves having a beer with a hardcore Harley-Davidson biker in black leather or a lawyer in pinstripes. Sundown opens at noon daily and serves snacks until closing at 2 a.m. There are six pool tables and a big-screen TV to pass the time between.

TAHONA TEQUILA BISTRO
1035 Pearl Street, Boulder
(303) 938-9600
www.tahonaboulder.com
In addition to authentic food inspired by the Yucatan, Tahona offers 80 specialty tequilas, freshly-squeezed margaritas, and other tasty tequila cocktails. Bar food specials are available from 4 p.m. to close every night. Don't miss their happy hour from 4 to 6 p.m. daily and after 10 p.m. Sunday through Wednesday, when beer, wine, well drinks, house margs, and shooters are among the featured drinks. This is a great

> Would Boulder be Boulder without The Sink? Nope. A funky pizza joint for sure, this place is a must-see!

place to have dinner and drinks, or a delightful after-dinner spot to sip that tequila you've always wanted to try.

WALNUT BREWERY
1123 Walnut Street, Boulder
(303) 447-1345
www.walnutbrewery.com
This very popular microbrewery is in a tastefully redecorated old warehouse and makes its own six fresh, delicious beers. Order a sampler and try them all. The diverse dinner menu is served until 10:30 p.m. every night (see our Restaurants chapter for details). The Walnut Brewery is open until 2 a.m. Thursday through Saturday and until 1 a.m. Sunday through Wednesday. Go early on weekends (before 6 p.m.) if you don't want to wait in a line that often stretches out the door and down the block. The Walnut Brewery also provides beer to go and catering services.

WALRUS
11th and Walnut Streets, Boulder
(303) 443-9902
The Walrus has been around for many years, undergoing various changes of personality and clientele from a fancy restaurant to a neighborhood bar. Currently it's a late-night college bar, with pizza, burgers, and appetizers served along with bar drinks and beer. There are six pool tables, air hockey, and foosball for fun. Last call every night is 1:15 a.m., and food is served until 11 p.m. on weekdays and 1 a.m. on weekends.

WEST END TAVERN
926 Pearl Street, Boulder
(303) 444-3535
www.thewestendtavern.com
www.bigredf.com
The West End Tavern has been a local favorite since 1987 and now it has a new look and a new menu. Recently named one of the top restaurants in the Denver area by *5280* magazine, the West End has a great antique wooden bar that is the perfect place to unwind at the end of a

long day. There is nothing like an afternoon on the rooftop deck savoring one of the tavern's 50 bourbon selections or one of their special mint juleps. Beers flow during game days with games enjoyed on three plasma TVs. The menu is unrivaled whether you are in the mood for an appetizer or a full lunch or dinner. Don't miss the hermit crab races on the first Thursday of every month at 11 p.m.! The kitchen is open daily from 11:30 a.m. to 10 p.m. Happy hour is Monday through Friday 3 to 6 p.m.

ZOLO GRILL
2525 Arapahoe Avenue, Boulder
(303) 449-0444
www.bigredf.com

According to Denver's *Rocky Mountain News*, Zolo is fresh and hip and one of the most popular spots in Boulder. We couldn't agree more. Since opening in Boulder in 1994, Zolo Grill has continued to draw patrons who swear by their spicy southwestern/New World cuisine. Dubbed the "absolute hottest restaurant in Boulder" by *5280* magazine, Zolo's menu includes a masterful blending of traditional Mexican, Native American, and New World cuisine. With zesty entrees that range from $12 to $27, Zolo also offers an extensive wine list, microbrews, margarita menu, and more than 80 tequilas. Zolo is open Monday through Saturday from 11 a.m. to 10 p.m. and Sunday from 10 a.m. to 9 p.m.

ACCOMMODATIONS

Boulder proper offers more than two-dozen places to stay, with nearly 2,500 rooms ranging from bargain-rate facilities to luxury hotels and romantic bed-and-breakfast inns. The choices expand when you head for the hills, where country cabins, great adventure ranches, and mountain retreats beckon. Many of the accommodations are popular way stations for travelers planning to continue on to Rocky Mountain National Park and Estes Park (see the chapters on those destinations for more information). In fact, Boulder itself is only 35 miles from Estes Park, which means roughly an hour's drive up, down, and around the mountains. Many country places are even closer, so for these, we've listed the approximate driving time to reach both Boulder and Estes Park.

Towering over the Denver-Boulder turnpike just minutes from the city, the Omni Interlocken Resort features a 27-hole championship golf course. The new St. Julien Hotel & Spa is centrally located in downtown Boulder.

GET YOUR RESERVATION EARLY

Where Boulder accommodations are concerned, it pays to start working on your reservations early. From May through October, it's wise to reserve a month in advance. Dates that sell out early include CU-Boulder fall football weekends (especially when the Buffaloes play Nebraska), graduation in mid-May, and the Bolder Boulder Memorial Day weekend, all of which pack the town. Since it's not a ski destination, Boulder's slowest season is November through February. Rates are usually lower then, too.

Whether you need a room two years from now or right away, the Boulder Convention & Visitors Bureau (303-442-2911 or 800-444-0447 or www.bouldercoloradousa.com) can send you an updated packet of information about Boulder, plus the latest hotel/motel rate sheet. The bureau does not operate a central reservations service, but on busy weekends it will assist visitors seeking a place to stay by calling around to see if anyone has canceled, making a room available. If you're desperate, this sometimes can help.

A WORD ABOUT SMOKING

Boulder policy-makers figured out early the harmful consequences of America's legal drug—tobacco—and established many smoke-free zones. In 1995 smoking was banned in all public places, and in 2006 a law was passed requiring that 75 percent of hotel rooms and all common areas in hotels be smoke-free. Many accommodations also prohibit or restrict smoking. Most bed-and-breakfast inns, for instance, don't allow any smoking indoors. While most hotels provide some smoking rooms, there are fewer and fewer all the time; so if you want the freedom to smoke, be sure to ask for a smoking room.

PRICE INFORMATION

Prices may vary throughout the year, dropping in late fall and winter. Some places offer rooms at various price levels. Some properties also offer discounted business rates for extended stays or discounts for AAA members, senior citizens, or others. Individual properties can provide more details. Unless indicated otherwise, assume that local lodging places accept cash, traveler's checks, personal and company checks (both in-state and out-of-state), and major credit cards.

Price-Code Key

Our price-code key, shown in dollar signs ($), is based on average daily summer (peak) rates for a standard room for two adults.

$.................less than $55
$$ ....$56 to $75
$$$ ....$76 to $100
$$$$ ....$101 to $125
$$$$$..........$126 and more

BED-AND-BREAKFASTS AND COUNTRY INNS

If you've never stayed at a bed-and-breakfast or a country inn (though often a distinction is not made between the two, in this area, a country inn is generally bigger), try one in Boulder. Each room is individually decorated with special treasures, antique furnishings, and paintings. Most rooms have private baths, often lavishly appointed. Many are in former mansions or mountain lodges. No, most Boulderites don't live this way, but plenty of us would like to. These homes are so peaceful and romantic, you may wish you could linger for years. Extra details of decor and service can add immeasurably to the richness of your stay. No wonder these are popular for honeymoons and anniversaries. Keep to yourself or relax in the living room and strike up a conversation with the staff and other travelers. Most bed-and-breakfasts offer what they now tend to call "continental-plus breakfast," with homemade breads or rolls, a choice of beverage, fresh fruit, and perhaps cereal. Some prepare a full breakfast each morning, with a hot entree and cereal available, too.

Bed-and-breakfasts rarely permit smoking or pets, and most inns don't allow children younger than age 12. If you book your family somewhere that does permit children, make sure the kids are well-behaved—and brace them for the absence of standard hotel offerings such as televisions and indoor, heated pools. If you might be arriving during one of Boulder's infrequent hot spells,

ask about air-conditioning. Some rooms have it, some don't need it, and others don't have it but need it.

Several of Boulder's best bed-and-breakfasts belong to an association called the Distinctive Inns of Colorado (800-866-0621), which can send you a directory including evocative photographs of many member properties.

City of Boulder

Many Boulder bed-and-breakfasts are near the center of the city, often in mostly residential areas. In a way, they make you an instant resident, for they give you a lovely, distinctive neighborhood to call your own during your stay. A central location means fun just outside your door. It can also mean traffic and other urban noise. Mention a desire for total quiet to the staff if you want a room where you won't notice traffic at all.

ALPS BOULDER CANYON INN $$$$$
38619 Boulder Canyon Drive, Boulder
(303) 444-5445
www.alpsinn.com
Voted the best 2006 Boulder Bed and Breakfast by the *Rocky Mountain News,* the Alps Inn is a rustic yet luxurious getaway in Boulder Canyon. Perfect for romantic weekends, weddings, and company retreats, the Alps Inn has 12 distinctive guest rooms with authentic Mission furniture. All rooms have private baths, fireplaces, air-conditioning, high-speed wireless, and other premium amenities. Guests are served a gourmet breakfast, afternoon tea, and evening desserts. A variety of indulgent spa services are also available, rounding out a perfect stay.

THE BRADLEY BOULDER INN $$$$$
2040 16th Street, Boulder
(303) 545-5200
www.thebradleyboulder.com
Luxurious rooms and cozy comfort await visitors to Boulder's newest bed-and-breakfast. The inn, which is located just one block from the Pearl Street Mall, has 12 sophisticated guest rooms, each with a private bath, fireplace, luxurious

linens, Jacuzzi spa, wireless Internet, and flat-screen TV. The mountain views are on the house. A delicious breakfast is served each morning, and wine and cheese is offered every afternoon. Guests also can enjoy free health-club privileges at Boulder One Fitness.

BRIAR ROSE BED & BREAKFAST $$$$$
2151 Arapahoe Avenue, Boulder
(303) 442-3007 or (800) 786-8440
www.briarrosebb.com

This was Boulder's first bed-and-breakfast, established in 1981, and it remains one of the coziest. This English-style inn has a landscaped courtyard and garden complete with lovely little pond and waterfall. Each of the nine guest rooms has Boulder-made featherbed comforters. Two of the rooms feature wood-burning fireplaces. Tea is served in the afternoon, and a homemade breakfast—delicious baked goods, granola, and fresh fruit—greets the guests every morning. The inn is within walking distance of Crossroads Mall, CU-Boulder and downtown, Naropa University, and the Village Shopping Center.

The Mountains

The peace and quiet of a mountain lodge can be incredible. Some of these places are just a short drive from Boulder. Others are way, way up where the spring flowers bloom in August. Some locations are even secrets—the owners will give you directions when you inquire. Many are open all year, but check in advance, for some close during winter.

ALLENSPARK LODGE $$$
184 Main Street, Allenspark
(303) 747-2552
www.allensparklodge.com

Six rooms with private baths, six rooms with shared baths, and three cabins with private baths and full kitchens make up this authentic 1933 log lodge. Construction is of ponderosa pine on the first two levels inside and out, with knotty pine inside on the top floor. Many of the furnishings are the same vintage as the buildings. There are

hot tubs, a gift shop, a wine and beer bar, and a TV in the great room near the flagstone fireplace. Views from this mountain lodge are tremendous, and Wild Basin and its wonderful hiking trails are nearby. Children younger than age 14 are welcome in the cabins, and older kids may stay in the lodge, too. It's about a 45-minute drive from Boulder and a 25-minute drive to Estes Park. The lodge includes a hot family-style breakfast in its rates.

BEST WESTERN LODGE AT NEDERLAND $$$
55 Lakeview Drive, Nederland
(303) 258-9463, (800) 279-9463
www.bestwesterncolorado.com/hotels/best-western-lodge-at-nederland

This oversize log lodge, in the heart of Nederland, is a convenient mountain retreat from Boulder. Accommodations include 23 nonsmoking rooms with king-size beds for couples, and rooms with two queen-size beds or a queen and a set of bunk beds for families. All rooms are equipped with hair dryers, coffeemakers, and small refrigerators; suites also have fireplaces. The spacious lobby has a fireplace, and there's an outdoor hot tub on the deck. There is no restaurant, but Nederland's most popular eating places are within a short walk. In winter, the Lodge at Nederland offers reasonably priced ski packages in cooperation with nearby Eldora Mountain Resort. It is also a great jumping-off place for snowshoeing, backcountry skiing, and summer hikes. The activities desk can arrange guided hikes, horseback trail rides, and other diversions.

BOULDER MOUNTAIN LODGE AND
CAMPGROUND $-$$
91 Four Mile Canyon Drive, Boulder
(303) 444-0882, (800) 458-0882
www.bouldermountainlodge.com

Twenty-two rooms, many with kitchenettes or full kitchens and all with whirlpool-jetted bathtubs, are available at this rustic motel with homey touches. The campground has 25 first-come, first-served sites with electricity and access to water for RVs (25-foot-maximum) or for tent campers.

The lodge is in the mountains, and the office is in an old narrow-gauge train depot. The property features a private fishing pond for kids, a heated outdoor pool (open seasonally), and hot tubs. Pets are welcome with a deposit. Their meeting room is great for company retreats and accommodates up to 30 people. The lodge is less than 10 minutes from Boulder and about an hour from Estes Park.

GOLD LAKE MOUNTAIN RESORT
AND SPA $$$$$
3371 Gold Lake Road, Ward
(303) 459-3544, (800) 450-3544
www.goldlake.com

This mountain hideaway can be a wonderful escape for honeymooners (or second honeymooners), or the perfect spot for a pleasant, close-by family retreat. Eighteen charming and distinctive cabins are tucked amid the pine trees. They feature artistically decorated accommodations ranging from single rooms to three-bedroom suites. All guests enjoy a Swiss-style continental breakfast. The resort's spa offers massages and facials, and you can book a spa package. The 35-acre lake is beautiful for catamaran sailing, canoeing, kayaking, and fly fishing in summer. In the winter there's ice skating, cross-county skiing, and snowshoeing; those who prefer the indoors can head for the billiard room. The lakeside hot tubs are a dreamy treat. Summer brings opportunities for horseback riding on mounts you can rent by the hour or day, great mountain biking on challenging trails, volleyball, and hiking. Children are more than welcome. Guests and visitors can dine in the excellent and stylish restaurant, Alice's. Gold Lake Mountain Resort is a 45- to 60-minute drive from either Boulder or Estes Park.

PEACEFUL VALLEY RANCH $$$$$
475 Peaceful Valley Road, Lyons
(303) 747-2881, (800) 955-6343
www.peacefulvalley.com

This family-owned, family-run guest ranch, on the site of an old homestead, is a "got everything" facility with 12 cabins, rooms in the main lodge, and various other guest buildings as well as a stable and indoor riding arena and other facilities. This is a classic dude ranch that can house more than 100 people, and conference facilities are available. Staying overnight is dandy, but longer stays are what most seek at Peaceful Valley. Half-week stays are around $845 per person, and full-week packages, including all meals, use of ranch facilities, and all recreational programs, begin at $1,375 per person during the summer. (The chef makes ranch-style meals such as prime rib and lemon-flavored catfish.)

The children's program is extensive. There's an indoor hot tub, indoor swimming pool, and children's petting farm as well as activities that include horseback riding, jeep tours, and square dancing. The mountainside chapel, with a view of the Indian Peaks behind the altar, is a gorgeous wedding site. In winter, Peaceful Valley offers sleigh rides; stocks cross-country skis, snowshoes, and snowmobiles; and maintains a small track on the property. The trailhead for extensive marked but ungroomed trails around Camp Dick lies just across the highway. This outstanding resort is just a bit less than an hour from Boulder and about 40 minutes south of Estes Park. No smoking or pets are allowed.

The Eastern Plains

These motels, bed-and-breakfasts, and country inns are open all year and offer good variety and reasonable prices.

BRIARWOOD INN $$
1228 North Main Street, Longmont
(303) 776-6622

The 17 rooms in this motel include 10 kitchenettes. The owner calls his the best backyard in town, with a quiet patio area, a fish pond, and a gazebo. Children are welcome. It's a half-hour drive to Boulder and about 45 minutes to Estes Park.

ELLEN'S BED & BREAKFAST IN
A VICTORIAN HOUSE $$$
700 Kimbark Street, Longmont
(303) 776-1676
www.ellensbandb.com

Two guest rooms, each with a private bath, are in this beautifully shaded, quiet, 1910 Victorian-style house, with eclectic furnishings including several interesting art deco pieces collected by the well-traveled owners. Full breakfast is included; there's a hot tub; and children and nice pets are welcome. It's a half-hour drive from Boulder and 45 minutes to Estes Park. No credit cards.

BOULDER TWIN LAKES INN $$$
6485 Twin Lakes Road
Gunbarrel/Boulder
(303) 530-2939, (800) 322-2939
www.twinlakesinnboulder.com

With 33 spacious, non-smoking studio suites, each with a mini-kitchen and cable TV, this is a great place for business travelers, people relocating or traveling with families. There's one common kitchen with a house-style range, an oven, and utensils for preparing full-scale meals. A membership at Synergy, a full-service sports club, is complimentary for guests. A cold breakfast buffet, served in the common kitchen from 6:30 to 10 a.m. daily and from 8 to 10 a.m. on weekends and holidays, is included in the rate. It's a 10-minute drive to Boulder and about an hour from Estes Park. The inn owners also rent one- and two-bedroom condominiums, normally on a monthly basis.

THE VICTORIA INN $$$
2400 West 17th Avenue, Longmont
(303) 772-4667
www.victoriainnapts.com

Each of this inn's 30 executive suites includes a full kitchen, full bath, and sitting room. They are set in three-story, blue Victorian-style buildings with contemporary furnishings. There's a heated outdoor pool and each unit has a wood-burning fireplace and stackable washers and dryers. It's a half-hour from Boulder and 45 minutes to Estes Park.

HOTELS AND MOTELS

Boulder hotels and motels all offer nonsmoking rooms (ask if you need a smoking room). Most have pools, but if it's cold, check when you call to see whether it's a heated indoor pool. The places we've listed have the usual hotel/motel amenities such as televisions and air-conditioning. Some are simple and sweet, others are lavish. Most don't allow pets. Unless noted, all take major credit cards.

Note that most hotels and motels in Boulder are wheelchair-accessible. Some of the mountain properties may have more difficulty accommodating a wheelchair. Call ahead to be sure.

BEST WESTERN BOULDER INN $$$
770 28th Street, Boulder
(303) 449-3800, (800) 233-8469
www.boulderinn.com

This motel's 112 rooms are right across the street from the south end of the CU-Boulder campus. Room options include units with two queen-size beds, or just one queen-size bed, or upgraded rooms that have a king-size bed and a wet-bar area. Admission to the nearby health club is included in the rate, as is continental breakfast daily and wireless access. The motor inn has a hot tub, sauna, and outdoor pool (open seasonally).

i   **Book early! That's the best advice when it comes to Boulder's accommodations. From May through October rooms fill up fast. So, keep the following very busy weekends in mind when making your plans: CU graduation in mid-May; the Bolder Boulder Memorial Day weekend, when more than 50,000 runners take to the streets; and CU-Boulder football games, especially when Nebraska is in town for a CU home game. Since it isn't a ski destination, Boulder's slowest season is typically November through February. However, it's always best to make your reservations early to make sure you get your choice of lodging.**

BEST WESTERN GOLDEN BUFF LODGE $$$
1725 28th Street, Boulder
(303) 442-7450, (800) 999-BUFF
www.bestwestern.com
This comfortable, well-located business and family motel has 112 guest rooms with king- or queen-size beds; some suites; and conference/banquet space accommodating up to 40 people. On-site is The Buff Restaurant, which is open for breakfast and lunch daily. There is a seasonal outdoor pool and an indoor hot tub, and free Internet access is also available.

RODEWAY INN & SUITES/THE
BOULDER BROKER INN $$$$$
555 30th Street, Boulder
(303) 444-3330, (800) 338-5407
www.boulderbrokerinn.com
Formerly known as the Boulder Broker Inn, this hotel has 118 guest rooms with free continental breakfast and wireless high-speed Internet access. Services include valet parking, room service, and bell staffs. There's also a seasonal outdoor pool and hot tub, and the hotel is equipped with banquet and meeting rooms. Just south of the campus, this hotel is a short walk or a CU-Boulder shuttle bus (take your pick) away from the university. It is also normally the location where passengers leaving and arriving via the Super Shuttle Boulder transportation service switch from smaller city vans to the larger vehicles that run hourly between Denver International Airport and Boulder.

BOULDER INTERNATIONAL YOUTH
HOSTEL $
1107 12th Street, Boulder
(303) 442-0522
www.boulderhostel.com
Visitors from all over the world have stayed at this hostel, which is a member of the American Association of International Hostels. Accommodations are scattered among several buildings on University Hill. The hostel has separate dormitories for men and women, where beds are as low as $17 a night, as well as private rooms for

couples and families that go for $50 a night for two people. Apartments are available for those wanting longer-term facilities. Each room has a phone, but televisions are located only in common areas. Cable TV hookups are provided, but you must bring your own apparatus. Kitchen and laundry facilities are on-site.

BOULDER MARRIOTT $$$$$
2660 Canyon Boulevard, Boulder
(303) 440-8877, (888) 238-2178
www.marriott.com
This business and meeting hotel opened in 1997 with 155 deluxe guest rooms and suites. It is tucked into a shopping center in central Boulder with magnificent views of the Flatirons, especially from the rooftop terrace. Facilities include underground parking, an indoor pool, a whirlpool, a health club and gift shop. JW's Steakhouse and a lounge are inside the hotel, which also houses a jewelry store, an art gallery, and the Essentials Beauty Clinic. The Boulder Marriott is within walking distance of shopping, restaurants, movie theaters, and the CU campus.

BOULDER OUTLOOK HOTEL &
SUITES $$-$$$$$
800 28th Street, Boulder
(303) 443-3322, (800) 542-0304
www.boulderoutlook.com
This hotel is conveniently located across the street from the CU-Boulder campus. The hotel welcomes a diverse collection of travelers and local guests, from families to business travelers. Families with children will appreciate the poolside rooms for easy access to the many activities there. Travelers with pets enjoy special amenities such as a complimentary "Fido Gift Pack," a fully enclosed dog run, and the in-room pet carriers. Quiet business corridors are designed for business travelers as are the special extras such as the executive-class rooms and the services of the on-site business center. All rooms have free wireless Internet access. Skinny Jay's Pizza & Pub is on the premises.

COLORADO CHAUTAUQUA CABINS   **$$$**
Ninth Street and Baseline Road, Boulder
(303) 442-3282
www.chautauqua.com
More than two dozen lodge rooms and about 60 cottages are available for rent. The one- to three-bedroom cottages offer full kitchens but no telephones, air-conditioning, TVs, or swimming pools. What you get here is a great deal on lodgings, one of the most beautiful locations in town, hiking and superb cultural events right outside your door, and a wonderfully nostalgic step back in time. Bookings start in November for the following summer. Ask about pets. For more information about Chautauqua Park, see the Attractions chapter.

COMFORT INN   **$$$**
1196 Dillon Road, Louisville
(303) 604-0181,
(800) 228-5150 (nationwide reservations)
www.comfortinn.com
The 68-room Comfort Inn is next to a 12-plex movie theater, just off US 36. Rooms have one or two queen-size beds, and there is also one luxury room with Jacuzzi and queen-size bed. Continental breakfast, included in all room rates, is served in the breakfast room. This motor inn also has a meeting room and an exercise facility; for those who want a more comprehensive workout, the Louisville Recreation Center is a short drive away. Free wireless high-speed Internet access is available in all rooms.

COURTYARD BY MARRIOTT   **$$$$**
4710 Pearl East Circle, Boulder
(303) 440-4700, (800) 321-2211
www.courtyard.com/denbd
This smoke-free business hotel has 12 suites and 137 rooms with either a king-size bed or two doubles; there are work desks and coffeemakers in every room and separate seating areas in the suites. Each room is wired for Internet access. The hotel offers conference rooms, the in-house Courtyard Cafe, and an indoor pool, whirlpool,

and workout room. It's right next to the Boulder Creek Path in a quiet location just east of Foothills Parkway (Highway 157) on Pearl Street.

COURTYARD BY MARRIOTT—
LOUISVILLE   **$$$$**
948 West Dillon Road, Louisville
(303) 604-0007, (800) 321-2211
www.marriott.com
Just off US 36, this hotel offers 154 guest rooms and suites, a heated indoor pool with a whirlpool, an exercise room, and in-room coffee service. There are also numerous banquet and reception facilities. The affordable restaurant features a full breakfast buffet served daily.

DAYS INN   **$$$**
5397 South Boulder Road, Boulder
(303) 499-4422, (800) 329-7466
www.dayshotelboulder.com
This motel is on a main thoroughfare, just off US 36 and near the Table Mesa Park-n-Ride. It is just about the most convenient lodging to the National Center for Atmospheric Research and the National Bureau of Standards and Technology. Some of its 76 rooms have mountain views. The hotel offers free high-speed Internet access. The Boulder Super Shuttle airport vans also stop here. The Eggcredible Café is on-site.

FOOT-OF-THE-MOUNTAIN MOTEL   **$$**
200 Arapahoe Avenue, Boulder
(303) 442-5688
www.footofthemountainmotel.com
Each of the motel's 18 rooms is in a red-trimmed log cabin, making this place a quaint and rustic charmer. The mountain against whose foot the property nestles is Flagstaff. On a quiet street near the pretty Eben Fine Park and the Boulder Creek Path, it is also just 9 blocks west of CU-Boulder and the downtown Pearl Street Mall. All rooms have refrigerators and free HBO. Pets are welcome.

HAMPTON INN $$$$
912 West Dillon Road, Louisville
(303) 666-7700, (800) HAMPTON
(nationwide reservations)
www.hamptoninn.com

The Hampton Inn is suited to multiday business or leisure stays. Each of its 80 spacious, traditionally furnished rooms has a king-size bed or two queen-size beds, along with a refrigerator, microwave, coffeemaker, hair dryer, two-line speaker phone, and television with Nintendo. All rooms feature fine designer furniture and working desks for business travelers. In addition, there is one hospitality suite for small meetings, an indoor swimming pool, a hot tub, and an exercise facility. Continental breakfast is included in all rates. It's within walking distance of restaurants, bars, and shopping.

HOLIDAY INN EXPRESS $$$
4777 North Broadway, Boulder
(303) 442-6600, (800) HOLIDAY
www.hiexpress.com

This North Boulder non-smoking hotel has 106 rooms, some with microwaves and refrigerators. Extras include a seasonal outdoor pool, an exercise room, a guest laundry, and complimentary deluxe continental breakfast. Free local phone calls and complimentary wireless high-speed Internet also are included. The property is a short walk from the intersection of US 36 (28th Street) and Broadway. Airport transportation is available through Boulder Super Shuttle.

HOMEWOOD SUITES BY HILTON $$$$$
4950 Baseline Road, Boulder
(303) 499-9922, (800) 225-5466
www.homewood-suites.com

The 100 apartment-style suites each include a full kitchen and separate living and sleeping areas. Other highlights are an outdoor pool, the fabulous view of the Flatirons, complimentary continental breakfast, and a free social hour, including food and drinks, on Monday through Thursday nights. Rooms feature a fully equipped kitchen, high-speed Internet access, granite countertops

and hardwood floors. Children are welcome, and pets are allowed. The Flatiron Athletic Club is just next door. The bottom line here is good, basic living for extended-stay guests and business travelers.

HOTEL BOULDERADO $$$$$
2115 13th Street, Boulder
(303) 442-4344, (800) 433-4344
www.boulderado.com

Built in 1909, this is a local landmark as well as the city's finest hotel. It offers old-style grandeur and is famous for the stained-glass canopy in its huge mezzanine. Robert Frost and Louis Armstrong are among its past guests. Its 160 lavishly decorated, Victorian-style rooms are divided between the historic older section of the hotel and the new wing. The VIP suites are the largest and fanciest lodgings. Each has a wrought-iron or four-poster bed, its own stereo, and a separate living room furnished with a Victorian-style desk and sofa. The hotel has over 8,000 sq. ft. of meeting space, two excellent restaurants and the Catacombs bar, a gift shop, and a sensational location just one block from the Pearl Street Mall.

LA QUINTA INN & SUITES LOUISVILLE/ BOULDER $$$$
902 Dillon Road, Louisville
(303) 664-0100, (800) NU-ROOMS
www.laquinta.com

This hotel has three spacious room choices, with in-room coffeemakers, 25-inch televisions, oversize desks, voice mail, dataport phones and free high-speed Internet access. There are 120 rooms total, some with microwaves and refrigerators. Summer visitors will enjoy the beautifully landscaped courtyard with gazebo, while winter visitors can take advantage of the heated pool and spa.

MILLENNIUM HARVEST HOUSE $$$$$
1345 28th Street, Boulder
(303) 443-3850, (800) 545-6285
www.millenniumhotels.com

This is Boulder's biggest hotel, with more than

269 high-quality rooms and great business facilities on 16 acres right next to the Boulder Creek Path. It's an easy walk from CU-Boulder and the Pearl Street Mall. It has resort-type recreation facilities, including indoor and outdoor swimming pools, 15 indoor and outdoor tennis courts, mountain bike rentals, and a workout room. The beautifully landscaped inner courtyard is a lively hangout after a Buffs game. The Thyme on the Creek restaurant is on-site as is Fuller's Griffin, the city's original cigar bar, and Coaches Corner Interactive Sports Bar.

NEW WEST INNS $
970 28th Street, Boulder
(303) 443-7800
www.newwestinnsboulder.com
Conveniently located across the street from the University of Colorado and right off of US 36, this motel offers 72 affordable rooms and 12 apartment units with kitchenettes, free wireless WiFi and cable TV with HBO. Kids stay free with a paying adult and pets are welcome. Nonsmoking rooms are available. Good for travelers on a budget yet close to all that Boulder has to offer.

OMNI INTERLOCKEN RESORT $$$$$
500 Interlocken Boulevard
StorageTek/Interlocken Loop
off US 36, Broomfield
(303) 438-6600
www.omnihotels.com
If it's a view you're after, this hotel along the Colorado Front Range (opened in 1999) will win you over. The Omni features 390 guest rooms, 13 suites, and a 34,000-square-foot conference center. Guests can dine in comfort at the Meritage restaurant or more informally at the hotel's sports bar; there's also 24-hour in-room dining. Other amenities include a 27-hole championship golf course with clubhouse and pro shop, a health club, and a full-service spa. Running, biking, and hiking trails surround the property, which also features a year-round outdoor swimming pool and whirlpool.

QUALITY INN & SUITES—
BOULDER CREEK $$
2020 Arapahoe Avenue, Boulder
(303) 449-7550, (800) 228-5151
www.QualiltyInnBoulder.com
Forty-six rooms compose this tidy and pleasant motel (formerly the Econo Lodge). All rooms have king- or queen-size beds and offer cable TV, dataports, coffeemakers, hair dryers, free local calls, and full baths. Just 6 blocks from downtown's Pearl Street Mall and minutes from the university, the property features a 33-foot indoor pool, hot tub, sauna, and fitness center. A complimentary hot breakfast buffet is served in the lobby each morning. Refrigerators and microwaves are available and pets are very welcome

QUALITY INN & SUITES—
LOUISVILLE $$–$$$
960 West Dillon Road, Louisville
(303) 327-1215, (800) 228-5151
www.qualityinn.com
This Quality Inn is close to shops, theaters, and restaurants, minutes from downtown Boulder, and less than a half-hour drive from downtown Denver and Coors Field. The spectacular Flatirons Crossing Mall, featuring Nordstrom and Macy's, is just a mile away. Not a shopper? Each of the inn's 61 guest rooms comes with either one king- or two queen-size beds, and four wheelchair-accessible rooms features a refrigerator, microwave, two-line speaker phone with dataport and voice mail, 25-inch TV, an in-room safe, a coffeemaker, and a hair dryer. When you're not at the fitness center, you can enjoy your continental breakfast with your

i Some Boulder-area motels allow pets in rooms if you check ahead and meet certain requirements, including Boulder Mountain Lodge, the Boulder Broker Inn, Foot-of-the-Mountain Motel, and Homewood Suites by Hilton. If you're traveling elsewhere in the United States, check out *Pets Are Permitted,* a book listing hotel/motel, kennel, and pet-sitting services nationwide.

complimentary newspaper or, later in the day, a cocktail next to the outdoor pool and Jacuzzi.

RAINTREE PLAZA HOTEL AND
CONFERENCE CENTER $$$$$
1900 Ken Pratt Boulevard, Longmont
(303) 776-2000, (800) 843-8240
www.raintreeplaza.com
This is Longmont's only full-service hotel. It housed the Emperor of Japan's entourage during the summer of 1994. There are 295 rooms, of which 86 are extended-stay rooms, each with a full kitchen, fireplace, and living room. The hotel also has a 42,000-square-foot conference center, a restaurant, and a heated, outdoor swimming pool. Guests get free breakfast and evening cocktails. The hotel is popular with business travelers, families, and conventions. It's a 15-minute drive to Boulder and an hour to Estes Park.

RESIDENCE INN BY MARRIOTT $$$$$
3030 Center Green Drive, Boulder
(303) 449-5545, (800) 331-3131
www.residenceinn.com/vbocg
This village-like, smoke-free complex has 128 studio suites, all with full kitchens and fireplaces, designed for extended stays or for families who want a comfortable, relaxing refuge. The Residence Inn provides a complimentary continental breakfast buffet daily and has an outdoor, seasonal pool and whirlpool. It offers easy access to central Boulder, and it's close to many of the high-tech and other companies there.

ST. JULIEN HOTEL & SPA $$$$$
900 Walnut Street, Boulder
(720) 406-9696
www.stjulien.com
In January 2005, Boulder was treated to a new world-class hotel and spa near downtown. In fact, the St. Julien is the first such hotel to open in the city in more than 100 years, and as a result, it has been greeted with open arms. Two hundred rooms, including 11 spacious suites, offer just about every amenity you can image. Luxurious bathrooms with soaking tubs and separate glass

showers and lavish duvets and linens are just a start. There is a 10,000-square-foot spa and fitness center in the hotel with a two-lane lap swimming pool and whirpool. The outdoor terrace, with its knockout view of the Flatirons, is a wonderful place to spend an afternoon visiting with friends. Have a delicious breakfast, lunch, or dinner at Jill's Restaurant, or stop by the T-Zero Bar to try one of the hotel's signature blackberry martinis. The hotel also caters to conferences and other special events such as weddings. Special packages are available as well.

UNIVERSITY INN $$$
1632 Broadway, Boulder
(303) 417-1700
www.boulderuniversityinn.com
This neat little inn at the corner of Broadway and Arapahoe Avenue has 39 rooms with refrigerators, cable TV with free HBO, a guest laundry and pool. It's within easy walking distance of both downtown and the university. Although the property is close to a busy intersection, the rooms are fairly quiet if you keep the doors and windows shut. A free continental breakfast is provided. Pets are welcome and each room has free high-speed wireless Internet service.

RV HOOKUPS AND
CAMPGROUNDS

If you're planning to stay in your RV or tent in Boulder, check our Sports chapter (see the "Camping" section under "Participatory Sports").

THE BOULDER COUNTY FAIRGROUNDS
9595 Nelson Road, Longmont
(303) 678-1525
www.co.boulder.co.us/openspace/fairgrounds
The fairground site has 92 campsites and can handle nearly 100 RVs. Costs change minimally from year to year. A site for an RV with no hookups or for one tent costs approximately $15 a night. A site with electricity is $20; one with water and electrical hookups is $25. The maximum stay is two weeks. Showers are available free for registered guests. The dump station fee is $5.

BOULDER MOUNTAIN LODGE AND CAMPGROUND
91 Four Mile Canyon Drive, Boulder
(303) 444-0882, (800) 458-0882
www.bouldermountainlodge.com
This campground has 25 first-come, first-served sites with electricity and access to water for RVs (25-foot-maximum) or tent campers. The fee ranges from $21 to $24 a night, with a two-week maximum stay. Shower facilities are available.

THE COLORADO DIRECTORY FOR CAMPGROUNDS, CABINS AND LODGES
5101 Pennsylvania Avenue, Boulder
(303) 499-9343, (888) 222-4641
www.coloradodirectory.com
This statewide directory service offers free information on campsites, cabins, lodges, bed-and-breakfasts, and fun things to do.

MEETING SPACES

In addition to the number of hotels, motels, and conference centers that offer space for meetings and other get-togethers, these places offer space for rent in and around town.

RODEWAY INN & SUITES/THE BOULDER BROKER INN
555 30th Street, Boulder
(303) 444-3330
www.boulderbrokerinn.com
There are several rooms on the second floor of the hotel with a maximum capacity of 250. There are also three private meeting rooms.

BOULDER CONVENTION & VISITORS BUREAU
2440 Pearl Street, Boulder
(303) 442-2911
www.bouldercoloradousa.com
A huge family reunion, a big convention, or a bonanza of a business meeting should start with a phone call here. Be sure to check on available space as soon as possible. Chamber members have access to meeting space for 50 or more at the Pearl Street location.

CU-BOULDER'S GLENN MILLER BALLROOM
CU Campus, Euclid Avenue and Broadway
Boulder
(303) 492-8833
This is a great space for a reunion, reception, or any kind of social gathering, and is therefore usually booked a year in advance. It has room for 1,200 people seated theater-style, 800 seated banquet-style with rectangular tables, or 450 seated at round tables.

HOTEL BOULDERADO
2115 13th Street, Boulder
(303) 442-4344
www.boulderado.com
An addition to this historic hotel houses a full-service meeting and conference center. It offers an elegant first-floor space that seats 350 and has a separate street entrance from the hotel.

MILLENNIUM HARVEST HOUSE
1348 28th Street, Boulder
(303) 443-3850
www.millenniumhotels.com
Centrally located, the Millennium's Grand Ballroom can seat 650 theater-style, and there are 10 other conference rooms of varying sizes.

OMNI INTERLOCKEN RESORT
500 Interlocken Boulevard
off US 36, Broomfield
(303) 466-9799
www.omnihotels.com
The newest conference facility at the Omni Interlocken Resort hotel (between Boulder and Denver, just off US 36) can accommodate 1,100.

RAINTREE PLAZA HOTEL AND CONFERENCE CENTER
1900 Ken Pratt Boulevard, Longmont
(303) 776-2000
www.raintreeplaza.com
Boasting easy access and plentiful parking, the Raintree offers a 42,000-square-foot conference center with seating for 1,100. There are also several smaller meeting rooms.

ST. JULIEN HOTEL & SPA
900 Walnut Street, Boulder
(720) 406-9696
www.stjulien.com
The St. Julien can offer space for everything from meetings to company retreats to receptions, with more than 16,500 square feet of meeting space in both inside and outdoor locations. The hotel chef will create epicurean delights for every function, and the underground parking garage provides parking for 650. The hotel concierge service is also available for meeting organizers.

A PLACE FOR YOUR PET

Some of the accommodations we've listed do not allow pets. But never just leave them in your car. Even with the windows left open a bit, Colorado's strong sun can zoom the temperature in the car to a fatal level within minutes.

CAMP BOW WOW
3631 Pearl St., Boulder
(303) 442-2261
www. campbowwowusa.com/colorado/boulder
Camp Bow Wow Boulder offers doggy day care and overnight dog boarding in a fun, safe and upscale environment for dogs to play, romp and receive lots of love and attention. The "camp" is open 365 days a year and has live Webcams so the residents' two-legged friends can check in.

COTTONWOOD KENNELS
7275 Valmont Road, Boulder
(303) 442-2602
www.cottonwoodkennels.com
Cottonwood calls itself "A Bed & Breakfast for Pets." This is one of the largest kennels in Boulder, boarding both dogs and cats. But it's always a busy place. Generally, if you're traveling during the time when the kids are out of school, call six months in advance for a kennel reservation. During non-holidays in the winter, give two weeks' notice. When Cottonwood fills, they offer other suggestions.

SHOPPING

The Boulder shopping scene has gone through some changes in the past few years. Items that are unusual, eclectic, handmade, imported, upscale, or sporty are available in abundance. If you're in the market for a couch or a housedress, however, the pickings are a bit skimpier. Once the shopping hub for the region, Boulder had been losing ground to neighboring communities and the big-box stores that are springing up in the region. The city's shopping scene has evolved once again with the opening of 29th Street. Built on the site of the former Crossroads Mall, 29th Street is Boulder's newest retail district. The addition of this unique outdoor shopping venue complements smaller businesses and only enhances and enriches the other shopping options available in Boulder. A variety of shops, restaurants with indoor and outdoor seating, and plazas and open space create a vibrant environment for shopping and gathering with friends. The new sixteen-screen Century Theater is located on the property as well.

SHOPPING AREAS

PEARL STREET MALL
Pearl Street between 11th and 15th Streets
Downtown Boulder
www.boulderdowntown.com

Boulder's Pearl Street Mall, also known as the Downtown Mall, was the city's original retail area and is still the heart and soul of the city. This photogenic, 4-block, open-air walkway is for pedestrians only—no dogs, no bikes, no skateboards, just leisurely strollers. It is lined with historic buildings that house numerous shops, galleries, microbreweries, offices, and sidewalk cafes, as well as newer buildings of a style and scale that harmonize with the old. During the warm months, street entertainers abound, including a rubber-jointed Rastafarian who obligingly packages himself into a plastic cube several times a day, jugglers, professional musicians, and kids with their first violin trying to pick up a few bucks. A pickup band of drummers gathers periodically in the bus shelter to pound out a beat, and a didgeridoo player periodically fills the night air with mournful tones.

The quality of entertainment generally is quite high. In addition to the buskers who play for what's dropped in the hat, an "out-to-lunch" weekly summer performance series brings formal live entertainment to the mall. Find a seat on one of the mall's benches and enjoy one of the most entertaining free shows to be found anywhere.

Don't let all the distractions make you forget to shop while you're downtown. Some of Boulder's most popular shoe and clothing shops, cafes, galleries, bookstores, and card and gift shops occupy prime spots along the mall and on adjacent blocks. A stroll along the mall will take you past everything from chain stores like American Apparel and Urban Outfitters to only-in-Boulder shops like Peppercorn, which stocks elegant kitchen, bath and bed items; El Loro, offering crystals and clogs; and Paper Doll, a gift shop that has wonderfully, interesting window displays for every holiday. Rocky Mountain Chocolate Factory seduces with rich whiffs through the open doors, and down the street you work it off on a rented bicycle built for two from University Bikes.

Since the mall was completed in 1977, Pearl Street, both east and west of the mall, has become an increasingly eclectic mix of service and retail businesses plus offices and restaurants. New buildings are going up all around the downtown, new businesses open almost daily, and sadly, some old favorites have closed down. To the east, look for The Envelope Please; the traditional Swiss Chalet for quality watches; and Willow, a shop that specializes in unique, handmade gifts. There's a fun mix of used bookstores, used clothing shops, and an interesting cluster of craft and gift stores.

The west end is a bibliophile's paradise, from the classy Boulder Bookstore at the end of the mall to the Trident coffeehouse and bookstore. The original Dot's Diner, a friendly, '50s-style restaurant in a former gas station, has been replaced by a new complex of housing, parking, and upscale shops that include the West End Gardener, West End Wine Shop, Spruce Confections, and Bedell and Co. Fine Antiques.

You can try your luck at finding on-street parking, but your best bet is one of the parking structures just off the mall at 14th and Walnut, 11th and Spruce, and 10th, 11th, 14th, and Walnut Streets, or one of the two new structures north and south of Pearl on 15th Street. Parking in the public garages is free on the weekends, and on Sundays the parking meters are free. Or, like a conscientious Boulderite, you can bike, walk, or take a bus or shuttle and not have to worry about where to store your car. (See Getting Here, Getting Around.)

The Mall itself is city property, managed by the Downtown Management Commission (303-441-4000). Downtown Boulder, Inc. (303-449-3774) acts as a sort of specialized chamber of commerce for businesses in the area.

29TH STREET
Between 28th and 30th Streets and Arapahoe Avenue and Walnut Street
(303) 444-0722

The long-awaited Twenty Ninth Street officially opened in the fall of 2006. The multipurpose site (formerly the Crossroads Mall) offers a one-of-a-kind shopping and entertainment venue with spectacular views of the Flatirons and the foothills beyond. Twenty Ninth Street is an inviting collection of retail, entertainment, and dining offerings all in an open-air environment. The successful integration of these three neighborhoods

is made possible with the clever use of streets, plazas, walkways, and spaces.

The property is anchored by Macy's and Century Theater's state-of-the-art 16-plex cinema, which opened in the summer of 2007. With almost 900,000 square feet of retail space, there is a store for everybody. For the computer buff there's the Apple Computer Store. Other retail establishments include M.A.C., Montbell, Ann Taylor Loft, and Anthropologie. For a fine-dining experience, visit the Cantina Laredo or L. There is a host of eateries to meet the needs of hungry shoppers! The project was designed to make the area accessible to all modes of transportation. In addition, there is ample indoor and outdoor parking.

ARAPAHOE VILLAGE/THE VILLAGE/ WATERSTREET
Between 28th and Folsom Streets, both sides of Arapahoe Avenue and Canyon Boulevard

In addition to some of the city's most popular retail shops, this complex of somewhat upscale strip malls has developed into a shopping and eating destination. Memorable restaurants include Alba, formerly known as the Full Moon Grill and Zolo Grill. More casual eateries in the area include Le Peep, Red Robin, and the Boulder-Chill. Goodies from Great Harvest Bread and The Brewing Market can fill in any remaining empty spaces. The wonderfully inviting Sunflower Market and Ellie's Eco Home Store are two new and exciting additions to the center.

This busy retail area is where you'll find the original McGuckin Hardware (if they don't have it, you don't need it), Studio Bernina and Elfriede's Fine Fabrics, Video Station (a locally owned video store whose employees seem to have seen every movie ever made and remember the details of each one), the addictively aromatic Ead's News & Smoke Shop, and the rare and exotic furnishings from Indochine. Children's shops clustered near a pleasant child's pocket park includes Rocky Mountain Kids, a clothing and shoe store for kids. If you ski or snowboard, a trip to Boulder is not complete without a visit to Boulder Ski Deals.

The Marriott Hotel dominates the east end of the Village and offers its own upscale contributions to the shopping, with everything from Essentiels Spa to Boulder Body Wear and the Boulder Jewelry Company (see the Accommodations chapter for more information on the hotel).

The WaterStreet shopping complex, on the north side of Canyon Boulevard between Folsom and 27th, features some of Boulder's most luxurious shops. Christina's Lingerie carries expensive underwear, while The Regiment Shops sell quality men's and women's outerwear. JJ Wells carries distinctive women's fashions and accessories. Walters & Hogsett (see the subsequent "Jewelers" section) offers elegant jewelry. Chain stores in the area include Safeway, Petco, Performance Bicycle Shop, Pier 1 Imports and Joann Fabrics.

You can reach this area in a variety of ways: the Boulder Creek Path is on the south edge (making walking and biking easy), auto access is a snap (but the parking lots fill up when hit movies are showing), and it's on major bus routes, including the super-convenient Hop.

The Hop buses run between three of the area's biggest shopping centers—Pearl Street Mall, University Hill, and Twenty Ninth Street. The fare is only $1.75, and the bus comes by every 10 minutes or less. It's a speedy, convenient way to explore Boulder's stores. And when you use The Hop, you're helping the environment!

28TH STREET AND 30TH STREET
Between Walnut Street and Iris Avenue
These two major north-south streets bracket Twenty Ninth Street, and a series of strip malls and freestanding stores stretch northward along the two arteries. Because most of them are fronted by parking lots, it's not easy to wander among them. But if you take the trouble, you can find most of Boulder's discount chains such as Target, Marshall's, and Ross, and interesting specialty shops strung out along 28th Street.

The Marshall Plaza Shopping Center is home to local outposts of nationally known chains

such as REI, Bed, Bath & Beyond; Radio Shack; Office Depot; Floyd's Barbershop and Blockbuster Video. Past Twenty Ninth Street and Target to the north is a huge Whole Foods market (which introduced Boulder shoppers to the concept of valet parking at a grocery store), Barnes & Noble books, and Vitamin Cottage.

Just up 30th Street is the tiny Willow Springs shopping center, whose shops include Rocky Mountain Soccer, Abo's, Chaz Salon and Boulder Ink, one of our city's handful of tattoo salons. Thirtieth Street merchants include Best Buy, King Soopers, Walgreen's, Office Max, Cloth Constructions (designer fabrics and wallpaper), and Concepts (home furnishings and gifts).

BASEMAR SHOPPING CENTER
Baseline Road and Broadway
Wild Oats health food market is the centerpiece of this L-shaped strip mall just south of the CU campus. Next door is The Egg and I and Starbucks. This center offers a nice mix of little shops and services, including Buffalo Lock and Key, which is quick at matching keys and getting into locked cars. Herb's Meats and Specialty Foods boasts a wide variety of beef, poultry, and game. The Taj restaurant serves a popular Middle Eastern buffet.

HOLIDAY NEIGHBORHOOD
North Broadway and Yarmouth, Boulder
Boulder's newest shopping district is known as the "Holiday Neighborhood". The name comes from the old '50s twin-screen Holiday Drive-In. The original sign was refurbished a couple of years ago and graces the entrance to the neighborhood on the south side. Transformed into an area rich with entrepreneurs, artists and homegrown businesses, Holiday is funky and hip. You'll find restaurants like Organic Orbit, 4580, Proto's Pizza, as well as Amante Coffee. Across Broadway you'll find the fun and laid back Terrace Maya restaurant, featuring an outdoor patio and yummy, authentic Mexican food. You'll find the perfect treasure for your home at The Amazing Garage Sale on the west side of Broadway as well.

THE MEADOWS SHOPPING CENTER
Foothills Parkway and Baseline Road

As Boulder has grown eastward, this strip mall has become busier and busier. More than 50 businesses are part of this large neighborhood shopping complex, located near several retirement and senior-living facilities. It includes a Safeway, along with Glacier Homemade Ice Cream and Gelato, Art Cleaners, and Rite Aid. Take a lunch break at Lee Yuan Chinese restaurant. Michael's craft store offers everything from candle wax and rattan by the bundle to baking supplies and picture framing. Nick-N-Willy's Pizza, Blockbuster and Big Daddy Bagels are longtime residents of this center as well. The Meadows branch library on the south side of the shopping center has a popular meeting room, in addition to the books and other materials of a well-stocked branch.

NORTH BROADWAY AND COMMUNITY PLAZA
Broadway and Alpine Avenue, across from Community Hospital

Imaginative looping and zigzag rooflines transform these 1960s-era shopping malls into trendy mini-plazas with a European feel. Pleasant little shops offer flowers, prescription drugs and natural remedies, haircuts, gifts, and more. All the restaurants here have outdoor dining areas—and there are many restaurants here. Moe's Bagels customers rub shoulders with diners at the BreadWorks or KT's BBQ. You can enjoy a casual breakfast at Marie's, a Boulder institution, or try a tasty lunch at Radda. Those enjoying a bowl of Thai noodle soup from the Noodles and Company can trade tastes (if they want) with those dining alfresco on sandwiches from the wonderful Ideal Market deli. Ideal is one of Boulder's favorite grocery stores because it combines old-fashioned ambience with the latest food fashions and friendly clerks. Other great shops include the Boulder Wine Merchant, European Flower Shop, the Ginger and Pickles toy store, Fleet Feet, and the Jacque Michelle boutique.

i The best parking for the downtown area is in the structures located at 14th and Walnut, 11th and Spruce, and 10th and 11th and Walnut Streets. When you're parked in any of these, ask for validation stickers as you pay at downtown stores. Every sticker is good for a half-hour of parking, so you can shop your way to reduced or free parking. In addition, a city-owned garage with wraparound retail is at 15th and Pearl, east of the Pearl Street Mall, and a private structure is 1 block north at 15th and Spruce Streets.

NORTH VILLAGE MART
Broadway and Quince Street

This is the kind of low-key, small-scale shopping area that any neighborhood would want. You won't find choices galore here, but you'll notice just how lovely and cozy a small neighborhood shopping center can be. The area fits its neighborhood well. Kids arrive from the bike trails to pick up videos, wander into the pet store, and stop for ice cream. Families and friends winding down after work fill the restaurants, which serve Chinese food, Italian food, and sandwiches. The Nomad Players, a well-regarded community theater group, performs in the Quonset just east of the center. North Boulder Market, which anchors this little shopping center, is a good basic grocery store, with one of the better meat departments in town and a more-than-adequate deli. A video outlet, liquor store, florist, and pet supply store round out the shopping opportunities.

TABLE MESA SHOPPING CENTER
Broadway and Table Mesa Drive

In addition to a King Soopers and the usual complement of restaurants and various stores, this South Boulder shopping center has many excellent outdoor stores, including Neptune Mountaineering, Play It Again Sports, and Weaver's Dive Center. Weaver's is for divers, but weavers go to Shuttles, Spindles and Skeins. The Cooking School of the Rockies holds classes, from practical to decadent, recreational to professional, and has a small retail section with gourmet cookware. Stop in and enjoy a pint of brew and a healthy lunch from locally owned restaurant/brewpub Southern Sun.

UNIVERSITY HILL
Broadway, north and south of College Avenue

Just west of campus and both affectionately and officially called "The Hill," this area caters mainly to the university crowd. The Hill developed in 1906 as a streetcar stop between the Boulder Depot downtown and Chautauqua Park. In 1928, it was the focus of Boulder's first business growth restriction, from homeowners who feared their neighbors would eventually sell out to stores. For that reason, The Hill's retail zone remains quite compact. The 3-block University Hill district is located in central Boulder, bordering the western edge of the University of Colorado.

The district includes 100 businesses and 29 commercial property owners, around the intersection of 13th and College Streets.

Declining sales prompted a face-lift in 1997, with street improvements and the addition of trees and artwork and a clock. (As you stroll, keep an eye out for the literary quotations embedded in the sidewalk.) Unfortunately, the sprucing up has not turned things around, and Hill merchants chipped in for a marketing study, completed in spring 2001.

The plan's recommendations, some of which are currently in the works, included:

- Creating a marketing fund for such efforts as a Hill business district Web site, specific marketing to the neighborhood and student populations, newsletters and neighborhood forums, collaborative promotions for the university population, and special events such as a Hill Farmers' Market or a foot race.
- More visible patrols by the police, supplementary security patrols, community court for enforcement of nuisance crimes, extending the Blue Light security network, creating weekend maintenance and seasonal clean-up days, and lighting improvements.

- Investigating direct access to the parking lot currently accessed from a side street, installing directional signs to The Hill along Broadway and at College Avenue, and installing gateway landmarks at key entrances to the district at the intersections of Broadway and College Street, and Broadway and 13th Street.
- Adjusting the zoning designation in the district to encourage new development, specifically allowing smaller new restaurants and rethinking height restrictions.
- Recruiting the types of new businesses The Hill wants: sit-down upscale restaurants, a family-friendly movie theater, a bank, an upscale grocery, a hardware store, and activities for those under 21.
- Creating a public/private partnership to market and manage The Hill.

Located slightly off campus, this eclectic, intimate business district boasts a fascinating mix of personalities. A variety of restaurants, shops and entertainment venues are virtually an extension of the University of Colorado campus. Coffee is available approximately every 10 feet, as is fast food of one type and another. The Colorado Bookstore is the largest business on The Hill, its huge glass windows covered over with brick after anti-war riots left them in shards (protestors against the war in Vietnam also closed U.S. Highway 36 connecting Boulder to Denver). Across the street is the venerable Jones Drug, and next door, the Pipefitter offers oddments. Art Hardware provides everything for the budding Picasso, and Albums on The Hill has an extensive collection of old and new CDs, tapes, and even vinyl records.

Parking is at a premium on The Hill, but its convenient location on the Hop and Skip routes make it easy to reach from the Pearl Street Mall and Twenty Ninth Street, as well as from north and south Boulder. Otherwise, it's best to walk or bicycle to this shopping area. You can sometimes find metered spaces on campus, which is a short walk away via a beautiful pedestrian underpass at Broadway and College Avenue that is worth a visit in its own right. If your interest in The Hill runs deeper than shopping, you can pick up a free booklet outlining a self-guided walking tour at the Hill Annex, a small "city hall" for students and visitors in the 1200 block of 13th Street, behind Buchanan's.

GUNBARREL SQUARE
Gunpark Road and Lookout Road
Gunbarrel
It's not extensive, but for the residents of Gunbarrel, who for many years had only a King Soopers grocery and tiny strip mall, the expanded shopping area of Gunbarrel Square is a welcome enhancement. Gunbarrel Square includes the Printed Page, a small but high-quality bookstore with a charming cafe. Other food offerings include pizza and subs, Akiyama Sushi Bar and Grill, and Serrano's Southwestern grill. Also here are a Mail Boxes, Etc., a flower shop, a liquor store, and even a private elementary school.

East County Shopping Areas
TWIN PEAKS MALL
Hover Road and Highway 119
Longmont
(303) 651-6454
www.twinpeaksmall.com
Nearly 10 million shoppers a year visit the 80 stores and 10 eateries at this traditional, regional, enclosed shopping center, which was renovated and expanded in 1997. (The name refers to the view west to two Rocky Mountain peaks.) The big draws presently include Sears, and Dillard's department stores. Another major draw is the United Artists 10-screen movie complex.

Twin Peaks features many of the national chain stores: Victoria's Secret, Foot Locker, Bath and Body Works, and Gymboree, as well as several jewelry and shoe stores. Woodley's Fine Furniture features locally made items. In addition to such sit-down restaurants as Red Robin and Chili's, there's a food court that serves up the usual burgers, pizza, and Chinese food.

LAFAYETTE
East on Arapahoe Road, Baseline Road, or South Boulder Road
Lafayette's main shopping areas are around the intersection of South Boulder Road and Public Road, which is also U.S. Highway 287. To the north, this is an area of small, unique, and charming shops, with the big-box stores just down the road. Antique hunters gravitate to the funky finds at West's Antiques, which is a full block long. Lafayette Florists offers the most bedding plants in the county; a visit is a rite of spring for many Boulder County residents. The Lafayette Flea Market uses sandwich-boarded boosters to draw customers into the rambling series of interconnecting spaces, with everything from antiques to unadulterated junk. Take a trip back a few decades by pulling into the Sonic drive-in on Waneka Parkway for a limeade and a chili dog, and run over to the Coal Creek Bowling Center for a game or two. Cannon Mine's Coffee or the newly opened Mojo is a great place to enjoy a cup of coffee any time of day. You can get a good bite of Mexican food at Efrain's, which serves the hottest green chile around.

LOUISVILLE
East on South Boulder Road or Louisville exit off US 36
Louisville's quaint and sleepy downtown has been eclipsed of late by the bright lights of the retail strip along McCaslin Boulevard. New big-box retail outlets, fast-food eateries, chain restaurants, a 12-plex theater, and hotels are being joined by clusters of smaller shops. On the west side of McCaslin you'll find Home Depot and Lowe's Hardware competing across the street from each other, and chain restaurants that include Spice China, Chili's, and Outback Steak House. The Village Safeway Shopping Center is at South Boulder Road and Centennial; Albertson's grocery is on West Cherry Street. Louisville Plaza, at South Boulder Road off of Highway 42, has King Soopers and a Blockbuster Video. The Centennial Center, at McCaslin Boulevard and Cherry Street, is near the movie complex and the hotels. In historic downtown, along Main Street, you'll find Wildwood Music and several casual, families-welcome eating places, includ-

ing The Huckleberry, The Blue Parrot restaurant, and Tulien's Vietnamese Restaurant. Thunderbird Barbers, complete with an American flag outside, offers a glimpse of Main Street past, as does the ad for 5-cent Coca-Cola painted on the small brick home of the Louisville Historical Society. Close by, the Old Louisville Inn, at 740 Front Street, features an antique bar and lots of character.

SPECIALTY SHOPS

Antiques

Boulder
BEDELL & CO.
767 Pearl Street, Boulder
(303) 939-9292
www.bedellandco.com
When visiting Boulder's West End, stop by this elegant antiques store. Bedell & Co. specializes in fine antiques and jewelry from the Victorian, Art Nouveau, Art Deco, and Arts and Crafts periods. They are noted for the largest selection of antique picture frames and bookends in Colorado and feature an extensive collection of American and European sterling silver, art glass, and lighting.

CLASSIC FACETS
942 Pearl Street, Boulder
(303) 938-8851
This unique little shop specializes in rare antiques—diamonds and colored stones, period jewelry from the 1700s to 1950s, and vintage designer costume jewelry. If you're looking to sell, your stuff better be good—consigners from 30 states and 9 countries send items to the exclusive shop; 90 percent of the offerings are rejected.

EIGHTH & PEARL ANTIQUES
740 Pearl Street, Boulder
(303) 444-0699
This store on the west end of the Pearl Street Mall is always worth popping into. Great finds, typically at good prices, await. The shop isn't hard to find, for on nice days they always have wonderful items out on the sidewalk.

Lafayette
CANNON MINE COFFEE AND ANTIQUES
210 South Public Road, Lafayette
(303) 665-0625
Have a coffee and pastry and experience firsthand the ambience created by the antiques sold in this unique shop. Like the chair you're sitting in? Make an offer. It's all for sale.

LAFAYETTE ANTIQUES
611 South Public Road, Lafayette
(303) 665-2212
Lafayette Antiques is a multi-dealer shop with collections including furniture, glassware, stoneware, and primitives.

LAFAYETTE FLEA MARKET
130 East Spaulding Street, Lafayette
(303) 665-0433
Good Housekeeping has called this one of the nation's best flea markets. Among the 500,000 items for sale are clothes, glassware, pots and pans, dishes, and antiques. It's open all year, in a clean, well-organized store with friendly salesclerks.

Longmont
FRONT RANGE FLEA MARKET
1420 Nelson Road, Longmont
(303) 776-6605
This nearly 30,000-square-foot flea market has something for everyone. There is large and small furniture, many usable household goods, decorating items, and even tools. Much of the furniture is new or nearly new. At the same time, antique glassware, old linens, rare furniture, and other collectibles are for sale, making it difficult to spend less than a couple of hours here. Owners call this store an "upscale flea market," and acknowledge what is currently in demand by stocking a large inventory. Each vendor rents a 10-foot by 10-foot space so the selection is constantly changing.

Lyons
LEFT-HAND TRADING COMPANY
401 and 405 Main Street, Lyons
(303) 823-6311
www.lefthandtradingcompany.com
Don't miss this gem. Left-Hand offers a huge inventory of antiques, Western collectibles, jewelry and Native American artifacts.

RALSTON BROTHERS ANTIQUES
426 High Street, Lyons
(303) 823-6982
Located north of Boulder, Lyons is worth the special trip, whether you're in the market for something specific or just browsing. Left-Hand Trading Company carries general antiques, including those with a Western flair and Indian artifacts. Ralston Brothers, in a historic stone building, specializes in vintage jukeboxes, radios, phonographs, light fixtures, toys, and restored furniture.

Nederland
OFF HER ROCKER ANTIQUES
4 East First Street, Nederland
(303) 258-7976
www.offherrockermercantile.com
It's a funky corner shop that feels like a rustic mountain museum. Old wash basins, oak furniture, and nifty used clothes go for bargain prices. On nice days, old rockers bedeck the boardwalk out front, rocking gently in the mountain breeze. The shop is known by watch collectors for its interesting array of old pocket watches in working condition. Local artisans supply such whimsical merchandise as tinkling wind chimes made from flattened antique spoons and forks.

Niwot
NIWOT ANTIQUES
136 Second Avenue, Niwot
(303) 652-2587
www.niwotantiques.com

WISE BUYS ANTIQUES
190 2nd Avenue, Niwot
(303) 652-2888
Northeast of Boulder, Niwot has several wonderful antiques stores, all within a short stroll of each other. Niwot Antiques is the town's giant. This is a cooperative of more than 40 dealers, many with particular specialties that appeal to collectors. Period antiques, Fiesta ware, fine china, art, Oriental rugs, clocks, and jewelry are among the treasures found here. Wise Buys offers fireplace mantels, millwork doors, and large pieces of furniture.

Art Galleries/Framing/Supplies
ANIMA MUNDI GALLERY
430 Main Street, Lyons
(303) 823-6085
Located in downtown Lyons, this gallery specializes in Fair Trade crafts and global folk art. The gallery houses fine art ranging from Peruvian textiles to contemporary Australian aboriginal paintings.

ART AND SOUL GALLERY
1615 Pearl Street, Boulder
(303) 544-5803
www.artandsoulboulder.com
A unique array of crafts and fine art, this international collection includes sculpture, paintings, fine woodworking, jewelry, and ceramics. It's located just off the east end of the Pearl Street Mall.

i ArtWalk, a collaborative effort between businesses and art organizations, takes place three times a year in Longmont. You can enjoy art exhibits, children's activities, live theater, and dance along Longmont's Main Street.

ART MART
1222 Pearl Street, Boulder
(303) 443-8248
www.artmartgifts.com
This is kind of a crafts supermarket, which bills itself as an "artist outlet store." It overflows with Southwestern objects, including jewelry, pottery, weavings, dream catchers, and all manner of other popular items. The large store also carries

clothing, candles, wood inlays, and myriad other crafts, along with a large collection of local and regional photography.

ART SOURCE INTERNATIONAL
1237 Pearl Street, Boulder
(303) 444-4080
www.rare-maps.com

This store specializes in antique maps and prints, books, and vintage Colorado photographs. Many are already framed, some are ready for your choice of frame, and all are fascinating. In addition to a great selection of 18th- and 19th-century maps, the gallery displays prints from the same era. Check out the public art just out front—a chess table and two chairs commemorating a Pearl Street Mall frequenter who didn't live to enjoy his dream of playing chess with his grandson on the Mall.

BOULDER ARTS AND CRAFTS COOPERATIVE
1421 Pearl Street, Boulder
(303) 443-3683
www.boulderartsandcrafts.com

This is the biggest and most diverse of the city's several crafts co-ops. It shows the works of more than 150 artists from Colorado and surrounding mountain states, displaying high-quality crafts in all media. Pottery, puppets, jewelry, photographs, weavings, stained glass, clothing, leather wallets stamped with leaves, whimsically painted wood tables and benches, hand-weaving, and other items make great gifts or accent pieces for your home. The co-op will also ship purchases anywhere in the continental United States.

EARTHWOOD GALLERY
1412 Pearl Street, Boulder
(303) 444-3838
www.earthwoodgallery.com

This is Boulder's newest art gallery featuring fine art and exquisite handcrafts by prominent local and national artists.

MARY WILLIAMS FINE ARTS
2116 Pearl Street, Boulder
(303) 938-1588
www.marywilliamsfinearts.com

This gallery shows old and new American works, including some with strong Western and Native American orientations. Fine prints and graphics on such themes as botanicals, natural history, and architecture from the 17th through 20th centuries abound. There's free on-site parking, a scarce commodity downtown.

MERCURY FRAMING
4692 Broadway, Boulder
(303) 938-0123
www.mercuryframing.com

Located in North Broadway, Mercury Framing provides quality, custom framing for artists, collectors, galleries and lovers of art. Watch for regular gallery openings in their cozy shop with some of Boulder's top artists.

MUSE GALLERY
365 Main Street, Longmont
(303) 678-7869
www.themusegallery.org

This cooperative gallery features shows by Longmont Council for the Arts plus work by member artists. The shows focus on a specific medium, such as oils, watercolor paintings, jewelry, clay and pastels, and mosaics.

OLD TIBET
948 Pearl Street, Boulder
(303) 440-0323
www.oldtibet.com

More than 200 Tibetan Thanka paintings are at the heart of this rich collection of Hindu and Buddhist art and religious items. You will find statues, ceremonial pieces, jewelry, books, singing bowls, bells and cymbals, clothing, music, incense, and beads. The shop is a generous supporter of the struggling country that has attracted the attention and concern of many Boulder citizens.

SMITH-KLEIN GALLERY
1116 Pearl Street, Boulder
(303) 444-7200
www.smithklein.com

This gallery houses contemporary art, including jewelry, hand-blown glass, and folk art animals, by both local and regional artists. A recent show featured a collection of hand-carved Zuni horse fetishes dating from the early 1900s.

VILLAGE CUSTOM FRAMING & ART
2525 Arapahoe Avenue, Boulder
(303) 413-9110
www.villageart.com

At Village Custom Framing & Art you will find both the picture framer and art dealer. They sell rare prints, antique engravings and prints, hard-to-find limited editions, stained-glass decorative objects, and engraved plaques and ornaments. If you are looking for a particular print from the publisher, they will assist you in finding the print at the best price. They employ a certified picture framer, ensuring that your project will receive the attention it needs.

Arts and Crafts Supplies

ART HARDWARE
1135 Broadway, Boulder
(303) 444-3063
www.arthardware.com

This is one of Boulder's top professional (and amateur) artists' supply center, with a full line of art and drafting supplies in a 14,000-square-foot building. The shop also does blue printing, large-format copying for architects and engineers, and custom framing. The store boasts free covered parking for customers, a real rarity on The Hill.

15TH STREET STUDIO
1708 15th Street, Boulder
(303) 447-2841

Specialty framing studio, also features gallery exhibits: works on paper including collages, monotypes, and limited edition lithographs; paintings on canvas and three-dimensional wood sculpture.

GUIRY'S
2404 Pearl Street, Boulder
(303) 444-3800
www.guirys.com

Guiry's, a retailer of quality house paints, art supplies, and home-decorating resources, is also an excellent source of high-quality art supplies. They carry everything from professional supplies to starter kits and educational materials.

MICHAEL'S ARTS AND CRAFTS
4800 Baseline Road, Boulder
(303) 494-2008

410 Marshall Road, Superior
(720) 304-3224

Michael's is a bustling warehouse chain store packed with craft items, from dried and plastic flowers to the right kind of muslin and paint sets for creating doll faces. Beads, Styrofoam, jewelry findings, and all sorts of kits appeal to crafters of all ages and skills. It's a big, reasonably priced place where kids and adults like to wander and take classes. There's a framing shop in the back.

SHUTTLES, SPINDLES AND SKEINS
635 South Broadway, Boulder
(303) 494-1071
www.shuttlesspindlesandskeins.com

This South Boulder shop has walls and walls of yarn in a fantastic array of colors for knitting and weaving. Uncarded wool, silk, flax, and camel hair are all perfect for making doll hair as well as for spinning. You can also find a few handmade items for sale that are truly masterpieces. This small, charming store has a cozy atmosphere that just says "welcome." The staff is very knowledgeable, and the shop offers both craft books for inspiration and classes to show you how to turn the inspiration into action.

WILLOW—AN ARTISANS MARKET
1500 Pearl Street, Boulder
(303) 443-0835

Formerly known as The Middle Fish Gallery, this whimsical boutique showcases unique, handcrafted items from more than 150 artists, most of them local.

Bakeries

Many of our better groceries stock locally produced breads, or you can go straight to the bakeries so you can luxuriate in bread aromas as soon as you open the door. Most have some sort of frequent-buyer program, giving you a free loaf after a dozen or so purchases, and many offer you a chance to sample the wares while you decide which loaf has your name on it.

ACOUSTIC COFFEEHOUSE AND BAKERY
95 East First Street, Nederland
(303) 258-3209
Located in a 100-year-old building, this rustic coffeehouse and bakery offers breakfast bagels, homemade quiches, sandwiches, and a Nutella cheesecake.

BREADWORKS
2644 Broadway, Boulder
(303) 444-5667
Newly expanded, Breadworks features traditional rustic breads in addition to a wide assortment of pastries. The new menu includes an assortment of soups, sandwiches, paninis, pizza, salads, and coffee drinks. Open daily. Outside seating available.

CAKES BY KAREN
2085 30th Street, Boulder
(303) 449-6254
www.cakesandlimousines.com
The name says only part of it. Photo cakes, custom wedding cakes, birthday cakes, and other sweet goodies certainly are the specialty here, but Cakes by Karen also can fill your need for balloons, party favors, decorating supplies—even a limo.

GREAT HARVEST BREAD COMPANY
2525 Arapahoe Avenue, Boulder
(303) 442-3062
This is part of a tightly controlled franchise operation that makes rich, chewy, healthful breads

and rolls. While other bakeries just put out sample bites, Great Harvest cuts whole slabs and invites you to slather your "taste" with butter and honey.

INDULGE BAKERY
1377 Forest Park Circle, Lafayette
(303) 926-1676
www.indulgebakery.com
As the name implies, this is indulgence at its finest. You'll want one of everything here. Choose from wonderful cakes, delicious pastries, and even yummy gelato.

PANERA
1855 29th Street, Boulder
(303) 544-1800
www.panera-colorado.com/locations.html
Panera arrived in Boulder when Twenty Ninth Street was developed. This bakery-cafe has a menu of freshly baked breads, pastries, sweets, bagels, tossed salads, soups, and sandwiches. The large comfy chairs offer an inducement to sit, relax, and watch the day go by.

SPRUCE CONFECTIONS
767 Pearl Street, Boulder
(303) 449-6773
Homemade charm and beautiful detail. This west end gem features delectable cakes, pies and pastries as well as soup, salad and sandwiches

THE STONE CUP CAFÉ AND GALLERY
442 High Street, Lyons
(303) 823-2345
www.thestonecup.com
A gathering place for hikers, bikers, kids, artists, and everybody else, this Internet cafe and art gallery serves fine teas, fair-trade coffees, and homemade baked goods. Dine outside and enjoy all the beauty Colorado has to offer.

A TASTE OF HEAVEN
537 Terry Street, Longmont
(303) 448-1047
Elegant desserts, breakfast pastries, and spectacular wedding cakes are the specialties of this

bakery on the east end of downtown Boulder. Lunch includes a variety of sandwiches named for local hot spots and salads that are popular with area businesses and meetings.

Bookstores

Considering the number of bookstores in town, it seems that everyone you see ought to have his or her nose buried in a book. Boulder bookstores were selling coffee and goodies, even meals, long before a corporate somebody stumbled upon the idea.

BARNES & NOBLE
2915 Pearl Street, Boulder
(303) 444-2501
www.barnesandnoble.com
This may be a big chain store, but it's working to offer a more personal touch that's gaining local respect. The store specializes in popular fiction and nonfiction but has a large sampling of more obscure works, too. People linger in the on-site coffee shop, and the store is the site of regular meetings of locals interested in both the creative and reading aspects of literature. There is also a nice selection of cards, magazines, books on tape, reading lights, and other gifts and accessories.

BEAT BOOK SHOP
1713 Pearl Street, Boulder
(303) 444-7111
www.abebooks.com/home/beatbookshop
If you want to turn the calendar back a few decades, check out this quirky store, which specializes in literature, poetry, biography, and books on film, sociology, and subculture, all with a distinct retro flair. It offers a commendable selection of first editions, too. The shop also stocks rare records and tapes, some fine art, and used CDs.

THE BOOKWORM
3175 28th Street, Boulder
(303) 449-3765
The unprepossessing location of this family-owned and -operated bookstore, tucked into an aging strip mall, does not reflect its status as the largest used bookstore in the county. The stacks and stacks of books just keep going and going and going—400,000 titles in all. There is an extensive mystery section, and there are romances to soften up the hardest pragmatist. Books on tape and videos are a growing collection. The shop also does a mail-order business.

THE BOULDER BOOKSTORE
1107 Pearl Street, Boulder
(303) 447-2074
www.boulderbookstore.com
This is Boulder's local showpiece and everyone's favorite bookstore. In 1993 the store moved into the historic Buckingham Building, receiving an award of merit from Historic Boulder for "historic preservation and restoration of the second-floor ballroom." The lovely high-ceilinged room with its antique stained-glass windows is the stage for visiting authors; more than 100 are invited to read and chat and autograph their works here each year. Notables have included Barbara Kingsolver, Ram Dass, Amy Tan, Frank McCourt, Whitley Strieber, and Isabel Allende. The 20,000-square-foot, four-story bookstore offers more than 100,000 titles and also has a large selection of magazines, journals, and various book-related items, plus exhibits of works by local artists. The store recently began stocking a small selection of used books, with proceeds going to local charities. It is also a strong supporter of local authors. The adjacent, but separately owned, Bookend Cafe is connected by an open door and makes a nice stop after browsing through the books.

THE COLORADO BOOKSTORE
1111 Broadway, Boulder
(303) 442-5051
www.coloradobkstore.com
Located next to the big outdoor clock and the pedestrian underpass on University Hill, this is a classic college bookstore. It sells new textbooks and plenty of used books (they buy and sell) and has a mezzanine devoted to general books. You

also can buy CU-Boulder sweatshirts, souvenirs, and school supplies. There's a small post office substation, and copiers, fax machines, prepaid phone cards, photo processing, and other services are available.

CU BOOK STORE
University Memorial Center
Euclid and Broadway, Boulder
(303) 492-6411
www.cubooks.colorado.edu
Located on the CU-Boulder campus, this store has it all if you're looking for CU-related gifts and clothing. Their selection of textbooks as well as general books is extensive. Books and supplies are located on the lower level, gifts and clothing on the main level. Check out the life-sized stuffed Ralphie buffalo.

EAD'S NEWS & SMOKE SHOP
1715 28th Street, Boulder
(303) 442-5900
www.eadsnews.com
Also under an outdoor clock, this is actually a mega-newsstand, with Boulder's best selection of magazines and out-of-town newspapers. It also carries an assortment of travel books, popular paperbacks, and adult-only books and magazines, and sells an aromatic selection of cigarettes, cigars, and pipe tobacco (but don't light up until you're outside).

LEFTHAND BOOK COLLECTIVE, INC.
1200 Pearl Street, lower level, Boulder
(303) 443-8252
www.lefthandbooks.org
This all-volunteer bookstore is Boulder's resource for progressive books on feminism, national and environmental causes, political thought, gay and lesbian studies, Marxism, and National Liberation. Periodicals cover political, economic, ecological, and Third World issues. They also carry gifts, greeting cards, magazines, and T-shirts.

LIGHTHOUSE BOOKSTORE
1201 Pearl Street, Boulder
(303) 939-8355
Below street level on the Pearl Street Mall, this store carries Boulder's largest selection of New Age books dealing with spirituality, self-help, religions from around the world, and exploring the inner self. It's well stocked with books, music, candles, Tarot cards, scarves, and crystals. Light filtering in from the street-side windows, the aroma of incense, and calming music from the store's New Age and traditional selections create an atmosphere conducive to browsing. The staff is especially helpful here, too.

PAGE TWO
6565 Gunpark Drive, Boulder
(303) 530-3339
This store carries stationery and gifts, along with a small selection of books, mostly local-interest and children's books. Their Christmas and Hanukkah card selection is one of the best in the city, and there are delightful seasonal gifts tucked in cupboards at the entrance. Page Two also houses a pleasant cafe.

RED LETTER SECOND HAND BOOKS
1737 Pearl Street, Boulder
(303) 938-1778
This is a readers' store. Step through the front door and you face a forest of books, stacked, spread, and shelved. The shop is jammed and crammed with a selection of used books, including travel, biography, and all sorts of fiction. It offers classics as well as modern works for buying, selling, trading, or simply browsing.

TIME WARP SCIENCE FICTION AND COMICS
3105 28th Street, Boulder
(303) 443-4500
www.time-warp.com
This is a word-of-mouth favorite among kids and has been nominated as one of the nation's best comic stores. Regionally, it has garnered "Best of

Boulder" and "Best of Denver" awards from the Boulder *Daily Camera* and Denver's *Westword*. Time Warp is known for both mainstream and underground comics.

TRIDENT BOOKSELLERS & CAFE
940 Pearl Street, Boulder
(303) 443-3133
www.thetridentcafe.com

Trident customers were enjoying a cuppa with their reading when coffee came in only one flavor. Inside, interesting-looking people huddle over tables, apparently engaged in the most existential of conversations. In the summer, the sidewalk tables are similarly filled, usually with a leashed dog or two reclining on the sidewalk. The bookstore has a potpourri of used books, new remainders, cards, and calendars. The sale table just inside the front door always displays interesting books on history, gardening, cooking, travel, spiritual topics, and more.

TROUBADOUR BOOKS
5290 Arapahoe Avenue, Boulder
(303) 444-2901
www.troubadourbookstore.com

Troubadour Books specializes in books and magazines for performing artists, students, writers, and teachers. They have a wide selection of magazines and general fiction and nonfiction books.

Clothing and Accessories

For Children

BRAVE NEW KIDS
3083 Walnut Street, Boulder
(303) 443-8333
www.bravenewkids.com

Brave New Kids is a locally owned manufacturer specializing in unique natural fiber clothing. If you are looking for comfort, utility, and style for kids, this is the store for you. The uncomplicated clothing makes it easy for the little ones to get dressed by themselves, and they sell hats that stay on! All garments are made in the USA.

CHILDISH THINGS
2071 30th Street, Boulder
(303) 442-2703
www.childishthingsconsign.com

Recycled children's clothing, toys, baby equipment, maternity clothes and accessories, and nursery furniture fill this friendly consignment shop. It's next door to Collage Children's Museum, so you can make shopping here part of an afternoon outing.

GYMBOREE
1755 29th Street, Boulder
(303) 245-8004
www.gymboree.com

Gymboree is the store to find the perfect outfit for a child up through 10 years of age. For a newborn you can find everything from sleepers to socks, toys, hats, and clothing so that the baby will be comfortable and stylish as well. Clothing and accessories for the older kids are practical, durable, and great to look at.

LITTLE MOUNTAIN OUTDOOR GEAR FOR KIDS
1136 Spruce Street, Boulder
(303) 443-1757
www.outdoorgearforkids.com

This store claims to be the only local outlet specializing exclusively in outdoor clothing gear and accessories for children. If you're a visitor, Little Mountain offers daily rentals on backpacks and baby joggers.

ROCKY MOUNTAIN KIDS
2525 Arapahoe Avenue, Boulder
(303) 447-2267

As you might expect from the name, this store sells fleece and other outdoorsy performance clothing, but it also carries pajamas, holiday outfits, and school clothes. There are clothes for infants through size 12, plus backpacks, baby joggers, and carriers for sale or rent.

For Adults

The best description we've heard of the "Boulder look" is "always ready for a hike." Certainly, casual attire is acceptable just about anywhere in town, for almost any occasion—and when the snow's flying, that philosophy gets kicked up another notch. Boulder abounds with clothiers catering to that outdoorsy look; however, when there's no way around the pantyhose, dressy clothing and office attire are available, too.

ALPACA CONNECTION
1326 Pearl Street, Boulder
(303) 447-2047
www.thealpacaconnection.com
Natural fiber clothing from around the world, including a large selection of hand-knitted wool sweaters from South America, is sold in this former movie theater on the Downtown Mall. You'll find natural fiber dresses and shirts, too.

BOULDER BODYWEAR
2660 Canyon Boulevard, Boulder
(303) 447-9100
www.boulderbodywear.com
If clothes were an element, Boulder Bodywear's stock would be water—flowing, skimming, falling. These clothes are cut for comfort but suitable for uptown.

CHELSEA
935 Pearl Street, Boulder
(303) 447-3760
www.chelseabella.com
Visit Chelsea for the latest in high style and fashion. The store offers a wide selection of clothing and accessories to meet daytime and evening needs.

CHICO'S
1215 Pearl Street, Boulder
(303) 449-3381
www.chicos.com
"Traveling clothes" is what comes to mind when you step into Chico's small space on the Downtown Mall. The clothing is simple, unstructured, built for comfort and style, and evocative of places foreign and natural.

CHRISTINA'S LINGERIE
2425 Canyon Boulevard, Boulder
(303) 443-2421
When you want to fling it all to passion, consider Christina's, which offers exquisite lingerie, well-fitting swimsuits, plus a staff that is truly helpful at telling you which styles flatter your figure.

COLLEGE CORNER
1310 College Avenue, Boulder
(303) 786-8243
This store on The Hill specializes in CU-Boulder sweatshirts, T-shirts, hats, and other memorabilia. Champion reverse-weave sweatshirts and CU-Boulder baseball caps are especially popular; the hats come in a dozen sizes ranging from kids to huge.

DRAGON FLY
1220 Spruce Street, Boulder
(303) 447-9777
Imagine a dragonfly hovering, iridescent, over a pond of shifting shadows and you have some idea of what you'll see in the window of this fascinating women's clothing store a block north of the Downtown Mall. Unique and lovely, the fashions are the sort that cause even a preoccupied passerby to stop for a closer look.

ELENA CICCONE
947 Pearl Street, Boulder
(303) 544-0554
www.elenaciccone.com
West end merchant Elena Ciccone features wonderful Italian fashions and accessories. Ciccone, who is in her seventh year in business in Boulder, has established herself as a Boulder go-to fashion expert. A must for locals and tourists alike.

FRESH PRODUCE SPORTSWEAR
1218 Pearl Street, Boulder
(303) 442-7507
www.fresh-produce.biz
Located on the Pearl Street Mall, this shop spotlights locally manufactured clothing—mostly easy-to-wear knits in colors reminiscent of a bowl of mints. The style is casual, fun, and natural.

JACQUE MICHELLE APPAREL AND HOME DECOR

2670 Broadway, Boulder

(303) 786-7628

This might be called a little "everything shop," selling items from T-shirts to locally made hats, cards, and arty things, and beautiful seasonal items, many reasonably priced. They will gift-wrap, too.

JILA DESIGN

2041 Broadway, Boulder

(303) 442-0130

www.jiladesign.com

Jila's sells original-design women's clothing, in gorgeous silks and rayons. Another Boulder original, Jila is now offering clothes in some national department stores, such as Nordstrom.

JJ WELLS

2460 Canyon Boulevard, Boulder

(303) 449-2112

www.jjwells.com

In a cluster of shops next to McGuckin's Hardware, JJ Wells carries a classic collection of women's clothing—classy pants, earth-toned sweaters, and dresses that make the transition from office to evening outing—by Eileen Fisher, Garfield & Marks, Isda & Co., Zelda, and others. Wardrobe consultants on the staff will help you select just the right accessories, from leather bags to belts to jewelry.

KINSLEY & CO.

2070 Broadway, Boulder

(303) 442-7260

www.kinsleyco.com

On The Hill for more than 50 years, this prime men's clothier (it also carries women's fashions for business, evening, and casual) moved to the Pearl Street Mall a couple of years ago. Kinsley carries custom clothing, Barbera and Hugo Boss suits, and high-quality accessories. They also house a connecting Orvis shop featuring high-quality outdoor gear for fishing, hiking, etc.

KNIT WIT

2025 Broadway, Boulder

(303) 444-6776

Knit Wit is a cute little store just off the Pearl Street Mall that offers elegant New York and L.A. styles. You can find both casual and dressy clothes and lots of matching accessories.

MAX CLOTHING STORE

1177 Walnut Street, Boulder

(303) 449-9200

www.maxfashion.com

If you are looking for that extra-special designer outfit with accessories to match, this is the store to shop.

MEOW MEOW

1118 13th Street, Boulder

(303) 449-7555

Geared toward the college and young professional crowd, Meow Meow offers contemporary dresses and separates from such designers as Betsey Johnson and April Cornell.

THE REGIMENT SHOPS

2425 Canyon Boulevard, Boulder

(303) 443-2713

www.theregimentshops.com

Traditional, yet updated, tailored business clothes such as Perry Ellis for men and blazer/skirt combinations for women draw Boulder professionals to this shop in the upscale strip mall called WaterStreet.

STARR'S CLOTHING AND SHOE CO.

1630 Pearl Street, Boulder

(303) 442-3056

Starr's has reasonably priced, rather sporty attire for men, women, and children. The store's fans in Boulder were relieved that redevelopment on the east end of the Downtown Mall didn't chase it out of town, just into a new location down the block.

TALBOT'S
2700 Arapahoe Avenue, Boulder
(303) 449-1556
Women who need professional clothes will find a large selection of suits and blouses with matching accessories in Talbot's large, free-standing store in Arapahoe Village, near the Safeway grocery.

TITLE 9 SPORTS
1801 Pearl Street, Boulder
(303) 996-0074
www.titlenine.com
Title 9 Sports is dedicated to supporting women in fitness and athletics. Their clothes and accessories are designed for comfort and practicality, and they look great, too.

URBAN OUTFITTERS
938 Pearl Street, Boulder
(303) 247-0828
Definitely not your dad's (or mother's) clothing store, Urban Outfitters is a jazzy, metallic, neon-colored space with the edgy fashions and accessories that keep the college crowd, and their younger siblings, coming back. The prices please parents and offspring alike

VIOLETTE
1631 Pearl Street, Boulder
(303) 443-3976
With over sixty years of experience under their belt, the owners of Pearl Street newcomer Violette were well prepared to open this lovely boutique. An experienced eye for fashion, design and value produced a wonderfully feminine clothing store that's also affordable.

WEEKENDS
1200 Pearl Street, Boulder
(303) 444-4231
For the outdoorswoman or outdoorsman who wants to look very, very good in the wild (or at home in front of the fire), Weekends offers a collection of sturdy trousers, cuddly sweaters, and soft-as-butter flannel shirts, all with irresistible style.

In summer, there are shorts and T's, along with jackets for the changeable high-country weather.

Consignment and Resale Shops
While there's plenty of good shopping to be done at our traditional retail outlets, some of the best bargains in Boulder show up on the shelves of these consignment and resale shops. They're the kind of places you want to check back with frequently, for you never know what will have just come in, and the best stuff never lasts long.

THE AMAZING GARAGE SALE
4919 Broadway, Boulder
(303) 447-0417
www.theamazinggaragesale.com
You'll find everything from furniture to household items, from antique to retro at this funky North Boulder establishment. Look for the chartreuse and red building on the west side of the street.

THE BUFFALO EXCHANGE
1717 Walnut Street, Boulder
(303) 938-1924
www.buffaloexchange.com
Current and retro vintage clothing is the draw here. If you've got stuff to sell, this place has liberal policies. They buy during all business hours. And rather than taking items on consignment, they buy outright for cash or credit toward a store trade.

CANDY'S VINTAGE CLOTHING AND COSTUMES
4483 North Broadway, Boulder
(303) 442-6186
www.candysvintageclothing.com
Poodle skirts, leather jackets from when bikers were bikers, boas, housedresses that somebody's mamma wore, clunky-soled shoes, sleek satin lingerie—a stop at Candy's is like checking out the contents of the closets down the street from Wally and the Beav's house. The shop carries women's and men's clothing from 1900 through the 1980s. There are also costumes for adults and children, vintage home furnishings, and linens and lace.

COMMON ERA 2000
1500 Pearl Street, Boulder
(303) 444-1799
This shop carries vintage clothing for both men and women, mostly from the '20s through the '50s, with shoes and accessories to match.

NO PLACE LIKE HOME
3550 Arapahoe Avenue, Boulder
(303) 440-9011
This is one of the cleanest used-furniture stores you'll ever see, with a nice selection of nearly new items. Those with a sharp eye can find some real bargains, but some of the furniture is surprisingly high-priced considering that it's secondhand. Turnover is rapid, so if you're on the lookout for something in particular, it's best to check fairly frequently. The best stuff borders on the antique; newer, lower-quality offerings are simply used. The store also carries some tableware, framed pictures, and other small objects. If you consign to them, they'll pick up. If you buy, they'll deliver.

RAGS CONSIGNMENTS
3129 28th Street, Boulder
(303) 440-5758
Rags (shortened a couple of years ago from Rags to Riches) specializes in (mostly) designer and brand name clothing for teens and women, along with an assortment of housewares. The store accepts consignments most days. Fantastic finds every day!

THE RITZ
959 Walnut Street, Boulder
(303) 443-2850
Around the corner from the Pearl Street Mall, the Ritz inventories a fabulous selection of classic '40s fashions, flouncy prom gowns from the '50s, elegant cocktail attire from various decades, and other unusual and vintage clothing. The store also sells and rents great costumes (Halloween and otherwise), including gorilla suits, creepy creatures from horror films, and masks of current politicians' faces.

Farmers' Markets and Food Co-ops
It's not surprising that health-conscious Boulder boasts more than its share of alternatives to the pre-packed, heavily salted fare preferred by most of the rest of the country. Here are some of our favorite spots for fresh and organic food.

i The west end of Pearl Street is always worth a visit. Officially starting at the intersection of 11th and Pearl Streets and continuing west for a few blocks, this shopping area has become its own quaint neighborhood. Browse shops such as the unique West End Gardener. The antiques store at the corner of Eighth and Pearl always has great finds.

BOULDER COUNTY FARMERS' MARKET
13th Street between Arapahoe Avenue and Canyon Boulevard
(303) 910-2236
www.boulderfarmers.org
As much of a happening and social event as a shopping opportunity, this market operates from 8 a.m. to 2 p.m. on Saturday and 10 a.m. to 2 p.m. on Wednesday from spring through fall. There's a mouthwatering selection of organically grown vegetables and fruits, and baked goods, as well as herbs, bedding plants, fresh flowers, and crafts. What began as an overflow area on the east side of 13th Street has developed into an alfresco dining experience featuring the best of some of Boulder's best restaurants and bakeries. (See the Attractions chapter for more details.)

LONGMONT FARMERS' MARKET
Northwest corner of Boulder County Fairgrounds, Hover Road and Boston Avenue
As Longmont is still surrounded by farm fields, it makes sense that a farmers' market prospers at the site of the county fairgrounds. Fruits and vegetables are eased out by pumpkins, bales of hay, and gourds as the season progresses. It's open from 8 a.m. to 1 p.m. May to October.

MOUNTAIN PEOPLE'S CO-OP
30 East First Street, Nederland
(303) 258-7500
This humble food store is a blast from the past. It is a cooperative, and members pay slightly lower prices. The co-op harkens back to the old-time, small-town neighborhood grocery but with a New Age twist. They carry a good selection of some of the tastiest organic and locally grown fruits and vegetables. There are also supplements, grooming supplies, coffee beans, grains, good breads, and other wholesome items and most necessities from toilet paper to Ben & Jerry's ice cream. A deli offers to-go items like burritos, fresh sandwiches, and salads.

Gadgets

THE BETTER BACK STORE
3043 Walnut Street, Boulder
(303) 442-3998
This store is hardly a frivolity to those in discomfort or pain. The inventory is extensive: back-strengthening exercise equipment, ergonomic office furniture, home furniture such as Ekornes Stressless Chairs from Norway and Backsaver recliners, cervical pillows, back cushions, lumbar belts and rolls, seat supports, massage equipment and creams, inversion units and boots, Backsaver snow shovels and other tools, ingenious purses that evenly distribute their weight, and video and cassette tapes. All these gadgets are designed to help you save your back or just to relax, feel good, and even prevent back problems.

MCGUCKIN HARDWARE
2525 Arapahoe Avenue, Boulder
(303) 443-1822
www.mcguckin.com
The slogan here is, "If we don't have it, you don't need it." It's just about true. This gigantic hardware superstore carries a do-it-yourselfer's dream of hand- and power-tools and stuff to do with them. You will find wood trim, door and window hardware, lighting fixtures and accessories, electrical and plumbing supplies, and the biggest selection of screws, nuts, bolts, clamps, washers, springs, gaskets, and every other gizmo and widget you can imagine. There are high-quality paint and housewares departments. One department makes keys and sells locks; another has video and audio tapes. Christmas decorations abound during the holiday season, and patio furniture moves in with the warm weather. Gardening tools and supplies, as well as seeds and annual and perennial plants, herald summer. McGuckin's also sells sporting equipment, including fishing and hunting supplies, backpacks, and camping equipment, and some outdoor books.

The spring and fall tent sales are three-day extravaganzas that include closeout and special-purchase merchandise at tremendous savings, as well as a blanket 10 percent off everything in the store. What sets McGuckin's apart from the big-box chains is personal service. A veritable army of green-vested salespeople waits to help, advise, guide, and point the way to the department you're looking for.

THE PEPPERCORN
1235 Pearl Street, Boulder
(303) 449-5847
www.peppercorn.com
If anything stops your stroll down the Downtown Mall, it's likely to be The Peppercorn's display windows, filled with an ever-changing array of gorgeous glassware, whimsical serving dishes shaped like rabbits or pumpkins or fantastical fish, avarice-inspiring table linens, and things you never knew existed and don't know how you've lived without. You can order by mail, but it's far more fun to personally visit this very pretty, full-to-bursting kitchen store with fine cookware, kitchen gadgets, table linens, a huge assortment of cookbooks, and gourmet foods. Need a mushroom brush? A butter mold? A madeleine pan? A replacement blade for your coffee mill? A spoon rest with a clever design? A set of Calphalon pots? A food processor in Mama Bear, Papa Bear, or Baby Bear sizes? The Peppercorn has them all—and oh-so-much more. Celebrity author-chefs sometimes do book signings and occasionally put on cooking demonstrations here.

THE WEST END GARDENER
777 Pearl Street, Boulder
(303) 938-0607

This is a delightful shop selling top-quality gardening tools, books, fountains, garden signs, wreaths, annuals and bulbs in season, and gifts and goodies for plant-lovers. It makes a putterer want to garden seriously, and a serious gardener strive to make the garden just perfect.

Gift Shops

HANGOUTS
1328 Pearl Street, Boulder
(303) 442-2533
www.hangouts.com

Mayan and Brazilian hammocks and hanging chairs in a rainbow of colors give this friendly mall shop its name, but venture inside and you'll also find imported sweaters, tie-dye T-shirts, and odd little trinkets from exotic locales. Stretch out in one of the floor-model hammocks and you won't want to leave the store.

THE PIPEFITTER
1352 College Avenue, Boulder
(303) 442-4200

A throwback to the '60s updated to the present, the Pipefitter carries pipes and smoking accessories, ethnic clothing and T-shirts, jewelry, candles and incense, posters and cards.

High Spirits

THE BOULDER WINE MERCHANT
2690 Broadway, in Community Plaza
Boulder
(303) 443-6761
www.boulderwine.com

This store is owned by two of the world's great wine experts, Wayne Belding and Sally Mohr. Both master sommeliers, with unerring noses for fine wine, Wayne and Sally and the store's experienced staff take very seriously the business of selecting, analyzing, recommending, and selling wine. Fewer than 30 master sommeliers are active in the United States, and another few dozen have

earned the title worldwide. The store sponsors two wine-appreciation classes each year and joins with local restaurants in presenting occasional very special dinners served with very special wines. The whole staff loves to help customers find a match for both palate and pocketbook.

HARVEST WINE AND SPIRITS
3075 Arapahoe Avenue, Boulder
(303) 447-9832

Harvest offers outstanding selections of imported and domestic wines, billed as the largest selection in the county. There are also microbrews, spirits, and fine cigars. This place is convenient for its location next to the King Soopers grocery store. The friendly, knowledgeable staff is always willing to help.

THE LIQUOR MART
Corner of 15th Street and Canyon Boulevard, Boulder
(303) 449-3374
www.liquormart.com

This is a supermarket-size liquor store, one of the largest in the United States. The variety is staggering, including hard liquor, beer, ale, wine, champagne, mixers, and soft drinks. If you want something exotic, you're as likely to find it here as anywhere in the state. The helpful staff is known for offering informed advice. If that's too much trouble, you can join Club Liquor Mart and receive a monthly selection of wine or a weekly six-pack of beer chosen by the store's staff. Buy a case of wine and get a 15-percent discount; you get 10 percent off when you buy a case of beer or liquor. For such a huge non-specialty store, The Liquor Mart's wine selection is surprising, both in its depth and its breadth. The store hosts frequent special dinners at local restaurants and joins with a local travel agency to sponsor a wine trip to Colorado's own wine country near Grand Junction.

SUPERIOR LIQUOR
100 Superior Parkway, Superior
(303) 499-6600
www.superiorliquor.com

At 20,000 square feet, this huge store has room

🔍 Close-up

It's xeriscape. Not zero-scape.

It's xeriscape (zer-rih-scape). Not zero-scape. It's beautiful plants that thrive in our dry, windy climate. It's not rocked-over yards or lawns addicted to herbicides, pesticides, and fertilizers. Boulder is a center for xeriscaping. At least a half-dozen books have been published by Boulder-area experts on water-wise gardening. And why not? Water use is critical in a climate that gets less than 17 inches of rain a year. What's more, after wandering Boulder's beautiful open-space trails, many gardeners develop a liking for this natural style. By comparison, the traditional green lawn is, well, boring.

Great area garden stores, filled with bedding plants, perennials, and ornamentals, include Lafayette Florists, The Flower Bin in Longmont, Sturtz and Copeland, and Fruehauf's. McGuckin Hardware has been voted by readers of Boulder's *Daily Camera* as the best place for garden supplies. It's also a good spot for finding plants if you like the flowers you see around the Village shopping center. (For more on marvelous McGuckin's, read this chapter's "Gadgets" section.) Boulder County has its own plant kingdoms. Most are on the way to Longmont, including the GreenSpot Nursery, and The Tree Farm. Mikl and Linda Brawner's Harlequin's Market is little but unique, down to the beautiful display of native and/or xeriscape plants in the Brawners' front yard next door. Wander their display garden and point to whatever gorgeous, thriving plant you like. Then ask Mikl or Linda to guide you to the potted version of the plant—small and inexpensive.

If you're shopping for garden space, consider this: 480-square-foot garden plots are available behind the North Boulder Recreation Center. The fee is $45, including water. (Gardeners must provide their own hoses.) Call (303) 441-3400. Or how about a free tree? If you move into a Boulder home with a bare front yard, you can apply to have the city plant a city-owned tree close to the street for you. For information, contact Boulder's Forestry Division at (303) 441-4406.

Now, about those garden books. Here are gems about Boulder area plants and gardens: *Pieces of Light* by Susan Tweit; *The Xeriscape Flower Gardener: A Waterwise Guide for the Rocky Mountain Region* by Jim Knopf; *Gardening in the Mountain West* by *Daily Camera* columnist Barbara Hyde; *Grow Native: Landscaping with Native and Apt Plants of the Rocky Mountains* by Sam Huddleston and Michael Hussey; *The Shortgrass Prairie* by Ruth Carol Cushman and Stephen R. Jones; *Personal Landscapes* by Jerome Malitz; and *The Undaunted Garden* by Lauren Springer.

for a wide variety of liquors, wines, and beers. Regulars can save by joining a Frequent Customer Program and earning rebates. There are weekly specials for all.

Home Furnishings

BARTLETT INTERIORS
2020 Pearl Street, Boulder
(303) 442-5194

It's a toss-up as to whether clients come here more for the stylish decorating advice or for the elegant and unusual upholstered and wood furniture, lamps, and window treatments. The inventory features many dramatic pieces that create a distinctive look. Cheap, it ain't.

BAYLEAF ON PEARL
805 Pearl Street, Boulder
(720) 565-2477

Featuring elegant gifts to delight the senses from high-quality aromatherapy candles to bistro tables and chairs straight from Paris.

CONCEPTS FURNITURE AND ACCESSORIES
1890 30th Street, Boulder
(303) 443-6900
Lean, clean lines, contemporary styling, and affordable prices make Concepts a favorite of college students setting up house in Boulder. The line includes upholstered pieces, dining and bedroom furniture, lamps, and accessories.

DECORASIAN
1500 Pearl Street, Boulder
(303) 938-1107
www.decorasianstyle.com
DecorAsian is the store for quality home decor from all over Asia. Whether you select an antique or reproduction, a functional or a decorative piece, you can rest assured that your purchase will be of the highest quality. If you happen to be looking for tribal ancestor figurines, Kazak rugs, or Chinese manuscript cabinets—visit DecorAsian.

HW HOME
1941 Pearl Street, Boulder
(303) 545-0320
www.hwhome.com
This store is dedicated to finding quality furnishings that are stylish and stand the test of time. Looking for that special accessory? Perhaps a silk pillow from Paris or candlesticks from the glassworks of the legendary Simon Pearce will work. Outfitting the bathroom? Don't forget the sensationally soft towels from Switzerland. HW Home also offers custom interior design services.

MOUNTAIN FURNITURE ARTS
4 East First Street, Nederland
(303) 443-2030
At Mountain Furniture Arts (formerly Boulder Furniture Arts and Country West), each piece of furniture is handcrafted to meet your specific needs. If you haven't been able to find the right size table for your home, Mountain Furniture Arts is the place for you.

NOW & ZEN
1638 Pearl Street, Boulder
(303) 530-9028
www.now-zen.com
Founded in 1995, Now & Zen creates natural lifestyle products. The growing preference for natural foods and natural fibers is carried forward by Now & Zen in the natural acoustic sounds and natural hardwood materials featured in all their products.

TIMBERLINE STUDIOS
2015 Pearl Street, Boulder
(303) 443-3610
Down-filled upholstered pieces, unique accents, a line of dining and bedroom sets—Timberline bills its stock as "eclectic furniture for the Colorado lifestyle." Design consultation is also available.

UNPAINTED FURNITURE
7161 Valtec Ct., Boulder
(303) 443-8229
If you're a do-it-yourselfer, head for this store, which carries Colorado's largest inventory of unfinished hardwood and pine furniture: china and corner cabinets, coffee and end tables, armoires and wardrobes, juvenile furniture, tables and chairs, rockers, chests, dressers, bookcases, and toy boxes. The staff has advice and the finishing materials you'll need, or if you want to spend the extra money and wait a few weeks, they'll do the finishing for you.

Z GALLERIE
1755 Twenty Ninth Street, Boulder
(303) 440-0495
www.zgallerie.com
Z Gallerie moved to Boulder with the opening of Twenty Ninth Street in 2006. The store offers a variety of high-quality, reasonably priced merchandise for the home, including furniture, lighting, artwork, tabletop items, textiles, and decorative accessories from around the world.

Jewelers

In addition to dedicated jewelry stores, you'll find jewelry in the Boulder Arts & Crafts Cooperative and other crafts stores, as well as in many of Boulder's art galleries.

BILL CRONIN GOLDSMITH
1235 Alpine Avenue, Boulder
(303) 440-4222
www.billcronin.com
Since 1979 this shop north of downtown has been manufacturing high-quality jewelry set with diamonds and other stones. Cronin's specializes in custom goldsmithing, helping local romantics create The Ring to their specifications.

CARLA MORRISON FINE JEWELRY DESIGN
2017 10th Street, Boulder
(720) 564-9285
www.carlamorrison.com
Carla Morrison brings her talent as a goldsmith and jewelry designer to Boulder. She has traveled around the world to observe and learn from other jewelry designers. Her designs are simple and elegant.

HURDLE'S
1402 Pearl Street, Boulder
(303) 443-1084
www.hurdlesjewelry.com
This is a very traditional jeweler, just what you'd expect to find in a historic downtown like Boulder's. And well it should be, for it was established back in 1947. There's even a little repair booth right in the window, armed with loupes, velvet cushions, and the teeny instruments necessary to perform surgery on delicate watches and jewelry. Hurdle's carries estate and new jewelry of all sorts as well as fine watches, including TAGHeuer from Switzerland.

THE LITTLE JEWEL
1225 Pearl Street, Boulder
(303) 443-3353
On the Pearl Street Mall, the Little Jewel lives up to its name by cramming its tiny dimensions with a lot of pieces in a lot of styles. There's some Southwestern turquoise and silver. There's some Italian gold. There are chains, earrings, bracelets, and wedding sets.

MASTER GOLDSMITHS
10th and Pearl Streets, Boulder
(303) 443-3424
www.mastergoldsmiths.com
Since 1971, Master Goldsmiths has been creating unique and custom-designed jewelry in gold and platinum. Ideal Cut diamonds are imported directly to the store.

PETER ROSEN JEWELRY DESIGNER
1600 Pearl Street, Boulder
(303) 443-2852
www.rosenjewelrydesigner.com
Since 1980, jewelry designer Peter Rosen has been creating unique pieces, each verified with his signature. The sculpted gold and silver pieces are adorned with precious and semiprecious stones.

THE RINGMAKER
2691 30th Street, Boulder
(303) 440-5507
www.theringmaker.com
With more than 1,500 pieces on display, selection is no easy task at this custom jewelry store that has been operating since 1944. In addition to wedding sets, rings, bracelets, necklaces, and earrings, you can get stones remounted and repairs on-site. Appraisals are also available.

WALTERS & HOGSETT
2425 Canyon Boulevard, Boulder
(303) 449-2626
www.waltersandhogsett.com
Gold, silver, and gemstones are featured at this highly regarded jewelry store. It stocks fine domestic and imported jewelry, watches, crystal, and silver. In addition to repairs, Walters & Hogsett offers an annual fall special on re-plating silver flatware and hollowware.

Miscellany

ALLEN SCIENTIFIC GLASS BLOWERS
1752 55th Street, Boulder
(303) 442-2141
www.allenglass.com
The Ph.D. crowd told us that this guide wouldn't be complete without including Ray Allen, called the "God of Scientific Glass." He can make anything out of glass and glass/metal transitions. You know . . . all those things you always wanted for your lab but couldn't find at a really good price.

BLAKE'S SMALL CAR SALVAGE
2559 Weld County Road, No. 5, Erie
(303) 665-4312
This junkyard is so darned pretty it was featured on the CBS Evening News. Car parts, fitting everything from a 1959 Anglias to a 1993 Geo Storm, are arranged by country. A Japanese flag flies near the Hondas; a German flag marks the BMWs. Small parts are stored picturesquely in yellow school buses and Chevy vans. The Colorado New Music Association came out here one fall and made, along with other instruments, drums from the hubcaps.

COLORADO BAGGAGE
Twenty Ninth Street, Boulder
(303) 449-8621
www.bagnbaggage.com
Going somewhere? This store has exactly the right bag, tote, suitcase, backpack, overnight kit, money belt, billfold, purse, jewelry case, or computer carrier to get your stuff there. Going nowhere? It's a great place to fantasize.

ELLIES ECO HOME STORE
2525 Arapahoe, Boulder
(303) 952-1004
www.elliesecohomestore.com
Visit Ellie's in the Village and find an amazing array of things for yourself, your family and your house that are either recycled, renewable or sustainable. This amazing store features products like cork flooring, recycled cotton insulation, nontoxic paints and finishes, wool carpeting and the like. You will also find items like Boulder laundry detergent, an extensive line of organic skin care products, organic linens for baby and natural pet supplies.

FASCINATIONS LOVE SHACKS & SUPERSTORES
2560 28th Street, Boulder
(303) 442-7309
Fascinations is an adult products (ahem . . .) store. The inventory is about what you'd expect but with a more playful, less shadowy corners feel.

H.B. WOODSONGS
2920 Pearl Street, Boulder
(303) 449-0516
www.hbwoodsongs.com
H.B. Woodsongs has been serving Boulder's acoustic community for more than 25 years. The business has now grown to three locations. The Boulder store's products include guitars and folk instruments, rentals, and accessories; world percussion instruments; and printed music, videos, and recordings. The store is still the home of Woodsongs Lutherie—a repair shop which specializes in the repair of stringed instruments and the amplification of acoustic instruments.

ROBB'S MUSIC
2691 30th Street, Boulder
(303) 443-8448
www.robbsbouldermusic.com
Robb's has digital pianos, electronic keyboards, guitars, drums, band instruments, and more. They offer great deals on used instruments and have experts who repair electronic instruments.

WILDWOOD MUSIC
804 Main Street, Louisville
(303) 665-7733
www.wildwoodguitars.com
This store specializes in both acoustic and electric guitars, including Fender, Martin, Gibson, Paul Reed Smith, Taylor, and Dobro. Wildwood has unbeatable prices.

Nature Stores

CRYSTAL GALLERIES LTD.
1302 Pearl Street, Boulder
(303) 444-2277
www.crystalgalleries.com
This store features a fine collection of minerals, crystals, fossils, and jewelry made from semiprecious gemstones. The glasswork of René Lalique, plus eggs, spheres, and bookends, are all in the inventory.

Photographic Equipment

JONES DRUG & CAMERA CENTER
1370 College Avenue, Boulder
(303) 443-4420
More than a drugstore, this Hill institution has a very good line of fine cameras, lenses, film, and photo accessories, including filters, bags, books, albums, and frames. In addition to processing film, Jones has a full selection of darkroom supplies and one of the best offerings of black-and-white enlarging paper in the state. The store also sells high-quality used equipment and has a very knowledgeable and helpful staff.

MIKE'S CAMERA
2500 Pearl Street, Boulder
(303) 443-1715
www.mikescamera.com
Boulder's only complete camera shop dedicated exclusively to photographic equipment, related items, and services, Mike's is a local icon. Its services include camera and video repairs, rentals (full spectrum), used camera sales, digital imaging, and photo and video industrial equipment—plus classes on how to use it all. There are also telescopes, picture frames, and bags. The staff is knowledgeable and helpful.

PHOTO CRAFT
3550 Arapahoe Road, Boulder
(303) 442-6410
www.pcraft.com
This shop is another favorite of the professionals, with custom photographic services, including giant photographic color murals and backlights suitable for trade show and store display. It also offers rush service and custom computer-imaging services.

Specialty-Food Shops

THE ASIAN DELI
2833 28th Street, Boulder
(303) 541-9377
Need some dried bonito flakes, pickled daikon radishes, lemongrass, or divine curries? This store has them all, plus Asian produce and freshly made Vietnamese spring rolls—cilantro and shrimp enclosed in a delicate rice wrapper.

THE CHEESE IMPORTER'S WAREHOUSE
33 South Pratt Parkway, Longmont
(303) 772-9599
www.cheeseimporters.com
The Warehouse is an importer for the Willow River Company and has bargains on wheels of foreign and domestic cheeses and bags of perfect, meltable dark chocolate, all set on industrial-strength shelving in a huge, refrigerated room. A small shop also carries other gourmet foods, coffee, tea, and cookware.

COLORADO CRAFT AND CAKE SUPPLY
1750 30th Street, Suite 12, Boulder
(303) 447-1557
If you are ambitious and want to decorate your own cakes, you can get all the supplies you need here. They sell powdered meringue for frosting and incredible cake decorations.

HERB'S MEATS AND SPECIALTY FOODS
2530 Baseline Road, Boulder
(303) 499-8166
A Boulder institution, this store is just what the name says. Herb's carries the freshest cuts of meat and a large variety of sauces. If you're particular, the perfect leg of lamb or pork roast can be found here.

MOUNTAIN MAN NUT AND FRUIT CO.
2525 Arapahoe Avenue, Boulder
(303) 546-0920
A locally owned store that carries gourmet candy such as double-dipped malted-milk balls, all kinds of nuts and dried fruits, trail mixes, peach salsa, and dried soups, plus teas, coffees, mustards, and jellies. They do gift baskets, too. In the Village Shopping Center, just around the corner from the movie theater, it's a perfect stop if movie popcorn and candy aren't your thing.

THE ORIENTAL FOOD MARKET
1750 30th Street, No. 84, Boulder
(303) 422-7830
This market carries all the ingredients you'll need for all manner of Asian cuisine, including Chinese, Japanese, Thai, Indian, Cambodian, Laotian, Vietnamese, Malaysian, Philippine, and Indonesian. The small deli serves primarily Indonesian specialties.

SALVAGGIO'S ITALIAN DELI
2609 Pearl Street, Boulder
(303) 938-1981

1397 Pearl St., Boulder
(303) 545-6800

1107 13th St., Boulder
(303) 448-1200
If you're a former Easterner, these delis can satisfy your craving for good, New York-style Italian fare. The store carries Italian cold cuts and cheeses, including fresh, water-packed mozzarella and fresh pastas and sauces.

WHOLE FOODS MARKET
2905 Pearl Street, Boulder
(303) 545-6611

1651 Broadway St., Boulder
(303) 442-0909

2584 Baseline Rd., Boulder
(303) 499-7636
www.wholefoods.com
Ever since it opened just off 28th Street, the city's biggest Whole Foods has been the place to be for shoppers who really love food. Now there are a couple different locations in Boulder. Past a huge selection of fruits and vegetables there are fish and meat departments that pride themselves on freshness. Aisles are filled with herbs, foods, cosmetics, and cleaning supplies with an environmental conscience, plus bulk supplies of munchies, cereal, honey, oil, and nut butters. Delis offer browsers samples of crackers, cheeses, meat, and olives. Among the other stores-within-the-store are a bread shop, a pizza shop, and a juice bar. There's a huge selection of prepared foods, from grilled eggplant to corn cakes to barbecued chicken.

Sporting Goods Shops
From one end of town to the other, Boulder is speckled with sporting goods shops, including a number of exceptional mountaineering and climbing stores. You don't have to leave Boulder to find such high-country gear as hiking boots; parkas; alpine and Nordic skis; snowboards; snowshoes; in-line skates; rock-climbing, camping, and backpacking equipment; and clothing and accessories for any terrain or activity. Most stores rent as well as sell clothing and equipment, and some of the best deals are end-of-season closeouts on rental equipment.

BICYCLE VILLAGE
2100 28th Street, Boulder
(303) 440-8525
www.bicyclevillage.com
Mountain bikes, road bikes, comfort bikes, clothing, accessories, car racks, and bikes for rent—Bicycle Village has it all. This is Colorado's largest Schwinn dealer.

BOULDER ARMY STORE
1545 Pearl Street, Boulder
(303) 442-7616
www.boulderarmystore.com
A Boulder favorite, this store is true to its name and features a full array of such army surplus items as ammo cases, camouflage clothing, combat boots, and canteens. It's a good place to shop

for backpacks, nylon climbing rope, hiking boots, sunglasses, hats and gloves of every description, freeze-dried food, water purification systems, solar showers, bandanas, and campfire coffeepots.

BOULDER RUNNING COMPANY
28th and Pearl Streets, Boulder
(303) RUN-WALK
www.boulderrunningcompany.com
A free running and walking gait assessment and analysis of your feet ensures that you pick the right footwear. You can check out the results by watching yourself on a video monitor as you try out different pairs.

BOULDER SKI DEALS
2525 Pearl Street, Boulder
(303) 938-8799
www.boulderskideals.com
This shop sells equipment and clothing for alpine and Nordic skiing and snowboarding. There's a full-service boot and ski repair shop and custom boot fitting. Mostly new but also some traded-in used equipment is available. The store also sells such accessories as hats, gloves, long johns, socks, sunglasses, goggles, and sunscreen. In summer, the shop partially switches over to in-line skating and water sports, including kayaking.

BOULDER SPORTS RECYCLER
4949 North Broadway, Boulder
(303) 786-9940
This is a great place to pick up used and closeout skis, in-line skates, and equipment for racquetball, hockey, baseball, golf, camping, football, water sports, biking, tennis, soccer, fishing, and weight-lifting. They also sell used sports clothing.

FLEET FEET
2624 Broadway, Boulder
(303) 939-8000
www.fleetfeetboulder.com
Specialty shoes for walkers and runners are available here, along with a thorough fitting to make sure they stay comfortable. The shop collects and posts information about area races and fun runs

and offers both an analysis of your gait and clinics on how to do it better.

LOUISVILLE CYCLERY
1032 South Boulder Road, Louisville
(303) 665-6343
www.louisvillecyclery.com
Road- and mountain-bike specialists help here with sales, rental, custom wheels, professional fittings, and suspension and repair service. They also carry high-quality clothing and gear for the whole family.

MONTBELL
1755 29th Street, Boulder
(303) 449-5331
www.montbell.com
Founded and based in Osaka, Japan, Montbell America was established in the fall of 2002 with the flagship store in Boulder. The company manufactures high-quality, lightweight outdoor clothing and equipment.

NEPTUNE MOUNTAINEERING
633 South Broadway, Boulder
(303) 499-8866
www.neptunemountaineering.com
The first among equals for hard-core climbers and mountaineers is this store in Table Mesa Shopping Center. This huge store is owned by Gary Neptune, a prominent U.S. mountaineer who has reached the summit of Mount Everest and other high peaks. Besides ice axes, ropes, and climbing shoes and boots, the store has a good selection of Nordic ski equipment and outdoor clothing. Its book department is one of the best around. Gary's private collection of mountaineering memorabilia, including rarities of immense historic value, is displayed throughout.

THE NORTH FACE
1711 29th Street, Boulder
(303) 499-1731
www.thenorthface.com
Located at the Twenty Ninth Street Mall, this is a national wholesaler/manufacturer that has

established one of its few retail stores in Boulder. The Berkeley, California–based company sells its tents, packs, sleeping bags, ski jackets, and other products to 800 shops across the country.

OUTDOOR DIVAS
1133 Pearl Street, Boulder
(303) 449-3482
www.outdoordivas.com
If you are a woman who skis, rides, stretches, bikes, hikes, paddles, climbs, runs, and swims, this is the store for you. Devoted entirely to the woman who likes to be outside!

PADDLE SHOP
1727 15th Street, Boulder
(303) 786-8799
This shop sells plenty of kayaking equipment but also rents and sells canoes and rafts. They also carry wet suits and all other related accessories. Kayak instruction and raft trips are available through the shop.

PRO PELOTON
2615 13th Street, Boulder
(303) 415-1292
www.propeloton.com
A peloton is the large pack of cyclists riding together in a long road race like the Tour de France. On the back side of the Community Plaza, this high-end shop specializes in serious road and racing bikes and everything you need to embark on heavy-duty cycling.

REI
1789 28th Street, Boulder
(303) 583-9970
www.rei.com
REI is a retailer of outdoor gear and the nation's largest consumer co-op. REI gear and apparel are available, along with other top brands for climbing, cycling, hiking, camping, snow sports, outdoor fitness, and paddling. Their sales staff is unsurpassed. They know about each and every product and can assist you in making an informed purchase.

ROCKY MOUNTAIN ANGLERS
1904 Arapaho Avenue, Boulder
(303) 447-2400
www.rockymtanglers.com
If the flash of a fighting fish's belly rising from a rushing stream makes your heart beat faster, this shop has what you need. Flies, and the supplies to make them, reels and rods, waders and boots, and fish knives are in stock. There are classes in fly-tying and information on where they're biting, and on what.

ROCKY MOUNTAIN RACQUET SPECIALISTS
2425 Canyon Boulevard, Boulder
(303) 442-1412
This is where Boulder's major tennis, squash, and racquetball enthusiasts go for the gear and duds. Racquets and balls, of course, are available, but so is name-brand clothing, footwear, and accessories such as eyewear and gloves. This store offers one-day racquet stringing and can also make custom grips. They have abbreviated hours during the winter, so call first.

ROCKY MOUNTAIN SOCCER
2767 Iris Avenue, in the Willow Springs Center, Boulder
(303) 938-9166
www.rockymountainsoccer.com
Soccer is a big deal in Boulder. Apparel and equipment such as shin guards, balls, and cleats are available here. It's a real mecca for soccer-holics and has meeting space available for groups who want to plan events centered around this round-ball sport.

SCUBA JOE DIVE AND TRAVEL
3015 Bluff Street, Boulder
(303) 440-8882
www.oceanfirstdivers.com
Scuba Joe is a dive and snorkel center with an in-store travel agency and convenient basic-through-instructor classes offered on weeknights or weekends.

SPORTS AUTHORITY
3320 28th Street, Boulder
(303) 449-9021
www.sportsauthority.com
Sports Authority offers a wide assortment of sporting goods from tennis and golf equipment to skiing, fishing, and hunting supplies. It is ideal for finding gear for team sports, exercise paraphernalia, logo clothing, athletic shoes, and low- to mid-priced sporting goods for skiers and other recreational athletes.

UNIVERSITY BICYCLES
839 Pearl Street, Boulder
(303) 444-4196
www.ubikes.com
You can't miss this shop—look for the clever outdoor mural of the bicyclist who appears to be breaking through the exterior wall. This store sells and repairs mountain and road bikes and promises "all the neat stuff you see in bike magazines." It's a handy location to rent a bike, for one or two, for a pedal around downtown.

WEAVER'S DIVE AND TRAVEL CENTER
637 South Broadway, Boulder
(303) 499-8500
www.weaversdive.com
Weaver's sells dive gear, wet suits, and swimwear. If you don't know how to dive, they'll teach you and help you get certified. If you dive, you can book a group or individual dive trip to some of the world's top underwater destinations. Weaver's has a full-service travel agency on-site.

Yard Sales

Lastly, perhaps some of the best shopping in town is at Boulder's yard and garage sales. Check the classified sections of the local newspapers, check out Craigslist, or just drive around town on summer weekends and keep an eye out for homemade signs on trees and utility poles. Many sales start on Fridays, but Saturdays are the big days—and a few dribble over into Sunday, too.

In south Boulder, the bridge across Bear Creek at Table Mesa Drive and the King Soopers entrance is always plastered with yard sale signs around the weekend. Downtown, the corner of Arapahoe Avenue and Ninth Street is often festooned with garage sale signs. With its transient population of students and upwardly mobile adults, Boulder's yard sales offer everything from skis, bicycles, snowboards, and sailboarding equipment to violins, art, and antiques.

If you're not too picky, dumpsters on The Hill yield a bounty in May when students are moving out and discarding everything that won't fit in a duffel bag.

FESTIVALS AND ANNUAL EVENTS

S pecial events make an evening or weekend sparkle, and Boulder has so many that it's hard to choose. The following listings are in approximate chronological order. Where possible, they include dates, times, and prices. Other events bloom with serendipity, so planners can't say exactly when and how much until the event draws near. You can find even more possibilities by checking our Attractions and The Arts chapters. Keep in mind, volunteers run many of these festivals, and you're welcome to lend a hand.

JANUARY

POLAR BEAR CLUB ICE PLUNGE
Boulder Reservoir, 51st Street, Boulder
(303) 441-3461
Pay around $15 to brave ice-crusted water, dance a jig, screech, then hurry to shore (or stay in as long as you wish). Rescue workers stand by in case anyone gets hypothermia from the morning dip. Plungers say, "It's intensely painful, in a pleasurable sort of way." For spectators, admission to this New Year's Day event is free

COLORADO MAHLERFEST
Macky Auditorium (on the CU-Boulder campus)
and Boulder Public Library (11th Street and Arapahoe Avenue), Boulder
(303) 530-2646
www.mahlerfest.org
Gustav Mahler fans and other classical music lovers rave about this one-of-a-kind concertfest, now in its 21st year. In 1988, Conductor Bob Olson gathered a volunteer orchestra to play Mahler's 1st Symphony. Each year another of Mahler's ten symphonies was performed, then a second cycle began, starting at the beginning. Traditionally in January, MahlerFest XXII will be held in May in 2009, with an all-day free symposium of lectures, and free song recitals at the Boulder Public Library and the Rocky Mountain Center for Musical Arts in Lafayette. Concert ticket prices range from $10 to $40.

NATIONAL WESTERN STOCK SHOW, RODEO, AND HORSE SHOW
I-25 on I-70, Denver
(303) 297-1166, ext. 810
www.nationalwestern.com
Denver proudly calls itself a "cow town" and proves it during the month of January, when the Stock Show comes to town. Since 1906 serious competition combined with showmanship have made this one of the largest stock shows in the world. More than 600,000 people attend. At one recent stock show, there were nearly 40 performances, including 23 rodeos by the Professional Rodeo Cowboys Association, two Mexican rodeos, two bull-riding events, seven horse shows, three Wild West shows, and two evenings of dancing horses. Other events include sheep shearing, mutton busting, barn tours, and a children's petting farm. Visit their Web site for ticket prices for specific events

LAFAYETTE QUAKER OATMEAL FESTIVAL
100 South Public Road, Lafayette
(303) 926-4352
www.discoverlafayette.com
When Lafayette business owners decided to initiate a unique annual festival, someone noted that January is "oatmeal month." Not surprisingly, Lafayette now boasts the "world's largest oatmeal breakfast buffet." Quaker Oats was more than happy to participate, and the annual festival now includes a 5K health walk, a health fair, kids'

activities, and lots of entertainment. Scheduled for January 10th in 2009, the all-you-can-eat breakfast has become a tradition in this town. Visit their Web site for up-to-date information on this event

FEBRUARY

CHOCOLATE LOVER'S FLING
Glenn Miller Ballroom (on CU-Boulder campus), Boulder
(303) 449-8623
www.bouldercountysafehouse.org
Eat all the chocolate you want and benefit a good cause on the Friday or Saturday evening closest to Valentine's Day at the Chocolate Lover's Fling. Admission (tickets are in the $125 per person or $250 per couple range) includes a popular silent auction. Feast your eyes on chocolate TV dinners, armadillos, cabbages, and castles. Boulder's best professional chefs vie with talented amateurs in categories ranging from "Sheer Artistry" to just plain yummy. Enter your creation, or just eat the entries. Profits go to the Boulder County Safehouse, which helps battered families.

BOULDER INTERNATIONAL FILM FESTIVAL
Boulder Theater, Boulder
(720) 273-8169
www.biff1.com
Typically held on Presidents' Day weekend, this world-class festival brings together storytellers, actors, and audiences from all over the world. The goal of the festival is to encourage young filmmakers to turn their visions into film reality.

MARCH

4-H CARNIVAL
Boulder County Fairgrounds
9595 Nelson Road, Longmont
(303) 776-4865
www.bouldercountyfair.org
This all-day family event on the first or second Saturday in March has a silent auction and over 40 game and food booths. Throw shaving-cream pies and walk through a maze of bright-colored calico walls. You might win a T-shirt by launching a stuffed toy lamb into a little pen. Admission is free. Concession booth proceeds support a variety of 4-H activities.

BOULDER BACH FESTIVAL
P.O. Box 1896, Boulder, CO 80306
(303) 652-9101
www.boulderbachfest.org
Only a handful of American festivals play nothing but J. S. Bach. This is one. Local professional musicians and well-known guest artists keep the music lively, playing those hummable tunes you might have thought were modern. Founded in 1981, the festival will be held in March in 2009. Additional concerts take place on an irregular schedule from September through May at locations that include the University of Colorado's Grusin Music Hall, University Lutheran Chapel, the Boulder Public Library Auditorium, and Denver's St. John's Cathedral. Ticket prices vary.

ST. PATRICK'S DAY PARADE
Walnut Street, Boulder
(303) 449-1922
As "the world's shortest St. Patrick's Day Parade," this is one of Boulder's wackiest events and a true Boulder tradition. After the parade, follow the revelers to local pubs for St. Patrick's Day cheer.

APRIL

CONFERENCE ON WORLD AFFAIRS
CU-Boulder campus, Boulder
(303) 492-2525
www.colorado.edu/cwa
International flags festoon the campus during this weeklong series of forums held the week after CU-Boulder's spring semester resumes following spring break. Over 100 speakers from all over the world jet to Boulder at their own expense to participate in this popular conference. Past participants have included the likes of R. Buckminster Fuller, George McGovern, Annie Leibovitz, and Ted Turner, just to name a few. Call ahead for session topics, or just wander into the University Memorial Center to pick up a schedule

and slip into one of the many discussions. All events are free and open to the public.

BOULDER COUNTY FARMERS' MARKET

13th Street between Canyon Boulevard and Arapahoe Avenue, Boulder
(303) 910-2236
www.boulderfarmers.org
Local farmers offer their fresh fruit, flowers, herbs, veggies, gourmet cheeses, wines, and more at the Farmer's Market that starts in April and runs into November. The market bustles with activity and is a fun place to meet up with friends for coffee and pastries while shopping for all sorts of goodies. Parking is free in adjacent city parking lots. The market runs Saturdays from 8 a.m. to 2 p.m. April 5 to November 1, with the addition of Wednesdays from 4 to 8 p.m. May 7 through October 1.

PUTTIN' ON THE LEASH

Coors Events Center, CU-Boulder Campus
(303) 442-4030
www.boulderhumane.org
The annual adoptable animal fashion show and auction fund-raiser for the Boulder Valley Humane Society is held in late April. Auction items have included ski packages, vacations in Mexico, and trips to swim with the dolphins off the coast of the Bahamas. It is held at the Coors Events Center on the CU campus. Tickets are around $50 per person but check the Web site in the spring for exact dates and ticket prices.

MAY

STRAWBERRY FESTIVAL ANTIQUES SHOW

Boulder County Fairgrounds
9595 Nelson Road, Longmont
(303) 776-1870
www.stvrainhistoricalsociety.org/
Antique.htm
This is one of three annual antiques shows hosted by the St. Vrain Historical Society and held in the exhibit hall at the fairgrounds. (The others are the Heritage Festival in July and Pumpkin Pie Days in October.) Antiques and collectibles are

available, but those who aren't buying are usually taste-testing the strawberry shortcake sold in the cafeteria. Admission at all three events is $3.

BOULDER CREEK FESTIVAL AND RUBBER DUCK RACE

Boulder Creek, Boulder
(303) 449-3825
www.bceproductions.com
This popular rite of spring has been rated the "Best Annual Children's Event" by *Daily Camera* readers. Throughout Memorial Day weekend, craft booths, music and dance, carnival rides, and food stands entertain the throngs who edge their way through the tightly packed festival area all the way from 6th to 13th Streets and between Canyon Boulevard and Arapahoe Avenue.

On Sunday, more than 5,000 yellow rubber duckies bobble from the Ninth Street and Canyon Boulevard bridge to the Peace Garden at 11th Street and Arapahoe Avenue—all in the name of fun and charity. The race benefits the Boulder Parks and Recreation Department, helping it expand its therapeutic program for children and adults with disabilities. It costs $5 to enter a duck, and prizes range from the trivial to major vacations.

Other activities, such as the kids' Fishing Derby, a sports expo, and a huge art and crafts show, help to draw approximately 150,000 people to the Central Park area before the fun ends Monday evening.

BOLDER BOULDER 10K RACE

From 30th and Iris Streets to Folsom Field
Boulder
(303) 444-RACE
www.bolderboulder.com
This Memorial Day tradition is rated one of the top road races in the nation and "Boulder's Best Annual Event" by *Daily Camera* readers. It's amazing how much fun it can be to run or walk more than 6 miles. More than 50,000 participants, from the most fleet-footed elite amateur runners in the A wave to first-time walkers in the ZZ, make this one of the nation's largest citizen races. An inter-

i The Bolder Boulder 10K is a moving party for 50,000-plus, with some of the world's most fleet runners, thousands of amateur runners, a whole bunch of walkers, and live entertainment to cheer people along the way.

national field of celebrity runners and top wheelchair athletes make this an important race on the national 10K calendar too. The Bolder Boulder's nonstop party atmosphere is exhilarating. In addition to aid and water stations, entertainment is provided along the route. All runners finish at CU-Boulder's Folsom Field, where thousands of spectators watch world-class professional racers compete after the amateur races are through.

The race fee varies depending on which race package you choose. Every runner is timed, so you will get your time and ranking calculated in a variety of ways after the race. You can register at local running stores or at race headquarters. Try to get your application in by early May. (If the race doesn't fill up, you can register on race morning, too, but the price is $10 higher.)

Nearly 50,000 runners make quite a pack, but the race never feels so crowded, for organizers stagger the starting times in successive waves to give everyone room. Along the way you'll see belly dancers, including the lady with the sword on her head, and high-stepping grandmas decked out in fringed cowgirl skirts. You'll hear everything from live jazz bands to bagpipers playing rock 'n roll. Don't fear wimping out. In the ZZ wave, the pace is a pleasant amble, and the cheers from the crowd are just as enthusiastic.

The citizens' race starts at 7:20 a.m. at 30th Street and Iris Avenue. The elite professionals, among the fastest in the world, start at noon so that citizen racers can watch the pros' final laps in Folsom Field. If you decide to watch, pick a spot anywhere along the course or at Folsom Field. Runners have included wedding parties and guys who leapfrog the whole way. Marines usually sign up for the "M" section and run in formation, entertaining the crowd with military chants along

the route. Blind runners and wheelchair racers inspire us all, as do the fleet-footed gazelle types and seniors running with their grandchildren.

JUNE

BOULDER JEWISH FESTIVAL
Pearl Street Mall, Boulder
www.boulderjewishfestival.org
This one-day, family-oriented event celebrates the Jewish culture with local artist exhibits, food, live entertainment, dance, and representatives from various Jewish organizations in Boulder County.

BOULDER OUTDOOR CINEMA
Boulder Museum of Contemporary Art
1750 13th Street, Boulder
(303) 444-1351
www.boulderoutdoorcinema.com
Bring a chair and your own popcorn and enjoy an informal cinema experience in the museum's parking lot. This outdoor walk-in theater screens "B" movies, cult classics, cartoons, and funny short subjects Saturday nights June through August. Prizes are awarded for best costume as it relates to the movie. The film, which starts at dusk, is projected onto an outside wall of the museum. The movies are free but there is a suggested donation of $5.

THE COLORADO SHAKESPEARE FESTIVAL
CU-Boulder's Mary Rippon Outdoor Theatre, Boulder
(303) 492-0554
www.coloradoshakes.org
This festival, started in 1958, has presented all the Shakespeare plays. It is now the fifth-largest Shakespeare company in the United States, according to the Shakespeare Theatre Association. The lushly costumed, lavishly acted plays are produced from mid-June through mid-August. A recent season featured three plays, *The Tempest, As You Like It,* and *The Merchant of Venice.* Because the Rippon's amphitheater-style benches are made of stone, the wise theatergoer brings or rents a soft cushion or a stadium chair. After the sun goes down, the

evening can turn cool, so toting a sweater, jacket, and even rain gear is smart, too. Single tickets range from $14 to $54 with discounts for seniors, students, and CU faculty and staff.

SUMMERFEST AT BOULDER HISTORY MUSEUM
1206 Euclid Avenue, Boulder
(303) 449-3464
www.boulderhistorymuseum.org
This free, family-oriented event allows visitors to experience the history of yesterday and today with a different theme every year. All sorts of activities make this a fun day for all ages. Located in the historic Harbeck-Bergheim House, the museum highlights Boulder's unique history. Museum hours are 10 a.m. to 5 p.m. Tuesday through Friday and noon to 4 p.m. on Saturday and Sunday.

TASTE OF LOUISVILLE
Louisville's shopping districts
(303) 666-5747
www.ci.louisville.co.us
Less-than-a-dollar samples from many Louisville eateries are part of this mid-June celebration, which includes 80 participating businesses. The weekend often includes country-dance lessons, face-painting and shuttle buses, which take revelers between this growing city's shopping areas.

THE COLORADO MUSIC FESTIVAL
1525 Spruce Street, Boulder
(303) 449-1397
www.coloradomusicfest.org
The festival features a first-rate, full orchestra that plays great classical music at the Chautauqua Auditorium throughout the summer. The CMF season starts with a special children's performance and includes a free Fourth of July outdoor concert. You can get a subscription or single tickets to festival concerts. Insiders often bring a picnic and blanket for a pre-concert dinner on the grassy lawn, and many cluster behind the auditorium and listen to the sounds of brass and strings that waft through the wooden walls. Single tickets range from $12 to $47.

WALK AND BIKE WEEK
2018 11th Street to 1739 Broadway, Boulder
(303) 441-3266
www.goboulder.net
Bike Week was a decade old when the city's alternate modes division added the "Walk" to the title in order to encourage participation by those who don't have a gift for cycling. The annual event is scheduled for the third week in June; Walk or Bike to Work Day is held on the Wednesday of that week. Prizes are offered to those who commute the farthest and to businesses with the most employees who bike or walk to work. More than 35 breakfast stations offer participants a quick bite to eat before they reach the office.

JULY

BOULDER CONCERT BAND
Summer Performances in the Parks
Various Boulder parks
(303) 442-3597
www.boulderband.org
When the weather turns warm, Boulderites head to the parks on Monday night to support the Boulder Concert Band. This premier adult community band, comprised of 70-plus volunteer musicians, performs marches, show tunes, Big Band standards, and sing-alongs sure to delight the whole family. Concerts are held at 7 p.m. every Monday night from late June through mid-August at such places as the North Boulder Park, Eben G. Fine Park, Salberg Park, the public library lawn, and the courthouse plaza.

FOURTH OF JULY
An overture of real thunder often ends just before the planned fireworks begin. The public gatherings are grand, but so is a quiet, foothills nook. From a high roost, you can see those giant, bright-colored dandelion puffs all the way from Denver. Once the sun sets, it can get cold. Bring a heavy sweater or blanket. Many other Boulder County communities, such as Longmont, Louisville, and Broomfield, have their own fireworks, often with community picnics and concerts.

BOULDER CONCERT IN THE PARK—FOURTH OF JULY

Chautauqua Park, Ninth Street and
Baseline Road, Boulder
(303) 442-3282
www.chautauqua.com

This Fourth of July outdoor concert by the Colorado Music Festival's nationally recognized summer orchestra features pop and sing-along music. Insiders bring picnic baskets and blankets, then linger here to watch distant fireworks. The concert starts at 5 p.m., and admission is free.

RALPHIE'S INDEPENDENCE DAY BLAST

Folsom Field (on CU-Boulder campus)
Boulder
(303) 442-1044
www.bouldercolorado.usa.com

Even without great fireworks, which are launched at dark, this evening extravaganza would be a kick, for the live entertainment is good, and the sing-alongs include popular rock and hokey camp songs. The Boulder Philharmonic Orchestra plays while families wait for darkness to descend. Admission is free, with a donation requested. It's best to get there early, because the place begins to fill up long before the sun sets.

BOULDER PEAK TRIATHLON

Boulder Reservoir
www.5430sports.com

Grab your bike, running shoes, and swimsuit! This annual event is held at the Boulder Reservoir and was established to raise awareness for the ALS Association. The race includes a 1.5K swim, a 42K bike ride, and a 10K run.

LOUISVILLE FOURTH OF JULY PICNIC AND FIREWORKS

Downtown Louisville and Coal Creek Golf Course
(303) 666-6565
www.louisvillechamber.com

Enjoy a community picnic, art festival, children's games, and a band concert in Memory Square Park, then "Fireworks on the Links," with the couples swinging on the temporary dance floor.

ETOWN

Boulder Theater, 2034 14th Street
Boulder
(303) 786-7030
www.etown.org

What is etown? It's a nationally syndicated radio show heard 52 weeks a year on more than 150 stations across the county, and it's produced in Boulder at the historic Boulder Theater. Most shows feature founder and host Nick Forster, a member of the bluegrass band Hot Rize, and his wife, Helen Forster. Weekly shows are taped before a live audience and feature many of today's top musical artists performing live, as well as thought-provoking interviews.

DOWNTOWN BOULDER ARTFAIR

Pearl Street Mall
(303) 449-3774
www.boulderdowntown.com

From fine art to fun art, this mid-July event on the Pearl Street Mall features works in all media and styles by 150 artists from across the nation. The fair is held on Saturday from 10 a.m. to 8 p.m. and on Sunday from 10 a.m. to 5 p.m.

COLORADO LIGHT OPERA

CU-Boulder Campus
Imig Music Building
18th and Euclid Streets, Boulder
303-492-8008

This university program features outstanding student vocalists. The 2008 season featured two favorite musicals: *A Little Night Music* and *How to Succeed in Business without Really Trying*. Productions are performed in the Music Theatre of the Imig Music building on the CU-Boulder campus.

CHAUTAUQUA SUMMER SILENT FILM SERIES

Ninth Street and Baseline Road
(303) 440-7666
www.chautauqua.com

Each year, five or six summer evenings are devoted to silent film classics accompanied by live music. To add to the historic atmosphere, the films are shown inside the cavernous Chautauqua

Auditorium in Chautauqua Park. Screenings are Wednesday at 7:30 p.m. Among the films shown in the past are *The Black Pirate,* starring Douglas Fairbanks, and *The Kiss,* starring Greta Garbo.

ROCKYGRASS BLUEGRASS FESTIVAL
Planet Bluegrass Ranch, Lyons
(303) 823-5215
www.bluegrass.com/rockygrass/
In a pretty creekside field, internationally known bluegrass fiddlers and banjo pickers entertain campers and picnickers. Bluegrass workshops, late-night campfires, and dips in the St. Vrain River add to the old-time ambience. In recent years, a three-day pass was $90. Tickets are also available by the day for this weekend event. The producer also presents the famous Telluride Bluegrass Festival in southwestern Colorado.

AUGUST

BOULDER COUNTY FAIR
Boulder County Fairgrounds
9595 Nelson Road, Longmont
(303) 772-7170
www.bouldercountyfair.org
The whole family will love the goats and rabbits at this down-home country fair, which draws more than 100,000 spectators. Sheep yell "Ma-a!" as 4-H parents do the final, pre-show shearing. The harness horses prance, their braided manes decorated with flowers. At the old-timers' rodeo on the last Friday, see bucking broncos and fancy riding. Admission to the fairgrounds is free, but call ahead to check fees for such events as the rodeo. The fair runs from the first through the second weekend in August.

ROCKY MOUNTAIN FOLK FESTIVAL
Planet Bluegrass Ranch, Lyons
(800) 624-2422
www.bluegrass.com
Sixties folk legend Arlo Guthrie is among those who have performed at this mid-August festival; others include Bruce Hornsby, Patty Larkin, and Cliff Eberhardt. It's sponsored by Planet Bluegrass,

the same folks who host the RockyGrass Bluegrass Festival and the Telluride Bluegrass Festival. These events are organized in a less-than-formal manner, attracting many families who camp in the surrounding area. In recent years a three-day pass was $90.

OLD TOWN LAFAYETTE ANTIQUES & COUNTRY PEACH FESTIVAL
401 South Public Road, Lafayette
(303) 666-7200
www.chamber.lafayette.co.us/co
This annual event in early to mid-August features dealers' booths with antiques and crafts all along the Old Town section of Public Road. It features peach cobbler, peach ice cream, and peach smoothies, as well as other food concessions and entertainment. Hours are 9 a.m. to 5 p.m.

SEPTEMBER

ECOARTS
(303) 449-2128
www.ecoartsonline.org
The year 2008 marked the third season of this three-week festival which focuses on current understandings in climate science and a sustainable future. The event features lectures, art exhibits, dance recitals, and tours. It's an interesting and entertaining way to bring attention to these subjects. A tour of the Ponnequin Wind Farm in Weld County was part of the series in 2008.

LOUISVILLE FALL FESTIVAL AND LABOR DAY PARADE
Downtown Louisville
(303) 666-5747
www.louisvillechamber.com/community
Louisville's Labor Day parade, one of Colorado's largest, attracts more than 25,000 people. The Saturday and Sunday of Labor Day weekend feature an art fair, carnival, music, and pancake breakfast. The Monday parade includes pets, the King Soopers Shopping Cart Drill Team, marching bands, and antique cars. The parade down Main Street starts at 10 a.m.

BOULDER CREEK HOMETOWN FAIR AND HARVEST FESTIVAL

Municipal Building Lawn, Canyon Street and Broadway, Boulder
(303) 449-3825
www.bceproductions.com
Held for the first time in 1998, this Labor Day weekend event is hosted by the same folks who produce the Boulder Creek Festival in May. With old-fashioned flair the event offers a chili cookoff, the Great Zucchini Race, hayrides, a speakers' corner, arts and crafts vendors, food vendors, and a dance hall. Hours are Saturday 10 a.m. to 10 p.m., Sunday 10 a.m. to 9 p.m., and Monday 10 a.m. to 7 p.m.

LONGS PEAK SCOTTISH-IRISH HIGHLAND FESTIVAL

Estes Park Fairground, Community Drive
Estes Park
(800) 90-ESTES
www.scotfest.com
You'll find kilts and caboodles of festivities at this festival, the biggest event of Estes Park's year. It's a celebration of Celtic heritage held the first weekend after Labor Day. Naturally bagpipes play a large part in the festival and bagpipers take center stage for the weekend parade. (See our Estes Park chapter for more information.)

CAUSE FOR PAWS WALK-A-THON

Boulder County Humane Society
2323 55th Street, Boulder
(303) 442-4030
www.boulderhumane.org
More than 1,000 people and their dogs participate in the annual event, which helps fund the Humane Society's programs. The mid-September walk meanders along a 3-mile route through downtown Boulder, follows the Boulder Creek Path along a 4-mile route, and returns along the same route to a People and Pet Fair. There's also a 5K Doggie Dash and pancake breakfast.

GOLDEN ASPEN TREES

Peak to Peak Highway (Highway 72),
north of Nederland, and other locations
The greatest fall festival is the natural one—the annual gilding of the aspen. Mother Nature never calls ahead to reserve a day for the best leaf-viewing, so watch local papers for reports of favorable turnings, sometime in September or October. The *Daily Camera* runs stories and maps. The aspens east of the Continental Divide generally turn gold, but sometimes pinkish foliage peeks out among the yellow. Often, a whole grove changes at once, for aspen are large, cloned families, connected by their roots. Because "quakies" have loose leaf stems, the shiny leaves really shimmer. The biggest aspen fields are along the Peak to Peak Highway outside of Nederland. Driving is fun. But even better, park at a trailhead and take a stroll. Rocky Mountain National Park boasts several astonishing stands of aspen. The park rangers can direct you to the best. Wherever you hike, the filtered golden light, the tannin scent of fall, and the sound of fluttering aspen leaves are unforgettable.

WALKER RANCH LIVING HISTORY

Walker Ranch, Flagstaff Road
(west of Chautauqua Park), Boulder
(303) 441-3950
www.co.boulder.co.us/openspace
The last two weekends in September, blacksmiths pound a ringing "whang" on red-hot iron while the bellows release a throaty sigh. Sunbonnet-clad women prepare victuals at a potbellied stove. They're volunteers, trained by Boulder County Parks and Open Space to live the old-fashioned way for a few days. The ranch is open 10 a.m. to 3 p.m. and has free everything, from watching the horses plow to sampling the homemade bread and hand-churned butter. This gorgeous area frequently has brilliant mountain bluebirds. The ranch is on the left, 7.5 miles west of Chautauqua Park, up Flagstaff Road.

BOULDER FALL FESTIVAL
Pearl Street Mall, Boulder
(303) 449-3774
www.dbi.org
Loosely styled after a European Oktoberfest, this celebration in late September has become a primo showcase for local and visiting craftsmen. It still includes flowing beer—though now more microbrews than German brews—plus bands, carnival rides, lots of food, and a petting zoo for the kids. It runs 11 a.m. to 10 p.m. on Friday and Saturday and 11 a.m. to 6 p.m. on Sunday.

OCTOBER

CELEBRATE LAFAYETTE
Public Rd., Lafayette
(303) 926-4352
www.discoverlafayette.com
A street fair, free pancake breakfast and live entertainment mark this one-day celebration of Lafayette. In 2008 the event also featured an expo called "Living Green: A Commitment to a Sustainable Environment."

BAND DAY
Folsom Field, U-C campus, Folsom and Colorado Avenues, Boulder
(303) 492-6584
www.bands.colorado.edu/concerts
An autumn regular for more than five decades, Band Day brings stirring high school bands from across the state to compete at Folsom Field. This event is free.

PUMPKIN PIE DAYS ANTIQUES SHOW
9595 Nelson Road, Boulder County Fairgrounds, Longmont
(303) 776-1870
www.stvrainhistoricalsociety.org
More than 80 dealers display antiques and collectibles at the exhibit hall, where there is plenty of parking and admission is free. This mid-October event was named for celebrations that brought special trains full of visitors to Longmont from 1899 to 1914. The cafe at the exhibit hall serves the pie and other treats. Hours are Saturday from 10 a.m. to 5 p.m. and Sunday from 11 a.m. to 5 p.m.

MUNCHKIN MASQUERADE
Children's Trick or Treat
Daily Camera, 11th and Pearl Streets
Boulder
(303) 449-3774
www.boulderdowntown.com
On the afternoon of Halloween, approximately 2,000 costumed kids traipse through downtown, on the Pearl St. Mall between 11th and 15th, with their parents and stop at "treat stops" for goodies. The parade runs from 2 to 5 p.m.

NOVEMBER

SOUPER BOWLDER PROMOTION
Boulder Arts & Crafts Cooperative
1421 Pearl Street, Pearl Street Mall
(303) 443-3683
www.boulderartsandcrafts.com
Hundreds of ceramic soup bowls donated by professional potters sell at this benefit for the Boulder County Mental Health Center and Boulder Shelter for the Homeless. Dried soup mixes from the Women's Bean Project (a workforce of otherwise unemployed women) are also offered.

BOULDER POTTERS' GUILD SHOW AND SALE
2108 55th Street, Boulder
(303) 447-031
www.boulderpottersguild.com
Here's a chance to purchase tasteful, handcrafted holiday gifts at reasonable prices. This mid-November show and sale runs 10 a.m. to 8 p.m. on Thursday and Friday, 10 a.m. to 6 p.m. on Saturday, and 10 a.m. to 4 p.m. on Sunday. There is no admission fee, and the kids can snack on delicious treats while you browse. This popular show has been held in several different locations in recent years, so call ahead or visit their Web site for directions.

NUTCRACKER BALLET
Macky Auditorium (on CU-Boulder campus), Boulder
(303) 492-8423
www.colorado.edu/Macky
The Boulder Philharmonic teams up with the Boulder Ballet for four packed performances of this favorite family ballet during Thanksgiving weekend. Everything's magic when local children play the mice, and rising local stars portray Clara and her prince. During intermission, kids can peek in the orchestra pit, where friendly musicians demonstrate instruments such as the celesta, which makes those little tinkly bell sounds for the Sugar Plum Fairy. Single tickets range from $10 to $50, with discounts for students and children.

WINTERSKATE
www.bceproductions.com
Grab your skates! There are now two WinterSkate locations in Boulder County, one in the Stein-baugh Pavilion in historic downtown Louisville, and at Flatiron Crossing Mall in Broomfield. Skate rentals, lessons, and group discount rates are available.

DECEMBER

LIGHTS OF DOWNTOWN DECEMBER PARADE
Pearl Street Mall, Boulder
(303) 449-3774
www.boulderdowntown.com
This eclectic parade on the first Saturday in December launches Boulder's holiday season. Like many parades throughout the year, the route circumnavigates the pedestrian center. The parade is both sweet and hokey. You'll see everything from Boulder's Girl Scout troops with battery-operated Christmas lights in their hair to the local Polar Bear Club members prancing about the cold streets barefoot and bathing-suited, hopping into a hot tub on wheels whenever they need to warm up again. Eco-elves prance by in curled-toe green slippers, passing out information about recycling; local marching bands play; and gleaming antique cars and fire trucks get festooned with ornaments. The parade starts around 6 p.m.

LOUISVILLE PARADE OF LIGHTS
Downtown Louisville
(303) 666-5747
www.louisvillechamber.com
Garlands swing from Main Street lamps, and cho-ral groups perform by City Hall. There are open houses and hayrides. More than 20 floats join the parade, which starts at 7 p.m. on the first Friday in December.

HOLIDAY FESTIVAL CONCERT
Macky Auditorium, CU-Boulder Campus
(303) 492-8423
www.colorado.edu/Macky
This early December event is so popular, the auditorium fills up for the dress rehearsal in addi-tion to the actual performance. Tickets go fast. University of Colorado College of Music students and faculty perform in a festively decorated Macky Auditorium. The program features Christ-mas favorites and seasonal music from various cultures. There are performances on Friday and Saturday nights and Sunday afternoon. Tickets are $12 for the rehearsal and prices range from $12 to $52 for the actual performance.

HISTORIC HOMES FOR THE HOLIDAYS
Various Boulder homes
(303) 444-5192
www.historicboulder.org
Grand homes deck their halls for the holidays, and everyone is invited to have a look during the first weekend in December. Mapleton Hill Victorians and Romanesque Uni-Hill homes are among those that have been part of the tour. The decorating by the owners and professionals is spectacular. This fund-raiser for Historic Boulder also includes a gift shop and drawings for door prizes. Ticket prices vary.

MESSIAH SING-ALONG
St. John's Episcopal Church, 14th and
Pine Streets, Boulder
(303) 666-9016
www.messiahsingalong.org
Professionals fly in to sing the solos, and the choir practices for weeks to lead a rousing rendition of Handel's *Messiah*. But the passion comes from the regular folks who fill the pews. Some are practically pros, while others have never sung before, but they all join in for the rousing "Hallelujah Chorus," which must be audible all the way to the heavens. There are two evening performances and one matinee the weekend before Christmas Eve. Tickets are $13.

EVENTS CENTRAL

Many other festivals and events occur in the Boulder area throughout the year. The *Daily Camera*'s "Friday Magazine" is loaded with entertainment information for the upcoming weekend. The quarterly publication *Boulder Magazine,* free at various locations in the city, is the most complete source for information. (See www.getboulder.com.) The chambers of commerce also have information on specific local events. Also check out the choices listed in our Boulder Attractions chapter. If you're looking for something to do, call any (or all) of the following organizations: **Boulder Chamber of Commerce** (303-442-1044, www.bouldercolorado.com), **Boulder County Fairgrounds** (303-678-6235, www.co.boulder.co.us/openspace), **Chautauqua Association** (303-442-3282, www.chautauqua.com), or **Downtown Boulder** (303-449-3774; www.downtownboulder.com).

ATTRACTIONS

Boulder's top five, must-see attractions are detailed here, followed by a smorgasbord of other treats if time and taste permit. Also see our chapters Festivals and Annual Events, Kidstuff, Sports, and Neighborhoods and Nearby Communities.

THE TOP FIVE

PEARL STREET MALL
Pearl Street from 11th to 15th Streets
Boulder

It has set the standard for pedestrian malls throughout the country and it still hasn't lost its appeal since its inception in 1977. In fact, "Pearl Street," as it is known to locals, is one of the best places in the city. Period.

The *Wall Street Journal* has called the Pearl Street Mall one of the nation's most successful pedestrian malls, and it has won national design awards. It's Boulder's people-watching spot, from kids climbing the bronze frog to college-age lovers buying gauzy new clothes to businesspeople grabbing a savory pie at the Empañadas window. Street musicians embroider the air with a saxophone's blue tones, steel-drum calypso, folk guitar, and more. Breathe deeply. The aroma of fresh pretzels might draw you to a kiosk in front of the courthouse; fresh popcorn or stir-fried something might bring you to a pushcart vendor; or a thick, dark river of perfume might sweep you into the Rocky Mountain Chocolate Factory.

In addition to matchless people-watching, the Pearl Street Mall offers abundant free entertainment—though, of course, the jugglers, clowns, and magicians appreciate tips. In the warm months, you can sit to have your portrait painted, your fortune told, or your neck and shoulders massaged; or you might pick a ringside seat in one of the many excellent restaurants with patio tables. Thanks to Boulder's clear skies and mild days, people-watchers often sit out even in winter.

Some of Boulder's finest restaurants, galleries, and shops are found on the mall. Discover them as you wander, or check the Shopping, The Arts, and Restaurants chapters.

Pearl Street's history does not always reflect such a stylish past. It started out Wild West style, with drunks horse-racing down the dirt lane that was the main street. And no proper lady walked a white poodle, for these dogs were popular among the "soiled doves" whose creekside homes advertised, "Men Taken In and Done For." To civilize the street, storekeepers built plank walks, but they didn't match sidewalk height between stores, so shoppers bobbed up and down along the way.

By the 1970s, Pearl Street was drearily, Midwesterny respectable. Aluminum facades hid brick storefronts, cars jammed streets, and FOR LEASE signs proliferated like mushrooms growing in decay. To halt the decline, planners suggested everything from a covered shopping mall to high-rises. Although it seemed so risky to restore the original buildings, tweak the Old West character, and create strolling space with sculptures, trees, and flowers, the mall has been a smash hit.

If you're a history buff, stop by the **Hotel Boulderado,** at 2115 13th Street, just north of the mall (303-442-4344; www.boulderado.com). This redbrick hotel, named after Boulder and Colorado, was built in 1909. The city's pride, it features Italianate porch corners, a cherry cantilevered staircase, and an Italian stained-glass ceiling. Robert Frost and Louis Armstrong were among the guests. But the Boulderado suffered decline, too. The glass ceiling crashed in a 1960s snowstorm; kitchen cooks hung bait over vats to drown rats; and vagrants slept in empty rooms. In the 1980s, Boulderado Concept Ltd. restored the grand old hotel. Wander inside. The Catacombs Bar in the basement has live blues, reggae, and jazz most nights of the week, and there's live music on the mezzanine on Friday evenings; it's reserved for private parties other times.

Another historic area on Pearl Street is the **Boulder Courthouse Square,** between 13th and 14th Streets. The location started as the town's baseball diamond and then was the site of Boulder County's grand Victorian courthouse, which burned down in the 1930s. Local architect Glenn Huntington designed the light-colored stone, art deco courthouse you see today. The lawn, which was extensively redesigned in 1996, is a popular festival spot.

A fountain built in 1935 by the Lions Club began operating again in 1999 after years of disrepair and neglect. Surrounded by tasteful landscaping and benches, it makes a wonderful spot to sit and have lunch.

Just east, at 2032 14th Street, is the **Boulder Theater** (303-786-7030; www.bouldertheater .com), a turn-of-the-20th-century opera house renovated in the 1930s as the gaudy little sister of the plain blond courthouse. The art deco facade is as lavish as a peacock's tail, and the restored interior has gorgeous, hand-painted, flowery murals. A live music venue for both local and national acts, the former movie house also offers dance, theater, and corporate events and can be rented for private parties. The theater is also home to the weekly etown live music/talk performances broadcast by National Public Radio to more than 150 cities.

From the Pearl Street Mall, it's an easy walk to **Central Park,** between Canyon and Arapahoe Streets east of Broadway. An art deco band shell, built in 1938 and restored in 1996, once again hosts concerts and civic events. A steam locomotive is a permanent fixture in the park and frequent festivals are held on the grounds.

On Saturday mornings from early spring through late fall and on Wednesday afternoons in summer, the **Boulder County Farmers' Market** takes place along 13th Street (see the subsequent "Boulder Creek Path" entry for details about this market). On the east side of the street is the **Boulder Museum of Contemporary Art** (see subsequent entry), and the **Boulder Creek Path,** the next must-see attraction, runs along the south side of the park.

BOULDER CREEK PATH
Parallel to Canyon Boulevard and/or Arapahoe Avenue, from Four Mile Canyon in Boulder Canyon east to Cherryvale Road

Boulder's most popular "architecture" is 12 feet wide, 7.5 miles long, and flat on the ground. This 1980s project lets commuters travel without cars and in the prettiest possible way. The Creek Path dips under 10 major intersections, transforming traffic's roar into a whispered "whoosh." More than a half-dozen wooden pedestrian bridges crisscross the stream, clattering merrily as bicyclists and in-line skaters pass. The bridges are designed to snap to the side and reduce debris if a big flood hits. The whole path was designed with a rising creek in mind. Major flooding is rare, but every few years, some overflow happens. The city's flower plantings along this route are a feast for the eyes.

Each year, nearly 2 million bicyclists, in-line skaters, walkers, runners—you name it—use the Boulder Creek Path. Other nonmotor-vehicle routes from all over the city connect so people can really get around without cars. Be alert, however. Some fierce bicyclists and in-line skaters ignore speed signs and can scare the daylights out of walkers. Especially in busy areas near downtown, keep an eye on kids, your dogs, and your own tendency to stray. Choose your chariot—bicycle, feet, in-line skates, or wheelchair—and head to the path.

The **Boulder Public Library**'s main branch (303-441-3100; www.boulder.lib.co.us), at 10th Street and Arapahoe Avenue, is a good place to start, and in fact, a stop to admire this gleaming facility is worthwhile, too. About 3,000 folks use it daily. Look for the dramatic glass entry on the Arapahoe Avenue side. Inside, the library has approximately 320,000 circulating books, an artists' register showing slides of local artwork, and a computerized media/browsing system. Books can be delivered to the homebound who can't get to the library, and another service transcribes text into Braille. Kid-pleasing attractions include a trout habitat, multimedia computers with interactive children's software, and storytelling hours. The library auditorium on the Canyon Boulevard side is the site of a free year-round film and concert series. The BoulderReads! program provides free, confidential tutoring for everyone from children to adults. There are seven computer terminals with free Internet access, but be prepared to wait, as they are extremely popular. The library is open 10 a.m. to 9 p.m. Monday through Thursday, 10 a.m. to 6 p.m. Friday and Saturday, and noon to 6 p.m. Sunday. There are also three branch libraries in Boulder; their hours vary from each other and the main library.

Just west of the library is the **West Boulder Senior Center** at Ninth Street and Arapahoe Avenue. After passing under Ninth Street, be sure to notice the sculpture of Chief Niwot (Niwot means "left hand") on the left. Continue westward to Sixth Street and Canyon Boulevard, where you'll find the **Children's Fishing Pond,** marked by an abstract metal sculpture that looks like leaping fish On your right is the **Boulder County Justice Center,** with courts for dreary things from speeding tickets to criminal cases, but also where civil marriage ceremonies are performed. Just beyond, west along the Creek Path, the **Xeriscape Demonstration Garden**. displays native plants that make environmentally wise gardening choices for Colorado's arid climate, an herb garden, and a "wheel" of lawns comparing bluegrass, two buffalo grasses, fescue, and blends

Continuing westward, the path opens out

> **i** No summer is complete without a stop at Boulder's Farmers' Market. It takes place on Wednesday and Saturday on 13th Street, between Arapahoe Avenue and Canyon Boulevard.

to **Eben G. Fine Park** at Fourth Street, a favorite shady picnic and Frisbee-throwing area, with playgrounds and a congenial family atmosphere At the park, you'll see a tunnel to the north, or right, under Canyon Boulevard. It leads to **Red Rocks/Settlers Park,** site of the 1858 campsite along Boulder Creek by the gold seekers who became Boulder's first citizens. Historical plaques explain some of Boulder's early history. Near more picnic tables, you'll see a steep trail up to the nearly vertical red rocks, naturally called Red Rocks, and a fine hilltop view of the whole area. Take care should you decide to scramble up the rocks for an even better vista

Back along the creek path and just west of the park is Boulder's kayak course. Even if you're not into white water, it's thrilling to watch kayakers and canoeists test their skills in the rapids during spring and early summer. Inner tube riders crawl into their black doughnut-shaped vessels here too for a bracing ride down to Broadway. Two historic markers along the path tell about the **Switzerland Trail** railroad line and **Farmers' Ditch,** two early landmarks in the development of Boulder County.

For a lovely walk into Boulder Canyon, keep going up the hill and to the west along the Creek Path (watch out for speeding downhill cyclists). After a while, the pavement ends, and the path dips under the canyon road and deposits you at the base of the **Elephant Buttresses** and the **Dome,** two of Boulder's most popular rock-climbing spots. In one vista, you'll see an old water flume and Lycra-clad rock climbers, a perfect combination on the Boulder firmament. Farther along the path, wild roses and purple asters bloom in summer beside the frothy creek, and wild plums and grapes ripen in the fall. The gravel path continues up along the creekside under the rustling cottonwoods and glinting ponderosa pines to **Four Mile Canyon,** about 1.5 miles away. The total distance from Eben Fine Park—the lower bridge at the east end of the park with a boulder marked 0 miles—to the end of the trail is 2.25 miles.

If instead you head east from the Boulder

Public Library, you'll soon get to **Central Park** at Broadway. There are small waterfalls, historic railroad cars, a band shell, and sometimes an outdoor sculpture exhibit. The Boulder Museum of Contemporary Art (see subsequent entry) is across the street, east of the park.

On Saturday mornings from spring through fall and Wednesday afternoons during the summer, the **Boulder County Farmers' Market**. stretches on both sides of 13th Street between Arapahoe Avenue and Canyon Boulevard. This assembly features a colorful parade of produce, flowers, homegrown and homemade goodies, and weekly cooking demonstrations by local chefs. This beguiling attraction features a changing cornucopia of produce and related wares and has become Colorado's most successful open-air market. Regulars use it as an opportunity to shop, stroll, nibble, and socialize. The location is perfect, close to the Pearl Street Mall and right next to Central Park. During the market's early weeks, vendors specialize in seedlings that you can take home and plant. At summer's peak, the street's packed with local fresh tomatoes, Western Slope peaches, Rocky Ford cantaloupe and honeydew melons, green beans, lettuce, fresh herbs, and more. Tamales, pirogen, and focaccia give the market a true international ambience. Fresh and dried flowers, lavender water, hot corn on the cob, honey, and delicacies from goat cheese to smoked trout tempt from many stands. Don't forget sweet ices, lemonade, and fresh-baked pastries—a big colorful crowd. The market opens in mid-April and runs through October. Saturday hours are 8 a.m. to 2 p.m. After May 1, a smaller version is also open Wednesday from 4 p.m. to 8 p.m. until early October. Downtown workers appreciate the lunch menu at the Wednesday market

The eclectic atmosphere of the farmers' market is a perfect complement to Boulder's unique **Dushanbe Teahouse,** located in the center of all this activity. In 1986, the residents of Boulder's sister city of Dushanbe crated and shipped this elegant teahouse to Colorado. Because there was no unanimity on where it should be built or who should foot the bill, the crates remained

warehoused for 11 years. Finally in 1997 the city council agreed (the vote was not unanimous) to spend $800,000 for construction of the teahouse at the 13th Street site. The funding helped bring artisans from Tajikistan to Boulder to complete the intricate assembly. The folks who run the cafe at the Naropa Institute now serve daily meals at the teahouse, which is also the venue for a variety of special community events.

After you enjoy a meal on the teahouse patio, you can return immediately to the Creek Path and continue east, past **Boulder High School** and its athletic fields, to a sunny, stone-bench alcove just west of the 17th Street bridge.

Just beyond is **Scott Carpenter Park,** south of Arapahoe Avenue on 30th Street (303-441-3427; www.ci.boulder.co.us). Carpenter, a Boulder native who became one of the early astronauts, named his spaceship the *Aurora 7* after a local school. The playground has a spacecraft theme, and the park also has an outdoor swimming pool and includes Boulder's state-of-the-art 14,000-square-foot concrete in-ground skatepark for skate boarders and in-line skaters. The park features an exciting street course with rails, curbs, free-flowing forms and bowls, and viewing benches made of old snowboards. The park's sledding hill, which served as the city's landfill many years ago, is one of Boulder's enduring winter meccas.

Farther east, just before Foothills Parkway, you'll pass the **CU-Boulder Research Park.** Landscape designers decided the standard lawn would take too much care, guzzle water, and look boring. So they planted something much better—low-maintenance, drought-tolerant meadows that attract butterflies and birds. The result is so lovely that it's almost too popular.

At the intersection of Arapahoe Avenue and Foothills Parkway is a prairie-dog town. Prairie dogs get a bad rap as vermin spreaders, but health officials say it's undeserved, and they are appropriate prey for raptors nesting nearby. Still, don't feed them; they are wild animals and should stay that way. Kids love how they stand like little soldiers, then yip before diving underground. Prairie dogs are a remnant of the shortgrass prairie ecosystem and are food for swooping hawks.

You can take the Creek Path northeast from here, to the tent-roofed stands of the **Stazio Ballfields,** at 2445 Stazio Drive, which are well-lighted and busy well into evening all summer long. Notice that the path veers away from the oldest cottonwood trees. Playing by the creek is fun, but human activity has caused creekside wildlife to decline. By keeping people farther away, critters, such as the red-eyed vireo and yellow warbler, have a better chance. If you ever hear a warbler sing, you'll thank creek planners for giving those birds privacy. As the Creek Path spreads its tentacles, you can take offshoots either to the north or south through residential as well as industrial areas, which is one reason why it is so popular for commuting.

CHAUTAUQUA PARK
Ninth Street and Baseline Road, Boulder
(303) 442-3282
www.chautauqua.com
At the turn of the 20th century, sites across the nation became gathering spots for summer cultural and educational institutes, all named "Chautauqua" after Chautauqua Lake in upstate New York, where the first such gathering was held. Dozens of Chautauquas once existed, but few remain. Boulder's was one of the rare Western locations. The **Chautauqua Auditorium and Dining Hall** (303-440-3776; www.chatauqua .com), built in 1898, and a charming nearby colony of wooden cottages comprise the last original site west of the Mississippi.

Chautauqua's main buildings, decked out in crisp gray, would still be a perfect setting for banjo-strumming gallants in flat-brimmed hats, but summer offerings now draw modern crowds with contemporary interests. There's a nod to the past with July's silent films, accompanied by live piano. The Colorado Chautauqua Association

Forum is a lecture series dating from 1898, but today's speakers address topics such as health issues, transportation, and world affairs.

The **Colorado Music Festival** (303-449-1397) has a full orchestra of musicians invited here for the summer and features internationally renowned guest artists as well as rising stars with promising futures. The vast majority of classical performances are instrumental, for the wooden auditorium tends to swallow voices. An orchestra or a powerful soloist can make the wonderful barn resonate with great sound. For ticket events, call the Box Office, (303) 440-7666, between May and September, or visit their Web site at www .coloradomusicfest.org.

Chautauqua Park has 60 cottages for rent from June through August and 16 year-round cottages. They vary in size, but all have a kitchen, bathrooms, living area, and one or more bedrooms. For the 2008 summer, rooms range from $104 to $194 per night, depending on the size of the cottage. The cottages fill up fast, so make your reservation as soon after November 1 as possible. The renovated and award-winning Missions Lodge is available for between $1,089 and $1,143 a night. This eight-bedroom, nine-bathroom facility is perfect for wedding groups or family reunions. Rent the whole place. Built in 1911, it's the only accommodation of its type in the entire state. To rent a cottage, call the Chautauqua Association, (303) 442-3282, or visit www .chautauqua.com.

Children like the **Chautauqua Park playground**, especially after they discover low-branched trees for playing hide-and-seek. (Only kids can scamper through. Moms and Dads have to hunch.) The **Chautauqua Ranger Cottage** (720-564-2000), near the big meadow on the west side of the park, is generally open 10 a.m. to 4 p.m. daily. Its small garden displays native plants, and the rangers dispense plenty of hiking information. The rangers can answer questions, and they're trained to handle emergencies. They also lead free interpretive hikes that depart from the Ranger Cottage at 8 a.m. Saturday mornings in summer.

Trails lead everywhere. The Boulder Moun-

i Historic Boulder (303-444-5192) offers walking-tour information for Boulder's historic neighborhoods.

tain Parks trail system includes everything from short, nearly flat strolls to steep hikes. One of the easiest, and shadiest, is the McClintock Trail, starting southeast of the Chautauqua Auditorium. You can head west on the Chautauqua Trail, cross the big meadow, and watch rock climbers. Or head west and south to the Mesa Trail. It's 3 up-and-down miles to the next major attraction, NCAR (see subsequent entry), and twice that far to the Mesa Trail's southern terminus just off the Eldorado Canyon Road.

NATIONAL CENTER FOR ATMOSPHERIC RESEARCH (NCAR)
West end of Table Mesa Drive, Boulder
(303) 497-1000
www.ncar.ucar.edu/ncar
Anyone who has ever gazed at the sky can find something of interest at NCAR (pronounced "en-car"). Founded in 1960 for research on the world's climate, NCAR draws scientists from all over the globe to study our wonderful blanket of air. Interesting displays present the fundamentals of the scientists' fields of expertise. Sky-watchers can learn about clouds, air currents, lightning, hail, tornadoes, and other weather phenomena, including global warming. I. M. Pei designed this mesa-top complex, which helped establish his reputation as a world-class architect. "The mountains," said Pei, "gave us scale trouble from the beginning. We had to return to elemental forms. The Rockies humbled us." Local red limestone was mixed into the concrete so it would blend with the Flatirons. The building's angular forms mimic keyhole doors at the Mesa Verde cliff dwellings. This building is considered one of the nation's finest public structures. Two galleries feature community art. The computers in the basement are some of the world's fastest and largest.

The center is open daily for self-guided tours; pick up a brochure in the lobby. Guided walking tours take place at noon throughout the year including weekends and holidays. No reservations are needed for the guided tours, but for more information call (303) 497-1174. If you want to bring a school class, scout troop, or any other group, tours must be arranged in advance by calling (303) 497-1173. The Walter Orr Roberts Weather Trail at NCAR is the only one of its kind in the country. Just west of the building, the 0.4-mile trail is not paved but is wheelchair accessible. There are signs posted at regular intervals along the trail explaining weather patterns that hikers are then able to observe. In addition, there are many short nature trails near NCAR that are spectacular for more ambitious hikers.

The NCAR is open 8 a.m. to 5 p.m. Monday through Friday and 9 a.m. to 4 p.m. weekends and holidays. Admission is free.

UNIVERSITY OF COLORADO AT BOULDER
Intersections of Baseline and Broadway/Folsom and Colorado/Broadway and College, Boulder
(303) 492-1411
www.colorado.edu
CU-Boulder's 600-acre campus is one of the nation's most beautiful. The buildings are a visual symphony of red tile roofs and warm, native-stone walls that make the entire campus harmonize, and the landscaping is splendid. Norlin Quadrangle is the 3-block-long, tree-lined lawn next to Broadway. Nearby are the oldest buildings on campus, including Macky Auditorium, Old Main, Hale Science Building, and the Koenig Alumni Center. Kittredge Pond, near Fleming Law School, and Varsity Pond, just off the intersection of Broadway and College, are "water features" created decades before such amenities got a trendy name. The big old trees, quacking mallards, and basking turtles help time stand still—even among the achingly with-it students all around.

For many, the main draw to the campus is the sports teams, and rabid fans might never get past **Folsom Field** or the **Coors Events Center.** Call (303) 492-8337 for information about Big 12 conference games, or see the Sports chapter for more information. For other folks, the campus is fun for exploring. Maps located throughout the campus pinpoint spots of interest, or call (303)

492-6301 for information about campus visits and tours. An hour-long information briefing followed by a one-hour tour is given at 9:30 a.m. and 1:30 p.m. Monday through Friday and at 10:30 a.m. Saturday. Be sure to visit the **University Memorial Center,** known on campus as "the UMC," at Euclid, just east of Broadway. The **Glenn Miller Lounge and Ballroom** are named after the CU jazz trombone player who popularized Big Band swing A short walk to the northeast is **Norlin Library** (303-492-8705; http://ucb libraries.colorado.edu/norlin), with more than 10 million books, periodicals, manuscripts, government publications, and more—the biggest such collection in the state. The **Colorado Centennial Foucault Pendulum** (303-492-6952) is at Duane Physical Laboratory, inside Gamow Tower, just south of Gate 2 of Folsom Field. It might seem that the 40-meter pendulum changes direction during the day, but it actually stays steady while the earth rotates underneath it. (At the equator, it would swing the same direction all the time.)

The domed **Fiske Planetarium** on Regent Drive is a campus landmark housing a great theater for star shows and featuring one of the finest stargazing machines in the world. Scientists use it to turn the celestial skies back so that they can compare ancient ruins to an ancient sky. Often, they discover important building features align with star patterns that occurred long ago. Regular visitors can enjoy laser light shows and talks—fun in those leaned-back chairs that coddle your neck while you're staring upward. Star shows are normally scheduled on Friday evenings and some Tuesdays and Saturdays. Adult admission is $6.00, and children and seniors pay $3.50 for the evening shows; the fee includes admission to the adjacent **Sommers-Bausch Observatory** afterwards, weather permitting. You can get recorded information on the current week's shows by calling (303) 492-5001. For more detailed information, call (303) 492-5002 or visit http://fiske .colorado.edu. At the observatory, the real sky, not a planetarium show, is occasionally open for public viewing. Astronomy students man the telescopes during a special heavenly show, like a spectacular comet, meteor shower, or eclipse; but in recent years, clouds have obscured the most heralded events.

The **Herbarium** (303-492-3216) houses nearly a half-million dried plant specimens from Colorado and around the world. It is located in the Claire Small building and is open to the public from 9 a.m. to 4 p.m. Monday through Thursday and 9 a.m. to 3 p.m. on Friday. Hours are curtailed over the summer break.

The **Heritage Center,** a CU-Boulder museum

i Some of Boulder's most popular stores have become attractions in their own right. Boulderites often take out-of-towners to McGuckin Hardware, The Peppercorn, and other distinctive retail establishments just for the fun of it. See the Shopping chapter for more information.

(303-492-6329; www.cualum.org/heritage), is in Old Main, which housed the whole university from 1876 through 1884. This authentic Victorian landmark has been renovated, and the beautiful chapel is an especially cozy area for small performances. The Heritage Center's top floor is noteworthy for its "Space Room" honoring CU-Boulder's 13 astronauts, and for its sensational collection of sports memorabilia. The distinguished alumni gallery in the center includes retired Supreme Court Justice Byron White, Miss America 1958 Marilyn Van Derbur-Atler, Robert Redford (granted an honorary degree), *M*A*S*H* actor Larry Linville, and the 1989 Nobel Prize won by CU-Boulder chemist Tom Cech. An architectural gallery shows the original models for CU, showing its rural Italian design. Hours are 10 a.m. to 4 p.m. Monday through Friday. Special tours can be arranged, and it's open before and after home football games. Admission is free.

University of Colorado Museum, at Broadway and 15th Street in the Henderson Building (303-492-6892; http://cumuseum.colorado.edu) displays dinosaur fossils that include a triceratops head and a pterodactyl, taxidermy specimens, and touchable items for kids, including a sea turtle shell you can try on for size. Established in 1902, the museum has grown to include a diversity of displays, notably in paleontology, anthropology, and botany. The museum hosts traveling exhibits as well. It is open 9 a.m. to 5 p.m. weekdays, 9 a.m. to 4 p.m. Saturday, and 10 a.m. to 4 p.m. Sunday. There are occasionally events that interfere with public hours, so call ahead. Admission is free but donations are appreciated.

For academic information about CU-Boulder, check the Child Care and Education chapter.

MORE MUSEUMS, HISTORIC BUILDINGS, AND SPECIAL PLACES

BOULDER COUNTY FAIRGROUNDS
9595 Nelson Road, Longmont
(303) 441-3927
Anytime you visit, something's happening at the fair. This big, big fairground hosts antiques and craft shows, barrel racing (for non-cowboys, that means racing horses in hairpin turns around barrels), national dog shows, bridge tournaments, circuses, motorcycle shows . . . the list goes on. Some events attract more than 100,000, and some are small. To reach the fairgrounds, head north to Longmont on Highway 119. Turn left at Hover Road, whose intersection is marked with big stoplights. Go north on Hover past the Twin Peaks shopping mall to Nelson Road. The fairground is on your right. Call for an event schedule.

BOULDER MUSEUM OF CONTEMPORARY ART (BMOCA)
1750 13th Street, Boulder
(303) 443-2122
www.bmoca.org
This not-for-profit museum has three exhibition spaces for rotating shows as well as performing arts and mixed media space. Local, national, and international artists and photographers have shown at BMoCA. In the past the museum hosted a very successful outdoor cinema program that attracted many first-time museumgoers. The

small museum is open Tuesday, Thursday and Friday 11 a.m. to 5 p.m., Wednesday 11 a.m. to 8 p.m., Saturday 9 a.m. to 4 p. m. and Sunday noon to 3 p.m. Admission is $5 for adults and $4 for seniors and students.

BOULDER HISTORY MUSEUM
1206 Euclid Avenue, Boulder
(303) 449-3464
www.boulderhistorymuseum.org
The three-story, blond-brick Harbeck-Bergheim House, home of the Boulder History Museum, was built by a New York merchant in 1899 as a summer home. Its most renowned feature is a spectacular 9-foot-tall Tiffany stained-glass window. A fun place to visit, the museum is an eclectic grandma's attic–type showcase of Boulder County history. Artifacts show how mining, ranching, and everyday life affected Boulder. A costume gallery, one of the largest collections in the state, is on the second floor. The museum and gift shop are open 10 a.m. to 5 p.m. Tuesday through Friday and noon to 4 p.m. weekends. Admission is $5 for adults, seniors $3, and children and students $2.

CALLAHAN HOUSE
312 Terry Street, Longmont
(303) 776-5191
www.ci.longmont.co.us/callahan
In the early 1900s, a Longmont businessman named T. M. Callahan hired an unemployed Longmont butcher who had gone bankrupt because he refused to pay off the hotel chef with a weekly bottle of bourbon. That butcher, J. C. Penney, went to work for Callahan's chain of "Golden Rule" notion stores, and the Wyoming Golden Rule he and Callahan started became the first store in the Penney chain.

The Callahan home was presented to the city of Longmont in 1938. It is now used for meetings, weddings, showers, receptions, dinners, and other social events. The interior is opulently Victorian, with pink tones, ornately carved wood, swirly plaster moldings, and exquisite light fixtures.

Callahan House is home to the St. Vrain Historical Society (303-776-1870), the Longmont equivalent to Historic Boulder. The society provides brochures for self-guided tours. These are available at the Longmont Museum or the carriage house behind the Callahan House. Group guided tours can be arranged by appointment. Call ahead for reservations and fees. Terry Street, by the way, is just west of Longmont's Old Main downtown.

CARNEGIE BRANCH LIBRARY FOR LOCAL HISTORY
1125 Pine Street, Boulder
(303) 441-3110
www.boulder.lib.co.us
This small, stately marble-columned building was Boulder's original library. Its original interior has been restored and contains local historic materials, including books, diaries, oral histories, tapes, genealogical papers, 200,000 photographs, 700,000 documents, and various materials donated by the Boulder Historical Society. If you are researching your house or property, this is the best place to start. Hours are 10 a. m. to 9 p.m. Monday through Thursday, Friday and Saturday 10 a.m. to 6 p.m., and Sunday noon to 6 p.m. Admission is free.

DOUGHERTY ANTIQUE MUSEUM
8306 North 107th Street, Longmont
(303) 776-2520
www.co.boulder.co.us/openspace/dougherty
The late Ray Dougherty didn't realize what he was starting when, as a teenager, he bought a reed organ. His wife, Dorothy Dougherty, says the hobby of collecting antique cars, farm equipment, and musical instruments just grew and grew (there's also a stagecoach). The antique autos have starred in many parades. That doesn't happen much anymore, because few have the knack for driving them. After all, you don't just turn the key when a car has a steam engine or needs a hand crank.

A mile south of Longmont on U.S. Highway 287 at the family farm, this exhibit is open from 11 a.m. to 5 p.m. Friday, Saturday, and Sunday from early June 2 through Labor Day. Admission is $5

for adults, $3 for ages 6 to 12, and free for kids age 6 and younger. Large groups are welcome if they call ahead.

FLAGSTAFF NATURE CENTER
Flagstaff Mountain Summit, Boulder
(720) 564-2000
www.ci.boulder.co.us
The small log cabin atop Flagstaff Mountain contains interpretive exhibits on Front Range ecology. Displays on local wildlife, plants, and history are interesting for all ages. Nearby is the landmark Flagstaff Amphitheater, built by the Civilian Conservation Corps and still the site of evening ranger presentations and, often, weddings. The area affords excellent views of the Boulder Valley and beyond.

To reach the center, follow Baseline Road to Flagstaff Road. The road leading to the large parking lot is well marked and to the right. Volunteers will cheerfully answer questions about exhibits and displays from 10:30 a.m. to 4 p.m. on Saturdays and Sundays, May through September.

HISTORIC BOULDER
1123 Spruce Street
(303) 444-5192
www.historicboulder.org
Historic Boulder's Web site includes a downloadable walking guide of historic Boulder neighborhoods including Pearl Street, Columbia Cemetery, University Hill, and the Whittier and Mapleton Hill neighborhoods. This group also organizes a Christmas house tour and a spring tour of fine local homes in various neighborhoods. Their October haunted house and meet the spirits events are extremely popular.

LAFAYETTE MINER'S MUSEUM
108 East Simpson Street, Lafayette
(303) 665-7030
This delightful refurbished 1890s coal miner's home was moved into town during the 1910 coal strike. Maintained by the Louisville Historical Society, the six-room house displays clothing, tools and other mining equipment and household items of the

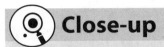 **Close-up**

See, Taste, and Smell the World of Celestial Seasonings!

Before even seeing the sign for Celestial Seasonings, you know you are getting close—just from the smell of mint in the air.

Boulder is one of those magical places where companies like Celestial Seasonings are born. And after virtually inventing the herbal and specialty tea business in the United States, Celestial Seasonings is still based in Boulder—still creating new teas to delight their customers. And you can take a tour of the home of Celestial Seasonings and see just how they make their teas.

Celestial Seasonings had its beginnings in 1969 in Aspen, Colorado, where 19-year-old Mo Siegel gathered wild herbs in the forests and canyons of the Rocky Mountains and mixed them into healthful teas. In 1970 Mo and his friend Wyck Hay found a bountiful harvest of wild herbs growing around Boulder. With friends and wives helping, they picked the herbs and produced 500 pounds of their first blend, called Mo's 36. It was packaged in hand-sewn muslin bags and sold to local health food stores. The partners also began buying herbs rather than picking everything themselves, and the dream of a national herbal tea company slowly began to materialize. This dream was reinforced when Red Zinger and Sleepytime teas were introduced in the early 1970s—they were immediate sensations. They remain two of the best-selling Celestial Seasonings teas.

The rest, as they say, is history. Celestial Seasonings grew out of its old facility and constructed a state-of-the-art facility in 1990. They opened their doors to the public for tours in 1991 and now have an average of 100,000 visitors each year.

USA Today listed the Celestial Seasonings tour as one of the top 10 tours in the country. Steve Spencer, guest relations manager, thinks it's because the tour is such a sensory experience. Their tour brochure asks guests to come to "see, taste and smell the world of Celestial Seasonings" and the art gallery, tea-sampling bar, and factory tour certainly live up to that promise.

---

time. Hours are 2 to 4 p.m. Thursday and Saturday and by appointment. Admission is free.

THE LEANIN' TREE MUSEUM AND SCULPTURE GARDEN OF WESTERN ART
6055 Longbow Drive, Boulder
(303) 729-3440
www.leanintreemuseum.com

Original paintings and bronze sculptures of the American West make up one of the nation's most important collections of Western art. The artwork, all created after the time of Russell and Remington, is the private collection of Ed P. Trumble, the man who founded the Leanin' Tree greeting card company in Boulder in 1949. Over a period of more than 50 years, Trumble purchased the work from artists he befriended as he grew the

company and licensed their work for the cards. He continues to add to the collection. A large sculpture garden of life-size or larger bronzes graces the museum entrance.

Since it opened in 1974, the museum has welcomed more than a million visitors. The gift shop sells all 3,000 Leanin' Tree cards, gifts, framed canvas reproductions of museum art, and other Leanin' Tree merchandise.

To reach the museum, take the Diagonal Highway (Highway 119) north to 63rd Street, and exit right. Go south on 63rd Street and turn right on Longbow Drive. Continue on Longbow Drive until you see the monumental elk sculpture and Indian on horseback on the right. Ample free parking. Open 8 a.m. to 5 p.m. weekdays and 10 a.m. to 5 p.m. Saturday and Sunday. Closed only

Factory tours are loved by all ages. After all, people love to see how things are made. The Celestial Seasonings tour takes visitors right on to the factory floor and very close to the operation, where they can feel a part of the process.

Just walking into the newly remodeled and expanded Tour Center tells you that this will be a fun experience. The center has a beautiful display of original paintings from Celestial Seasonings tea boxes, cabinets containing a collection of unusual teapots, and a full sampling bar featuring more than 90 kinds of tea.

Sample hot and iced teas, watch a video on the history of the company, and witness the milling department where they clean, cut, and sift the herbs, teas, and spices. Then it's on to the "Tea Room," where the guide explains the difference between green, white, and black teas.

It's the Mint Room, however, that may be the eye-watering, sinus-clearing highlight of the tour. The incredible aroma of peppermint and spearmint will overwhelm your senses.

The packaging line is next, where before your very eyes, thousands of colorful boxes cruise through the room on the conveyor system to be filled with tea, closed, wrapped, cased, and finally lifted by the robotic palletizer onto a pallet.

"Ours is a multisensory experience," says Spencer. "Guests not only see the process, but they also have the opportunity to taste over 90 varieties of tea and herb teas, from Sleepytime and Red Zinger to new products like Imperial Peach White Tea and True Blueberry."

On your way out don't miss the gift shop. There you can purchase many teas that are difficult to find, as well as teapots, cups, mugs, and lots of items for a "tea lifestyle."

Tours are conducted daily. Groups of eight or more require reservations. Children must be age five or older to go into the factory. Call (303) 581-1202 for information or to schedule a group tour.

on Thanksgiving, Christmas Day, and New Year's Day. Admission is free. Tours at the museum are self-guided. Call (303) 729-3440 for information.

LONGMONT MUSEUM AND CULTURAL CENTER
400 Quail Road, Longmont
(303) 651-8374
www.ci.longmont.co.us/museum/about/index.htm
Founded in 1936 as part of the St. Vrain Historical Society, the Longmont Museum and Cultural Center is an outstanding local attraction. The museum includes four exhibit galleries. The Longmont Gallery and the Longs Peak Room contain long-term exhibits on the history and culture of Longmont, the St. Vrain Valley, and the West,

and include interactive exhibits for all ages. Two additional galleries, the Colorado Gallery and the St. Vrain Gallery, host changing art, history, and science exhibits throughout the year. A variety of excellent educational programs are offered. The museum is open Tuesday through Saturday 9 a.m. to 5 p.m., Wednesday until 8 p.m., and on Sunday from 1 to 5 p.m. The facility is closed on Mondays and city holidays. Admission is free.

LOUISVILLE HISTORICAL MUSEUM
1001 Main Street, Louisville
(303) 665-9048
www.ci.louisville.co.us/museum.htm
Coal mining gave birth to Louisville, and artifacts from the town's early days plus household and personal items fill this small museum. The

museum features special exhibits from time to time. Hours are 10 a.m. to 3 p.m. Tuesday through Thursday, and the first Saturday of each month. Admission is free.

LYONS REDSTONE MUSEUM
340 High Street, Lyons
(303) 823-5271
www.rockymtretreats.com/lyons.htm
Take a scenic drive from Boulder north to Lyons, the town whose sandstone quarries have yielded so much of the building material you see at the University of Colorado and elsewhere in Boulder County. This restored 1881 schoolhouse features displays on the town's history. Check out the museum's genealogy files and gift shop. Hours are 10 a.m. to 4 p.m. Monday through Saturday, 12:30 to 4 p.m. Sunday. Admission is free, but donations are welcome. This museum closes during the winter months.

OLD MILL PARK
237 Pratt Street, Longmont
(303) 776-1870
www.stvrainhistoricalsociety.org
The oldest log cabin in Boulder County is situated in a privately owned, tree-lined park. A real mill wheel turns at the pond. The park can be reserved through the St. Vrain Historical Society for weddings and meetings. Old Mill Park is open daily to the public for free 8 a.m. to 5 p.m. except during private events. Group tours are given by appointment.

TOWER OF COMPASSION
Missouri Street and South Pratt Parkway
Longmont
No phone
This 60-foot-tall pagoda was donated to the city in 1972 by the Kanemoto family, who settled in Longmont in the early 1900s to work in sugar-beet fields. Their family farm later was developed as residences and this city park. The tower was inspired by a family visit to Japan and the Kanemotos' gratitude to the people of Longmont. Its five levels represent love, empathy, understanding, gratitude, and giving selflessly of oneself—all elements of true compassion.

BUSINESS AND SCIENCE ATTRACTIONS

CELESTIAL SEASONINGS TOUR
4600 Sleepytime Drive, Boulder
(303) 530-5300
www.celestialseasonings.com
If you are planning a trip to Boulder, this needs to be on your "to do" list. Each year, 50,000 people enjoy a 45-minute tour of the nation's largest manufacturer of specialty and herb teas. The tour includes an assembly line where tea gets packed in those pretty little boxes, and there are taste-testing opportunities. Employees' children create safety posters, and the walls are festooned with sayings from the tea boxes. This is a New Age business to its very bones, now with a sleek all-business overlay that belies its counterculture origins in Boulder's haute hippie era.

Free tours are offered Monday through Friday every hour from 10 a.m. to 4 p.m., Saturday from 10 a.m. to 3 p.m., and on Sunday from 11 a.m. to 3 p.m. Arrive early to get tickets, as tours are given on a first-come, first-served basis. Children must be age five or older to go on the factory portion of the tour. Groups of eight or more must make reservations. You can also visit the Tea Shop and Emporium, the herb garden and lunchtime cafe, whether or not you take the tour. Shop hours are 9 a.m. to 6 p.m. Monday through Friday, Saturday 9 a.m. to 5 p.m., and 11 a.m. to 5 p.m. Sunday. To reach the plant, take the Longmont Diagonal Highway (Highway 119) to Jay Road. Turn right (east), go a mile to Spine Road, turn left, and continue a half-mile to Sleepytime Drive and Celestial Seasonings. Admission is free.

i Tall, bearded, dwarf, border, or median . . . no matter what type of iris you prefer, one thing's for sure: the sight of the blooming iris fields at Long's Iris Gardens on north Broadway is breathtaking.

LONG'S IRIS GARDENS
3240 Broadway, Boulder
(303) 442-2353
www.longsgardens.com

For nearly a century, the Long family has chugged an old tractor out to tend their iris fields. The 2,000 varieties range from pretty mongrels to prize-winning queens. You can go to the big yellow farmhouse in early May to mid-June, depending on the year's weather, to buy iris plants—at 2115 13th Street, just north of the mall, or you can dig your own plants. (The Longs will provide supplies so you can dig your own iris clumps.) The delicate scents and the rows of colorful, fluttering petals can make any day better. Digging-season hours are generally 9 a.m. to 5 p.m. daily. An iris clump costs less than $5. The farm is close to town, on Broadway, just south of Iris Avenue (guess how that street got its name). Catalogs come out in April.

NATIONAL OCEANIC AND ATMOSPHERIC ADMINISTRATION (NOAA)
325 Broadway, Boulder
(303) 497-4091 for tour information

Boulder is nowhere near the beach, but it's a center for incredibly sophisticated weather forecasting and oceanic research, thanks to high-powered scientists and their computers that study world weather. Until March of 1999 scientists were spread out over a half-dozen sites in Boulder. New buildings and additions now highlight the center. A real coup was securing the National Weather Service, which relocated to Boulder after 100 years in Denver. The National Institute of Standards and Technology is also on this campus. There are exhibits in the lobby, guided tours, school tours, and a school classroom. Call the tour information number for updated information. Tours are sometimes suspended due to security concerns.

KIDSTUFF

"I'm b-o-o-r-r-e-d!!!" If you have kids, it's an all-too-familiar refrain. But what to do? Here are ideas for when you get a little bored with your children's boredom. (Also check the Festivals and Annual Events, Attractions, and Day Trips and Weekend Getaways chapters.)

ATTRACTIONS

THE BUTTERFLY PAVILION & INSECT CENTER
6252 West 104th Avenue, Westminster
(303) 469-5441
www.butterflies.org
No matter how many times children visit, they never tire of the Butterfly Pavilion. After touring the display of living insects, visitors enter a greenhouse that's the home of exotic tropical butterflies. The large and colorful butterflies often land on children, producing squeals of delight and a charming sense of awe. In one corner you can watch the last two stages of metamorphosis as butterflies emerge from their chrysalises. A gift shop and cafeteria are adjacent to the Pavilion. Admission is $7.95 for adults, $5.95 for seniors, and $4.95 for children ages 3–12. Up to two children ages two and younger are admitted free with a paying adult. The Pavilion is open every day from 9 a.m. to 5 p.m. The facility is closed Christmas Eve, Christmas Day and New Year's Day.

COLOR ME MINE
1938 Pearl Street, Boulder
(303) 443-3469
www.colormemine.com
Boulder doesn't have many rainy afternoons, but this is a sure bet if you find yourself with a little time on your hands and you want to help your children express their creativity. Kids can pick from ready-to-be-painted pottery in sizes ranging from small enough to hold in your hand to too large to carry. Most children want to paint a miniature animal or a plate they can use for a "personalized dining experience" once they get it home. The pottery is fired after it's painted, meaning it will be a week before the finished piece is available for pickup.

CU WIZARDS!
Various locations, CU Campus
(303) 492-6952
www.colorado.edu/sciencediscovery/
cuwizards
Typically on the last Saturday of the month, September through June, the University of Colorado presents its CU Wizards! program. Wizards give free morning lectures that pack science lecture halls with laughing, learning kids. This is a great, informal introduction to astronomy, chemistry, biology, and physics for students in grades five through nine. Each program lasts about an hour and includes several lively demonstration experiments. The shows begin at 9:30 a.m.

GATEWAY PARK FUN CENTER
4800 28th Street, Boulder
(303) 442-4386
www.gatewayfunpark.com
Ask Boulder kids to name one of their favorite spots, especially for a birthday party, and Gateway Park will be the answer you get. The park is a great place to let your kids run free while they enjoy the video arcade and snack bar, the go-karts, miniature golf, batting cages, and the human maze. The roller hockey rink is always popular. For parents with younger kiddos, Gateway also has a play area for children younger

than age seven, including kiddie carts and a kiddie train. There's a fee for each activity, with a discount for children younger than age seven.

GYMBOREE
2525 Arapahoe Avenue, Boulder
(303) 546-0081
For little tykes only, this is a great place for toddlers to play, and the equipment is designed to keep them busy enough that parents have time to chat and possibly meet other new parents. There are regular free introductory sessions.

LOIS LAFOND AND THE ROCKADILES
Boulder
(303) 444-7095
www.loislafond.com
This group packs young fans in wherever they play, entertaining their audiences with funky, high-quality songs with kid-pleasing lyrics. They appear at such events as Halloween parades in the metro area, the Taste of Colorado in Denver, Boulder's Out to Lunch series, and others. Watch for them!

MUNSON'S FAMILY FARM
75th Street and Valmont Road, Boulder
(303) 442-5330
Before frost hits, you and the kids can tromp into the field and twist a pumpkin off the vine. Choose amongst giants and jack-o'-lantern pumpkins, pie pumpkins, and winter squash, including Delicata, a sweet, buttery-tasting winter squash that the Munsons say they've made famous. Munson's farm stand at this corner is a great place to let the kids help you buy produce all summer.

PEARL STREET MALL
On Pearl Street from 11th to 15th Streets, Boulder
(303) 449-3774
The gravel-lined pits and small climb-upon boulders (just west of the courthouse) make the Pearl Street Mall as popular a playground for children as it is for adults. Permanent climbing sculptures in the 14th Street block feature a snail, beaver,

and bunny rabbit that never fail to delight toddlers. The well-maintained flower gardens are a visual delight.

THE POTTERY CAFE
2460 Canyon Boulevard, Boulder
(303) 413-9300
www.potterycaffe.com
This is the place to paint your own pottery, buy beads, and drink espresso all at the same time. As a result, it's the perfect hangout for kids and adults alike. Wait one week for your pottery to be fired and voilà, you have beautiful artwork the whole family can enjoy creating.

CLASSES

BOULDER PARKS AND RECREATION PROGRAM
1777 Broadway, Boulder
(303) 441-3388
www.ci.boulder.co.us/parks-recreation
This is the largest program in the city, with children's classes in everything from arts and crafts to yoga. They include one-day workshops, multiweek sessions, and options in between. Gymnastics, dancing, and swimming are popular. Or try child/parent pottery classes given at the city's Pottery Lab. A new brochure is published four times a year and is available free at all three of the recreation centers. Don't dawdle with the registration—many of these classes are extremely popular and fill up quickly.

BOULDER ROCK CLUB
2829 Mapleton Street, Boulder
(303) 447-2804
www.totalclimbing.com
Great practice for eventually scaling the Flatirons, this club has an indoor rock-climbing wall and a variety of children's programs. They start with "ABC for Kids" for children ages two through six to help develop physical, mental, and social skills. There are separate programs for youths ages 6 through 14. Summer camps are offered as well.

BOULDER SUZUKI STRINGS

2705 Stanford Avenue, Boulder
(303) 499-2807
www.bouldersuzukistrings.org

This group specializes in string instrument instruction for kids from age four through high school. Boulder Suzuki Strings offers private and group lessons, note reading, performances, recitals, and workshops.

CU SCIENCE DISCOVERY

3400 Marine Street, 446 UCB
University of Colorado, Boulder
(303) 492-7188
www.colorado.edu/sciencediscovery

This is a wonderful program for children. It introduces kids to all facets of science—from computers to rocket building, to studying the great outdoors. There are after-school programs during the school year and terrific camps during the summer.

i Grab some wheels and head to the Boulder Creek Path. Don't have wheels? In-line skates or bikes can be rented at many bike shops.

MUSIC TOGETHER

(303) 530-0434
www.musictogetherboulder.com

Boulder children and their families enjoy these music classes that include singing, instrument play, rhythm chants and movement activities in a non-performance-oriented setting. Classes are offered near downtown and in north Boulder locations.

NORTHERN COLORADO FENCERS

1949 33rd Street, Boulder
(303) 443-6557
www.ncfencers.org

Always wanted to give this a try? Northern Colorado Fencers boasts nationally and internationally ranked fencers who give high-quality instruction to children; lessons include respect for the rules and safety.

THE PEANUT BUTTER PLAYERS

1370 Miner's Drive, Lafayette
(303) 786-8727
www.peanutbutterplayers.com

Voted the "Best of Boulder in Kids' Entertainment" by Daily Camera readers, this children's theater company has been delighting audiences with musicals for 23 years. For a modest fee you can enroll your child, but be prepared for an extensive rehearsal schedule—the director expects a professional performance and makes kids toe the line. Regardless of his or her experience, every child gets a speaking part, even if it's only one line. Summer programs are on a grand scale.

STIR IT UP COOKING

1140 South Lashley Lane, Boulder
(303) 494-2665
www.stiritupcooking.com

Carol Wiggins, the owner, started her cooking career by teaching gingerbread classes. When she witnessed the joy cooking brought to kids, she created Stir It Up Cooking. She offers classes for kids, teens, and families. Kids love the birthday parties offered by Stir It Up!

LIBRARIES

BOULDER PUBLIC LIBRARY—MAIN BRANCH

1000 Canyon Boulevard at Ninth Street
between Canyon Boulevard and
Arapahoe Avenue, Boulder
(303) 441-3100
www.boulder.lib.co.us

Most Boulder-area libraries offer abundant reading nooks, computers, and storytelling times. This is the city's crown jewel, an eye-popper with an outstanding selection of books, publications, videos, and other materials. The espresso shop on the second floor offers a view of the creek that is stunning any time of year. The main library is open 10 a.m. to 9 p.m. Monday through Thursday, 10 a.m. to 6 p.m. Friday and Saturday, and noon to 6 p.m. Sunday.

BOULDER PUBLIC LIBRARY—
GEORGE REYNOLDS BRANCH
3595 Table Mesa Drive, Boulder
(303) 441-3120
www.boulder.lib.co.us/branch/grb.html
A branch library serving south Boulder, it offers easy access and an extensive video- and audio-tape section. It's open from 10 a.m. to 9 p.m. Tuesday through Thursday, 10 a.m. to 6 p.m. Friday and Saturday, and 1 to 5 p.m. Sunday.

BOULDER PUBLIC LIBRARY—
MEADOWS BRANCH
4800 Baseline Road at Foothills Parkway
Boulder
(303) 441-4390
www.boulder.lib.co.us/branch/meadows
.html
This library branch serves residents who live east of downtown. Adjacent to the Meadows Shopping Center, it features a nice children's section, and with fewer patrons the staff always has time to help. The library is open from 10 a.m. to 9 p.m. Monday through Wednesday, 10 a.m. to 6 p.m. Friday and Saturday, and 1 to 5 p.m. Sunday. This branch is closed on Thursdays.

LAFAYETTE PUBLIC LIBRARY
775 West Baseline Road, Lafayette
(303) 665-5200
www.cityoflafayette.com/library
This contemporary 30,000-square-foot library opened in October 1997 and is 10 times the size of the original library. The large and knowledgeable staff can help you access books, audio books, computer programs, and the Internet. Lafayette's library is open Monday through Thursday 10 a.m. to 9 p.m., Friday and Saturday 10 a.m. to 5 p.m., and Sunday 1 to 5 p.m.

LONGMONT PUBLIC LIBRARY
409 Fourth Avenue, Longmont
(303) 651-8470
www.ci.longmont.co.us/library
Longmont's library was built in 1993 on the site of the original Carnegie Library. The new library contains a children's section and a separate teen section. There is a large CD, video-, and audio-tape section; periodicals and easy parking are other pluses. This library is open Monday through Thursday 10 a.m. to 9 p.m., Friday and Saturday 9 a.m. to 5 p.m., and Sunday 1 to 5 p.m. The library alters its hours during the summer months.

LOUISVILLE PUBLIC LIBRARY
951 Spruce Street, Louisville
(303) 335-4849
www.ci.louisville.co.us
Louisville's library has a long history, dating back to 1923, when the Chinook Campfire Girls made it their project to collect books that would eventually be housed in the town's library. It wasn't until 1980 that the library had a permanent home, and just 10 years later the collection moved again. In 2006 the collection was moved again to an even larger facility. It hasn't seemed to bother residents, who visit so often the library has one of the highest circulation statistics for a library of its size in the state. There are children's and young adult sections plus the usual audio and visual offerings. The library is open Monday through Thursday 10 a.m. to 8 p.m., Friday and Saturday 10 a.m. to 6 p.m., and Sunday 1 to 5 p.m.

MUSEUMS

THE CHILDREN'S MUSEUM OF DENVER
2121 Children's Museum Drive
(just off I-25), Denver
(303) 433-7444
www.cmdenver.org
If you're up for a drive or heading in that direction anyway, this is the biggest, most comprehensive children's museum around. It features a stunning variety of laboratories, interactive displays, a miniature grocery store where youngsters can shop or act as cashiers, and a terrific toddler area. You'll find this museum open Monday through Friday 9 a.m. to 4 p.m., Wednesday 9 a.m. to 7:30 p.m. and from 10 a.m. to 5 p.m. on Saturday and Sunday. Admission is free for kids younger than age one; $5.50 for seniors and $7.50 for all other ages.

LONGMONT MUSEUM & CULTURAL CENTER
400 Quail Road, Longmont
(303) 651-8374
www.ci.longmont.co.us/museum
This museum specializes in self-structured, hands-on science, history, and art activities. Permanent features are a puppet area, pioneer dress-up theater, and reading area; rotating activities include a water table, an electronic board, and "Tub-O'Bubbles," where kids can create giant soap bubbles with wands. There is no admission fee, but donations are always appreciated. It is open Tuesday 9 a.m. to 5 p.m., Wednesday 9 a.m. to 8 p.m., Thursday through Saturday 9 a.m. to 5 p.m., and Sunday 1 to 5 p.m. The museum is closed on Mondays and holidays. A nominal fee is charged for special events.

UNIVERSITY OF COLORADO MUSEUM
Broadway and 15th Street, Boulder
(303) 492-6892
cumuseum.colorado.edu
The CU museum has a kids' corner and numerous kids' activities and special events. This place is definitely one of Boulder's best-kept secrets. Find the real triceratops head, and try on the sea-turtle shell. This museum is open Monday through Friday from 9 a.m. to 5 p.m., Saturday from 9 a.m. to 4 p.m., and Sunday from 10 a.m. to 4 p.m. Admission is $3 for adults and $1 for seniors and children ages 6 through 18. Children younger than age six and CU students can visit for free.

WOW! (WORLD OF WONDER) CHILDREN'S MUSEUM
110 North Harrison Avenue, Lafayette
(303) 604-2424
www.wowmuseum.com
Call it a positive feature of the population growth in eastern Boulder County—another children's museum! WOW is designed for toddlers and school-age children and their families. It offers a variety of interactive and informative educational and creative exhibits and programs that stimulate learning. A very clever pirate ship, for instance, turns out to be a dress-up room. Opened in 1996, the museum features both permanent and traveling exhibits. There are three party rooms, a snack area, and a gift shop. This museum is open from 9 a.m. to 5 p.m. Tuesday and Wednesday; 10 a.m. to 6 p.m. Thursday through Saturday, and from noon until 4 p.m. Sunday. Parents are admitted free, while children pay $7 for all-day admission. There are also frequent-visitor cards, memberships, and group rates.

PARKS

CAVE PARK (ARAPAHOE RIDGE PARK)
1220 Eisenhower Drive, Boulder
(303) 413-7200
www.ci.boulder.co.us/parks-recreation
Cave Park, also known as Arapahoe Ridge Park, offers the best and most creative array of playground equipment around. It's next door to Eisenhower Elementary, but large enough for everyone.

CHAUTAUQUA PARK
Ninth Street and Baseline Road, Boulder
(303) 442-3282
www.chautauqua.com
Chautauqua Park boasts a great expanse of lawn, away from traffic, as well as playground equipment that includes a child-size playhouse. The huge grassy area is great for kids and Frisbee-chasing dogs. In summer months the Chautauqua Dining Hall is the perfect place to grab a bite to eat; it has convenient restrooms, too.

SCOTT CARPENTER PARK
30th Street and Arapahoe Avenue, Boulder
(303) 441-3427
www.ci.boulder.co.us/parks-recreation
Rated "Boulder's Best Park" by *Daily Camera* readers, this park was named after a local astronaut and features a climbing apparatus resembling a rocket ship. The playground was completely refurbished in 1998 with new equipment that adheres to the "space" theme. The Boulder Skatepark is also here. Open to kids eight years old and older, it lets skateboarders test their skills on the 10-foot

vertical half-pipe, or play it safe on the 6-foot or 4-foot mini-ramps and street course. Admission is free; helmets and pads are required and can be rented for a small fee. In winter, the park is Boulder's most popular sledding area. After a winter storm, the sledding hill is small enough to be manageable but big enough to be exciting.

VIELE LAKE
1360 Gillaspie Drive, Boulder
(303) 441-3448
Complete with canoes, paddleboats, and lots of Canada geese, this man-made lake is a central feature of this south Boulder neighborhood. For students who attend the nearby Fairview High School, it's a nice place to take a break. There's no swimming allowed.

SPORTS

Biking

If your child lacks a bike, isn't it time to buy one? "Pl-e-a-s-e? Pretty please?" The bike trails in Boulder are so wonderful, wheels can be the highlight of a child's vacation or life in Boulder. But make sure children wear helmets. In fact, set a good example and wear one yourself, and ride with the kids until you're sure they understand trail safety and bicycling rules. Although most riders are polite and considerate of children, paths can get crowded, and a few rude racers are ruthless.

Boulder Creek Path and its tributaries are perfect for bicycling and in-line skating (also see "Hiking"). Many places nearby rent in-line skates and bikes.

BOULDER BIKESMITH
2432 Arapahoe Avenue, Boulder
(303) 443-1132
www.boulderbikesmith.com
Should your child's two-wheeler "bite the dust" on Boulder's bike path, head for this shop, adjacent to the Boulder Creek Path. Trained experts on staff can help with bike service, the sale of new or used bicycles, and, as a last resort, in-line skate rental. They are open every day from 9 a.m. to 6 p.m.

UNIVERSITY BICYCLES
839 Pearl Street, Boulder
(303) 444-4196
www.ubikes.com
This is a great downtown location from which you can rent kids' bikes, bike trailers, tandem bikes, and trail-a-bikes, a style of hybrid tandem with an adult-size bike in front and a kid-size one in the rear. One way or another, you can get the whole family on wheels.

Hiking

For more information on trails in the area, see the Sports chapter.

BOULDER CREEK PATH
Broadway and Canyon Boulevard
Boulder
(303) 441-3388
www.ci.boulder.co.us
A stroll along the path—keeping mindful of fast-moving cyclists and in-line skaters, please—can take on exploratory aspects with small detours down the creek along the way, to the murky but well-intentioned trout-viewing windows near the Millennium Harvest House Bridge, or to the duck-pond overlook between Ninth Street and the Justice Center. Freelance musicians might be playing in the park between Broadway and 13th Street. Be sure to read the interpretive signs along the way.

CITY PARKS AND ADMINISTRATION/OPEN SPACE AND MOUNTAIN PARKS
3198 Broadway, Boulder
(303) 441-3440 (Open Space)
www.ci.boulder.co.us/openspace
After the paved Creek Path, a logical next step might be some of the area's easiest unpaved trails. Short-legged, short-burst-of-energy little hikers often do best with modest walks along relatively flat trails. From the Bobolink trailhead at Baseline and Cherryvale Roads, it's a little more than .75 mile to the East Boulder Community Center, and about 1.3 miles to South Boulder Road. The Baseline-EBCC

section features a series of interpretive signs on grasslands, wetlands, and river ecology.

The Teller Farm Trail runs 2.2 miles through a picturesque rural area between Arapahoe (the signed trailhead is off a dirt road between 75th and 95th Streets) and Valmont Road (the trailhead is near 95th Street). Partway along the trail is a small lake (fishing permitted). The nearby White Rocks Trail, whose trailhead is also near Valmont Road and 95th Street, is about 4 miles long, and its first stretch is really flat. Maps are available from the parks department.

With older children who have more stamina, the options multiply. Red Rocks is a good place to start. This short, steep trail, accessible from a well-marked trailhead at the mouth of Boulder Canyon, makes a suitable first challenge with some optional rock scrambling on top. Trails in the Boulder Mountain Parks; Walker Ranch, way up Flagstaff Road; the Rabbit Mountain open space near Lyons; Brainard Lake and the Indian Peaks Wilderness west of Ward; and Rocky Mountain National Park are among the abundant nearby options for various levels of stamina and interest. (See our Parks and Recreation chapter and our Rocky Mountain National Park overview.) If it's windy, a trail right against the foothills can provide some shelter from big gusts. If it's snowy, choose a flat one. If it's hot, find a creek with shade, or drive up to the mountains. Remember to watch little ones closely near any creeks with fast-moving waters.

WALDEN AND SAWHILL PONDS
75th Street between Jay Street and
Valmont Road, Boulder
(303) 678-6200
www.ci.boulder.co.us/openspace
This is a beguiling 113-acre complex of ponds reclaimed from old gravel pits—an example of nature's ability to heal a scarred landscape. The ponds, with their aquatic vegetation and fish, have become an attractive habitat and breeding area for waterfowl, painted turtles, muskrats, and other fauna. Two miles of ultra-gentle trails, picnic areas, and fishing areas make these ponds a fine family destination.

Ice Skating
CU ICE ARENA AND SKATE SHOP
CU campus, Broadway and College, Boulder
(303) 492-7255
www.colorado.edu/sacs/rec-center/facilities
CU-Boulder's indoor ice-skating rink gives skaters a great view of Sunshine Canyon. It is free to students and members, otherwise the cost is $5, plus $1 for skates. You must be a guest of a student or member to use this facility or be signed up for public lessons. Recreational skating hours vary from day to day.

GOLD LAKE MOUNTAIN RESORT AND SPA
3371 Gold Lake Road, Ward
(303) 459-3544
www.goldlake.com
At Gold Lake one-day packages include not only ice skating but also a brunch, use of the hot tubs, and the chance to do other winter sports including snowshoeing and cross-country skiing. Rental equipment is available. Packages start at $30.

YMCA ICE ARENA
2800 Dagny Way, Lafayette
(303) 664-5455
www.ymcabv.org
A membership or day pass grants access to the indoor ice rink at this YMCA Arapahoe Branch in Lafayette. Learn-to-skate, youth, and adult leagues and recreational skating available. This facility offers recreational skaters ice time several days a week and is a great place for kids' birthday parties. Be sure to call ahead for party reservations and current rates.

Skiing
ELDORA MOUNTAIN RESORT
2861 Eldora Ski Road, Nederland
(303) 440-8797
www.eldora.com
This resort is tailor-made for family skiing with easy and challenging downhill trails plus lots of ski and snowboarding instructors. This is an excellent learning environment for children. Lessons are available for kids age four and older. In

conjunction with the Mom's Monday, a series of women-only classes on Monday afternoons, Eldorables provides two-hour lessons and rental equipment for four- to six-year-olds. The Nordic Center is adjacent to the downhill ski areas. In addition to beautiful, wind-sheltered trails, it offers cross-country skiing lessons. Instructors set up the kids' lessons so everything's a game, and because there's so much movement, children tend to stay warmer than they do during downhill skiing.

Swimming and Boating

BOULDER RECREATION CENTERS
At the East, North, and South Boulder Recreation Centers, adult city residents pay $6.25, senior citizens age 60 and older pay $4.50, and children and teens younger than age 18 pay between $3.50 and $4.00 per visit. Punch cards purchased in advance will reduce the fee for those who plan to visit regularly. There are also annual passes and a corporate pass program. Online information for all of Boulder's recreation centers is available at www.ci.boulder.co.us.

EAST BOULDER RECREATION CENTER
5660 Sioux Drive, Boulder
(303) 441-4400
The "Lazy River" is very popular with small children, and the tall waterslide can surprise even the most-adult adult. Lap lanes are also available. This center is open Monday through Friday from 5:30 a.m. to 9:30 p.m., Saturday from 7:30 a.m. to 6 p.m., and Sunday from 8:30 a.m. to 8 p.m.

i The local recreation centers, which are open to the public for a fee, have great swimming pools, "lazy rivers," and wading areas.

NORTH BOULDER RECREATION CENTER
3170 Broadway, Boulder
(303) 413-7260
The city's oldest recreation facility has undergone a major remodel and is now a state-of-the-art facility. Its family swim on Sunday afternoon is inexpensive and often a lifesaver for parents or children who find themselves winter-weary and/or housebound. This center is open Monday through Thursday from 6 a.m. to 9:30 p.m., Friday from 6 a.m. to 6:30 p.m., Saturday from 6:30 a.m. to 7 p.m., and Sunday from 7:30 a.m. to 8 p.m. The North Recreation Center started a program in the fall of 1997 for kids ages 7 through 12. Called "Fridays with BPR," it allows kids to participate in a variety of activities from 7 to 10 p.m. on Friday nights, after parents have registered their children and paid the $15 fee. The center promises a safe, secure environment with a police officer on the premises. The popular program offers swimming, laser-tag games, blackout wallyball, alien art, dancing, swimming and diving contests, and other activities.

SOUTH BOULDER RECREATION CENTER
1360 Gillaspie Drive, Boulder
(303) 441-3448
The South Center was renovated in 1998 to include a new lap pool, new locker rooms, an improved weight room, and an elevator. Young runners can take several mostly traffic-free jogging routes from here. This center is open Monday through Thursday from 6 a.m. to 9:30 p.m., Friday from 6 a.m. to 8 p.m., and Saturday and Sunday from 8 a.m. to 5 p.m.

BOULDER RESERVOIR
5100 North 51st Street, Boulder
(303) 441-3461 or (303) 441-3468
This is a summer-only magnet for families (see the Parks and Recreation Centers chapter). Highlights are a sand beach and rentals of non-powered watercraft including canoes, rowboats, paddleboats, and Sunfish. The reservoir is open from 6 a.m. until dusk for sailboarding, sailing, and waterskiing. Swimmers are admitted from 9 a.m. until 7 p.m. Daily admission at the reservoir is $6 for adults, $4 for kids ages 4 through 18, and $4 for seniors; children younger than age 4 get in free. Money-saving resident and nonresident passes are available.

BROOMFIELD RECREATION CENTER/ AQUATIC PARK
280 Lamar Street, Broomfield
(303) 464-5500
www.ci.broomfield.co.us/recreation
With a six-lane pool and typical amenities, this center is very popular. It is open Monday and Wednesday 5:30 a.m. until 9 p.m., Tuesday and Thursday 7 a.m. to 9 p.m., Friday 5:30 a.m. to 7 p.m., and Saturday 8 a.m. to 4 p.m. Closed Sunday. Admission for resident adults ED: price for nonresident? is $3.50; seniors pay $2.75, teens (13-17) pay $2.75, and kids (4-12) are charged $2.50 per visit. Non-resident fees are $4.50 for adults, $3.75 for seniors, $3.75 for teens, and $3.50 for kids. Annual passes are available. The outdoor aquatics park is a real summertime treat. The aquatics park is open during the summer only.

LAFAYETTE BOB L. BURGER RECREATION CENTER
111 West Baseline Road, Lafayette
(303) 665-0469
www.cityoflafayette.com
This center has it all—a huge waterslide, a "lazy river," and a children's pool. Even when their fingertips look like prunes and their lips are blue, children beg to stay "just a little longer." This center is open from 5 a.m. until 9 p.m. Monday through Thursday; 5 a.m. until 7:30 p.m. on Friday; 8 a.m. until 6 p.m. on Saturday, and 10 a.m. until 6 p.m. on Sunday. The admission fee for adults is $4.50; seniors pay $2.75; children ages 3 through 12 pay $2.50; and youths ages 6 through 17 pay $3.00.

LOUISVILLE RECREATION CENTER
900 West Via Appia, Louisville
(303) 666-7400
www.louisvillerecreation.com
This center's six-lane pool allows adults to swim while kids frolic in the children's pool, which features an impressive 160 foot waterslide. Louisville's center is open Monday through Thursday 5:45 a.m. to 9 p.m., Friday 5:45 a.m. to 7 p.m.,

Saturday 7 a.m. to 6 p.m., and Sunday 8 a.m. to 6 p.m. Adults pay $5.00 per visit; seniors pay $3.00, kids ages 13 to 18 pay $3.50, and those younger than age 13 pay $3.00.

SCOTT CARPENTER POOL
30th Street and Arapahoe Avenue, Boulder
(303) 441-3427
www.bouldercolorado.gov
This is Boulder's largest public swimming pool, open in summer only, with three wide lap lanes, a 151-foot waterslide, a snack bar, a toddler pool, and plenty of space to sunbathe. The pool hours vary year to year. Single-entry admission is $6.00 for adults, $4.00 for seniors age 60 and older, $3.50 for teens ages 13 through 18, and $3.00 for children ages 3 through 12. A punch card or an annual pass will reduce the fee. Swimming lessons are offered weekday mornings.

SPRUCE POOL
2102 Spruce Street, Boulder
(303) 441-3426
www.bouldercolorado.gov
Boulder's oldest public swimming pool, this central Boulder gem was once called the Hygienic Swimming Pool. Open during summer months only, it has a colorful mural, waterslide, and grassy sunbathing spot that make it a family favorite. The pool hours change from year to year. Single-entry admission is $6.00 for adults, $4.00 for seniors age 60 and older, $3.50 for teens ages 13 through 18, and $3.00 for children ages 3 through 12. A punch card or an annual pass will reduce the fee. Swimming lessons are offered weekday mornings.

WANEKA LAKE PARK
1600 Caria Drive, Lafayette
(303) 665-0469
www.cityoflafayette.com
This 147-acre community park has a 1.2-mile fitness trail and a path around the lake for walking, biking, running, fishing, and cross-country skiing in winter. Paddleboat, canoe, and rowboat rentals

are available. There is also playground equipment and plenty of picnic tables to enjoy the views of the lake and nearby mountains. There is no swimming allowed in Waneka Lake.

Team Sports

High school and college sports abound in Boulder, and pro teams are no farther away than Denver. See our Sports chapter for further information.

BOULDER JUNIOR SOCCER
2400 Central Avenue, Boulder
(303) 443-1618
www.novasoccer.com
Soccer is a great way for youngsters to learn cooperation and team spirit and for newcomers to make friends. This is the biggest program around, with spring and fall seasons for schoolchildren as young as kindergartners. Nova is for strong older players.

BOULDER COUNTY FORCE
2769 Iris Street, Suite 115, Boulder
(303) 443-8877
www.bcforce.com
This has been one of Boulder's premier soccer camps for more than 20 years. Force offers programs for children ages 5 to18.

YMCA
2850 Mapleton Avenue, Boulder
(303) 442-2778
www.ymcabv.org
The "Y" has baseball programs in spring and summer, basketball in winter and spring, and soccer, volleyball, flag football, and in-line hockey in fall. Children are grouped according to age. Girls will find as many activities and as enthusiastic coaches as the boys.

SUMMER CAMPS

A week or more out of the house can go a long way toward relieving the tedium of a bored child's summer. Overnight camps, day camps, and camps that provide both options abound in the Boulder area. Camps are great for learning about everything from computers to archery, outdoor skills to swimming. Area newspapers publish special camp issues in spring.

ALEXANDER DAWSON SUMMER CAMPS
10455 Dawson Drive, Lafayette
(303) 665-6679
www.dawsonschool.org/SummerCamps
Dawson's camps cater to the athletes, academics, and artists in your family. They have a multitude of programs to satisfy any kid's curiosity and needs. There is a juniors camp specifically for five and six year olds. The camps are held on the Alexander Dawson campus.

BOULDER PARKS AND RECREATION
3198 Broadway, Boulder
(303) 413-7200
www.ci.boulder.co.us
Boulder Parks and Recreation offers many day-camp-type options, from playground programs to a Teen Adventure Program with kayaking and overnight camping, plus programs for people with disabilities.

CAMP SHAKESPEARE
277 University of Colorado, Boulder
Intersection of Broadway and Euclid Avenue
or the intersection of Broadway and
University Avenue
(303) 492-0554
www.coloradoshakes.org
Celebrating its 11th year in 2009, Camp Shakespeare is for kids ages 10 through 18. The camp focuses on the skills needed for acting in Shakespeare productions. Participants also take a variety of workshops ranging from costuming, vocal production, stage combat, and movement. This camp is very popular, and advance registration is strongly advised.

COLORADO MOUNTAIN RANCH (TROJAN RANCH)
10063 Gold Hill Road, Boulder
(303) 442-4557
www.coloradomountainranch.com
The Walkers' family-run mountain ranch, also known as Trojan Ranch, is more than 50 years old. The camp offers both weeklong overnight sessions and day sessions, both featuring Western riding, swimming in a heated pool, Indian lore, archery, gymnastics, drama, and confidence-building outdoor adventures.

THE FRONT RANGE NATURAL SCIENCE SCHOOL
Thorne Ecological Institute
1466 West 63rd Street, Boulder
(303) 499-3647
www.thorne-eco.org
Founded in 1954, this children's environmental education program gets high marks for offering classes that include lots of outdoor exploration. Classes are offered year-round, but the summer program is the most popular.

RENAISSANCE ADVENTURES
302 Pearl Street, Boulder
(303) 786-9216
www.renaissanceadventures.com
These camps, which focus on active outdoor Renaissance-theme theater games, have been offered to children ages 6 through 14 since 1995. Participants are the heroes of a mythic quest to solve mysteries and riddles, brainstorm creative solutions to puzzling dilemmas, swashbuckle with foam swords, and negotiate peace treaties.

ROCKY MOUNTAIN THEATRE FOR KIDS
Boulder
(303) 245-8150
www.theatreforkids.net
So you wanna be in show business? At this camp, children ages 5 through 15 take to the stage in a thorough curriculum that includes theatrical performance, character building, improvisation, mime, creative movement and dance, and audition skills. All performances take place in a professional theater.

SCIENCE DISCOVERY SUMMER CAMP
3400 Marine Street, Boulder
(303) 492-7188
www.colorado.edu/sciencediscovery
This camp, sponsored by CU-Boulder's Science Discovery Program, is a well-regarded program that offers a wide variety of classes for kid ages 4 through 16. Classes include excursions to Colorado wonders such as the Great Sand Dunes and Dinosaur National Monuments and Cortez Cultural Center. The program is so popular participants are chosen by a lottery system. There are local programs and overnight options. Activities include hiking, paleontology, river rafting, and mountain biking.

UNIVERSITY OF COLORADO BASKETBALL CAMPS
Coors Events Center, Boulder
(303) 492-6877, (303) 492-6086
www.cubuffs.com/camps
Girls and boys of all ages flock to these camps to work with the head coaches of both the CU women's and men's basketball programs. Kathy McConnell-Miller and Jeff Bzdelik and their staff and players hold day and overnight camps, most of them three days long, on the CU campus. There are several specialty camps available including a father-son camp.

UNIVERSITY OF COLORADO SOCCER CAMPS
University of Colorado 372, Boulder
(303) 735-0530
www.cubuffs.com/camps
This camp gives boys and girls ages 10 through 18 the fundamentals needed to play the game of soccer. Each program is dedicated to the age and level of participants.

WILD BEAR CENTER FOR NATURE DISCOVERY
20 Lakeview Drive, Nederland
(303) 258-0495
www.wildbear.org

Wild Bear summer camp is based at the Nederland Elementary school. They have programs for kids 5 through 12 years old. The Junior Rangers are for six and seven year olds who like to get their hands dirty. They discover the wild animals on the trails surrounding the elementary school and cultivate their own biodome!

YMCA OF BOULDER VALLEY
2850 Mapleton Avenue, Boulder
(303) 442-2778
www.ymcabv.org

The Y offers an extensive variety of camps: nature, sports, teen adventures, teen leadership, bicycling, fine arts, making memories, and mountain camp. All are licensed and staffed by professionals. In addition, the Y runs excursions to Denver-area fun spots such as Water World and staffs daylong summer camps at many schools.

DAY TRIPS AND WEEKEND GETAWAYS

From the mountains to the plains, the area around Boulder offers a wealth of possible day-trip activities, from cultural and historic sites to outdoor recreation, shopping, dining, and just enjoying the beautiful scenery. Among the places covered in this chapter are the Air Force Academy in Colorado Springs, the gambling casinos of Central City and Black Hawk, the ski resorts of Summit County and Winter Park, and the museums and other attractions of Denver. We've provided some history and vital information about each, along with details on special events, dining, and shopping opportunities. Among the popular activities in the mountains are skiing, Alpine-sliding, and sleigh-, hay-, and horseback riding. Athletes with disabilities can learn to ski, rock climb, and take on other challenges at Winter Park, site of the National Sports Center for the Disabled. For hiking, backpacking, bicycling, and cross-country skiing (and other participatory sports), also see our Sports chapter.

Denver's Zoo, with its Tropical Discovery exhibit, and the Denver Botanic Gardens will cheer you with lush greenery and tropical creatures even during the cold winter months. Drive up Pikes Peak in the summer and you can say you've been on top of one of Colorado's "Fourteeners"—the 54 mountains in the state that reach 14,000 feet or higher. Or take a leisurely sail across scenic Lake Dillon or Grand Lake.

Whatever your inclination, the area offers activities that are fun, challenging, inspirational, educational—or perhaps all of the above.

Accommodations Price-Code Key

Accommodation listings include dollar signs ranging from one to five ($–$$$$$) indicating the price range for a one-night stay, double occupancy, during the summer season.

$	$55 or less
$$	$56 to $75
$$$	$76 to $100
$$$$	$101 to $125
$$$$$	$126 or more

Restaurants Price-Code Key

Restaurants are listed with dollar signs ranging from one to five ($–$$$$$) indicating the average cost of dinner for two, excluding appetizer, alcoholic beverages, dessert, tax, and tip.

$	$20 or less
$$	$21 to $40
$$$	$41 to $60
$$$$	$61 to $100
$$$$$	$101 or more

DENVER

Believe it or not, Denver actually has some attractions that Boulder doesn't, though Boulderites hate to admit it. Driving time between Boulder and sprawling Greater Denver can vary depending on which part of the city you visit. All the attractions listed here are in the center-city area and an hour's drive or less from Boulder. It's fun to spend a day in the "big city" visiting museums, shops, restaurants, or galleries, or going to the Colorado Symphony or a show.

Some of Denver's top attractions are the Denver Botanic Gardens, the Denver Zoo, the Museum of Natural History, the elegant Brown Palace hotel (which serves high tea), and the Black American West Museum and Heritage Center. There's also good shopping on Larimer Street, the 16th Street Mall, Cherry Creek at the Tabor Center, and the lavish Park Meadows Mall—and lots of good restaurants, too.

i Those planning a day trip to Denver from Boulder or elsewhere should wait until the morning rush hour is over—usually around 9 a.m. Likewise, time your return for either before 3 p.m. or after dinner—unless you want to get caught in the traffic jam on I-25.

If you're a parent looking for fun activities to do with your children, make sure you see the following "Denver for Kids and the Young at Heart" section. For the complete Insiders' scoop on Denver, check out the *Insiders' Guide to Denver.*

Getting There

Take U.S. Highway 36 from Boulder to the I-25 exit. The interstate, with six lanes in some places, can be a bit intimidating for non-city drivers. It helps to have someone else along for navigation. Once on I-25, stay to the middle/right, because some of the far right lanes are "exit only" to such places as Denver International Airport or Limon in eastern Colorado. Follow I-25 for a few miles as it nears downtown Denver and watch for the sign for the Speer Boulevard South exit, which comes up quickly after the sign (not to be confused with the Speer Boulevard North exit). Take the exit and head for the tall buildings over Speer Boulevard. There are signs for the Denver Art Museum on Speer Boulevard past Colfax Avenue.

Or avoid the hassle of traffic and parking and take the RTD bus, which leaves from the RTD station in Boulder at 14th and Walnut Streets (and other stops along Broadway). The bus goes to the Market Street station in downtown Denver, right at the 16th Street Mall. There are numerous trips daily. In Denver, a free shuttle takes riders up and down the 16th Street pedestrian mall. The far end of the mall (and the shuttle stop) is only a few blocks from the capitol and the Denver Art Museum. For RTD route and schedule information, call (303) 299-6000 or visit their Web site at www.rtd-denver.com. A one-way ticket to Denver is $4.00. Tickets can be purchased on the bus, but you must have exact change.

In Denver, the Gray Line (303-289-2841 and www.grayline.com) runs a daily tour of the city. After leaving the pickup point, the bus stops at two parks, the Denver Museum of Natural History, the zoo, and the Botanic Gardens. It travels through the main part of downtown and up to the Capital Hill area. The tour is three hours long and departs daily at 8:30 a.m. and at 1:30 p.m. Tickets can be purchased at departing points but they prefer a call ahead of time to have an idea how many folks they'll be picking up. They also pick up at most hotels in the downtown area.

To get to the Denver Zoo and the Denver Museum of Natural History by car, take I-25 to I-70 eastbound. Follow I-70 to the Colorado Boulevard exit, then proceed south on Colorado Boulevard for 2 miles to 23rd Avenue and turn right. The zoo is on 23rd Avenue between Colorado Boulevard and York Street (look for signs). The museum is nearby in City Park at Colorado Boulevard and Montview.

To get to the museum from downtown Denver by car, go east on 17th Street (which eventually becomes East 17th Avenue) and turn left (north) onto Colorado Boulevard. Look for signs for the museum and the zoo.

For the Denver Botanic Gardens, from downtown take 14th Street east to York Street, turn right (south) onto York Street and go 4 blocks; free parking is on the left, and the gardens are on the right.

To reach the Black American West Museum and Heritage Center, go northeast on Stout Street (a block over from California Street) from downtown Denver out to 31st Street.

Attractions

BLACK AMERICAN WEST MUSEUM AND HERITAGE CENTER

3091 California Street, Denver
(303) 482-2242
www.blackamericanwestmuseum.com

Black Americans played an important role in the settling of the West; documentation at this unique museum shows that roughly a third of the West's cowboys were black. There were also many black businessmen, miners, pioneer doctors, politicians, soldiers, and teachers—a fact that historians have generally overlooked. At this museum, numerous photos and displays explain the role of black Americans as early settlers in Denver and Colorado. Every six months there's a changing exhibit with such subjects as the history of jazz in Denver or black churches in Denver. Summer hours are from 10 a.m. to 5 p.m. Tuesday through Saturday; winter hours are from 10 a.m. to 2 p.m. Tuesday through Saturday. Admission is $8 for adults, $7 for seniors, and $6 for children ages 5 through 12; children age 4 and younger are admitted for free.

THE DENVER ART MUSEUM

100 West 14th Avenue, Denver
(720) 865-5001
www.denverartmuseum.org

The Denver Art Museum has one of the best and most extensive collections of Native American crafts in the United States plus works of Picasso, Georges Braque, Matisse, Frederic Remington, Winslow Homer, Thomas Hart Benton, and many others. You'll find a cafe and restaurant and gift shop here as well. The newest addition to the art museum, the Hamilton Building (designed by Daniel Libeskind), debuted in October 2006. Hours are Tuesday through Thursday 10 a.m. to 5 p.m., Friday 10 a.m. to 10 p.m., Saturday 10 a.m. to 5 p.m. and Sunday 12 noon to 5 p.m. The museum is closed on Mondays and major holidays. Admission is $10 for adults, $8 for seniors and college students, $3 for youths ages 6 through 18, and free for museum members and

children age 5 and younger. General admission is free on the first Saturday of every month.

DENVER BOTANIC GARDENS

1005 York Street, Denver
(303) 331-4000
www.botanicgardens.org

Enjoy 23 outdoor acres full of beautiful flowers, trees, and shrubs, including a Japanese garden and an alpine rock garden, just 10 minutes east of downtown Denver. You'll find an indoor conservatory with special tropical and orchid areas plus a library and gift shop, too. There's increasing focus on Japanese-style designs, native prairie areas, and rock gardens. The curator of the Rock Alpine garden, Panayoti Kelaidis, is a Boulder native who has gained a national reputation for his daring eye and superb plant knowledge. For anyone who wants to learn what grows beautifully in this climate, the Botanic Gardens is a required stop. Although most visitors choose to see the brilliant summer flowers, winter, Colorado's longest season, is a good time to visit—especially to experience the 50-foot-tall tropical forest. For anyone with the winter blues, this lung-full of Hawaii is a sure, if temporary, cure. Hours are 9 a.m. to 5 p.m. daily from September 15 through May 11. From May 12 through September 14, hours are 9 a.m. to 8 p.m. Saturday through Tuesday and 9 a.m. to 5 p.m. Wednesday through Friday. Summer admission rates (May 1 through September 15) are $10.50 for adults, $7.50 for seniors, and $6.00 for students with ID and youths ages 4 through 15. Admission is free for children younger than age 4. Winter admission rates are a dollar less than the summer rates.

DENVER MUSEUM OF NATURE AND SCIENCE AND IMAX THEATER

2001 Colorado Boulevard, Denver
(303) 370-6357
(303) 322-7009 (reservations)
(303) 370-8257 (hearing-impaired TDD)
www.dmns.org

Besides dinosaurs, the museum features exhibits of Colorado's birds and animals and a fantastic collection of other natural history exhibits and dioramas. The museum also features the following exhibitions: *Space Odyssey, Discovery Zone, Egyptian Mummies, Gems and Minerals,* and the *Hall of Life.* From time to time the museum also hosts spectacular world-traveling exhibitions such as *Ramses II* and *Aztec. Prehistoric Journey,* an award-winning dinosaur exhibit popular with kids, is a permanent attraction that includes walk-through "enviroramas." The museum is open daily from 9 a.m. to 5 p.m. The museum's IMAX Theater, with its four-story screen, shows educational and entertaining movies. Call for showtimes. Admission to the museum is $11 for adults and $6 for youths ages 3 through 18 and seniors. There are also combination museum, IMAX, and planetarium tickets available.

DENVER ZOO
2300 Steele Street, Denver
(303) 376-4800
www.denverzoo.org
Today, visitors to the Denver Zoo can view almost 4,000 different animals, representing 700 species. The naturalistic habitats Predator Ridge, Tropical Discovery, Dragons of Komodo, and Primate Extravaganza enhance the lives of some of the world's endangered species. The zoo is open every day of the year. Zoo hours from November 1 through March 31 are 10 a.m. to 4 p.m., and hours from April 1 through October 31 are 9 a.m. to 5 p.m. Admission from April through September is $12 for adults, $9 for seniors, and $7 for children ages 3 through 11; children younger than age 3 are admitted for free. From November through March the admission is reduced by $2 for seniors and kids and $3 for adults. Call for free days for Colorado residents. The zoo's cafeteria serves light meals and snacks.

Restaurants
On the 1400 block of Larimer Street and along the 16th Street Mall, a potpourri of restaurants offer ethnic foods, sidewalk cafes, and lots of ambience. See the price-code key at the beginning of this chapter. The following are some favorites:

BISTRO VENDÔME $$$–$$$$
1424-H Larimer Square, Denver
(303) 825-3232
www.bistrovendome.com
Named one of Denver's 25 Very Best Restaurants by *5280* magazine in 2005 and an "A" list Theater Restaurant (one of five chosen nationally) by *Bon Appétit* in 2003, this French bistro serves hearty cuisine in a casual and authentic atmosphere. The bistro's full-service bar offers more than 65 French wines representing each region of France and a collection of pastis and champagne cocktails.

CAPITAL GRILLE $$$$–$$$$$
1450 Larimer Square, Denver
(303) 539-2500
www.thecapitalgrille.com
The Capital Grille has been voted the best steak house in many categories. The restaurant is nationally acclaimed for dry-aging steaks on the premises. Other classic steak house offerings include fresh seafood, chops, and large North Atlantic lobsters. The atmosphere is relaxed and elegant with professional and gracious service.

LIME $$
1414-C Larimer Square, Denver
(303) 893-5463
www.limecantina.com
Lime features creative Southwestern cuisine in an energetic urban atmosphere. It has earned accolades for its margaritas and fresh, handcrafted fare that follows family recipes. Lime's is the perfect dinner destination for professionals and downtown shoppers.

MCCORMICK'S FISH HOUSE AND BAR $$–$$$
The Oxford Hotel
1600 17th Street, Denver
(303) 825-1107
www.theoxfordhotel.com
McCormick's serves all types of American food plus seafood, which is their specialty. The popular eatery serves breakfast, lunch, and dinner daily, with a special weekend brunch on Saturday and Sunday.

WAZEE SUPPER CLUB   **$$$**
1600 15th Street, Denver
(303) 623-9518
www.wazeesupperclub.com
This is a classic LoDo institution serving up burgers, wonderful pizza, a large beer selection, and plenty of neighborhood character for more than two decades. It's open daily for lunch and dinner.

THE WYNKOOP BREWING CO.   **$–$$**
1634 18th Street, Denver
(303) 297-2700
www.wynkoop.com
A few blocks from Larimer Square, the Wynkoop provides an interesting dining and drinking experience. This was Denver's first brewpub, founded in 1988, and it's housed in a historic 19th-century building. Though the Wynkoop can be a bit noisy and crowded, the choice of ales and pub fare at reasonable prices and the lively atmosphere more than compensate. It's open daily for lunch and dinner.

Accommodations

Since Boulder is so close to Denver, most people just make it a day trip. But should you decide to have a little Denver holiday, many downtown hotels offer special weekend-getaway packages. Call the Colorado Hotel and Lodging Association reservations service line at (303) 297-8335 for information. See the price-code key at the beginning of this chapter.

THE BROWN PALACE   **$$$$$**
321 17th Street, Denver
(303) 297-3111
www.brownpalace.com
The Brown Palace is Denver's most famous hotel. It is quite elegant but expensive, starting at $189 per night for a standard room during the week to $1,575 per night for a suite. The hotel has three restaurants: Elyngton's and The Ship Tavern are casual; The Palace Arms is an acclaimed formal dining room. Churchill's, a cigar lounge, serves cocktails. Drinks are also available in the lobby and

The Ship Tavern, and lunch and afternoon tea are served in the beautiful Victorian-style lobby.

THE QUEEN ANNE INN   **$$$**
2147 Tremont Place, Denver
(303) 296-6666
www.queenannebnb.com
Just north of downtown in a historic neighborhood, the Queen Anne occupies two adjacent Victorian buildings, built in 1879 and 1886 in the Queen Anne style of architecture. Single rooms are in the $135 to $215 range, which includes breakfast. There are 14 rooms, all with private baths. The inn is popular with honeymooners and for weddings.

> **i** Spend an evening strolling along Denver's Larimer Street, off the 16th Street Mall, with its variety of sidewalk cafes, lively restaurants, and quaint shops.

Shopping

Denver has a number of popular shopping areas, some within walking distance of each other and others not. Downtown in the historic district are Larimer and Writer Squares. Farther afield are Cherry Creek and the Park Meadows Shopping Center.

CHERRY CREEK SHOPPING CENTER
3000 East First Avenue, Denver
(303) 388-3900
www.cherrycreekmall.com
With some 160 specialty stores—mostly high-end—Cherry Creek attracts 16 million visitors annually. Stores include Ann Taylor, Anthropologie, Abercrombie and Fitch, Apple, Cartier, Cole Haan, Lacoste, Ralph Lauren, Louis Vuitton, Neiman Marcus, Macy's, and Nordstrom. North of the mall are several blocks of trendy establishments including art galleries, restaurants, and a multitude of furniture stores.

LARIMER AND WRITER SQUARES
15th and Larimer Streets, Denver
(no main number)
Historic Larimer Square, at Larimer and 15th Streets, is packed full of upscale clothing boutiques, art galleries, cafes, and other shops, as is Writer Square, just across 15th Street. Looking for antique and estate jewelry? Victoriana, an interesting shop on Writer Square, is worth a visit. Find unusual artistic greeting cards at Avant-Card. Ann Taylor, the popular women's clothing and accessory shop, is also in Larimer Square (1421 Larimer).

PARK MEADOWS SHOPPING CENTER
8401 Park Meadows Center Drive
Littleton
(303) 792-2533
www.parkmeadows.com
The Park Meadows Shopping Center is in Douglas County (and not actually Denver proper). One of the big draws is Nordstrom. There's also Denver's first Dillard's department store. Other popular shops are Crate and Barrel and Restoration Hardware, with all types of gourmet kitchen and unusual decorating items. Park Meadows' entertainment section has four virtual theaters at a complex called Starport, where you can do things like virtual hang gliding. There are also movie theaters and a massive food-court area. For those who prefer finer dining, there's the California Cafe with upscale, nouvelle cuisine; Bella Restaurante for Italian food; and Alcatraz Brewing Co., a brewpub.

THE 16TH STREET MALL
16th Street between Market Street and
Colfax Avenue, Denver
(no phone)
There are lots of inexpensive souvenir-type shops along the 16th Street Mall. It's fun to walk up 16th Street or take the free shuttle. This is the place for a quick cup of coffee, finding a tacky Denver souvenir, or people-watching, but not serious shopping.

THE TABOR CENTER
1201 16th Street, Denver
(no main number)
The greenhouse-like Tabor Center, at the 16th Street Mall's north end, houses ESPN Zone, Paradise Pen, and Flag World, plus miscellaneous clothing and other shops.

Denver for Kids and the Young at Heart

Attractions
ON THE ROAD TO DENVER

ARVADA CENTER FOR THE ARTS AND HUMANITIES
6901 Wadsworth Boulevard, Denver
(720) 898-7200
www.arvadacenter.org
The Arvada Center offers participatory fairy-tale theater for children many weekday mornings and some Saturdays. Kids are often invited to come on stage to join the acting. The evening adult dramas and concerts, which cost from $13.50 to $55, are excellent, and the free museum has art and cultural displays.

BOONDOCKS FUN CENTER
11425 Community Center Drive, Northglenn
(720) 977-8000
www.boondocksfuncenter.com
The Boondocks Fun Center in Northglenn has seven acres of pure fun! There is miniature golf, laser tag, batting cages, go-karts, bumper cars, and the Max Flight roller coaster. For the young ones, they have Junior Racer and the Kiddie Cove. Pricing is based on the attraction; attraction packages are available. Boondocks is open Monday through Thursday and Sunday from 10 a.m. to 10 p.m. and Friday and Saturday from 10 a.m. to midnight. Hours vary in the summer. Tickets are $7 for adults and $5 for kids. Children under 2 are free.

THE BUTTERFLY PAVILION & INSECT CENTER

6252 West 104th Avenue, Westminster
(303) 469-5441
www.butterflies.org

This amazing place is about 20 minutes south of Boulder on the Church Ranch Boulevard exit off US 36 to Denver. Half of the center is a fascinating display of living insects, the other part is a greenhouse for exotic tropical butterflies. At the insect center, visitors can handle a live tarantula, see scorpions that glow in the dark, and learn about exotic cockroaches of the world. In the Butterfly Pavilion, 70 percent humidity and lush tropical foliage simulate the Costa Rican rain forest and butterflies flit around freely, hitchhiking on visitors.

There's also a nifty gift shop full of butterfly-themed items, plus a cafeteria. The center was created by the Rocky Mountain Butterfly Consortium and is a nonprofit organization. Its purchase of the insects from various tropical countries helps create a viable industry for sustaining tropical forests. The Butterfly Pavilion purchases butterfly chrysalises and hatches its own butterflies. Those who visit in the morning can see these beauties emerging from their chrysalids and cocoons. Outside, the facility has gardens of native wildflowers and prairie grass planted to attract local butterflies, so it's a great place for gardening ideas, too. Open daily from 9 a.m. to 5 p.m.; admission is $7.95 for adults, $5.95 for seniors, and $4.95 for kids ages 3 through 12. Kids younger than age three are admitted for free.

i Water World gives you the most splash for your money, and it's only 20 minutes from Boulder.

CASA BONITA

6715 West Colfax Avenue, Denver
(303) 232-5115
www.casabonitadenver.com

For sheer kitsch value, Casa Bonita is an experience not to be missed. It's the favorite dining experience of many youngsters. The Mexican food is passable, the doughnut-sweet sopapillas are tasty, but the main draw is the entertainment. At the indoor lagoon, a dramatic troupe presents plays that usually end with heavily costumed actors splash-landing in the pool. A dark cave maze is popular for hide-and-seek, and troubadours wander among the tables singing "Happy Birthday" when requested. The experience is hokey beyond belief and adored by children. A meal generally costs less than $10; children age 12 and younger eat for less than $5. Casa Bonita is open 11 a.m. to 9:30 p.m. Sunday through Thursday and 11 a.m. to 10 p.m. Friday and Saturday.

HYLAND HILLS WATER WORLD

1800 West 89th Avenue, Federal Heights
(303) 427-7873
www.waterworldcolorado.com

The 64 acres of water rides and 40 attractions make Water World America's largest family water park. *USA Today* rated its Voyage to the Center of the Earth one of America's top 10 attractions. To get here, take US 36 to the Pecos exit, close to Denver. Turn north (left) and drive until you see those blue canopies on the hilltop. Water World offers several safe introductions to white-water rafting. For those missing surf, Water World's big wave pools make plenty. Add an entertaining wading area for tots and grade-schoolers, plus many theme rides, and you've got wet for kids of all ages. Beach Boys music bops from the loudspeakers. A day of splashing costs $33.95 for individuals taller than 48 inches and $28.95 for those shorter than 47 inches. Tots smaller than 40 inches are admitted free. Water World is open daily in the summer from 10 a.m. to 6 p.m., weather permitting, and accepts major credit cards but no personal checks.

DOWNTOWN DENVER

THE DENVER ART MUSEUM

100 West 14th Avenue, Denver
(720) 865-5000
www.denverartmuseum.org

From the fantasy fortress facade outside to the hands-on displays, kids' corner, and videotape nooks inside, kids will particularly enjoy this museum. Count on spending an hour, maybe 90 minutes, with the kids in tow. Hours are Tuesday through Thursday and Saturday 10 a.m. to 5 p.m., Friday 10 a.m. to 10 p.m., and Sunday noon to 5 p.m. The museum is closed on Mondays and major holidays. Admission is $10 for adults, $8 for seniors, $3 for youths ages 6 through 18, and free for museum members and children younger than age 5.

THE DENVER MINT

320 West Colfax Avenue, Denver
(303) 405-4761
www.usmint.gov

Any kid who likes money will love the Denver Mint, between Delaware and Cherokee Streets (tour entrance on Cherokee). It began when Coloradans made their own money. In those days, real U.S. currency was hard to find this far west, and locals tired of weighing gold dust to exchange for food. Later, this private enterprise became an official U.S. mint. Teeth-rattlingly loud machines stamp coins from sheet metals. People hush as they pass a safe displaying 27.5 pounds of gold in six 400-troy-ounce gold bars. The bars are surprisingly small, like $3 bars of good chocolate in shiny yellow wrappers. They're a fraction of Denver's gold, which is one of three stashes nationwide (West Point and Fort Knox are the other two). Tours take place weekdays from 8 a.m. to 2 p.m. on a first-come, first-served basis. Tours are free, but slots fill quickly during the summer, so it's best to get your ticket by mid-morning. The coin sales area operates during the same hours as the tours and is accessible only by taking the tour. The mint is closed on weekends and holidays.

THE MOLLY BROWN HOUSE

1340 Pennsylvania Street, Denver
(303) 832-4092
www.mollybrown.org

Rent the movie *The Unsinkable Molly Brown,* starring Debbie Reynolds, then tour this landmark. It's just a few blocks from Denver's gold-domed capitol. Molly Brown was a diamond-in-the-rough whose husband made a gold strike. Denver society snubbed Molly, but she became a heroine when the *Titanic* sank in the freezing North Atlantic. Molly was on board that fateful day, and she saved many by pulling them into her lifeboat. Her mansion is 10,000 square feet of Victoriana. From September through May, the museum opens Tuesday through Saturday at 10 a.m. and Sunday at noon. From June through August, the museum opens Monday through Saturday at 10 a.m. and Sunday at noon. The history-filled 45-minute guided tour is $7 for adults, $6 for seniors age 65 and older, and $4 for children ages 6 through 12. The last tour is at 3:30 p.m.

WEST OF DOWNTOWN, NEAR I-25

THE CHILDREN'S MUSEUM OF DENVER

2121 Children's Museum Drive, Denver
(303) 433-7444
www.cmdenver.org

Near Elitch Gardens Amusement Park (see subsequent listing) is a square green building that appears to be wearing a burgundy pyramid cap. This is the Children's Museum, which offers hands-on exhibits such as a science lab and a Wild Oats Community Market where kids can play shopping. The museum is open Monday, Tuesday, Thursday and Friday from 9 a.m. to 4 p.m., Wednesday from 9 a.m. to 7:30 p.m. and Saturday and Sunday from 10 a.m. to 5 p.m. Entry fee is $7.50 for ages 2 to 59, $5.50 for age one and adults age 60 and older. Children younger than age one are admitted free. Call for show and schedule information for the Children's Theatre.

COORS FIELD

20th and Blake Streets, Denver
(303) ROCKIES
www.rockies.mlb.com

Home to the Colorado Rockies, this 50,000-seat stadium is extraordinarily detailed, down to 40 plate-size blue columbines on the exterior. (The columbine is Colorado's state flower.) A ball game with kids is delightful here. They'll love the hot dogs, pizza, sodas, and snacks. You can find Rocky Mountain Oysters for sale, too. (Those are fried bull testicles, in case you're munching one right now and wondering what you just ate.) Rockies Larry Walker, Todd Walker, and Jeff Cirillo often hit home runs, and the mascot, Dinger the Purple Dinosaur, is always performing antics somewhere. Obviously, baseball is not just for kids. It's a great place for a date on a summer evening, watching the sun set behind the stadium. You might even catch a fly ball and have a fun story to tell your co-workers at the watercooler. The Rockies still have the "Rockpile," where you can come on game day and buy tickets. Tickets in advance are generally $4 to $75; call (303) ROCK-IES. From I-25, take the Park Avenue West exit to reach the stadium. (See the Sports chapter for more information on the Rockies.)

FORNEY TRANSPORTATION MUSEUM
4303 Brighton Boulevard, Denver
(303) 297-1113
www.forneymuseum.org
The Forney collection consists of antique cars, buggies, and trains including *Big Boy*, the largest steam engine in the world. The famous pilot, Amelia Earhart, drove the Gold Bug Kissel roadster. You will also see Prince Aly Khan's Rolls Royce and the now infamous "Amphicar", the world's first amphibious vehicle produced in Germany from 1961–1968. The museum is open 9 a.m. to 5 p.m. Monday through Saturday and is closed on Sunday. Admission is $7.00 for adults, $6.00 for seniors, $4.50 for children ages 11 through 15, and $3.50 for children ages 5 through 10. Children younger than age five are admitted for free.

INVESCO FIELD AT MILE HIGH
1701 Bryant Street, Denver
(720) 258-3000
www.invescofieldatmilehigh.com
At Mile High, which is what loyal fans insist on calling this stadium, despite the name change, sports events are a special occasion, with or without kids. This is where the Broncos battle other National Football League teams, and often practically every seat in the stadium is occupied. That's part of the reason voters in 1998 agreed to

pay additional taxes in order to build the Broncos the new, modernized stadium that opened in August 2001. (See the Sports chapter for more information.)

PEPSI CENTER
1000 Chopper Circle, Denver
(303) 405-1100
www.pepsicenter.com
The Pepsi Center, located in Denver's central downtown area, officially opened on October 1, 1999. It replaced McNicholls Sports Arena, which was demolished in the fall of 1999. The Pepsi Center is home to about 160 sporting and entertainment events, including the National Basketball Association's Denver Nuggets and the Colorado Avalanche of the National Hockey League. Pepsi Center features include two dramatic, six-story atrium entranceways; views of the Central Platte Valley, downtown Denver, and the Rocky Mountains; a 236-seat club-level restaurant; 95 fully furnished luxury suites; and plenty of parking. The center is easy to reach off I-25; exit South Speer Boulevard to Auraria Parkway.

ELITCH GARDENS AMUSEMENT PARK
2000 Elitch Circle (off Speer Boulevard)
Denver
(303) 595-4386
www.elitchgardens.com
This is Denver's oldest and grandest amusement park, in a new location near lower downtown Denver. Families can enjoy the live restaurant entertainment and the progression from kiddie rides to hair-raising ones. The new location lacks the 100-year-old trees and turn-of-the-20th-century elegance of the former site, but with 67 acres, it's more than twice the size of the old park. The 1925 carousel with wooden horses is there. Twister, the famous wooden roller coaster, has been rebuilt, which relieves most parents, because although the old roller coaster was safe, sometimes you wanted to take a hammer on the ride and whack in a few extra nails. Like the old Twister, the new one is listed as one of the top 10 in the country by American Coaster Enthusiasts. The landscaping includes formal gardens, shaded

areas, and several thousand young trees. Elitch's is open 10 a.m. to 10 p.m. daily. Daily tickets are no longer available. A family four-pack season pass for four or more is $74.99 and an individual season pass is $79.99. You may choose to just buy a day pass for $34.99. Elitch Gardens is easy to find. To get there, take I-25 to Speer Boulevard South and head for the roller coasters.

EAST OF DOWNTOWN

In Denver, you'll find many child-pleasing attractions about 10 minutes east of downtown. We've discussed the addresses, hours, and fees of these in the previous section on Denver Attractions. Here's a look at them from a kid's point of view. Please refer to the individual listings on these attractions on previous pages for details.

With 23 lovingly landscaped acres, the **Denver Botanic Gardens** has room for serious gardeners and kids who need to frolic. At the **Denver Zoo,** the Tropical Discovery and the Primate Panorama exhibits are full of animals that would need overcoats out in a Colorado December. The polar bears and sea lions make any summer day seem cooler. They're most fun to watch from underwater portholes.

Next to the zoo is the huge **Museum of Nature and Science.** Just follow the crowd toward the Hall of Life and the wonderful mineral displays. They include twinkling gems, gold-filled boulders, and a quirky series of statuettes, all made of different colored stones. We grown-ups talk the kids into lingering in the Explore Colorado Hall, which has beautiful renditions of Colorado's prairie and alpine forest. Changing exhibits always pack in people.

While at the museum, enjoy the **IMAX Theater,** with 30 speakers to help the sound track thunder into your solar plexus while you watch cliff-hangers about sharks, volcanoes, and other wonders.

Shopping and Dining in Denver with Your Kids

Denver's premier shopping area is east on Speer Boulevard at Cherry Creek. Here you will find a variety of shops and fast-food restaurants. Some specific ones are listed below. With kids, downtown shopping is most fun around the Tabor Center, Larimer Square, and LoDo (pronounced low-dough), as lower downtown is known. It's not hard to find places to eat with kids. Most shopping areas have casual eateries.

KAZOO & COMPANY
2930 East Second Avenue, Denver
(303) 322-0973
www.kazootoys.com
The store is a full-service toy store specializing in educational items for children, parents, and teachers. The two-story store has a large selection of toys, puzzles, games, and creative items to suit the imagination of your child.

THE TABOR CENTER
1201 16th Street, Denver
(303) 572-6865
The food court in the Tabor Center, downtown by Larimer Square, offers Mexican food, cheesecake, Panda Express, and many other choices.

TATTERED COVER BOOK STORE
1628 16th Street, Denver
(303) 436-1070
www.tatteredcover.com
This is Denver's biggest bookstore, and the lower level has a comfortable reading sofa where older kids can peruse books while you browse. If you're double-teaming your kids, one of you can read with them while the other shops. They offer book signings on a regular basis and are open seven days a week.

TIMBUK TOYS
2780 South Colorado Boulevard, Denver
(303) 756-2522

200 Quebec Street, Denver
(303) 366-1755
www.timbuktoys.com
If you are looking for a wide selection of specialty toys priced moderately to expensive, this is the toy store for you. The store is well organized, and

the aisles are wide enough to accommodate strollers and wheelchairs.

THE WIZARD'S CHEST
230 Fillmore Street, Denver
(303) 321-4304
www.thewizardschest.com
Find all types of magic tricks and toys at this entertaining shop in Cherry Creek. Look for the big castle on the east side of Fillmore.

Family Accommodations
DENVER INTERNATIONAL
YOUTH HOSTEL $
630 East 16th Avenue, Denver
(303) 832-9996
www.youthhostels.com
The ultimate bargain accommodation, the youth hostel requires guests to pitch in and do a chore or two here as part of the deal. Like other youth hostels, the doors are locked during the day. Check-in time is between 8 and 10 a.m. and 5 and 10:30 p.m. There are about 30 beds total distributed among various dormitory-style rooms, plus kitchen and bathroom facilities. No frills, but clean and basic accommodations, and you're guaranteed to meet the guests from around the world.

HOLIDAY CHALET $$$–$$$$$
1820 East Colfax Avenue, Denver
(303) 321-9975
www.holidaychalet.com
Originally the home of the Bohm family and built in 1896, this immaculate and friendly hostelry is ideal for families and even accepts pets. It has a unique, historic charm with stained-glass windows and a crystal chandelier to add to the ambience. The 10 rooms/suites are all sunny and have their own personality with various nooks and crannies. Though Colfax Avenue is a bit noisy, the thick walls of the old mansion provide a quiet refuge. The rooms are three different sizes and each has a TV, VCR, kitchen, and bathroom. Prices range from $94–$160 per night and include a full breakfast.

LOEW'S GIORGIO HOTEL $$$–$$$$
4150 East Mississippi, Denver
(303) 782-9300
Kids might enjoy the looming *Star Wars* quality of this ultramodern hotel, which has a surprising northern Italian country-villa interior decor. The large property has 180 rooms and 20 suites, and the price includes complimentary continental breakfast and access to a fine sporting club. Though the hotel caters more to a business clientele, it offers weekend packages for families.

MELBOURNE INTERNATIONAL HOTEL &
HOTEL $
607 22nd Street, Denver
(303) 292-6386
For those seeking a private room at bargain prices, here's the place. Rooms have a refrigerator and some have private baths. Dorm rooms are also available. The hostel has a convenient downtown location and is clean and basic—definitely for the more adventurous and outgoing traveler or family. Check-in is from 7 a.m. to midnight, but those checking in after 7 p.m. should call first.

COLORADO SPRINGS
Getting There
Just two hours south of Boulder is Colorado Springs. To get there, take I-25 through Denver, and keep going south through the rolling foothills until you're at the foot of Pikes Peak mountain—and Colorado Springs. Try to avoid Denver rush hour, which can add a half-hour to the trip. If you squeak through Denver on weekends or when the traffic is lightest, some commuters who nudge the speed limit a bit say you can slip into town in about 90 minutes.

Top attractions in Colorado Springs are the United States Air Force Academy, Cave of the Winds, the Cheyenne Mountain Zoo, Garden of the Gods, and the Broadmoor Hotel. For quick, up-to-date information on the area, call the Colorado Springs Visitor Center at (719) 635-7506 or (800) 888-4748.

We'll tell you about these many special attractions next. But first, some perspectives from the past.

History

Before 1900, the Denver Rio Grande railroad wanted to establish communities near the remote Colorado foothills in order to profit from buying and selling goods along its train route. In 1871, it backed the Fountain Colony, with 150 buildings and 800 residents. The promoter, Gen. William Jackson Palmer, wanted a genteel, well-bred crowd, so he advertised "villa sites" to wealthy English compatriots. Thus began a community that would grow into Colorado's second-largest city, Colorado Springs, with nearly a half-million people.

One Englander said the brand-new community was a "very high-toned sort of new town" run by a "very tony company on teetotal lines." It was a tourist attraction and resort health spa for wealthy tuberculars.

Colorado Springs has gracefully reached much of its potential. But years ago, early settlers who had been assured they were moving to tree-lined avenues and fenced English farmlands got a big surprise when they saw the windswept plain. One irate Englishman, stepping out of his train in a March snowstorm, huffed in a furious, highbrowed Edwardian "haccent," "And h'is this the H'italian climate of H'america?"

The resort town diversified into many other businesses. Tourism, defense, and high-tech are big employers. North American Air Defense Command (NORAD) is dug deep into hollowed-out Cheyenne Mountain. South of town is Fort Carson, an active Army base. Colorado Springs is the site of the Winter Olympic Training Center and excellent colleges such as the Air Force Academy, Colorado College, and the University of Colorado at Colorado Springs.

Colorado Springs and Boulder share similar aspirations of being well-planned, beautiful, wealthy utopian communities. But if you could imagine social and political outlook as the pendulum of a great clock, then Boulder's liberal tendencies would pull the pendulum left, while the conservative outlook of Colorado Springs would swing the pendulum far to the right. This typecasting isn't set in stone. But it's a fair comparison that has stood the test of time. For instance, Boulder opposed Amendment 2, which denied "special rights" for gays; Boulder residents viewed the amendment as a hate vote against homosexuals. A Colorado Springs group called Coloradans for Family Values initiated that amendment. While many of the positions they take earn praise because they focus attention on family responsibility, this coalition also has raised concerns because of its hostility toward homosexuals and its growing demand to include Christian doctrine in public schools.

Attractions

AIR FORCE ACADEMY
I-25, Exit 156B, Colorado Springs
(719) 333-2025
Colorado's leading human-made attraction is the Air Force Academy at the base of Rampart Range. Under normal circumstances the visitor center is open 8 a.m. to 6 p.m. daily in the summertime, and it closes an hour earlier the rest of the year. But in the wake of the September 11, 2001 tragedy, the academy was closed to visitors until further notice. Call for current information.

Four thousand cadets train at the academy to become astronauts, pilots, engineers, scientists, and tactical leaders. The campus includes 143 acres of athletic fields, a 2,500-seat ice rink, and a 6,000-seat basketball arena. What's more, the setting is memorable. More than 18,000 acres of the campus are a wilderness refuge, thick with Colorado's scrubby native oak, Gambel's oak, pine trees, and other native plants.

When the campus was established in 1954, 340 architectural firms competed to design the buildings. The Chicago firm Skidmore, Owings and Merrill Architects and Engineers won. Their modern ideas stunned Congress. The chapel was described as an "accordion." That seems funny today, when most people consider that chapel a masterpiece. Overall, the buildings are as crisp as their crew-cut era. But their futuristic tone might make them appropriate for *Star Trek*'s Star Fleet Academy, too.

The visitor center displays space suits of graduates and shows free 14-minute informational movies every half-hour. Cadets lead a free campus tour.

The crown jewel is the chapel, with 17 gleaming aluminum spires that rise 99 feet into the clear blue sky. Ribbons of stained glass separate each spire and create a rainbow of color inside. The arrangement inside says something about the '60s worldview of American religion. The Protestant chapel on the main floor seats 1,200. The Catholic chapel, seating 500, is on the lower level, and in the back is a 100-seat Jewish worship area, with a nondenominational area behind. Generally, chapel hours are 9 a.m. to 5 p.m. Monday through Saturday and 1 to 5 p.m. Sunday (in summer, chapel hours are extended to 6 p.m. daily). There are weekly Protestant, Catholic, Jewish, Islamic, and Buddhist services. But the chapel occasionally closes for special services, such as funerals and weddings—and there are a lot of cadet weddings.

CAVE OF THE WINDS
U.S. Highway 24 West, Manitou Springs
(719) 685-5444
www.caveofthewinds.com
Just west of Colorado Springs, these caves are open 9 a.m. to 9 p.m. daily in summer; 10 a.m. to 5 p.m. the rest of the year. More than 200,000 people a year choose the standard 45-minute guided tour, which costs $14 for adults and $7 for kids older than age 6. Or, dress in clothing you won't mind getting muddy, bring a flashlight, and join the Lantern Tour, where an experienced guide goes climbing and crawling with you into danker, darker, mysterious places. The Lantern Tour lasts approximately one and a half hours. You will venture deep underground, exploring raw cave passages while listening to folklore and details of the history and geology of the Manitou Grand Caverns. The tour costs $18 for adults and $9 for children ages 6 through 15. Children younger than age six are not allowed.

For those who get flutter-nerved just thinking of that Lantern Tour, relax. The regular tour probes caves just deep and narrow enough to feel a little creepy sometimes, but they're perfectly safe. In some areas, tourgoers walk single file, but most corridors open into large cave rooms wondrously lit to show off the stalactites hanging from the ceiling and the stalagmites growing, century by century, from the floor. Hokey lighted areas get silly names from the guides. In one spot, the crusty gray rock has been rubbed smooth by the oil from millions of human hands, revealing a honeyed glow like alabaster.

CHEYENNE MOUNTAIN DIRECTORATE
(NORAD—North American Air Defense Command)
250 Vandenburg Street, Peterson
Peterson Air Force Base
(719) 554-6889
Following the September 11, 2001 tragedy, NORAD was closed to visitors until further notice. Call for current information. When the facility is open to the public, tours often fill six months ahead of time, so call early, for reservations are required. A bus takes visitors to the mountaintop auditorium for a briefing, slide show, and explanation of the mission of Cheyenne Mountain. Then visitors ride a bus through a tunnel to the NORAD Command Center—the entire complex is underground. Inside the facility visitors can walk around in a restricted area. Visitors also see an industrial area with reservoirs and turbines that power the facility. For obvious reasons, this is a high-security tour and you'll be asked for a photo I.D. and Social Security number.

CHEYENNE MOUNTAIN ZOO
4250 Cheyenne Mountain Zoo Road
Colorado Springs
(719) 633-9925
www.cmzoo.org
West of the Broadmoor Hotel, this is one of the largest privately owned zoos in the nation. It started in 1938 as Spencer Penrose's own collection and grew from there (Penrose built the Broadmoor Hotel). More than 145 species are at

the 75-acre zoo. Perhaps the 6,800-foot altitude invigorates the animals. Maybe it's the generally spacious pens. Whatever, the zoo is known for producing babies, including endangered species, such as tiny, golden tamarind monkeys, black rhinos, red pandas, snow leopards, and Andean condors. The most popular animal is the African elephant, followed by the orangutans in their large climbing area. The zoo is open 9 a.m. to 6 p.m. (last admission is at 4 p.m.) Memorial Day weekend through Labor Day, and 9 a.m. to 4 p.m. the rest of the year. Admission is $14.25 for adults; $12.25 for ages 12 to 17 and 64 and older; $7.25 for children ages 3 to 11. The entrance fee also gives you access to the Will Rogers Shrine of the Sun and beautiful vistas. From I-25, take exit 138 west to the Broadmoor, then turn right and follow the signs.

GARDEN OF THE GODS
I-25, Exit 146, Colorado Springs
(719) 634-6666
www.gardenofgods.com
This drive-through garden has 2.5 square miles of eroded red rocks that are remnants of ancient mountain ranges. The highest rock is 350 feet high, and the strange natural "sculptures" include formations known as Kissing Camels and Balancing Rock. To reach these spectacular natural formations take exit 146 and continue west until it dead-ends. Then take a left onto 30th Street. The park is open 8 a.m. until 8 p.m. daily between May 1 and October 31 and 5 a.m. to 9 p.m. from November 1 to April 30. The visitor center is open 8 a.m. to 8 p.m. in the summer, with shorter winter hours.

PIKES PEAK COG RAILWAY
515 Ruxton Avenue, Manitou Springs
(719) 685-5401
www.cograilway.com
Since 1891, the bright-red train cars have made the three-hour round-trip by following Ruxton Creek through the aspen and Englemann spruce forests of Pikes Peak. In addition to wheels and tracks, a cog train has a center cog gear that pulls the train up the mountain, useful against

slipping in steep spots. To get there, take US 24 to the Manitou exit. Go west on Manitou Avenue to Ruxton Avenue and turn left. In summer trains depart daily every hour and 20 minutes, with the first at 8 a.m. and the last at 5:20 p.m. Tickets cost $30.50 for adults; $17 for children ages 5 to 11 (July 1 to August 18: $32.50 and $18). Younger children ride free if they sit on your lap.

THE PIKES PEAK HIGHWAY
2 miles west of Colorado Springs on US 24
www.pikespeakcolorado.com
This scenic drive is generally open May through November. It's a long, slow way up, with many hairpin turns to the peak of Pikes, one of Colorado's highest mountains. At 11,578 feet, trees shrink to ground-huggers that might take 100 years to grow an inch. Here, you might spy yellow-bellied marmots. The 14,110-foot Pikes Peak is a boulder-strewn, windswept summit. Take a jacket, even if the temperature in Colorado Springs is more than 90 degrees. And stop at the Summit House, which has been selling delicious doughnuts and hot chocolate since the turn of the last century.

Since 1891, the Manitou and Pikes Peak Railway—the world's highest cog railroad, the highest Colorado railroad, and the highest train in the United States—has taken passengers to the 14,110-foot summit of Pikes Peak, which is the 31st-highest mountain in Colorado.

SANTA'S WORKSHOP
US 24, 10 miles west of Colorado Springs
(719) 684-9432
www.santas-colo.com
If you thought the North Pole was a few thousand miles away, here are new directions. This outpost, just 10 miles west of Colorado Springs, is open in the summer from 10 a.m. to 5 p.m. daily. Weather permitting, it's open in the fall from 10 a.m. to 5 p.m., except for Wednesdays and Thursdays. Generally, it stays open through Christmas Eve. This sweet little amusement park has 24 safe rides for

little kids, a full-size Ferris wheel (the 7,500-foot altitude makes it the highest wheel in the world), and a colorful cottage in which Santa Claus waits in his rocking chair. Kids can have their picture taken with a truly plump Santa, whose curly white beard is real. In summer, he often wears knickers with suspenders and a colorful shirt, or red trousers and boots with a colorful shirt. When it gets cold, Santa dons his red jacket. The cost for admission is $16.95 for ages 2 through 59; children younger than age 2 and seniors older than age 60 enter for free.

THE WINTER OLYMPIC TRAINING CENTER
1 Olympic Plaza, I-25 Uintah Exit 143
(719) 632-5551
www.olympic-usa.org
You may see Olympians—such as Amy Van Dyken, four-time gold medal swimmer, and John McCready, a member of the men's gymnastic team—training at the two sports centers here. Free tours are offered daily every hour on the hour from 9 a.m. to 4 p.m. (during summer, they're every half-hour). Groups of eight or more are asked to make group reservations. Otherwise you can just show up and take the tour, which includes a 15-minute film on the Olympics or the Olympic movement. The best times to see athletes training are on the 9 a.m. and the 4 p.m. tours. The center is closed Thanksgiving, Christmas Eve, Christmas, New Year's Day, and Easter.

Restaurants

The Broadmoor Hotel's many fine restaurants are described in the hotel entry in the next section on Accommodations. Other Colorado Springs choices are listed below. See the price-code key at the beginning of this chapter.

CHAMPPS AMERICANA $$
1765 Briargate Parkway, Colorado Springs
(719) 548-0113
http://restauranteur.com/champpscos
Decorated with memorabilia, Champps Americana is a popular hangout for all ages. Enjoy

soups, large salads, poultry, steak, burgers, and chops. Open for dinner.

THE DALE STREET CAFE $
115 East Dale Street, Colorado Springs
(719) 578-9898
A former Victorian home, this charming cafe offers Southern French and Northern Italian cooking, including homemade pizzas, pastas, soups, salads, and desserts. There are also grilled items and two fresh fish specials daily. Dale Street is open Tuesday through Saturday for dinner, Tuesday through Sunday for lunch and 10 a.m. to 3 p.m. on Sunday for breakfast.

GIUSEPPE'S DEPOT $$
10 South Sierra Madre Street,
Colorado Springs
(719) 635-3111
Kids especially like Giuseppe's, an old railroad station that has been converted into a restaurant. You can see freight trains go by, and there's a view of the mountain range, too. Ribs, steak, chicken, spaghetti, pizza, and a children's menu are available. The restaurant serves lunch and dinner daily.

LA CASITA PATIO CAFE $
4295 North Nevada Avenue,
Colorado Springs
(719) 599-7829
Right next to I-25, this pink stucco restaurant has great personality, down to the black velvet paintings, metalwork frames, and murals of tropical birds. Beer-soaked barracho beans, known as drunken beans, are a house specialty. Try the chicken or beef fajitas. La Casita serves breakfast, lunch, and dinner daily. Hours are Sunday through Thursday 7 a.m. to 9 p.m., Friday and Saturday 7 a.m. to 10 p.m.

THE PEPPERTREE $$
888 West Moreno Avenue, Colorado Springs
(719) 471-4888
www.peppertreecs.com
Here, the chef will prepare a pepper steak flamed

with brandy right at your table—or steak Diane, chateaubriand, or veal sweetbreads. The cuisine is continental and excellent. The atmosphere is very romantic, on top of a hill with a view of the city. Peppertree is open daily for dinner only from 5 to 9 p.m.

Manitou Springs Restaurants

This cute community just west of Colorado Springs offers lots of good restaurants.

THE BRIARHURST MANOR INN $$
404 Manitou Avenue, Manitou Springs
(719) 685-1864
www.briarhurst.com
Chef-owned and operated, this inn occupies the landmark home of the founder of Manitou Springs. Built in 1878, the mansion has seven different dining areas. The varied menu offers rack of lamb, chateaubriand, and trout. The steak tartar and alligator pears (an avocado stuffed with crabmeat and served with a special sauce) are great appetizers. The Briarhurst is open nightly for dinner. The restaurant hosts regular murder-mystery dinners with the last one of 2008 on December 27. Call for more information.

THE CRAFTWOOD INN $$$
404 El Paso Boulevard, Manitou Springs
(719) 685-9000
http://restauranteur.com/craftwood.com
This inn is another mansion, built in 1908. Regional Colorado cuisine is served, including venison, antelope, and wild boar. Ostrich and buffalo are also on the menu, plus vegetarian entrees, seafood, and other meats. The seven vegetables served with the meal are cooked separately to perfection then combined in a colorful medley. Entrees usually are served with wild rice or quinoa. There's a unique wine list along with views of Pikes Peak and a very romantic atmosphere. The Craftwood Inn is open nightly for dinner.

THE MISSION BELL INN $
178 Crystal Park Road, Manitou Springs
(719) 685-9089
www.missionbellinn.com

Come here for good Mexican food. The specialty is green chile with pork. Burritos come stuffed with green chile, and flautas are rolled with beef and onions, then baked with red chile.

Accommodations

Many Colorado Springs accommodations are also attractions. Read this section, even if you're not planning to stay overnight. These places take Visa and MasterCard. See the price-code key at the beginning of this chapter.

THE BROADMOOR HOTEL $$$$$
1 Lake Avenue, Colorado Springs
(719) 634-7711, (800) 634-7711
www.broadmoor.com
For Old World elegance, check into the Broadmoor Hotel. With more than 3,000 acres of delights, the Broadmoor, built in 1918, has 700 rooms in four different buildings. The exterior is Italian Renaissance. Authentic Chinese lion statues guard the entry. The renovated interiors have rich hunter green and burgundy decor. Although freshly decorated, the atmosphere feels straight from the Kennedy Camelot era. You might imagine Jackie, in a Chanel suit and pillbox hat, pulling on white gloves as she heads toward the Broadmoor's shops. A beautiful addition is a bridge across the lake that connects the main hotel with the Broadmoor West building for the convenience of the guests. Paddleboats can still glide under it, followed by the Broadmoor's famous white and black swans.

Three 18-hole championship golf courses, 12 tennis courts, a 90,000-square-foot golf/tennis clubhouse and spa, bicycle rentals, horseback riding, fly fishing, and hot-air balloon rides are all here. The children's program is famous, and hiking trails are right out the door.

Nine restaurants make the dining choices exquisitely difficult. The fanciest is the Penrose Room, with views of both city and mountains. This Edwardian salon offers such continental cuisine as chateaubriand served on silver place settings by tuxedo-clad waiters. The average price of dinner with wine and dessert is $200 for a couple. Charles Court is casual and contemporary, with one of the best wine lists in the country. Dinner for two here is around $150. Some specialties include baked double Colorado lamb chops with goat cheese and mustard seed crust; Prince Edward Sound grilled salmon; seared Colorado native bass; elk with lingonberry compote; and black-diamond rattlesnake quesadillas. The Tavern offers traditional fresh seafood, prime rib, and pasta, as well as an assortment of entrees cooked on the wood-burning open grill over pine, applewood, mesquite, and other flavor-enhancing woods. The average price for two is around $100. A babysitting service provides caregivers that come to the room. But if you wish to take them along, kids prefer Julie's sidewalk cafe, which serves sandwiches, salads, and ice cream.

Twenty-five specialty shops include Ralph Lauren, for women; Broadmoor Kids' Shop for infant and toddler wear; a year-round Christmas store; Cheyenne Gourmet for cooking enthusiasts; the Signature Shop for souvenirs; and the Espresso/Newsstand. The Golf Pro Shop and Tennis Shop are very popular.

During the summer, the average price for two people staying overnight is $400 to $530 for a regular room, with discount rates in the quieter seasons. For $3,170 you can have a night in the Penrose Suite. The sixth-floor suite features a parlor, sunporch, 20-seat dining room, and three bedrooms. Julie Penrose, wife of the Broadmoor's builder, Spencer Penrose, lived here in her later years. The furnishings include antiques she collected.

At Christmas, a package deal includes a room, dinner, and a show called *Colorado Christmas*, with carols sung by talent from Nashville's Opryland. There's also a movie theater on the grounds with first-run movies.

To get here, take exit 138 off I-25. This is the Circle Avenue exit. Go right (west). Circle Avenue changes into Lake Avenue, and at the end is the Broadmoor.

CRIPPLE CREEK

About 50 miles southwest of Colorado Springs

is the gaming town of Cripple Creek, with gambling, melodrama, and more. If you decide to go there, then find you want some peace and quiet to contrast with the hubbub, check out these two places. See our price-code key at the beginning of this chapter.

Accommodations

HOSPITALITY HOUSE TRAVEL PARK $–$$
600 North B Street, Cripple Creek
(719) 689-2513, (800) 500-2513
www.cchospitalityhouse.com
Owners Stephen and Bonnie Mackin say you can come here and get well—the place used to be a hospital. It has been renovated, and furnished with period furniture and modern amenities such as TVs. The property also has a hot tub and areas for volleyball and horseshoes. It's very relaxed and has a Victorian feel. Hotel prices range from $48 to $109. There are 50 spots with full hookups for RVs, along with tent spaces. Camping costs around $18 while RV hookups run about $24.

i Those going to Cripple Creek (near Colorado Springs) should go a bit farther to the charming town of Victor—at the end of the same road (Highway 67). It's only another 6 miles and Victor is where most of the mining in the area took place. It retains the historic character of the times more than Cripple Creek with its many casinos. Stroll around the small downtown area and enjoy the antiques shops—and don't miss the handmade broom and wax shop.

THE VICTOR HOTEL $$$
Fourth and Victor Streets, Victor
(719) 689-3553, (800) 748-4595
http://victorhotelcolorado.com
If you want to stay near Cripple Creek, consider The Victor Hotel. This award-winning Victorian hotel was built in 1899 and underwent a complete renovation in 1992. It currently has more than 20 rooms, which generally cost around $80 a night for two people. Take US 24 southwest of

Colorado Springs to Highway 67 and proceed about 18 miles.

THE GAMBLING TOWNS: BLACK HAWK AND CENTRAL CITY

Getting There

About an hour southwest of Boulder, on scenic Peak to Peak Highway, you enter tiny Gilpin County. The easiest route is to take Canyon Boulevard west to Nederland, then head south from Nederland on Highway 119. Enjoy the aspens and great mountain views. Pretty soon, you'll reach the biggest towns in the county—Black Hawk and Central City. These are Boulder's closest gambling centers, with colorful extras such as brightly painted buildings, historic cemeteries, nearby ghost towns, and one of the finest musical theaters in the west—the Central City Opera.

Those coming from Boulder might want to consider taking the Boulder County Express (303-829-1966)—an especially good way to travel if you're thinking of drinking while you're up in the mountains. Groups or individuals can go anytime at a cost of $25 per person round-trip; senior packages are available. You will be reimbursed $15 in cash from the Mardi Gras Casino in Blackhawk if you put 50 points on a player's card. All round-trips include casino packages for Colorado Central Station in Black Hawk. These packages consist of blackjack money, free drink coupons, and other extras—making the shuttle trip virtually free. There are daily shuttles normally leaving at 8:30 a.m. from Boulder, as well as shuttles on demand. Group charters of any size can be arranged in advance. Individuals or small groups should call for a reservation the night before or early on the morning of the trip. Colorado Central Station casino (see subsequent listing) offers transportation from Golden and Denver as does People's Choice (303-289-2222).

Love, Hate, or Whatever

Depending on your preferences, you'll either love these gambling towns or hate them. If you love them, you'll enjoy the easy entertainment in a beautiful mountain setting, with quaint touches of mining and mountain history.

But you may hate gambling, seeking, instead, a quaint mountain setting with a bric-a-brac of small mom-and-pop stores owned by third-generation mountain families. This section will describe what the mountain towns offer gamblers. Then it explains what Gilpin County has for those who want something in place of, or in addition to, the one-armed bandits. But first, to understand how legalized gambling has changed the area, consider its history.

i Take a trip to Black Hawk and Central City for the history as well as the gaming. A great place to start is the Gilpin History Museum, 228 High Street, Central City; (303) 582-5283.

History

Placer mining revealed gold south of Boulder, and dozens of mountain towns boomed. Central City and Black Hawk were among them. Up here, the Wild West was not so awfully woolly. Public drunkenness was the biggest crime problem (as it is again today), and miners felt comfortable sleeping in unlocked cabins with their gold dust under their pillows. One congregational preacher reported that, rather than being rude and wicked, a few Central City residents were well-educated and cultivated enough to be among the more pleasant families that "demand and appreciate good preaching."

The pros of a boomtown were showing when Central City built the Teller House Hotel in 1872, one of the most lavish hotels west of the Mississippi at that time. It had a luxurious bar and a tall diamond-dust mirror that was carried over precarious mountain roads by an oxen team. The Teller House drew Mae West and Mark Twain. Sarah Bernhardt and Edwin Booth appeared at the opera house in the 1880s. But the mining operations that fueled these fancy places were not so attractive. Mining sluices ruined the countryside. Trees were toppled to build peaked-roof houses on the sloping hills, leaving the mountains barren for decades.

By the end of World War II, the mother lodes were barren and most Gilpin County mining centers were ghost towns. A few, however, experienced a new boom. "We still get the gold," quipped Central City's mayor in the 1950s. "We get it from some 450,000 tourists a year."

Historian Robert G. Anthearn, author of *The Coloradans,* scorned Central City when he wrote in 1976 that it had become a "classical example of fakery in the world of tourist traps." He lamented, "That once charming little town was turned into the Coney Island of the Rockies."

Well, it was tawdry, but it didn't have gambling then. Before gambling, the colorful little hillside homes sheltered grizzled miners and third-generation families. The area limped downhill on fading tourism. Buildings were condemned, and many residents commuted to Boulder or Denver for work.

Colorado residents voted for gambling in 1990. The measure passed, with limitations. Bets had to stay low, and gambling would be legal in only three places—Black Hawk, Central City, and Cripple Creek. Interestingly, the measure was written so that even if one of the towns hated gambling, the state vote could impose it on them. (Since then, the law has been changed so that a town must want gambling before a state vote can bring it into the gaming community. So far, Coloradans have not voted for more gambling.)

Gilpin County voters went along with the state's gambling fever in 1990, hoping to save their towns. Many believed gambling would bring renewed tourism to the little shops and help restore the historic buildings. What they've discovered is that maintaining a community alongside a gambling center is a learning process. Businesses that tried to stick a slot machine next to their gift items couldn't compete with national casino chains that put slot machines wall-to-wall. Expenses such as buying slot machines and paying gambling taxes required deep pockets for getting started, and many local businesses went under. People who owned buildings in easy-to-reach areas made

good money by selling. Those who lived out of the way had a harder time selling, even though their regular livelihood was being smothered. So, with some people making fortunes and others losing modest savings, many of the area's pre-gambling residents left. Meanwhile, residents who stayed discovered that gambling profits did not just stay in their towns. The money went to state taxes and out-of-state investors.

As old-timers left, authentic charm left too. Local services dwindled. In Central City and Black Hawk today, don't count on buying gasoline (you can buy gas at the KOA campground on Highway 46, about 6 miles north, back toward Nederland). And those buildings that locals hoped would be restored often were gutted, with only the facade, or a copy of the facade, remaining.

People who view gambling more positively point out another set of facts. Many old buildings were beyond repair, and re-creating them has given the town a fresh, glitzy kind of charm. Those gutted interiors had been changed many times in the past already. Streets and utilities are in better repair, and the towns are prettier for walking. As for services, there weren't any basic services in Central City at the time gambling came in. Black Hawk had a little grocery store and two gas stations, which are gone. Some casinos sponsor local athletic teams and provide matching grants to local schools. Some residents who were struggling before now have nice new homes out of town. Shops can open and close almost weekly, according to the Black Hawk/Central City Chamber of Commerce, so it's hard to keep track of the businesses in town. Therefore some shops listed in this book may no longer exist, but new ones may have taken their places.

Without gambling, rural parts of Central City and Black Hawk might have faded into ghost towns. And after the newness of gambling wears off, perhaps diversity will return. Right now, the hunger to build yet another slot palace fuels development. Black Hawk has captured 53 percent of all the gaming revenues in the state. Central City and Cripple Creek fight for the remaining revenues. Central City has been blighted with the "extra-mile" syndrome: People either don't realize it's a mile away from Black Hawk or don't want to drive the extra mile. They see all the casinos in Black Hawk and think they've arrived at both destinations.

Central City has a lot more to offer than just casinos—richer history, the opera house, and the Gilpin History Museum, which gives visitors a good grasp of the city's colorful past. (See subsequent listings.) Be sure to visit the museum, especially if the kids are along, to learn about the area's mining history—it's only a block from the gaming area.

A Gambler's View of Black Hawk/Central City

Colorado's limited stakes tend to keep the focus on fun. Bets are $5 and less. Only poker, blackjack, and platoons of one-armed bandits are allowed at the nearly 40 parlors, and the maximum hours are 8 a.m. to 2 a.m.

Try setting aside some money—anywhere from $1 to $100—and see how long you can play before you lose it. One friend sets the limit at $20 for a night. Another goes for $50. They both recall times when they have played into the wee hours and managed to take home more than they brought, then other days when they have lost all their change in the first half-hour.

Slot machines gulp quarters everywhere. Some casinos offer good deals on food and entertainment. Central City and Black Hawk are less than a mile apart, linked by shuttle buses and plenty of on-the-street attendants. Altogether, the two towns have only six main streets, so it's easy to poke around. In general, Black Hawk gamblers seem more serious, drinking and looking intently at their cards, while Central City is a little more lighthearted. As one gambler puts it, you wander until you find where your luck seems best.

While we hate to end with a caution, here goes. For most people, gambling is just plain fun. But psychologists note that the problem of gambling addiction is growing. If this happens to you, be one of the lucky ones who seek help. Gambler's Anonymous (303-754-7119) in Denver is a source of assistance.

Casinos

BULLWHACKERS CASINO
101 Gregory Street, Black Hawk
(800) GAMBULL
www.bullwhackers.com

SILVER HAWK
100 Chase Street, Black Hawk
(303) 271-2500
Under the same ownership, the Bullwhackers and Silver Hawk casinos could be described as fancy in a cheesy sort of way. Bullwhackers offers transportation to and from Denver and Westminster (the RTD Park and Ride at Wadsworth, and the Boulder Turnpike, which is US 36).

CENTURY CASINO AND HOTEL
102 Main Street, Central City
(303) 582-5050
www.centurycasinos.com
Don't miss this traditional casino with a superior selection of the most popular penny game and your favorite table games. The casino offers lodging and quality restaurants.

COLORADO CENTRAL STATION
Highway 119, Black Hawk
(800) THE-ISLE
www.isleofcapricasinos.com
The game of Hold'em 88 was invented here. Now being offered in at least a half-dozen casinos, Hold'em 88 is a simpler version of Texas Hold'em, the most popular form of poker played at casinos. In Colorado, where $5 is the maximum amount allowable for any single bet, the Hold'em 88 player can lose no more than $10 on a single game. In Texas Hold'em, which has four betting rounds and up to five raises per round, a single game can cost a player more than $100. Set in an authentic railroad depot, this casino boasts at least 10 tables of blackjack and 7 poker tables, along with 600 slot machines.

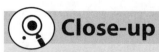

Close-up

Take a Grand Tour of Historic Central City

GILPIN COUNTY HISTORY MUSEUM

There are so many historic sights to see in Central City, but the best bet is to start at the Gilpin County History Museum. The museum, operated by the Gilpin Historical Society, opened in 1970 in a former stone schoolhouse. Skilled Cornish stonemasons constructed the two-story building, which once housed all of Central City's classrooms and later became the county high school in 1870.

The seven large rooms contain many possessions of the county's early pioneers. A re-creation of a Victorian parlor and dining room boasts a pump organ, Brussels carpets and period furnishings, a pioneer kitchen, and labor-saving devices. The Main Street display has a barbershop, a lawyer's office with Gov. John Evans's desk, a grocery store, a pharmacy, a doctor's office, a stationery and bookstore, a salon containing a roulette wheel once owned by Maxcy Tabor, and a re-creation of Baby Doe Tabor's cabin.

The mining display depicts the various mining processes and minerals from the 1867 mining exhibition in Paris. A history of the Chinese in Central City is also located here, along with a well-stocked gift shop featuring numerous books. The second floor features history on the local fire department, Native American artifacts, and a post office replica. A carpenter's shop and children's clothing and toys are also displayed.

In 2007 the keynote exhibit will focus on the 75th anniversary of Central City Opera's reopening. Opera dioramas, clothing, and props will be displayed. Twelve original works created by artist Herndon Davis will also be exhibited. Davis is the artist who painted the famous *Face on the Barroom Floor* in the Teller House.

Gilpin County History Museum, 228 High Street, Central City, (303) 582-5283, www.gilpinhistory .org. Hours: 11 a.m. to 4 p.m. daily Memorial Day weekend through Labor Day; other times by appointment. Admission: adults $5, children younger than age 12 admitted for free. A combination ticket with the 1874 Thomas House is available for $8.

THE THOMAS HOUSE

The 1874 Thomas House is a Greek-Revival residence owned by Central City's Thomas Family for 90 years. It reflects period interest in European classical styling, with such features as Doric columns, entablature pediment windows, applied plasters, and a secluded patio terraced with a Cornish mortarless rock wall. The outhouse was reconstructed in 2006.

Originally a one-room miner's cabin, the house was once owned by one of the Hendrie brothers, who jointly owned a Central City foundry. In 1897, George Billings, owner of the Billings Millwork Company in Denver, gave the house to his daughter, Marsha, as a wedding gift, and it remained in the family until 1987. The Gilpin Historical Society purchased the home, complete with its original furnishings, articles of clothing, and kitchen supplies.

The house is filled with advertising art and salesman's samples (Ben Thomas was a vice-president of the Sauer McShane Mercantile Company) and works of art done by Marsha.

FORTUNE VALLEY HOTEL AND CASINO

321 Gregory Street, Central City
(800) 924-6646
www.fortunevalleycasino.com

Fortune Valley is one of the newest casinos in this area and offers one of the largest selections of slots, video poker, video keno, live poker, and live blackjack in the state. It has earned the only three-diamond rating for a casino/hotel property in Colorado. The hotel boasts three restaurants, a deli, a steakhouse and a buffet.

Among the other items in the house are handmade quilts, dresses, hats, beaded bags, and a large assortment of hair combs and hatpins worn by Marsha. It is truly a house frozen in time and an excellent example of a Victorian middle-class home.

Thomas House Museum, 209 Eureka Street, Central City, (303) 582-5283, www.gilpinhistory.org. Hours: 11 a.m. to 4 p.m. Saturday, and Sunday Memorial Day weekend through Labor Day; other times by appointment. Admission: adults $5, children younger than age 12 admitted for free. A combination ticket with the 1870 Gilpin History Museum is available for $8.

TELLER HOUSE AND MUSEUM

The Teller House Hotel was built in 1872 as a grand Victorian hotel during Central City's boom days. It later became known for the mysterious face on the barroom floor painted by Denver artist Herndon Davis in 1936.The walls of the Face Bar are decorated with 10 murals depicting classical figures, each incorporating an intentional anatomical mistake.

The historic landmark, owned by the Central City Opera House Association since 1935, was originally touted as the finest hotel west of the Mississippi and hosted such notables as President Ulysses S. Grant. A path of silver bullion bricks was laid from Grant's carriage to the hotel's front door as a welcome mat during his 1873 visit.

The second-floor museum features furniture from the Tabor mansion in Denver, furnishings owned by Gov. John Evans, Colorado's second territorial governor, and a Wooton desk. The first floor has a gift shop selling numerous books and opera articles. The gift shop and tours of the Teller House are operated by the Gilpin Historical Society.

Teller House and Museum, 120 Eureka Street, Central City, (303) 582-5283. Hours: 10 a.m. to 5 p.m. daily Memorial Day weekend through Labor Day; other times by appointment. Admission: $4. Combination tickets that include the Opera House are $7.

CENTRAL CITY OPERA HOUSE

Built in 1878, the Central City Opera House is the centerpiece of the Central City Historic District and the site of the famous summer opera performances. The 2009 season runs from June 27 through August 2. A complete schedule may be found at www.centralcityopera.org. Tickets range from $50 to $99. Tickets may be ordered on the Web site or by calling (303) 292-6700.

The 550-seat opera house, designed by Robert Roeschlaub, Colorado's first licensed architect, is a Victorian jewel with an elaborate painted ceiling, excellent acoustics, and new, theater-style seating. Anne Evans and Ida Kruse McFarlane saved the property from decline in 1932. It re-opened later in 1932 with Lillian Gish starring in *Camille*. Other notable performers have been Buffalo Bill, Mae West, Shirley Booth, Myrna Loy, and Beverly Sills. The Gilpin Historical Society conducts tours of the Opera House.

Central City Opera House, 124 Eureka Street, Central City, (303) 582-5283. Opera information: (303) 292-6500. Hours: 10 a.m. to 5 p.m. daily Memorial Day weekend through Labor Day. Admission: $4. Combination tickets that include the Teller House and Museum are $7.

THE GILPIN HOTEL CASINO
111 Main Street, Black Hawk
(303) 582-1133
www.thegilpincasino.com
At the Gilpin, the eight poker tables play Texas Hold'em, Hold'em 88, Omaha, and occasionally Stud. There's also off-track betting for dog and horse races. The Gilpin Hotel started slot machine tournaments in Colorado, and they still have the biggest. This historic building has the original Victorian-style facade from 1869. It's brickwork adorned with ornate hardwood. The Mineshaft

Bar has been a local hangout for more than 100 years. It's full of memorabilia and offers nightly live entertainment that sometimes includes karaoke singing. There's free valet parking across the street. Lucille Malone's restaurant is named after the hotel's resident ghost. After Lucille's fiancé died after being run over by a wagon in front of the hotel, the distraught schoolteacher hurled herself off a balcony. Locals say she's been hanging around ever since.

Black Hawk/Central City
When You're Not Gambling

Some gambling friends complain that Black Hawk and Central City get boring after you've spent all your pocket change and are waiting for your friends to lose theirs. After all, this isn't Vegas. Some slot parlors don't even have a TV ball game. Fortunately, many casinos are catching on. Some places offer sports television and good restaurants, and if you step away from the casinos, you'll find other reasons to see these mountain towns.

CEMETERIES
West on Eureka Street, Central City
Ten cemeteries let you glimpse more mining-era history. Was the idea that Woodcutters, Masons, and Catholics would go to separate heavens? Judging from the separated plots, it looks that way. Actually, in those days, not everyone could afford a burial. So people were buried in plots bought by their fraternity, charity, or lodge. Children's tombstones bear witness to the worldwide flu epidemic of 1919, plus smallpox and other diseases that wiped out entire families.

CENTRAL CITY OPERA HOUSE
124 Eureka Street, Central City
Tickets and information:
Central City Opera House Association
400 South Colorado Boulevard, Denver
(303) 292-6700, (800) 851-8175
www.centralcityopera.org
Central City Opera is a beautiful, historic opera house built in 1878. The summer troupe is one of the oldest opera companies in the country, with a distinguished national reputation. All performances are in English, well-sung and wonderfully acted. Everyone stays in historic Victorian character, including the uniformed ushers, who ring brass hand bells when it's time to take your seat. The theater is beautifully decorated, right down to the handpainted murals of Pegasus and cafe chairs engraved with the names of famous benefactors. Every seat is good. You're close enough that the actors and actresses come across as real people who feel life so strongly, they've just got to sing about it. See our entry on the Central City Opera in The Arts chapter for details.

A dinner and ticket package is also offered, with catering provided by chef/restaurateur Kevin Taylor (from Rouge at the Teller House), at the Opera House. This includes a cocktail hour at 5 p.m. followed by a seated dinner at 6 p.m. Price is about $135 per person or $250 per couple. For tickets and information, call (303) 292-6700.

> **i** You can still find two funky little places to pan gold, Vick's Gold Panning and The Old Timer Panning (across from the Gold Dust Lodge), about 2 to 5 miles from Black Hawk on Highway 119. They don't have phones, so just drive down to see if they're open.

GILPIN COUNTY HISTORY MUSEUM
228 High Street, Central City
(303) 582-5283
www.gilpinhistory.org
Housed in the first stone schoolhouse west of the Mississippi, the museum displays about 10,000 artifacts arranged in period rooms such as a Victorian parlor and kitchen. Business memorabilia dating from mining days are here, including items from the doctor's office, the law office, bank, and more. A general store and hand-drawn firefighting equipment are on display, plus an early schoolroom from Russell Gulch. There's also a carriage display, doll collection, and mining tools. It's open daily Memorial Day to Labor Day from

11 a.m. to 5 p.m. and costs $5 for adults. Children age 12 and younger are admitted for free.

NEVADAVILLE GHOST TOWN
1 mile north of Central City

A mile above Central City is a real live—well, maybe not live—ghost town. In the 1800s, 4,000 people lived here, operating 20 quartz mills and several stores and hotels. Few historic structures still stand. But nothing's left of many other Gilpin County boomtowns. Lost cities include Deadwood Diggings, Dogtown, Eureka, Gambell Gulch, Gold Dirt, Glory Hole, Hoosier City, Quincy, Springfield, Trail's End, and Wide Awake.

ST. JAMES METHODIST CHURCH
123 Eureka Street, Central City
(303) 582-5882

Founded in 1859, this is the state's oldest church building. The stone structure was erected by Cornish masons in 1871. The stained glass is lovely; the pipe organ was installed in 1899. The church seats 350, and it's active today. It's open for free tours 11 a.m. to 4 p.m. daily in the summer.

THE THOMAS HOUSE
209 Eureka Street, Central City
(303) 582-5283
www.gilpinhistory.org

This is an 1874 Greek-Revival Victorian house. It's mostly yellow with white trim. However, Marsha Thomas was a free thinker, and on a trip back East she bought a gallon of salmon-colored paint for the porch. During every world war, the government ordered gold mining to stop in an effort to stabilize the economy, so in World War I Central City took a dive. Ben Thomas, vice president of the local mercantile store, no longer had any business. In 1917, the Thomases locked the house and relocated to Denver. Marsha visited for summer operas, but they never moved back. All the furnishings—from spices to fine art to the 13 different varieties of clocks—are intact from 1917. The corset of 4-foot, 11-inch Marsha hangs beside the long johns of 6-foot-plus-tall Ben. Because Marsha was so short, Ben cut the

legs off the kitchen's wood-burning stove so it would match her height. The house is open 11 a.m. to 4 p.m. Saturday and Sunday in summer only, with $5 admission for adults. (If you tour the Gilpin History Museum, too, the total cost is only $8 for both.)

Restaurants

Many of the casinos feature fast food—there's a Burger King in Colorado Central Station—but several offer very inexpensive buffets, too. For fine dining, it's wise to get a reservation. Below are a few recommended restaurants. See the price-code key at the beginning of this chapter.

FITZGERALD'S SHAMROCK CAFE $$
101 Main Street, Black Hawk
(303) 582-3203
www.fitzgeralds.com

This very green Irish-themed restaurant with comfortable booths and tables serves just about everything from corned beef and "shamrock stuffed potatoes" to salads, steaks, prime rib, hamburgers, pork chops, meat loaf, salmon, and pasta. It's open daily for breakfast, lunch, and dinner.

ROUGE AT THE TELLER HOUSE $$$$
120 Eureka Street, Central City
(303) 582-0600
www.ktrg.net

Rouge at the Teller House (brought to you by the Kevin Taylor Restaurant Group) is a modern mountain chophouse. The menu offers steak, seafood, and chops with clever, enticing makeovers. Appetizers and lighter fare are available at the Atrium, the Gardens, the Face Bar, and the Little Kingdom Room. The Kevin Taylor Restaurant Group and the Central City Opera have partnered to offer new seasonal dining options. Open only during the summer months, it closes Labor Day weekend.

Accommodations

See the price-key code at the beginning of this chapter.

**FORTUNE VALLEY HOTEL AND
CASINO** $$–$$$$$
321 Gregory Street, Central City
(303) 582-0800, (800) 924-6646
www.fortunevalleycasino.com
One of Central City's newer casino/hotels, it has
118 rooms, giving a big boost to the accommo-
dations options in this little county. It's the only
casino/hotel in Central City. Tony Roma's is the
on-site restaurant.

THE GOLD DUST VILLAGE $$
Highway 119, Black Hawk
(303) 582-5415
www.thegolddustlodge.com
On the main highway in Black Hawk, this lodge
offers 25 nicely decorated, comfortable rooms in
a convenient location.

**HOOPER HOMESTEAD
GUEST QUARTERS & SPA** $$$–$$$$$
210 Hooper Street, Central City
(303) 582-5828
www.hooperhomestead.com
Located on a beautiful historic hilltop location,
this is where you can find peace and relaxation
away from the crowds and noise of the casi-
nos. Take advantage of the Goddess Spa, which
includes aromatherapy wrap and spa treatment,
or enjoy a full-body deep tissue massage or a
heated stone massage. Rooms are priced from
$85 to $299. A continental breakfast is included
with rooms and suites. The Hooper Homestead
is child friendly.

SKI COUNTRY (BOTH SUMMER AND WINTER)

Winter Park and Summit County offer some of
the nation's best skiing and summer recreation.
Both are within a two-hour drive of Boulder. The
individual ski areas, resorts, and towns appear
on the following pages, with separate contact
numbers for each. There are also separate listings
for getting there, attractions, restaurants, accom-
modations, and recreation.

Please note that we list prices for accom-
modations instead of using the price-code key
in the Ski Country section. That's because rates
are rarely less than $100 per night, especially
during ski season, and can go upwards of $1,000
per night at the most luxurious condominium
complexes.

Winter Park

The town of Winter Park, 2 miles north of the
Winter Park ski area, offers numerous restaurants
and lodging places. It's set in a beautiful valley
surrounded by high peaks. Continuing northwest
on U.S. Highway 40 brings you to the small towns
of Fraser and Tabernash. Fraser often reports the
coldest temperatures in the country, so some
Coloradans call it "Freezer". But it's a beautiful
area with broad open meadows and spectacular
views. If you look up toward the Continental
Divide to the east, you might be able to spot
the jutting rock formation known as the Devil's
Thumb, north of Fraser, for which the nearby
cross-country ski resort was named. Continuing
north will eventually bring you to the town of
Granby and to the intersection with U.S. Highway
34, which leads to Grand Lake, on the western
boundary of Rocky Mountain National Park.

Getting There

Winter Park is 70 miles west of Denver. From
Boulder, drive south on Broadway (Highway 93)
toward Golden and, at the new Golden bypass,
follow the signs for I-70 West. Or you can take U.S.
Highway 6 up Clear Creek Canyon, which follows
the old Colorado Central Railroad bed and depos-
its you right on I-70 headed west. Follow I-70 and
exit onto US 40 West at Empire and continue
over Berthoud Pass, which is well-maintained all
winter. There are two entrances to the ski area:
Mary Jane offers expert skiing with challenging
mogul runs; the main Winter Park base is better
for beginners and intermediates. The town of
Winter Park is 2 miles farther on US 40. Fraser is 3
miles past Winter Park.

THE SKI TRAIN
Union Station, 17th and Wynkoop Streets
Denver
(303) 296-I-SKI
www.skitrain.com

During winter, the Ski Train provides another, more interesting way to get to Winter Park. It requires going into Denver, making the trip a bit longer than driving directly, but you won't have to deal with traffic or icy mountain roads. The Ski Train departs from Denver's Union Station at 7:15 a.m. and takes skiers within walking distance of the lifts. It goes through some 30 tunnels, including the 6.2-mile-long Moffat Tunnel, drilled a mile below the Continental Divide—a nifty ride and worth experiencing, especially with children. The Ski Train leaves Winter Park at 4:15 p.m., just after the lifts close. The trip takes two hours each way. The Coach Car fare is $59 for adults and $49 for kids for a round-trip during the winter months. The same trip is $85 in the Club Car, including continental breakfast and après-ski refreshments. Discounted lift tickets are available on the train. The Ski Train runs Saturdays and Sundays from mid-December until late March plus additional days during Christmas–New Year's week and on Thursdays and Fridays in mid-February.

Downhill Skiing

In winter, skiing and snowboarding, of course, are the main attractions at Winter Park.

WINTER PARK: THE RESORT AND AREA
677 Winter Park Drive
(970) 726-5514, (303) 892-0961
www.skiwinterpark.com

Winter Park operates on USDA Forest Service land, as do most Western American ski areas, but it is unique in that the city of Denver owns its assets, which are run by a nonprofit corporation. It is Colorado's fifth-largest ski area in terms of skier visits. Skiers and snowboarders can move among four interlinked mountains: the original Winter Park, Mary Jane, Vasquez Ridge, and Parsenn Bowl.

Twenty lifts, including seven high-speed express quads, access 1,414 acres of skiable terrain. Children's programs are exemplary, including day care for youngsters ages 2 months to 5 years and ski instruction for 3-year-olds to teens.

In recent years, the price for a one-day lift ticket was approximately $59 to $79 for adults. Discounted tickets are available at Front Range grocery stores and ski shops.

If you don't know how to ski or snowboard, January is a good month to learn. Winter Park offers instruction ranging from $40 to $70 per lesson. Discovery Park, a mid-mountain learning-area slope with its own slow-moving chairlift, is like a ski area within a ski area, where novices can practice comfortably.

Winter Park is also well-known for its disabled skiers program and is the site of the National Sports Center for the Disabled, located at 677 Winter Park Drive (970-726-1540). Founded in 1970, the center has 39 full-time employees, including instructors and coaches, and 1,000 volunteers who work with people with many different types of disabilities—cerebral palsy sufferers, amputees, paraplegics, and others—and provide nearly 11,000 private, customized lessons each winter. The center has expanded its scope to include snowboarding and snowshoeing lessons as well as a substantial program of adaptive summer sports.

Cross-Country Skiing

DEVIL'S THUMB CROSS-COUNTRY CENTER
3530 County Road 83, Tabernash
(970) 726-8231
www.devilsthumbranch.com

This center offers 105 kilometers of great groomed trails for beginners to advanced cross-country skiers. There are flat trails for beginners and smooth wide lanes for ski-skaters plus lovely rolling meadows and some steep downhills for thrills. A trail pass is $18 for adults. Seniors older than age 60 and kids under 12 are $8.

SNOW MOUNTAIN RANCH
1101 County Road 53, Granby
(970) 887-2152, (303) 443-4743
www.ymcarockies.org

In addition to various winter activities for kids and families, Snow Mountain has 100 kilometers of groomed trails, including 3 kilometers illuminated for night skiing. Single-day rail passes are $10 for YMCA members, $5 for children ages 6 through 12, and seniors 61-69. Seniors 70+ are free. Fees for nonmembers range from $15 - $8

Other Winter Activities
DASHING THROUGH THE SNOW
1400 County Road, Tabernash
(970) 726-0900
www.dashingthruthesnow.com

These are one-hour tours that leave daily from 12:30 to 5 p.m. Enjoy hot chocolate by a roaring bonfire or dessert sleigh rides that take you to a cabin where you enjoy hot chocolate and wonderful desserts. Private rides are available as well.

DOGSLED RIDES OF WINTER PARK
King Crossings Road at the Railroad Crossing
(970) 726-8326
www.dogsledrides.com

Dogsled teams take riders through 1,000 acres of pristine backcountry. Sleds pulled by 8- to 10-dog teams—all purebred Siberian huskies—can attain 30 miles per hour on downhill stretches. The cost for a 45-minute ride varies at different times of winter, but figure on about $87 per person; reservations are required.

GRAND ADVENTURE BALLOON TOURS
P.O. Box 1124, Winter Park, CO 80446
(970) 887-1340
www.grandadventureballoon.com

This is a wonderful opportunity to see the majestic Colorado Rockies from above. Flights depart at sunrise and are approximately one hour, depending on wind direction and fuel consumption. There is no flying if winds exceed 6 mph. The entire trip takes three hours. Rates are $225 per person. Child care is provided for $20 for children younger than age four.

SNOWCAT TOURS
Departures from the Balcony House,
at the base of Winter Park
(800) 729-7907
http://oldsiteskiwinterpark.com.activites/
snowcattours.html

Nonskiers can enjoy the ambience of the slopes by taking a two-hour mountain tour. They have frequent departures.

SOMBRERO RANCH
Winter Park
(800) 979-0332
www.skiwinterpark.com/todo/grandcounty

Sombrero Ranches offer the only sleigh rides in Winter Park. Let the team of Belgians or Percherons guide you through the meadows along the Fraser River. The entire trip, including 15 minutes by the campfire, lasts for one hour. Private sleigh rides are also available. Rides depart at 1:30, 3:30, and 5:30 p.m. Arrive 30 minutes before your scheduled ride.

WINTER PARK ICE-SKATING RINK
Cooper Creek Square, Winter Park
(970) 726-4118
www.winterpark-info.com

Bring the whole family and enjoy free ice skating here; skate rentals are available nearby at the Ski Broker and SportsStalker. Call the Winter Park/Fraser Valley Chamber of Commerce (303-422-0666 or 970-726-4118) for information on snowmobile tours and rentals and other winter diversions.

Summer Activities, Events, and Attractions
ALPINE SLIDE, ZEPHYR EXPRESS, AND OTHER WINTER PARK ATTRACTIONS
Winter Park Resort, 677 Winter Park Drive
(970) 726-4221
www.skiwinterpark.com

The Alpine Slide is Colorado's longest, and a big summer attraction for young and old.

With special bike mounts, Winter Park's Zephyr Express chairlift takes mountain bikers to the top, where they can ride 45 miles of steep, exciting single-track trails and gentler jeep roads. Rental bikes are available.

Also at the resort you'll find miniature golf, a human maze, a climbing wall, a zip line, mountain scooters, and chairlift rides to the top of the mountain. In recent years, full-day park passes for all activities were $49, and morning or afternoon half-day passes were $44. Passes for anyone younger than age 5 or older than age 70 are free. Summer hours are 10 a.m. to 6 p.m. (5 p.m. in September, weather permitting).

ARAPAHOE NATIONAL FOREST
Ranger District Office
(970) 887-4100
Visitors to the national forest will enjoy fishing, hiking, horseback riding, jeeping, and rafting. The Winter Park Chamber of Commerce (970-726-4118) has information about outfitters.

BICYCLING
(970) 726-4118
www.skiwinterpark.com/biking/index.htm
Bicycling is a popular participant sport and Winter Park accommodates cyclists with 600 miles of marked, mapped, and maintained trails. There are 10 bike shops in the Fraser Valley. Free town rides are held every Thursday evening and free women-only rides take place on Wednesdays throughout summer. Trail maps are available online.

THE HIGH COUNTRY STAMPEDE RODEO
John Work Arena, 1 mile west of Fraser
(970) 406-1335
The rodeo takes place every Saturday evening from early July to late August. The junior rodeo gets under way at 5:30 p.m., followed by the pros. Bull riding, bronc busting, barrel racing, and other popular events are held. In recent years admission was $10 for adults and $6 for children. A low-cost barbecue dinner is also available.

THE POLE CREEK GOLF CLUB
6827 County Road 5, Tabernash
(970) 887-9195
www.PoleCreekGolf.com

Golf Digest named this the best public course in Colorado. It offers golfers 18 holes of gorgeous greens. In recent years greens fees were $85 and $65 (for high and low seasons, respectively).

WINTER PARK RESORT MOUNTAIN BIKE RACE SERIES
239 Winter Park Drive, Competition Center
(970) 726-1590, (303) 316-1590
www.skiwinterpark.com/biking/index.htm
The resort hosts this annual series, which is composed of six events with different formats, including hill climb, circuit racing, and point-to-point racing. It's held from early June to early August. Two hundred and fifty competitors age 8 and older take part in each event. The entry fee is $35 in advance or $45 on race day.

WINTER PARK RESORT MUSIC FESTIVALS
Winter Park Resort, 677 Winter Park Drive
(800) 903-7275
Winter Park also hosts two major music events in July: The KBCO World Class Rock Festival and The Winter Park Jazz Festival, featuring nationally known bands.

Restaurants
The price-code key for restaurants appears at the beginning of this chapter.

CARVER'S $
93 Cooper Creek, Winter Park
(970) 726-8202
Tucked into a log cabin behind Cooper Creek Square, Carver's offers excellent baked goods and an eclectic menu that includes burgers and pasta, sandwiches, and lots of vegetarian fare, all moderately priced. Breakfast and lunch are served daily, and dinner is served Thursday through Sunday.

CROOKED CREEK SALOON & EATERY $
401 Zerex Avenue, Fraser
(970) 726-9250
www.crookedcreeksaloon.com

This is a family-style Mexican and American restaurant that is best known for giant burgers and fiery wings. There are also steaks and pasta. It's open daily for lunch and dinner with the bar open until 2 a.m. One margarita, two margarita, three margarita, floor.

GASTHAUS EICHLER $$
78786 US 40, Winter Park
(970) 726-5133
www.gasthauseichler.com
This place is noted for Austrian and German specialties. Try the veal dumplings, bratwurst, or goulash. It serves breakfast to overnight guests only, and lunch and dinner to the public. Reservations are suggested.

HERNANDO'S PIZZA AND PASTA PUB $
78199 US 40, Winter Park
(970) 726-5409
This is a local favorite for homemade pastas, including delicious lasagna, as well as good pizza and a summer beer garden. Hernando's is open for lunch and dinner during the summer, dinner only during the winter months.

THE SHED $
78672 US 40, Winter Park
(970) 726-9912
This is a longtime Winter Park favorite, now serving hearty breakfasts and Southwestern-style dinners. The weekend buffet is popular with skiers. It's closed on both Tuesday and Wednesday.

WINTER PARK: THE RESORT
AND AREA $–$$$
677 Winter Park Drive
(970) 726-5514, (303) 892-0961
The Winter Park ski area has dining options both at the base and on the mountain. The Coffee and Tea Market in Winter Park's Balcony House is open for breakfast and lunch, and the nearby West Portal Station day lodge has self-service snack and lunch service as well as the Derailer Bar. The Mary Jane Center features a cafeteria, a sit-down restaurant called The Club Car, and Pepperoni's Pizza and

Sports Bar. The beautiful and monumental Lodge at Sunspot, at the top of the Zephyr Express chairlift, offers snacks and lunches at The Provisioner, a self-serve facility; table service is available in the Dining Room, which is also open for dinner Thursday, Friday, and Saturday evenings in winter, with access via gondola. Reservations are recommended. Other on-mountain eating facilities include Snoasis, mid-mountain at Winter Park; and Lunch Rock and Sundance Cafe, snack bars atop Mary Jane and Vasquez Ridge, respectively.

Accommodations
Reservations are necessary in this popular area for most accommodations. You can make them through **Winter Park Central Reservations** (800-979-0332) or by calling individual properties.

DEVIL'S THUMB RANCH RESORT
3530 County Road 83, Tabernash
(800) 933-4339
www.devilsthumbranch.com
This is a quiet, beautifully located retreat ski lodge open year-round. It is equally nice for cross-country skiing on 100 kilometers of track in the winter and horseback riding, hiking, fly fishing, and mountain biking in the summer. Cabin rentals are consistent for both summer and winter months. Three miles north of Fraser (before the bridge entering Tabernash), turn east (right) off US 40 onto County Road 83; after another 3 miles take the right fork in the road. Rates range from $315 to $895 per night.

GASTHAUS EICHLER
78786 US 40, Winter Park
(970) 726-5133, (800) 543-3899
www.gasthauseichler.com
This small, European-style hotel offers rooms that are warm and cozy, with all of the modern conveniences. The down comforters and lace curtains add to the European flavor. The restaurant serves authentic German cuisine, and the guest list often includes many from Europe, creating a lively, international atmosphere. Rates start at around $69 without meals and $250 with meals.

THE GRAND VICTORIAN
78542 Fraser Valley Parkway
Winter Park
(970) 726-5881, (800) 204-1170
This is the first among equals when it comes to Winter Park's growing selection of charming bed-and-breakfast inns. Secluded in a grove of lodgepole pines, this romantic neo-Victorian offers lodging in three sumptuous fireplace suites. The rates include a gourmet breakfast and afternoon drinks and hors d'oeuvres.

THE IRON HORSE RESORT
101 Iron Horse Way, Winter Park
(970) 726-8851
www.ironhorse-resort.com
This ski-in, ski-out property has 130 rooms, all with full amenities, including fireplaces. A full-service restaurant, with room service, and heated indoor and outdoor pools are other pluses. In addition to winter ski packages, golf packages are offered during summer months. Call for current rates.

SUPER 8 MOTEL
78665 US 40, Winter Park
(970) 726-8088, (888) 726-8088
Right in town, the Super 8 has 60 rooms, all with two queen-size beds and some with refrigerators. Rooms run to around $135 during winter and $70 in summer. Room rates here increase dramatically during the ski season and on certain festival weekends.

ZEPHYR MOUNTAIN LODGE
201 Zephyr Way, Winter Park
(970) 726-8400
www.zephyrmountainlodge.com
Zephyr Mountain Lodge offers ski-in, ski-out lodging with luxury condominiums situated at the base of the resort. They offer a state-of-the-art fitness room, four outdoor hot tubs, free high-speed Internet in every room, and heated, underground parking. Room rates start at about $155 per night and range to $1,130 per night for a suite.

Summit County
The four Summit County ski areas of Breckenridge, Copper Mountain, Keystone, and Arapahoe Basin collectively attract more skiers and snowboarders than any other ski destination in North America. They offer an incredible range of great terrain. During summer, Summit County offers hiking and backpacking in the Arapahoe National Forest; fishing and boating on Lake Dillon; whitewater rafting on the Blue River; and an excellent network of bike trails and several good golf courses, as well as a calendar full of special events and festivals. Forest information is available from the Dillon Ranger District Office (970-262-3486).

The Summit County towns of Breckenridge, Dillon, Silverthorne, and Frisco—and the resort developments of Keystone and Copper Mountain—also offer outstanding restaurants and accommodations, all in proximity to the Greater Denver area and Boulder.

Getting There
Road condition or traffic slowdowns excepted, all Summit County ski areas are less than a two-hour drive from Boulder. Drive south on Broadway (Highway 93) toward Golden and, at the Golden bypass, follow the signs for I-70 West. Or take US 6 up Clear Creek Canyon directly to I-70 West. Follow I-70 to the Eisenhower Tunnel. For Arapahoe Basin, exit at US 6 West over Loveland Pass. For all the other resorts, proceed through the tunnel. Keystone is reached by taking the first exit after the tunnel, which is US 6 East. For Breckenridge, take the Frisco exit and drive south on Highway 9 for about 9 miles. Copper Mountain is directly off I-70, at exit 195, just before the highway climbs up to Vail Pass.

Breckenridge
Breckenridge, the town, is the oldest and largest of the Summit County communities and home to the Breckenridge Ski Resort. The town was founded in 1859 when gold was discovered in the area. It remains a picturesque and historic renovated mining town. The main street is still lined with some of the handsome Victorian homes that housed the first prosperous citizens,

along with numerous restaurants, cafes, shops, and art galleries. Every summer the National Festival of Music at Breckenridge mounts a two-month season of classical music.

DOWNHILL SKIING

BRECKENRIDGE SKI RESORT

1599 C Summit County Road 3
Breckenridge
http://breckenridge.snow.com

Breckenridge, the ski area, is huge and wide-ranging. Peak 8 is the original ski area, with a complex network of interlaced trails for all ability levels. It also offers access to high, above-the-treeline bowls and chutes as well as Peak 7, a steep mountain that is patrolled but not groomed and has no lift service—extreme terrain by anyone's standards. Peak 9 offers the greatest concentration of beginner and novice terrain and access to Peak 10, fabled for moguls, steeps, and open glades. You can ski from mountain to mountain and back again, crisscrossing Breck's 1,600-acre playground via different routes each time. There are excellent children's facilities at both the Peak 8 and Peak 9 bases. Breckenridge has long welcomed snowboarders with a half-pipe, terrain features, and just plain good riding.

Breckenridge has 135 trails on 2,031 acres with 20 lifts. In recent years, at-the-window tickets were about $80 for adults (one-day passes), with discount tickets available at King Soopers and Safeway. Children's lift tickets (ages 5 to 12) are about $40. Discounted tickets are also available online.

CROSS-COUNTRY SKIING

THE BRECKENRIDGE NORDIC CENTER

1200 Ski Hill Road, Breckenridge
(970) 453-6855
www.breckenridgenordic.com

The Breckenridge Center has more than 23 kilometers of groomed track set in the valleys below Peaks 7 and 8. The Breckenridge and Frisco (see entry later in this chapter) Nordic Centers are under the same management and share an interchangeable trail pass. Both offer instruction and rentals of cross-country skis and snowshoes.

OTHER WINTER ACTIVITIES

BRECKENRIDGE RECREATION CENTER

880 Airport Road, just off Highway 9
Breckenridge
(970) 453-1734
www.townofbreckenridge.com

This outstanding facility offers indoor lap and recreational pools, a kiddie fountain, tennis and racquetball courts, a running track, fitness facilities, a climbing wall, and a variety of programs. There are also outdoor tennis, basketball, and volleyball courts, a skateboard park, and a playground. It is open 6 a.m. to 10 p.m. on weekdays, 7 a.m. to 10 p.m. on Saturdays, and 8 a.m. to 10 p.m. on Sundays. Nonresident adults pay $10; youths ages 13 to 17 and seniors age 60 and older, $6; children ages 3 to 12, $5; toddlers 2 years of age and younger get in free.

ICE SKATING AT MAGGIE POND

Village of Breckenridge, 535 South Park
Avenue, Breckenridge
(970) 547-5726 (Maggie Ski Rental Shop)

There's ice skating on Maggie Pond at the village of Breckenridge, behind the Bell Tower Mall. Cost is $12 for adults and $8 for children. At the time of this printing they are not sure when they will open in 2009, possibly as late as March. Please call for details.

SLEIGH RIDES/SNOWMOBILING/DOGSLED RIDES

Breckenridge Guest Services and
Activity Center
150 West Adams Street, Breckenridge
(970) 453-2918
www.brecksleighrides.com
www.snowmobilecolorado.com

Skiing is the No. 1 activity in winter in Summit County, but other options, snow-related and otherwise, abound. Winter sleigh rides, snowmobiling, dogsled rides, and other activities can be arranged by the Breckenridge Activity Center. In addition to making reservations, it can provide information on prices, hours, and availability of off-slope activities. Contact Good Times (970-453-7604) to arrange snowmobile tours, sleigh rides, and dogsledding trips.

SUMMER ACTIVITIES, EVENTS, AND ATTRACTIONS

THE BRECKENRIDGE GOLF CLUB
200 Clubhouse Drive, Breckenridge
(970) 453-9104
This club offers outstanding golf at America's only Jack Nicklaus–designed municipal course. High-season greens and cart fees are about $110 for 18 holes.

BRECKENRIDGE STABLES
1799 Ski Hill Road (above the Super Slide on Peak 8), Breckenridge
(970) 453-4438
This stable offers rides over the Ten Mile Range and prides itself on its gentle horses. A 90-minute ride is $50, half-price for children age 6 and younger.

NATIONAL REPERTORY ORCHESTRA
111 South Main Street, Breckinridge
(970) 453-5825
www.nromusic.com
This festival of classical music usually begins June 10 and continues through August. The orchestra performs at the beautiful Riverwalk Center, which was completed in 1993. Tickets are $22 to $32 per person.

SUMMIT COUNTY HISTORICAL SOCIETY
111 North Ridge Street, Breckenridge
(970) 453-9022
www.summithistorical.org
The society conducts a variety of walking tours, mainly in summer but also in winter on request.

WASHINGTON GOLD MINE/LOMAX PLACER GULCH
469 Illinois Gulch Road, Breckenridge
(970) 453-9022
301 Ski Hill Road, Breckenridge
(970) 453-9022

COUNTRY BOY MINE
(970) 453-4405
0542 French Gulch Road, Breckenridge
www.countryboymine.com
You can tour some of Breckenridge's mines or pan for gold (panning is around $10) and take a step back in mountain time; call for more specific info. The price is about $19 for adults and $12 for kids. For directions, call the Breckenridge Guest Services at (970) 453-5579, they're open every day from 9 a.m. to 6 p.m.

RESTAURANTS

The price-code key for restaurants appears at the beginning of this chapter.

BLUE MOOSE RESTAURANT $$
540 South Main Street, Breckenridge
(970) 453-4859
The Blue Moose offers a casual atmosphere with a wide range of American-style food served at breakfast and lunch.

THE CAFE ALPINE $$
106 Adams Street, Breckenridge
(970) 453-8218
The charming Victorian setting complements the eclectic menu, which includes steak and seafood. The Alpine is open for lunch and dinner during the summer, for dinner only during winter months.

MI CASA MEXICAN RESTAURANT AND CANTINA $
600 South Park Avenue, Breckenridge
(970) 453-2071
Mi Casa has traditional Mexican specialties served at lunch and dinner. Specials also include Mexican-style pork chops and steak.

MOUNTAIN SAGE CAFE AND GOLD PAN SALOON $
105 North Main Street, Breckenridge
(970) 547-4628
Enjoy a Tex-Mex breakfast, or cheap pizza and bar food later in the day. There are also burgers, veggie wraps, and steaks.

RELISH $-$$
137 South Main Street, Breckenridge
(970) 453-0989
www.relishbreckenridge.com
Located on the Riverwalk on the former site of
Pierre's, Relish is fairly new to Breckenridge. The
restaurant features simple yet elegant dinner
entrees, as well as smaller choices at very affordable prices. You'll find lovely cocktails and appetizers during their daily happy hour from 4 p.m.
to 6 p.m. They are open nightly for dinner from
5 p.m. to 9 p.m.

THE ST. BERNARD INN $
103 South Main Street, Breckenridge
(970) 453-2572
The St. Bernard specializes in classic Northern
Italian food and also offers contemporary cuisine.
The inn is open for lunch and dinner; there's a
lounge, too.

ACCOMMODATIONS

With lodging for nearly 25,000 visitors, Breckenridge ranks as one of Colorado's major resort
towns, offering all types of overnight options
in many price ranges. Call the Breckenridge
Resort Central Reservations (888-251-2417) for
information or reservations at the town's many
condominiums, bed-and-breakfasts, and other
accommodations.

BEAVER RUN RESORT
620 Village Road, Breckenridge
(800) 265-3560
www.beaverrunresort.com
A ski-in, ski-out establishment on Peak 9, this is
Breckenridge's largest property, with lodging
ranging from hotel rooms to three-bedroom
suites. The fully equipped resort has indoor and
outdoor swimming pools, hot tubs, fitness facilities, shops, restaurants, and even an indoor miniature golf course.

FOUR PEAKS INN
407 South Ridge Street, Breckenridge
(888) 251-2417
www.gobreck.com
This 1880s Victorian bed-and-breakfast is located
200 yards from Peak 9 lifts. The inn is centrally
located and is perfect for couples and families.
A gourmet breakfast and afternoon snacks are
included in the price.

GREAT DIVIDE LODGE
550 Village Road, Breckenridge
(970) 453-4500
www.greatdividelodge.com
Formerly the Hilton, the lodge offers full hotel
services, including complimentary van service.
Rooms have two queen-size beds, a king-size
bed, or a king-size bed with a sleeper sofa. An
on-site restaurant provides room service, and a
lounge, indoor swimming pool, workout room,
sauna, and hot tub are on the premises. Prices
for rooms begin at $225 per night in winter and
$160 in summer.

Copper Mountain
Copper Mountain is a self-contained resort that
was constructed more than half a century ago
and has since won kudos for its outstanding trail
and slope design as well as its compact and congenial village. It has the distinction of being the
site of Club Med's first and only North American
ski village.

DOWNHILL SKIING

COPPER MOUNTAIN RESORT
209 Ten Mile Circle, Copper Mountain
(I-70, Exit 195)
(888) 219-2441, (866) 841-2481
www.coppercolorado.com
Copper Mountain, which celebrated its 50th anniversary in 1997, is treasured for its well-laid-out
terrain and congenial ambience. Copper Mountain
is famous for its logical layout. As you are looking
at the mountain, with I-70 at your back, most of
the easy terrain is in the middle, most of the inter-

mediate runs are in the middle or on the right, and most of the challenging turf is to the left. Copper Peak, 12,441 feet, is (after Arapahoe Basin) Colorado's second-highest lift-served summit. Spaulding Bowl, Union Bowl, and Resolution Bowl have long been favorites with powder-loving skiers and snowboarders, but in 1995–1996, the area built the first of two lifts in Copper Bowl and catapulted into the top rank of Summit County ski areas. All the bowls are steep snow pockets, treasured by advanced skiers and riders.

Copper Mountain now boasts 21 lifts (including three high-speed express chairlifts), 2,601 vertical feet, and 2,433 acres of skiable terrain—the most in Summit County. If you start at the village center, you have the choice of two high-speed express lifts, American Flyer or American Eagle, that shuttle skiers toward Copper Peak and Union Peak, respectively. These two summits, the snow-kissed slopes cascading down on all sides and the valley between them offer a sensational array of ski and snowboard terrain for all ability levels. The Union Creek area, with a separate day lodge, is one of Colorado's best novice areas. If you're a new skier who needs practice, you can ride the K and L lifts and ski nearly 1,000 vertical feet of gentle terrain free of charge during part of the ski season.

Copper's well-regarded day-care facility is in the Mountain Plaza Building. The children's ski school, which offers ski lessons for kids age 3 and up as well as snowboarding instruction for older children, is headquartered in its own building, with ski school desk, kids' equipment rentals, and food service under one roof.

At-the-window, one-day tickets cost about $65 for adults, $50 for seniors aged 60–69 and $35 for children ages 6 through 14 and those 70 and above; kids age 5 and younger are admitted free. They also offer a patriot ticket rate of $50 for military members and their immediate family. Discount tickets are available at King Soopers, Safeway, Albertson's, Diamond Shamrock, Total, Christie Sports, and other locations. The Copper Card enables you to buy up to four lift tickets discounted to the lowest available price every time

you visit. It also offers additional discounts on food at the resort and on goods and services at Copper and elsewhere in Summit County. You can obtain more information from the resort or call the Summit Chamber of Commerce at (970) 668-2051.

CROSS-COUNTRY SKIING

Twenty-five kilometers of machine-set tracks and skating lanes start at Union Creek and wind through the wooded valleys of the Arapahoe National Forest.

SUMMER ACTIVITIES, EVENTS, AND ATTRACTIONS

During the summer months, Copper Mountain offers golf, horseback riding, mountain biking, paddleboat rides, tennis, and free scenic chairlift rides. Over Labor Day weekend, the resort hosts Michael Martin Murphey's WestFest—three days of country-western music, crafts, and food. Call (970) 968-2882 or (800) 458-8386 for details.

COPPER CREEK GOLF COURSE
104 Wheeler Place, Copper Mountain
(888) 219-2441, (866) 841-2481
At 9,650 feet, this is the highest-altitude 18-hole championship golf course in America. It is said that balls will fly 15 percent to 20 percent farther here than at sea level. Greens fees are about $50 for 9 holes, $80 or so for 18. Golf packages are available.

THE WHEELER-DILLON PACK TRAIL
Copper Mountain Stables
355 Beeler Place, Copper Mountain
(970) 968-2232
This trail begins across the highway from Copper Mountain and climbs steeply into the rugged Gore Range. It offers a challenge for hikers, backpackers, and horseback riders. Pack trips can be arranged through the stable.

RESTAURANTS

The price-code key for restaurants appears at the beginning of this chapter.

BEACHSIDE PIZZA AND PASTA $

I-70, in the Copper Junction Building
(970) 968-2882

This eatery is at the base of the American Eagle lift. Lunch and dinner are served during the winter months, but the restaurant is typically closed during summer months.

SALSA MOUNTAIN CANTINA $

Snowbridge Square, Copper Mountain
(970) 968-6394

Traditional Mexican fare, plus hamburgers and daily specials that include lasagna and seafood, are served here. It's open daily for lunch and dinner.

ACCOMMODATIONS

COPPER MOUNTAIN RESORT

209 Ten Mile Circle, Copper Mountain
(970) 968-2882, (800) 458-8386
www.coppercolorado.com

All of the overnight lodging at Copper Mountain is in condominiums. Units range from compact studios to luxurious four-bedroom townhomes. Depending on the season, the price for a single room can range from $125 to $275, while a four-bedroom townhome would run about $750 to $1,400 per night. Multiday packages, including excellent family values, are available. All resort guests have free access to the excellent Copper Mountain Racquet & Athletic Club.

Keystone

The town of Keystone is the site of two ski resorts: Keystone and its sister, Arapahoe Basin.

DOWNHILL SKIING

ARAPAHOE BASIN SKI AREA

US 6, Keystone
(888) 272-7246
www.arapahoebasin.com

Arapahoe Basin is America's highest ski area, with a base altitude of 10,800 feet and a summit elevation of 12,450 feet. Rugged terrain, fabled steeps, open bowls, and high, tree-free snowfields make it paradise for advanced and expert skiers and snowboarders. The lifts can run into summer (in 1995, A-Basin finally closed on August 10).

Both A-Basin and Keystone have child-care facilities. Arapahoe Basin's nursery accepts children as young as 18 months. It offers ski lessons from age 3 and snowboarding lessons from age 8.

A-Basin has 61 trails with 490 skiable acres and 5 lifts. Fifteen percent of the trails are beginner, 45 percent are intermediate, and 40 percent expert. A one-day pass during the early season (until December 12th) is $49 for an adult, $25 for a child. High season tickets will be somewhat more. Tickets can be purchased in advance at King Soopers, Safeway, and Christie Sports.

KEYSTONE RESORT

US 6, Keystone
(800) 842-7415
www.keystoneresort.com

Keystone is a self-contained resort with skiing on three contiguous mountains: Keystone Mountain, primarily for novice and intermediate skiers; North Peak, with its excellent mogul runs; and The Outback and The Outback Bowl, with powder-holding glades and steeps. Thanks to a huge and efficient snow-making system, Keystone is traditionally the first Colorado ski area to open for the season. Mid-October openings are not uncommon, and Halloween skiing is a tradition. In the 2000–2001 season, Keystone also welcomed snowboarders to a sensational snowboarding park in Packsaddle Bowl. It's the only Summit County area (and one of the few in Colorado) to offer night skiing and snowboarding, nightly until 9 p.m. during most of the season.

Keystone has 91 trails and 21 lifts and offers great deals on night skiing. A single-day ticket is about $92. Children ages 5 to 12 ski for about $49 per day. A $10 discount is offered to seniors ages 65 and above. On the Front Range tickets are available at King Soopers and Safeway. Keystone's child-care center, which remains open in the evening during night skiing, takes babies as young as 2 months old, and parents may use complimentary pagers to stay in touch with the center.

Skiing lessons are offered to kids age 3 and older; snowboarding instruction begins at age 8.

CROSS-COUNTRY SKIING

ALPINE INSTITUTE
US 6, Keystone
(970) 496-4275
www.keystone.snow.com

The Alpine Institute is near the stables on Soda Ridge Road about a mile west of the main lodge. Directed by ebullient former Olympian Jana Hlavaty, it offers outstanding instruction programs and guided ski tours. Nearly 35 kilometers of prepared trails lace through the Snake River Valley and high on the mountain, accessible from North Peak.

OTHER WINTER ACTIVITIES

ICE SKATING ON KEYSTONE LAKE
Keystone Resort, US 6, Keystone
(970) 496-7103
www.keystone.snow.com

Keystone Lake is the largest maintained natural-ice surface in the country. For rink use and rentals the cost is $18 for adults; $14 for ages 12 to 17; $11 for ages 11 and under.

SUMMER ACTIVITIES

KEYSTONE GOLF COURSE
Off US 6, Keystone
(970) 496-4386 (Keystone Resort Activity Desk)

Designed by Robert Trent Jones Jr., this golf course is known for both scenery and challenge. After exiting onto US 6, look for signs to the golf course (take Soda Ridge Road to the end, then go left onto Keystone Ranch Road). The Activity Desk takes tee-time reservations. Greens fees are about $130 per person, including cart. Keystone lodging guests pay $120 per round, and golf packages are available.

RESTAURANTS

ALPENGLOW STUBE $$$$$
US 6, Keystone
(970) 496-4386

In The Outpost at the top of Keystone's North Peak, this restaurant serves elegant, Bavarian-influenced contemporary cuisine for lunch and dinner. Lunch is served only during ski season, dinner is served year-round, and reservations are required. The fixed-price meals include appetizer and dessert.

DER FONDUE CHESSEL $$$$
US 6, Keystone
(970) 496-4386

Der Fondue Chessel, in The Outpost, is a self-serve restaurant offering Swiss specialties. It serves dinner only, to the oompah of live entertainment. For both options at The Outpost, you can ski in during the day, and in the evening, you ride out on the enclosed gondola from the top of Keystone Mountain. Der Fondue typically closes for a month when the ski season ends, from approximately mid-May to mid-June. Call ahead to make sure the restaurant is open on summer evenings.

KEYSTONE RANCH $$$$$
US 6, Keystone
(970) 496-4386

Down in the valley, the elegantly rustic ranch has garnered accolades for its six-course dinners and an outstanding wine list. Only dinner is served and a reservation is recommended. The fixed-price meals include appetizer and dessert. There is year-round dining here, but only on certain evenings, so call ahead for information.

SKI TIP LODGE $$$$
US 6, Keystone
(970) 496-4950

Once a stagecoach stop and Summit County's original ski lodge, this lodging spot is reminiscent of an Old New England Inn. Its quaint and charming restaurant serves excellent American and continental cuisine. Breakfast is served to overnight guests only; the restaurant is open to the public for dinner year-round.

ACCOMMODATIONS

A pedestrian village at the base of the River Run gondola offers additional lodging options at the Keystone Resort. The properties can accommodate about 1,500 more visitors.

KEYSTONE LODGE
US 6, Keystone
(800) 222-0188

The original Keystone development centered around Keystone Lake and the surrounding woods. The lodge offers luxurious mountain- and lake-view rooms. Keystone also offers nearby condominium and private home rentals of various sizes, styles, and prices. Call for rates.

Frisco, Dillon, and Silverthorne

Frisco and Dillon were once mining towns, though the original Dillon is now at the bottom of Lake Dillon, a reservoir, and what you see was either moved before it was filled or rebuilt since then. The reservoir was filled between 1960 and 1965. Silverthorne has become known as a major outlet shopping center, with more than 80 manufacturers' outlets. All three now have numerous stores, restaurants, and accommodations (including condos) convenient to all the Summit County ski areas.

CROSS-COUNTRY SKIING

THE FRISCO NORDIC CENTER
18454 Highway 9, Frisco
(970) 668-0866

The Frisco Center has 35 kilometers of trails groomed daily, with much of the system also offering great views of Lake Dillon and a particularly congenial log day lodge. The Breckenridge and Frisco Nordic Centers are under the same management and share an interchangeable trail pass. Both offer instruction and rentals of cross-country skis and snowshoes.

WHITE RIVER NATIONAL FOREST
Dillon Ranger District, 680 Blue River Parkway, Silverthorne
(970) 468-5400

Several Nordic routes are accessible from the road to Montezuma or directly from this old mining camp. Peru Creek is a good trail for novices, while the routes to the St. John and the Wild Irishman Mine trails are popular with intermediate skiers and snowshoers. All are open to the public free of charge.

SUMMER ACTIVITIES

BIKING
Summit County Chamber of Commerce and Frisco Visitors' Center
(800) 530-3099
Dillon Town Hall
(970) 668-2403
www.summitchamber.org
Summit Information Center
(970) 262-0817

Mountain biking is king all over Colorado, but in Summit County, riding along the paved Blue River Bikeway connecting Breckenridge and Frisco is a milder option. The route parallels Highway 9, winding through meadows and forests. If you can handle the uphill, take the paved Ten Mile Canyon National Recreation Trail from Frisco up to Copper Mountain, or put your bike on a free Summit Stage bus and coast down. From Copper Mountain, you can also continue on the Vail Pass Bikeway, a 20-mile route (one-way) that climbs over 10,600-foot Vail Pass and down into Vail Village. These are beautiful rides anytime but especially in early fall when the aspen trees are turning gold. For trail maps contact either of the above telephone numbers.

BOATING ON LAKE DILLON
300 Marina Drive, Dillon
(970) 468-5100

This is a 3,000-acre reservoir offering opportunities and charters for all types of boating, including fishing and sailboats. The Dillon Marina is open from the end of May through October.

RESTAURANTS

THE ARAPAHOE CAFE $

626 Lake Dillon Drive, Dillon
(970) 468-0873

Breakfast, lunch, and dinner are served daily in a cozy log cabin. Early in the day you'll find omelets, hamburgers, and salads, and by evening steak, seafood, and pasta.

THE MINT $

341 Blue River Parkway, Silverthorne
(970) 468-5247

This restaurant is in one of Summit County's oldest buildings (one of those rescued from the bottom of the lake) and is a good family-dining spot. You cook your own steak or chicken on the grill.

OLD DILLON INN $

Highway 9 in Silverthorne, north of I-70
(970) 468-2791

For a great margarita—though you'll have to fight the crowds—go to the Dillon Inn. The restaurant serves primarily Mexican food at the dinner hour only and has a 19th-century bar and lively music.

THE SNAKE RIVER SALOON $–$$

23074 US 6, Dillon
(970) 468-2788

Open daily for dinner only, this is a popular spot for après-ski, with steak and seafood and not-to-miss late-night entertainment on weekends.

ACCOMMODATIONS

CHATEAUX D'MONT

0175 County Road 8, Dillon
(888) 222-9298

Close to the Keystone Resort, the Chateaux costs $700 to $900 per night for a truly deluxe two- or three-bedroom condo within walking distance of the lifts and featuring a private hot tub on a glass-enclosed balcony. Amenities include a welcome grocery package, fresh flowers, plush terry-cloth robes, nightly turndown, complimentary newspaper, and concierge service.

THE ARTS

Despite its small-city size, Boulder offers a big-city arts scene, ranging from local artists with national reputations to the summer Colorado Music Festival with musicians from around the world. The internationally renowned Colorado Dance Festival and the Colorado Shakespeare Festival also attract top talent. The Boulder Museum of Contemporary Art (BMoCA) and the University of Colorado galleries show work by both locally and nationally known artists. In addition to exhibitions, BMoCA and Naropa University (see the Child Care and Education chapter) sponsor innovative arts events and community theater; dance and music groups provide a varied mix of entertainment.

Proximity to Denver expands the arts horizon with the Denver Art Museum, Colorado Symphony, Denver Center Theatre Company, and a number of small theater companies. Even closer, the Arvada Center for the Arts and Humanities offers theater, music, dance, and visual art by Colorado's best and nationally known artists. The nearby communities of Longmont, Louisville, Lafayette, Lyons, Central City, Golden, and Nederland offer their own historical museums, music and theater groups, and art exhibitions as well.

The following are just the highlights of the area's arts offerings. Note that we have listed museums in our Attractions chapter. You may notice that many of the groups have the same address. That's the Dairy Center for the Arts, a 40,000-square-foot space that used to house the Watts-Hardy Dairy. The empty building was purchased as a home for small arts groups, and today about 15 such groups make their home there.

DANCE

BOULDER BALLET
Dairy Center for the Arts
2590 Walnut Street, Boulder
(303) 442-6944
www.boulderballet.org
Founded in 1981, the Boulder Ballet is Boulder County's only classical ballet company. Boulder Ballet is a company of local professionals and amateurs and visiting professionals. The ballet collaborates annually with the Boulder Philharmonic Orchestra to present two full-length productions—*The Nutcracker* ballet, a winter tradition so popular the performances sell out every year, and spring performances such as *Springtime in Paris* and *The Emperor's (Really) New Clothes*.
As a member of the Peak Association of the Arts, the Boulder Ballet also provides ballet instruc-

tion through the PeakArts educational wing, the Boulder Arts Academy. In addition, the Ballet tours Boulder County schools presenting "Steps in Time," an interactive educational program for young people.

Performances are held in a variety of places, including Longmont's Vance Brand Auditorium and Macky Auditorium in Boulder.

BOULDER JAZZ DANCE WORKSHOP
CU-Boulder campus
(303) 449-0399
www.bcn.boulder.co.us/arts/idt/idt.html
Founded in 1978 by Lara Branen, then a graduate student at CU-Boulder, this two-week August workshop includes public performances. This now-independent group returns to Boulder each year, where CU-Boulder's Theatre and Dance Department lends its facilities. The workshop is

open to the public, offering classes in jazz dance, hip hop, jazz funk, and modern dance, as well as ballet barre, a mat class based on the principles of Joseph Pilates, and special classes emphasizing partnering and turns for students age 16 and older.

Following the summer workshop, there are performances by students, faculty, and the company in residence, Interweave Dance Theatre of Boulder, which is composed of some 30 dancers. Thirty to 40 percent of the workshop participants come from other states and countries, including Mexico, Italy, and elsewhere. Participants can receive up to two college credits at CU, and housing is available. Sign up early—the program fills very quickly.

CLEO PARKER ROBINSON DANCE
119 Park Avenue, West Denver
(303) 295-1759
www.cleoparkerdance.org
This 36-year-old dance company–cum–school and theater is dedicated to providing cross-cultural, African-centered performances and classes. Its fall and holiday performances are at the Denver Center for the Performing Arts. Jazz and modern-dance aficionados will relish this internationally renowned group. Well-known performers from around the world visit the school and theater, and the ensemble goes on extended tours. An annual July event is the International Summer Dance Institute, which hosts great master instructors from all over the world. The instructors teach all types of dance, music, theater, storytelling, and cultural rituals to children and adults. The company also operates the Season of Schools program that introduces more than 50,000 students in Denver metro schools to dance. One of Denver's greatest holiday traditions is the annual December concert, "Granny Dances to a Holiday Drum." There's usually an annual spring performance as well. The school also runs Project Self-Discovery, an outreach program for at-risk youth. Call for information and current schedules for these excellent performances, classes, and workshops.

COLORADO BALLET
1036 14th Street (ticket office);
1278 Lincoln Street (administrative office), Denver
(303) 98-MUSIC (tickets)
www.coloradoballet.org
Born from a ballet school in Denver, the Colorado Ballet was established in 1961, making it one of Colorado's oldest arts institutions. The company now includes 30 professional dancers from around the world and 25 apprentice dancers. In 1997, Colorado Ballet II was created to provide upper-level students at the company's Colorado Academy of Ballet an opportunity to gain performance experience.

The Colorado Ballet performs such classics as *La Sylphide* and *The Nutcracker* each Christmas season, but also offers more innovative works such as those of George Balanchine. The 2008 season included *The Nutcracker, Swan Lake* and *A Midsummer Night's Dream*. The performance season is from September through March. Series tickets are available.

COLORADO DANCE FESTIVAL
2590 Walnut Street, Boulder
(303) 442-7666
Now the third-largest dance festival in the nation, the Boulder-based Colorado Dance Festival (CDF) is partially funded by the National Endowment for the Arts. CDF has earned international recognition with its innovative programs and renowned performers, including such top names as Trisha Brown and the late, great tap dancer Honi Coles. The CDF also founded the Boulder-based International Tap Association (303-443-7989).

In 2001, the festival's 19th season, more than 400 dancers from around the globe gathered for intensive training with a faculty of 40 from five continents. The program has something for beginners to experienced professionals.

In addition to performances and classes, CDF continues with its energetic Youth Dance Project, which gives young dancers ages 12 to 18 a chance to study with renowned professional dancers; the lecture-demonstration Informances; and the Family Series of matinee performances that give the audience a chance to take a turn onstage.

COMMUNITY DANCE COLLECTIVE
2020B 21st Street, Boulder
(303) 447-2566

The collective offers rehearsal space and classes, as well as performances in folk, ballet, modern dance, and jazz for all ages. The organization is the oldest nonprofit dance group in Boulder. Call for a schedule.

FREQUENT FLYERS PRODUCTIONS
Dairy Center for the Arts
2590 Walnut Street, Boulder
(303) 444-5569
www.frequentflyers.org

If dance sometimes resembles floating, flying, and swooping through air, Frequent Flyers Productions really makes it so. The company uses trapezes to set dancers free of gravity. It all began in 1988 with a chilling performance inspired by Anne Rice's vampire novels. Now, the company offers workshops and classes for adventurous folks age 10 and older, along with periodic performances (the vampire program has become a Boulder staple at Halloween, drawing a repeat audience with many in full white-faced, fanged, black-clad regalia).

The company's annual Aerial Dance Festival brings together aerial artists from around the world for a week of performance, experimentation, teaching, and discussion. Faculty demonstrated their talents on the trapeze, stilts, ropes, and harness and bungies.

THE NAROPA UNIVERSITY PERFORMING ARTS SERIES
2130 Arapahoe Avenue, Boulder
(303) 546-3538
(303) 786-7030 (ticket office)

A private, nonsectarian liberal arts college with roots in Buddhism, Naropa opened its doors in 1974. It concentrates mainly on avant-garde and new dance, offering classes, workshops, and performances. A spring cultural festival combines dance with music, costume, food, films, and storytelling from around the world. Call the ticket office for other events and classes.

UNIVERSITY OF COLORADO DEPARTMENT OF THEATRE AND DANCE
CU-Boulder campus
(303) 492-7355
(303) 492-8181 (tickets)
www.colorado.edu/TheatreDance

Throughout the school year this talent-filled university department presents a number of innovative performances, including ballet, modern, African-American, and other dance forms. In the summer, all resources are focused on the Colorado Shakespeare Festival (see details in the "Theater" section). There are student performances all year-round, with the main one presented in late fall; a faculty performance takes place in late spring. Call for a current schedule.

i Among the best local entertainment values are CU-Boulder's Program Council Films and the more art-oriented International Film Series. Both are held on campus. The Program Council features recent first-run movies; the International Film Series has excellent award winners from all over the world that you'll have a hard time finding at a regular theater. Look for a free schedule in the Boulder Public Library and at area bookstores. See the listing in this chapter for more information.

FILM

In addition to the special film series listed below, Boulder has a variety of theater options. The brand new Century theater, a 16 screen, state-of-the-art complex located at the new 29th Street Mall has brought Boulder theatergoers back to our fair city after a much-felt absence. A 12-plex of theaters at the Louisville exit off US 36 gives moviegoers a different option, and a 24-plex farther south off Highway 36 offers stadium seating

🔍 Close-up

Pull Up a Lawn Chair and Take In a Film

Boulder's Outdoor Cinema rocks. That's what all the locals say. Where else can you pull up a lawn chair, dig into your picnic dinner, and watch a movie under the stars? Located at 1750 13th Street in downtown Boulder, directly behind the Boulder Museum of Contemporary Art, this outdoor summer venue comes complete with Digital Surround Sound. All movies are shown on a screen that's 18 feet high by 30 feet wide, and the variety of films caters to families. The 2006 season included such films as *Corpse Bride, Triplets of Bellville, Office Space*, and *The Big Lebowski*. With approximately 21 films shown each summer on Friday and Saturday nights, the place is popular indeed. The gates open at 7 p.m. and the movies start at 9 p.m. Admission is free but donations are appreciated. Be sure to check the online calendar at www.boulderoutdoorcinema.com because some shows feature pre-show entertainment, which is always extra fun. For additional information, you can call (303) 444-1351.

and butter-your-own popcorn. In the summer, the Almost Free Outdoor Cinema unrolls a screen and turns the parking lot behind BMoCA into an open-air theater featuring everything from classic films like *Yellow Submarine* to the campy *Monty Python's Meaning of Life*. Every Saturday night between early June and early September, fans bring blankets, lawn chairs, even couches and coffee tables, and fill in the time during reel changes with costume and trivia contests.

BOULDER INTERNATIONAL FILM FESTIVAL
1906 13th Street, Boulder
(303) 449-2289
www.biff1.com
This festival, sponsored by the Colorado Film Society, is held annually on President's Day Weekend in Boulder and has developed a reputation as one of the most influential young film festivals in the U.S., with an extraordinary number of new-but-unknown feature films, documentaries and shorts that have gone on from early screenings at BIFF to significant box-office success and multiple Oscar nominations. Over 13,000 filmmakers, national media, special guests and film enthusiasts attended the four-day BIFF 2008. Various Boulder venues provide the public with film screenings throughout the four-day festival. Check the Web site for venues, showtimes and prices.

The festival has been proud to host and celebrate some of independent film's most talented players, including legendary Indie filmmakers Michael and Mark Polish "The Polish Brothers" (*Twin Falls Idaho, Northfork, The Astronaut Farmer*), Golden Globe–nominated actress Maria Bello (*A History of Violence, The Cooler, Thank You for Smoking*), Academy Award–nominated writer and director Susannah Grant (*Erin Brockovich, 28 Days, Catch and Release, In Her Shoes*), Director Jon Poll (*Charlie Bartlett*, Producer—*The 40-Year Old Virgin*) and renowned Hollywood screenwriter John August (*Big Fish, Go, The Nines*) along with many other independent filmmakers, directors, producers and stars including Academy Award–nominee Eric Roberts, and Patrick Warburton *Seinfeld*).

BOULDER PUBLIC LIBRARY FILM PROGRAM
Main Branch Auditorium, Ninth Street and Canyon Boulevard, Boulder
(303) 441-3197
www.boulder.lib.co.us/films
Since 1974, this free film program has offered everything from Asian anime and the French classic Diabolique to documentaries and series on such topics as Depression Era Musical Comedies. The library also shows mainstream Hollywood movies. Call for information, or visit the library to pick up the latest schedule. Movies are shown in the library's comfy, cozy auditorium and start at 7 p.m.

CHAUTAUQUA SUMMER SILENT FILM FESTIVAL
Ninth Street and Baseline Road, Boulder
(303) 440-7666
www.chautauqua.com
Moviegoers of all ages will feel like kids at summer camp inside Chautauqua's barn-like auditorium. This summer-only program shows historic silent films from the 1920s and earlier, such as Charlie Chaplin's *The Kid* and Marion Davies in *The Patsy*, many with live piano accompaniment.

INTERNATIONAL FILM SERIES
Muenzinger Auditorium, Muenzinger Plaza
CU-Boulder campus (west of Folsom
Stadium near the corner of Colorado
Avenue and 18th Street)
(303) 492-1531
www.internationalfilmseries.com
Connected with the CU-based Rocky Mountain Film Center (RMFC), this series is the West's longest-running continuous forum for international and art-film screenings and has entertained university and Boulder audiences for more than 50 years. The First Person Cinema is affiliated with the RMFC and features visiting artists throughout the academic year. It includes avant-garde works by independent and personal filmmakers such as Stan Brakhage, Fred Worden, and Caroline Leaf, as well as wonderful, entertaining films from all over the world that aren't available in mall theaters or video stores. The spacious, steeply sloping Muenzinger Auditorium offers every moviegoer a perfect view for the right price—$5 ($4 for CU students). The 24-hour hotline above lists each week's events. Some films are also shown in the Film Studies Theater in ATLAS and elsewhere on campus.

UNIVERSITY OF COLORADO PROGRAM COUNCIL FILM SERIES
Forum Room in the UMC, and Chemistry
140 in the Chemistry Building (next building
over from UMC), 16th Street and East Euclid
Avenue, CU-Boulder campus
(303) 492-5458
www.colorado.edu/programcouncil

These free and bargain-priced films offer some of the best entertainment around. Catch up on first-run movies you might have missed at the local theater last year. A high-tech Dolby stereo cinema sound processor makes the sound system in the university's Chemistry 140 auditorium one of Boulder's best. Pick up a film schedule at the University Memorial Center (UMC), Boulder Public Libraries, city recreation centers, and local supermarkets. The screen is dark during the summer.

MUSIC

ARS NOVA SINGERS
(303) 499-3165
www.arsnovasingers.org
This group of 40 a capella singers presents music from the Renaissance and 20th and 21st centuries, including works by Colorado's finest composers, and performs in churches in Boulder and Denver. Founded in 1985, Ars Nova was one of the first choirs from Colorado funded by the National Endowment for the Arts and the only one to receive funding for three consecutive years. In 1998, the choir performed its first international tour, and it was later invited to perform at the statewide memorial service for the victims of the Columbine High School shootings, also attended by Vice President Al Gore. Ars Nova presents annual Christmas concerts in Boulder and Denver at area churches. The ensemble has performed the complete *Responsoria* by Renaissance composer Carlo Gesualdo, Gyorgy Ligeti's *Lux Aeterna,* Charles Ives's cantata *The Celestial Country,* and many experimental and avant-garde choral works. The Ars Nova Singers have been heard in radio broadcasts throughout the United States, Canada, South America, and Europe. The group has released several CDs. Ticket prices vary.

ARTIST SERIES
Macky Auditorium, Grusin Music Hall, and
Imig Music Building, CU-Boulder campus
(303) 492-8008
www.cuconcerts.org
The University of Colorado-Boulder's Artist Series has been going strong for some 70 years, with

a full season of varied performances. The 2009 season includes performances by the Colorado Symphony with Alisa Weilerstein, the Great Tennessee Monkey Trial with L.A. Theater Works and the Vanguard Jazz Orchestra. The Takacs String Quartet, composed of the series' Hungarian artists-in-residence, also performs. The Artist Series is held in the university's Macky Auditorium, Grusin Music Hall, and the Music Theatre in Imig Music Building, and includes performance art, jazz, classics, dance, folk, and ethnic performances. Tickets prices range from $15 to $60.

ARVADA CENTER FOR THE ARTS AND HUMANITIES
6901 Wadsworth Boulevard, Arvada
(303) 431-3939
www.arvadacenter.org
About a 30-minute drive south of Boulder, the more than 25-year-old Arvada Center is a sophisticated venue for music of all types, from popular to classical, with nationally known groups and performers. During performances, the upper gallery is open so that audience members may view the work of nationally known artists and craftspeople. Summer concerts are in an outdoor amphitheater. The previous seasons have included performances by such varied artists as the Ahmad Jamal Trio, A Roomful of Blues, Eileen Ivers Immigrant Soul, and The Russ Morgan Orchestra, among others. Tickets run from $8 to $55. The center also offers year-round theater, concerts, and dance performances, a historical museum, a children's theater, and classes in ceramics, dance, writing, acting, visual arts, and more.

BOULDER BACH FESTIVAL
(303) 652-9101
www.boulderbachfest.org
It began in 1981 as a one-weekend festival; now the Boulder Bach Festival has evolved into a year-round series of concerts highlighting the famous composer's work. The annual three-day Bach Festival is in January. Lecture series, master classes, youth competitions, and an enrichment program for local elementary schools round out

the offerings. The very unstuffy company puts on a lively New Year's Eve performance with a champagne reception. There are also children's concerts in March and May, and a fall concert in the more than 100-year-old Ryssby Church west of Longmont.

BOULDER PHILHARMONIC ORCHESTRA
2590 Walnut Street, Boulder
(303) 449-1343
www.boulderphil.org
Beginning its 51st season in 2008, the Boulder Philharmonic Orchestra, founded in 1958, is a critically acclaimed, fully professional orchestra. Each season the orchestra presents dynamic programming featuring timeless masterpieces, promising new works, and both accomplished and emerging guest musicians and performing artists.

In past seasons, the guest performance list has included Yo-Yo Ma, Itzhak Perlman, Mstislav Rostropovich, Anne Sophie Mutter, and Sarah Chang. By popular demand, the orchestra performs at a variety of venues under its community outreach program with concerts at local parks, the Boulder Public Library, and the Farmers' Market, in addition to its main concert schedule performed at Macky Auditorium on the CU campus. An opening concert gala event is held in the fall as a benefit for the orchestra. The Boulder Arts Academy, with instructors from the Boulder Philharmonic and some 700 students, offers group classes and private lessons and has large ensembles.

CENTRAL CITY OPERA
Eureka Street, Central City
(303) 292-6700, (800) 851-8175
www.centralcityopera.org
One of Colorado's favorite outings, the Central City Opera, now in it's 78th season, features operatic works sung in English in this old mining town, now a glitzy gambling haven. This summer troupe is one of the oldest opera companies in the country, with a distinguished national reputation. The CCO also offers daytime cabaret opera and special youth performances. The opera house was built in 1878 in an effort to bring

culture to the formerly rough and rowdy mining town. Performances are frequently sold out, so call ahead for reservations for the summer-only program. In 2001, Central City Opera became the first American opera company to stage Benjamin Britten's regal, romantic *Gloriana*. First performed in 1953 for the coronation of Elizabeth II, Britten's compelling portrait of Elizabeth I was joined by the regional premiere of Mark Adamo's *Little Women* and a revival of Giacomo Puccini's *La Boheme* for Central City Opera's 69th season.

Reserved parking is available, and a shuttle bus takes operagoers from the parking area (a half-mile away) right to the opera house's front door. The bus leaves about every 10 minutes during the two hours before and after the opera, so there's plenty of time for a meal, gambling or sightseeing in Central City. Tickets range from $43 to $99.

i Boulder is bursting with activities in the arts. It has become a mecca of sorts for art forms of every conceivable type. A visit to Boulder just isn't complete without a picnic in Chautauqua Park before a performance of the Colorado Music Festival, or an evening under the stars at the outdoor Colorado Shakespeare Festival. Film festivals, theater performances, museums, and a wide variety of galleries are sure to please just about everyone. There is something on tap every night of the week, from the smallest local theater productions to performances by top recording artists.

CHAUTAUQUA SUMMER FESTIVAL CONCERTS
Main Office, South of Ninth Street and Baseline Road, Boulder
(303) 440-7666 (summer only)
(303) 545-6924, ext. 18
www.chautauqua.com
Summer in Boulder wouldn't truly be summer without Chautauqua, which features a series of popular-music concerts and performances in addition to the classical Colorado Music Festival. This

historic music venue has been an institution since 1898, when Boulder's Chautauqua first opened as part of a national movement that brought the arts to numerous summer camps around the country. Today, many concertgoers enjoy dinner on the lovely old veranda of the picturesque Chautauqua Dining Hall or bring a picnic to enjoy under the shady trees on the green. The Summer Festival Concerts have featured such groups and performers as Shawn Colvin, Rosanne Cash, Los Lobos, Peter Kater, Michelle Shocked, Richard Thompson, Joan Armatrading, Laurie Anderson, The Persuasions, and the delicately named Mother Folkers. Some folks picnic into the night and enjoy the music (for free) from outside the concert hall. Dance fans can see performances by Cleo Parker Robinson and Danielle Helander. Chautauqua makes it a point to feature quirky performances such as the Reduced Shakespeare Company, "the Bad Boys of Abridgement," and The Barbershoppers, a large barbershop chorus. Among the many others who have appeared here are Karla Bonoff, Spaulding Gray, and Hunter S. Thompson.

COLORADO CHILDREN'S CHORALE
910 15th Street, Denver
(303) 892-5600
www.childrenschorale.org
Children from all over the Denver metro area audition to get into one of the five chorales. The CCC presents popular and traditional music such as *Carmina Burana* and special compositions written for the chorale by resident composers. There are annual U.S. and international tours by the group. A December Christmas concert features traditional holiday music, and there's a special spring concert in May. The chorale has recorded two CDs that are available for sale.

COLORADO MUSIC FESTIVAL
1525 Spruce Street, Suite 101, Boulder
(303) 449-1397 (year-round)
(866) 464-2626 (TicketsWest)
www.coloradomusicfest.org
From late June through mid-August each year, classical musicians from around the country and

world come to Boulder to participate in the Colorado Music Festival at Boulder's historic Chautauqua. Founded in 1976, the series is organized around themes such as "Renaissance to Gen X," "American Music," "Romantic Refresher," and "Baroque to Bel Canto." There are several children's and family concerts, too. A Boulder Fourth of July tradition is the Colorado Music Festival's free concert on the Chautauqua lawn, highlighted with foot-thumping John Philip Sousa marches. The festival's music director, Michael Christie, is just one year older than the festival founded by Giora Bernstein. Season tickets are available in advance, or concertgoers can pay at the door.

COLORADO SYMPHONY
821 17th Street, Suite 700 (admin. office),
Boettcher Hall, Performing Arts Complex,
14th and Lawrence Streets, Denver
(303) 893-4100
www.coloradosymphony.org
Many Boulderites gladly make the trek to Denver to enjoy the Colorado Symphony, under the direction of Jeffrey Kahane, at Denver's delightful Boettcher Hall. Choices include a regular concert series and special holiday concerts, plus Family, Masterworks and Popular Classics, and Pops concert series. The Colorado Christmas concert features the Colorado Children's Chorale and Colorado Symphony Chorus. Past highlights include an evening of Copland with mezzo-soprano Marietta Simpson and a program of percussion with Colin Currie.

In the past, the Pops series has featured Yo-Yo Ma, a three-day Jazz in America series with guest Dr. Billy Taylor, the Lincoln Center Jazz Orchestra with Wynton Marsalis, pianist Fabio Bidini, and Hot Latin Nights with Doc Severinson as conductor and on trumpet.

Tickets are sold through the Denver Center for the Performing Arts. Single tickets may be purchased in person, at the Denver Center Box Office at 14th and Curtis Streets, Monday through Saturday from 10 a.m. to 6 p.m., or on the symphony's Web site. A fee is assessed on purchases made by phone or through the Internet. No fee is charged on orders placed in person.

COORS AMPHITHEATRE
6350 Greenwood Plaza Boulevard
Englewood
(303) 220-7000
About an hour's drive from Boulder, this popular outdoor concert hall on Denver's south side offers nationally known groups that aren't likely to visit Boulder. Enjoy these summer-only concerts either from reserved seats or while picnicking on the lawn. Tickets are available at the box office or at www.ticketmaster.com.

LONGMONT SYMPHONY
519 Main Street, Longmont
(303) 772-5796
www.longmontsymphony.org
Under the direction of Robert Olson, the Longmont Symphony celebrated its 40th season in 2006. Performances are held in Longmont's Vance Brand Civic Auditorium. The 2008 concert season included Russian Masterpieces, Sumptuous Violin and a special candlelight concert in December featuring soprano Maurenn Sorennson. The orchestra also teams with the Boulder Ballet for performances of *The Nutcracker* in December. Tickets for all performances are available by calling the symphony box office at (303) 772-5796.

PUBLIC LIBRARY CONCERT SERIES
1000 Canyon Boulevard, Boulder
(303) 441-3100
www.boulder.lib.co.us
This free series at the Boulder Public Library Auditorium (Canyon Boulevard entrance) offers music lovers a wealth of listening, from Bach to ragtime. Piano and harp soloists, string quartets, members of the Boulder Philharmonic, and local musicians are among the varied performers.

RED ROCKS
Morrison Street, Morrison
(303) 640-7334 (recorded information and events)
www.redrocksonline.com
For more than 60 years this spectacular natural-rock open-air amphitheater is the venue for most top performers who come to the Denver area.

Performances by Crosby, Stills, Nash & Young; R.E.M.; the Dead; Coldplay; Toby Keith; and Counting Crows are just a few of the bands that have played (sometimes yearly) at this magnificent venue. Red Rocks information and tickets are available through Ticketmaster at www.ticketmaster.com. Check local newspapers for a rundown of the performers appearing at Red Rocks, or visit the Red Rocks Web site. Ticket prices vary and are available with no service charge at the Pepsi Center and the Denver Performing Arts Complex in downtown Denver (cash only and in person).

THEATER

ARVADA CENTER FOR THE ARTS AND HUMANITIES
6901 Wadsworth Boulevard, Arvada
(303) 431-3939
www.arvadacenter.org
The Arvada Center opened its stage doors in 1976 and has been an equity theater since 1992, bringing professional talent into an intimate setting. The center was expanded and renovated in 2005/2006 and is better than ever. Shows run Tuesday through Sunday with matinees. The Arvada Center also has a huge education program offering more than 100 classes for both children and adults in everything from acting, performing arts, and music to ceramics and the humanities.

BOULDER'S DINNER THEATRE
5501 Arapahoe Avenue, Boulder
(303) 634-6459
www.theatreinboulder.com
From *Paint Your Wagon* and *South Pacific* to the hilarious *Midlife*, Boulder's Dinner Theatre is the only local venue for popular musicals. It has won a number of awards for its professional performances with excellent sets and staging. The theater offers cocktails and a choice of delicious dinners (the prime rib is great!) served by its talented singers and performers. Tickets cost $35 to $55 per person and are discounted for seniors and children for some performances.

THE COLORADO SHAKESPEARE FESTIVAL
Mary Rippon Theatre
CU-Boulder campus
(303) 492-0554
www.coloradoshakes.org
Film actor Val Kilmer took part in these Shakespeare productions one year, and other top performers, such as film and TV star Jimmy Smits, have likewise been attracted to this highly regarded annual summer festival. Held at the outdoor Mary Rippon Theatre, this is another local institution. It includes both traditional and modern renditions of the bard's work. The 2009 season promises to be just as wonderful as seasons past with productions of *Hamlet, Much Ado about Nothing* and *To Kill a Mockingbird*. Theatergoers can order a box dinner and dine on the green before the show. Be sure to fit in a stroll through the Shakespeare Gardens, planted each year with herbs, flowers, and even vegetables mentioned in the summer's plays. There are evening and Sunday matinee performances. Single tickets range in price from $7 to $54, with discounts for children and seniors.

DENVER CENTER THEATRE COMPANY
1050 13th Street, Denver
(303) 893-4100
www.denvercenter.org
The Denver Center for the Performing Arts attracts big Broadway shows with national touring companies, but the Denver Center Theatre Company, now in its 30th season, is the local theater company that performs at the center. Featuring a varied menu of entertainment ranging from works by Dickens and Shakespeare to the life of Janis Joplin, the company has received many awards, including, in 1998, the Tony Award for Outstanding Regional Theater.

LONGMONT THEATRE COMPANY PERFORMING ARTS CENTER
513 Main Street, Longmont
(303) 772-5200
www.longmonttheatre.org
A short drive from Boulder via the Longmont

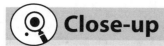 **Close-up**

The Denver Art Museum: Art and Dramatic Architecture

In October 2006 the Denver Art Museum unveiled its new expansion—the Frederic C. Hamilton Building. Designed by renowned architect Daniel Libeskind, it is a careful symphony of angles and cuts. Covered with gleaming titanium panels, it is definitely a must-see.

Libeskind says he found his inspiration for the building's design in the natural beauty of the area, from the peaks of the Rockies to the geometric rock crystals in the surrounding foothills. "I was inspired by the light and the geology of the Rockies, but most of all by the wide-open faces of the people of Denver," says Libeskind. Approximately 9,000 titanium panels cover the exterior of the building, reflecting Colorado's abundant sunshine.

The original museum building, now known as the North Building, was innovative when it opened in 1971. Designed by Italian architect Geo Ponti, the building was daring with its castle-like facade and one million reflective glass panels on the exterior. It was only natural that the new expansion take on a similarly bold design.

The Frederic C. Hamilton Building has added more than 30,000 square feet of gallery space for permanent collections, three temporary exhibition spaces, art storage facilities, and public amenities.

Diagonal Highway (Highway 119), the Longmont Theatre Company, founded in 1959, offers musicals, drama, comedy, children's performances, a Christmas show, and a Shakespeare Festival. Call for a current schedule of performances. The 2006–2007 season included such performances as *Dearly Departed*, *Oliver*, and *Wait Until Dark*. Tickets run $13 to $15 and are available by phone, at the box office, or online. They also offer two-for-one tickets for matinees and five-pack tickets at discounted prices.

THE NAROPA UNIVERSITY PERFORMING ARTS CENTER
2130 Arapahoe Avenue, Boulder
(303) 546-3538
www.naropa.edu/tour/pac.html
Not limited to theater per se, Naropa has speakers, poetry readings, and various performances. There are student-run shows, inter-arts faculty concerts (including music, art, dance, and theater), faculty and student readings every semester, and annual Balinese and African concerts. The university offers workshops, dance performances, and art exhibits, too. Call for a schedule of events.

NOMAD THEATRE
1410 Quince Street, Boulder
(303) 774-4037
www.nomadstage.com
Since 1951, Nomad has been providing community theater in a Quonset hut "Just a little off Broadway"—Boulder's Broadway, that is. The theater was completely renovated in 1998. Former Boulderites, Joan Van Ark of *Knot's Landing* and Larry Linville of *M*A*S*H*, both got their acting start with the Nomad, which hosts some excellent serious and not-so-serious drama.

OPERA COLORADO
695 South Colorado Boulevard, Denver
(800) 641-1222, (303) 893-4100
www.operacolorado.org
Opera Colorado's season consists of three operas presented in March, April, and May. The 2008-2009 season highlights include Puccini's *Madame Butterfly*, Bizet's *The Pearl Fishers* and Mozart's *Cosi Fan Tutti*.

THE PEANUT BUTTER PLAYERS (PBP)
Harlequin Center for the Performing Arts
990 Public Road, Lafayette
(303) 786-8PBP
www.peanutbutterplayers.com
Formerly based in the Toadstool Playhouse, one of Boulder's funky landmark buildings, this theater company of local youngsters ages 5 to 18 offers year-round performances. The luncheon theater here is just like adult dinner theater, except the performance is at lunchtime and the performers are a lot shorter. There are classes during the school year and a day camp in summer that teach such things as music, puppetry, pantomime, dance, makeup, voice dialects, clowning, and theater crafts. Each summer PBP puts on a major production at Boulder High School with about 250 children. Call for ticket prices and reservations.

UNIVERSITY OF COLORADO DEPARTMENT OF THEATRE AND DANCE
CU-Boulder campus
(303) 492-7355
www.colorado.edu/TheatreDance
Considered by local critics to present the most consistently good and reliable performances, the CU-Boulder Theatre Department won the 1993 Denver Drama Critics Circle award for Best Season for a Company. Throughout the school year, this university department holds numerous performances at campus theaters. The 2009 season will include *Twelfth Night, Boom Boom Yum Yum, Butterfly Kiss* and *Shakespeare Unplugged*. The department also offers performances by students in the master of fine arts degree program, and student dance performances. Call for more information or a complete schedule.

UPSTART CROW THEATRE COMPANY
Dairy Center for the Arts
2590 Walnut Street, Boulder
(303) 442-1415
www.theupstartcrow.org
Performing since 1979, this ensemble presents classical plays in their complete and uncut versions, as well as more current productions. The 2008 season included *Lady Windermere's Fan* by Oscar Wilde, *The Two Noble Kinsmen* by Shakespeare and *The Seagull* by Chekov.

VISUAL ARTS

Admission to the following galleries and shops is free unless otherwise noted.

ART & SOUL GALLERY
1615 Pearl Street, Boulder
(303) 544-5803
www.artandsoulboulder.com
Art & Soul is one of Boulder's best galleries, with a sophisticated yet fun and funky collection of unique and contemporary jewelry, fine art, and crafts. The innovative gallery represents both local and national artists. The *Boulder Weekly* Readers Poll recognized Art & Soul as "Boulder's Best Gallery" 2001 through 2004. The gallery is open seven days a week.

ARVADA CENTER FOR THE ARTS AND HUMANITIES
6901 Wadsworth Boulevard, Arvada
(303) 431-3080
www.arvadacenter.org
The Arvada Center hosts 12 to 15 art exhibits a year. Nationally known artists and Colorado's best artists and craftspeople show their work in the excellent gallery. There is also a permanent historical exhibit on the area's early days. The gallery is open 9 a.m. to 6 p.m. Monday through Friday, 9 a.m. to 5 p.m. Saturday, and 1 to 5 p.m. Sunday.

BOULDER ARTS & CRAFTS COOPERATIVE
1421 Pearl Street, Boulder
(303) 443-3683
www.boulderartsandcrafts.com
The co-op has 45 members and shows the work of more than 200 artists, including nationally known artists and participating members and consignees from Colorado and surrounding mountain states. Nowhere else in the area will you find such a concentrated collection of top-quality pottery, puppets, jewelry, photographs, fiber art, stained glass, woodwork, and other

items. The co-op has an extensive and spectacular selection of jewelry made from precious metals, as well as contemporary fashion jewelry. There are handcrafted clothes that are works of art on hangers, and whimsical painted wooden furniture, too. Opened in 1971, the member-directed co-op celebrated its 35th year in 2006. A Visiting Artist Series brings the work of outside talent to exhibit in the gallery from late May through early November. There is also a series of shows that benefit local nonprofit organizations. The co-op is open daily 10 a.m. to 6 p.m., 10 a.m. to 9 p.m. during the summer.

i Chautauqua Park's buildings are on the National Register of Historic Places, and the Chautauqua Auditorium was voted by musicians as one of the top 10 places in the country to perform.

BOULDER MUSEUM OF CONTEMPORARY ART (BMOCA)
1750 13th Street, Boulder
(303) 443-2122
www.bmoca.org
Located across the street from Boulder's Central Park, BMoCA provides a dynamic venue for a variety of innovative art exhibits, including the work of local, national, and international artists. The museum was founded in 1972 by a group of artists to promote the visual arts in Boulder. Over the years the facility expanded and now houses three gallery spaces and a 100-seat black-box theater. Admission is $5 for adults and $4 for students and seniors and is free for children under 12.

BOULDER PUBLIC LIBRARY
1000 Canyon Boulevard, Boulder
(303) 441-4397
www.boulder.lib.co.us
Besides the library's permanent art collection in both wings, there are ongoing exhibitions by contemporary regional artists in various media in an area called The Exhibit Space (entrance on Canyon Boulevard). With a ceiling height of 11 feet, 10 inches, and 160 linear feet of exhibition

walls, it's one of the largest display spaces in Boulder. Most artists represented are well-known Colorado painters and sculptors, though some national traveling exhibits are also displayed. Another worthwhile stop is at the display cases on the bridge, where all types of interesting exhibits are shown monthly. The Boulder Public Library Meadows Branch, 4800 Baseline Road (303-441-4390), also has a display space, featuring such items as raku pottery and Hawaiian leis and ceremonial capes made of feathers. If you're interested in historic photographs, check out the Carnegie Library, 1125 Pine Street (303-441-3110), which has digitized about 7,000 of its best photographs so people can view them on a computer screen without touching and possibly damaging them. Call each branch for specific hours.

BOULDER STAINED GLASS STUDIOS
1920 Arapahoe Avenue, Boulder
(303) 449-9030
Specializing in glasswork in Boulder for more than 25 years, the studio offers custom design and fabrication, and both architectural and period work. The general approach is architectural, though there's a selection of beautiful glass items, including blown-glass vases, jewelry, clocks, and imaginative pieces by various Colorado artists. The studio is known for its high-quality contemporary and period leaded, etched, and beveled stained glass. It primarily promotes glass crafts by Colorado artisans. The studio is open 9 a.m. to 5:30 p.m. Monday through Friday and by appointment.

CU ART GALLERIES
Sibell-Wolle Fine Arts Building (east of UMC at Broadway and Euclid), CU-Boulder campus
(303) 492-8300
www.colorado.edu/cuartgalleries
At CU Art Galleries, the large group shows of student work are especially fun and zany—a little bit of New York in Boulder. The gallery also hosts exhibitions by nationally known artists, and there are 5,000 pieces in its permanent collection. Be sure to check out the Sibell-Wolle galleries, which, in addition to student work, also regularly feature impressive work by national and interna-

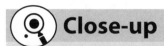 **Close-up**

Where to See Cowboys and Indians? Only at The Leanin' Tree Museum and Sculpture Garden of Western Art

A favorite of out-of-town visitors and locals alike, the Leanin' Tree Museum and Sculpture Garden of Western Art exhibits more than 250 original paintings and 150 bronze sculptures. These works comprise the personal collection of Ed P. Trumble, who founded the Leanin' Tree fine art greeting-card company in Boulder in 1949.

Give yourself plenty of time when you visit the museum, which opened in 1974 in the Leanin' Tree corporate headquarters. It is the largest private collection of Western art in the nation open to the public with no admission charge. The artwork is by artists whom Ed Trumble met as he was seeking Western art to reproduce on greeting cards at a time when there were no galleries or museums exhibiting Western-themed art and modern art had eclipsed it in importance. Trumble traveled the West in the 1950s and 1960s to find artists still painting in the traditional, representational realist style. He found them working at other trades to earn a living and painting only in their spare time. As Trumble licensed their work and began to sell reproductions of it on greeting cards and prints throughout the nation, interest in this Western art genre was reborn. After years of visiting the artists in their homes to view their paintings and license their art, Trumble developed lasting friendships. It was from these friends that he acquired paintings and bronze sculptures, piece by piece, as he could afford it, over a period of more than 50 years.

American Western art is a unique genre that began in the 1800s with landscape painters painting in a realistic style to capture the vast wildness of the frontier of America. As the frontier was pushed west from the Hudson River, beyond the Mississippi and to the Pacific, it was painters who gave Americans a glimpse of their growing nation. In the century it took us to settle the West, American artists produced magnificent paintings and bronzes of the wondrous landscapes, wildlife, Native Americans, and cowboys that play such a large part in our history. Modern Art, introduced in the early 1900s, soon replaced Western art. Now the two genres exist side-by-side since the development of color printing has made artworks of any period of art history available, from a few dollars to many thousands, to art lovers all over the world.

Western art is now only a portion of the art reproduced on Leanin' Tree cards, and only a handful of the museum works are on cards and prints. The work of more than 500 artists, photographers, cartoonists, and designers is licensed by Leanin' Tree, a private Colorado corporation. The brand now includes a Christian line of cards, beautiful watercolors, New-Age fantasies, angels, seascapes, raucous cartoons, 1900s photos, horses, Native American themes, and many others. The cards and other merchandise with the distinctive Leanin' Tree logo are sold at retail establishments in all 50 states and in 40 foreign countries.

tional artists. In summer the galleries are open 10 a.m. to 4:30 p.m. Monday through Friday and 2 to 4:30 p.m. Saturday; call for winter hours. Closed Sunday year-round.

THE DENVER ART MUSEUM
100 West 14th Avenue, Denver
(720) 865-5000
www.denverartmuseum.org

With its newest building designed by famed architect Daniel Libeskind, the Denver Art Museum has two unique structures in the state. The original museum, with its silhouette of see-through geometric shapes, was designed by Italian architect Geo Ponti and resembles a giant paper cutout. The new adjacent structure, the Frederic C. Hamilton Building, opened in October 2006 and is an architectural gem. In one elegant gesture, an acute angle cantilevers over the street below, truly expressing the power and strength of the new structure. Inside the museum is one of the best collections of art in the West, including an internationally acclaimed pre-Columbian art collection. You also can enjoy works by Picasso, Matisse, Frederic Remington, and Winslow Homer. The museum offers an extensive array of family and children's programs and classes. Visit the Web site for up-to-date collection information and new museum amenities. Hours are Tuesday through Thursday and Saturday 10 a.m. to 5 p.m., Friday 10 a.m. to 10 p.m., and Sunday noon to 5 p.m. The museum is closed on Monday. Tickets are available online and at the door and vary in price.

FISKE PLANETARIUM
Regent Drive, CU-Boulder campus
(303) 492-5001 (star shows)
(303) 492-5002 (administration and information)
http://fiske.colorado.edu
Stargazers and sci-fi fans will enjoy the small gallery outside the planetarium's star-show auditorium, which often displays astronomical or futuristic artwork. Take the kids and take it all in—art exhibit and a star show, workshop, or lab. The planetarium is open 8 a.m. to 5 p.m. Monday through Friday and offers public shows on Friday evenings and some Tuesdays and Saturdays. A tour of the gallery is free; star shows are $3.50 for kids and seniors, $6.00 for adults; laser shows are $5.00.

THE LEANIN' TREE MUSEUM AND SCULPTURE GARDEN OF WESTERN ART
6055 Longbow Drive, Boulder
(303) 530-1442
www.leanintreemuseum.com
This museum houses the nation's largest privately owned Western art collection that is open to the public and free of charge. The artwork, all created since 1950, includes original paintings and bronze sculptures. Two monumental (15-foot) bronze sculptures grace the museum's courtyard and grounds. The collection is a result of Leanin'

Tree founder Ed Trumble's long friendship with Western artists. Admission is free; the museum is open 8 a.m. to 5 p.m. weekdays, 10 a.m. to 5 p.m. Saturday and Sunday. For more information, see the Attractions chapter.

Western architecture buffs will love the Boulder Museum of History, which provides exhibits showing the history of Boulder's neighborhoods and gives detailed information on how to tour Boulder, offering several routes and various recommended walks. Be sure to ask about Boulder's two world-class landmarks: the National Center for Atmospheric Research for its building, and the University of Colorado for its landscaping.

MARY WILLIAMS FINE ARTS
2116 Pearl Street, Boulder
(303) 938-1588
www.marywillamsfinearts.com
This gallery specializes in antique prints and original art from the 19th and 20th centuries. You'll find fine prints and graphics with botanical, natural history, and architectural themes. If you want a John James Audubon, a Currier and Ives, or an Edward S. Curtis on your walls, here's where you'll find one. The gallery also features local and national contemporary artists.

OPEN STUDIOS
125 Artist Studios throughout Boulder
(303) 444-1862
www.openstudios.org
The first two weekends in October from 12–6 p.m. are intriguing and fun thanks to Boulder's own Open Studios Tour. Each fall, 125 of Boulder's best artists open their studios to the public and feature demonstrations and works for sale. You can buy a map/calendar at numerous locations throughout the city and be on your way. Look for the familiar yellow and turquoise signage that directs you to each studio. Check out their Web site for more details and a list of artists.

REMBRANDT YARD
1301 Spruce Street, Boulder
(303) 301-2970
www.rembrandtyard.com
Rembrandt Yard, located in the heart of downtown, is a gallery and working artists' studio. There are typically seven to eight resident artists whose works are displayed in the gallery spaces. Special exhibitions are held in the galleries as well. Rembrandt Yard also offers workshops and classes and provides lovely rental space for special events.

SMITH-KLEIN GALLERY
1116 Pearl Street, Boulder
(303) 444-7200
smithklein.com
This contemporary space offers an extensive collection of old and new jewelry, statues, hand-blown art glass, and traditional and contemporary paintings and sculpture. It also features work by contemporary Native American artists. Smith-Klein is open daily.

WILLOW—AN ARTISANS MARKET
1500 Pearl Street, Boulder
(303) 443-0835
You can always find the perfect gift—for yourself or someone else—at Willow, formerly known as the Middle Fish. Full of whimsical and unique crafts from local and national artists, the Willow is located just off the Pearl Street Mall. Handcrafted items include jewelry, ceramics, fiber work, greeting cards, and so much more.

PARKS AND RECREATION CENTERS

From the Boulder Creek Path and mountain parks to the reservoir and recreation centers, our city is rich with recreational facilities, both indoor and out, public and private. Boulder offers a total of 56 urban parks and more than 100,000 acres of open space and mountain parks, a one-acre reservoir, a golf course, two outdoor pools, three athletic complexes, a 7.5-mile linear creekside park, three recreation centers, and an extensive program of classes and activities. Following is a description of some of Boulder's most popular parks and their special features. Details on additional outdoor recreational activities can be found in our Sports chapter.

PARKS

City Parks

BOULDER CREEK PATH
Parallel to Canyon Boulevard and/or Arapahoe Avenue from Four Mile Canyon in Boulder Canyon east to Cherryvale Road (approximately 7.5 miles)

Certainly the most popular and accessible park and the best way to see Boulder is the Boulder Creek Path, which cuts through the heart of the city, following the creek's tumbling path down Boulder Canyon and out to the eastern plains. The Creek Path hugs Canyon Boulevard down to Broadway then veers off south under Arapahoe Avenue. It meanders back under Arapahoe after 30th Street. For a close-up look at what goes on inside the creek, from mountains to plains, stop off at the Boulder Public Library and check out the creek fish tank, complete with colorful rainbow trout. You can also take a peek under the water at the observatory on the creek near Folsom Avenue.

Bicyclists, walkers, and in-line skaters crowd this scenic path, shaded by some of Boulder's oldest cottonwoods and willows. The path branches off into various other routes and is accessible at sidewalk intersections throughout its length. Many Boulderites use the Creek Path to commute across town, so be sure to stay to the right or you might be run down by those on wheels. Stop and enjoy the scenery or have lunch at one of the many benches.

The creek itself provides recreation, too. There's a kayak course near the mouth of the canyon, catch-and-release fishing, and in the summer tubers bob from Eben G. Fine Park to Central Park. The water is too shallow and swift for swimming, but waders brave the chilly flow to reach a mid-creek perch on a rock.

While you're enjoying the rushing water, keep in mind that in the 1970s the Corps of Engineers suggested that Boulder might want to cut channels in the creek to reduce flood danger. Boulder, typically, took another path, bringing in huge boulders to re-create the creek's natural profile of burbling rapids and quiet pools for resting fish. The city is gradually buying property along the path of the creek to allow the inevitable flood waters to spread with a minimum of destruction.

The Boulder Creek Path is described in detail in the Attractions chapter.

CENTRAL PARK
Broadway and Canyon Boulevard
Boulder
No phone
www.ci.boulder.co.us/parks-recreation

There's always something going on in this pretty park in the heart of downtown, with its historic

PARKS AND RECREATION CENTERS

passenger train, creekside picnic tables and lawns, bandshell, and plentiful green grass for lounging and watching the passing crowds. Right on the Boulder Creek Path and across from the Boulder Museum of Contemporary Art and the Boulder Dushanbe Tea House, the park is also adjacent to the Saturday and Wednesday Farmers' Market along 13th Street.

EBEN G. FINE PARK
Third Street and Arapahoe Avenue
Boulder
(303) 413-7200
www.ci.boulder.co.us/parks-recreation
Green grass, rushing cool water, lofty trees, creekside picnic tables and grills, a covered shelter, and playground equipment make this mouth-of-the-canyon park a popular retreat from the heat. The Boulder Creek Path passes by on its way up the canyon. The rustic shelter, with generous picnic tables and its own grill, can be rented for parties. Call the number listed above.

FOOTHILLS COMMUNITY PARK
Eighth and Cherry Streets, Boulder
No phone
www.ci.boulder.co.us/parks-recreation
This 69-acre site was purchased in 1985 with money from a voter-approved bond issue. The south portion of the park between Locust and Cherry Streets opened in 2001. It has two playgrounds, two outdoor hockey rinks, and open, grassy areas for sledding, Frisbee, ball playing, and just running around. The park is also linked to Open Space trails and to the Foothills Community Gardens, one of three community gardens in Boulder.

SALBERG SHELTER
19th and Elder Streets, Boulder
(303) 413-7200
www.ci.boulder.co.us/parks-recreation
This small park in the north-central part of town has a crafts building, playground, and plenty of space to play Frisbee or stretch out under the trees and take an afternoon nap. The shelter, with

restrooms, a lighted stage, tables and chairs, and a grill, can be rented year-round by calling the Parks and Recreation Department at the listed number.

SCOTT CARPENTER PARK
Arapahoe Avenue and 30th Street
Boulder
(303) 441-3427 (pool)
www.bouldercolorado.gov
Named for Boulder's own astronaut, this is a favorite warm-weather spot for kids, with its outdoor pool and playground featuring a rocket jungle gym commemorating the feats of its namesake. Open swim is from 1 to 5 p.m. Monday through Friday, 1 to 6 p.m. Saturday and Sunday between Memorial Day weekend and Labor Day. Admission for residents on a per-visit basis is $6.00 for adults, $4.00 for seniors age 60 and older, $3.50 for teens ages 13 through 18, and $3.00 for kids ages 3 through 12. Annual and multi-entry passes are available.

SKATEPARK
30th Street and Arapahoe Avenue
Boulder
(303) 441-3410
www.ci.boulder.co.us/parks-recreation
Next door to Scott Carpenter Park is a street-course for skateboarders, in-line skaters, and BMX bicyclists. The unsupervised park is free and open dawn to dusk. There are rails, curbs, bowls, and free forms to challenge the most daring air-eater. It's skate-at-your-own-risk; helmets and pads are strongly recommended. The park was designed by nationally known skateboarder and skatepark designer Michael McIntyre with advice from Boulder area skateboarders. BMX bikes have the run of the facility 7 to 10 a.m. daily. And graffiti artists are welcome to demonstrate their abilities on a graffiti wall just north of the Skatepark.

SPRUCE POOL
2102 Spruce Street, Boulder
(303) 441-3426
www.bouldercolorado.gov
This outdoor pool is a particular favorite of summer lap swimmers, who stop by before and after

work or over the lunch hour for a wet workout. Open swims are from 1 to 5 p.m. Monday through Friday and 1 to 6 p.m. Saturday and Sunday from mid-June to early September. In addition to lap lanes, there is a separate kiddie pool and a great slide. Sunbathers can stretch out on a grassy hill that borders the pool. Red Cross–certified swim lessons are available. Fees for residents and non-residents are the same as for the Scott Carpenter Park pool, listed previously.

Dog Parks

AIRPORT AND VALMONT ROADS
5660 Sioux Drive
Howard Heuston Park, 34th Street
and Iris Avenue, Boulder
Boulder residents love their dogs, and they love their parks. The two passions have been combined with the creation of two fenced parks just for dogs and their owners. The parks are open daily from dawn to dusk and are surrounded by 4-foot chain link fences so dogs can safely run off-leash. A 3.5-acre park at Valmont and Airport Roads in northeast Boulder is on a portion of the otherwise undeveloped Valmont City Park. Water spigots are available for thirsty pooches. The second park is on 1.5 acres in an undeveloped portion of the East Boulder Community Park, next to the East Boulder Community Center at 5660 Sioux Drive. This park gives dogs access to a portion of a pond. Only licensed and unaggressive dogs may visit the parks. In addition, there is an unfenced dog exercise area at Howard Heuston Park at 34th Street and Iris Avenue. Dogs visiting this park must respond to voice commands.

Mountain Parks and Open Space

BOULDER OPEN SPACE AND
MOUNTAIN PARKS
P.O. Box 791, Boulder, CO 80306
(303) 441-3440
www.ci.boulder.co.us/openspace
Way back in 1898, long before Colorado's Front Range became one of the fastest developing regions in the country, Boulder's prescient citizens bought their first piece of land for preserva-

tion. In the years since, the city has bought up a sweep of mountain backdrop and a ring of high plains prairie that shapes the city, protects it from encroachment by its fast-growing neighbors, preserves precious ecosystems, and gives residents a refuge for passive recreation and contemplation. That 65,000 acres of open space and mountain parks land is the envy of other cities that are just now recognizing the value of undeveloped land.

An excellent introduction to the mountain parks is the drive up Flagstaff Mountain. The hairpin-turn, two-lane drive offers spectacular panoramas along the way, as well as pull-offs, trails, and picnic spots. Keep your eyes on the road and let your passengers describe the human flies climbing on the rock formations. To get there, take Baseline Road west, follow its curve to the right and up Flagstaff Mountain. (The elegant Flagstaff House restaurant along the way is open for dinner only.)

A glut of visitors from other cities in the region has put a strain on the popular area. To reduce that number, and recoup some of the cost of maintaining the area, the city requires cars not registered in Boulder County to pay for parking both on Flagstaff Mountain and in Gregory Canyon (the area below Flagstaff). Annual permits are $15; daily permits are $3 and may be purchased at six self-service stations along Flagstaff Road. Be warned: Rangers do patrol the lots and ticket cars without permits.

More than 120 miles of hiking trails lace the mountain backdrop and the plains below. Popular mountain trailheads begin at Chautauqua Park, Flagstaff Mountain, the National Center for Atmospheric Research, and Eldorado Springs. You can hike to Bear Peak, Green Mountain, Mount Sanitas, and to the Devil's Thumb—all of which are popular, substantial hikes taking from several hours to most of the day, depending upon your level of fitness. (Some specific locations and suggested hikes are described under "Hiking" in the Sports chapter.)

Among the flat, popular trailheads are: Bobolink, a favorite of dog walkers, offering a shady stroll along South Boulder Creek, located at Cherryvale and Baseline Roads; Boulder Valley Ranch, a long prairie path popular with horseback riders, past one of the working ranches leased from the city, located a mile east of U.S. Highway 36 on Longhorn Road; and Doudy Draw trailhead, a meandering trail through ponderosa pine and the South Boulder Creek riparian corridor, past historic homesites (and a great place to find bear signs or even spot a black bear), located 1.8 miles west of Highway 93 on Eldorado Springs Drive.

Trail maps are available from the Open Space and Mountain Parks Department; Boulder Chamber of Commerce, 2440 Pearl Street (303-442-1044, www.boulderchamber.com) and Boulder Map Gallery, 1708 13th Street (303-444-1406, www.bouldermapgallery.com).

Rangers and naturalists offer a series of free hikes and educational programs on topics ranging from the truth about rattlesnakes to where to find (but not disturb) wild irises to the best spots for bass fishing. They even offer an evaluation of canine citizenship to help owners determine if their dogs are well-trained enough to handle the distractions of a hike off-leash, where allowed.

CHAUTAUQUA PARK
Ninth Street and Baseline Road, Boulder
(303) 442-3282
At the base of the Flatirons, Boulder's first park opened as a summer camp and retreat for visitors from Texas in 1898 and was originally called Texado Park. Perched on a hill overlooking the city, the park features a sweeping grassy area below the camp's cottages (some for rent and some owner-occupied) and communal buildings; it invites casual summer sports such as Frisbee throwing and badminton. An auditorium hosts a summer concert series and popular movie series. Many concertgoers bring their own picnics to enjoy under the shady cottonwoods. A dining room serves meals year-round. There are two playgrounds and several hiking trails into the foothills.

State Parks
ELDORADO CANYON STATE PARK
Highway 170, Eldorado Springs
(303) 494-3943
www.parks.state.co.us
One of the best rock-climbing areas in the United States, this canyon is lined with spectacular rock walls rising to 1,500 feet, the patient work of South Boulder Creek. It's a great place to watch some world-class rock climbing on the 500 routes or to do a bit of hiking, biking, or fishing. In the early 1900s, daredevil Ivy Baldwin made unique use of the towering canyon walls, walking a high wire from the Bastille to the aptly named Wind Tower. Ike and Mamie Eisenhower reportedly honeymooned in the canyon, when it was operated as a private resort. The park is open until dusk. The entrance fee is $3 for walk-ins, $7 per vehicle, and $60 for an annual state parks pass, $30 for those 64 and over ($12.50 for those age 62 and older or with a permanent disability). Check the maps at the park entrance and ranger station for information on the length and level of difficulty of the various trails.

On the way to the park you'll pass Eldorado Artesian Springs (303-499-1316, ext. 5), a privately owned historic resort (see the History chapter). The thermal pools and snack bar are open from 10 a.m. to 6 p.m. daily from Memorial Day through Labor Day. Cost per day is $8 for adults, $5 for kids ages 3 through 12 and for seniors age 60 and older; children younger than age 3 are admitted free. The park is 8 miles south of Boulder. Take Highway 93 to Highway 170 and head west.

RECREATIONAL FACILITIES
Boulder Recreation Centers
The city of Boulder operates three excellent recreation centers. Daily admission for adults is $6.25; children ages 3 to 12, $3.50; ages 13 to 18, $4.00; seniors older than age 60, $4.50. Admission is reduced by purchasing a punch card, for which prices vary by age group, number of punches, and residency. There is also an annual pass, costing about $490 for a single resident adult and

varying based on age and residency. The centers are open daily; call for specific hours of operation. Reservations must be made two days in advance for the handball, racquetball, and tennis courts. Child care is available for children ages 6 months to 5 years for $6.50 per hour. Call each center for child-care schedules. Child-care space is limited, so it's smart to call first.

BOB BURGER RECREATION CENTER
111 West Baseline Road, Lafayette
(303) 665-0469
www.cityoflafayette.com
The Lafayette Recreation Department, winner of the National Medal Award, serves our community by offering a wide variety of fitness and recreational opportunities. Classes and activities are affordably priced and open for public enjoyment. The Recreation Center is housed on 20 acres of parkland. This multi-use area features a 4-field youth sports complex, an inline hockey rink and the city's outdoor classroom. These amenities provide the community with a wonderful focal point for great family recreation. Fees are: Children ages 2–5 pay $2.50, ages 6–17 pay $3, ages 18–54 pay $4.50, and those over 55 pay $2.75.

EAST BOULDER RECREATION CENTER
5660 Sioux Drive, Boulder
(303) 441-4400, (303) 441-4150
(senior center)
www.ci.boulder.co.us/parks-recreation
Boulder's newest recreation center combines a senior center and recreation center. The Senior Center wing includes a cafeteria, a common area, an arts-and-crafts room, and computers with Internet access for public use. The recreation facility features a 25-yard indoor lap pool and leisure pool with waterslide and children's play area; gymnasium with adjustable basketball hoops; extensive weight rooms with free and body-master weights, rowing machines, and stationary cycles; a climbing wall; an aerobics room; and a dance studio. Outdoors you'll find tennis, basketball, and racquetball courts, as well as a wheelchair-accessible playground. Kayakers make use of the pond.

ERIE COMMUNITY CENTER
450 Powers Street, Erie
(303) 926-2550
www.ci.erie.co.us
This gorgeous new recreation center opened in 2007 and is a fantastic addition to the burgeoning east county towns. The center features state of the art equipment as well as an indoor climbing wall for the young and young at heart! The building was designed with sustainability and energy conservation as a priority. Key features include an aquatics area with lap pool, leisure pool with play features, whirlpool, 2-story figure-8 pool slide with splash tank, lazy river, and outdoor water feature and spray area, gymnasium, fitness areas on two levels, including cardiovascular (all with integrated 15" LCD screens), fitness/group exercise studio (1,340 sq ft) with sprung timber floor and mirrored walls, 32' climbing pinnacle and 12' bouldering wall, elevated indoor running track, racquetball courts and so much more. The center is open Monday through Friday, from 5:30 am until 10 pm and on Saturday and Sunday, from 8 am until 6 pm. Fees are: $4.50 adults, $2.70 seniors and $2.25 for kids ages 4 through 17.

LOUISVILLE RECREATION CENTER
900 West Via Appia, Louisville
(303) 666-7400
www.louisvillerecreation.com
The facility offers a 6-lane, 25-meter pool with diving well, a 160-foot water slide, adventure splash down pool, solarium and sundeck, sauna whirlpool steam room, racquetball courts, two free-weight rooms, circuit weight room, gymnasium, cardiovascular training area, wallyball court, aerobic studio, multipurpose rooms, senior center, outdoor playground, 10-lap–per-mile indoor track, sand volleyball court, locker rooms, indoor cycling classes, 57,400-square-feet outdoor inline hockey rink, skate park, and four outdoor lighted tennis courts. Center fees: Children 3–12 pay $3.00, 13–18 pay $3.50, 19 and over pay $5.00, and those 60 and over pay $3.00. Group rates are for 10+ people: $2.00 for kids and $4.00 for adults.

NORTH BOULDER RECREATION CENTER

3170 Broadway, Boulder
(303) 441-3444
www.ci.boulder.co.us/parks-recreation

This heavily used center reopened in spring 2003 after a major overhaul. The renovated center has a leisure pond with a twisting body slide; a separate 25-yard lap pool with a ramp for swimmers with disabilities; an expanded weight room and yoga center; a children's garden; an enhanced gymnastics center with a foam pit, vaulting space, and area for "air tumbling"; expanded locker rooms; and a new family locker room.

SOUTH BOULDER RECREATION CENTER

1360 Gillaspie Drive, Boulder
(303) 441-3448
www.ci.boulder.co.us/parks-recreation

This center has a pool with a wheelchair ramp, a hot tub, a sauna, locker rooms, showers, classrooms, a gymnasium, an expanded weight room, a racquetball/handball court, outdoor sand volleyball courts, and four outdoor tennis courts. On Sundays, a huge inflatable pyramid is put in the pool for kids to play on. Neighboring Viele Lake offers canoeing and paddleboating, as well as a fitness course around the lake.

OTHER RECREATION OPTIONS

BOULDER RESERVOIR

5100 51st Street, off north side of the
Diagonal Highway, Boulder
(303) 441-3456 (boathouse)
(303) 441-3468 (gate)
www.ci.boulder.co.us/parks-recreation

For those craving a beach, this is the closest thing to it in Boulder County. Tons and tons of sand were trucked in to create the beaches for the reservoir, and more is added periodically. Swimmers, sailors, sailboarders, canoeists, kayakers, and water-skiers make this a busy place on summer weekends. Various watercraft are for rent, including sailboats and Windsurfers; call the boathouse for rates. Grills and picnic tables provide a nice spot for summer barbecues on the swimming beach. The reservoir hosts sailboat races, volleyball tournaments, and a national in-line skating competition. The chilly reservoir is also the scene of the annual Polar Bear Dip on New Year's Day (see the Festivals and Annual Events chapter). Waterskiing, sailboating, and sailboarding classes are available. One-day summer admission to The Res is $6.00 for adults age 19 and older, $3.50 for teens ages 13 through 18, $3.00 for children ages 4 through 12, $4.00 for seniors ages 60 to 64, and free for seniors 65 and older and children younger than age 4. Season passes are available; call the gate for information. The one-acre reservoir is open year-round, but services are provided weekends only in the spring (Memorial Day weekend to the second Monday in June) and fall (third Monday in August through Labor Day weekend), seven days a week during the months in between. There is no admission charge during the rest of the year. Boulder Reservoir is 1.5 miles north of Jay Road via the Diagonal Highway (Highway 119).

MAPLETON CENTER THERAPY POOL

311 Mapleton Avenue, Boulder
(303) 441-0436

If a bathtub-style dip is more your style, try out the therapy pool at the Mapleton Center of Boulder Community Hospital. The indoor pool is kept at a balmy 94 degrees. It is used by patients at the rehab hospital but is also open to the public for open swim—call (303) 441-0542 for hours—and lessons. Drop-in fees are $9.25 for ages 18 to 59 and $6.75 for adults older than age 60; punch cards are available. Children younger than age 12 are not allowed in the open swim, but swim classes are offered for kids and adults.

YMCA OF BOULDER VALLEY

2850 Mapleton Avenue, Boulder
95th Street and Arapahoe Avenue, Lafayette
(303) 442-2778
www.ymcabv.org

There are three Y facilities in Boulder County, offering everything from an indoor running track to an outdoor swimming pool to the county's only public indoor ice-skating rink. The main facility is in Boulder at 2850 Mapleton Avenue. It offers a full range of facilities and classes, including racquetball/handball courts; a 25-yard indoor pool; a full gym; indoor running track; Jacuzzi, Cybex, Nautilus, and Hydrogym equipment; an aerobics studio; a picnic area and playground; a nursery and child-care facility; and single-sex saunas. Admission for nonmembers is $12 for teens and adults; $6 for kids younger than age 18. Adult membership is $50 to join and $47 per month; family membership is $50 to join and $71 per month.

The Arapahoe Center is a 55,000-square-foot facility located near the intersection of 95th Street and Arapahoe Avenue. This Y includes a full gymnasium, locker rooms, an indoor track, free weights, an in-line skating rink, aerobic space, and the only public indoor ice arena in Boulder County. All new Techno-Gym fitness equipment will be arriving in December 2008 as well as a kinesis studio and a mind, body, spirit studio (yoga and pilates) with a brand new, state of the art "reverberating floor" (first in Colorado!). The drop-in fee is $12 for adults and $7 for teens to use all of the facilities. Call (303) 664-5455 for more information.

SPORTS

Many people move to Boulder specifically for what's contained in this chapter: bicycling, hiking, camping, skiing, rock climbing, running, and other outdoor sports. Boulder has been called "the sports town" by *Outside* magazine, and you'll share the trails, parks, and facilities with some of the nation's and world's best athletes, who come here to train.

Non-Olympians also abound, and you'll find them poking around in sporting goods shops and at meetings of the various clubs and organizations for bicycling, skiing, rock climbing, and hiking listed in this chapter.

If you're a spectator rather than a participant, you'll be in the minority, but you'll have plenty of exciting games to watch. Football fans cheer for CU-Boulder's Buffaloes, who are members of the NCAA Division I Big 12 Conference and former national football champions, and the National Football League's Denver Broncos. If you like basketball, you can follow CU's women and men Buffaloes, as well as the National Basketball Association's Denver Nuggets. Other sports teams in our area include the Colorado Rockies Major League Baseball team, the Colorado Avalanche National Hockey League team (formerly Quebec's Nordiques, the Avalanche have firmly endeared themselves to Coloradans by winning the 1996 and 2001 Stanley Cup), and various college teams. The Rockies and Avalanche are both based in Denver.

PARTICIPATORY SPORTS

Bicycling

Boulder provides more than 90 miles of bikeways, from marked on-street bike lanes to separate paths reserved for nonmotorized travel, including cycling, in-line skating, walking, skateboarding, and running. Bicyclists are very active in lobbying for their facilities (in fact, several members of the City Council ride their bikes to and from council meetings). The city sponsors a 15- or 24-mile bicycle-around-the-city event to encourage citizens to get acquainted with the city's bicycle accommodations. Local organizations include Boulder Bicycle Commuters (www.boulderbicyclecommuters.org), Boulder Mountainbike Alliance (www.bma-mtb.org), and Bicycle Colorado (www.bicyclecolo.org).

Rentals and Information
Bikes can be rented at various shops around town, including University Bicycles, 839 Pearl Street, downtown (303-444-4196); Boulder Bikesmith, 2432 Arapahoe Avenue, Arapahoe Village Shopping Center (303-443-1132); and Louisville Cyclery, 1032 South Boulder Road, Louisville (303-665-6343). Average rates for a cruiser are $16 for four hours (city or mountain bike) and $22 for a full day.

Bike paths weave all around and through Boulder, and a map is a good bet if you don't want to get lost. The transportation department's Bicycle and Pedestrian Map is available from Go Boulder, the city's alternative transportation program, 1739 Broadway, second floor (303-441-3266); the Boulder Chamber of Commerce, 2440 Pearl Street (303-442-1044); and also at the bicycle shops listed previously. Other resources for bicycling information are the University of Colorado Bike Office (303-492-6486) and the local clubs for cycling enthusiasts listed previously.

Bicyclists are treated as vehicles and must obey the same traffic laws as cars. That means no riding on sidewalks, yielding to pedestrians, obeying traffic signals, and riding on the right side of the road. You must have a rear reflector and a front light when riding after dark. The county Sheriff's Office has gotten very serious about enforcing rules against bicyclists riding abreast and blocking traffic lanes. A helmet isn't required but is highly encouraged.

Boulder's Bike Paths

The city's plentiful bike paths are the obvious place to start pedaling.

BEAR CREEK GREENWAY
**Northeast corner, Broadway and
Table Mesa Drive**

South Boulderites can enjoy a beautiful bike path that heads northeast from Martin Park, on the corner of Broadway and Table Mesa Drive. Access the path at the far northeast end of the park. Called the Bear Creek Greenway, the path winds along Bear Creek under highways and eventually over Foothills Parkway, where cyclists have the choice of heading farther east on the Centennial Bike Path or heading north across Arapahoe Avenue and connecting with the Boulder Creek Path.

BOULDER CREEK PATH
Various locations

Cruise right onto the very popular Boulder Creek Path, the backbone of the city's bike path network. The path, which also accommodates pedestrians and in-line skaters, is most easily accessed at Central Park (Broadway and Canyon), Eben Fine Park (Fourth and Arapahoe), the Millennium Harvest House Hotel (1345 28th Street, just south of Arapahoe), or Scott Carpenter Park (30th Street south of Arapahoe Avenue). Most major intersections crossing Arapahoe Avenue have a sidewalk ramp onto the bike path.

Head east or west—both directions offer a great ride and scenery. Going west, the paved section ends about a half-mile into Boulder Canyon, and a wide packed-gravel path continues a little more than 2 miles (from Eben Fine Park) up to Four Mile Canyon, where the Creek Path ends. It's not a steep or difficult ride to the end of the

path, but those new to Boulder's elevation might be a bit breathless as the trail gradually climbs the canyon, paralleling the highway. It's best ridden on a mountain bike, but skinny tires can make it, too, with care on the gravel and "curbs" at the bridges.

For those who prefer no hills, ride east, where the Creek Path sweeps out onto the plains past 30th Street and CU-Boulder's Research Park for a panoramic view of the Front Range, past duck ponds, cottonwoods, and prairie dog towns. See the Attractions chapter for a detailed description of the path.

> **i** The trail systems in Boulder are fantastic, with a trail for every ability. Grab a map and go!

Paved Roads (Skinny Tires)
AROUND BOULDER
FLAGSTAFF MOUNTAIN
Macho cyclists can tackle Flagstaff Mountain—a real muscle-buster right in town, due west on Baseline Road. You'll be hunched over the handlebars on the way up, but the zoom down provides some beautiful vistas of the Boulder Valley, and the Chautauqua Dining Hall (303-440-3776) waits at the bottom of the hill.

BEYOND BOULDER
JAMESTOWN
For a good mountain ride, head for Jamestown (17 miles from Broadway and Canyon). Take Broadway up Left Hand Canyon (8 miles north of town) and then, after 6 miles, up James Canyon Drive. (Look for mile markers in the canyon.) The picturesque Jamestown Mercantile Cafe (303-442-5847) offers breakfast, lunch, and snacks.

LOUISVILLE
To reach Louisville (12 miles from Broadway and Canyon), go south on the bike path along the east side of Broadway to Marshall—south of Boulder—through Marshall and over Highway

170. Cross U.S. Highway 36, make a right onto Dillon Road, then a left onto 96th Street.

LYONS

The very popular ride to Lyons is a little hilly. To reach Lyons (16 miles from Broadway and Canyon), ride north on Broadway (US 36), which has a wide shoulder part of the way, all the way to Lyons, and turn left at the railroad track. Andrea's (303-823-5000) is a dandy breakfast or lunch spot (closed Wednesdays).

NEDERLAND

The 17 miles up Boulder Canyon to Nederlands is a strenuous ride. Be cautious—the curving canyon road with its narrow shoulder and speeding cars can be quite hazardous for cyclists. Choose less busy times such as midweek and midday for this ride.

NIWOT

The ride to Niwot is relatively flat and pastoral, winding past ponds and pleasant countryside (16 miles from Broadway and Canyon). Go north on Broadway to Nelson Road and turn right (for a shorter ride turn right on Neva Road before Nelson). Follow Nelson Road to Highway 73, turn right and go to Niwot Road and turn left; proceed into Niwot. Treppedas Gourmet Market Cafe (303-652-1606) offers a variety of great lunch goodies.

WARD

The truly tough can ride all the way up Left Hand Canyon to Ward (23 miles one way from Broadway and Canyon)—all steady climbing from the start of Left Hand Canyon. If you can make it over the final hill out of Ward to the Peak to Peak Highway (Highway 72), great meals, homemade pie, and local ambience await you at the Millsite Inn (303-459-3308), just north of Ward.

UNPAVED ROADS (FAT TIRES)

Bicycles aren't allowed off-trail on publicly owned lands around Boulder, but there are 120 miles of trails in the city's open space and mountain parks

and another 80 miles of trails on county open space, many of them open to bicyclists.

The Boulder Mountain Bike Alliance, a citizen's nonprofit organization formed in 1991 to provide "a positive voice for mountain biking," hosts social rides two or three times a week during the summer and encourages riders to volunteer time for trail maintenance. Call (303) 667-2467 for more information.

A few suggested off-road mountain bike trails follow.

AROUND BOULDER

COMMUNITY DITCH TRAIL

The Community Ditch Trail is a 4-mile dirt service road of moderate difficulty that travels through grasslands, mesas, and land with evidence of early farming and mining activity. Taken from the Marshall Mesa trailhead, this ride is a huff and a puff up the mesa, but riders will be rewarded with spectacular views of the mountains and a delightful flat ride along the flower-lined (in spring) mesa and the Community Ditch, which in warm weather invites a swim.

You'll find the trail south of Boulder, at the Doudy Draw trailhead on the south side of Highway 170, 1.7 miles west of Highway 93, or at the Marshall Mesa trailhead, 0.9 mile east of Highway 93 on the south side of Marshall Road.

Cross Highway 93 (Broadway) and continue along the ditch winding back among the cottonwoods. To make a nice loop back to Boulder, head for the Doudy Draw trailhead at the junction of Community Ditch Bridge. At Doudy Draw trailhead you can choose between a side trip into Eldorado Springs (turn left on the paved highway) or turn right to return to Highway 93 to Boulder or the Marshall Mesa Trailhead. Eldorado Springs (about 2 miles) provides a chance to refuel with spring water, swim (in the summer) at Eldorado Springs Resort, graze at the snack bar, or gaze at the daring rock climbers in the state park (303-494-3943) climbing the impressive Bastille and other formations. To return to Boulder or the Marshall Mesa trailhead, ride back out to Highway 93 on the Eldorado Springs road, crossing at the light and continuing straight into the tiny settlement of Marshall. The trailhead is just a little farther east on Marshall Road. If you choose the reverse direction, starting at the Doudy Draw trailhead, go left (east) at the junction of Community Ditch Bridge and the dirt road you're on. The trail crosses Highway 93 and goes to the Marshall Reservoir inlet and up a steep hill to the Marshall Mesa Trailhead.

EAST BOULDER TRAIL
Access Teller Farm South Trailhead, on Arapahoe Road, 1 mile east of 75th Street
The 7-mile East Boulder Trail has a difficulty ranking of moderate. A 2.2-mile level section of the trail goes through a wildlife preserve and past Teller Lake. Then, a 2.7-mile section climbs a mesa on dirt trails and service roads to the Gunbarrel Farm. The Gunbarrel Farm section travels along a dirt service road with moderate grades and turns east at 1.2 miles into the White Rocks area.

GREENBELT PLATEAU TRAIL
This gentle trail rolls across a mesa top through open grasslands with beautiful views of the foothills. At 1.3 miles, bicyclists may choose to take the dirt path to Community Ditch Trail or continue on the service road to Highway 93. This trail is ranked as easy and covers 1.6 miles on gravel surface road. The Greenbelt Plateau Trail is south of Boulder, on the north side of Highway 128, just east of Highway 93.

IN THE MOUNTAINS
Most mountain biking in the local high country requires an outstanding pair of lungs and legs, since it's mostly uphill and at high altitudes.

GOLD HILL
For a ride right out of town, go west on Mapleton Avenue, which becomes unpaved in Sunshine Canyon and continues to the historic mining town of Gold Hill, about 10 miles uphill. From there you can continue to Nederland and return down Boulder Canyon. Or, start the ride at the mouth of Boulder Canyon along the Creek Path,

which ends in 2 miles at Four Mile Canyon (County Road 118). Then, proceed up Four Mile Canyon and turn right at the sign for Gold Hill— also about 10 miles uphill from the mouth of Four Mile Canyon.

ROLLINS PASS
For those in really top shape, try Rollins Pass, one of Colorado's premier mountain biking (and four-wheel-drive) routes. This former railroad bed crosses the Continental Divide. Cars used to be able to make this exciting drive over rickety railroad trestles perched above thousand-foot drops, until the Needle's Eye tunnel caved in. Today, the tunnel, 1.5 miles from the Divide, is the end of the road for vehicles, but mountain bikers and hikers can bypass the tunnel and continue on the roadbed over the pass and all the way down the other side to Winter Park, if desired. To reach Rollins Pass Road, drive west up Boulder Canyon (Highway 119) to Nederland, then south on Highway 72 to Rollinsville. Turn right (west) onto the dirt road marked with signs to Tolland and East Portal and drive 8.5 miles to the East Portal and Moffat Tunnel. The Rollins Pass road begins there, as marked. Bicycling over the pass is an all-day affair requiring another vehicle on the Winter Park side and lodging reservations or plans—not to mention advanced physical fitness.

SOURDOUGH TRAIL
Accessible from the Peak to Peak Highway (Highway 72) west of Nederland, the Sourdough Trail is 17.5 miles long but has different segments at various trailheads. The trail was constructed with help from the Colorado Mountain Club mainly for ski touring and mountain biking, and features pleasant rolling terrain through the pines. From Camp Dick Campground to Beaver Reservoir is 2.3 miles. From Beaver Reservoir to Brainard Road it's 7.4 miles, and from Brainard Road to Rainbow Lakes Road, 7.8 miles. All access to the various connections to the Sourdough Trail is via the Peak to Peak Highway. Camp Dick Campground is on Middle St. Vrain Road, 5.8 miles north of Ward and 0.5 mile west of Peaceful Valley. One

Sourdough trailhead is on the left-hand side of County Road 96 just east of Beaver Reservoir, 2.5 miles north of Ward and 2 miles west on CR 96. The Red Rock trailhead is on the right-hand side of County Road 102, just east of Red Rock Lake, 2.5 miles west on Brainard Lake Road. Another Sourdough trailhead is on the right-hand side of Rainbow Lakes Road (County Road 116), 4.7 miles south of Ward (7 miles north of Nederland) and 0.4 mile west on CR 116.

SWITZERLAND TRAIL

The historic Switzerland Trail, a former single-gauge railroad track, makes for some scenic riding with spectacular mountain views and reasonable climbing grades. Most riders start at the town of Sunset and go south toward Bald and Sugarloaf Mountains. To reach Sunset, head up Four Mile Canyon (see "Gold Hill," listed previously), and stay on CR 118 past Salina and Wallstreet until you reach Sunset, 17 miles from Boulder. Go right to reach Gold Hill or left to Glacier Lake.

Camping

Camping beneath the pines in the cool, clear air of the high country—and perhaps near a gleaming mountain lake or stream—is one of the Rockies' greatest joys. The USDA Forest Service, state of Colorado, and city of Boulder maintain many such sites. (For information on camping in Rocky Mountain National Park, please see that chapter later in this book.)

Boulder County
ROOSEVELT NATIONAL FOREST

The following campgrounds are within the national forest. For information about federal regulations within Roosevelt, call (970) 295-6600.

GOLDEN GATE CANYON STATE PARK
10 miles south of Nederland on Highway 72
2 miles east on Gap Road
(303) 582-3707
www.parks.state.co.us/parks/goldengate canyon
Golden Gate offers many miles of hiking plus backpacking, fishing, and camping at 7,900- to 10,500-foot elevations. You'll find 155 sites, including some in the backcountry. Fees are $18 per night for RV or motor-home sites with electricity, $14 for drive-in tent sites with showers, $8 for walk-in hut and tent sites. There's a one-time reservation fee. Golden Gate is open year-round, weather permitting. A day pass costs $6. For reservations, call (303) 582-3707.

The park's north entrance is 10 miles south of Nederland on Highway 72 and 2 miles east on Gap Road. For the south entrance drive 3 more miles, then 4 miles east on Highway 46.

KELLY DAHL
3 miles south of Nederland on Highway 119
(877) 444-6777
www.fs.fed.us
This campground offers a scenic view of the Continental Divide and limited hiking. There is a small playground, but no electrical hookups, dump stations, or showers. There are 46 sites at an elevation of 8,600 feet. The season lasts from late April or early May through October 31 or the first snow, whichever comes first. The fee is $16 with water.

OLIVE RIDGE CAMPGROUND
15 miles south of Estes Park, or 1.5
miles north of Allenspark, on Highway 7
(877) 444-6777
www.fs.fed.us
Nestled close to lush Rocky Mountain National Park, this campground offers access to the park as well as horse rentals at nearby stables. There are 56 sites at an elevation of 8,400 feet. The season is mid-May through late September. Half the sites can be reserved; there's a $9 reservation fee. Site fees are $16 to $19.

PAWNEE CAMPGROUND
5 miles west of Highways 119/72 on CR 102
(at Brainard Lake)
(877) 444-6777
www.fs.fed.us
This extremely popular (and heavily used) camp-

ground offers beautiful views, fishing, and non-motorized boating with access to the wilderness area. The 55 sites lie at an elevation of 10,400 feet, and the brief season lasts from the first Friday after the Fourth of July through Labor Day. Half of the sites may be reserved; the rest are first come, first served. There is a $9 reservation fee. The site fee is $16.

PEACEFUL VALLEY CAMPGROUND AND CAMP DICK
15 miles west of Lyons on Highway 7, left at the junction with Highway 72, 6 miles farther
(877) 444-6777
www.fs.fed.us
Peaceful Valley is a pleasant, pine-shaded campground with 18 sites at an elevation of 8,500 feet. The season is mid-April through mid-October. Half of the 18 sites may be reserved for a reservation fee of $9. Site fees are $16 to $19.

To reach Camp Dick campground, located a mile west of Peaceful Valley, follow the dirt road to the 46 sites at an elevation of 8,600 feet. Horses are available for rental nearby. The season is from Memorial Day through mid-October depending on the weather. The fee is $16.

RAINBOW LAKES
6.5 miles north of Nederland off Highway 72
(877) 444-6777
www.fs.fed.us
Rainbow Lakes campground is set near several small but lovely lakes. There is no available running water, but good fishing is nearby in the Indian Peaks Wilderness Area. There are 18 sites at an altitude of 10,000 feet, available on a first-come, first-served basis. The season runs from mid-June through mid-October, or the first snow. The fee is $6.

City of Boulder Open Space and Mountain Parks
BUCKINGHAM CAMPGROUND
12 miles northwest of Nederland
(303) 444-6600
The campground is at an elevation of 10,160 feet and is accessible to Indian Peaks Wilderness. Buck-

ingham's 8 sites, available on a first-come, first-served basis, are heavily used. Camping is allowed only in the designated sites, as the surrounding vegetation is easily damaged. The season runs from early June until snow season. No ground fires or charcoal fires are permitted; only gas grills or camp stoves may be used for cooking. No reservations are required, and there's no fee charged for camping, but no water is available.

Buckingham Campground is at the Fourth of July trailhead, 12 miles northwest of Nederland. Take County Road 107 west through Eldora to County Road 130 (a rough road) and proceed to its end.

Climbing
Boulder is internationally known for its great rock-climbing areas, particularly the Flatirons and Eldorado Canyon in the state park (see the Parks and Recreation Centers chapter for more information). With proper equipment and training, rock climbing can be a relatively safe sport, and rock jocks dancing up the cliffs at Eldorado Canyon might even make it look easy. Tempted as they might be, however, those without proper training and equipment should stay on the ground. Every year Colorado witnesses several fatalities involving inexperienced scramblers without equipment—especially around the Flatirons and Boulder Falls (in the Boulder Canyon). The book *Flatiron Classics* by Gerry Roach, a famous local mountaineer and climber, has detailed route information for experienced climbers who want to climb the Flatirons and other popular routes. *Rock Climbing Colorado* by Stewart M. Green is a very thorough book that covers the whole state, describing 1,500 routes.

Those interested in learning to climb have many options, some of which we've listed below.

COLORADO MOUNTAIN CLUB
633 South Broadway, Boulder
(303) 554-7688
www.cmc.org
The CMC, as it is known, offers mountaineering classes that will take you from rank beginner

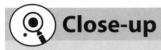 **Close-up**

Camping and Backcountry Travel

Various wilderness areas and national forests have their own sets of use regulations, but the following general guidelines apply to all areas. Remember: Even when we are careful, our presence and actions have an impact on the natural world. As our human population grows, negative impacts become more and more severe.

BACKCOUNTRY TRAVEL

Travel quietly and in small groups. Avoid disturbing others.

Spread out impact by exploring less heavily visited areas.

Leave your pets at home to keep from bothering wildlife and other visitors.

Stay on maintained trails whenever possible. Do not take shortcuts; doing so destroys vegetation and causes erosion.

Be especially careful when trails are muddy, and minimize horse use when trails are wet.

On narrow trails, walk single file rather than several abreast, and try to avoid congregating in large groups in sensitive areas.

Don't pick wildflowers or dig up plants; it's illegal in all parks, and permission is needed on private land. Be judicious in picking fruit so that you leave enough for wildlife.

Comply with signs regarding vehicles and mountain bikes, which are prohibited on many trails because of erosion problems. Refrain from using bikes on muddy slopes, where deep ruts develop quickly, and yield to other trail users.

If you are photographing or observing wild animals and they become nervous, you are too close. Back away.

Give right-of-way to horses, keeping to the downhill side. The same rule applies to all large mammals, who will become stressed if you remain above them.

Avoid disturbing nesting birds, and comply with closures designed to protect plants and animals.

Leave gates as you find them unless signs instruct otherwise.

to advanced mountaineer. Learn all the basics of rock climbing and mountaineering in these courses. CMC also offers advanced mountaineering courses, as well as many scheduled trips both locally and internationally. Many of the classes and outings are free, and the prices of others are very reasonable.

EAST BOULDER RECREATION CENTER
5660 Sioux Drive, Boulder
(303) 441-4401
www.ci.boulder.co.us

The city offers rock-climbing and mountaineering courses for adults, teens, and children as part of its Adventure Program. There's a climbing wall at the East Boulder Community Center.

ERIE COMMUNITY CENTER
450 Powers Street, Erie
(303) 926-2550
www.erieco.gov
New on the climbing scene, the Erie Community Center offers free climbing and lots of lessons on their 32-ft. climbing pinnacle.

CAMPSITE SELECTION

In heavily visited areas, use existing campsites to confine impact to a small area.

In less-visited areas, choose a site well away from streams and lakes and out of sight of other users. Eliminate all traces of your camp.

Carry out all trash. Do not bury it.

If you must use soap for washing or bathing, use biodegradable products, stay at least 150 feet from any water sources, and pour the water into absorbent ground.

STOVES AND FIRES

Use a gas stove for all cooking. Wood is scarce in the high country and an essential part of the ecosystem. Gas is quicker, cleaner, and won't leave a scar of charred and sterilized soil.

Campfires are becoming controversial. If you absolutely must build a fire, use only dead and down wood. Use existing fire rings and keep the fire very small. Use only as much wood as will burn completely.

Never leave fires unattended, even for a moment. When you leave, make certain that the fire is dead and cold. Clean out fire rings so they will be ready for the next visitor.

SANITATION

Bury human waste in a small cat-hole about 6 inches deep and dug in organic soil (not just leaves or rocks) away from heavy-use areas and at least 150 feet from any water.

Soiled toilet paper, diapers, and sanitary napkins should be carried out.

Place all trash in trash cans. In Colorado's climate, organic wastes such as orange peels, egg shells, and paper can take more than 100 years to decompose if left outside.

If you feel like doing a good deed, carry out litter left by others.

This safety and environmental information comes from the American Medical Association's *Encyclopedia of Medicine, A Roadside Guide to Rocky Mountain National Park* by Beatrice Elizabeth Willard and Susan Quimby Foster, *A Climbing Guide to Colorado's Fourteeners* by Walter Borneman and Lyndon Lampert, and the *Boulder County Nature Almanac* by Ruth Carol Cushman, Stephen Jones, and Jim Knopf. The latter three are excellent resources for detailed information on these areas of Colorado.

NEPTUNE MOUNTAINEERING

633 Unit-A, South Broadway, Table Mesa
Center, Boulder
(303) 499-8866
www.neptunemountaineering.com

Another excellent resource for climbing and mountaineering information, books, and equipment (though no instruction is offered) is this shop owned by Gary Neptune, a prominent U.S. mountaineer who has stood on the top of Mount Everest and many other peaks worldwide.

The shop hosts talks by adventurers and authors fresh from conquering peaks around the world, free or for a minimal fee. The museum located in the shop includes boots and crampons from Sir Edmund Hillary's first ascent of Mount Everest, a Russian oxygen bottle brought back from Everest, and antique ice axes, alpenstocks, pitons, and carabiners dating back more than 100 years. It's the most extensive collection of its kind in the country.

ℹ️ Even people who have no intention of ever climbing a rock wall themselves might enjoy watching others do so. A short drive or walk up Boulder Canyon (on foot up the Creek Path from Eben Fine Park, it's less than a mile) takes you to the Elephant Buttresses and the Dome (just past where the Creek Path goes under Canyon Boulevard), two of Boulder's most popular rock-climbing spots. On the Dome, watch climbers tackle a route called the "Disappearing Crack"—you'll see why. A bench along the creek invites spectators.

TOTAL CLIMBING
2829 Mapleton Avenue, Boulder
(800) 836-4008
www.totalclimbing.com
Total Climbing has an indoor climbing wall and offers instruction. A full range of lessons and outdoor clinics are available, as is rental equipment. The club's building has 10,000 square feet of climbing surface, 35-foot lead walls, and a 2,000-square-foot bouldering cave.

Fishing

Many lakes and streams in the area offer good fishing for both warm- and cold-water species. The Fish Observatory on the Boulder Creek Path just behind the Millennium Harvest House Hotel at 1345 28th Street is a fun place to see the local species of Boulder Creek. There are windows built below water level for viewing. Look for brown, brook, and cutthroat trout. The Boulder Public Library at Ninth Street and Arapahoe Avenue also offers a living stream habitat display showing the fish and plant life found at various levels of the creek.

Some easy-to-reach area streams that offer good trout fishing include the Middle and South forks of St. Vrain Creek; Left Hand Creek between Left Hand Reservoir and Buckingham Park; North Boulder Creek between Highway 72 and Boulder Falls; Middle Boulder Creek from its headwaters

to 28th Street (with special restrictions in city limits); and South Boulder Creek from its headwaters to Baseline Road (with special restrictions between Walker Ranch and South Boulder Road). Golden Gate Canyon State Park is a good place to take kids fishing, and also offers camping and numerous hiking trails (see details under the "Hiking" section). Some favorite spots in and around Boulder are Wonderland and Thunderbird Lakes, Walden Pond (there's a special area for seniors and people with disabilities), and Sawhill Pond. You'll get a detailed map and information on these areas when you buy your fishing license at one of the locations listed in the following section, under "Licenses."

The Colorado Division of Wildlife (303-291-7227, http://wildlife.state.co.us) offers a weekly fishing conditions report that lists areas that have been recently stocked, and reports of where they're biting and where they're not.

BARKER RESERVOIR
17 miles up Boulder Canyon, on Canyon Boulevard, Nederland
Barker Reservoir in Nederland attracts many anglers at its western end, where Boulder Creek empties into this scenic reservoir on the east side of Nederland. Anglers can catch some of the stocked rainbow trout, about a foot long. The water level fluctuates quite a bit, depending on the season and downstream water needs. No boats of any kind are allowed on this reservoir, which is owned by the Public Service Company of Colorado and supplies some of the drinking and irrigation water to towns below.

BOULDER RESERVOIR
5100 North 51st Street 1 mile north of Jay Road, Boulder
(303) 441-3468
www.ci.boulder.co.us
Out on the eastern plains, with a nice mountain vista, Boulder Reservoir is loaded with crappie, catfish, and largemouth bass. It's open year-round. The best place for bank fishing is the deep water near the dam embankment at the eastern

end. Boating is prohibited on weekends unless you are a Boulder resident. Drive toward Longmont on Highway 119 to reach 51st Street.

BRAINARD AND RED ROCKS LAKES
5 miles up Highway 119, Ward
These beautiful mountain lakes attract many anglers looking for rainbow trout, brookies, and brown trout. Fishing is permitted with flies and lures only. To reach these lakes, drive up Boulder Canyon to Nederland and head north on Highway 72; the turnoff is just past Ward, 200 yards on the left. Or, drive up Left Hand Canyon north of Boulder past the Greenbriar Inn. Turn left (west) and proceed up the canyon through Ward and on to Highway 72. Turn right and look immediately to the left for the Brainard turnoff. Brainard Lake is 5 miles up CR 102.

DIAMOND LAKE/INDIAN PEAKS
For those who desire more solitude (which you won't find at Brainard Lake), hike up to beautiful Diamond Lake, from the Fourth of July trailhead. To reach Fourth of July trailhead, travel west from Nederland for about 7 miles on CR 107—you'll pass through the rustic town of Eldora—then continue up CR 130 (a rough, dirt road) for about 5 miles. It's about a 2.5-mile hike up to Diamond Lake from the trailhead.

GROSS RESERVOIR
Flagstaff Road
Gross Reservoir is another favorite of local fishermen looking to hook trout and bass. To reach it, drive west on Baseline Road, which becomes Flagstaff Road as it twists and turns up Flagstaff Mountain above Boulder. The reservoir is a few miles from the top of the road.

Licenses
Required fishing licenses cost $56 for nonresidents, $26 for residents (free for seniors), and are good for one calendar year. Five-day and one-day licenses are also available for $21 and $9 for nonresidents. They are available—along with maps—at McGuckin Hardware, 2525 Arapahoe Avenue in Boulder (303-443-1822) and at Ace Hardware Store, 20 Lakeview Drive, in Nederland's shopping center (303-258-3132). For more information contact the City of Boulder Open Space Department (303-441-3440), Boulder County Parks and Open Space (303-678-6200), or the Colorado Division of Wildlife (303-297-1192).

Fitness Centers
Boulder has numerous private health clubs and fitness centers, many of which are open to nonmembers.

FLATIRON ATHLETIC CLUB
505 Thunderbird Drive, Boulder
(303) 499-6590
www.flatironathleticclub.com
Flatiron offers an enormous array of classes and equipment. For $15, if you go with a member, you can enjoy all the facilities for the day, including a lap pool and coed hot tub; tennis courts; saunas; a steam room; handball, squash, and racquetball courts; volleyball; aerobics classes; an indoor running track; and a complete weight room. There are also Pilates and spinning equipment and classes, and massage therapy.

> **i** Want to learn a new sport or have an adventure? The City of Boulder Parks and Recreation Department offers everything from kayaking and rock climbing to tango lessons. Call (303) 413-7200.

FRONT RANGE BOXING ACADEMY
3801 Pearl Street, Boulder
(303) 546-9747
www.frontrangeboxing.com
Front Range offers a relaxed atmosphere where you can work one-on-one with a trainer to master that quick jab, or just get a workout with the punching bag. Nonmembers can drop in for $10 (the trainer is extra).

THE PILATES CENTER
4800 Baseline Road, The Meadows
Boulder
(303) 494-3400
www.thepilatescenter.com
Sisters Amy Alpers and Rachel Segel founded this Pilates center and teacher training certification school in 1990. Nonmembers are welcome to stop in for an evaluation lesson, a mat class, private lessons, and group classes. Fees vary.

ONE BOULDER FITNESS
1800 Broadway, Suite 190, Boulder
(303) 447-8545
www.oneboulderfitness.com
Nonmembers pay $15 for a day of working out in the strength training facility, on the cardio equipment, attending a variety of aerobics or cycling classes, and finishing up with a sauna, steam or a massage.

RALLYSPORT
2727 29th Street, Boulder
(303) 449-4800
www.rallysportboulder.com
In addition to its local members, RallySport is open to members of other clubs affiliated with IRSHA, the International Racquet, Health and Sports Association. This club has a full range of facilities including racquetball, squash, handball, tennis, volleyball, and wallyball courts plus all types of classes, weight-training equipment, and indoor and outdoor pools. There's a well-run child-care facility on-site.

Golf

Golfers have a reasonable selection of public courses to choose from in Boulder and the surrounding area. Most of the courses listed here have driving ranges, equipment rentals, snack bars, pro shops, and lessons.

COAL CREEK GOLF COURSE
585 West Dillon Road, Louisville
(303) 666-7888
www.coalcreekgolf.com

Coal Creek has 9- and 18-hole courses, a driving range, a snack bar and lounge, pro shop rentals, and a lovely view of the Front Range of the Rockies. Greens fees for residents are $24 and $40 ($26 and $47 on Fridays, weekends and holidays) for 9 and 18 holes. The pars are 36 and 72 for 9 and 18 holes. Carts are $10 and $17 but generally are not necessary.

EAGLE TRACE GOLF CLUB
1200 Club House Drive, Broomfield
(303) 466-3322
www.eagletracegolfclub.com
Eagle has an 18-hole course, driving range, putting green, bar, pro shop, and rentals. The par is 35 or 36 (depending on what tees you're playing from) on the 9-hole layout and 71 on the 18-hole course. See their Web site for fee details.

FLATIRONS GOLF COURSE
5706 Arapahoe Avenue, Boulder
(303) 442-7851
The city of Boulder operates the Flatirons Golf Course. Greens fees are $20 for 9 holes, $32 for 18 on weekends. Par is 35 and 70. There's a driving range, and golf carts available for rent.

GOLF HAYSTACK
5877 Niwot Road, Boulder
(303) 530-1400
www.golfhaystack.com
The course of choice of "duffers" (according to one local, who includes himself in that category), Haystack is excellent for beginners, and there's no need to reserve a tee time—just show up. The easy 9-hole course is par 32, and greens fees range from $10 to $15. No motorized carts are available, only pull-carts. There is an excellent driving range with cover, so rain doesn't halt play.

INDIAN PEAKS GOLF COURSE
2300 Indian Peaks Trail, Lafayette
(303) 666-4706
www.indianpeaksgolf.com
Indian Peaks offers 9 and 18 holes, a driving range,

snack bar and lounge, pro shop, and equipment rentals. Nonresident fees are $25 and $45 every day. Residents pay $23 and $39. The par is 36 or 72, and golf cart rentals are $9 or $15.

LAKE VALLEY GOLF CLUB
County Road 34, north of Boulder
(303) 444-2114
www.lakevalley.com
Also in Boulder, this is an 18-hole championship course. Par is 70. After paying the annual dues, members never pay greens fees. Unaccompanied guests pay $50 weekdays for 9 holes, including a cart and practice balls, or $70 for 18. On weekends and holidays, nonmembers pay $55 for 9 holes with a cart and practice balls, $85 for 18 holes.

SUNSET GOLF COURSE
1900 Longs Peak Avenue, Longmont
(303) 651-8466
www.ci.longmont.co.us/golf/sunset
Sunset has both 9- and 18-hole options, a pro shop, instruction, and rentals. Fees for Longmont residents are $14 for 9 holes and $21 for 18 holes. Junior and senior weekday rates are $11 and $16. Par is 34 and 68 for 9 and 18 holes, respectively. Golf carts rent for $16 and $24 but usually are not necessary on this layout, which is a pleasure to walk.

TWIN PEAKS GOLF COURSE
1200 Cornell Drive, Longmont
(303) 651-8401
www.ci.longmont.co.us/golf/twinpeaks
Twin Peaks offers 9 and 18 holes, a driving range, pro shop, snack bar, and a restaurant. Instruction and rentals are available. Residents pay $16 for 9 holes on weekdays and $26 for 18 holes, $17 and $28 on weekends. The par is 35 for both the front and back nines. Golf carts ($16 and $24) are generally not necessary because the course is so flat.

Hiking and Backpacking

If recreation is Boulder's raison d'être, then hiking is, perhaps, the biggest raison. Most people moved to Boulder to be near the mountains, and in Boulder trails are literally just out your back door. On the toughest trails and even mountaintops you'll see lean runners in flimsy nylon shorts and singlets, equipped with only water bottles.

There are so many places to hike around here, it's hard to know where to begin. But in town, the logical place to start is the mountain parks. Again, for serious hikers, a map is the best bet for choosing the scenic destination, distance, and degree of difficulty accordingly. Maps of open space and mountain parks trails are available at most sporting goods stores. Eldorado Canyon State Park, south of Boulder (see the Parks and Recreation Centers chapter), also has spectacular scenery and good hiking trails. See this chapter's "Hiking in the Mountains" (to follow) and "Camping" (previous) sections for information on overnight getaways in the wild. For more information on city of Boulder mountain parks call (303) 441-3440 or visit the Web site at www.ci.boulder.co.us/openspace.

Hiking in Boulder
BEAR PEAK
NCAR Trailhead
For a fairly strenuous hike of four to six hours—or more (depending on your conditioning)—climb Bear Peak (8,461 feet). It's 7 miles round-trip with an elevation gain of 2,200 feet and many steep sections of trail. But the view from the top is worth it, and if you're there in the early fall, you'll see tens of thousands of ladybugs clinging to the rocks at the summit, where, amazingly enough, they winter in the rock crevices. Don't disturb them as they prepare for their hibernation. They will emerge in spring to mate and lay eggs. There are several routes up Bear Peak. One good way is from the NCAR trailhead (described later in the chapter) to the Mesa Trail (past the large water tank on the hill and then down the hill). Turn left onto the Mesa Trail, which descends and joins Bear Canyon Road below. Turn right onto the road and look for the Fern Canyon Trail sign, and follow that trail to the summit of Bear Peak. This is the shortest, but steepest, route. Another alternative is the earlier trail turnoff via Bear Canyon,

which affords great views to the west. Just below the summit on the Bear Canyon Trail, a sign points to the Fern Canyon Trail to the northeast. Toward the top, the trail becomes quite steep, and some rock scrambling brings hikers to the summit. A nice loop can be made by going up one trail and down the other.

GREGORY CANYON
West on Baseline Road (base of Flagstaff Mountain)

Several fine hikes start in Gregory Canyon at the base of Flagstaff Mountain, where Baseline Road becomes Flagstaff Road. Catch the Flagstaff Mountain Trail (3 miles round-trip, 1,100 feet elevation gain) at the mouth of the dirt road into Gregory Canyon, across from the curving Armstrong Bridge. The trail zigzags back and forth across the paved road to the summit of the mountain. Continue upward, past a fork that leads down to Panorama Point. A small parking lot on the south side of the road from the trail marks a popular bouldering (rock-climbing) area that includes Monkey Wall, Crown Rock, Alamo Rock, Tree Slab, and Pebbles. Though many folks drive up, the hike provides a close-up of rock climbers, wildflowers, native shrubs, and wildlife. Flagstaff Summit Nature Center is open weekends in summer from 10 a.m. to 4 p.m. Once you reach the top, look for Boy Scout Trail, which leads a short distance west to May's Point and Artist's Point with fantastic views of the Continental Divide. Another trail at Flagstaff summit called Rangeview leads down to Realization Point, also with spectacular views of the Divide, North and South Arapaho peaks, Mount Audubon, Mount Meeker, and Longs Peak.

MALLORY CAVE
NCAR Trailhead

There are various options for longer hikes at the NCAR trailhead (see following entry)—including a connection to Bear Canyon and the Mesa Trail. For an interesting longer hike (3.2 miles round-trip), look for the Mallory Cave Trail just south of the NCAR Mesa Trail junction and north of Bear Canyon. Please observe the trail closures, which

are allowing revegetation as well as protecting endangered wildlife nesting areas. Mallory Cave is a nesting site for the bats that you may see sweeping over this area at dusk, scooping up a tummyful of insects. This trail weaves through a forest of ponderosa pines, leading to a meadow of yucca and low shrubs. Follow the small trail to a huge lichen-covered boulder at the entrance to a stone "staircase" between the rock slabs. Look for a sign at the fork indicating a left turn for the cave, which has been notoriously hard to find for many hikers. The final approach is a shimmy up a 50-foot, 40-degree-angle rock chimney with plenty of hand- and footholds but challenging nonetheless. The cave is shallow, but the vista is grand. At the age of 18, E. C. Mallory rediscovered this cave, which was known by locals but never recorded. Mallory later graduated from the University of Colorado and worked as a miner and eventually a chemist for the United States Geological Survey. For many years he kept the cave a secret.

NATIONAL CENTER FOR ATMOSPHERIC RESEARCH (NCAR)
1850 Table Mesa Drive, Boulder

For a really short hike, but one with a great view, stroll out behind the National Center for Atmospheric Research (NCAR—pronounced "en-car"), at the west end of Table Mesa Drive (see the Attractions and Area Overview chapters for details on the research center). The Walter Orr Roberts Nature Trail (0.4 mile round-trip), named for NCAR's founder, is perfect for those with limited time or who don't want to walk much. It's also wheelchair-accessible. The drive up the NCAR mesa is beautiful, and you're sure to spot some grazing deer along the way. The nature trail is a pleasant ramble along the mesa top, offering great views and a fine introduction to the local flora, fauna, and terrain.

The NCAR building, known as the Mesa Laboratory, was designed by the internationally acclaimed architect I. M. Pei (who also designed new sections of the Louvre in Paris and the National Gallery in Washington, D.C.). It's made of Lyons sandstone mixed with concrete to tint it pink and blend with the Flatirons rock formations. The design is reminiscent of Anasazi ruins like those of Mesa Verde in Southwestern Colorado. If it looks familiar, you may be remembering Woody Allen's comedy *Sleeper*, which was filmed partially at NCAR.

i You don't have to venture far out of town to hike. Take a walk on the wild side along Boulder Creek. Choose any summer afternoon and witness one of the city's most popular spots. Bird watchers gather in quiet pocket parks, bicycles breeze by the joggers, and people of all ages enjoy the serenity and the sheer beauty along the green banks.

ROYAL ARCH, ENCHANTED MESA, McCLINTOCK NATURE TRAIL VIA MESA TRAIL
**Ninth Street and Baseline Road
(Chautauqua Park)**
The Mesa Trail—also a popular running trail—begins just below the Bluebell Shelter at Chautauqua Park and leads 6 miles south to Eldorado Springs, with close-up views of the Flatirons and Front Range and sweeping vistas of the plains. The steep, strenuous 3-mile (round-trip) hike to the Royal Arch from Chautauqua is a local favorite. Access it south of Bluebell Shelter at the end of Bluebell Road in Chautauqua Park. The trail quickly climbs almost 1,500 feet on the slopes of Green Mountain to the natural sandstone arch, which offers superb vistas.

An easier trail, and one suited for young children or tired adults, is the McClintock Nature Trail (2.5 miles round-trip) at Enchanted Mesa. Begin at the picnic shelter next to Chautauqua Auditorium in Chautauqua Park and descend to cross Bluebell Creek and arrive at a fork. Take the right branch that climbs to intersect the Enchanted Mesa Road at an old apple tree. Cross the road and continue uphill along the creek. Look for interesting interpretive signs on the area's natural history. The trail then reaches the Mesa Trail, where you turn left (south) and continue .75 mile

to a large trail intersection. Take the left fork, passing a covered reservoir to reach the Enchanted Mesa Road, which is closed to traffic. Pines and wildflowers invite a picnic on the mesa top, and this gentle trail also makes a nice moonlight hike. Enchanted Mesa Road intersects McClintock Trail at Bluebell Creek, and this makes a return loop to Chautauqua, downhill all the way back.

Hiking in the Mountains
Called the Snowy Range by the area's first settlers, the spectacular snow-covered mountains just west of Boulder—among them, skyscraping Mount Audubon, North and South Arapaho Peaks, Mount Toll, and others—are part of the Indian Peaks Wilderness Area. Many soar above 12,000 feet and several above 13,000 feet. This 73,391-acre area west of Boulder contains some of Colorado's best scenery and highest peaks. The wilderness area, so designated in 1978, encompasses parts of Arapaho and Roosevelt National Forests. Indian Peaks shares a boundary with Rocky Mountain National Park to the north and Rollins Pass to the south.

BRAINARD LAKE
Past Ward on Highway 72
The USDA Forest Service trails throughout the Indian Peaks Wilderness Area are interchangeable as hiking, backpacking, and cross-country skiing trails. Some of our favorites are in the Brainard Lake area, just past Ward on Highway 72. Drive up Boulder Canyon to Nederland and head north on Highway 72; the turnoff is 200 yards past Ward on the left. Or, drive up Left Hand Canyon, north of Boulder past the Greenbriar Inn. Turn left (west) and proceed up the canyon through Ward and on to Highway 72. Turn right and look immediately to the left for the Brainard turnoff. Brainard Lake is 5 miles up CR 102.

Two popular hikes at Brainard Lake are Mount Audubon (13,223 feet, 8 miles round-trip, and 2,750 feet of elevation gain), an arduous all-day climb, or much easier Long Lake, a 3-mile loop around the lake. Once at Brainard Lake, drive past the lake and look for the Long Lake and Mitchell Lake parking areas for these trailheads. The Long

Lake Trail is a level stroll around this beautiful lake with spectacular views, colorful wildflowers, and wheelchair accessibility. Hikes from this area to Mitchell Lake (1 mile, one way), Blue Lake (2.5 miles, one way), and 12,550-foot Pawnee Pass via Lake Isabelle (4.3 miles, one way) are all spectacular and easy to follow (though not all are easy to ascend) on the well-marked trails. Due to the area's great popularity and heavy use, there is now a $3 per vehicle charge, good for five days; or an annual pass is available for $15. The fee goes toward protecting the area.

DIAMOND LAKE, NORTH AND SOUTH ARAPAHO PEAKS, AND ARAPAHO PASS
Fourth of July Trailhead
This trailhead leads to spectacular hikes to Diamond Lake, South Arapaho Peak, Arapaho Pass, Fourth of July Mine, and Dorothy Lake. Fourth of July trailhead is just north of Hessie (see next entry) via the same road through the town of Eldora. To reach these trailheads from Boulder, drive to Nederland via Boulder Canyon. From the southwest end of Nederland, follow Highway 72 to the town of Eldora, where CR 130 begins at the west end of town. Follow this dirt road to the Hessie fork and take the right branch, which is a very rocky and bumpy 5-mile ride to Buckingham Campground (also called Fourth of July Campground). From the campground, take the right fork up to the parking lot at the trailhead. From the trailhead (10,121 feet) it's a 3-mile climb to Arapaho Pass at 12,061 feet. One mile from the trailhead is a turnoff to Diamond Lake, another 1.3 miles away at 10,960 feet. The Diamond Lake Trail dips down the valley and crosses the North Fork of Middle Boulder Creek. The trail crosses several small streams and continues upward to a big, wet meadow full of wildflowers. A trail junction sign directs hikers to the left for Devil's Thumb Trail and Jasper Lake, but continue going straight for Diamond Lake, which sparkles like the gem for which it was named. By continuing on the Fourth of July Trail (instead of taking the Diamond Lake Trail), hikers reach the Fourth of July Mine at 1.5 miles, a worthwhile destination in

itself, with interesting old mining equipment and a great view of Arapaho Pass on the Continental Divide. At the mine, there's the option of turning right and continuing up the Arapaho Glacier Trail to the glacier overlook and on up South Arapaho Peak (13,397 feet and 3.5 miles one way from the start of the trail). North Arapaho Peak (13,502 feet) is another .75 mile along a connecting ridge with some exposure.

These peaks should be attempted only by strong, experienced climbers with proper equipment. It's also important to get an early start to avoid the regular afternoon lightning storms. (The rule of thumb in summer is to be off a peak and headed back down by noon.) By continuing straight up the trail at Fourth of July Mine, hikers can reach Arapaho Pass in another 1.5 miles along a barren, rocky old wagon road. Listen for the whistles of marmots and pikas along the way, and look for these appealing, high-altitude critters. Marmots are similar to groundhogs, and pikas are guinea pig-size creatures related to rabbits, not rodents. Arapaho Pass is usually extremely windy, but the view is sublime, looking over the Continental Divide down the western slope to Caribou Lake and Coyote Park. Another short jaunt of 0.5 mile to the left leads to scenic, snowfield-crowned Dorothy Lake, at a chill 12,061 feet with usually an iceberg or two. Take care to avoid trampling the tiny tundra flowers around the lake—rock hopping is best.

HESSIE AND FOURTH OF JULY TRAILHEADS
CR 130
South of the Brainard Lake area in the Arapaho Peaks area you'll find two very popular trailheads: Hessie and Fourth of July, 8 and 12 miles, respectively, west of Nederland. To reach these trailheads from Boulder, drive to Nederland via Boulder Canyon. From the southwest end of Nederland, follow Highway 72 to the town of Eldora, where CR 130 begins at the west end of town. So popular are these trails—and with good reason—that it's hard to find a parking place on weekends, so weekday hiking is recommended. The left fork leads to the old town site of Hessie, 1.5 miles west of Eldora,

now just an old cabin or two. The short road to Hessie (and the trailhead) is usually underwater and not passable by ordinary passenger cars. So park where permitted along the road. Observe the NO PARKING signs, because they're strictly enforced, and cars are towed. Reach the Fourth of July trailhead via the right fork of CR 130.

LOST LAKE
Hessie Trailhead
The 4-mile round-trip hike to Lost Lake is especially nice in the fall with the changing aspen leaves. The trail is a gravelly road that climbs through aspen groves. When it sort of levels out for a bit, listen for the roar of water, take a short detour to the left (not marked), and look for a gorgeous series of cascades culminating in a thundering waterfall. Continue on the trail to a junction sign at a bridge. Don't take the Devil's Thumb Bypass Trail; instead, cross the bridge and continue up the left-hand side of the creek past another beautiful falls. The trail leads to Woodland Flats, a large, open meadow with fine views of Devil's Thumb and the mountains. Don't miss the sign at this point for Lost Lake to the left; it's another 0.5 mile up to this pretty, wildflower-lined lake and the site of much early mining activity. Reach the Fourth of July trailhead via the right fork of CR 130.

Backpacking
Hiking trails are interchangeable as backpacking trails, but backpackers will need permits to stay overnight in the Indian Peaks Wilderness Area, which includes many of the trails described previously. Certain trails are also off-limits for backpacking, so check with the District Ranger Office (see subsequent information) before heading for the hills. The following are various trails in the Indian Peaks area and elsewhere that offer access to good backpacking destinations. Also see the preceding "Camping" section for more details. Information on the Indian Peaks Wilderness is available from the USDA Forest Service Boulder Ranger District (see below under "Permits and Regulations"). Entire books have been written just on Boulder-area hiking and backpacking trails, with detailed descriptions and interesting

historical notes; look for them at local mountain sporting goods shops. An especially good book is *Boulder Hiking Trails* by Ruth Carol Cushman and Glenn Cushman. Another good one is *50 Front Range Hiking Trails* (including Rocky Mountain National Park and the Indian Peaks Wilderness Area) by Richard DuMais. Hikes in Rocky Mountain National Park are described in the chapter on the park in this book.

GOLDEN GATE CANYON STATE PARK
10 miles south of Nederland on Highway 72
(303) 582-3707
This 14,000-acre state park offers many miles of hiking plus backpacking, fishing, and 155 camping sites at lower altitudes than the Indian Peaks Wilderness Area. It's a lovely spot in the fall with the changing colors. Don't forget your camera when you visit Panorama Point, which offers a view of 100 miles along the Continental Divide. (See admission fees in the preceding "Camping" section.)

INDIAN PEAKS WILDERNESS
There are numerous backpacking options in the Indian Peaks Wilderness. The Arapaho Pass Area begins at the Fourth of July trailhead (see above under "Hiking in the Mountains") and offers many choices on both sides of the Continental Divide. The trail climbs 3 miles to the 11,900-foot pass and drops down on the other side to Caribou Lake, where it continues southwest over Caribou Pass to Columbine Lake. To reach Fourth of July trailhead, travel west from Nederland on Highway 72 to the town of Eldora. County Road 130 begins at the west end of town. The Fourth of July trailhead is 5 miles farther (take the right fork at the Hessie intersection).

PAWNEE PASS (INDIAN PEAKS)
The climb to Pawnee Pass (12,541 feet) starts at Brainard Lake on the extremely popular Isabelle Lake trailhead, on the right side of Long Lake, but the crowds thin as the going gets rougher and higher. This 4.5-mile hike is quite steep for the last 2 miles. An interesting backpacking loop leads over the pass to Monarch Lake and returns to the

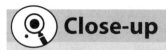 **Close-up**

Mountain Safety and Environment

Colorado's Rocky Mountains can take the unwary and unprepared by surprise. Remember: Going above or near timberline is the same as visiting the Arctic regions of the world. Mountain weather can change from a warm, sunny day to hail, snow, thunder, and lightning in minutes. It can snow at any time of the year. Summer daytime temperatures in Rocky Mountain National Park on Trail Ridge, Fall River, and West Slope roads average in the 50s (10 degrees C). The record high temperature in the alpine tundra is 63 degrees (17 degrees C). Wind chill can make these temperatures seem much lower—and it's usually windy in the mountains.

Visiting the high mountains can be a safe and extremely rewarding experience, as long as people are prepared and aware of the following dangers. As usual, prevention is the best way to make your trip safe and enjoyable.

1. **Hypothermia.** More of a threat to backpackers, day hikers, and skiers, hypothermia occurs from prolonged exposure to the cold and a resulting drop in body temperature. It's more common among elderly people. Symptoms include a slowed heart rate, puffiness, pale skin, lethargy, and confusion. In severe cases, breathing slows and intravenous liquids are required. Hypothermia is a killer and has claimed many victims in the mountains. Always bring a hat, rain and wind gear, and extra warm clothing (layers are best) when going into the mountains. Staying well-hydrated by drinking liquids frequently also helps to prevent hypothermia. Keep a hat on if it's chilly—most body heat is lost from the head.

2. **Dehydration.** Colorado's dry climate, combined with exertion at high altitudes, can cause dehydration: a drop in the body's water level and often a drop in the body's level of salt. Symptoms include severe thirst, dry lips, increased heart and breathing rates, dizziness, and confusion. The skin is dry and stiff. There's little urination, and what is passed is dark. Salt loss causes headaches, cramps (often in the legs), lethargy, and pallor. Drink liquids frequently in the mountains. If you're feeling thirsty, your body's telling you that you're already about a quart low on water. Take salty snacks such as pretzels, chips, and crackers. Rehydration drinks, such as Gatorade, are also good aids to take along.

3. **Lightning.** Lightning is much more dangerous above timberline. Every year lightning claims a number of lives in Colorado's high country. If a storm develops, stay off ridges and peaks. Keep away from trees, boulders, isolated buildings, and metal objects. The safest place is in your car. A tingling sensation at the base of the neck or scalp and hair standing on end with static electricity are both signs that lightning is about to strike near you. Move rapidly to your car. Do not stand still, no matter what. If you are unable to return to your car, squat and wrap your arms around your knees, keeping your head low. Do not lie or sit on the ground (because if lightning strikes you or the ground and travels through your body, you want it to have a way out—an open circuit).

To estimate your distance from a lightning strike, count the seconds between the flash and the accompanying thunder and divide by five to get the distance in miles. It takes five seconds for the sound to travel a mile.

4. **Altitude sickness.** Symptoms include headache, dizziness, nausea, shortness of breath, and impaired mental abilities. Breathing into a paper or plastic bag for five minutes reduces these symptoms. In severe cases, fluid can build up in the lungs, causing breathlessness, heavy coughing, and heavy phlegm. If untreated, these symptoms can lead to seizures,

hallucinations, coma, brain damage, and death. There is 40 percent less oxygen in the air above 8,000 feet (2,438 meters) than at sea level. To avoid altitude sickness, refrain from strenuous activity for the first few days at high altitude. Move slowly above timberline, eat lightly, and drink fluids frequently. Alcoholic beverages may aggravate the symptoms. Move to a lower elevation if symptoms persist. People with respiratory or heart problems should check with a physician before going to high elevations.

5. **Sunburn.** Sunburn is much more severe at high altitudes because the reduced atmosphere is less able to filter out the sun's harmful ultraviolet radiation. With 5 percent more ultraviolet light per 1,000 feet, Colorado has 25 percent more damaging sun rays than Florida's beaches. Skiers and other winter sports enthusiasts need to be especially careful, because reflection from snow can cause severe sunburn. Skiers have been known to get sunburned inside their nostrils. In summer, to avoid burning, wear a long-sleeved shirt and a brimmed hat. Use sunscreen with at least a 15 SPF (sun protection factor) rating year-round.

6. **Dangerous currents and floods.** Though they look shallow and serene, mountain streams have strong currents, slippery rocks, and cold temperatures that have been contributing factors in many drownings. Be especially careful when fishing or allowing children to play near streams. Sudden rains can raise stream levels rapidly and even cause flash floods. If rain continues, move to higher ground.

7. **Giardia.** Don't drink water from streams and lakes. Tempting though it might be, many mountain streams and lakes contain bacteria and a microscopic organism called Giardia lamblia, which can cause long-term intestinal problems. The organism is transmitted into water by cysts in human, domestic animal, and wildlife feces. Dogs and cats can catch and transmit Giardia. Symptoms of Giardia include violent diarrhea, gas, cramps, loss of appetite, and nausea. Carry your own water bottle filled with tap water. Campers and hikers should boil all stream or lake water for 10 or more minutes, or use water-purification kits or the now-popular (and expensive) microfilters (portable pumps that filter water). A microfilter must filter down to four microns to filter out Giardia.

8. **Ticks.** Not usually a problem in the higher mountains, wood ticks appear in the spring after vegetation begins to leaf in the Lower and Upper Montane zones—the areas below 9,500 feet (2,896 meters). They can appear as early as February in forested and shrubby areas and remain active into late summer. They are rare in the subalpine zone and above the tree line (above 9,500 feet). Applying insect repellent and wearing long pants and long-sleeved shirts help prevent tick bites. The best precaution is to check frequently for ticks on your clothing, hair, and body, because it takes several hours for a tick to attach. After being outdoors, undress in a shower or tub or on a ground cloth outside your tent. Inspect clothing carefully before putting it back on. Destroy ticks, but do not crunch them with your fingers.

Wood ticks can transmit Colorado tick fever and the more serious (but fairly uncommon) Rocky Mountain fever. Consult a physician if you have localized swelling, a rash, enlarged lymph glands, or a fever in the days or weeks after a tick bite. Lyme disease is uncommon in Colorado, but it does occur from nonnative ticks that somehow hitch a ride into the state.

To remove an attached tick, disinfect the area. Grasp the tick firmly with tweezers close to its head. Gently remove it by pulling it upward and out from the skin. Never twist or jerk on it. Putting nail polish, cooking oil, or petroleum jelly on the tick before removing it can make it release its grip more easily.

east side of the Divide over Arapaho Pass—you'll need two cars or a drop-off and pickup arrangement to complete this one.

Permits and Regulations

You must have a permit to backpack anywhere in the Indian Peaks Wilderness Area from June 1 to September 15. Permits and detailed maps and routes are available at the Boulder District Ranger Station of the USDA Forest Service, 2140 Yarmouth Avenue, (303-444-6600; recorded information line: 303-541-2519). Permits are not required for individual backpackers, but are required for organized groups. Backpacking group size is limited to 12; permits cost $5 for up to 14 nights. Dogs are allowed in Indian Peaks (but not Rocky Mountain National Park) but must be on a 6-foot (maximum), hand-held leash at all times. (There's a $50 fine for violation of the leash law.) It's important to observe this regulation because the great number of hikers with dogs has caused considerable disturbance to wildlife and other hikers, particularly in recent years. Backpacking permits for Indian Peaks are available on weekends (when the Boulder District Ranger Station is closed) at Nederland's Ace Hardware, 20 Lakeview Drive (in the shopping center). National forest maps of Indian Peaks are also sold at area climbing, hardware, and sporting goods stores.

Horseback Riding

What could be more western than riding a horse? Most stables are out of town a bit, on the plains, or in the mountains.

PEACEFUL VALLEY LODGE AND GUEST RANCH
Peak to Peak Highway (Highway 72), 8 miles north of Ward
(303) 747-2881
www.peacefulvalley.com
Peaceful Valley offers nonguest pack trips, breakfast rides, and guided trail rides from mid-May through mid-October, based on availability. All-inclusive six-day packages run $1,375 to $1,875 for an adult, less for kids. A three-day package is $745 to $1,045.

Hunting

To be honest, Boulder County isn't going to be your best bet for hunting. Most of the open land around Boulder is city or county open space, where hunting is not allowed, and in fact, even killing a rattlesnake can get you in big trouble. Locations, seasons, and regulations for hunting particular animals are complicated (too much so to outline here), so it's necessary to get the appropriate information for hunting elk, deer, bear, mountain lion, grouse, rabbit, squirrel, etc. Pamphlets and information are available wherever hunting licenses are sold, such as McGuckin Hardware, 2525 Arapahoe Avenue (303-443-1822) and the Colorado Division of Wildlife, 6060 Broadway in Denver (303-291-7227); call (303) 291-7530 for hunter education and (303) 291-7529 for big-game information.

In-line Skating

The Boulder Creek Path is the most popular spot for in-line skating, but any of the city's bike paths are good (check our previous "Bicycling" section). Rates to rent in-line skates are around $5 an hour and $15 to $20 a day. You can rent in-line skating equipment at:

CUTTING EDGE SPORTS
1817 Highway 42, Louisville
(303) 666-4550
www.cescolorado.com
Cutting Edge specializes in sales, rental, and service on all kinds of bikes, skis, and skates.

Kayaking, Canoeing, and Rafting

Canoeing and kayaking are mainly done at Boulder Reservoir and Boulder Creek, although the pond at the East Boulder Recreation Center draws an occasional craft. Boulder kayakers practice at a course set up on Boulder Creek (in memory of an avid kayaker). For extended river trips, they head to the Arkansas River near Buena Vista (a few hours' drive from Boulder), or over to Utah and other states. If you want to take a longer paddling trip, you'll have to travel elsewhere.

ACQUIRED TASTES INC.
(800) 888-8582
www.atraft.com
This reputable Boulder guide service specializes in white-water excursions on the Arkansas River, with one-, two-, and three-day trips available from mid-May through August.

Paragliding

A silent glider ride over the Front Range is an experience of a lifetime. For those who want nothing to stand between them and the great blue sky—other than a chute of sheer nylon—there's paragliding.

FLY AWAY PARAGLIDING
Golden
(303) 642-0849
www.flyawayparagliding.com
Owner Bill Lawrence, who has competed in two national championships, is a tandem-rated instructor and has been flying for a decade. He originally trained in Switzerland. He runs trips out-of-state but mostly works out of Boulder. His company specializes in pilot training and small classes.

Rugby

Rugby aficionados can contact the more than 30-year-old Boulder Rugby Club at the BRFC Hotline (303-575-5698, www.boulderrugby.com) for information about practices and games.

Running

Anywhere you look in Boulder, you'll see people running. Runners choose just about any location: the Boulder Creek Path (see our Parks chapter), quiet streets through town, the Mesa Trail (see the "Hiking" section in this chapter), various open space trails, and even mountains. For more information contact the following shops and clubs:

THE BOULDER ROAD RUNNERS
P.O. Box 1866, Boulder, CO 80306
www.boulderroadrunners.org
Formed in 1979, this group offers organized runs and programs for runners of all ages and abilities.

For serious runners there are training and running groups and speed workouts; for information, call president Rich Castro at (303) 49-6650.

BOULDER RUNNING COMPANY
2775 Pearl Street (at 28th Street)
Boulder
(303) 786-9255
www.boulderrunningcompany.com
This running store offers a great selection of running shoes, clothing, and other accessories. Talk to the staff about local runs

Sailing, Sailboarding, and Powerboating

With Boulder's capricious Chinooks and occasional gale-force winds, sailing and sailboarding can be exciting experiences here. The mountains may be our most popular attraction, but water-lovers can find plenty of places to catch a wave.

BOULDER RESERVOIR
51st Street, 1.5 miles north of Jay Road via the Diagonal Highway (Highway 119)
(303) 441-3456 (boathouse)
www.ci.boulder.co.us
In the summer, sailboats and sailboards can be rented at Boulder Reservoir through the city of Boulder–operated boathouse. The city also offers instruction at the reservoir. Classes are offered in sailing as well as sailboarding.

UNION RESERVOIR
461 Weld County Road 26, Longmont
(303) 772-1265
Another popular sailing spot (only wakeless boating allowed) is Union Reservoir. From Boulder, take the Diagonal Highway (Highway 119) east to Weld County Road 1, and follow the signs. Or, from Longmont take Ninth Avenue east to County Line Road, turn right and follow the signs. The gate fee for vehicles is $6.

Skiing

Since skiing, in all its variations, is so popular with Colorado residents and visitors, we've presented information on the sport in several places in this book. For a brief review, see the subsequent sections. For more information—prices, related activities, lodging—on Ski Country, see the Attractions and Day Trips and Weekend Getaways chapters.

Downhill Skiing
ELDORA MOUNTAIN RESORT
2861 Eldora Ski Road, Nederland
(303) 440-8700
www.eldora.com

It's not Vail or Aspen, but it's only 21 miles from Boulder and there are no mountain passes or giant ski-traffic jams to slow you down. Eldora is a great little ski area right in Boulder County. It has 12 lifts: 2 quads, 2 triple, 4 double, and 4 surface. With a top elevation of 10,800 feet, Eldora has 1,400 feet of vertical gain—and beautiful views from the top. You'll probably get more skiing in and less standing in lift lines at Eldora than at the bigger resorts. There's a ski school, rentals, a lodge, races, leagues, Nordic and telemark trails, and even an RTD bus from Boulder that makes numerous daily trips right to the resort.

OTHER SKI AREAS
Keystone, Arapahoe Basin, Breckenridge, Copper Mountain, and Winter Park are within a two-hour drive of Boulder (see the "Ski Country" section of the Day Trips and Weekend Getaways chapter). For information on these and other Colorado ski areas, call Colorado Ski Country USA, Monday through Friday, (303) 825-SNOW (recorded information) or (303) 837-0793 (administrative office). Discount lift tickets to the aforementioned areas are available at King Soopers and Safeway, among other places.

Rocky Mountain Skiing by Claire Walter (one of this book's former co-authors and contributing editor for Skiing magazine) is a great resource book for the entire Rocky Mountain region and is available at local bookstores.

Cross-Country Skiing
Before you head to the mountains, you can warm up and practice right in Boulder. The Boul-

der Nordic Club (BNC), in cooperation with the Boulder Parks and Recreation Department, sets a nice track around North Boulder Park (Ninth and Dellwood Streets), whenever there's enough snow on the ground. Skiing at the park is free. The Boulder Nordic Club is full of very serious skiers, most of whom compete in the various citizens' races throughout Colorado and beyond. BNC provides information on local skiing conditions at (720) 352-7808.

Farther away—but still just an hour's drive into the mountains—lie our favorite spots in the Brainard Lake area: East Portal from Rollinsville (see directions to Rollins Pass Road in this chapter's "Biking" section), and the Hessie and Fourth of July roads at the west end of the town of Eldora and Peaceful Valley (north of Nederland and Ward on Highway 72; see the previous "Hiking" section for more directions to these areas).

The Colorado Mountain Club (CMC; 303-279-3080) and Flatirons Ski Club (303-449-8335) are good clubs to contact for additional information. They both provide a great way to meet other skiers and explore local ski trails for those new to the area. Ski rentals, books, maps, and trail information are available at Neptune Mountaineering (303-499-8866). Please refer to this book's Shopping chapter for more details on this shop.

Excellent sources for local cross-country skiing are Peak to Peak Ski Trails of the Colorado Front Range by Harlan N. Barton and Backcountry Skiing by Brian Litz.

BRAINARD LAKE
Many national forest summer hiking trails are used for cross-country skiing in the winter. For absolute beginners who want no hills or spills, the Brainard Lake Road offers nearly level terrain to the lake with no surprises and great scenery. Just follow the road up past the closure—2.2 miles to the lake.

Left Hand Reservoir at Brainard Lake is more challenging, but the wide trail offers plenty of margin for error. Begin on the south side of the Brainard Road below the gate closure and follow the trail signs up a roadbed about 2 miles to the

🔍 Close-up

Spend a Day on the Slopes, Not in Your Car

Boulder might not be a ski destination town, but you don't have to venture far from the city to take advantage of world-class skiing and riding. Just 21 miles up Boulder Canyon you can find fresh powder at Eldora Mountain Resort, where skiing, snowboarding, cross-country skiing, skate-skiing, and snowshoeing are all available.

A great family resort, Eldora Mountain first opened for skiing in 1962 and has been a favorite of locals ever since. And it holds its own against the bigger resorts farther up in the Rockies. Eldora certainly measures up in both terrain and services. With an average of 300 inches of snow per year and the state's best snowmaking system, it's no wonder it's so popular. Eldora boasts 680 acres of skiable terrain with its base area at an elevation of 9,300 feet above sea level. The view from the top, at 10,800 feet, is breathtaking.

There is something for everyone here. Snowboarders delight in the 20-foot-tall, 600-foot-long Super Pipe, one of the longest in the state. Eldora's Nordic Center and 45 kilometers of cross-country trails meander through beautiful alpine clearings and peaceful pine forests with trails designated for classic cross-country skiing, skate-skiing, or snowshoeing.

Name your sport and Eldora Mountain resort has a lesson for you at affordable prices. Likewise with rentals. The youth programs are outstanding and many kids ride the RTD up the mountain after school. Four restaurants at the resort round out a picture-perfect day on the slopes or trails.

Believe it or not, lodging here is easy. As a matter of fact, because of Eldora's unique proximity to Boulder, finding lodging during the winter months and the peak holiday season is no problem. In fact, many of the Boulder-area hotels have special winter rates, and occupancy is generally low at this time of year. This little-known fact is contrary to other winter resort communities in Colorado.

---

reservoir. There are thrilling downhill runs back on the wide trail.

The Colorado Mountain Club South Trail begins on the south side of Brainard Road 50 yards west of the closure gate and is a bit longer and narrower through wooded areas. Climb a short hill and ski the rolling 2.5 miles to Brainard Lake.

For intermediate to advanced skiers comfortable on narrow, steep hills and turns, there's the Waldrop North Trail, about 5.5 miles round-trip, accessible just north of the closure.

Buchanan Pass Trail begins at the curve on Highway 72 (5.8 miles north of Ward) at Peaceful Valley. Follow the trail on the north side of the creek west of Camp Dick campground. An 11-mile loop can be made by returning on the Middle St. Vrain four-wheel-drive road (some snowmobiles), but you can ski whatever distance you like.

The Sourdough Trail is 17.5 miles long but has different segments at various trailheads. From Camp Dick Campground to Beaver Reservoir, it's 2.3 miles. From Beaver Reservoir to Brainard Road, it's 7.4 miles, and from Brainard Road to Rainbow Lakes Road, 7.8 miles. The trail was built mainly for ski touring and mountain biking, and is pleasant rolling terrain though the pines. All accesses to the various connections to the Sourdough Trail are on the Peak to Peak Highway (Highway 72), west of Nederland. Camp Dick Campground is on Middle St. Vrain Road, 5.8 miles north of Ward and 0.5 mile west of Peaceful Valley. One Sourdough trailhead is on the left-hand side of CR 96 just east of Beaver Reservoir, 2.5 miles north of Ward and 2 miles west on CR 96. Another Sourdough trailhead is on the right side of Rainbow Lakes Road (CR 116), 4.7 miles south of Ward (7 miles north of Nederland) and 0.4 mile west on CR 116. The Red Rock trailhead is on the right side of CR 102, just east of Red Rock Lake, 2.5 miles west on Brainard Lake Road.

ELDORA MOUNTAIN RESORT NORDIC CENTER
2861 Eldora Ski Road, Nederland
(303) 440-8700
www.eldora.com

Eldora Mountain Resort's Nordic Center is one of Colorado's largest and most popular cross-country centers, with 45 kilometers of marked and groomed trails. There's a cozy log cabin lodge with refreshments, rentals, and lessons. At Eldora, there's also access to the free national forest Jenny Creek Trail. Climb up the Ho-Hum downhill run next to the Little Hawk lift, turn right, and look for the trail signs. The trail weaves up and down through the woods and then descends on a narrow trail (which is bad when icy) to the Jenny Creek Road. You can turn around here or follow the creekbed, eventually leading up to Yankee Doodle Lake (9 miles round-trip from the Eldora parking lot). Or, at the Jenny Creek Road, take another trail to the right, the Guinn Mountain Trail, which leads up a steep, difficult climb to the distant Guinn Mountain cabin (10.5 miles round-trip), operated by the Colorado Mountain Club. Skiers can bring camping gear to spend the night; call the subsequently listed CMC number for information.

Snowboarding

All of Colorado's ski areas except Aspen Mountain allow snowboarding, rent the equipment, and offer lessons. Snowboards are now generally available for rent at skiing and mountaineering equipment shops, and a whole new genre of snowboard (and skateboard) specialty shops have sprung up to accommodate the growing popularity of this sport. One-day snowboard rentals cost around $25. Ask about high-performance equipment. Some shops that rent and demo snowboards include:

BOULDER SKI DEALS,
2525 Arapahoe Avenue
Boulder (303-938-8799)
www.boulderskideals.com

CHRISTY SPORTS,
2000 30th Street
Boulder (303-442-2493)
www.christysports.com

CRYSTAL SKI SHOP
3216 Arapahoe Avenue
Boulder (303 449-7669)
www.crystalskishop.com

Snowshoeing

The growing popularity of snowshoeing is also evident on all the local trails in winter. One needs no real lessons for this simple sport. Just strap on the snowshoes and start walking. Snowshoes provide you with the ability to leave the crowds on the trails and make your own route—and the cross-country skiers would appreciate it if you did. Snowshoes can be rented at most local mountaineering and ski rental shops (listed in the previous "Skiing" section), at a cost of around $12 a day.

Please note: Snowshoers sharing forest trails with cross-country skiers should make their own tracks, wherever possible, and avoid walking in existing ski tracks. This is because cross-country skis work best in ski tracks and don't work well on snowshoe paths. People without skis or snowshoes should not walk in either tracks—it ruins them both, making it frustrating and miserable for skiers and snowshoers alike.

Swimming

Until the really big one hits California, and the Pacific Ocean laps the foot of the Rockies, pools and reservoirs are the main swimming options around Boulder. The three city of Boulder–operated recreation centers (see "Recreational Facilities" in the Parks and Recreation Centers chapter) all have indoor pools. East Boulder

Recreation Center has a waterslide and lazy river with inner tubes for kids, plus a mushroom waterfall. Outdoor pools are open during summer months only at Scott Carpenter Park and Spruce Pool (also city-operated and listed in the Parks chapter). Boulder Reservoir's sandy swimming beach helps relieve ocean homesickness a bit (no sharks, only carp).

ELDORADO ARTESIAN SPRINGS
Eldorado Springs
(303) 499-1316
www.eldoradosprings.com
Just a few miles south of Boulder in Eldorado Springs, look for the resort in this scenic canyon setting. The pool at the springs of this historic resort offers therapeutic mineral water. The thermal pools and snack bar are open Memorial Day through Labor Day from 10 a.m. to 6 p.m. daily. Rates are $8 for adults, $5 for kids and seniors.

HYLAND HILLS WATER WORLD
1800 West 89th Avenue, Federal Heights
(303) 427-7873
www.waterworldcolorado.com
If you are up for a 30-minute drive, there's a world of water waiting at Water World—a kiddie pool with fountains and slides, a wave pool, massive waterslides, and a circular lazy river where you can float peacefully around and around. All-day admission is $33.95 for adults and $28.95 for children no taller than 47 inches.

Tennis

Free public tennis courts are usually in great demand and short supply in Boulder. Courts can be reserved for $8 for 60 minutes through the city-operated North (303-413-7260), South (303-441-3448), and East Boulder Recreation Centers (303-441-4400), and the city offers instruction at various levels. The Boulder Tennis Association (303-442-4282) has tennis ladders and formal and informal tournaments. There's a smattering of free courts around Boulder at various parks and schools, including:

ARAPAHOE RIDGE,
1280 43rd Street (two courts)

BASELINE MIDDLE SCHOOL,
700 20th Street (two courts)

BOULDER HIGH,
1604 Arapahoe (two courts)

CENTENNIAL MIDDLE SCHOOL,
2005 Norwood Avenue (eight courts)

CHAUTAUQUA PARK,
Ninth Street and Baseline Road (one court)

FAIRVIEW HIGH,
1515 Greenbriar Boulevard (eight courts)

MANHATTAN MIDDLE SCHOOL,
290 Manhattan Drive (four courts)

MARTIN PARK,
36th Street and Dartmouth Avenue (two courts)

TOM WATSON PARK,
63rd Street and IBM Drive (four courts with lights)

WILLIAMS VILLAGE
30th Street and Baseline Road (two courts)

SPECTATOR SPORTS

College Sports

Basketball
UNIVERSITY OF COLORADO
Athletic Ticket Office, Folsom Field, Colorado Avenue, Boulder
(303) 492-8337
www.cubuffs.com
The women's and men's teams belong to the Big 12 Conference and play home games at the CU Coors Events/Conference Center, on Regent Drive in Boulder on the CU campus; it holds 11,198 fans.

The regular season runs from December to March. Call to order tickets, or for season tickets write to the Athletic Ticket Office, Box 372, Boulder, CO 80309.

Football
UNIVERSITY OF COLORADO
Athletic Ticket Office, Folsom Field,
Colorado Avenue, Boulder
(303) 492-8337
www.cubuffs.com
The Golden Buffaloes belong to the Big 12 Conference in NCAA Division I and play home games at Folsom Field, which seats 53,750. The regular season runs from September through November. For season ticket information, call the Athletic Ticket Office at (303) 492-8337 or visit the CU Web site.

Volleyball
UNIVERSITY OF COLORADO
Athletic Ticket Office, Folsom Field,
Colorado Avenue, Boulder
(303) 492-8337
www.cubuffs.com
The Buffs belong to the Big 12 Conference and play home games at the CU Coors Events/Conference Center on the CU-Boulder campus. The season runs from September into November. Tickets are $5 for general admission, and $2 for seniors and children. Call or visit their Web site for further ticket information.

Other College Sports
UNIVERSITY OF COLORADO
Other varsity sports teams at CU-Boulder include golf, cross-country skiing, track and field, tennis, and skiing, and there are numerous club sports. For information about varsity sports schedules visit www.cubuffs.com.

Professional Sports
Baseball
COLORADO ROCKIES
Coors Field, 2001 Blake Street, Denver
(303) 292-0200
http://colorado.rockies.mlb.com

The Rockies belong to Major League Baseball's National League West Division and play their home games at the snazzy Coors Field in Denver (seating capacity 50,249). The regular season runs from April through September. Tickets are available by calling (800) 388-ROCK; for group tickets (25 people or more) and general customer service, call (303) ROCKIES; write to the Colorado Rockies Baseball Club, P.O. Box 120, Denver, CO 80201, or visit their Web site.

Basketball
DENVER NUGGETS
Pepsi Center, Speer Boulevard and
Chopper Place, Denver
(303) 405-1100
(303) 893-DUNK (ticket office)
www.nba.com/nuggets
The Nuggets belong to the National Basketball Association's Western Conference and play home games at the impressive Pepsi Center (capacity 19,099). The regular season runs from November into April.

Football
DENVER BRONCOS
Invesco Field at Mile High,
2755 West 17th Avenue, Denver
Denver Broncos Ticket Office,
1900 Eliot Street, Denver
(720) 258-3333
www.denverbroncos.com
With the completion of the bizarrely named 85,000-seat Invesco Field at Mile High in 2001, the Broncos now play on new turf. The Broncos belong to the National Football League's American Conference Western Division. The team won consecutive Super Bowls in the late 1990s, making it one of the most popular teams in the Rockies.

The regular season runs from September through December. For ticket information call the listed number. Season tickets are sold out for the foreseeable future, with a waiting list of more than 5,000 names. Single game tickets, if available, are offered the week prior to each game at the Broncos Ticket Office.

Ice Hockey
COLORADO AVALANCHE
Pepsi Center, Speer Boulevard and
Chopper Place, Denver
(303) 405-1111
www.coloradoavalanche.com

Yes, Coloradans are nuts about their 2001 Stanley Cup Champions—and hoping for another championship season. The Colorado Avalanche (formerly the Quebec Nordiques) belong to the National Hockey League and play home games at the Pepsi Center. The regular season runs from October through April, with the playoffs sometimes lasting into June. Call or visit their Web site for more information about ticket prices and game schedules. Tickets are also available online through Ticketmaster (303-830-8497).

Soccer
**COLORADO RAPIDS MAJOR LEAGUE
SOCCER CLUB**
Dick's Sporting Goods Park
6000 Victory Way, Commerce City
(303) 727-3500
www.coloradorapids.com

Part of the new and burgeoning Major League Soccer, the Rapids play home games at the Dick's Sporting Goods Park with a seating capacity of 18,000. The regular season runs from April through October. Tickets are available at King Soopers stores. Call for discount and special group rates.

NEIGHBORHOODS AND NEARBY COMMUNITIES

As long as you aren't set on oceanfront property, you just might fall in love with a home in one of Boulder's varied neighborhoods. This chapter is for those who enjoy checking out how other people live. It highlights neighborhoods in Boulder and around the county. Boulder's older neighborhoods get the spotlight first. We follow with a description of mountain places, then cities on the plains. If you want more practical information on settling down, check our Real Estate and Relocation chapter.

HISTORIC BOULDER NEIGHBORHOODS

If you like historic homes, the first place to call is Historic Boulder (303-444-5192, www.historic boulder.org). If you are up for some walking, they can give you information on self-guided tours through Boulder's historic neighborhoods. It's a good excuse to get out and enjoy the usually fine weather while you're gaining an appreciation for the town's past.

Whittier Historic District

The Whittier Historic District is northeast of the Pearl Street Mall. If you're driving, you may have a first encounter here with the raised pedestrian crossings and traffic circles scattered through Boulder neighborhoods to slow speeders and discourage through traffic in residential areas. The trick with traffic circles is to bear right and yield to other cars, bicyclists, and pedestrians already in the circle.

Whittier is a fascinating mix of styles, from the grande old dame to a tiny rental with a couch on the front porch. *Mork & Mindy*'s house, the turreted, gray Victorian at 1619 Pine Street, is a private residence, but you can enjoy it from the sidewalk (the residents lost patience with fame when fans of the show started walking in their front door). At 16th and Spruce Streets, a giant owl guards the home of artist Bob Bellows, who creates sculptures from old farm tools. The "feathers" around the owl's beak are spoons. Some homes are painstakingly authentic; others have been altered with abandon. A city policy of "in-fill" development to increase residential density near downtown produced many backyard alley houses in the Whittier neighborhood.

Step inside the Hotel Boulderado at 13th and Pine Streets if you like historic interiors. Another to check is the whimsical Arnett-Fullen house at 646 Pearl Street. Among a long line of residents of the Arnett-Fullen House were sisters Marion and Ethel Mann, who took their rope-twirling expertise to New York City's vaudeville circuit, where they learned a few tricks from fellow performer Will Rogers in the basement of Madison Square Garden.

Mapleton Hill Historic District

Located northwest of Broadway and Pearl Street, Mapleton took its name from the stately maple trees that line the island running down the middle of Mapleton Avenue. Those 100-plus-year-old maples are dear, for this city started as a windblown prairie, and as they age, the city is planting young trees to replace them to maintain the distinctive character of the neighborhood. When lifelong Mapleton resident Judge Horace Holmes died, neighbors planted several new trees in his honor.

The simple stone house at 1019 Spruce Street is Boulder's oldest surviving house. The area is frequently on Historic Boulder's lavish fund-raising Christmas tour of homes; if you are hoping for a peek inside, that's your best chance. This neighborhood is a favorite strolling location, and on warm summer evenings the streets and flagstone sidewalks are filled with a quiet crowd enjoying its hometown feel.

At the corner of Mapleton and Ninth Street is Mapleton Elementary School, the heart of the neighborhood since it opened in 1888. Step inside and check out the photos of student bodies shod in everything from button shoes to Adidas.

University Hill

This historic area continues to attract many university staff, faculty, and students. Its location, tucked between the foothills and the university, is one of the area's greatest pluses, and its greatest source of frustration. Specifically, the neighborhood is reluctant host to thousands of cars that can't find a space on campus, and rental homes can end up overstuffed with students looking for affordable housing.

It's walkable from downtown, but keep in mind you're going to put in some distance, uphill. Head south on Ninth Street from Canyon Boulevard, past the grandly conceived and minimally executed sculpture park, and cross Boulder Creek and the creek path, where you'll see two interesting buildings. The main Boulder Public Library is on your left, and Highland Office Park, a beautiful renovation of an old school, is on your right. The library was designed as a green building, with lots of ambient light and lights in the stacks that turn on and off automatically in response to motion detectors. Live trees in the children's library soar two stories, so adults in the reference department above are in the treetops. During the 1960s and 1970s, Highland was the funky home of the Free School, which taught tie-dyed adult students to throw pots and create stained glass. Today, it's an upscale office building with an old-money ambience. Farther up Ninth Street at Euclid Avenue is

an unusual redbrick home with the look of a castle, partially obscured by a wood fence. Legend has it that two Boulder brothers who fell in love with the same woman held a house-building contest. The woman chose this octagonal house, which has not a single square room—and the innovative guy who came with it.

i **Boulder neighborhoods are very diverse. Take a self-directed driving tour to see the historic homes up in the Mapleton and Whittier areas, the 1950s-style ranches in Martin Acres, and the modern homes perched on the mountainside in Pinebrook Hills. It's an afternoon well spent.**

Turn left (east) to 1206 Euclid, where you'll find the Boulder Museum of History set in a beautifully landscaped park. The museum was built in 1899 as a summer "cottage" for a New York stockbroker. If this is a cottage, that New Yorker's regular home must have filled 3 blocks. It now features a Tiffany window, fascinating snippets of Boulder history, and a gift shop. Locals swear the third-floor ballroom is periodically frequented by ghostly revelers and that the spirits of beloved dogs of a previous owner still prowl the grounds. One block south, at 12th and Aurora Streets, is the serene white building known as Marpa House. With the look of a foreign embassy, complete with flagpoles, Marpa House is a communal residence and meditation center for Boulder's Buddhist community.

Three blocks west, at 970 Aurora, is The Academy retirement community, a blend of new and old. The original building on the site was an isolated Catholic girls' school when it was built— the young students fell asleep to the serenade of coyotes and the howl of the unrestrained wind. The building later housed offices and classrooms for the University of Colorado until CU decided to sell. While sitting empty, it lost its roof and upper floors to fire and became a crumbling home to raccoons, squirrels, and occasional homeless squatters. In 1998, the building was renovated as the centerpiece of a retirement community aimed at former CU faculty. In this area, you will also encounter sorority and fraternity houses, some stately, some in need of a good spruce-up. To the south, at the northwest corner of 12th Street and Baseline Road, is a home designed by local architect Glen Huntington, whose stately brick buildings set the tone for 1930s University Hill.

Chautauqua Park

Technically, Chautauqua is the name of the historic park and residential area that fills the triangle between Baseline Road, the Flatirons, and a hilly neighborhood of contemporary homes. However, the name Chautauqua has spread to encompass the surrounding neighborhood as well. In the summertime you can still rent a little old wooden summer cabin at Chautauqua Park, a remnant of the days when Texas schoolteachers and their families summered in Boulder to escape the heat. Street names honor mountain flowers, such as the daisy-shaped gaillardia and the nodding blue lupine. South of the big Chautauqua auditorium, site of musical and dance concerts and a summer silent movie festival, it's a short hike up Enchanted Mesa. With the purchase of this meadow of grasses and strong-limbed ponderosa pines in the 1960s, Boulder became the first town in the nation to buy open space through a sales-tax bond. Enchanted Mesa is one reason Boulderites can gaze out their windows and see pine forests, rather than houses, in the foothills. Also check the Chautauqua Rangers' Station on Kinnikinick Road, where you can get information on Boulder Open Space and Mountain Parks. It's staffed part-time every day; take your chances on it being open or call (303) 441-3440 for the latest hours.

CONTEMPORARY BOULDER NEIGHBORHOODS

While you can hoof through Boulder's oldest neighborhoods, you'll probably want to drive to see the newer ones. Many people complain that Boulder is a difficult driving town because it does not always follow a standard grid pattern. If you're lost, remember that if you are facing the mountains, you are facing west. North-south streets are numbered from the mountains, starting with 3rd; Broadway takes the place of 12th Street downtown.

Flagstaff Road

Some of Boulder's most futuristic homes were designed by the late Boulder architect Charles Haertling. The easiest to spot are just up Flagstaff Road. To get there, follow Baseline Road up Flagstaff Mountain. A tenth of a mile past the fire danger sign is a home of round white towers beside one with sand-colored, pyramidal roofs. These are two of Haertling's 52 creations. Haertling, considered one of America's finest architects, often used dramatic and fluid forms. If you are ever invited inside a Haertling home, go gladly, for he designed with reverence for Boulder's vistas. If you haven't driven up Flagstaff Road before, by all means, keep going. The panorama of Boulder Valley is gorgeous, and if you have a map, you can spot most landmarks from up there. If you don't have a Boulder County license plate on your car, you'll have to pay a $3 parking fee at the overlook parking area. The red roofs you are seeing are the University of Colorado, whose architect imported the red tile roofs of his Italian homeland. The largish bodies of water farther to the east are cooling ponds for the coal-fired Valmont Power Plant, where undisturbed fish are said to grow to phenomenal size in the warm water. If you continue up Flagstaff Road past the park boundary, you'll pass widely scattered homes in diverse styles, from one that resembles a French château to monumental log houses.

Return down the mountain to Baseline and turn left onto Sixth Street. Then turn left again at Cascade to Willowbrook Road, then left once more. On your right is a white house that some call a spaceship. It's the Volsky house, a 1960s-era Haertling design that earned him a feature in *Life* magazine.

🔍 Close-up

An Inside Look at Boulder's Historic Homes

To the delight of history buffs and those interested in historic preservation, Historic Boulder, Inc., Boulder's first permanent preservation organization, offers two home tours designed to give visitors an inside glimpse of Boulder's past. The Historic Homes for the Holidays house tour, held every December, is a sampling of some of Boulder's most delightful historic homes, all dressed up for the holidays. From bungalows to mansions, the tour covers homes located in a variety of Boulder's older neighborhoods. In addition to being educational, the tour is a great way to get into the holiday spirit. On the flip side, October brings Historic Boulder's Ghost Walk and Meet Spirits Tour of Columbia Cemetery. During the Ghost Walk, haunted historic homes with their resident spirits are on display in addition to psychics presenting readings on the homes, and things that go bump in the night.

Martin Acres

If you've had your fill of fancy homes, check out Boulder's first tract-home neighborhood, south of Baseline Road, north of Table Mesa Drive and east of Broadway. Most of the homes in Martin Acres were built in 1955, when $13,000 bought a three-bedroom ranch house. They now sell for about 15 times that price, and are still among Boulder's most affordable homes. The trees are now more than 40 years old. Some renovations are, well, sort of like a kid's party hat on a businessman. But more and more are enthralling transformations. Martin Acres proves that homes from a plain area, filled with interesting people, add character to a neighborhood. Like many Boulder neighborhoods, traffic is the primary concern in the neighborhood. Martin Park residents can get reduced-cost bus passes, and the Bear Creek bike path is a lovely way to visit without adding pollution or parking problems.

Table Mesa

More 1970s-vintage, and generally pricier than Martin Acres, this is an area of split-levels and raised ranches below the National Center for Atmospheric Research. Table Mesa lies west of Broadway and south of Table Mesa Drive. The Table Mesa Shopping Center is convenient for residents here, as are many mountain trails. The South Boulder Recreation Center on Gillespie

Drive butts up against a lovely park encircling what, in the arid West, passes for a lake—Viele Lake. It's an easy, lovely stroll around the lake, particularly if you are fond of geese. One note: Don't wear your finest shoes.

If you long for unobstructed views, follow Broadway south to the stoplight at Greenbriar Boulevard. Turn right, and head west past Fairview High School into a neighborhood of earth-toned homes called Shanahan Ridge. Townhomes, condominiums, and single-family homes pack the street's north side. The south is open space—a whole valleyful. Residents awaken to meadowlark songs. One of Boulder's finest achievements is leaving open space near residential areas. People pay a premium to live near open, natural areas. Check out the fresh green growth on the Shanahan Ridge open space, where a prescribed burn in 2000 cleared out dangerously dense undergrowth.

Dominating South Boulder is the I. M. Pei–designed National Center for Atmospheric Research. This is one of America's finest public buildings, and in typical Boulder fashion, it is also the gateway to easy and popular nature trails, some of them accessible to wheelchairs. NCAR is open to the public for free guided tours at noon Monday through Saturday from June through September; winter tours are at noon Mondays and Wednesdays. You can also take a self-guided tour between 8 a.m. and 5 p.m. Monday through

Friday, 9 a.m. and 4 p.m. weekends and holidays. The library and cafeteria are also open weekdays. Call (303) 497-1174. To reach it, drive west on Table Mesa Drive and up to the mesa; keep your eyes open for the deer that roam the mesa (and don't forget to rent Woody Allen's *Sleeper* afterward for an I-was-there experience—also check out the Wonderland Hill neighborhood, later in this section, for another *Sleeper* reference).

Knollwood Neighborhood

This lovely little neighborhood is tucked away so carefully, many longtime Boulder residents don't know it's there. Driving west on Mapleton Avenue, cross Fourth Street and find the sign on your left announcing Knollwood Drive. The long building near the entrance, embracing a boulder, is another Haertling home. Careful of a winter visit, though, as the steep streets can be difficult when icy.

Newlands Neighborhood

More than 10 years ago this now-trendy place to live didn't even have an official name. But the Newland family once owned the land, and what was once just a collection of houses around North Boulder Park is now one of the hottest real estate markets. This neighborhood is west of Broadway from approximately Alpine Avenue on the south to Hawthorn Avenue on the north (from Alpine to the north, east-west street names are pretty much alphabetical). A landscaped island at the intersection of Ninth and Evergreen Streets welcomes visitors to the neighborhood. A sculptor resident donated the statue of a crouching, nude woman in the center of the island; his neighbors have had mixed reactions to the public art. Note the bungalows, some original and others spectacular renovations and "scrape-offs," where an owner demolishes the old house and builds a bigger one on the site. There is also a subsidized housing unit in the area, but you won't recognize it as such. Approximately 4,900 subsidized units are sprinkled around Boulder, in small, unobtrusive pockets, often close to Boulder's trendiest areas.

A very active neighborhood organization is working hard to build a sense of community here, with activities that include a cooperative child-care and play group, the Junkengrooven swap meet, May Day and Fall Fest picnics, and regular guest presentations for the neighborhood meetings.

Pine Brook Hills

Some of Boulder's grandest modern homes can be found on Linden Avenue in what is called Pine Brook Hills. Back on Broadway, go north past Iris Avenue and turn left (west, toward the mountains) onto Linden. These designer homes can't be missed, as many are perched on hillsides with commanding views. Up Linden Avenue is South Cedar Brook Road, and at its very top are the last two homes Haertling designed before he succumbed to cancer in his 50s. You can probably find these homes yourself, but here's a clue. One is round and white. The other's roof mimics an aspen leaf, gently curling upward in the wind.

Wonderland Hills

This area was Boulder's first planned multi-unit development and its sense of neighborhood is often appealing to newcomers. To reach the entrance, return to Broadway, going north again, to Poplar Avenue and Wonderland Hills. Several bike paths wind through the neighborhood. In landscaped areas, weeping crab apples, native red-twig dogwoods, and evergreens make homes seem more secluded than in many areas with much larger yards. Within a two-minute walk of the smallest condo are Boulder-style mansions. Did you spot the white "barnacle" house also featured in Woody Allen's futuristic film, *Sleeper*? It's another Haertling home.

Also clinging to this hillside is the huge structure referred to as "the volcano house." Innocuous on the outside, the bizarre home indulges its owner's childhood fantasies, from a faux volcano with on-command eruptions into bubbling hot tubs, to a fireman's pole connecting the living room with the downstairs foyer. There's even a mini movie theater where every seat is a lounger. The owner has been generous about sharing the ambience with civic groups holding fund-raisers, so do good and you may get a chance to try out the "snow room"—walls painted with snow scenes and a snowmaker to shower you with the white stuff in the dead of summer.

Go anywhere you want now, and you'll find a new neighborhood. This "point of interest" tour has focused on the older side of Boulder. East of Broadway are many more homes, generally less than 20 years old and more affordable. Dakota Ridge, north of Wonderland Hill, appeals to young families looking for a recently built home. These areas are ripe for homeowners eager to add their style to a highly creative town.

BEYOND BOULDER

Mountain Towns

To get an overview of mountain living, take Canyon Boulevard west out of town and head up Boulder Canyon. Turnoffs to Four Mile Canyon, Magnolia Road, and Sugarloaf Road lead to more areas containing mountain homes of various styles. If you continue 17 miles up the canyon, you will reach Nederland and the Peak to Peak Highway (Highway 72), which leads to other mountain communities. Most of them are along this scenic highway, made up of Highways 119, 72, and 7. These paved roads are beautiful all year, from the sparkling pine-scented days of summer to the shimmering golden world of an aspen grove in fall to a crisp winter day softened with a comforter of snow. These scenic roads can be steep and curvy, so keep your lower gears in tune and don't let the occasional commuter in a hurry rush you along, as the views along the way are worth the time. Not all mountain towns are listed here, so keep your eyes open to discover one on your own.

ALLENSPARK
8,250 feet, pop. 400
32 miles from Boulder
Founded by Alonzo N. Allen as a mining town, Allenspark was once a stagecoach stop between Ward and Estes Park. Today, Allenspark is a peaceful retirement and vacation community nestled in pine forests on the eastern edge of Rocky Mountain National Park. The style tends to rustic cabins and barns full of trail horses. It has a volunteer fire department and a post office, and offers lodges, cabins, and restaurants. The Fawn Brook Inn (303-747-2556) is a fine-dining spot, worth the drive from Boulder. Its hours vary according to the season, so call ahead. To reach Allenspark, go to Ward and Nederland and head north on the Peak to Peak Highway (Highway 72). From Lyons, take Highway 7.

ELDORADO SPRINGS
5,760 feet, pop. 650
15 miles from Boulder
This is the closest "mountain" community to Boulder. The gold in these hills comes from the orange and yellow lichens that color the walls of Eldorado Canyon State Park, one of the nation's premier rock-climbing areas. The springs area was the winter home of a Ute Indian tribe. In the early 1900s, these same springs sustained a 40-room resort. Trombone player Glenn Miller used to leave studies at CU to play with the Eldorado Springs resort band. Sweet-faced movie star Mary Pickford was a visitor, and soon-to-be-president Dwight Eisenhower and his bride, Mamie, vacationed here. A quarry once yielded Eldorado Canyon's beautiful red rock. It has closed, but that mining scar remains, a reminder of the trade-offs between promoting industry and natural grandeur.

To see Eldorado Springs, drive south on Broadway. Three miles past Table Mesa Drive, turn west on Highway 170. After 3 more miles, you'll meet a riffraff of cabins, precariously balanced along a steep mountain stream. Welcome to the bumpy dirt roads that some residents say add character and discourage tourists. Most Eldorado Springs residents are romance-smitten commuters. You can see their influence in the flowers that wink in rock gardens, in the misty wash of rainbow colors on a potter's garage, in the blue cow bells cascading near a shake-shingle entry. Drive past the pool and head over the rutted wooden trestles of that one-way bridge. Continue past the caramel-colored chalet called "L'il'

Abner," past the 1950s-style, minty green place named "Jitterbug," and by that upscale cottage called "Chelsea Morning."

Eldorado Springs pool, fed by underground springs, is a favorite summer swimming hole, the warm water delivered from more than a mile below. The springs also provide clear Eldorado Artesian Springs water, available for home delivery or in local grocery stores.

JAMESTOWN
7,000 feet, pop. 240
18 miles from Boulder
Gold, silver, and fluorspar once brought 10,000 miners to "Jimtown," a town whose name was later "upgraded." Douglas Fairbanks Sr. was born in this shady town. The Jamestown Mercantile Building is a classic false-front store from the mining-town days. There's a public elementary school and strong sense of family values in town, including a desire to keep the children safe. So watch for the speed bumps as you enter and leave. Jamestown is northwest of Boulder. Take U.S. Highway 36 to Left Hand Canyon, turning into the mountains and, at the big fork, jogging right.

LYONS
5,375 feet, pop. 1,600
17 miles from Boulder
The red sandstone around Lyons has been the source of much quarry rock, locally called flagstone. Fifteen sandstone buildings, including the Old Stone Congregational Church, are in Lyons's historical district. This dark-brown flagstone church, square with a short steeple, is just north of Main Street, on High Street. The quarries that provided the stone for these buildings still operate around Lyons and are excellent choices if you want flagstone for your patio, classic Colorado stones for your home, or beautiful boulders for your garden. Lyons itself has a small-town atmosphere, with cottonwood trees shading the sparkling St. Vrain River, towering blue spruce trees standing beside turn-of-the-20th-century bungalows, and plenty of pretty contemporary homes. Vacation cabins and high-tech companies are here, plus many good restaurants and antiques

shops, some decorated to give a Germanic/Slavic feel to the shopping areas.

Bring your swimsuit and make time to visit Meadow Park on the town's western edge; here the St. Vrain accommodates swimmers with an excellent swimmin' hole with overhanging rocks perfect for cannonballing. There are also baseball diamonds, playgrounds, and lots of places to climb, hike, and picnic.

The prettiest way to reach Lyons is to take 28th Street or Broadway north from Boulder—the two converge into US 36. The route winds beside the foothills, and less than 20 miles from Boulder it dead-ends into Highway 66. Turn left here, pass roadside shops and eating places, and you're in Lyons. The Town Hall is at 432 Fifth Avenue (303-823-6622).

NEDERLAND
8,236 feet, pop. 1,270
16 miles from Boulder
Nineteen miles up Canyon Boulevard, just past the big blue lake formed by Barker Dam, is Nederland, the largest mountain town near Boulder. Here, the aspen trees shimmer next to pretty plots of colorful mountain flowers during the summer, with mountainsides of pine trees and aspen in every direction. Nederland has a good mix of shopping, tourist-oriented businesses, and basic services. This is a friendly, easygoing community that includes mountain people who wanted to be close to high alpine fields, hippies who came here decades ago to found communes, New Age yuppies, and Boulder intellectuals who retreated from the city below. All this makes for an eclectic, worldly, remote but close-enough-to-it-all mountain town. If you want some fun reading about Nederland history, find a copy of local author Marlys Millhiser's *The Mirror*. This fantasy novel describes a Boulder woman who trades places in time with her Nederland grandmother, then discovers the rigors of being a miner's wife, the challenges of driving a wagon team up a treacherous dirt canyon road, and the red light district that even tiny Nederland supported.

Near Nederland are the Indian Peaks Wilderness and the Eldora Mountain Resort, with its downhill and cross-country skiing. The shops are comfortably close together, picturesque, and easy to amble through. Annie's Cafe is a good neighborhood restaurant (see Restaurants). All this means that Nederland has settled, by fits and bounds, into the intriguing community its beginnings hinted at. Originally a gold-, silver-, and tungsten-mining area, Nederland had more than 3,500 residents at the height of the mining boom in 1874. Today, gambling in Black Hawk and Central City, south on Peak to Peak Highway, plus Boulder's spillover prosperity, have fueled Nederland's latest boom. Many residents work in Boulder or elsewhere in the "lowlands" to the east.

Summer events usually include a Kinetic Wind Festival, a Native American Pow Wow, and a replay of the pioneer days. Check in at the visitor center on West First Street, where the RTD bus stops. Across from the visitor center is Town Hall (303-258-3266).

PINECLIFFE
7,960 feet, pop. 475 (winter)
525 (summer)
20 miles from Boulder
Retired miners and nature lovers live in this enclave southeast of Nederland on Highway 72. Some are upscale commuters, and some people live "off the grid." That means they're in homes without city power, water, or sewage hookups. "Off the grid" can mean rough-hewn cabins or a high-tech home complete with photovoltaic cells to provide solar electricity and heat.

WARD
9,253 feet, pop. 165
23 miles from Boulder
An 1890s gold strike brought 4,000 people to this greatest gold camp of northern Colorado. Ward merits a footnote to Colorado history, for this is where silver baron (and briefly U.S. Senator) Horace Tabor served as a postmaster toward the end of his life, which he passed in unaccustomed poverty. During the boom, $5 million in gold was taken from veins around Ward, but by 1930 the mines died out, and only three residents stayed behind. Hippies arrived in the 1960s, and many of

them have never left; persistent rumors put heiress Patti Hearst in a commune near Ward when she was on the run with the SLA. It's still a place of shaggy hair and beards to match, fringed vests, and love beads. On weekends, intrepid Lycra-clad bicyclists perch outside the general store, with great pride, sucking up cold mineral water and swapping stories about their 23-mile ride from Boulder to reach the hilly streets of Ward. Tourists gaze at the rustic buildings, their colors as faded as sand-washed jeans, within the thick mountain forests. The old Ward School, now the town hall and post office, is typical of wood-framed rural schoolhouses.

Ward has an honor-system public library and a general store. The Millsite Inn (see the Restaurants chapter) sits above town on the Peak to Peak Highway (Highway 72), about 8 miles north of Nederland. The beautiful alpine hiking area around Brainard Lake is just west of Ward.

> **i** Can you believe that Boulder once was a windswept prairie? All those lovely trees have been planted by the people who decided to stay.

Towns of the Plains
All the towns around Boulder have modern 'burbs, fed by a series of building booms since the 1960s. Here you'll find Boulder County's more affordable housing. Although these towns are more development-friendly and growth-oriented than Boulder, they are beginning to pay more attention to such quality-of-life enhancements as open space. The prosperity of these towns is evident in their golf-course competitions and swimming-pool wars. Actually, these aren't wars, but they reflect a trend toward family-oriented community centers.

Stunned by the rate of growth in their towns, east county residents have been increasingly insistent that natural areas be preserved. To keep seeing eagles flying overhead, even as these communities grow, their citizens are beginning to raise more open-space purchase funds. It might not happen in time to save all the favorite local nature walks, but sentiment is growing to preserve more.

These communities have a range of personalities. Rock Creek is nothing but newer homes, a huge growth on the side of tiny, historic Superior. Other towns are as old as Boulder, complete with traditional downtowns and beautiful Victorian neighborhoods. Lafayette, Louisville, and Longmont offer the contrast between modern developments and older parts of town known for their quaint atmosphere and lovely trees.

BROOMFIELD
5,200 feet, pop. 53,691
8 miles from Boulder

When the Pony Express needed to get overland mail from Julesburg, Scottsbluff, or Fort Laramie to Denver, carriers changed horses at Broomfield. Travel gave the farming town fame again in 1952, when Broomfield became the site of a toll station on the new Boulder/Denver Turnpike (now known as US 36). The road was especially popular during Saturday CU-Boulder football games. In 1967, it became the nation's first toll road to pay for itself, approximately 13 years ahead of schedule.

That history of a town at the crossroads became a bureaucratic headache as the town found itself in four counties and five different school districts. In 2000, Broomfield became its own county, the first time since 1902 that a city and county was created in Colorado. The city is busily creating the government structure, and the buildings, to support that status.

Meanwhile, growth continues at a phenomenal rate. The city's population increased from 24,000 to more than 53,691 in the past decade. The huge campus-like Interlocken high-tech office park continues to expand. The park is wired with fiber-optic cables to keep the high-tech tenants connected to the world. Interlocken is zoned for at least 25 percent open space, including wetlands and natural grasses, plus a golf course next to a hotel.

Flatirons Crossing Mall opened in 2000, with 1.5 million square feet of retail and restaurant space that draws shoppers from all around the region.

As Broomfield grows it is attempting to preserve some open space as well—more than 2,000 acres so far. The Bay, Broomfield's outdoor aquatic park, attracts bathers from around the region. For more information contact the city (and county) of Broomfield, 1 DesCombes Drive, (303) 469-3301.

ERIE
5,020 feet, pop. 16,800
8 miles from Boulder

The town was first settled around 1867 by a Methodist pastor who named it after his hometown of Erie, Pennsylvania. Like its namesake, Colorado's Erie is a former coal town. An area of tilled farm fields and subdivisions, Erie is the site of the 119-acre Tri-County Airport. Some homes near the airport have hangars and taxiways to the airport in their backyards, mirroring the garages and driveways they have in the front. Its major industries are landfills and junkyards near town. Sound boring? Quite the opposite. This is Boulder County, remember! Blake's Small Car Salvage has been on national television for being one of the prettiest junkyards around. (See the Shopping chapter for more on this spot.) And a nearby business, Construction Recycling, recycles more than 80 percent of the building scraps it receives.

As housing prices push residential development east from Boulder to Lafayette, Louisville and Superior, Erie is beginning to feel the ripple. This neat little town is warm and friendly and is welcoming newcomers with new housing and retail developments.

You can reach Erie by taking Arapahoe Road east out of Boulder past U.S. Highway 287. You'll be on a dirt road for a while, which dead-ends. Turn left (north). Go about 1.5 miles and you're in Erie. The Town Hall is at Lincoln School, 645 Holbrook Street (303-926-2700).

GUNBARREL
5,145 feet, pop. 10,080
7 miles from Boulder

Great mountain views and fancy homes around a golf course/country club are hallmarks of this large neighborhood of subdivisions. It was first developed in 1963 as a 558-acre subdivision to house the employees of a huge IBM plant across the Diagonal Highway. With Big Blue cutting back on its staff and other high-tech firms moving into the area, Gunbarrel has developed into a more varied community.

The commercial part of Gunbarrel, which includes Celestial Seasonings, IBM, Leanin' Tree, and a small shopping center, is part of the city of Boulder. Much of the residential area is in unincorporated Boulder County. Even though the city of Boulder twice has offered to annex the neighborhood, residents prefer the autonomy of being in the county.

Take the Diagonal Highway (Highway 119) north toward Longmont. Just out of Boulder, turn right onto Jay Road. Keep going. To see the fancy houses, turn left on a street such as Carter Road. To get deeper into Gunbarrel, continue on the Diagonal to 63rd Street and turn right (south). The homes and enterprises of Gunbarrel are both to your right and left. The Boulder Country Club, with a golf course backing up against the yards of dozens of homes, is in the heart of Gunbarrel Greens, south off of Lookout Road. Sorry, members only.

HYGIENE
5,100 feet, pop. 265
14 miles from Boulder
In the 1880s, farmers battled grasshopper plagues and other woes to settle this fertile area. The town earned its name when people suffering from tuberculosis moved to a local sanitarium called Hygiene House. Fresh air and sunshine revived many, as the elements still do today. Hygiene is about a mile west of Longmont in an area full of towering old cottonwoods, Siberian elms, ancient lilac hedges, and farm homes with horses mowing the grass. It's at the intersection of North 75th Street and Hygiene Road. A local hangout is Clark's Food Store, the little shop with a rickety, tilting porch awning that hangs like half-closed eyelashes above the front door. Here's a town where the neighbors know each other, and if you decide to hang out for a while, you can be sure they'll talk about you.

LAFAYETTE
5,260 feet, pop. 24,888
11 miles from Boulder
Lafayette Miller ran a farm, a stagecoach, and a hotel. After he died, Mary Miller discovered coal on their late homestead. In 1890, she named a new town after her husband. Coal and farming were the main industries for 50 years. Today, the town is a burgeoning residential community for the high-tech industry, with brand-new home tracts, green patches of lawn, and hopeful baby trees. To reach Lafayette, head 11 miles east on either Baseline Road or South Boulder Road through Louisville.

"Old Town" Lafayette has its tidy little bungalows and big street trees. Efrain's is a good Mexican restaurant (see the Restaurants chapter). The city offices (303-665-5588) are at 1290 South Public Road, the northeast corner of "Four Corners," a business district at the intersection of US 287 and South Boulder Road. The Lafayette Chamber of Commerce (303-666-9555) is in the old historic district at 309 South Public Road.

Local sentiment favors keeping small-town charm even as affordable and upscale subdivisions boom. There's a move to protect favorite open areas such as Waneka Lake, where people can paddle rented canoes to a blue heron's marshy shallows. So far, the city has 167 acres of developed parks and more than 1,000 acres of open space. You can find a map of these places at the recreation center on 111 West Baseline Road (303-665-0469).

The YMCA of Boulder Valley has opened a 55,000-square-foot complex including an ice-skating rink, fitness center, gymnasium, indoor running track, and other facilities on Arapahoe Road and 95th Street to entertain the burgeoning population. The Indian Peaks Golf Course is within city limits.

Lafayette is home to a community of Hmong families, refugees from Laos. It also has one of the nation's few co-housing communities, the Nyland Community Association (303-494-2778). It features 42 passive-solar homes built around a common area and the "community house" with guest rooms, activity rooms, a child care center, and a dining hall open to residents who don't want to cook evening meals in their homes. Cars are parked outside the community. Only pedestrians are allowed inside.

LONGMONT
4,979 feet, pop. 77,900
12 miles from Boulder

Longmont, named after Longs Peak, which in turn was named after Major Stephen Long, started as a 30,000-acre farming community and sugar beet center. The city celebrated its 135th anniversary in 2006. It is the county's second-largest town and is sometimes called Boulder's twin. Sure enough, it offers many services similar to Boulder's, including a hospital, school district, daily newspaper, branch of the County Clerk's Office, state Motor Vehicle Division office, and other services. But these twins are not identical. For one thing, Longmont is kind of modest about how pretty it is, and publicity for local events is often low-key. For another, the two towns come from opposite ends of the political spectrum.

From the old Main Street shopping district to the Boulder County Fairgrounds at 9595 Nelson Road, which hosts dog shows, antiques shows, and the Boulder County Fair in August (see the Festivals and Annual Events chapter), Longmont retains a conservative farming-town hospitality even as it grows and grows. With the exception of Boulder, more homes were sold in Longmont during the first half of 1996 than in any other town in the county, and sometimes it seems that the fields surrounding the town have been planted with house seeds instead of grain. This house crop is sprouting overnight, with town houses here, single-family homes there and a naked, surprised look to many of these late-20th-century homesteads, as they wait for the saplings in their front yards to catch up and shade their peaked roofs.

To reach Longmont from Boulder, head northeast on Highway 119 (also called the Diagonal Highway or just the Diagonal for short). Except during rush hour, it's about a 20-minute drive. To get a feeling for the Victorian houses and tree-canopied streets near Main Street and Third

Avenue, check the Callahan House. New houses are in developments all around town. Municipal offices (303-776-6050) are at the Civic Center, at Third Avenue and Kimbark Street. The Longmont Chamber of Commerce (303-776-5295) is at 528 Main Street.

LOUISVILLE
5,350 feet, pop. 19,400
11 miles from Boulder

Louis Nawatny founded this town in 1878, after discovering coal 200 feet below a settler's farm. Twelve mines eventually thrived in Louisville, providing high wages for sometimes-dangerous work. In the early 1900s, labor organizer Mother Jones spoke to coal miners in the town. During this time, European miners, who occasionally worked as strikebreakers, came to town.

Although the statue of a miner that stands outside city hall is still the town's trademark, Louisville is a coal-mining town that has transformed itself into the epitome of a modern suburb. Centura Avista Adventist Hospital is located in Louisville. It specializes in maternity and neonatal care. The Coal Creek Golf Course was listed by *Golf Digest* magazine as one of the top 25 new golf courses in 1990. When the golf course first went in, next to US 36, there was concern that errant golf balls would hit cars, but it has not been a problem. The highway interchange is booming, with Louisville's first modern hotels, small shops and huge chain outlets, a 12-plex theater, and practically every chain restaurant you can imagine.

Louisville's population has more than tripled since the 1970s, making it one of Colorado's fastest-growing communities, but the goal is now to stabilize the population and put some effort into preserving open spaces. Most of the population growth has come from young families, with kids galore. Still, Louisville strives to maintain small-town charm with events such as a Fourth of July Community Picnic and a Labor Day food celebration (see the Festivals and Annual Events chapter). Louisville's city offices are at 749 Main Street (303-666-6565).

NIWOT
5,095 feet, pop. 4,444
5 miles from Boulder

The unincorporated town is named after Chief Niwot, whose name means "left hand" in the Arapaho language. The original downtown, which was comprised of supply shops and a school for local farmers, is now filled with antiques shops and surrounded by housing developments. The old town center also boasts the Niwot Auction, a big bimonthly mecca for antique hounds, and an annual auction festival in the summer.

To reach Niwot, take the Diagonal Highway (Highway 119) north toward Longmont. One mile after IBM is Niwot Road. Hang a right, and you're there. It's about a 10- to 15-minute drive from Boulder. Boulderites visit for the antiques and, around Christmas, to mail gifts from the town's small post office.

i Take a stroll in old town Niwot. The quaint restaurants and shops are a true delight.

SUPERIOR
5,400 feet, pop. 10,483
9 miles from Boulder

If you had been struck by an unlikely urge to visit the town of Superior more than a decade ago, you would have found a tiny hamlet of small homes housing 255 souls. Today, you're even more likely to bypass the small old town for the bright lights of a commercial strip and the broad avenues of a huge development called Rock Creek, built on land annexed by Superior in 1987 and given water rights in 1990. Rock Creek sprawls across more than 3 square miles of rolling grassland. By 2010, it could eventually include up to 8,000 homes and 15 million square feet of commercial space, extending east along US 36 all the way to the Interlocken Office Park at Broomfield and south to Highway 128. Some large homes stand beside the meticulously landscaped, wide boulevards, decorated with statuary and leading to tennis courts and a swimming pool. There are also townhomes and numerous smaller single-family homes on more modest lots.

The town is still catching up with much of this growth. Until 1999, Rock Creek's only commercial development was two gas stations. Now there are a slew of new businesses, most of them of the "mega" variety.

The town hall, at 24 East Coal Creek Drive (303-499-3675), is a good information place, as are Rock Creek's real estate offices and show houses. Superior is just south of the Superior/Louisville interchange on US 36.

REAL ESTATE AND RELOCATION

In recent years, Colorado generally and Boulder specifically have been among the hottest housing markets in the nation. For a while, the housing market was so hot that Boulder home buyers had a half-hour to run through a home, then sign up before the next buyers beat them to it. Factors including rapid growth of well-paying jobs, the high demand for housing, and a low supply of available homes continues to rank Boulder at the top for average single-family home prices among the metro-area counties. In the past few years buyers scrambled, and there were many reports of people making two or three offers on houses before they could actually call one their own. Even those moving from high-priced locales such as San Francisco found themselves paying $60,000 more than they had planned. "We expected this to be a cakewalk," said one newcomer from the West Coast. "We made offers on five houses before we got one." Home prices in surrounding communities such as Longmont, Lafayette, and Louisville have climbed sharply even without the benefit of the Boulder postmark. In 2001, home prices in Boulder and the surrounding area finally slowed. Once considered a hotbed for sellers, by mid-2003 it was considered a buyer's market for the first time in two decades. Renters benefited too, with landlords offering incentives and dropping prices $50 to $100 from the previous tenant's payment. The nation's struggling economy has also taken a toll on homeowners. In mid-2003, there were 30 percent more homes for sale in the Denver metro area than at the same point a year earlier. Despite the slowdown, the county remains one of Colorado's most expensive.

This chapter provides a general sense of home prices and rental costs in Boulder County. It also includes bargain-hunting tips, ideas on what to look for in a Boulder home and neighborhood, and a list of real estate resources. If you're looking for a Boulder home, happy hunting!

THE HOMEBUYER'S MARKET

Quality of life, the cachet of a Boulder address, and something called the "Danish Plan" are what have driven local house prices into the stratosphere. Boulder was one of the first cities in the nation to adopt a residential growth-control ordinance (called the Danish Plan after City Councilman Paul Danish), which limits the number of permits for new construction that are issued annually. The law of supply and demand is in effect in Boulder, and with limited new construction coupled with a strong economy, property values have soared, and the issue of "affordable housing" has become a community hot button.

The strict growth controls, in place since the mid-1970s, depress the number of homes that are for sale in Boulder in any given month. However,

Boulder, along with the rest of the country, has felt the effects of the recent housing market slump. In November 2006, single-family home resales averaged $638,264. Two years later in September of 2008, that number dropped to $513,537. The average selling price of condominiums and town houses in September 2008 was $302, 560.

It used to be that you could buy a lot more house outside the city limits, but that has changed somewhat. If you are looking for the lifestyle or Boulder mystique, you will have to pay for it. As the saying goes, location, location, location. Boulder encompasses a wide range of houses and housing styles, from historic cottages, between-the-world-wars Tudor mansions, postwar ranch houses, and new subdivisions with contemporary homes.

Housing costs considerably less in Boulder County's other communities. The majority of new homes are now built in Erie, Lafayette, Longmont, and Superior. According to the Boulder Area Realtors Association, the average price of homes in September 2008 was $393,571 in Broomfield, $331,581 in Erie, $384,400 in Louisville, and $465,533 in Superior. Generally, rural lots in both the mountains and plains offer good deals, but price swings are enormous. And if you're thinking about building, you need to take into consideration zoning and the cost of water and utilities. When rural sellers put high price tags on agricultural land, they most likely expect a city to annex the land; when county land does get annexed, the annexing city can change its zoning to allow much greater density. The market price depends, as always, on location, maintenance, and (this being Boulder) the way your horoscope is interacting with current mortgage rates. The Boulder market is softest on the upper end and hottest for condominiums, but no matter what the price, special homes on special lots still sell fast.

Locals, whether tire-kickers or serious buyers, and newcomers alike flock to the open houses (or "open homes," as they are pretentiously called these days) held year-round, rain or shine, on Sunday afternoons. Check the Saturday and Sunday newspapers, or be alert for "Open House" signs if you are out for an afternoon drive to scout neighborhoods. A real estate agent will be on hand to answer questions, pass out leaflets on the property, and perhaps give a very soft sell on the home you're looking at. It's an easy way to comparison shop without the commitment of being taken around by an agent to look at homes by appointment.

REAL ESTATE RESOURCES

So you're sure you want to move to Boulder County, but where do you start? You can get information on buying or renting in Boulder County from the local chambers of commerce and from the area's Board of Realtors. The Boulder Chamber of Commerce, for instance, issues

a useful relocation packet, as do many real estate agencies. City halls, listed in our Boulder Neighborhoods chapter, can provide general local information. Recreation centers and most grocery stores display free publications about places to live. *Homes & Land of Boulder County* and *Where to Live in Boulder County* are the two biggest and slickest. You can also check out one or more of these groups: Boulder Chamber of Commerce, 2440 Pearl Street, Boulder (303-442-1044, www.boulderchamber.com); Boulder Area Board of Realtors, 4885 Riverbend Road, Suite A, Boulder (303-442-3585, www.baraonline.com); Office of Human Rights Department of Housing and Human Services, 4800 North Broadway (720-564-4610, www.boulderhousing.org).

Real Estate Firms

With the booming real estate market, it seems as if there's an agency on every corner. Most of the bigger agencies serving Boulder County provide newcomer relocation services as well as matching you with a place to live. The Boulder Area Board of Realtors (see contact information listed previously) can provide you with a list of real estate agencies, and you'll find others in the phone book, the local newspaper, and such free periodicals as *Where to Live in Boulder County*. Here are a few of the largest firms:

COLDWELL BANKER RESIDENTIAL BROKERAGE
2700 Canyon Boulevard, Boulder
(303) 449-5000
www.coloradohomes.com

COLORADO LANDMARK REALTORS
2530 Broadway, Boulder
(303) 443-3377
www.coloradolandmark.com

PRUDENTIAL BOULDER REALTORS
4710 Table Mesa Drive, Boulder
(303) 494-7700, (800) 383-6805
www.prurmrboulder.homesandland.com

RE/MAX ALLIANCE
4770 Baseline Road, Boulder
(303) 499-9880, (800) 373-1282
www.homesincolorado.com

RE/MAX OF BOULDER
2425 Canyon Blvd. Suite 110, Boulder
(303) 449-7000
www.boulderco.com

WRIGHT-KINGDOM, INC.
4875 Pearl East Circle, Boulder
(303) 443-2240
www.wrightkingdom.com

ABOUT HOME BUILDERS

With boom times come large, California-style subdivisions put up by major developers and builders. Boom times also bring the need for more schools, more utilities, more roads, and more services. Communities are leveling "impact fees" at builders, and these fees are built into the price of new construction. Home Builders Association of Metropolitan Denver (303-778-1400, www.hbadenver.com) can supply a list of its members, including some large firms building in Boulder County.

HOUSE-HUNTING TIPS

Whether you plan to be a yuppie commoner living in a simple condominium or the royal owner of a grand mansionette, the following tips will help you find just the right home in or near Boulder. Spend time looking, and keep location in mind. The closer to a city center, the more you pay, for it puts you closer to the activities and services that make Boulder and other cities so inviting. The lot itself matters—a good mountain view, a babbling creek, adjacent city open space, a golf course, good entertainment, or a public park all add value. So does beautiful, mature landscaping. That's why a tiny Boulder condominium with all these location features might cost more than a spacious single-family home in outlying areas.

On the other hand, Boulder doesn't have many "wrong side of the track" homes, or acres and acres of homogenized housing, although vast housing tracts are blanketing former farmland surrounding outlying communities. One great feature of this city is how mansions can exist right next to apartment buildings, quirky little bungalows, and subsidized public housing. This magical mixture happens because many Boulder neighborhoods add diversity in neighbor-friendly ways. Drive with a real estate agent through sought-after Mapleton Hill, Whittier, University Hill or North Boulder neighborhoods. Look closely, and you'll see how diversity can help a neighborhood thrive. Even in developments where every house seems to have been cloned from the one next door, a mix of high and moderately priced housing often develops as the trees have grown and people have renovated their properties, whether in modest areas like Martin Acres or more prepossessing ones like Table Mesa. You can find exclusive "mono-communities" in and around Boulder, but if the only thing stopping you from choosing a more eclectic mix is a fear that it would lower your house value, relax. Diverse neighborhoods that are well-loved in Boulder do just fine.

However, an eclectic neighborhood might not be your cup of tea. Perhaps you prefer a brand-new house in a brand-new neighborhood, where you are no more of a newcomer than anyone else. Area developers and Realtors showcase their offerings through annual tours.

WHAT TO LOOK FOR IN A BOULDER HOUSE

Boulder has a cool, semiarid climate, which means most energy goes into heating, not cooling. Insulation matters. Because it's so sunny, passive solar can do wonders. This doesn't mean you must settle for a 1970s-style solar home, with a long wall of south-facing glass and sun-blasting black-painted oil drums. Energy-efficient homes can blend into any style and still keep January gas bills low. One regular-looking Boulder home earned a national energy efficiency award. Its owner, Craig Cristensen, has no heater at all. He relies on passive solar heat, super insulation, and a 1,000-gallon hot water storage tank, so that even if a rugby team burst in and asked for showers during a cloudy February week, enough solar-heated water would be on hand to douse them all.

Some homes are energy-efficient but not all. Check winter utility bills before buying. A few summer days get awfully hot, but heat spells tend to be short, and summer nights cool. As long as a home is positioned to keep out the fiercest summer rays, either with deep eaves or shade trees, most residents don't miss air-conditioning.

Keeping the garden green is a problem in the dry heat of summer. A sprinkler system is a plus, and a modern, water-saving drip system is a super-plus. While some of Boulder's older, most desirable neighborhoods boast the mixed blessing of large, non-indigenous shade trees that provide atmosphere and character but are not really suitable for the region's climate, xeriscaping is a plus in contemporary homes. Xeriscaping is the art and science of landscaping with indigenous drought-tolerant plants that is increasingly popular in the Southwest and Mountain States. See the Shopping chapter's Close-up on xeriscaping.

WANT TO LIVE IN THE MOUNTAINS?

One of Boulder's most distinctive characteristics is that it is a true city with remote mountain living close by. Is a mountain house your dream? Mountain living is not for the fainthearted. Residents keep their snow chains handy. One winter day, the snow on Magnolia Road hid a steeply tilted skating rink. One woman's sporty truck skidded off near the top and plummeted nearly 100 feet. The truck's bed hit first and collapsed like an accordion. Maybe NASA should study the event to improve their hard-landing techniques, for the lucky lady walked out of that truck alive.

Notice a rocky mountainside covered with charred black sticks marking the 1989 Black Tiger Gulch wildfire. As smoke billowed miles away, one mountain couple packed favorite Navajo rugs in the station wagon. They joked that the scare would end in a few hours, and they'd be unpacking. Suddenly they heard a train-like roar and felt blistering heat. The fire had leapt up their ridge. If they had to do it over again, they would have packed the family photo album instead of those rugs. They raced down their bumpy mountain road and will never forget how it felt to breathe searing, hollow air, the oxygen sucked out by the firestorm. That fire caused $10 million in damage and destroyed 39 homes. Another fire in 1990 burned 2,200 acres and 10 homes. Such fires are a natural part of mountain ecosystems. On dry, windy summer days, even big bomber planes, dropping payloads of slurry, cannot slow the flames.

Icy roads and forest fires are nothing compared to your love of nature? Suppose one dusky evening, a mountain lion eats your dog. The kids are horrified. You're just glad it was the dog. So you build a fence. A mountain lion can jump most fences. And you've blocked land that was open to migrating deer, mountain lions, and everything natural up there. Endangered wildlife is one reason Boulder County has decided to slow mountain developments. A mountain home can be wonderful, but unless you're committed to the mountain lifestyle, you can always visit. The average price for a house in the mountains during 2006 was $373,465.

On the other hand, if you realize the trade-offs you're making and the negative impacts you might create, you can do plenty to minimize the problems. Before you build a home, ask your architect about low-impact choices. If you move into an existing home, you can remodel with attention to firefighting materials. Consider replacing cedar shingles with tile, slate, metal, or asphalt (if you build new, you won't be permitted to use cedar shakes). Stucco, brick, and stone siding do not burn and will protect the interior better than a wood exterior. Be sure dead brush is kept away from your home. Such changes minimize flammability.

Pop into an eco-shop, such as Planetary Solutions, 2030 17th Street (303-442-6228, www.planetearth.com), which offers materials and consulting services for environmentally sound building. Take a course in environmentalism from the University of Colorado (303-492-8308, www.colorado.edu/envirostudies) or the Naropa Institute (303-440-0410, www.naropa.edu). Check with the Colorado Division of Wildlife (303-297-1192, www. wildlife.state.co.us) to see how to live with animals. The Thorne Ecological Institute, 1466 North 63rd Street (303-499-3647, www .thorne-eco.org), is another resource. Train your children about mountain safety, and keep your pets—especially cats—indoors. Mountain lions consider cats tasty tidbits, and cats themselves are miniature mountain lions whose hunting has led to the decline of many rare birds.

A FEW, FEW WORDS ABOUT CRIME

Some Boulder County residents leave their doors unlocked. Others have security systems on everything except their running shoes. Most people take care walking at night, especially when in deserted areas of CU-Boulder, downtown, or the Creek Path. Others head into the dark at 5 a.m. all by themselves and have a grand time listening to the morning birds. Boulder County's biggest law-enforcement concerns involve speeding cars and loud parties. Yes, the county has crimes, including murder and abduction. But there are some, well, endearing criminals, too.

Take the fleet-footed Gunbarrel burglar. Under cover of night, he slipped into homes along golf course greens. He stole silver; he stole jewels. Fifty officers and a helicopter tried an ambush. The SWAT team's fastest sprinter cornered him, but that burglar leapt the fence like a deer. Finally, in 1992, they nabbed him with a backpack full of jewels. Turns out he was a marathon runner. He had girlfriends around the world. They didn't know about each other but had enjoyed his dazzling gifts. Over seven years, the bold, handsome runner had burglarized 244 homes. Golf course communities sleep better now that he runs his laps in prison.

THE RENTERS' MARKET

Of Boulder's nearly 96,727 residents, 28,000 are CU-Boulder students, and a good majority rent off-campus. They're not the only ones. In the nonstudent population, almost 55 percent of Boulder city residents rent. That's higher than the overall rate in the United States, where less than 35 percent of all households live in rented dwellings. Many people moving here rent first while searching for something to buy. Others can't afford to buy and remain renters for years. Many who move from Boulder hang onto their homes while they look elsewhere or contemplate returning. Others move up in the market, then use their former digs as an investment.

So brace yourself. Between 1990 and 2000, the rent for a two-bedroom apartment went up 40 percent, and the rent for a single-family home increased more than 100 percent, compared to 20 percent in the United States overall. Much of this is fueled by an extraordinarily low vacancy rate, which is approximately 1.2 percent. Rents tend to be higher near CU and lower in the county. In recent years, you could get a studio or efficiency in the city for about $602, a one-bedroom apartment for $720, and a two-bedroom apartment for about $970. Reduced rents are available through CU married-student housing and Boulder family assistance programs, but waits for such spaces can run years, so apply early.

i Other things being equal, a new house in the Boulder area costs more than a comparable older one—except in select historic neighborhoods where the rule is, "the older, the better."

Popping into town and finding a place right away is not a sure thing, except in spring or early summer, when relatively few students are in residence and there are more apartment vacancies. Many rental agencies prefer at least 45 days advance notice, and they can match you with a place best if you visit for a few days so they can show you around. To be on the safe side, it's best to rent only a dwelling that is licensed and inspected by the city's inspection office.

The city of Boulder has adopted landlord/tenant laws, which cover such things as security deposits, when a lease is required, when the landlord can raise the rent, and so on. Check these laws before you rent, for your own protection. The Community Mediation Service, 2160 Spruce Street (303-441-4364, www.ci.boulder.co.us), issues a Landlord/Tenant Handbook that covers these subjects and also can help resolve disputes including landlord/tenant relations. Colorado doesn't have many renter-protection laws, so if you rent outside the city your lease is where your rights and responsibilities will be spelled out. Read it while wearing your fine-print glasses. Also, some areas allow only three unrelated people per dwelling, and if you're caught cheating, you can be fined until the situation is corrected, so review the terms in your lease carefully.

Rental Resources

HOUSING HELPERS
2865 Baseline Road, Boulder
(303) 545-6000
www.housinghelpers.com

This company offers a number of services, including rental information, roommate or housemate matching for a modest fee, and help with subleasing. There is also a free referral service that helps you select a Realtor, based on the requirements you outline.

UNIVERSITY OF COLORADO OFF-CAMPUS HOUSING
University Memorial Center, Room 336227
(CU-Boulder campus), Boulder
(303) 492-7053
www.colorado.edu/OCSS

This referral service helps students find rooms, apartments, houses, and roommates. It also provides free copies of Boulder's tenants rights and responsibilities, free model leases and subleases, and general information about renting in Boulder.

CITY OF BOULDER HOUSING PARTNERS
4800 North Broadway, Boulder
(720) 564-4610
www.boulderhousing.org

Subsidized housing in the city is available by application to the Housing Authority. There's a one-year wait for a one-bedroom apartment to a two- to three-year wait for a four-bedroom place. The market, however, is very changeable, so it doesn't hurt to call.

BOULDER COUNTY HOUSING AUTHORITY
3482 North Broadway, Boulder
(303) 441-3929
www.co.boulder.co.us/cs/ho

In the county, the waiting list for subsidized housing is two to four years, depending on the house size. The wait is shortest for those who are residents of Boulder County, or who are employed or attend college here.

QUESTIONS OF AFFORDABILITY

An ongoing dilemma in Boulder is the issue of housing affordability. The effort to preserve open space limits the addition of new homes, and people's sentimental attachment to the present character of their block often leads to strong opposition to increased density. Managing these issues is like squeezing a balloon: locate new housing away from open space and fearful neighborhoods, and housing prices balloon. That's why more and more people with moderate incomes either choose much smaller places than they originally envisioned or buy homes a long drive from their jobs. Some people say, "Big deal. Things always cost more in a city, but it's worth it." Or they say, "Big deal. Commutes of nearly an hour are common near urban centers." Other people fear that our very success will destroy what's best about Boulder. If the topic of affordability interests you, attend one of the frequent city meetings at which planning experts from around the nation share ideas.

RETIREMENT

In many ways, Boulder so epitomizes the youth culture that many people don't realize it is a splendid place to retire as well. Excellent community services, an increasing commitment to public transportation, and a benign four-season climate make it congenial for retirees. But "retirement" doesn't automatically equate with "inactivity," and many so-called "retirees" put working folks to shame when it comes to their range of interests.

A "retired" engineer studies ethics at CU-Boulder and works summers at a greenhouse. When his children were young, this high-level manager left escalating salaries and a thirst for fancier things. He and his wife spend more time with their sons now. The dad loves both his scholarly pursuits and his plants. Among the area's other "retirees" is a fifty-something former satellite communications expert who retired early, moved to Boulder, and started hiking, backpacking, and knocking off "fourteeners" (Colorado's 54 peaks that are 14,000 or more feet above sea level). And then there's the eighty-something famous Boulder author who writes less these days because she's so busy managing her very successful stock portfolio. The "Chronologically Gifted" who hike or bike miles might seem intimidating to seniors who plan to age more conventionally. Keep in mind these super seniors impress people a third their age, too. When we grow up, can we do it too? What's their secret?

About 8 percent of Boulder residents are age 65 or older, compared with 12 percent nationwide. (Boulder's large student and early post-grad population explains much of the difference.) Although Boulder offers many retirement complexes aimed at the senior market, most older residents opt for more individuality. Two city-sponsored senior centers and even a community Internet link provide a sense of connection with most recreational opportunities and services.

Long-term older residents have shared ideas for improving Boulder. The saltier ones say, "confine the cat" or "send joggers to South America." They are still nostalgic for 19-cents-per-gallon gasoline, passenger trains, and manners. But many say the good old days are now, and 78 percent of the seniors who responded to a *Daily Camera* survey said they're happy. In many cases, especially in Boulder's more traditional neighborhoods, seniors mix comfortably with other age groups.

AGENCIES AND SERVICES FOR SENIORS

Centers

These are the best one-stop shops for senior-related offerings. People who equate senior centers with "old" tend to avoid them, but the centers provide useful services and opportunities for seniors to connect with their peers. When asked why they use the centers, women report that they're interested in learning and improving their lives. Men more often list the challenge of staying active. The county has six urban centers with comprehensive resources and three rural centers open for limited hours and with limited on-site staffing. They can connect you with reduced-cost medical, tax, and legal aid.

Many of the nearby communities aren't large enough to have their own senior centers, so instead they offer the following resource clearinghouses for seniors in Boulder County:

ALLENSPARK AREA CARE COORDINATOR
Allenspark Fire Hall
Highway 7, Allenspark
(303) 747-2592
www.co.boulder.co.us/cs

LYONS AGING SERVICES RESOURCES
Bloomfield Community Room
722 Fifth Avenue, Lyons
(303) 823-9016
www.co.boulder.co.us/cs

NIWOT SENIOR RESOURCES (BRANCH OF BOULDER COUNTY OFFICE OF THE AGING)
Eagle Place Community Building
6790 North 79th Street, Niwot
(303) 652-3850
www.co.boulder.co.us/cs

BOULDER EAST SENIOR CENTER
5660 Sioux Drive, Boulder
(303) 441-4150
www.bouldercolorado.gov (senior services)
Located at the East Boulder Recreation Center, this facility is operated by the city of Boulder. Because of its location, this is the first choice for seniors who want to combine exercise with socialization and classes. An open floor plan allows the east center to host fairs and art shows, and with the adjacent volleyball courts, seniors create their own tournaments. Classes include ballroom dancing, tai chi chuan, and modern investing.

BOULDER WEST SENIOR CENTER
909 Arapahoe Avenue, Boulder
(303) 441-3148
www.bouldercolorado.gov (senior services)
Centrally located just west of the downtown public library, this is Boulder's original senior center. Described as a "traditional" facility, many seniors drop in here to socialize. Hot lunch is served daily, and dinner is served on Tuesday nights. Information on places to live, medical screenings, and assisted-care options is available here. Classes range from watercolor painting to the art of playing snooker.

BROOMFIELD SENIOR CENTER
280 Lamar Street, Broomfield
(303) 464-5526
www.broomfield.co.us/senior/index.shtml
Hot lunch is served weekdays and a sunset dinner is scheduled monthly at this center, which is located in the same building as the Broomfield Recreation Center. Fitness classes are available on-site, and arts and crafts classes also are offered.

LAFAYETTE SENIOR CENTER
103 South Iowa Street, Lafayette
(303) 665-9052
www.cityoflafayette.com
Local entertainers visit this senior social hub regularly, and special events are often scheduled on Saturdays. Local seniors really enjoy the Eat, Meet 'N' Greet Café located in the center. Travel excursions to the mountains, special events, drop-in activities, daily classes, and educational seminars are also offered.

LONGMONT SENIOR CITIZENS CENTER
910 Longs Peak Avenue, Longmont
(303) 651-8411
www.ci.longmont.co.us
Longmont is a traditional center offering regular exercise programs, card games, craft workshops, educational programs, and day trips. Longmont's Meals on Wheels prepares its food at this site.

LOUISVILLE SENIOR CENTER
900 West Via Appia, Louisville
(303) 666-7400
www.louisvillerecreation.com
Seniors bring their gym clothes to this center, located inside the Louisville Recreation Center. Specialists from the local hospital offer educational courses on staying healthy, and any holiday is an excuse for a special feast. Lunch is served every weekday (reservations required). Day trips to wineries, dinner theaters, and casinos are scheduled monthly. Classes range from arts and crafts to tax preparation and computer training.

Education

If you missed out on educational opportunities in your youth, Boulder is the ideal place to be a senior. Many Boulder agencies and private groups offer discounted or age-geared classes to seniors.

BOULDER PARKS AND RECREATION

3198 Broadway, Boulder

(303) 413-7200

www.ci.boulder.co.gov

The city department offers senior yoga, swimming, and tennis classes. The senior centers (listed previously) have offerings, too. Other programs include tennis tournaments and a Boulder Creek walking group. Very popular is the 55/Alive Driving Class—a way to brush up on driving skills, learn new driving laws, and, often, get a break on insurance.

CU SENIORS AUDITORS PROGRAM

1202 University Avenue, Boulder

(303) 492-8484

www.cualum.org/seniorauditor/auditor guide.html

A senior may audit virtually any class for $5 to $60.

Nutrition

When you're a senior, grocery shopping and meal preparation may be more challenging than they used to be. Perhaps it's the hassle of getting to the supermarket, or the difficulty of cleaning up after your meal. For those who would rather leave the cooking or shopping to someone else, Boulder has two options:

i The City of Boulder Housing and Human Services division produces a quarterly magazine for seniors that lists special events, classes, dining opportunities, information on day trips and overnight travel programs, drop-in activities, sports, clubs and organizations, and community happenings. This free publication, *Boulder Senior Services,* is available at senior centers, public libraries, and grocery stores. For information call (303) 473-1905 or visit www.ci.boulder.co.us/hhs.

ELDERSHARE

6363 Horizon Lane, Longmont

(303) 652-3663

www.communityfoodshare.org

Operated by Community Food Share, this service delivers basic groceries twice a month to hundreds of seniors throughout the county.

MEALS ON WHEELS

909 Arapahoe Avenue, Boulder

(303) 441-3908

www.mowboulder.org

This is Boulder's most frequently requested senior service. It enables people of all ages to eat regular, nutritious meals, even when they're short on money or are unable to handle food preparation and cleanup. A hot meal is delivered at noon, Monday through Friday, with the cost per meal based on an individual's monthly income. This agency serves the elderly, chronically ill, disabled, and those convalescing from illness, accident, or surgery.

Transportation

Senior centers in Boulder County offer trips to the Denver Center for the Performing Arts, gambling towns, and Denver's Cherry Creek Mall. But it's often the need to get around town that presents the greater challenge. Boulder's commitment to alternative transportation makes it less car-dependent than many Western cities, but there is still plenty of room for improvement. The following services can meet daily transportation needs.

THE HOP, THE SKIP, THE JUMP, THE LEAP, THE BOUND, AND THE DASH

1739 Broadway, Park Central Building Boulder

(303) 441-3266

Six colorful shuttle buses are operated jointly by the Regional Transportation District (RTD) and the Transportation Planning Group, the city's alternate modes division. The Hop takes people between major shopping areas and CU-Boulder. The Skip, a 22-passenger bus operating every 10 minutes, will take you anywhere along Broadway.

The Jump offers service between Boulder and Lafayette via Arapahoe; The Leap is a Pearl Street shuttle between 55th Street and the downtown bus station; and The Bound—painted with Superman-inspired graphics—travels along 30th Street between Baseline and Jay Roads. The DASH is the latest addition to the Community Transit Network and connects Boulder to Lafayette and Louisville via South Boulder Road. With the introduction of the new services, bus travel in Boulder is much faster and more pleasant. See the Getting Here, Getting Around chapter for more transportation information.

REGIONAL TRANSPORTATION DISTRICT (RTD)
14th and Walnut Streets, Boulder
(303) 299-6000
http://rtd-denver.com
It costs only 85 cents for seniors to ride RTD buses. An RTD shopping bus goes from the senior housing sites to grocery stores. Most buses accommodate wheelchairs.

SPECIAL TRANSIT
4880 Pearl Streets, Boulder
(303) 447-9636
www.specialtransit.org
Special Transit provides wheelchair-accessible, door-to-door service. This nonprofit group charges $2 each way within the city, $4 between various cities in the county. It's quite a discount—the real cost of this subsidized service is closer to $16 per person. Those using the service must register first and call a week in advance to schedule a ride.

Special-Interest Organizations and Volunteer Opportunities

Most Boulder seniors consider retirement a chance to do as they please. For others it might mean their first backpack trip to Nepal or that longed-for second career. Many find retirement lonely or just plain boring. In Boulder there are many work and volunteer opportunities for seniors who want to remain active.

AUDUBON SOCIETY
1966 13th Street, #230, Boulder
(303) 415-0130
www.audubon.org
Community education opportunities are offered through the society's Human Population and Habitat Program. The Boulder County chapter schedules daily and extended field trips for those interested in birding and offers a list of what birds to look for in this area. A Christmas bird count is held during a 24-hour period in December; it enlists more than 100 birders and 30 teams who help conduct the local bird census, part of an annual nationwide effort.

BOULDER ROTARY CLUB
Spice of Life Events Center,
5706 Arapahoe Avenue, Boulder
(303) 554-7074
www.boulderrotary.org
This service organization works to "build a better community" by hosting fund-raising events and distributing the money to local nonprofit agencies, including Safehouse and Special Transit. The Rotary offers more than $10,000 in scholarships to CU students and funds a study-abroad program for selected CU juniors. Two of the Boulder groups meet weekly for lunch; the third group meets for breakfast.

50+ EMPLOYMENT OPPORTUNITIES PROGRAM
2520 55th Street, Boulder
(303) 301-2900
www.wfbc.org
A service of Workforce Boulder County, this program connects people with job-retraining programs and employment possibilities.

RETIRED AND SENIOR VOLUNTEER PROGRAM (R.S.V.P.)
951 Arapahoe Avenue #10, Boulder
(303) 443-1933
www.rsvpboulder.org
More than 2,000 registered volunteers in the county participate in this program, both older

residents and "junior" volunteers, meaning those younger than age 55. One out of every 10 people age 60 or older volunteers each year through R.S.V.P., which celebrated its 35th anniversary in 2007. People join because they want to give back to their community while staying active and productive. The Handyman Program, which does fix-it-up jobs for seniors, attracts seniors as volunteers, too.

THE SERVICE EXCHANGE OF BOULDER COUNTY
2345 Bent Way, Longmont
(303) 678-3228
www.bcn.boulder.co.us/community/
servexchange
Service Exchange is a volunteer-matching service. Volunteers earn service credits (hours) for their work, and then cash them in when they need expertise or assistance from another volunteer.

VOLUNTEER CONNECTION
2885 Aurora Avenue, Boulder
(303) 444-4904
www.volunteerconnection.net
Are you stuck in a rut? This service organization has current information on hundreds of volunteer opportunities that could make the difference in your life—while you make a difference in the community. The calendar section of the *Sunday Camera* lists current volunteer opportunities available through Volunteer Connection.

RETIREMENT LIVING

Often Boulder seniors live in single-family homes, much to the benefit of local neighborhoods. It helps keep the streets safer when retired people are in and out during the day, and it can make for great intergenerational interactions. A child's first job might be watering an older neighbor's lawn or shoveling snow, and seniors may be unofficial substitute grandparents when the real ones live far away. When a favorite local retiree broke her hip, kids came by with flowers. "Guess what!" she told them with a grin. "I have metal parts now. That means I'm a bionic woman!" Her humor

delighted them, as does seeing her back on morning walks. Another Boulder senior, when asked by a young neighbor what's the worst thing about growing old, replied, "Where did I put it?"

When they tire of yard work or keeping up a big house, many seniors do the Boulder yuppie thing and move to a town house or condominium. Most housing inquiries at the senior centers regard finding affordable independent-living quarters, preferably with no stairs and near bus routes and shopping. But Boulder offers assisted-living options for seniors, too, as well as facilities that offer a range of levels of care.

Assisted Living

The waiting list for assisted-living options can be long—6 to 12, even 18, months. If you want affordable housing with assisted-living services, start checking as soon as you can.

ALTERRA STERLING HOUSE
2240 Pratt Street, Boulder
(303) 682-1066
www.assisted.com
Alterra Sterling House opened in 1998, offering studio units and one-bedroom apartments that look out onto a courtyard. Services include laundry, housekeeping, a 24-hour staff, all meals and special diets, medication assistance, activities, transportation to shopping and medical appointments, and assistance with personal needs. The facility is "committed to quality of life and care while respecting privacy and dignity." Alterra Sterling strives to create a sense of family and community by offering a library, living room, TV room, and crafts room. Rates range from $2,550 to $3,180 per month, depending on level of need.

ALTERRA WYNWOOD AT RIDGE POINT
3375 34th Street, Boulder
(303) 473-0333
www.assisted.com
This assisted-living facility, which opened in 1994, has 76 apartments and a 24-hour personal-care staff. The monthly costs are: studio, $2,650; one-

bedroom, $3,400 to $3,600; and two-bedroom, $4,135. The rate structure is based on the level of care required. Fees include three meals per day, housekeeping and laundry services, medication assistance, and transportation to outside appointments and recreational activities. RISE (Restoring Independence, Strength and Energy) is a physical fitness program that allows residents to work with a personal trainer; there's a Wellness Spa, too. The facility also offers a daily program for those with memory impairment.

THE BEATRICE HOVER ASSISTED-LIVING RESIDENCE

1380 Charles Drive, Longmont
(303) 772-8102
www.hovercommunity.org
This facility accommodates 55—8 in double suites and the rest in private rooms, all with private baths. Opened in the early 1990s, the residence provides three meals per day, housekeeping and laundry services, medication assistance, and a van to take residents to doctors' appointments and outside activities. The rate structure is complex, based on the accommodation's size and location and three levels of service (the third, daily assistance with bathing and dressing, is considered the last step before skilled nursing care is needed); costs range from approximately $2,800 to $3,200 per month. The 121-unit independent-living facility called Hover Manor is nearby.

THE LEGACY AT LAFAYETTE

225 Waneka Parkway, Lafayette
(303) 666-0691
http://legacyatlafayette.com
Opened in 1997, this 40-room facility offers both a private-pay and Medicaid rate structure. Services include medication management, 24-hour personal care assistance, life enrichment programs, three nutritious meals daily, weekly housekeeping, laundry service, transportation, and a whirlpool and spa. There are four living options: small and large studios, and small and large one-bedroom apartments. Monthly rates range from $3,500 to $4,100. The Legacy is close to shopping in central Lafayette.

> **i** By paying $30 per year to enroll at the 55+ HomeCare (303-441-0444), Boulder County residents can receive 12 months of preventative health care, including routine blood-pressure checks, review of prescription medicine, individual wellness counseling, and skin-cancer screening.

Independent Living

Some retirees move to independent-living facilities to simplify their lives so they can travel and pursue more hobbies while increasing the availability of medical care. Take the woman who moved to one of Boulder County's independent-housing properties with assisted-care and nursing facilities on the grounds. When she announced that she was renting out the old family home, her children were aghast. She replied, "Well, it's about time. After all, I am going to be 90 this year." She now hosts her women's group in the meeting room of her living center.

Heed this—the independent-living housing market is tight. Although you can get into some places quickly, the waiting list for others is four years long. Here is a partial list of independent living facilities.

BOULDER MERIDIAN

801 Gillaspie, Boulder
(303) 494-3900

GOLDEN WEST – FLATIRONS TERRACE

930 28th Street, Boulder
(303) 939-0842

PRESBYTERIAN MANOR

1050 Arapahoe Avenue, Boulder
(303) 444-0642

VILLAS AT THE ATRIUM

Brooksdale Senior Living
3350 30th Street, Boulder
(303) 444-0200

Multilevel Facilities

While various specialized levels of senior housing, including independent and assisted living, respite care, and nursing homes, are available in Boulder, several multilevel facilities provide a range of options and give people the opportunity to move to increasing levels of care if and as needed.

THE ACADEMY
970 Aurora Avenue, Boulder
(303) 938-1920
www.theacademyboulder.com
Built in 1892, this former private girls' school survived the 20th century against all odds. Originally known as Mount St. Gertrude Academy, it was used for classes by the university after the Sisters of Charity closed the school. A fire in 1981 caused severe damage and CU chose not to restore the building. Several proposals for redevelopment were promoted and swiftly rejected by either city planners or the surrounding neighborhood. Finally, in 1996, the plan for a retirement community was approved.

There are three historic buildings on the site, including a chapel, conservatory, and the Academy, which now houses 18 apartments. There are a total of 33 apartments, 9 assisted-living units, and 9 bungalows. The buildings are so beautifully restored that when visitors toured the new facility as a stop on Historic Boulder's 1998 Christmas tour, guests of all ages were ready to move in. The rooms are spacious, with lots of light, and many have beautiful views of the Flatirons. Former Colorado Senator Dorothy Rupert and her husband, Richard, were on the waiting list even before the Academy opened.

BALFOUR RETIREMENT COMMUNITY OF BOULDER COUNTY
1855 Plaza Drive, Louisville
(303) 926-1000
www.balfourcare.com
This beautifully landscaped home was designed by award-winning Colorado architects who specialize in retirement housing. In addition to concierge service, the facility offers three meals per day, a private dining room, weekly housekeeping service, scheduled transportation, health promotion and exercise programs, medication management, an in-house beauty salon, a massage therapist, a library, and Internet access. Shopping, restaurants, doctors' offices, hospitals, and cultural events are nearby.

FRASIER MEADOWS MANOR
350 Ponca Place, Boulder
(303) 499-4888
www.frasiermeadows.com
A continuing-care retirement community since 1960, Frasier offers 200 independent-living and 15 assisted-living units. There are one- and two-bedroom apartments with a three-month waiting list. Amenities include a flexible meal plan, laundry service, housekeeping, transportation, a rehabilitation program, a computer center, a beauty shop, and recreational opportunities. The units cost between $1,336 and $3,950.

GOLDEN WEST
1055 Adams Circle, Boulder
(303) 444-3967
www.seniorhousing.net/ad/goldenwest
Golden West was established by the First Christian Church and has been around for more than 30 years. There are currently 255 senior apartments and 56 assisted-living units in three adjacent, interconnected elevator-equipped buildings. On-site are a library, computer center, recreation room, wellness center, beauty salon, sitting and guest rooms, a gift shop, and coin laundry facilities. Recreational activities for all residents include exercise classes, educational programs, musical programs (the Kitchen Band is popular), crafts classes, slide presentations, and the Residents' Council.

CHILD CARE AND EDUCATION

Don't you wish someone could lead you by the hand into the child care facility or school of your dreams? Boulder offers many good options for child care and education on all levels. This chapter starts with a rundown of the main child care information centers and reviews how to screen child care options. It explains how to find a sitter fast, and then goes on to provide tips on checking out nannies, day-care centers, and preschools. The chapter ends with an overview of Boulder's public and private schools, including its universities. For fun places to go with children and information about summer camps, see the Kidstuff chapter.

CHOOSING CHILD CARE

Information Centers

First, head to **Boulder's Children's Services,** 2160 Spruce Street (303-441-4357, www.ci.boulder.co .us/cyfhhs). Children's Services offers the county's most comprehensive lists of everything: more than 500 family child care homes, nannies, day-care centers, preschools, babysitting co-ops, public and private school information, financial assistance for housing and food, parenting classes, and more. It also has a library of helpful books and videos. This city-run agency is open 8 a.m. to 5 p.m. Monday through Friday.

If money is a problem, Children's Services also runs a reduced-rate child care program and can also tell you which centers/preschools offer a sliding fee or tuition reduction.

There are also other resources for families with young children. The **Colorado Preschool and Kindergarten Program** (www.cde.state .co.us/cdefinance/sfCPP.htm) subsidizes the tuition for kids who qualify. **Head Start** (303-441-3980, www.co.boulder.co.us/cs/hs/index.htm) operates in Boulder, with preschool enrichment for qualifying 3- to 5-year-olds. The **Parenting Place** in Boulder (303-449-0177) offers low-cost centers with support groups, education, and play groups. You can bring children as old as 5 with you.

Finding a Sitter

You need a sitter, and Children's Services is closed. If the play starts in five minutes, good luck. Boulder might be a spontaneous kind of town, but good sitters get booked fast. Some services advertise that they can provide a sitter with just 24 hours' notice, but don't count on it. It's best to make arrangements for a sitter at least a week in advance.

Before you call a sitter, it's good to prepare a list of questions regarding qualifications. If the sitter you're considering is a teenager or preteen, have they completed the certification course offered by the YMCA? If they are not in the neighborhood, do they drive or will you be responsible for picking them up and getting them home? If your child is a baby, does the sitter have experience with infants? What about rates? Is the sitter prepared to make dinner and play games or help with homework? Does the sitter have references— other families that will vouch for his or her babysitting skills? A list of questions will make it easier to find a suitable match for your family's needs. College students interested in babysitting are listed through **CU-Boulder's Student Employment Office** (303-492-7349), which takes calls 9 a.m. to 5 p.m. Monday through Friday during the school year and until 4:30 p.m. in the summer.

Workforce, Boulder County's 50+ Program (303-301-2909, www.wfbc.org) makes referrals for pre-screened senior sitters, primarily retirees looking for jobs. **Rent-a-Mom** (303-322-1399, www.rentamom.com) has a nanny program. Their pre-screened employees can drive and generally are hired for an evening or up to two weeks. The **YMCA** (303-442-2778) offers a list of teenagers who have passed a Red Cross babysitting course.

If you are visiting Boulder and need a sitter, the hotel's front desk or concierge can probably help. If you've just moved to town and need to find reliable sitters or child care, ask the mom you see on Pearl Street Mall, call neighborhood churches and schools, and talk with workmates. Ask, ask, ask. It's just like home (or your last home). Sometimes, you find a good sitter fast. Sometimes, you've got to keep trying.

i If you have chosen a child care center but want to make one final check on its reputation, ask the State Department's Office of Child Care Services in Denver (303-866-5958, www.cdhs.state.co.us) to share its licensing files. These files contain complaints and reviews about the center.

Nannies and Au Pairs

A "nanny" can be anyone from a local college student to a grandmother who regularly cares for your child, either live-in or coming to work in your home every day. An "au pair" is a live-in caretaker, often from Europe. Generally between 18 and 25 years old, the au pair lives with you for a year, providing child care in exchange for modest pay, room, and board. Check with Denver's Child Care Services (listed above).

Day-Care Homes and Centers

Every parent wants the best possible environment for their children. Poor-quality child care can harm a child's self-esteem, ability to learn, and ability to thrive later in life. *Working Mother* magazine regularly lists Colorado in the top 10 states for the quality of child care, but many experts believe we must set higher standards

nationwide. A report by local early childhood expert Mary Culkin has highlighted infant/toddler care as an area of special concern. She found wide variation in the nurturing and interpersonal interaction at child care centers, vital indicators of care quality. What's more, the cost of a center did not always correlate with the quality of care provided. That's why visiting prospective daycare centers is an excellent idea.

Full-time child care costs depends on where you live. Longmont is less; Boulder is more. Smaller caregiver/child ratios, better caregiver training, more nutritious snacks, and age-appropriate play materials all add up. Check with Children's Services if you need information about sliding-scale fees. And keep your screening questions handy to help narrow your search.

The following child care centers and preschools are currently accredited by the National Association for the Education of Young Children. This group provides a national, voluntary, professionally sponsored accreditation system for preschools, kindergartens, and child care centers. They base their decisions on interaction among staff and children, staff and parents, location, staff qualifications, health, safety and physical environment. The Boulder centers are: **Boulder Day Nursery** (303-442-7605, www .boulderdaynursery.org), **The Acorn School for Early Childhood Development** (303-938-8233, www.theacornschool.org), **Boulder Montessori School** (303-494-5814, www.bouldermontes sori.org), **Children's Creative Learning Center, UCAR Child Care Center** (303-443-5595), **Commerce Children's Center** (303-497-5063), **JOY-CARE Infant/Toddler Center** (303-443-1462, www.boulderdaycare.com), and two locations of **Miss Catherine's Creative Learning Center** (303-530-1820, www.misscatherines.com). The **CU-Boulder Family Housing Center** (303-492-6185) also has national accreditation, but it is only available to University of Colorado students, staff, and faculty.

The city of Boulder offers a complete directory of local child care centers. Boulder families may access the Community Resource and Referral Service by calling either (303) 441-3544 or (303) 441-3564. Information is also available at their office at 2160 Spruce Street in Boulder. **The Children's Services Community Resource and Referral Service** is open Monday through Friday 8 a.m. to 5 p.m. There are other accredited centers in some neighboring communities such as **The Tiny Tim Center** in Longmont (303-776-7417), and the **Cottage Schools** with two locations in Longmont on Hover Road (303-651-3522) and on North Terry Street (303-651-3780).

Keep in mind that in addition to the accredited day-care centers listed here, many excellent, nonaccredited day-care homes provide a warm, safe environment with just a few children. Many top-notch day-care centers and preschools have not gone through the fees, paperwork, and visits required for official accreditation. For these reasons, check other places, too, and use our short list to compare.

Extended Care for Older Kids and Other Family Issues

Most local schools offer before- and after-school care and enrichment programs for students whose parents can't be there when their kids come home from school, but who don't want them home alone. If your older child has outgrown such programs, you might connect them with employment or volunteer opportunities. Church groups, **Boulder Youth Services** (303-441-4357, www.corra.org), and your local school are other places that can help.

Jobs for youngsters, especially those younger than age 16, are hard to come by—and vacation periods can stretch interminably for teens with little to do. One of the area's finest summer job program is the **Boulder Junior Rangers** (303-441-3440, www.ci.boulder.co.us/openspace). Since it began in 1966, more than 4,000 teens ages 14 to 17 have undertaken a variety of construction and maintenance projects in the Boulder Mountain Park System. Digging, hauling, planting, and cleaning have not only provided teens with a modest summer income but also have given them insight into conservation and

ecology. At age 18, Junior Rangers may graduate to Assistant Senior Rangers, and at age 21 they may become Senior Rangers, supervising teams of 10 to 12 Juniors. The YMCA's **Youth Employment Center** (303-442-2778, www.ymcabv.org) operates as a clearinghouse for jobs from lawn-mowing and babysitting to tutoring younger children. They've helped find work for teens as young as age 13.

If your teens are looking for evening entertainment, keep in mind that many local music clubs and pool halls ban anyone under the legal drinking age (21), even if they aren't planning to drink. That explains the popularity of places such as Red Robin (see the Restaurants chapter) for younger teens, and coffeehouses for older teens.

Youngsters often take advantage of the programs and facilities available at the YMCA and North, South, and East Boulder Recreation Centers (see the Parks and Recreation Centers chapter), which have excellent swimming programs, gyms, and other attractions. The three Boulder recreation centers offer free access to gymnasiums for teens every weekday afternoon.

If a family is in real trouble, Children's Services (see "Information Centers" in this chapter) is a source of information about organizations, classes, counseling, and other options to help resolve ongoing family conflicts and even abuse issues.

i **For the county's most comprehensive lists of nannies, day-care programs, and schools, call or visit Boulder's Children's Services Division, 2160 Spruce Street (303-441-3180, www.ci.boulder.co.us).**

SCHOOLS

Public Schools

Two school districts serve Boulder County—Boulder Valley and St. Vrain.

The **Boulder Valley District** (303-447-1010, www.bvsd.org) includes Boulder, Broomfield, Gold Hill, Jamestown, Lafayette, Louisville, and Nederland. More than 29, 700 students attend area schools. Average class size is 25 students. Most teachers have more than 10 years of teaching experience and hold master's degrees. Some schools offer before- and after-school meals and care, enrichment programs, and summer sessions. The annual budgeted cost per pupil as of May 2006 was $8,989.

The **St. Vrain Valley District** (303-776-6200) serves Dacono, Erie, Firestone, Frederick, Hygiene, Longmont, Lyons, Mead, Niwot, Peaceful Valley, and Raymond.

Even though Boulder public schools place quite high in national and statewide rankings, controversies have stirred the system in recent years. Such issues as middle school versus junior high school, individualized learning versus back-to-basics, phonics versus whole language for beginner readers, a disquieting pattern of threatened and rescinded teacher layoffs, and other thorny problems have taken an inordinate amount of community energy. Complicating what appears to be chronic district-wide dissension, the Boulder Valley Schools' "site-based management" approach means that each school sets its own policies within the framework of district goals.

Boulder's Open Enrollment policy means that you have a choice between sending your child to your neighborhood school, a different neighborhood's school, or one of the focus or alternative schools popping up around Boulder. So check around to see which suits you and your youngster.

Boulder students do much better than those in the rest of Colorado—not surprising, considering that Boulder parents are among the most well-educated in the nation. The average SAT score for Boulder's college-bound students is 45 points higher than the national norm. The ACT

i Scholastic Aptitude Test (SAT) scores for Boulder Valley Students in 2008 averaged 580 on the verbal test (502 national average); and 594 on the math test (515 national average).

scores are comparable. St. Vrain's SAT and ACT scores are also higher than the state and national averages. But what do those scores mean? Back-to-basics proponents say the SAT and ACT test firm knowledge and that high scores are necessary to get into a good college. Others believe that worshipping the Dow Kid Instructional Average can skew education into nothing but a testing drill.

When choosing a school, there are other important matters to consider. What's the school's curriculum? How many children will be in your child's class? What's the ratio of adults to kids? Are parents encouraged to help in the classroom? What's the school's teaching style? Do the desks face forward and do the teachers fill the walls with chemical element charts, or do kids study in a reading nook with old sofas and decorate the walls with their own creations? Testing scores won't tell you which schools are as homogenous as Wonder Bread and which have a richer cultural diversity. Test scores won't tell you what it's like to be at the school. Visits and talks are crucial, for your school is a community, where you and your children can make friends, build memories, and learn about life.

Public Focus Schools

Some children thrive in any situation, like hardy garden plants. Others need a special environment before they bloom. If you've got a unique bloomer, check out the city's focus and alternative schools, often called "magnet" schools. Some provide more structure than a traditional classroom. Others offer more open-ended explorations. There are programs with specially trained staff for bilingual children or children with unusual developmental needs. A few include Family Resource Schools, outreach programs that are as good as having a wonderful aunt or uncle around, ready to help plan after-school activities and improve the school's community.

You'll get the best information about magnet schools if you visit. Each one has distinctive features and programs. See the beautiful rain forest mural kids designed at **University**

Hill Elementary (303-442-6735, www.bvsd.org). **Platt Middle School's Choice Program** (303-499-6800, www.bvsd.org) boasts one of the most interesting science rooms around.

Peak to Peak charter school offers a liberal arts, character-based, college preparatory curriculum; **Horizons K-8 School** (303-447-5580, www.bvsd.org) is a member of William Glasser's Quality School Network and is committed to maintaining high academic and behavioral expectations. **High Peaks Elementary** (303-494-1454) is a focus school based on the Core Knowledge curriculum.

Fairview High School (303-499-7600, www.fairviewhighschool.net) offers an International Baccalaureate (IB) program for juniors and seniors. It is designed with more rigorous, internationally regarded academic standards. Fifty-seven students received an IB diploma in 2007. **New Vista High School** (303-447-5401, www.bvsd.org) is designed to cultivate students' unique talents and gifts, as well as their ability to be responsible for their own learning. It graduated its first class in 1996, sending 50 percent of its students on to college and boasting one National Merit Scholar.

Boulder's **Summit Middle School** (303-499-9511, www.summitmiddleschool.org) was founded in 1996 by parents, but operates under the auspices of the school system. This is a tuition-free, public charter school offering grades 6 through 8 a rigorous, academic curriculum designed to meet the needs of students wanting greater challenges.

Another specialized program is the Boulder Valley's **Arapahoe Campus** (303-447-5284, www.bvsd.org), which offers high school students education in trade skill programs. There's also **Halcyon** (303-499-1121), a day-treatment program for troubled adolescents; it includes around 30 staff people working with approximately 10 students.

Call Boulder Valley School District for more information, and when you do, perhaps you'll learn about even more new focus schools (schools that offer a special, nontypical way of teaching, operated by the school district) or charter schools (schools that offer a special, nontypical way of teaching, funded by the school district but managed by the citizens forming the school) in the works. On one hand, the diversity such schools offer gives people more choices and helps teachers learn from a rich variety of styles. However, there are fears that too much diversity could spread resources thin and create factions that turn attention toward bitter arguments on style rather than letting teaching occur in a nonpolitical, caring environment.

Twin Peaks Charter Academy (720-652-8201) in the St. Vrain district is for elementary students, grades K through 8. An alternative high school program is offered at **Olde Columbine High School** (720-494-3961). The **Career Development Center** (303- 772-3333) is at the same location, 1200 South Sunset. This vocational school is for adults and high school students who take electives in the CDC building. Courses include welding, automotive and building trades, health and dental, agriculture, horticulture, accounting, office systems and other specialties.

Private Schools

You can find private schools run by religious organizations and schools as nondenominational as a pin-striped suit. At some, kids aren't expected to read until they're past third grade. At others, the academic drills start in preschool. Boulder's Children's Services lists private schools in Boulder County. In addition to the local schools below, there are some private schools in Denver that Boulder-area residents attend, despite the commute.

ALEXANDER DAWSON SCHOOL
10455 Dawson Drive, Lafayette
(303) 665-6679
www.dawsonschool.org
Alexander Dawson offers a tried-and-true basics academic approach for grades K through 12. The sprawling campus east of Boulder includes tennis courts, art rooms, a pottery studio, and a theater. The buildings look as clean as new pennies, and the staff takes a rigorous, academic approach,

offering courses from Latin through Advanced Placement Biology, plus interscholastic sports and a creative-writing magazine.

BOULDER COUNTRY DAY SCHOOL
4820 Nautilus Court North, Boulder
(303) 527-4931
www.bouldercountryday.org
Preschool through fifth grade are taught at this very traditional, academically oriented program. French and Latin are part of the curriculum. Computers, art, music, and drama are taught here, too. Classes have no more than 10 students in the preschool and no more than 15 in the elementary grades. Students wear uniforms, and the principal greets them by name as they arrive each morning, holding an umbrella for them if it's raining. The fourth- and fifth-grade teachers send home biweekly progress reports about how each child is doing.

BRIDGE SCHOOL
The Abbey, 6717 South Boulder Road, Boulder
(303) 494-7551
www.bridgeschoolboulder.org
The Bridge School, a private secondary schools for grades 6 through 12, is designed for motivated, intellectually curious learners. The school also seeks youngsters with good character and a willingness to take risks and challenge themselves. The high school curriculum includes computer competency, an interdisciplinary approach to science, senior seminars in English (including one on literature written before 1914), foreign languages, art, and physical education. Community service is also part of the graduation requirement.

FRIENDS SCHOOL
5465 Pennsylvania Avenue, Boulder
(303) 499-1999
www.friendsschoolboulder.org
The average class size for preschool is 14 and for elementary about 20, with two teachers per classroom. Lots of hands-on materials, a custom curriculum for each student, and a caring atmosphere characterize Friends School.

JARROW MONTESSORI
3900 Orange Court, Boulder
(303) 443-0511
www.jarrow.org
Located on three acres in a pretty, quiet part of North Boulder, Jarrow Montessori offers a toddler program for kids ages 18 months to 3 years, a primary program for 3- to 6-year-olds, then an elementary program through sixth grade. Different age groups are blended in each classroom. This is a certified American Montessori Society school, with child-guided education. Education here goes from concrete, hands-on experiences to abstract associations.

SACRED HEART OF JESUS SCHOOL
1317 Mapleton Avenue, Boulder
(303) 447-2362
www.shjboulder.org
This Catholic school has a preschool child care program, then an elementary school from kindergarten through eighth grade. It's well regarded for its traditional academic program and religious course work. Lots of parents volunteer here, helping to add to the community atmosphere. Nearly 400 children attend.

SEPTEMBER SCHOOL
1902 Walnut Avenue, Boulder
(303) 443-9933
www.septemberschool.org
Hands-on learning and creativity distinguish this high school (grades 9 through 12) of about 100 students. The teaching staff is dedicated and excellent, including professional scientists and musicians with a knack for communicating with students as peers. The four-building campus includes a small, former church at Canyon and 19th Streets.

SHEPHERD VALLEY WALDORF SCHOOL
6500 West Dry Creek Parkway, Niwot
(303) 652-0130
www.shepherdvalley.org
Boulder's second Waldorf School opened when the demand at Shining Mountain (see next entry) exceeded space available. This Niwot-area school

has preschool through eighth grade. The school relocated in 1999 to a new building on a 38-acre farm site. This allows for a farm and garden atmosphere, making it unique in Boulder for those seeking Waldorf instruction. If you're not familiar with Waldorf schools, see the following entry.

SHINING MOUNTAIN WALDORF SCHOOL
999 Violet Avenue, Boulder
(303) 444-7697
www.smwaldorf.org
From preschool through high school, this school offers a rich blend of arts, music, and drama interwoven with academic curriculum. For a chemistry experiment, students might draw what they observe as well as describe it in words. Primary class lessons can include lore about traditional fairy tales, folk stories, and weaving. People who are not familiar with a Waldorf school should give it a visit to observe the warm, comfortable pace at which children learn and the richness of materials available. The philosophy behind Waldorf is more than 75 years old, and in addition to regular accreditation, teachers receive two years of training in Waldorf methods.

The Final Decision

If only Boulder had just one little red schoolhouse, you wouldn't have to agonize over what will be best for your child. Here's a comforting story: One teacher, substituting throughout Boulder County, wore jeans to a school where the children called her by her first name and she read storybooks to them from a rocking chair. She loved the friendly environment but worried that its open-ended structure let some kids slide. At another school, she wore a business suit, the kids called her "Mrs.," and she lectured from a desk. While academic performance was more easily measured here, she worried that creativity was stifled. Which school was better? She rated them equally good. But at the more casual school, she wove in more structure. At the more traditional school, she slipped in creative moments. If you know a school's program and your child's needs, the fit doesn't have to be exactly, always perfect.

You're a parent. You're a wonderful part of your child's life. You can help provide balance, just as this excellent teacher does.

Extra Help

Boulder also has resources for children who need assistance in boosting study skills. Options include **Sylvan Learning Center,** 1600 38th Street (303-449-1700), which offers help with general study skills, reading, writing, and math, as well as motivation and other issues related to improving grades and enhancing self-esteem.

School officials also can refer you to private tutors for your child. Some tutors advertise in the local classifieds, and the university is also a reservoir of older students, education majors, and specialists in other disciplines.

COLLEGES AND UNIVERSITIES

Boulder students can choose from a wealth of higher education opportunities. In addition to the colleges and universities right in the city, there are numerous other schools within commuting distance of Boulder, including those in Denver: the **University of Denver** (303-871-2000, www .du.edu), the **University of Colorado at Denver** (303-556-3287, www.cudenver.edu), **Regis University** (303-458-4100, www.regis.edu), and **Metropolitan State College** (303-556-3058, www .mscd.edu). **Colorado State University** (970-491-1101, www.colostate.edu) is in Fort Collins, roughly an hour north of Boulder. The **Colorado School of Mines** (303-273- 3000, www.mines .edu) and **Red Rocks Community College** (303-914-6255, www.rrcc.cccoes.edu) are in Golden, about a half-hour's drive south of Boulder.

Institutions of Higher Education in Boulder

FRONT RANGE COMMUNITY COLLEGE
2190 Miller Drive, Longmont
(303) 678-3722
www.frontrange.edu
Two-year degree and certificate programs are available in a variety of subjects. Some programs

are specifically designed for students who intend to continue their education at a four-year college or university. Tuition is about half the cost of a four-year college.

THE NAROPA UNIVERSITY
2130 Arapahoe Avenue, Boulder
(303) 444-0202
www.naropa.edu

Naropa is an accredited college offering undergraduate and graduate programs in the arts, social sciences, and humanities. The school was founded in 1974 by Chogyam Trungpa Rinpoche, and its educational philosophy is rooted in the Buddhist contemplative tradition. Approximately 1,000 degree-seeking students attend Naropa. Students can earn bachelor's degrees in music, psychology, dance/movement studies, dance therapy, religious studies, writing and literature, environmental studies, early childhood education, and interdisciplinary studies. Master's degrees are available in psychology, theater, Buddhist studies, fine arts, contemplative education, environmental leadership, and writing and poetics. The institute also offers a performing arts series and many workshops, and annually holds the Naropa Summer Institute, drawing faculty and students from around the world. Many courses and workshops are open to the community at large.

UNIVERSITY OF COLORADO AT BOULDER
Office of Admissions, Regent Administrative Center 125, Campus Box 6, Boulder
(303) 492-6301
www.colorado.edu

With all those red-roofed buildings, CU-Boulder is known as one of the nation's prettiest campuses. It's also close to recreational activities and home to top teams such as the CU Buffs football team and CU women's basketball, both of which make attending CU-Boulder lots of fun. But for academics, it offers excellent opportunities, too.

CU-Boulder is most renowned for its science programs. CU professor Thomas Cech won the 1989 Nobel Prize in chemistry. In 1995 professors Carl Wieman and Eric Cornell were awarded the

Fritz London Award for their work in low temperature physics. In 2005 John Hall became the fourth University of Colorado at Boulder faculty member to win a Nobel Prize. More CU undergraduate and grad-school alumni have become astronauts than graduates of any other school, including the service academies. With such a history, it's no surprise that CU-Boulder got more than $266.2 million in outside research funds in 2007.

Boulder is the largest campus in a four-campus system. Other campuses are CU-Denver on the three-college Auraria campus; CU-Colorado Springs; and the Health Sciences Center, including the University Hospital, in Denver. Approximately 26,900 students attend CU-Boulder, with 24,473 undergraduates and 4,515 graduates. Psychology, biology, and English are among the most popular undergraduate majors. Classics and dance are among the smallest.

As a state school, CU gives tuition breaks to in-state residents, who make up nearly 65 percent of the student population. Nondegree candidates may pay to attend university classes as part of the university's continuing education program. People older than age 55 can audit most classes for a nominal fee, with the professor's permission; call (303) 492-8484 for details.

Continuing Education

One of the most valuable lessons an educated person can learn is to keep on learning. If you have that attitude, you're going to love Boulder. Young and old, dabblers and those intent on gaining a specific new skill, many local residents take courses from time to time. To get one of the enticing catalogs listing available offerings, call the phone numbers in the following section, or explore the Web sites. Or, if you're already in Boulder, head to the library, a recreation center, or a major grocery store, where these catalogs are usually available for free.

BOULDER PARKS AND RECREATION
3170 Broadway, Boulder
(303) 441-3412
www.bouldercolorado.gov

All three of Boulder's recreation centers offer skill-building courses. Gymnastics for kids and pottery for adults are very popular, as are the dance classes for both age groups. Other courses include yoga, martial arts, guitar, cooking, sign language, investing, and white-water kayaking. Most of these classes take place at the recreation centers. When the parks and recreation offerings first get published each season, the registration phones can be busy for a long time. Sometimes it's quicker to go to any of Boulder's three recreation centers and register in person.

i Thirteen astronauts are alumni of the University of Colorado at Boulder. Other degree holders include the late Supreme Court Justice Byron White, 1958's Miss America Marilyn Van Derbur Atler, film actor/director Robert Redford, and *M*A*S*H* actor Larry Linville.

CU-BOULDER CONTINUING EDUCATION
1221 University Avenue, Boulder
(303) 492-5148
(800) 331-2801 (out-of-state)
http://colorado.edu/continuingeducation
This fabulous program offers 300 courses each semester, including everything from full-credit, college-level courses taught by CU-Boulder professors to noncredit pursuits such as beginning computer courses and art/ poetry workshops. Noncredit classes often are taught by professionals—some just starting out in their fields and willing to share boundless enthusiasm, others nationally famous who will always love teaching. Classes usually take place right on the CU-Boulder campus, in the evenings and on weekends.

REGIS UNIVERSITY BOULDER CAMPUS
6235 Lookout Road, Suite H, Boulder
(303) 458-7420
www.regis.edu
Through the School for Professional Studies, adults can complete bachelor of science degrees in business administration, computer information systems, religious studies, and many more

subjects by taking accelerated evening classes. Master's degrees are offered in science and management and in computer information science.

ALTERNATIVE SCHOOLS

In addition to schools offering continuing education classes for adults, there are more than 30 schools in Boulder offering training and certification in holistic and spiritual fields. A list of some of the most established schools follows.

BOULDER COLLEGE OF MASSAGE THERAPY (BCMT)
6255 Longbow Drive, Boulder
(303) 530-2100
www.bcmt.org
The Boulder School of Massage Therapy is a leading massage therapy education center. In 2008 the school celebrated its 33rd year as a nonprofit institution. BCMT's diploma program includes in-depth training in a variety of approaches to massage therapy. The program includes human sciences, ethics, movement studies, career development, and professional internships. More than 2,500 students have graduated from BCMT, which has an average annual enrollment of 250.

COLORADO SCHOOL OF ENERGY STUDIES
1721 Redwood Ave., Boulder
(303) 443-9847
www.energyschool.com
This center offers professional training and is accredited by the American Polarity Therapy Association. Polarity therapy is a comprehensive health system based on understanding the human energy field; it's founded on the work of Dr. Randolph Stone.

CULINARY SCHOOL OF THE ROCKIES
637 South Broadway, Suite H, Boulder
(303) 494-7988
www.culinaryschoolrockies.com
Culinary School students can refine their wine-tasting skills, watch famous chefs from around the world demonstrate their favorite techniques, or learn hands-on everything, from professional

French cooking to sushi rolling and gingerbread-house baking. A professional chef's course includes a trip to France. The Culinary School has a store with a big kitchen area. Call for classes and times.

GUILD FOR STRUCTURAL INTEGRATION
3107 28th Street, Boulder
(303) 447-0122, (800) 447-0150
www.rolfguild.org
Dedicated to the traditional teaching of Dr. Ida P. Rolf, GSI offers basic training in the Rolf method of structural integration, continuing education, advanced training, and introductory courses in anatomy and physiology and massage.

HAKOMI INSTITUTE
3296 Cripple Creek Trail, Boulder
(303) 499-6699
www.hakomiinstitute.com
Hakomi Integrative Somatics (HIS) is a body-centered psychotherapy influenced by the techniques of Gestalt, bioenergetics, and Feldenkrais, and by the spiritual principles of Taoism and Buddhism. The institute offers training in healing developmental and traumatic wounds.

HOMEOPATHY SCHOOL OF COLORADO
2995 Valmont Rd., Boulder
(303) 440-3717
www.homeopathyschool.org
The Homeopathy School of Colorado offers a two-year program of in-depth homeopathic study. The curriculum is designed to prepare participants for a professional career and the national exam given by the Council for Classical Homeopathy. HSC is a nonprofit organization,

and its program is approved and regulated by the Division of Private Occupational Schools, Colorado Department of Higher Education.

ROLF INSTITUTE
5055 Chaparral Court, Boulder
(303) 449-5978
www.rolf.org
The Rolf Institute was founded in 1971 and graduates about 75 to 100 students each year from its Boulder school. Developed by Dr. Ida P. Rolf in the 1940s, Rolfing is a series of 10 specific and individualized hands-on sessions designed to realign the body's structure.

THE SCHOOL OF NATURAL COOKERY
P.O. Box 19466, Boulder, CO 80308
(303) 444-8068
www.naturalcookery.com
Established in 1983, this vegetarian cooking school is internationally recognized for its programs for both nonprofessional and professional students. A strong curriculum in the art of preparing whole grains, beans, and vegetables includes the techniques of meal composition and improvisation.

SCHOOL OF NATURAL MEDICINE
3000 Folsom Street, Boulder
(303) 588-6887
www.purehealth.com
The School of Natural Medicine was established in 1977 by Director Sharan, also a founder of the British School of Iridology in Cambridge, England. SNM offers natural physician training in iridology, herbal medicine, naturopathy, and transcendence natural medicine.

HEALTH CARE AND WELLNESS CENTERS

Many people come to Boulder for the inherently healthful and congenial lifestyle, but even healthy, happy people have babies and sometimes get sick or hurt. This section lists referral services, then describes major medical facilities to assist you with your health care needs. We also give you an Insiders' look at how to choose from Boulder's large selection of alternative care providers—in case you're in Boulder County partly because you want to get even healthier.

In Boulder, however, it's not only people who have medical alternatives, but also their furry friends. Boulder's love affair with pets is evidenced by the many options for animal health care listed at the end of this chapter.

EMERGENCY

Call 911 if you are any place in Boulder County and need help fast. Not only can you get help, but our 911 is designed to automatically locate you unless you're calling from a party line.

PHYSICIAN AND DENTIST REFERRAL SERVICES

After hello, a new neighbor's first question is usually about a doctor, dentist, or orthodontist. Once you know what kind of physician you need, word of mouth is often a good bet for finding someone you're comfortable with. If you don't have a neighbor, friend, or coworker to ask, start by checking the Yellow Pages under "Physicians" or "Dentists" or call one of the area's referral services. The **Boulder County Medical Society** (303-527-3215, www.bcms.net) lists around 400 doctors. Four of the larger medical clinics also offer referrals. The **Boulder Medical Center's Patient Services** (303-440-3015, www.bouldermedicalcenter.com) lists more than 50 physicians and has two satellite clinics in Louisville, including one at Centura Avista Hospital. **Centura's Health Advisor** (303-777-6877, www.centura.org) is a 24-hour phone line providing referrals, health care information, and community information. **Longmont Clinic**

(303-776-1234, www.longmontclinic.com) lists around 40 local physicians. **Kaiser Permanente** (303-338-3800, www.kaiserpermanente.org) is a large health maintenance organization; it can also refer its own patients to more than 450 of its associated physicians in the Denver/Boulder area.

HOSPITALS

BOULDER COMMUNITY HOSPITAL
1100 Balsam Street, Boulder
(303) 440-2273 (general)
www.bch.org

With 265 beds, Community is the largest full-service hospital in Boulder County. It takes pride in its emergency, maternity, cancer (full radiation service), and open-heart surgery centers, among other specialties. It emphasizes high-quality and family-centered care. According to the Colorado Hospital Association's data, Community has one of the state's best records for successful inpatient care, short length of stay, and low-cost service.

The care is first-rate here, and the atmosphere tends toward the friendly and relaxed. Labor and delivery rooms might include old-fashioned rocking chairs and other homey touches, with lots of encouragement for family and new baby to happily bond. A friend who's had surgery in the cancer care center reports that her room's stereo system was top-notch. She's a professional hospital worker from out of state, and she gives the cancer unit an "A+" for the personal attention she received. With advance notice, pet visitation is allowed (be sure the pet's with a trained handler and you have a recent copy of its vaccination record). While there are sort of official visiting hours, the staff tends to be pretty relaxed about visitors if you would like them more often.

Boulder Community opened a new, comprehensive 54-bed hospital in 2003, at an east Boulder site on Arapahoe Avenue and the Foothills Parkway. The three-story, 200,000-square-foot facility has a 24-hour emergency department, intensive care unit, cancer center, surgery, radiology and laboratory services and a state-of-the-art cancer center. Maternity care and pediatrics are major components of the campus as well.

A satellite clinic in Lafayette is Community Medical Center, at 1000 South Boulder Road (303-666-4357).

Behavioral-health services at Mapleton include inpatient psychiatric care and day-treatment programs for adults and adolescents. The hotline for emergency evaluation is (303) 441-0400.

CENTENNIAL PEAKS BEHAVIORAL HEALTH SYSTEMS
2255 South 88th Street, Louisville
(303) 673-9990, (800) 842-4673
Centennial has facilities and programs for children, adolescents, adults, and seniors. There are 72 beds for inpatient care, and day-treatment and outpatient programs for anyone with emotional, behavioral, or substance-abuse problems. The Counseling and Assessment Center, a free consultation service, can help determine whether someone needs therapy and suggests where to get assistance from counselors, social workers, support groups, or psychiatrists.

CENTURA HEALTH AVISTA ADVENTIST HOSPITAL
100 Health Park Drive, Louisville
(303) 673-1000 (general),
(303) 673-1111 (emergency)
www.avistahosp.org

This hospital, commonly referred to simply as Avista Hospital, was built in 1990 in booming Louisville and originally had beds for 58 patients. Because of the incredible growth in this region of Boulder County, Avista has undergone a $32-million expansion project that nearly doubled its size. This well-regarded, full-service hospital offers 24-hour emergency service, single-room family-centered maternity care, a nursery, a pediatric unit, a cardiac unit, inpatient and outpatient rehabilitation services, and diagnostic services including whole-body MRI and CAT scan . . . the works.

EXEMPLA GOOD SAMARITAN MEDICAL CENTER
200 Exempla Circle, Lafayette
(303) 689-4000
www.exempla.org
This 202 bed hospital sits on 77 acres in Lafayette. The expansive facility offers 24-hour emergency services, adult critical care, a blood donor center, radiology services . . . and everything else you can think of. With mountain views and walking trails on its campus, this facility is a nice addition to the medical community in the area.

LONGMONT UNITED HOSPITAL
1950 Mountain View Avenue, Longmont
(303) 651-5111 (general)
(303) 651-5000 (emergency)
www.luthcares.org
This 142-bed hospital has a full range of services, from a whole-body CAT scanner to emergency services, home health care, a therapy pool, maternity care, psychiatric services, and an adult day-care program. In 1996, the hospital built a medical office building next door and leases space to physicians and other medical providers.

The Mapleton/LUH Rehab is on the hospital grounds. Patients who need minimal rehabilitation as they head home can get transitional care. Longmont United added a cancer care unit in 1995, with full chemo- and radiation-therapy services.

A satellite clinic in Niwot is United Medical Center of Niwot, at 6857 Paiute Avenue (303-652-9135). A second satellite clinic in Lyons is United

Medical Center of Lyons, located at 549 Mountain Avenue (303-651-5100). The unit offers urgent care and family practice.

MAPLETON CENTER
311 Mapleton Avenue, Boulder
(303) 440-2273

The Seventh-Day Adventists built their tuberculosis sanitarium here nearly a century ago. The location is beautiful, near Mount Sanitas Trail and the peace of the foothills. Today the hospital is a division of Boulder Community, offering rehabilitation services for victims of strokes, accidents, brain injuries, developmental disabilities, and more, as well as behavioral health services for people suffering from psychiatric disorders, chemical dependency, alcoholism, depression, drug abuse, eating disorders, and teen behavior problems.

"Easy Street," a special part of the rehabilitation facilities, has stores, curbs, cars, and restaurants so patients can practice real-world situations again. For patients working on balance, there is equestrian therapy and a low-ropes course. In past years therapy for head-injury patients has included a hike up 14,000-foot Pikes Peak to improve physical coordination and self-confidence. A warm-water, nonchlorinated therapy pool is open to anyone; call for hours and fees. A satellite facility, at 6685 Gunpark Drive, Suite 130 (303-530-3062) in Gunbarrel, offers physical therapy, speed and occupational therapy, and pediatric rehabilitation.

HOSPICE

HOSPICE OF BOULDER COUNTY
2825 Marine Street, Boulder
2594 Trailridge Drive, Lafayette
(303) 449-7740
www.hospicecareonline.com

This hospice, established in 1978 and one of the first in the nation, offers an interdisciplinary program of home care, counseling, educational services, and bereavement support to meet the needs of terminally ill patients and their family members. Services are provided in patients' homes and in nursing homes; there's no inpatient facility. Care for the terminally ill is provided regardless of a person's ability to pay. The hospice also has a volunteer training program.

COUNTY HEALTH DEPARTMENT CLINICS

Boulder County residents come to clinics for low-cost immunizations, well-child care, confidential HIV testing, senior clinics, environmental health screening, and more. There's a free directory of services available through the **Boulder County Public Health Department** (303-441-1100, www.co.boulder.co.us/health). Clinics are located in Boulder at 3482 North Broadway (303-413-7500), in Longmont at 529 Coffman Street, Suite 200 (303-678-6166), and in Lafayette at 1345 Plaza Court (303-666-0515). The Arc (as it's informally called) is the county's **Addiction Recovery Center,** at 3470 North Broadway (303-441-1275), offering detox and treating substance abuse and co-dependency. The center also operates an impaired-driver prevention program (303-441-1279).

The **Boulder County AIDS Project,** at 2118 14th Street in Boulder (303-444-6121, www.bcap.org), offers information about prevention and treatment along with a food bank, counseling, and buddy systems for clients with HIV. The **Mental Health Center of Boulder County,** 1333 Iris Avenue, Boulder, has a crisis line, (303) 447-1665, and a general line, (303) 443-8500, and a Web site, www.mhcbc.org. The **Boulder Rape Crisis Team**'s 24-hour crisis line is (303) 443-7300.

The **Boulder Heart Institute,** at 2750 Broadway in Boulder (303-440-3222, www.bouldermedicalcenter.com), offers services ranging from a basic cardiac risk-factor screening to various types of cardiac wellness programs and state-of-the-art exercise testing to assess athletes' fitness levels.

The **People's Clinic** is a health care clinic offering comprehensive adult, pediatric, and prenatal care for low-income residents. The Clinic is in Boulder at 3303 North Broadway (303-449-6050).

FINDING HOLISTIC HEALTH CARE

As early as 1896, patients admitted to Boulder's Colorado Sanitarium were given Swedish massage, hydrotherapy treatments, and a vegetarian diet as a cure for illness. Advertised as a resort, the sanitarium encouraged people to come for "refreshment of the mind, body, and spirit," and to that end operators offered their own line of whole-grain cereals and health foods. Many tubercular patients were drawn West to such facilities and soon recovered from what was believed a fatal condition. What was then viewed as radical medical treatment is now tame by comparison to other offerings from Boulder's holistic health community. In Boulder the word "wellness" is used as much as or more than "health care" or "medicine," and the line between conventional medicine and alternative approaches is blurred.

i Practitioners of alternative medicine are regularly listed in or advertise in *Nexus* (www.nexuspub.com), Colorado's holistic health, metaphysics, and natural lifestyles directory and magazine. The bimonthly publication is free at health-food stores and is supplied to 300 outlets in Boulder and Denver.

Holistic doctors believe in treating the whole person, rather than the symptoms of illness. Naturally there is some skepticism about alternative therapies from those who practice traditional medicine, but unless an illness is life-threatening, exploring options can be a first step toward taking control of your health.

Selecting the right therapy and a suitable practitioner can be overwhelming without a few basic guidelines. Holistic medicine defines "complete therapeutic systems" as those based on a philosophy or set of beliefs that include a comprehensive range of treatments. Some examples are Ayurvedic medicine, Chinese medicine, herbal medicine, homeopathy, indigenous medicine, naturopathic medicine, and nutritional therapy. (Chiropractic and osteopathy are sometimes called complete systems but just as often fall under the physical or bodywork category.)

Ayurvedic medicine is central to the culture of India and dates from 3000 B.C. A variety of healing and prevention techniques are part of Chinese medicine, including the use of herbs, acupuncture, and t'ai chi ch'uan. Once the only source of medicine for ancient cultures, herbal medicine dates from ancient Egypt but has only recently regained credibility in Western cultures. Homeopathy is based on the 19th-century "Law of Similars" and uses the substance causing an illness, in minute quantities, to cure that same illness. Indigenous medicine, or shamanism, employs a variety of healing techniques found in most tribal communities. Naturopathic medicine is sometimes called "commonsense" medicine because it relies primarily on four components for good health: fresh air and clean water, balanced diet, exercise, and "right living." Finally, nutritional therapy originates from naturopathic medicine, where diet is emphasized as the key to good health.

Not all people seeking a more holistic approach to health want to embrace a complete system of therapy. Perhaps you're suffering from chronic tension or lack of vitality and just want to try a new bodywork therapy. In that case, Boulder is the right place to be. Acupressure, aikido, Alexander technique, Breema, dance therapy, Feldenkrais, Hellerwork, massage, neuro-muscular therapy, polarity therapy, reflexology, Reiki, Rolfing, yoga, and Zen shiatsu are just a few of the offerings available.

There are also techniques that are often, but not always, used in conjunction with the larger, complete "systems" of healing. They include applied kinesiology, aromatherapy, biofeedback, color therapy, crystal and gem therapy, flower essences, hydrotherapy, hypnotherapy, iridology, magnetic therapy, sound therapy, and visualization therapy, to name a few. Practitioners of these techniques also abound in Boulder.

If you feel like an oddball for choosing alternative health options, consider this: Nearly half the population is said to use at least one remedy not prescribed by a doctor; over one-fifth have visited a complementary health care practitioner. And the number of adults using some form of alternative therapy continues to rise.

If you decide it's worth your money to seek alternative health care, you're not alone, but it will take some research. Finding the right practitioner is complicated by Colorado's vague licensing requirements, which might someday change. For the uninitiated, it's easy to confuse a certified dietitian with one who has one or two years of nonfederally certified training or with a registered dietitian who has several years of university training. The same is true with naturopathic physicians. Some have attended federally accredited, four-year programs that have the same basics as medical school, then have had specialized training in the science and counseling skills that can help a person stick with a good diet, exercise, and weight-reduction stress. Others who call themselves naturopathic physicians have taken no more than a six-month correspondence course. Clearly, screening and getting as much information as possible about a practitioner's competence is recommended. Don't be afraid to ask health care providers about qualifications. Which program did they attend? What was the program's accreditation—federal or state? How many years of study did they undertake, and what are they qualified to do? Can they provide references?

If you are seeking an expert in wellness counseling, choose carefully. Listen for word-of-mouth recommendations. The *Daily Camera*'s Monday "FIT" section features current articles on health and wellness and includes a large section for alternative practitioners to advertise their specialties. It's a great way to compare treatment philosophies and glean names of reputable professionals. Read the local holistic journals such as *Nexus* (www .nexuspub.com), which is available at many grocery stores, especially the health-food stores.

Here's the most important aspect of choosing alternative care: Patients of holistic doctors are required to take responsibility for their own wellness, an uncomfortable role for many of us raised on conventional medicine. Don't expect a magical quick fix for improving your health through lifestyle changes, but be aware that confidence in a practitioner is intrinsic to success.

The **Helios Health Center** (303-499-9224, www.helioshealthcenter.com) is an example of physicians and health professionals teaming up because they appreciate the way conventional and alternative health care can complement each other. Center director Pierre Brunschwig is both a board-certified acupuncturist and homeopath. He supplemented his conventional education by working with noteworthy leaders in the field of holistic medicine. Helios is an example of physicians and health professionals teaming up because they appreciate the way conventional and alternative health care can complement each other. In fact, one of Helios's doctors is a board-certified acupuncturist and homeopath as well as an M.D.

For a sampling of schools offering training and certification in holistic and spiritual fields in Boulder, see the Child Care and Education chapter.

WELLNESS FOR PETS

Boulderites love their pets. Owners regularly bring their dogs along to outdoor cafes and especially while running or hiking. In fact, residents feel so strongly about "pet rights" that they approved a ballot measure in 2000 to replace all references in municipal codes from "pet owner" with "pet guardian."

> **i** Boulder County is home to two yoga ashrams, or resident communities: the Eldorado Mountain Yoga Ashram in Eldorado Springs and the Shoshoni Yoga Retreat south of Rollinsville. Both communities share the same Hindu and Buddhist-derived spiritual lineage.

It's no surprise then that so many options exist for keeping pets healthy. **VCA-Allpets Clinic,** at 5290 Manhattan Circle (303-499-5335, www.vcai.com), stands out because it offers 24-hour veterinary care. This pet clinic has a welcoming fire hydrant out front for the dogs and separate entrances and waiting areas for clients with dogs and cats. For those in central or north Boulder, the **Boulder Emergency Pet Clinic,** at 1658 30th Street (303-440-7722), may be more convenient. This critical care and trauma center has a doctor on duty all night, every night, and no appointment is necessary.

Other vets specialize. The **Boulder Valley Cat Clinic,** at 2825 Wilderness Place (303-444-6369), deals with feline medical and behavioral problems, offers a low-cost vaccination clinic, and boasts of "no barking dogs." **Baseline Animal Hospital,** at 108 W. Baseline Rd. in Lafayette (720-214-0270) treats not only cats, dogs, and exotics

> **i** The Humane Society of Boulder Valley (303-442-4030, www.boulderhumane .org) is a state-of-the-art animal shelter that cares for more than 7,000 animals annually. The city is home to approximately 25,000 dogs and 20,000 cats.

but horses and everything in between. Google "Vets in Boulder" for a complete listing.

In Boulder there are also holistic veterinarians who treat sick pets with such techniques as chiropractic, osteopathy, or acupuncture. Holistic veterinarians believe in the animal's ability to heal itself and almost never use antibiotics when confronting illness. One such clinic in Boulder is the **Natural Animal Holistic Wellness Center** at 685 S. Broadway (303-494-7877, www.boulders naturalanimal.com).

MEDIA

The story goes that when one of Boulder's early citizens decided the rough mining town needed a newspaper to encourage a sense of community, he simply drove his wagon to a nearby town, loaded up that town's newspaper press, and Boulder had its newspaper. Apparently the notion took, and Boulder has been blessed (or cursed, depending upon your perspective) with a wealth of newspapers ever since. Currently, the town supports one daily, one semi-daily, alternative weeklies, and a number of special-interest newspapers. Boulder was one of the first cities in the nation (outside of the New York metro area) where the *New York Times* became available for home delivery. And the Denver dailies show periodic fascination with the odd little town to the north.

In addition to several local radio stations, the city also has cable television channels for city information, citizen input, and CU programming. Denver's four local television stations also include Boulder in their coverage area.

NEWSPAPERS

A quick glimpse at the newspaper stands on the city's street corners should satisfy the curiosity of any serious news hound. From the larger Denver-based papers to the Boulder-area dailies and magazines reporting local news, sports, and entertainment, Boulder has it all.

Dailies

COLORADO DAILY
2610 Pearl Street, Boulder
(303) 443-6272
www.coloradodaily.com

Published since 1897, this free and informative paper continues to serve the university community and Boulder. It's published five days a week, with an extra-large weekend edition on Friday. The paper covers local, regional, and national news with an opinionated style, plus sports and entertainment, and has a very vocal editorial and letters to the editor section. There are also classified advertisements. It's available on campus and at drop sites around town.

DAILY CAMERA
1048 Pearl Street, Boulder
(303) 442-1202
www.dailycamera.com

The *Camera,* Boulder's only complete daily newspaper, provides local coverage of Boulder, neighboring towns, and Boulder County as well as some state news. Regular daily sections and pages present local, national, and international news, business news, and entertainment news. The *Camera*'s award-winning sports section is competitive with Denver dailies and covers local preps, CU, and Denver's professional teams and features several informative special sections.

The *Sunday Camera* includes separate sections for business, lifestyles, and entertainment; a TV guide; color comics; news-focus stories; local guest opinions; and the *New York Times* crossword puzzle. Among the weekday special-interest sections are "Business Plus"; a food section; "Get Out," with local recreation information; and "Friday Magazine," covering entertainment in Boulder, Denver, and along the Front Range.

Camera writers, photographers, ads, sections, and the whole paper continue to win awards from various state and national organizations.

Weekly

BOULDER WEEKLY
690 South Lashley Lane, Boulder
(303) 494-5511
www.boulderweekly.com
Specializing in investigative news, and arts and entertainment, this edgy tabloid has columns, interviews with local people, plus entertainment news, a classified section and other special sections, and possibly the most adult ads of any paper in the county. The paper is free at numerous local drop sites.

Biweekly

BOULDER COUNTY BUSINESS REPORT
4865 Sterling Drive, Suite 200, Boulder
(303) 440-4950
wwww.bcbr.com
This hefty biweekly newspaper is a leading information source on local and regional trends in real estate, high technology, finance, tourism, and business. A subscription is $44.97 per year. Or you could just pick it up free at one of several local drop sites.

MAGAZINES

BOULDER MAGAZINE
1919 14th Street, Suite 709, Boulder
(303) 443-0600
www.bouldermag.com
Published three times a year—summer, fall, and winter/spring—this handy guide has all kinds of local information and interesting articles on local people, places, and things to do. The magazine is free at numerous local drop sites including most hotels and restaurants. Look for the glorious color photo cover.

NEXUS: COLORADO'S HOLISTIC JOURNAL
1680 Sixth Street, Suite 6, Boulder
(303) 442-6662
www.nexuspub.com
For more than 20 years, Nexus has been devoting its tabloid-size magazine to information about holistic health and natural living "in Colorado and

beyond." Readers will be amazed at the variety of therapies available locally. Nexus is published six times a year and includes information on physical health, spirituality, alternative education, complementary medicine, and art. Its lovely color covers are produced by area artists and probably end up on many a reader's walls. Subscriptions are $21 per year (six issues), or pick up Nexus for free at 300 locations in health-food stores, bookstores, restaurants, shops, and universities around Boulder and Denver.

WOMEN'S MAGAZINE
2610 Pearl Street, Boulder
(303) 443-6272
http://boulderwomensmag.com
Published monthly by the Colorado Daily, this delightful new addition to the city began publication in May 2002. Every issue features a prominent Boulder woman on the cover. Other features cover such topics as health, fashion, business issues, and decorating ideas. The monthly "Men We Like" feature is always a fun read. This publication is free and is distributed throughout Boulder.

RADIO STATIONS

The numerous Front Range radio stations whose broadcasts are received in Boulder are listed here, along with the more popular local stations. The quality of reception is very much dependent on where you are when you're listening (those pesky mountains, again).

ADULT ALTERNATIVE
KTCL 93.3 FM (Modern rock and new music), www.area93.com
KVCU 1190 AM (Independent music from all genres),
www.colorado.edu/student groups/KVCU

ADULT CONTEMPORARY
KOSI 101.1 FM, www.Kosi101.com
KXPK 96.5 FM, www.thepeak.com

Boulder's Community Broadcast Association, Inc., KGNU 88.5 FM, provides the real flavor of Boulder with all types of music, plus talk shows on environment, spirituality, alternative news, and a Grateful Dead Hour. Call (303) 449-4885 for a complete program.

BIG BAND
KEZW 1430 AM (Nostalgia, Big Band, and easy listening), www.kezw.com

CHRISTIAN
KPOF 910 AM (Christian/talk), www.kpof.org
KRKS 94.7 FM (Christian/talk), www.krks.com

CLASSICAL
KVOD 90.1 FM (Classical, public radio news), www.cpr.org

COMMUNITY
KGNU 88.5 FM in Boulder/Denver; 93.7 in Ward and the mountain regions; 89.1 in Ft. Collins (Pacifica, ethnic and world music, much attention to local affairs), www.kgnu .org

COUNTRY
KYGO 98.5 FM, www.kygo.com
KLMO 1060 AM (Country, Paul Harvey, and ABC News)

HISPANIC
KXPK 96.5 FM, www.thepeak.com

JAZZ
KJCD 104.3 FM (Smooth jazz), www.cd1043.com
KUVO 89.3 FM, www.kuvo.org

NEWS/TALK
KHOW 630 AM (News, local and syndicated talk), www.khow.com

KKZN 760 AM (Business and talk), www.am760.net
KVCU 1190 AM (Student-run University of Colorado station), www.radio1190.org

OLDIES
KTUN 105.1 FM, www.ktunradio.com
KIMN 100.3 FM, www.mixatwork.com

PUBLIC RADIO
KCFR 1340 AM (Colorado Public Radio, classical, National Public Radio, and local news), www.cpr.org
KCFC 1490 AM, www.cpr.org

ROCK
KBCO 97.3 FM Boulder, www.kbco.com
KQMI 99.5 FM (Classic rock), www.995themountain.com
KRFX 103.5 FM (Classic rock), www.thefox.com
KBPI 106.7 FM (Classic and progressive rock), www.kbpi.com

SPORTS
KLZ 560 AM (Sports), www.560espn.com
KOA 850 AM (News, talk, sports), www.850koa.com
KKFN 950 AM (Sports/talk), www.thefan950.com

TOP 40
KALC 105.9 FM (Alice), www.alice106.com

TELEVISION STATIONS

Besides the broadcast stations listed below, there are more than 30 cable stations, including Channel 8, the city of Boulder station. The city channel has all types of programs on local issues, such as the environment, seniors, arts, city council meetings, Boulder Valley School Board meetings, sports, and leisure, and information programs on science, travel, and much more.

Channel 54 is Community Access TV of Boulder, with talk shows, performance, community interest, and even local cooking programs. CATV offers inexpensive classes to train citizens to produce and edit their own videotapes for presentation on Channel 54. It also provides the audio for Radio Reading Services of the Rockies, which broadcasts audio versions of the *Daily Camera, Denver Rocky Mountain News, Denver Post,* and *Colorado Daily* newspapers, plus BBC News and local weather.

BROADCAST TELEVISION STATIONS
KWGN Channel 2 (CW), http://cw2.trb.com
KCNC Channel 4 (CBS), www.kcncnews4.com

KRMA Channel 6 (PBS), www.krma.org
KMGH Channel 7 (ABC), www.thedenver channel.com
KUSA Channel 9 (NBC), www.9news.com
KBDI Channel 12 (Community/PBS), www.kbdi.org
KVDR Channel 31 (Independent/Fox), www.fox31.com

CABLE/SATELLITE TELEVISION
Comcast (800) 266-2278, (303) 930-2000
DIRECTV (800) 280-4388
Dish Network (800) 843-4742

WORSHIP

In the early part of the 20th century, Boulderites often referred to their growing community as "the Athens of the West," and the city's willingness to embrace religious diversity is reflected in that lofty motto.

The Presbyterians were the first to bring worship services to what we now call the Boulder Valley, followed quickly by the Congregationalists, the Baptists, the Episcopalians, the Methodists, and the Roman Catholics. The church sanctuaries seemed large enough when built in the late 1800s, but with the country moving west, nearly all of the faiths quickly outgrew their modest worship halls and built larger churches. Architecturally impressive, many of the truly beautiful downtown Boulder churches were built with local materials.

Boulder is known, however, as much for its eclectic spirituality as its traditional religious offerings. An annual listing compiled by *Nexus,* Colorado's holistic journal, shows more than two dozen "unconventional" spiritual groups meet regularly. This metaphysical emphasis alongside the time-honored religious faiths is one of the best aspects of Boulder.

This chapter begins with some history and an overview of some current events involving Boulder's religious communities. It then describes worship centers located downtown—easy for both tourists and newcomers to reach. It ends by describing other groups that are part of the rich texture of Boulder worship.

FROM PIONEER CHURCHES TO EARTH-CENTERED WORSHIP

In 1859 a Methodist circuit preacher delivered Boulder's first sermon to 50 people. Churches of other denominations followed, their spires leading pioneers across the prairie. The First Congregational Church, now site of the Carnegie Library on Pine Street, had Boulder's first full-time pastor, building, and church bell. A few churches of historical significance still stand. Known as the Little White Church, Longmont's **St. Stephen's Episcopal Church** at 470 Main Street was built in 1881. Worship services are now held at a newer and larger sanctuary, at 1303 South Bross Lane, that is also called St. Stephen's Episcopal Church. Also in 1881, Colorado's original Swedish community built the **Swedish Evangelical Lutheran Church of Ryssby,** on 63rd Street south of Nelson Road (303-774-7761). They styled it after traditional Swedish churches but built it with local sandstone. Members still hold special midsummer and Christmas ceremonies that include Scandinavian traditions. For the winter service, they decorate the simple chapel with evergreen boughs and candles that make halos on winter-frosted panes. The church is very popular for weddings, and the bride and groom often leave in a horse-drawn buggy.

If you enjoy religious history, check with **Historic Boulder,** at 1123 Spruce Street (303-444-5192). This nonprofit group can provide you with information on sacred places. They also keep lists of historic buildings in which people may hold weddings. The vista from the Flagstaff Mountain Amphitheater, for example, makes it a favored wedding site. Boulder's proximity to the foothills, with easy access to nature trails, has created many special places for people to explore their spirituality without man-made structures or traditional ceremonies.

But worship is about more than creating, or finding, special places. The **First Congregational Church** was Boulder's first church. At the dedication ceremony in 1870, the minister encouraged his parishioners to attend every Sunday, but admonished them to "leave the tobacco at home!" Church members helped raise funds to bring CU to town, and for many years, its ministers taught philosophy at the new university. Grandma Dartt was a Seventh-Day Adventist who trudged through young Boulder's saloons, distributing temperance tracts and religious information. In 1895, the Seventh-Day Adventists began building a tuberculosis sanatorium where Mapleton Avenue heads up Sunshine Canyon. A popular hiking trail, Mount Sanitas Trail, is named after the health center, and the Mapleton Rehabilitation Clinic stands there today. The **Seventh-Day Adventist Church** is nearby at 345 Mapleton Avenue (303-442-1522).

If many of Boulder's worship halls were built with sandstone, then their souls are built of wood, tin, lead, and iron. The pipe organs at many of the downtown churches were crafted with loving care and pinched pennies. The three-manual Casavant organ at First Presbyterian is often played for Bach concerts. The Roosevelt organ at First United Methodist sat unused at a Denver church before it was moved to Boulder. By far the largest church organ in the city is enjoyed by parishioners at the First Congregational Church, but even this instrument pales in comparison to the giant at Macky Auditorium on the CU campus. Built in 1923 from contributions by Boulder citizens, the 100-rank organ is housed under the stage and would cost at least $1.5 million to replace. Other notable downtown church organs include the Austin at St. John's Episcopal Church, the hand-built pipe organ at Trinity Lutheran, and the three-manual McManis organ at the First Baptist Church.

The issue of the separation of church and state crops up periodically in this city. During the 1960s the State Board of Education backed religious and civic groups that asked that schools refrain from Christmas pageants. These days, schoolkids may sing songs from many religions at "winter festivals," and the focus is on informing people about various faiths. Still, seemingly small events create a large furor where issues of church and state are concerned. Before Christmas 1995, a big fuss developed after people started hanging little angel ornaments from a tree on public land, and the following spring, law enforcement officials were taken to task for marking sites of fatal vehicular accidents with white crosses as part of a safety awareness campaign.

ℹ️ **The Swedish Evangelical Lutheran Church is all that's left of what was once the town of Ryssby, founded in 1869 by settlers from Ryssby, Sweden. The name refers to a clearing in the forest. The small chapel is now popular for weddings and is decorated for Christmas services.**

WORSHIP CENTERS

Newcomers should check the *Daily Camera*'s Saturday religion calendar. The variety of offerings will meet nearly everyone's spiritual needs or desire for spiritual exploration.

Near the Pearl Street Mall

It's no surprise that most of Boulder's oldest—and many of the largest—houses of worship are downtown, within walking distance of the Pearl Street Mall, which has been the civic center of town for a long time. The following is just a sampling of the worship centers downtown.

First Presbyterian, at 1820 15th Street (303-442-3523), has an estimated 2,400 members, with 2,000 attending Sunday services. The original sanctuary celebrated its 100th year in 1995. A major renovation in 1998 added nearly 300 new seats in the main chapel and a 30,000-square-foot children's wing. Members describe it as a reformed, evangelical church with a big, warm congregation. It has large teen, singles, and college groups plus other smaller groups. The church provides space for performances by local music groups. It offers a weekly preschool, summer camps, snow camps, and weekly school programs in everything from crafts and cooking to family conflict resolution.

> **i** Boulder Shambhala Center is one of the largest communities of practicing Tibetan Buddhists in the West.

Sacred Heart of Jesus, at 2312 14th Street (303-442-6158), is a Roman Catholic church with more than 1,200 registered households and lots of people who drop in. Sacred Heart School, across the street, is affiliated with the parish (see the Child Care and Education chapter). The large community-outreach program includes a lunch program for transients and distribution of food baskets. The church offers daily masses in English and a weekly Spanish mass.

Boulder Shambhala Center, at 1345 Spruce Street (303-444-0190), is a center for Tibetan Buddhism called "Vajrayana," which translates as "diamond vehicle." The center includes 600 adult members, making it one of the largest communities of practicing Tibetan Buddhists in the West. The top floor, a shrine room, is full of traditional Tibetan red and gold. People are welcome to drop by in the afternoon. Members say that although Buddhism may sound exotic, it's very ordinary; it's about living your life well, with compassion and wisdom.

St. John's, at 1419 Pine Street (303-442-5246), is a traditional Episcopal Church with very contemporary sensibilities. Among Boulder Episcopalian churches, it's the only "AIDS-aware faith community"—and is one of the few such communities of any denomination. The congregation, which now numbers about 1,000, was founded in 1873 and is one of the oldest in town. The present church, where the big Messiah Sing-along happens each December (see the Festivals and Annual Events chapter), dates from 1902.

The **First Baptist Church,** at 1237 Pine Street (303-442-6530), was founded in 1872, making it another one of the oldest churches in town.

With more than 250 members, it is known for its Chancel Choir and Handbell Choir, which present concerts and cantatas.

First United Methodist Church is at 1421 Spruce Street (303-442-3770). The **Christian Science Reading Room** is on the Pearl Street Mall, at 1434 Pearl Street (303-442-0335). It is an extension of the First **Church of Christ, Scientist** nearby at 2243 13th Street (303-444-1770). The **First Congregational Church,** at 1128 Pine Street (303-442-1787), across from the original Congregational church site, is a medium-size, liberal church with about 850 members. On the opposite corner is **Trinity Lutheran Church-ELCA,** at 2200 Broadway (303-442-2300).

Around the County

The **Unitarian Universalist Church,** at 5001 Pennsylvania Avenue (303-494-0195), mirrors Boulder's liberalism. The church welcomes people of all races, ages, abilities, sexual orientations, cultures, and religious backgrounds to its adult services and children's classes.

Flatirons Community Church, at 400 W. South Boulder Rd in Lafayette (303-664-5524, www.flatironschurch.com), attracts large crowds to their popular services that include contemporary Christian music and lively sermons.

VineLife Community Church, at 7845 Lookout Road in Longmont (303-449-3330), is a non-denominational/evangelical/charismatic church started in 1982. More than 1,000 people attend Sunday services, which often include music and homey, inspirational stories and sermons. Teaching Biblical insights and positive family-raising skills are important parts of the ministry, and the church prides itself on its active and involved children's and youth ministry as well.

The **Boulder Valley Christian Church,** at 7100 South Boulder Road (303-494-7748), is an independent evangelical Christian church with 500 members. Christmas and Easter music programs are popular events.

Unity of Boulder, at 2855 Folsom Avenue (303-442-1411), is a New Age, Christian church. It has grown considerably since 1975, when minis-

i In First United Methodist Church (1421 Spruce Street) is a replica of an ancient labyrinth, painted on the basement floor of the downtown church. People are invited to walk the pathways as a tool for contemplation and meditation.

ter Jack Groverland came to town. He's a dynamic speaker, and sermons are full of both laughter and seriousness. The Unity newsletter goes out to 2,600 people, and 1,000 people attend two different Sunday services. Nearly 3,000 people have taken the church's Course in Miracles, a yearlong class that starts each quarter. The church houses a metaphysical bookstore and gift shop.

St. Malo Religious Retreat and Conference Center, a Catholic conference facility at 10758 Highway 7, near Allenspark (303-747-0201), is where Pope John Paul II rested on his 1993 trip through Colorado. **St. Catherine's,** better known as the "Chapel on the Rock," is at the same location. During the summer, it is open to the public, with Sunday masses occasionally held from Memorial Day to Labor Day.

The **Sacred Heart of Mary,** at 6739 South Boulder Road (303-494-7572), was built in 1873 and is the oldest Catholic church in Boulder County. It started as a Prairie Church and still has an old cemetery in the back. Its priest describes it as a progressive, medium-size congregation with about 700 families, meeting in a beautiful church. The church offers classes in adult education and centering prayer. Drop-ins are welcome at daily mass.

For many years the Benedictine Catholic **Abbey of St. Walburga** was located next door to Sacred Heart of Mary. Due to growing development and traffic in this once-tranquil area, the Abbey moved in 1996 to a quieter location in Larimer County, at 32109 North U.S. Highway 287, Virginia Dale (970-472-0612). The old Abbey is now home to a private secondary school.

Around 8 percent of the Boulder population is Jewish, according to Allied Jewish Federation surveys. The Jewish community is very active in

civic and local affairs. Area synagogues include **Congregation Bonai Shalom,** 1527 Cherryvale Road (303-442-6605), a conservative synagogue of nearly 150 households, nestled near a pretty stream, and **Congregation Har Hashem,** 3950 Baseline Road (303-499-7077), a reform congregation with more than 400 families. Both offer programs for youths, singles, and families, and Hebrew school education. In 1998, Har Hashem built a beautiful new sanctuary and seven new children's classrooms to accommodate its growing membership. The **Jewish Renewal Community of Boulder** (303-271-3540) is part of an international cross-denominational movement. Approximately 150 members meet for services in members' homes and also hold monthly community Shabbats.

The **Second Baptist Church of Boulder,** 5300 Baseline Road (303-499-4668), has a great musical presence. The Community Choir is open to any church member who likes to sing; the church also has a Men's Chorus; and Angels Without Wings, a chorus for children ages 3 to 13. The Shekinah Glory Choir is a young adult choir of superb voices that has performed all around the Denver area. **Boulder Meeting of Friends** (303-447-2168), a Quaker group, gathers at 1825 Upland Avenue for Sunday morning meetings. The **Boulder Mennonite Church,** at 3910 Table Mesa Drive (303-443-3889), has a strong emphasis on family, service, and faithful daily living. It founded the Victim-Offender Reconciliation Program, in which volunteers are trained to mediate in the community court system in property-related teen offenses. The **Islamic Center of Boulder** is at 1530 Culver Ct. (303-245-8121).

The **New Church of Boulder Valley,** 1370 Forest Park Circle (303-443-9220, www.boulder newchurch.org), is based on the teachings of Emanuel Swedenborg, an 18th-century Swedish scientist and theologian. A worldwide organization more than 200 years old, this Christian faith abides by Swedenborg's mission to bring the world into a new era of religious understanding.

In Boulder many choices are also available for those who wish to explore their spirituality either through self-examination or meditation. The **Shoshoni Yoga Retreat,** 21614 Highway 119 (303-642-0116), has log cabins, massage and health therapy rooms, and hiking trails. Many come to practice yoga or meditation or for spiritual renewal. Shoshoni members who founded Rudi's Restaurant, a well-regarded natural-food restaurant, have published a vegetarian cookbook, *The Shoshoni Cookbook.* **Dances of Universal Peace** (303-440-5714) offers attendees a chance to learn key phrases and gestures from many different religions through participatory song and dance. **Followers of Baha'i,** 437 Pine Street (303-443-6422), have been meeting in Boulder for more than 20 years. The **Ridhwan Foundation,** 5869 Marshall Drive (303-494-2613), teaches the "Diamond Approach" and has 250 local members. Members of the **Gurdjieff Foundation** (303-554-8120) meet regularly to study and practice the teachings of G. I. Gurdjieff. **Followers of Eckankar,** 1800 30th Street, Suite 208 (303-443-1610), meet monthly for classes and book discussions. The **Church of Gaia,** 8563 Flagstaff Road (303-443-1096), is an Earth-centered church offering training in such Native American traditions as sweat lodges, pipe circles, vision quests, and other ceremonies. Those interested in learning more about Native American worship can also find programs at the more than 20-year-old **Naropa University** at 2130 Arapahoe Avenue (303-444-0202). The **Society for the Greater Community Way of Knowledge** (303-938-8401) teaches how to live with certainty, strength, and wisdom in an emerging world.

CU-Boulder also has a Department of Religious Studies (303-492-8041) and offers ethics classes through the Philosophy Department (303-492-6132).

ROCKY MOUNTAIN NATIONAL PARK

A trip over Trail Ridge Road in Rocky Mountain National Park is a peak experience, literally. The nation's highest mountains, sparkling lakes and streams, abundant wildlife, and stunning wildflowers will leave visitors breathless from both the beauty and the altitude.

Trail Ridge Road transports visitors to a world of different life zones, climates, and vegetation—a trip comparable to driving more than 2,500 miles from Denver to Fairbanks, Alaska. But this world is compressed into just a 50-mile drive over the highest continuous highway in the United States, following the path etched by generations of Native Americans. Trail Ridge Road is one of the few paved roads in the world where a doctor's permission is recommended for those with medical problems. Every 300 feet of elevation equals one degree of latitude or 70 statute miles north. The road provides stunning views of peaks with memorable names—Never Summer Mountains, Mummy Mountain, Lumpy Ridge, Storm Peak, Chief's Head Peak, Isolation Peak, Twin Sisters. Keep your camera handy for the many scenic pullouts. If you ever contemplated investing in a wide-angle lens, this is the trip to make it worthwhile.

From spectacular vistas of endless snowy peaks to tiny, gem-like flowers that grow high above the tree line (one-third of the park's 415 square miles is above this level), Rocky Mountain National Park is without a doubt one of the nation's—and the world's—treasures.

You're almost sure to see grazing deer and elk and, if you're lucky, maybe some Rocky Mountain bighorn sheep, the park's symbol. Above timberline by boulder fields, listen for the whistle of the pikas—cute, furry animals that look like rodents but are related to rabbits. You may spot a yellow-bellied marmot, a large rodent similar to a groundhog, sunning on a rock. Gray jays or spiffy black-trimmed Clark's nutcracker birds will swoop down looking for handouts (but don't feed them, it's illegal and not good for them). It is rare to encounter bears and mountain lions since they are wary of humans; if such a meeting should occur, remember to stand tall, back away slowly, and whatever you do, don't turn and run.

Leave the crowded roadsides, walk a mile or two along one of the park's 355 miles of trails, and you'll begin to feel like one of the first humans ever to set eyes on this beautiful wilderness area.

HISTORY

As with the rest of Colorado, the first humans wandered through the area that is now Rocky Mountain National Park some 10,000 to 12,000 years ago. Part of what is now the park's Trail Ridge Road was once part of the Ute Trail, a major route across the mountains for American Indians.

The first Europeans who visited the area were French fur traders collecting animal pelts. The area became U.S. territory in 1803 as part of the Louisiana Purchase. Mineral deposits in the area proved unproductive, so there was never great mining activity.

Because of the astounding beauty, the area was destined to be a tourist attraction from its earliest days. For centuries, American Indians had visited the area and considered it sacred. Braves visited the area west of present-day Estes Park for vision quests and supposedly climbed Longs Peak to trap bald eagles for their feathers. By the time the settlers arrived, the Ute, having driven out the Arapaho, occupied the area.

After chasing the California Gold Rush in 1849, Joel Estes came looking for Colorado gold in 1859. Estes and his family homesteaded a beautiful parklike valley in 1860. Other settlers arrived slowly to try ranching and farming at elevations below 9,000 feet. Indian agent and soldier Kit Carson built a cabin on the eastern edge of the park in Tahosa Valley.

More visitors began arriving in 1864, determined to meet the challenge of climbing Longs Peak, northern Colorado's highest mountain. William Byers, who was editor of the *Rocky Mountain News* in Denver, was one of the early climbers. He and two friends stayed with the Estes family when they made their attempt at the climb. Although they were unsuccessful, Byers went back to Denver and wrote glowing accounts of the area, calling it Estes Park after his host. In 1868 Byers returned with Major John Wesley Powell (the renowned one-armed explorer of the Colorado River and Grand Canyon), and the two made the first recorded climb to the summit of Longs Peak. Byers wrote another story about Longs Peak and Estes Park, attracting more tourists, hunters, and adventure seekers. Around the area, settlers were finding a good income by housing the increasing number of tourists in their cabins. Later they began building rustic lodges (and even a nine-hole golf course). These lodges eventually evolved into dude ranches, which were popular in the early 20th century.

Had he stayed, Joel Estes might have become one of the richest men in the area, but the long, snowy winter of 1866 did him in. Later that year Estes sold off his claim and cattle for a yoke of oxen and headed south. Griffith Evans bought the Estes homestead, which he operated as a makeshift hostel until he added some cabins and opened a full-scale dude ranch in 1871.

By the 1870s, the area was becoming known around the world for its spectacular scenery. British writer and world traveler Isabella Bird visited the area in 1873 and stayed at the Evans ranch. Her adventures and travels in the area were published in 1879 in the extremely popular book, *A Lady's Life in the Rocky Mountains*. By 1882 the book was in its seventh edition; it's still a best seller at the park gift shops.

Lord Dunraven (the Fourth Earl of Dunraven, Viscount of Mount Earl and Adare) also visited the Evans ranch. It was common for European gentry to visit the United States, and this Irish nobleman and avid hunter liked Estes Park so much that he secretly acquired more than 15,000 acres through third-party purchases and other under-the-table deals, as it was illegal for foreigners to homestead. He then created a private hunting sanctuary for himself and his European hunting cronies. The earl even announced in the Rocky Mountain News that "admission to Estes Park, his game preserve, was by invitation only." But eventually the area's beauty defeated even the earl, because it attracted many others who disputed the legality of his claims.

Meanwhile, in 1876, Lord Dunraven invited Western landscape painter Albert Bierstadt to Estes Park to capture its beauty on canvas and to help the earl select a spot for his English Hotel. A lake and moraine in the park are named for the painter, whose exhibited works attracted even more attention—and tourists—to the area.

At his English Hotel near Lake Estes, Dunraven entertained such guests as Buffalo Bill Cody, Kit Carson, General William Tecumseh Sherman, and other notables in the early 1880s. Initially it catered mainly to foreign clientele—the earl's hunting buddies. Its name was later changed to the Estes Park Hotel, which operated until it burned to the ground in 1911.

Settlers continued to homestead and began contesting the earl's land claims. Dunraven eventually leased the land to ranchers and left. Failing to establish exclusive rights to the preserve and challenged about the legality of his claim, Dunraven stopped visiting Estes Park in 1881. He leased his land and hotel to Theodore Whyte, his property manager, and in 1904 the land was purchased by well-known inventor Freelan O. Stanley (inventor of the Stanley Steamer). Diagnosed with tuberculosis, Stanley, like many of his time, came to be cured in the dry mountain air (and eventually was restored to good health).

In 1905 the town of Estes Park was platted at the confluence of the Fall and Big Thompson Rivers on land sold by John Cleave. Like many locals, Cleave said he "couldn't stand to see the danged place overrun by tenderfeet tourists," so he moved away.

Construction in Estes Park came from logging operations in Hidden Valley, Hollowell Park, and Wild Basin. On the western side of the park, the Kawuneeche Valley, other logging operations provided materials to build dude ranches and develop Grand Lake village, west of the Continental Divide from Estes Park.

Designation of Rocky Mountain National Park

The ever-growing tourism prevalent by the early 1900s and use of the area by individuals and businesses raised concern among residents about preserving the area's pristine beauty.

In 1905 President Theodore Roosevelt had added the area as part of the new national forest system, but many felt that greater protection and preservation were needed, among them H. M. Wheeler, who had opened a national forest office in Estes Park in 1907.

i Don't hassle with driving! Ride the Rocky Mountain National Park shuttle to access many destinations and loop hikes along the Bear Lake Road corridor. Running between many of the park's trailheads, the buses are based at the Park & Ride shuttle bus parking lot, across from Glacier Basin Campground on Bear lake Road. Visit www .nps.gov/romo/planyourvisit/shuttle-bus-route.htm for more information.

Wheeler suggested creating a "wildlife reserve" in the nearby mountains. Enos A. Mills, a 20-year resident of Estes Park and a naturalist, writer, conservationist, and innkeeper, helped promote the park even further. Around 1909 Mills began campaigning to preserve the area. Other citizens joined Mills, among them the well-known

Stanley. The group formed the Estes Park Protective and Improvement Association to protect and preserve the area's scenery and wildlife.

Mills was so eloquent that President Roosevelt commissioned him to tour the country promoting the preservation of wild lands. The national park concept was first formalized in 1872 when Ulysses S. Grant designated Yellowstone as the first national park. The stated objectives of national parks were first to preserve natural and historical objects including wildlife, scenery, and ecosystems, and second to promote the enjoyment of these resources by the public.

Finally, in 1915, after years of debate on the size and boundaries of the park, President Woodrow Wilson signed a bill passed by Congress making Rocky Mountain National Park the nation's 10th national park. The new park encompassed 415 square miles of forest, aspen groves, alpine tundra, rich wetlands, and 76 peaks soaring above 12,000 feet. Soon after, the first park superintendent was installed, and rangers were hired to enforce the new restrictions on hunting and cattle grazing.

During the next decades, evidence of human settlement in the park, such as the briefly booming silver mining town called Lulu City in the late 1870s, was removed, and natural vegetation was painstakingly restored.

In 1975 Rocky Mountain National Park was named the 21st biosphere reserve in the world. The biosphere reserve system was established by the United Nations Man and Biosphere Programme to observe and monitor changes in natural ecosystems, especially those resulting from human activities. There are more than 320 biosphere reserves worldwide in 80 countries.

Since 1974, Congress has been pondering a recommendation by then-President Richard Nixon that 239,835 acres of the park be designated as wilderness, prohibiting expansion of roads and buildings in that area; the designation would not affect current activities in the park. Although the designation has not yet been made, National Park Service policy requires that the park be managed as a wilderness until Congress takes action. In 1980, 2,917 acres of the Indian Peaks Wilderness Area were added to Rocky Mountain National Park. And in 1990 it gained an additional 465 acres when Congress approved expansion of the park to include the Lily Lake area.

VISITOR CENTERS

Perhaps the park's early promoters and protectors realized how popular it would become. Today, more than three million visitors come to Rocky Mountain National Park every year. Six visitor centers at the park accommodate this yearly crush of humanity.

The **Beaver Meadows Visitor Center** is 2.5 miles west of Estes Park on U.S. Highway 36 and is open daily year-round. Call the staff at (970) 586-1206 for weather, camping, and other specific information; call (970) 586-1333 for a recorded message; those with hearing impairments can call (970) 586-1319. An orientation film of the park is shown on the half-hour. There are Saturday evening programs at 7 p.m. the rest of the year. Nightly programs are offered from mid-June to mid-August, beginning at 7:30 p.m. Check the Web site, www.rmnp.com for updated hours.

On the west entrance to the park, the **Kawuneeche Visitor Center** (970-586-1513) sits 1.3 miles north of Grand Lake on U.S. Highway 34, and is also open daily year-round. One of Kawuneeche's most popular exhibits is a 3-D topographical map of the park. Programs are presented at 7 p.m. each Saturday from mid-June to mid-August. Fall, winter, and spring Saturday evening programs are offered the second Saturday of each month at 7 p.m.

The **Moraine Park Museum** lies 5 miles west of Estes Park on Bear Lake Road and is open daily from mid-May to Labor Day. You'll find ranger-led programs and a 0.5-mile nature trail beginning at the museum.

Fall River Visitors' Center is on US 34, 5 miles west of Estes Park, at the Fall River entrance to the park. It is open April through October and features wildlife exhibits as well as a Discovery Room where children can dress up as firefighters or old-time rangers.

Most spectacularly situated of all is the **Alpine Visitor Center** at 11,796 feet atop Trail Ridge Road. It is 25 miles west of Estes Park and is open daily from June through September, weather permitting. Next door, a park concessionaire operates Trail Ridge Store and a snack bar, where diners can enjoy a simple meal along with a panoramic view. Call the main park number (970-586-1206) for information about the Alpine Visitor Center.

Lily Lake Visitor Center, 6 miles south of Estes Park on Highway 7, is open daily from June to Labor Day, depending upon snow conditions, and open weekends during May and September. There is a wheelchair-accessible trail around the nearby lake.

Besides providing education about the park's different ecosystems, plus maps and directions, the centers remind visitors of the park's regulations:

1. No pets are allowed on trails or away from roadways. Pets must be leashed at all times.
2. Feeding or touching wild animals is prohibited, along with hunting or harassment of wildlife. This includes stalking wild animals for photographs, which frightens them and makes them less viewable for other visitors.
3. Picking wildflowers or plants is prohibited. Removing, disturbing, damaging, or destroying natural features, including rocks and pinecones, is illegal.
4. Fishing requires a valid Colorado state fishing license. Only artificial lures may be used (but children 12 years of age and younger may use bait, in open waters only).
5. Camping is restricted to designated areas.
6. A permit is required for all overnight stays in the backcountry. There are restrictions on the use of pack animals.
7. Gathering firewood is prohibited. Fires may be built only in picnic areas and campsites with grates. Either bring your own wood or ask at the ranger stations or park headquarters about purchasing some.
8. Vehicles must remain on roads or in parking areas. Parking any vehicle or leaving

property unattended for more than 24 hours without prior permission is prohibited.

9. Hitchhiking is prohibited.
10. Trail bikes, snowmobiles, and all other vehicles are restricted to roads. Snowmobiles are permitted only on the west side of the park.
11. Firearms are to be kept unloaded.
12. All your own trash must be removed from picnic areas and campsites and disposed of in trash cans and recycling receptacles.
13. Having open containers of alcoholic beverages in a vehicle on park roads and in parking areas is illegal.

Entrance to the park is $20 per vehicle and $10 for walk-ins and bicyclists; passes are good for a week. An annual pass to Rocky Mountain National Park costs $35, and an annual pass to all national parks is $80.

RECREATION

Bicycling

Bicycling in the park is allowed only on roads, and these are heavily used by cars. Since the roads climb from about 9,000 feet to more than 12,000 feet, riding is quite strenuous throughout. No off-road or mountain biking is allowed on any of the trails.

For a challenging ride on a gravel road, follow Old Fall River Road, the first auto route over the Continental Divide, which is described by park officials as a "motor nature trail." The road is open to bicycles early in the summer season before it opens to vehicles. It climbs 9.4 miles

i Rocky Mountain National Park has one of the nation's highest paved roads, Trail Ridge Road, which traverses miles of tundra similar to what you'd find above the Arctic Circle. Look for elk, deer, and birds not found elsewhere. (But don't feed the wildlife—it makes it more difficult for them to survive in the wild.

before joining Trail Ridge Road at the summit of 11,796-foot Old Fall River Pass (see more information under "Driving," later in this chapter).

Bicycling over 50-mile-long Trail Ridge Road is only for the fittest of the fit, and even they will want to spend the night on the other side at Grand Lake before returning. Trail Ridge Road crosses the Continental Divide, and at its highest point is 12,183 feet, making it one of the world's most spectacular bike rides. But this road, too, is heavily traveled by cars.

Bear Lake Road is a strenuous 10-mile climb of 1,500 feet from the Beaver Meadows Entrance Station to Bear Lake at 9,475 feet.

Remember that you will be riding at a high altitude and be prepared for early afternoon thunderstorms, cold temperatures, icy roads, and thin, thin air.

Camping

To reduce the impact on the park, car camping is allowed only in five roadside campgrounds. Camping reservations can be made five months in advance for individuals and groups at three of the campgrounds, and campgrounds are frequently packed full from mid-June to mid-August, so plan ahead. The maximum stay in the park is 7 days during summer and 14 days during winter (only Moraine Park, Timber Creek, and Longs Peak campgrounds are open year-round). At Longs Peak Campground, the limit is three days, and only tents are allowed. Although they can't go on trails with you, pets are allowed in campgrounds (leashed at all times). Reservations can be made online at www.rmnp.com or by calling (877) 444-6777.

Permits are required for all backcountry camping; call the Backcountry Office at (970) 586-1243; fees for backcountry camping vary.

Remember, you are bedding down in someone else's home; make sure all food is stored in airtight containers in the trunk of your car or suspended high in a tree if you are in the backcountry, to avoid a midnight visit from a black bear.

The campgrounds listed below offer a great way to enjoy the park at close range. There are no electrical, water, or sewer connections in any of the campgrounds. Sewer dumping stations are located at Moraine Park, Glacier Basin, and Timber Creek campgrounds. Public telephones are located at Moraine Park, Glacier Basin, Timber Creek, and Aspen Glen. For general information about the park and specific information on recreation, rentals, campgrounds, or even ticks, call the public information office at (970) 586-1206. For emergencies, call (970) 586-1399 or 911.

Aspenglen: Aspenglen is open mid-May through late September on a first-come, first-served basis. It is located immediately inside the Fall River entrance of the park and has 54 sites for tents, motor homes, or recreational vehicles. The water is turned on in mid-May and turned off in late September.

Glacier Basin: Located 9 miles from Park Headquarters off US 36 on Bear Lake Road, this campground has 165 sites. Reservations are required. The site accommodates tents and recreational vehicles up to 27 ft. (it has dump stations, but, like all the park's campgrounds, no hookups). The season is typically mid-May through Labor Day.

Group Sites: The park has 15 group sites in Glacier Basin (see previous paragraph for location) that accommodate groups of 10 to 50 people. They are open mid-May through Labor Day, with water turned on and off the same times. Dump stations are provided, and there is a public phone. Reservations are strongly recommended.

Longs Peak: This smaller campground is 11 miles south of Estes Park and a mile west on Highway 7. It offers 26 tent campsites (no RVs or motor homes) on a first-come, first-served basis. It's open all year, with water turned on in mid-May and turned off mid-September.

Moraine Park: The park's largest campground, Moraine Park has 247 sites and is located 3 miles west of park headquarters off Bear Lake Road. It's open all year and accommodates recreational vehicles and tents. Water is turned on mid-May and turned off mid-September. Reservations are required May 22 through Labor Day.

Sprague Lake Handicamp: This campsite is designed to accommodate visitors with disabilities. From the campsite parking area 7 miles from Park Headquarters, a half-mile wheelchair-accessible nature trail leads to the tent campground for a maximum of 10 people and 5 wheelchairs. There is a three-night limit. For reservations, contact the park at (970) 586-1243.

Timber Creek: Also open all year, Timber Creek is 10 miles north of the Grand Lake entrance to the park and has 100 sites accommodating tents and recreational vehicles. Water is turned on mid-May and off in mid-September. The campground operates on a first-come, first-served basis, with no reservations.

Climbing

The park's climbing challenges are renowned and unlimited. The famous 900-foot Diamond cliff is ranked as one of the top 10 best rock climbs in the world. The diamond-shape granite wall sits atop the east face of Longs Peak—every inch of the sheer face is above 13,000 feet. More than 35 climbing routes challenge the most adventurous climbers.

As with other activities in the park, low-impact techniques are emphasized—motorized drills are prohibited, and climbers are urged to use brown chalk, neutral-colored webbing, and to follow established routes. Those staying overnight may not build fires and must remove all debris to keep the area pristine for the wild things that live there and other humans who visit. Registration is not required for technical climbers, but be sure to tell a reliable friend or relative of your climbing plans, should you be overdue. If you prefer both feet on the ground, you might catch a glimpse of technical climbers practicing their skills on Lumpy Ridge just north of Estes Park.

i Longs Peak in Rocky Mountain National Park is the northernmost of "the fourteeners"—Colorado's highest peaks, 14,000 feet or more. Longs Peak has an elevation of 14,255 feet and is the 15th-highest peak in the state.

Permits are required for overnight bivouacs and are available at park headquarters, the West Unit Office, and at most ranger stations for the 269 backcountry sites. Advance reservations are advised; call the Backcountry Office at (970) 586-1242 or write to the Backcountry Office, Rocky Mountain National Park, Estes Park, CO 80517.

Driving

The main park drive, Trail Ridge Road, is the highest continuous highway in the United States. It runs 50 miles from Estes Park to Grand Lake over the Continental Divide and was built in 1932. The road climbs through the evergreen forests amidst the eerie, gnarled krummholz—wind-sculpted trees (krummholz means "crooked wood" in German)—and up to the alpine tundra above the tree line, comparable to being in the Arctic Circle.

Depending upon weather conditions, the road is generally open from Memorial Day until mid-October. Allow three or four hours for this scenic drive, with stops at the numerous overlooks for stupendous vistas of glacier-carved peaks, snowfields, and cirques, and perhaps a snack at the Alpine Visitor Center on top. Take the short half-hour round-trip Tundra Walk to see the tiny delicate flowers that have adapted to this harsh environment, some of the 900 species of flora found in the park. Be sure to stay on paths because the alpine tundra is fragile and some of the flora is extinct outside the park.

The Bear Lake Road makes another scenic drive, leading to a lovely high mountain basin. Traffic during summer months through the park is quite heavy. A shuttle bus runs in the Moraine Park and Bear Lake areas during the peak summer season—June through Labor Day. Parking lots at Bear Lake and Glacier Gorge Junction will be full between 10 a.m. and 3 p.m. on summer days, so plan accordingly.

Old Fall River Road runs from Horseshoe Park Junction to Fall River Pass. Expect a leisurely pace on the 15-mile-per-hour road as it runs one-way uphill west of Endovalley Picnic Area. A gravel road with many switchbacks, it gives visitors an idea of early travel across the mountains, since it was the first road over the Divide in northern Colorado. A guide booklet describing interesting sights along the way is available at the visitor centers. You can make a loop up Old Fall River Road and return on Trail Ridge Road. Old Fall River Road is west of Estes Park on US 34 at the Fall River Entrance Station. The road is paved for the first 2 miles from the entrance. Take note of the alluvial fan along the way, caused by a flood in 1982. RVs and trailers are not allowed on Fall River Road because of the narrow switchbacks. The road is closed in winter.

Driving Tips

1. There are no service stations in the park. Enter with a full tank of gas.
2. Observe posted speed limits—roads are narrow, winding, and heavily used.
3. Travel in early morning or late afternoon. Wildlife is more active at these times, and the light is more beautiful. At midday, traffic can be bumper to bumper.
4. Downshift to lower gears when going up or down steep grades. This will reduce engine stress and keep your brakes from burning out. Manually downshift automatic transmissions. Go down hills in a lower gear than you use to go up.
5. Tap brakes gently and repeatedly on downhills to reduce brake wear and possible overheating (or failure).
6. Be sure to look first and signal at turnouts and parking areas. Watch for oncoming traffic. Sound the horn on blind corners to alert oncoming drivers, if necessary.
7. When you stop, always set the emergency brake, and park in gear if you have manual transmission.
8. Lock your car when unattended; place valuables out of sight or take them with you.
9. Stay in your own lane. Don't drive in the middle to avoid being near the edge. The roads were designed with plenty of room, and you'll only cause an accident by driving down the center.
10. Don't be surprised if your car doesn't perform normally at high altitudes. Cars tuned

for lower elevations may overheat or act as though they're not getting enough gas. Drive in a lower-than-usual gear to keep RPMs up and to avoid overheating. Don't pump the accelerator, as it will cause flooding and make matters worse. On warm days some cars may get vapor lock in the fuel line. If this occurs, try to get the car off the road at the nearest pullout. Stop the engine and allow it to cool. If there is snow or cold water nearby, put it on the fuel pump and the line leading to the carburetor. Let the car cool for 15 minutes before trying to start it again.

Fishing

Fly fishers will find four species of trout in the mountain streams and lakes of the park: German brown, rainbow, brook, and cutthroat. The only trout native to the park are the greenback cutthroat and the Colorado River cutthroat; the others were stocked by early settlers and spread throughout the region.

Valid Colorado fishing licenses are required for anglers age 16 and older for all fishing in the park; use of live bait is prohibited except for children age 12 and younger. See the fishing regulations at park headquarters, one of the ranger stations, or the "Fishing" section in the Sports chapter. No fishing is allowed in Bear Lake, and some lakes and streams on the east side of the park are closed to protect the greenback cutthroat trout, which is being reintroduced to its native habitat.

Only 48 of the park's 156 lakes have reproducing populations of fish. Cold temperatures and lack of spawning habitat make high-country lakes a bad bet.

Sprague Lake at the east edge of the park is good for catching pan-sized brook trout; however, it's right next to the road and is heavily used. From Estes Park, drive west on US 36 to the Beaver Meadows Entrance Station. Turn left (south) at the first intersection after the entrance, and continue on the Bear Lake Road for about 6 miles.

For a day's outing—a combination hiking and fishing trip—go to Peacock Pool. Begin at the East Longs Peak trailhead and hike about 4 miles up the trail to a spur that leads to Peacock Pool, 11,360 feet high. This is a hard hike but offers spectacular views. Another 1.5 miles from Peacock Pool is Chasm Lake, with deep water, but according to latest reports, no fish, though it's a scenic spot right under the spectacular Diamond, the east face of Longs Peak. The Longs Peak trailhead is 9.2 miles south of Estes Park on Highway 7; turn right at the sign.

Hiking and Backpacking

With 355 miles of trails, Rocky Mountain National Park is prime hiking and backpacking country. There's something for everyone, from wheelchair users to backpackers. Below are some day hikes, rated accordingly. It's best to get a map at one of the visitor centers for detailed descriptions, including distance, elevation, and type of terrain, or visit www.rmnp.com.

Very Easy

The Bear Lake Nature Trail is a half-mile paved path circling Bear Lake. A brochure available at the trailhead describes the subalpine landscape. Elevation is 9,475 feet. Leave from the Bear Lake parking area.

The Sprague Lake Nature Trail, known as the Five Senses Trail, is a half-mile trail around Sprague Lake, at 8,710 feet in altitude. It is also wheelchair-accessible. Take the road to Bear Lake, and turn off at the sign for Sprague Lake.

Easy

Trails from Bear Lake to Nymph, Dream, or Emerald Lakes present a little more challenge, at 3.6 miles round-trip.

The Gem Lake Trail, a round-trip hike, makes for a pleasant walk and begins outside the park on Devil's Gulch Road.

Moderate

Bear Lake or Glacier Gorge to Mills Pond or Black Lake are good 6- to 10-mile round-trip hikes that take a few hours, as does Bear Lake or Glacier Gorge to Sky Pond.

The hike to Chasm Lake is a bit more strenuous at 4.2 miles one-way, but the gorgeous view of the Diamond on Longs Peak and the beautiful lake make it worth the effort. Start at the Longs Peak trailhead, off Highway 7, north of Meeker.

Long or Difficult

The trail from Bear Lake to the top of Flattop Mountain is a little more difficult. The hike to Thunder Lake starts at Wild Basin, off Highway 7 between Allenspark and Meeker, and you should plan on it taking most of the day.

For Ypsilon Lake, start at the Lawn Lake trailhead at Horseshoe Park on Fall River Road. Don't forget your lunch and rain gear.

A Classic

Longs Peak has always been considered America's Matterhorn. At 14,255 feet high, it is the highest peak in the park and the northernmost "fourteener" in the Rockies (these are peaks of at least 14,000 feet). The dramatic peak has fascinated writers, artists, climbers, and explorers since the first recorded American sighting in 1820 by Stephen Long. The Arapaho are believed to have climbed Longs to obtain eagle feathers on its summit. In 1868 two famed nonnatives made it to the top: one-armed Colorado River explorer John Wesley Powell and Denver newspaperman William Byers.

Climbing Longs is still an exciting accomplishment today. It's an all-day affair—usually taking about 14 hours round-trip. It should be attempted only by strong hikers who are already acclimated to the altitude. The climb should not be attempted by novices. It's crucial to be off the peak and on the way back down by noon to avoid the daily summer thunderstorms and dangerous lightning, which has claimed the lives of many hikers. Remember that fresh snow is possible any day of the year.

The most popular (and only non-technical) route is the East Longs Peak Trail, usually called the Keyhole Route, which starts at the Longs Peak trailhead and climbs 8 miles and 4,855 vertical feet to the top. The first 6 miles are the easiest and follow an ever-climbing trail through beautiful forests of pine and aspen up to timberline with fantastic views. If you start early enough (say, 3:30 a.m.) you can reach timberline in time to watch the sunrise over Boulder. Those who want to bail out before this point can take the well-marked turnoff to Chasm Lake, at around 4 miles, to a gorgeous lake right beneath the 1,000-foot vertical Diamond on Longs' sheer, spectacular 1,675-foot east face (a popular world-class technical-climbing route). Chasm Lake is 4.2 miles from the trailhead.

But if you continue on the Keyhole Route, at mile 6 you reach the boulder field and hop from boulder to boulder for 1 mile up to the Keyhole, a prominent rock formation. To the left of the Keyhole is the chilly-looking Agnes Vaille Shelter Cabin. Vaille made the first successful winter ascent of the east face with Walter Kiener in 1925 but collapsed from exhaustion on her way back and froze to death while Kiener went for help.

After passing through the Keyhole, at 13,100 feet, the hard part begins. The route is marked by red and yellow paint circles over the rocky Ledges, which have intimidating drop-offs. The Ledges lead to a 600-foot steep couloir of loose gravel and running rivulets called the Trough (or "stairway from hell," as many hikers have renamed it). After climbing the Trough and negotiating the huge boulder at the top, you pass through the notch and cross the Narrows—more rock ledges with even more dizzying exposure. The Narrows lead to the Homestretch, a short, steep couloir to the top, not really difficult, but at this point in the game, a bit much. The Homestretch requires some hand-holds but has solid footing unless slicked by rain. At the top of Homestretch, you have reached the huge summit of Longs, which encompasses four acres. Enjoy the view, do a few push-ups to show how really tough you are, and take a look down the Diamond face, but don't stay too long if noon is approaching. If there is any snow—possible well into July—ice axes are necessary for safely climbing the Ledges, Trough, Narrows, and Homestretch.

Despite the rigor of the undertaking, don't expect to have the trail to yourself. On some summer days, hikers have complained that the view they saw most was the backside of the hiker ahead of them.

The Longs Peak trailhead is 9.2 miles south of Estes Park on Highway 7; turn right at the sign. Those who don't want to do it all in one day can backpack part of the way up Longs and camp in the boulder field, a spectacular but rather inhospitable campground—cold and windy and around 12,000 feet in elevation—among the boulders. But you'll need to reserve your permit well in advance by writing to the Backcountry Office, Rocky Mountain National Park, Estes Park, CO 80517. There are numerous backcountry sites and zones for individuals and groups throughout the park. For more information, maps, or reservations, call the Backcountry Office at (970) 586-1242, write to the address previously listed, or just show up. You can also visit www.rmnp.com/RMNP-Things-Backcountry.html for additional information.

Horseback Riding

Horses, mules, llamas, and other pack and riding animals are not allowed to travel cross-country in the park, but there are more than 260 miles of trails available for animals. Horses and guides can be hired at a number of liveries outside the park.

Skiing and Snowshoeing

Though most visitors to the park come in summer, winter offers great cross-country skiing and snowshoeing opportunities. January, February, and March provide the best conditions, sandwiched between the spotty coverage of early winter and the avalanche danger of late winter. Bear Lake and Wild Basin are the park's most popular cross-country skiing areas. The visitor center on US 36, 2.5 miles west of Estes Park, is staffed daily from 8 a.m. to 5 p.m. except Christmas Day. Rangers lead cross-country tours from Kawuneeche Visitor Center on Saturday afternoons, and snowshoe hikes are offered Wednesday, Saturday, and Sunday at Bear Lake. Rangers can answer questions and provide trail maps detailing 40 miles of marked trails around Bear Lake and 88 miles of mainly unmarked trails around Wild Basin. There's a $10 entrance fee per vehicle (don't forget your chains if you don't have snow tires), and $5 for skiers, walkers, or cyclists at all times. For more information call the park at (970) 586-1206.

Equipment can be rented in Estes Park (see "Cross-Country Skiing" in the Estes Park chapter of this book). Precautions to take to heart: don't ski or snowshoe alone; return to the trailhead well before dark; and pack in extra food and water to keep your hardworking body fueled, extra clothing, a map and compass, a flashlight, waterproof matches, a space blanket, and a first-aid kit. Here are a few of our favorite sites:

Glacier Basin Campground: (Easy) Drive 5 miles up Bear Lake Road. Park on the west side of the road at the large parking area (which is the shuttle-bus parking area during summer months) and walk across to the east side to begin skiing on the main trail from the campground, which heads southwest for a mile on level terrain to Sprague Lake. There are many trails in and around the campground as well.

Black Lake: (Intermediate to Difficult) Begin at the Glacier Gorge Junction parking lot, which is about 11 miles up Bear Lake Road. Follow the signs southwest toward Alberta Falls and The Loch. After the intersection of Icy Brook and Glacier Creek, turn south and follow Glacier Creek to Mills Lake. Continue past Mills and Jewel Lakes along the creek. When you leave the trees, continue up the open slope to Black Lake and enjoy the spectacular view of Longs Peak to the east, McHenrys to the west, and Chief's Head Peak to the south.

Wild Basin Trailhead: (Difficult) Drive 13 miles south from Estes Park on Highway 7 (past the Longs Peak Trail at 9.2 miles) to the Sandbeach Lake trailhead. Turn right and drive another mile to the National Park Service parking lot. The Sandbeach Lake Trail starts at the large sign in the parking area and climbs northeast through the pines 4.2 miles to Sandbeach Lake.

PROGRAMS AND TOURS

Park rangers offer a variety of fun and educational programs and guided tours throughout the year. Among our favorites are the full moon walks. The Trail Ridge Road tours, held Wednesdays in July and August, are also fun. Reservations are required for some of the programs; call (970) 586-1206.

The nonprofit Rocky Mountain Nature Association, created in 1931 to encourage the use of Rocky Mountain National Park as an outdoor classroom and research area, offers almost 100 classes in the park. Classes have such intriguing names as "100 Million Years in a Day," "Rivers of Ice," "Uppity Women of the Rockies," "Close-up Photography Techniques," "Herbal Medicines," and "Story of Moose." For kids, there are "Fishy Business," "Surviving in the Wild," "Native American Leather and Beads," and others. Fees are quite reasonable. Call (970) 586-0108 for more information, or visit www.rmna.org.

i Rocky Mountain National Park is a wildlife watcher's dream come true. Elk can be seen anytime, while bighorn sheep are commonly seen from May through mid-August. Moose frequent willow thickets along the Colorado River in Kawuneeche Valley on the park's west side. Otters, mule, bats, marmots, and birds galore are also common in the park.

Due to snowshoeing's soaring popularity, the park now offers **snowshoe tours** with park rangers. Reservations are required and may be made no sooner than seven days in advance. These tours are free of charge. For tours from the Grand Lake side, call (970) 627-3471. For tours from the east side, call (970) 586-1223.

SAFETY

A visit to Rocky Mountain National Park can be the experience of a lifetime, but don't forget that this is not a climate-controlled theme park—it is the real, wild world with unaccustomed dangers. Don't be afraid to enjoy it, but do use some foresight and common sense.

Altitude sickness: The flu-like symptoms of altitude sickness—nausea, headache, dizziness, rapid heartbeat, breathlessness—may be your body's way of telling you to head to lower ground. Follow its advice. To minimize the effects of the high altitude, avoid alcohol and tobacco, drink lots of fluids, eat frequently and lightly, and rest.

Animals: The park is richly inhabited. As guests here, human visitors must learn the acceptable rules of behavior. Never feed the wildlife; a human diet is not suitable for them and making beggars of them is dangerous for both species. Photographers should take a long lens and shoot from inside a car or from the roadside; aggressive photographers who approach animals may be fined $50. Keep food locked away in airtight containers in your car trunk when in bear country. If you encounter a black bear, stand still or slowly back away; never approach a bear, particularly a female with cubs. If you encounter a mountain lion, stop, pick up small children, stand tall, back away, yell. Do not run (running is your signal to the lion that you are game).

Avalanche: Open slopes, particularly after a recent wind or snow storm, can be triggered by as little as a footfall into a massive avalanche. Visitors traveling in such areas should travel in groups, wear electronic transceivers, and carry shovels and poles to use as probes. If you are swept up in an avalanche, discard equipment and swim toward the top of the moving snow.

Giardia: No, it's not just from bad restaurants. Giardia, a microscopic organism that can cause diarrhea, cramps, weight loss (the bad kind), and bloating, lives in the digestive systems of humans and wildlife. It can also flourish in that crystal stream, mountain lake, or enticing snow field. If you must drink the water, boil it for at least five minutes, or use a filtration system capable of removing microorganisms.

Hypothermia: There's a saying in the Rockies—"If you don't like the weather, wait five minutes." A sunny day can suddenly turn overcast, windy, cold, even snowy. Exposure to wet and cold can lead to hypothermia, a lowering of the body's core temperature. Symptoms are confusion, drowsiness, shivering, and slurred speech. A warm, nonalcoholic drink and warm, dry clothing are the treatment; coming prepared for any weather is the prevention.

Snowfields: There's nothing more thrilling than zipping down the slick face of a snowfield or glacier in the middle of summer, either on a tube or sled, or by the seat of your pants. But the thrill can turn to fear when you discover just how difficult it can be to stop. For safety and preservation reasons, snow play and sledding are permitted only at Bear Lake and Hidden Valley, but look for warning signs in those areas as well.

Storms: The high peaks of Rocky Mountain National Park are a favorite target when Thor starts practicing his aim with lightning bolts. Thunderstorms are frequent in early to mid-afternoon. If you're up top when a storm begins, get off ridges or peaks and avoid exposed rocks and trees. If you're on horseback, dismount and put a little distance between you and your horse. Better yet, start out early in the morning so you're down well before practice time.

Sunburn: The high elevation means that you are less protected than normal from ultraviolet radiation, and that dazzling snow also increases the risk of a severe burn. UV-protectant sunglasses, a hat, and covering clothing are a good idea, with heavy-duty sunscreen on exposed skin. Don't forget to slather the kids.

Ticks: Visitors are warned not to take anything from the park, but sometimes it's difficult not to. Ticks, tenacious members of the spider family, love nothing more than hitching a ride on a warm, blood-pumping body passing by. They are plentiful in early spring and summer. To discourage the hangers-on, spray on insect repellent before setting out, keep your ankles covered with thick socks, and if you are wearing pants, tuck them into your boots or socks. Check for ticks periodically throughout your visit to the park, especially in places where your clothing ends, such as your collar, the end of your sleeves, and your pants or shorts legs. If you find one, carefully remove it with tweezers, being sure to get the whole body; remaining embedded parts can cause infection or serious illness like Rocky Mountain spotted fever and Colorado tick fever (fortunately, no cases of Lyme disease have been reported in the park).

Water: A beautiful mountain stream can sweep you off your feet—literally. Keep in mind that during spring runoff, even a shallow stream can pick up enough force to knock down adults and carry them away.

Watermelon snow: You know not to eat the yellow snow, but did you know that pink snow is bad news, too? This snow, called watermelon snow because of its color and taste, is actually a colony of algae that can send you running for the nearest port-a-potty.

ESTES PARK

Estes Park (elevation 7,522 feet) lies 63 miles northwest of Denver and 34 miles northwest of Boulder at the eastern entrance to Rocky Mountain National Park and is the year-round home of more than 10,000 hardy souls (15,000 in summer). It exists primarily as a base camp and service area for visitors to the park, offering hotels, restaurants, shopping, equipment rentals, tours, and other diversions for tourists with a nearly endless choice during the summer months. Since more than three million visitors come to Rocky Mountain National Park every year—and most of them during summer—things can get a bit hectic along Estes Park's main drag. But those visitors left the town with $7.18 million in sales tax dollars in 2008.

In winter, some of the shops close, and their owners head south, but many others stay open, particularly the art galleries. Some restaurants have abbreviated hours during winter. But winter and other "low-season" months may be the best time to get the flavor of this small town, which is beautifully situated at the base of spectacular Longs Peak and Rocky Mountain National Park.

Estes Park has quite an interesting history all its own. Joel Estes gave his name to the area—which he described as the most beautiful spot he had ever seen—when he topped a ridge and looked down on the valley that is surrounded by 54 peaks 12,000 feet and higher.

Another notable newcomer attracted by the beauty of the mountain valley was Thomas Wyndam-Quin, fourth Earl of Dunraven. Following a series of hunting trips, the earl in 1874 began acquiring land, through means legal and otherwise, with the intention of creating a grand estate.

In 1877, Dunraven built a hunting lodge in a beautiful setting, calling it the Estes Park Hotel. Locals, who resented the acquisitive foreigner, referred to it as the "English Hotel." Estes Park homesteaders began to join forces against the earl's purchases and eventually Dunraven moved on to more hospitable areas. The remains of the buildings he left behind have been removed from the park as it is returned to its natural state.

Victorian traveler and writer Isabella Bird wrote extensively and lovingly about the scenic beauty of Estes Park in the fall of 1873. For those interested in the area's history and a fascinating glimpse of life for the first settlers, her book *A Lady's Life in the Rocky Mountains* is required and entertaining reading.

Stephen King wrote more horrifyingly about the malevolent spirits inhabiting the fictional Overlook Hotel (actually the Stanley Hotel, where King lived when he wrote the novel) and their effect on a family hired to "winter over" in the empty hotel. King was so unhappy about the movie version of *The Shining,* starring Jack Nicholson, that he returned to the Stanley to film a television series closer to the novel.

On July 31, 1976, real horror came to Estes Park when the burbling Big Thompson River was transformed by mountain storms into a deadly gusher powerful enough to pick up and carry cars, boulders, homes, bridges, and trees as it crashed down on the tourist-packed town. At least 139 people were killed (7 were listed as missing), and 88 people were injured, making it the largest natural disaster in Colorado history. The flood destroyed 361 homes and 52 businesses.

Estes Park has rebuilt, but the flood left as its legacy a heightened awareness of the inextricable connections between humans and the land on which they perch.

Indeed, the history of Estes Park and Rocky Mountain National Park are so deeply intertwined that one would probably not exist without the other. Major employers are the Park R-3 School District, the Estes Park Medical Center, the town itself, the Holiday Inn, the YMCA of the Rockies, the Harmony Foundation (a drug and alcohol rehab center), the park, and Estes Valley Recreation and Park District. The average age of residents is 45, 10 years older than the average age of Colorado residents. The average income is $49,422, with the average house selling for $339,288.

Some visitors enjoy connecting with the quieter, community side of an area. Others suddenly need a community service. These days, many visitors stand transfixed by the beautiful surroundings and decide to make Estes Park their permanent home. This chapter provides information for both tourists and newcomers, including details on medical care and worship, real estate and retirement, schools and child care, as well as information on accommodations, attractions, restaurants, and sports. The following sections are arranged alphabetically.

For information about almost anything in the area, call the Estes Park Convention & Visitors Bureau at (800) 443-7837 or (800) 44-ESTES or visit www.EstesParkCVB.com or www.estes-park .com. The area code for Estes Park is 970 and calls from Boulder are long distance.

ACCOMMODATIONS

Estes Park has so many motels, bed-and-breakfast inns, lodges, and cabins, visitors will have a large choice and range in quality and atmosphere. But reservations are a good idea during the crowded summer months and a must over holiday weekends. Choose a modern motel, a rustic lodge or cabin, or a place right out of history. All of these accommodations accept major credit cards, with the exception of the cabins at Estes Park Center/ YMCA of the Rockies. Smoking is prohibited at many inns and bed-and-breakfasts; if you're a smoker it makes sense to ask in advance.

Price-Code Key

Our code reflects what you'll pay on average for a double room.

$	less than $50
$$	$51 to $80
$$$	$81 to $100
$$$$	$101 to $150
$$$$$	$151 and more

ALPINE TRAIL RIDGE INN $$-$$$
927 Moraine Avenue
(970) 586-4585
http://alpinetrailridgeinn.com
This tidy blue-trimmed white motel is right on the highway, but its clean and pleasant rooms are a good value. There's a heated swimming pool, and family and kitchen units are available. Enjoy good meals at the Sundeck Restaurant right on the property. Smoking is not allowed at the inn.

ASPEN LODGE AT ESTES PARK $$$$$
6120 Highway 7
(970) 586-8133, (800) 332-6867
http://aspenlodge.net
Located 7.5 miles south of Estes Park, this beautiful 3,000-acre ranch is a full resort offering hayrides, swimming, fishing, tennis, racquetball, horseback riding, wildlife van tours, mountain biking, hikes, and a great children's program for kids ages 5 through 12 that includes Indian lore and nature rambles. It's the largest log lodge in the state, according to the owners. There are cozy cabins, a hot tub, saunas, and winter sleigh rides. Three-, four-, and seven-day packages make this

all-inclusive resort quite affordable, with all meals and activities included. Smoking is prohibited at this property.

THE BALDPATE INN $$$$$
4900 Highway 7 South
(970) 586-6151
www.baldpateinn.com
In January 1996, the Baldpate was placed on the National Register of Historic Places.

Family-owned and operated as a bed-and-breakfast, this classic mountain inn and historic local landmark is unsurpassed in charm and history. Built from local wood and stone in 1917, it's the quintessential rustic mountain getaway. The inn is 7 miles south of Estes Park across from the Rocky Mountain National Park Visitor Center at Lily Lake. Guests can stay in the Mae West and Jack Dempsey Rooms, where these and many other stars stayed. The Baldpate Inn has 12 rustic rooms and 3 cabins with colorful homemade quilts, calicos, gingham, and alluring log-cabin decor. One cabin is decorated as a honeymoon suite. There are five massive stone fireplaces and a library. The inn has the world's largest public key collection and an amazing photograph collection.

A three-course breakfast is included in the room rate, and the dining room serves delicious meals with homemade pies, pastries, breads, and soups. Smoking is not allowed. The Baldpate Inn is open Memorial Day until October, weather permitting.

BLACK CANYON INN $$$
800 MacGregor Avenue (Devil's Gulch Road)
(800) 897-3730
www.blackcanyoninn.com
This historic mountain lodge offers one, two and three-bedroom condos and a seasonal log cabin on fourteen secluded acres. It's a great place for weddings.

ELKHORN LODGE AND
GUEST RANCH $$$–$$$$$
600 West Elkhorn Avenue
(970) 586-4416
www.elkhornlodge.org

Be a part of history when you stay at the Elkhorn Lodge. The Elkhorn has been a guest ranch and lodge for the past 132 years, and it remains charming. It is located at the base of Old Man Mountain, a sacred Native American vision-quest site. There is something for everyone at Elkhorn, including rooms in the main lodge; the Coach House, which is perfect for large families; 10 cottages; 13 cabins; 5 Alpine houses; and 5 lower-cost units. There are stables on-site and hiking, biking, camping, and fishing right outside your door. Visit their Web site for all the possible options.

ESTES PARK CENTER/YMCA OF
THE ROCKIES $–$$$$
2515 Tunnel Road
(800) 777-9622
www.ymcarockies.org
There's something for almost everyone (except maybe honeymooners) at the Y. This enormous facility, just outside Estes Park, can accommodate 3,469 guests and runs numerous camps and programs. The Y is the place for families or other groups and it offers everything from rustic cabins that sleep four to 10 lodge rooms that sleep four to six. There's a miniature golf course, tennis courts, a livery, a craft shop, a library, a museum, a post office, and a theater. Concerts are given regularly. It's open year-round. Pets are allowed in the cabins but not in the rooms. Smoking is not allowed in any buildings. No credit cards.

FAWN VALLEY INN $$$$$
2760 Fall River Road
(970) 586-2388, (800) 525-2961
Only a half-mile from Rocky Mountain National Park, these year-round condominiums are set on more than eight acres along the Fall River. They feature complete kitchens and fireplaces, and there's a heated outdoor pool. Some suites have Jacuzzis. Smoking is not allowed.

HOLIDAY INN—ROCKY MOUNTAIN
NATIONAL PARK INN $$$
101 South Saint Vrain
(970) 586-2332, (800) 803-7837
www.foreverloding.com

Estes Park's only fully enclosed, full-service hotel with a large indoor heated pool, whirlpool, fitness room, and arcade. Full-service meals are provided by LongZ Mountain Grill. The Holiday Inn is located just 3 blocks from downtown Estes Park and the riverwalk, and adjacent to the Estes Park Conference Center. Like other Holiday Inns, kids age 12 and younger eat free here and there's no extra charge for kids age 19 and younger.

MISTY MOUNTAIN LODGE $$-$$$$
232 East Riverside Drive
(970) 586-4100
www.mistymountainlodge.com
This attractive and very reasonably priced lodge is a great value right in town. It's set against a hillside, away from the crowd across the river. There are multiroom suites, kitchens and fireplaces, a hot tub, and great off-season rates. Smoking is not allowed.

ROMANTIC RIVERSONG BED AND BREAKFAST INN $$$$$
Lower Broadview Road
(off Mary's Lake Road)
(970) 586-4666
www.romanticriversong.com
Reservations are a good idea at this lovely, secluded bed-and-breakfast set on 27 acres right along the Big Thompson River. Guests like it so much they return year after year, often booking a year in advance. For a stay during the high season, reservations need to be made about 15 weeks in advance. During the rest of the year it's not nearly as busy. Each of the rooms is custom-decorated either with lovely antiques or whimsical handmade furniture. One room has the beautiful 200-plus-year-old bed of the owner's grandmother; another has a delightful bed made of gracefully arching willow twigs complete with (decorative) nesting birds. There's a river stone–faced Jacuzzi in one room and fireplaces in most rooms. The list of amenities goes on and on at this lovely old home. Gourmet breakfast comes with the price of the room. This is a no-smoking inn.

THE STANLEY HOTEL AND CONFERENCE CENTER: A GRAND HERITAGE HOTEL $$$$$
333 Wonderview Avenue
(970) 586-3371, (800) 976-1377
www.stanleyhotel.com
The stately queen of the area's hotels, and listed on the National Register of Historic Places, the Stanley is truly a classic. The inspiration for Stephen King's book *The Shining*, the Stanley was also the scene for shooting the 1997 TV miniseries of the same name. King returned in 1996 as screenwriter and executive producer and stayed six months for the shooting. During the filming for the new version, the hotel lobby and MacGregor room were restored to a more authentic turn-of-the-20th-century look by the film directors and Grand Heritage (the company that owns the Stanley), going from white walls back to natural woods and patterned wallpapers.

The hotel was purchased by the Chesapeake Group. Grand Heritage, the previous owner, financed a $3.6-million restoration of the Stanley completed in spring of 1997, maintaining the hotel's turn-of-the-20th-century decor. Rooms have canopy beds, Victorian wallpaper, and other period details. Those feeling extravagant should ask for the Stephen King Suite. Though there are no skeletons in the closet, it's where the Emperor and Empress of Japan stayed during their visit a few years ago, and other VIPs have lodged there as well.

Historic tours of the hotel are offered year-round, five times a day (see the "Attractions" section of this chapter for more information). The Stanley also hosts free concerts every Sunday, "fairy tale weddings," dinner theater, holiday galas, Big Band dancing, the Colorado Music Festival during summer, and the famous "The Shining" Halloween Ball. Limited smoking is allowed at the Stanley.

STREAMSIDE ON FALL RIVER $$$-$$$$$
1260 Fall River Road
(970) 586-6464, (800) 321-3303
www.streamsideonfallriver.com
Describing itself as a "Village of Cabin Suites,"

these cabins are for those who want to "rough it" in luxury. They have skylights, fireplaces, wall-to-wall carpeting, private decks, gas grills, steam rooms, and jetted tubs. The cabins are on a wooded hillside on Fall River about a mile from Estes Park. The 16-acre site offers fishing and solitude. The cabins are listed among the 19 "Best of Estes," by an *Estes Park Trail Gazette* survey. Special packages are available. Smoking is not allowed.

SUNNYSIDE KNOLL RESORT   **$$$$$**
1675 Fall River Road
(970) 586-5759
www.sunnysideknoll.com
This is a resort for couples committed to romance. Each unit has a fireplace, cable television, and a VCR, and many have Jacuzzis for two situated with a fireplace view. There is also a heated outdoor pool and two outdoor hot tubs.

THE ARTS

Estes Park offers the full range of choices for those interested in high-quality art. Shops, galleries, and boutiques dot the main streets with a plethora of Native American art and representations of Rocky Mountain National Park in every medium. Besides the visual arts, the performing arts that may be enjoyed here include theater and classical, jazz, and contemporary music concerts. Larger performing-arts events and festivals generally take place during the summer.

Performing Arts
CHAMBER MUSIC SOCIETY OF ESTES PARK
(Cultural Arts Council)
(970) 586-9203
www.estesarts.com
This society of some 100 chamber-music-loving members sponsors concerts all year in the Estes

i   **Well before he became a famous author, a teenage Stephen King applied for a writing position at Boulder's** *Daily Camera* **newspaper. He was rejected.**

Park area, inviting different musicians from around the state and nation. The society also sponsors an annual Chamber Music Festival, held over a weekend in fall. Past festivals have featured the American Chamber Players and The Mendelssohn Trio. Information is available on concert locations, dates, and prices from the Cultural Arts Council at the number listed above.

THE ESTES PARK MUSIC FESTIVAL
(970) 586-9519
www.estesparkmusicfestival.org
Musicians from all over the state come together to play in concerts given by this group. Winter concerts are played at the Stanley Hotel, while summer events are held at different venues throughout town. Boulder's Colorado Music Festival chamber orchestra takes part in the concert series as well.

MUSIC IN THE MOUNTAINS
Rocky Ridge Music Center, Highway 7
12 miles south of Estes Park
(970) 586-4031
www.rockyridge.org
Rocky Ridge offers chamber music and opera. Student and faculty recitals take place here on Fridays and Sundays around 3 p.m. from late June until the end of August. Call for current ticket prices.

THE STANLEY HOTEL
333 Wonderview Avenue
(970) 586-3371, (800) 976-1377
www.stanleyhotel.com
For year-round entertainment check the Stanley Hotel, which presents theater and fine arts performances. In fact, the hotel claims to put on more performances than any other private property in the West. The Stanley also hosts free concerts on Sundays. There's a year-round jazz series and a Friday-night dance program. Call for the current schedule of events.

Visual Arts

ART CENTER OF ESTES PARK
517 Big Thompson Avenue
(970) 586-5882
www.artcenterofestes.com
Representing local and regional artists from the Rocky Mountain area, the Art Center exhibits sculpture, fiber arts, fine jewelry, photography, and more. Classes, art workshops, and education courses are offered as well. It is open daily from 11 a.m. to 4 p.m.

EAGLE PLUME GALLERY
9853 Highway 7, Allenspark
(303) 747-2861
www.eagleplume.com
The Eagle Plume Gallery and Museum of Native American Arts has been a local landmark since 1917 and is a favorite stop. Located 10 miles south of Estes Park on Highway 7, it has a huge collection of art and artifacts, including rugs, jewelry, pottery, baskets, and beautiful beadwork of the Plains Indians. Active in the Native American rights movement, founder Charles Eagle Plume graduated from the University of Colorado in 1932 and was later awarded an honorary Doctorate of Humanities from CU-Boulder.

EARTHWOOD ARTISANS/EARTHWOOD COLLECTIONS
141 East Elkhorn Avenue/
145 East Elkhorn Avenue
(970) 586-2151, (970) 577-8100
www.earthwoodartisans.com
These two galleries, located near each other in downtown Estes Park, represent more than 230 artists. They offer a large selection of photography, pottery, paintings, blown glass, fiber work, and much, much more. In 2003 they were named one of the top 100 galleries of American art and handcraft in the United States. They also have a gallery in Boulder.

GALLERIES OF ESTES PARK ASSOCIATION
www.estes-park.com/go/arts.html
The association publishes the *Estes Park Gallery Guide,* listing the town's shops and galleries. For information, write to the association; contact the Cultural Arts Council, P.O. Box 4135, 160 Moraine Avenue, Estes Park, CO 80517, (970) 586-9203; or visit their Web site.

THE GLASSWORKS STUDIO AND GALLERY
323 West Elkhorn Avenue
(970) 586-8619
www.garthsglassworks.com
This is the only hot-glass studio and gallery in the area. There are free public glass-blowing demonstrations daily, year-round, by owner Garth Mudge, who displays the delicate artwork.

ATTRACTIONS

All of these beautiful mountains could keep you happy for years. But even the most dedicated nature lover sometimes needs a change. There's a lot to see in Estes Park, since much of the early Colorado history was made here by settlers such as Alexander MacGregor and F. O. Stanley—not to mention 19th-century writer Isabella Bird and Enos Mills, the "Father of Rocky Mountain National Park."

Keep in mind, too, that Boulder County is just a stone's throw from the Estes Valley. Some Boulder County attractions are closer to Estes than they are to the city of Boulder. Even events smack on Boulder's Pearl Street Mall are less than an hour away, making them fair game for your fun. Also see the Festivals and Annual Events and Attractions chapters.

DICK'S ROCK MUSEUM
490 Moraine Route
(970) 586-4180
Dick's has been in the same location for more than 30 years, celebrating the varieties and uses of rock from the region. The free museum displays jewelry, fossils, crystals, slabs of rock waiting for shaping, and a 24-inch diamond saw hefty enough to do the job. There are pictures of a bunny, a kissing couple, and other images formed in the natural swirls of rock, a rock farm where everything is carved from rock, and rock "butterflies." Hours vary; call ahead.

ENOS MILLS CABIN
At the base of Twin Sisters Mountain
(970) 586-4706

The Enos Mills Cabin operates as a nature center and museum today, but it was the home of the well-known "Father of Rocky Mountain National Park." A naturalist, writer, and inn owner in Estes Park, Mills campaigned nationally for the establishment of the national parks in general and specifically for Rocky Mountain National Park. His cabin, built in 1885, is at the base of Twin Sisters Mountain and has several nature trails on the property. Tours of the house include a glimpse of Mills's books, photos, and the other memorabilia on display. Copies of his books are for sale. Open 11 a.m. to 4 p.m. Monday and Tuesday in the summer. Call for winter hours.

ESTES PARK BREWERY
470 Prospect Village Drive
(970) 586-5421
www.epbrewery.net

Open summers from 11 a.m. until midnight, with shorter hours off-season, the brewery offers a free video tour and samples of the nine microbrews it produces. A pub and a restaurant are on-site. See the "Nightlife" section of this chapter for details.

ESTES PARK CENTER/YMCA OF THE ROCKIES
2515 Tunnel Road
(970) 586-3341
www.ymcarockies.org

The YMCA of the Rockies is a huge facility with log cabins, lodges, and a leisurely pace that makes you automatically switch to strolling gear. It offers loads of family-oriented activities. During the winter, when the town is quieter, you can purchase a day pass to use the YMCA's facilities, which include an indoor gym, a roller rink, an indoor swimming pool, plus outdoor volleyball, basketball, and tennis courts. There's also a library and museum.

During the summer, more than 4,000 people stay at the YMCA of the Rockies. (If you'd like to be among them—or to stay during the winter— check the previous "Accommodations" section of this chapter.) Using the facilities in this busy season is limited to those staying as guests or those with proof of membership in a hometown YMCA. Once you've shown that proof, a number of programs are open for your enjoyment. In addition to winter offerings, there's an outdoor mini-golf course here. Complimentary family programs usually give you six options each day, ranging from survival classes and Indian lore to games of water balloon volleyball and campfire songs. For a fee, YMCA registered guests and hometown YMCA members can also enjoy Y-organized horseback riding, mountain bike rentals (including kids' sizes), and white-water rafting.

The Lulu W. Dorsey Museum (970-586-4331), on the YMCA grounds, explores the history of the facility, which has buildings dating from the early 1900s.

ESTES PARK HISTORY MUSEUM
200 Fourth Street
(970) 586-6256
www.estesnet.com/Museum

This interesting museum shows the history and heritage of the area's first settlers, including an 1859 photograph of just-arrived first settler Joel Estes and 6 of his 13 children. Look for the original National Park Headquarters building out back next to an old homestead cabin. The museum includes a Stanley Steamer, pioneer artifacts, historical photos, and documentation of the founding of Rocky Mountain National Park. In May through October, the museum is open from 10 a.m. to 5 p.m. Monday through Saturday, and from 1 to 5 p.m. Sunday. From November through April it's open Friday and Saturday 10 a.m. to 5 p.m. and Sunday 1 to 5 p.m. Admission is free but donations are appreciated.

ESTES PARK PUBLIC LIBRARY
335 East Elkhorn Avenue
(970) 586-8116
www.cat.estes.lib.co.us

Looking for Internet access? The library has it, plus CDs that can be checked out. This library is also kid-friendly. It loans toys in addition to books and has a parent-child center with educational activities that change monthly. The library is open 10 a.m. to 9 p.m. Monday through Thursday, 10 a.m. to 5 p.m. Friday and Saturday, and 1 to 5 p.m. Sunday.

MACGREGOR RANCH MUSEUM AND EDUCATION CENTER
180 MacGregor Lane, off Devil's Gulch Road
(970) 586-3749
www.macgregorranch.org
The MacGregor Ranch Museum and Education Center is a working ranch commemorating the Alexander Q. MacGregor family, one of the valley's largest and most influential ranching families. MacGregor battled the infamous Lord Dunraven over an illegal land claim at Estes Park. Dunraven had bought up all the land for his private hunting reserve. The museum displays domestic items, furniture, silver mining and ranching equipment, plus photos of life in the area in the 1870s through the mid-20th century. Historical photos and documents of MacGregor's battle with Dunraven also are on display. Admission is free, but donations are encouraged. Open Tuesday through Friday from June through August (closed weekends). The facility is open to school groups year-round. It's a half-mile north of Estes Park off Devil's Gulch Road.

THE STANLEY HOTEL
333 Wonderview Avenue
(970) 586-3371, (800) 976-1377
www.stanleyhotel.com
The inspiration for Stephen King's *The Shining* (see the "Hotels" section of this chapter), the Stanley continues to be a testament to a grand era. Ghosts aside, the Stanley stands on its own as a showstopper and has hosted the rich and famous since its construction in 1906 by F. O. Stanley, inventor of the Stanley Steamer automobile. Diagnosed with tuberculosis and given little time to live, Stanley came to Colorado for the curative value of the pure mountain air and lived another 30 years. During those years he built his classic hotel and helped promote the establishment of Rocky Mountain National Park.

Among the Stanley's treasures are a 1909 Steinway piano in the music room and a shiny, green Stanley Steamer with brass trim and wooden fenders in the hotel lobby. Stanley proclaimed it was an excellent mountain car because it didn't stall, and to prove his point he once drove the car up the steps of the U.S. Capitol.

Tourists are welcome to visit, and historic tours are offered year-round five times daily; participants are asked for a $5 donation. The tours go through all of the public rooms and down into the tunnel underneath the hotel, which is built on solid rock. Visitors will see fool's gold glittering in the rock that supports the original hotel beams. There's a small museum on the ground level. Many community events take place at the Stanley. You can also stay as a guest.

EDUCATION AND CHILD CARE

Preschools and Child Care Centers

During the winter, it's easier to find child care. But as summer brings wildflowers to the mountains, it brings visitors into Estes Park Valley. If you might need summer child care, even for a week or a few days, day-care centers recommend you start looking at least by midwinter.

To connect with child-related programs in the valley, visit the Estes Park Public Library, 335 East Elkhorn Avenue (970-586-8116). Parents can check out stuffed animals for their children there, and it also offers a list of babysitters who can come to your home or hotel room. Most are teenagers who have gone through a Red Cross Training Program for first aid and CPR. The library also sponsors summer reading programs for children. Call the Larimer Country Social Services Program in Estes Park (970-577-2150) to request a list of licensed day-care centers and homes, plus applications for reduced-fee services.

CIRCLE OF FRIENDS MONTESSORI PRESCHOOL
650 Community Drive
(970) 586-3341
www.cofmontessori.org
This school has 20 to 30 children, 20 of whom attend full time. There's a parent-toddler program offered in spring for children ages 18 months to 3 years. There is also a kindergarten program.

MOUNTAIN TOP PRESCHOOL & CHILD CARE
1250 Woodstock
(970) 586-6489
Full- and half-day care is provided with a preschool program. Drop-ins are available.

Private Schools

EAGLE ROCK SCHOOL AND PROFESSIONAL DEVELOPMENT CENTER
2750 Notaiah Road
(970) 586-0600
www.eaglerockschool.org
This is a year-round, tuition-free, ungraded residential high school. It has been developed and funded by the American Honda Corporation as a public service. A beautiful setting, excellent staff, and facilities for science, arts, and physical education are here. It focuses on young people who are not experiencing success in their current school settings and are willing to commit to growth and change. Individualized learning opportunities are offered to 100 students, who are accepted through a careful application process.

Public Schools

The Park School District R-3 (970-586-2361) includes almost 450 square miles and the towns of Estes Park, Allenspark, Glen Haven, Pinewood Springs, and the eastern slope of Rocky Mountain National Park. The district employs around 200 people, serving the more than 1,200 school-age children in the valley.

Though small, Park School District R-3 offers art, music, gifted and talented programs, special education, and reading and sports programs. Volunteers contribute nearly 150 hours each month.

The district runs an Aquatic Center, open to the community during nonschool periods. Computer and industrial technologies are part of many classrooms. Around 40 percent of teachers have master's degrees. The pupil/teacher ratio is 16.5 to 1. Nearly 95 percent of Park District children graduate from high school, and 80 percent of these go on to higher education.

For more information write or visit the following schools:

- Park School District R-3 (administrative office), 1501 Brodie Avenue, (970) 586-2361, www.estesschools.org
- Estes Park High School, 1600 Manford Avenue, (970) 586-5321
- Estes Park Middle School, 1500 Manford Avenue, (970) 586-4439
- Estes Park Intermediate School, 1505 Brodie Avenue, (970) 586-7406
- Estes Park Elementary School, 650 Community Drive, (970) 586-9529

FESTIVALS AND ANNUAL EVENTS

This is just a small sampling of the many Estes Park events held throughout the year. Contact the Estes Park Visitors Center for an up-to-date listing prior to visiting the area. (970) 577-9900, www.estesparkcvb.com.

January

FROST GIANT 5K OR 10K RACE
Municipal Building, 170 MacGregor Avenue
(970) 586-8191
www.estesnet.com
You might be a mild-mannered human, but you'll become an Estes Park frost giant if there's a little humidity and freezing weather, for your breath will add lacy frozen filigrees to your eyebrows and hair. If you join the 200 or so runners and walkers who participate, you'll puff up a scenic road to MacGregor Ranch and circle back for a total of either 5 or 10 kilometers (roughly 3 or 6 miles). The 5K race starts around 11 a.m.; the 10K starts at noon.

February

IMAGINE THIS!
Estes Park High School, 1600 Manford Avenue
(970) 586-9203
www.estesarts.com

The rest of this event's title is "See It! Hear It! Do It! Be It!" This is the single biggest arts event of the year, sponsored by the Cultural Arts Council of Estes Park, which represents all the arts in the area. Artists, musicians, jugglers, and actors give youngsters and adults a chance to create art at more than 26 hands-on activities areas. There's also a silent auction of original artwork, gift certificates, and merchandise. In the evening a benefit performance of dancers, musicians, and other artists from the Estes Valley keeps the entertainment going. Since the event is the main friend- and fund-raiser of the year for the nonprofit Arts Council, a donation of $1 is requested at the door.

March

DOG WEIGHT PULL
Estes Valley
(800) 44-ESTES

In Jack London's *Call of the Wild*, Buck pulls a 1,000-pound sled over a wager of gold. This isn't quite as dramatic, but it's more the real thing—a four-state, regional dog-pull contest held the last weekend in February. Dogs pull weighted sleds and wagons; winners are those who pull the most weight over the course in a minute. Dogs wear special harnesses to prevent injury, and weights are added incrementally. Small challengers have included a 10-pound poodle mix. A 200-pound Irish Wolfhound was among the largest. The little guy and the bruiser don't face off; they're in different classes and compete against dogs their own size.

WOMEN'S HISTORY MONTH
Various locations
(970) 586-9203
www.estesarts.com

The Cultural Arts Council of Estes Park celebrates female artists and performers with a series of exhibits and programs that run into April. Call for a schedule.

April

ESTES PARK MUSIC FESTIVAL WINTER CONCERTS
Stanley Concert Hall, Stanley Hotel
333 Wonderview Avenue
(970) 577-9900
www.estesparkcvb.com/calendar

These wonderful weekend concerts feature a variety of internationally known musicians. Call or visit the visitor bureau Web site for the exact date.

May

DUCK RACE
Downtown Estes Park
(970) 586-9519
www.rotaryclubofestespark.org

On the first Saturday in May, thousands of floating yellow plastic ducks, each tagged with a sponsor and charity choice, raise more than $20,000 at this annual event. To help you remember the date, the Rotary Club sponsors it on Kentucky Derby Day. But ducks aren't as quick as a thoroughbred. They start at Nicky's Restaurant, 1350 Fall River Road, and depending on the runoff, bobble downtown on the Fall, then, nearly two hours later, reach the Wheel Bar, 132 East Elkhorn Avenue. The mayor and police chief pull out the winning duck and distribute great prizes, such as trips to Disneyland and Hawaii. Sponsoring a duck costs around $20. Watching is free. Proceeds go to local charities.

ART WALK AND JAZZ FESTIVAL
Downtown Estes Park
(970) 577-9900
www.estesarts.com

More than 20 galleries feature special exhibits and artists' demonstrations as part of the Art Walk, a self-guided studio and gallery tour held Friday through Sunday. Children's art activities are offered, and live jazz concerts put an extra spring in the step of revelers in downtown Estes Park. This festival usually happens the second weekend in May.

ART MARKET
Downtown Estes Park
(970) 586-5882
www.artcenterofestes.com

More than 90 local, regional and national artists gather to showcase their art in this fun weekend event.

June

LAKE ESTES FISHING DERBY
Lake Estes Marina, U.S. Highway 36
near Lake Estes
(970) 586-8191

Every three weeks during summer, the Division of Wildlife drops 400 fish at many points along the Estes Valley river system, making trout plentiful. They double-stock the rivers and lake for this event, and the town buys some extra-big fish to tempt anglers. What's more, the Cline Trout Farm in Boulder donates some fish for the weekend (the first one in June). All this means contestants in the 8 a.m. to noon fishing derby are likely to pull in fine catches.

WOOL MARKET
Stanley Park Fairgrounds, Community Drive
(970) 577-9900

Tourists are welcome to enjoy this working wool market, the largest natural fiber show in the country. Around 10,000 wander among the market's animal shows. Events start the Thursday prior to the second weekend in June, with workshops and seminars on spinning, weaving, dyeing, raising animals, shearing, and grading wool. Throughout the weekend, you can enjoy spinning and weaving contests and a children's tent. See llamas, angora rabbits, alpacas, and sheep, or consider buying one of the beautiful sweaters, yarns, or other wool-related items. Admission is free.

TEDDY BEAR PICNIC
521 Lone Pine Drive
(970) 586-6483

The Talking Teddy Store has sponsored this picnic since 1983. Cute silly events may include a dentist who talks to children about care of their bear's teeth (and children's teeth). Cele-bear-ties, such as Smokey Bear and Celestial Seasoning's Sleepytime Bear, have appeared. There are prizes for the largest bear family, biggest bear, and cutest bear costume. Sandwiches, cake, and beverages might be on hand for nibbling. The picnic starts mid-morning and lasts until the teddies get tired. Admission is free.

SCANDINAVIAN MIDSUMMER FESTIVAL
Bond Park, Downtown Estes Park
(970) 586-6073
www.estesmidsummer.com

The local Scandinavian Club's festival includes traditional celebrations for the year's longest day in late June. On Friday, they erect a maypole (may is a Swedish word for dressing in green), and onlookers decorate it with greens and live flowers. Norwegians, Danes, and Finns used to start a bonfire in a Viking longboat to scare away the evil spirits on this long, long day. The Scandinavian Club hasn't found any people in Estes willing to burn up boats. So enterprising club members hammer one together and launch it near the Lake Estes Marina. The fire reflects on the water, reminding celebrants of Norwegian fiords brooding under tall mountains. Revelers then dance into the evening. All weekend, professional dancers in bright-colored folk costumes invite onlookers to learn new steps. You also can attend workshops, where sages share Scandinavian history. Food booths offer Swedish pancakes with bright red lingonberries. Or nibble potatas korv—a beef, pork and potato sausage. Crafts for sale include wheat-weaving items, painted-wood folk paintings, and rosemaling items, which are painted with traditional flower designs. Admission is free.

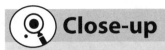 **Close-up**

Insider Secret: Estes Park Is Best in the Fall

The elk rut, the golden aspen leaves that rustle in gentle breezes, and the warm temperatures that signify "Indian Summer" are only part of the reason Coloradoans find autumn the perfect time to visit Estes Park. While most other communities pack away special events when children head to school, Estes Park entertains thousands. As a matter of fact, there's a special event every weekend from mid-August through October's Columbus Day weekend.

An Auto Extravaganza of collectible cars occurs the third weekend in August. Model Ts, lots of hot rods from the '60s, whatever the theme, this is a chance to see vintage vehicles up close. A Heritage Festival with storytelling, mountain men, thespians, and a nighttime street dance is also held that weekend in August. Labor Day weekend brings alpacas to the fairgrounds and a three-day crafts fair to the downtown area.

One of Colorado's most spectacular events happens the weekend after Labor Day. Imagine the haunting yet exhilarating sound of bagpipes, the resonance of brogues, plenty of malt beverages, and the rhythmic beat of Scottish footsteps on a dance floor converging for the Longs Peak Scottish Irish Highland Festival. About 60,000 attend the activities that include a parade down Elkhorn Avenue (Estes Park's main street), athletic competitions, international jousting, and concerts.

During the third weekend in September five annual events occur. Handcrafted work is on display in a juried fine arts show and sale. A chamber music concert always coincides with the fine arts show. Indie documentary and feature films are shown at the Film Festival. In addition, there's a 4.5-mile race sponsored by Boulder Bolder and a team penning competition at the fairgrounds.

Autumn Gold: A Festival of Brats, Bands & Beer showcases professional area musical talent on the last weekend in August. And don't miss the weekend closest to October 1, when elk in Estes Park are regaled, imitated, watched, and otherwise celebrated during the annual two-day Elk Fest, an event highlighting these magnificent animals.

Columbus Day weekend ends the eight-weeklong special activity period (although another of Estes Park's most prominent events is held the weekend after Thanksgiving). Retailers officially end their summer season with this "sale" event to make way for new merchandise.

So, head up to Estes Park this fall. To learn more about the festivals and Rocky Mountain National Park activities, call the Estes Park Convention & Visitors Bureau at (970) 577-9900 or toll-free at (800) 44-ESTES or log onto www.EstesParkCVB.com.

July

ESTES PARK FIREWORKS DISPLAY
Lake Estes
(970) 586-6104
www.estesparkresort.com

Locals arrive around 8 p.m. on the Fourth of July, generally gathering in the Stanley Village Shopping Center or near Lake Estes. Outdoor bands entertain the crowds. Around 9:30 p.m., the fireworks shoot up at the edge of the lake, so the reflections bloom in the water below. If you position yourself well, you get to see all this drama with the mountains as a backdrop. The event is free.

ROOFTOP RODEO
Estes Park Fairground, Community Drive
(970) 586-6104
www.estesparkresort.com

The rodeo started in 1923 as the Estes Park Stampede, stopped during WWII, but revived right afterward and has been galloping ever since, hanging onto its designation as one of the country's oldest rodeos. A parade through downtown starts it off. Team roping, bulldogging, broncos, barrel racing, and steer wrestling are part of the week's events, which are sanctioned by the Professional Rodeo Cowboys Association. A carnival offers plenty of rides. Cowboy poets read on a stage with a campfire scene. Sometimes, the poet brings his harmonica or strums a guitar.

Prices vary depending on who's in the main corral. By the way, it's not called "Rooftop Rodeo" because you have to watch from a roof. The name is to remind people of the 7,200-foot elevation and the United States' highest paved highway, Trail Ridge Road.

August
COWBOY SING-ALONGS
Downtown Estes Park
(970) 586-4431, (800) 44-ESTES
www.estesparkcvb.com/calendar
This fun chance to yodel your love for the sagebrush is held Thursdays, Fridays, Saturdays, and Sundays from mid-June through mid-August at 7 p.m. in Bond Park.

MUSIC IN THE MOUNTAINS
Rocky Ridge Music Center, Highway 7
12 miles south of Estes Park
(970) 586-4031
www.rockyridge.org
The center focuses on both chamber music and opera. Student and faculty recitals take place here on Sundays around 3 p.m. from late June until the end of August. Call for current ticket prices.

September
FINE ARTS AND CRAFTS FESTIVAL
Bond Park
(970) 586-9203
www.fineartsguild.org
Artists and craftspeople from all over the state set up about 95 booths that sell and display pottery, bronze and wood sculpture, folk art, needlework, jewelry, photography, and oil paintings. The local volunteer fire department puts on this event, and

it benefits the Muscular Dystrophy Association and the fire department.

LONGS PEAK SCOTTISH-IRISH HIGHLAND FESTIVAL
Estes Park Fairground, Community Drive
(970) 586-6308, (800) 443-7837
www.scotfest.com
This four-day festival in early September, which will celebrate its 33rd anniversary in 2009, is a 10-ring circus. It's so grand, *USA Today* has listed it as one of the nation's top 10 things to do. At least two and sometimes three top ceremonial bands come to play in the tattoo concerts, which include drums, bugles, and bagpipes. The festival hosts world champion pipe bands, including Simon Fraser University of Canada, Field Marshall Montgomery of Ireland, Victoria Police of Australia, and City of Victoria of Canada. The White House Drum and Bugle Corps has performed here, as have the Governor General's Foot Guard from Canada, and the Royal Highlands Scot Guards. Celtic folk musicians arrive for competitions. Irish step-dancers display their dazzling footwork. Evening concerts thrill Celtic hearts all over town.

i In the fall one of the area's top evening attractions is the eerie but beautiful mating call of the elk. (The elk bugle at dawn and dusk.) To discourage individual drivers and traffic jams at Horseshoe Park and other popular listening spots, Rocky Mountain National Park offers bus trips for the public to listen to these impressive animals bugle. Call the Estes Park Chamber of Commerce (800-443-7837) or park headquarters (970-586-1206).

Music isn't the only drawing card at this festival. There's jousting, dancing, a dog show, whiskey tasting, and seminars on topics Scottish. Highland games include tossing a stone the size of a shot put, throwing a caber, which is a large log roughly shaped like a telephone pole, and other heavy athletics. Highlanders demonstrate how to shoot antique cannon, and how to fly-fish with lures. Dr. James Durward, founder of this festival, points out that lure fishing had to start in Scotland. After all, a thrifty Scot isn't going to dig up a new worm every time he casts his line!

Altogether, about 3,000 performers participate in this event, and approximately 70,000 people come to see it. Those who like to shop can buy quilts, sweaters, and other crafts related to these island peoples. Hungry revelers can buy scones, which are slightly sweet biscuits; Scotch eggs, hard-boiled then rolled in bacon crumbs; sausages; hot dogs; and pastie, sort of a non-flaking turnover with hamburger inside. Don't forget the shortbread. When you're full, you can quaff it down with Scotch or Irish libations. There's plenty of soda on hand for the lads and lassies.

Ticket prices are $20 in advance. All the money earned by the festival goes back into the festival and other local nonprofits. Tickets may be purchased online at www.scotfest.com.

FINE ARTS AND CRAFTS SHOW
Bond Park, Estes Park
(970) 586-9203
www.estesarts.com
Sponsored by the Fine Arts Guild of the Rockies, this mid-September event is a juried, national art show. More than 80 booths display everything from pottery and small items to paintings and photography. Estes Park is working to become more of an arts community by bringing in national traveling art shows. This show has been an annual event for more than 20 years and is a pleasant way to pass the afternoon.

October
STANLEY GHOST STORIES
Stanley Museum
517 Big Thompson Ave.
(970) 577-1903
www.stanleyhotel.com
Stephen King wrote his horror classic *The Shining* after being inspired by a stay at the Stanley Hotel. Once you see what a lovely, elegant place the Stanley is, you'll be even more impressed by how creepily King remade it in his pull-up-the-covers-and-keep-the-lights-on story. Ghost stories from the hotel abound and these will get you in the spirit for Halloween! Call for days and times. Adults get in for $5 and children are $2.

Throughout the Fall
BULL ELK BUGLING
Rocky Mountain National Park
(970) 586-1206
Anyone who expects the bull elk's mating call to sound like a royal French horn is in for a surprise. These huge animals belt out a whistling squeal. It might strike you as wimpy, but boy, does it ever carry! The haunting call can travel across valleys and reach high mountain meadows. Forest rangers say the best time to witness (and hear) elk bugling is throughout the fall in the morning, from sunrise to an hour after, and then at dusk, starting about an hour before sunset. Three areas tend to provide good viewing: Moraine Park, Horseshoe Park, and Upper Beaver Meadows. To view wildlife, don't leave the designated trails and roadways. While bull elks rarely charge tourists, there are incidents of rangers charging visitors . . . and the fine they charge for harassing wildlife can be stiff. The Bighorn Brigade will be around to answer questions and remind you to stay out of the meadows. If you prefer smaller crowds, come on a weekday. You can also find seminars on helpful subjects like photography. Call for a schedule.

QUAKING ASPEN
Rocky Mountain National Park
(970) 586-1206
Mother Nature gives us hot, dry years when the leaves turn gold early, and she also bestows cool, moist summers when the green leaves never quite believe it's time to change. Because the golden aspen season varies, call the park's information office to learn the best time (generally mid-September through mid-October) and viewing places, which tend to be around Bear Lake Road and Moraine Park. Park officials say aspen stands outside the park can be even more spectacular. The highway to Allenspark is designated

a scenic byway, with huge aspen stands. Highways 119 and 72, heading south to Nederland and Central City, are good, too. Wherever you drive, find a chance to step out on a trail and walk. Get the aspens between you and the sunlight to take in their luminescence and brilliant color. Listen to the fluttering leaves. Smell the tannin. While strolling, you may notice elk coming down from the high country to beat the winter snows. Rangers request that you don't pick any aspen leaves, since our thin mountain soil needs their nutrients. To preserve the park's beauty for the future, remember to leave with only your memories and photographs.

November

CHRISTMAS PARADE
Estes Park Fairground, Community Drive
Estes Park
(970) 586-4431, (800) 44-ESTES
www.estesparkresort.com
When the downtown Christmas lights come on, the parade begins. It starts around 5:30 p.m. the Friday after Thanksgiving, heads through the main shopping district, and ends at the Chamber of Commerce around 7 p.m. Santa's sleigh is always the last float in line. Onlookers dress in winter woolens, parkas, and blankets. On a mild evening, a jacket will do. If it's cold, some people wear everything they've got. No matter what the thermometer says, the sight is heartwarming—and free. Stores downtown stay open to sell Christmas goods and warm refreshments.

December

CHRISTMAS HOLIDAY CONCERT
Hempel Auditorium, YMCA of the Rockies
(970) 577-9900
This holiday concert typically features the Estes Park Chorale, the Mountain Men and Estes Park MountainAires.

HOLIDAY HOME TOUR THROUGHOUT ESTES PARK VALLEY
(970) 586-5800
www.estesparkcvb.com
Proud owners of fine Estes Park homes decorate for Christmas, then open their doors on a Saturday in mid-December, so you can wander inside. Usually the tour is from 11 a.m. to 4 p.m.

ORATORIO SOCIETY CONCERT
Mountain View Bible Fellowship
1575 S. St. Vrain
(970) 586-9405
The Oratorio Society and Estes Park Chamber Orchestra perform at this concert which usually starts around 3 p.m. on a Sunday in mid-December.

Events Central

Here are the phone numbers and locations of the main event centers in town.

CULTURAL ARTS COUNCIL (CAC)
160 Moraine Avenue
(970) 586-9203
www.estesarts.com
The CAC represents all the arts in the area with the broad goal of enhancing the quality and accessibility of the arts in the Estes Valley. Call or write to these folks for music, art, or theater events and programs.

ESTES PARK VISITOR INFORMATION CENTER
500 Big Thompson Avenue
(970) 586-4431, (800) 44-ESTES
www.estesparkcvb.com
Stop here for local information. To reach the center when coming from Boulder on US 36, go to the second stoplight and make a right. The center is right across from the Taco Bell on U.S. Highway 34. Hours from mid-May to early October are 9 a.m. to 8 p.m. daily. Hours from early October to mid-May are 9 a.m. to 5 p.m. Monday through Saturday; 10 a.m. to 4 p.m. Sunday.

ESTES PARK CENTER/YMCA OF THE ROCKIES
2515 Tunnel Road
(970) 586-3341
www.ymcarockies.org

To reach the YMCA from Boulder, take US 36 to the second stoplight. Take a left at Elkhorn Avenue. At the second stoplight, turn left onto Moraine Avenue. Follow the signs to the YMCA. The tree-lined road winds through a lot of country-side, but you'll soon be there.

Even if you're not staying at the YMCA, it can be a good place to call. They don't publicize their events very much, because they've got a built-in audience. But they often welcome nonguests. For instance, the public is welcome to attend the Christian Artists Music Seminar Concerts held from June through August and featuring all types of music.

STANLEY ESTES PARK FAIRGROUND
Community Drive
(970) 586-6104
The fairground is off US 36 near Lake Estes. To get there, you take either US 34 or 36 to the east side of town. Right after you pass Lake Estes, turn south onto Community Drive. You'll see arenas, the stables, the covered building for special events, and the ballfields. Numerous events take place here.

THE STANLEY HOTEL
333 Wonderview Avenue
(970) 586-3371, (800) 976-1377
www.stanleyhotel.com
Once you're in downtown, you'll see the big white Stanley Hotel on a hill northeast of town. The Stanley Concert Hall is up there too. You can't miss it; but if you do, just pull over anywhere and ask for directions. Everybody knows the Stanley. Call to check on the schedule of events.

MEDICAL CARE AND DENTAL CARE

ESTES PARK DENTAL
343 South St. Vrain Avenue
(970) 586-9330
www.estesparkdental.com
If you need treatment for a toothache, this is the place to call. Other possibilities appear in the Yellow Pages under "Dentists."

ESTES PARK MEDICAL CENTER
555 Prospect Avenue
(970) 586-2317
www.epmedcenter.com
This medical center is a 15-bed critical access acute care facility with 24-hour emergency care and medical/surgical services. Emergency helicopter service can transport patients to specialized hospitals. Also see the chapter on Health Care and Wellness.

TIMBERLINE MEDICAL
131 Stanley Avenue, Suite 202
(970) 586-2343
www.timberlinemedical.com
This family practice also operates an urgent care center for treatment of injuries and illnesses that require immediate care but don't call for hospitalization. It is open 8 a.m. to 5 p.m. weekdays, 9 a.m. to 1 p.m. Saturday. The center is closed on Sunday and holidays.

NIGHTLIFE

Estes Park isn't big on nightlife, but there are a few choices for not-too-weary travelers or residents.

ESTES PARK BREWERY
470 Prospect Village Drive
(970) 586-5421
www.epbrewery.net
The brewery has a pub, family restaurant, and outdoor deck, and serves pizza, sandwiches, burgers, and salads. During summer it's open from 11 a.m. to midnight daily. (Check for winter hours, which may vary.) There are free samples of the nine microbrews sold on tap and by the bottle. The Renegade Red has won a gold medal at the Great American Beer Festival.

LONIGAN'S SALOON NIGHTCLUB & GRILL
110 W. Elkhorn Ave.
(970) 586-4346
www.lonigans.com
This is the spot where the locals hang out so you know it's good. Built in 1907, this Irish pub is located in the heart of downtown Estes Park. It's

a great place for drinks as well as good food. It's open at 11 a.m. for lunch and the fun continues until 2 a.m.

THE OLD GASLIGHT PUB
246 Moraine Avenue
(970) 586-0994
DJs provide the varied mix of music on weekends, and there's plenty of room for dancing. Dinner specials include fish and chips, Italian dishes, and other favorites. The bar has some British beers on tap and local microbrews.

PARK THEATRE
130 Moraine Ave.
(970) 586-8904
www.historicparktheatre.com
Enjoy first-run movies every night from May through September at this historic theater which has just started an annual film festival.

PARK VILLAGE PLAYHOUSE
900 Moraine Avenue
(970) 586-2885
Visit this playhouse to enjoy good, old-fashioned melodrama. The curtain goes up at 8 p.m., doors open at 7 p.m.; reservations are suggested. Other concerts and shows are held here as well.

THE STANLEY HOTEL
333 Wonderview Avenue
(970) 586-3371, (800) 976-1377
www.stanleyhotel.com
The Stanley presents theater and fine arts performances that vary with the season and include free concerts and holiday events. Call for the current schedule of events and ask about special honeymoon and "romance" packages.

WHEEL BAR
132 East Elkhorn Avenue
(970) 586-9381
www.thewheelbar.com
This local landmark has been owned and operated by the same family since 1945. The comfortable neighborhood bar offers bottled beers,

microbrews on tap, and cocktails at happy-hour prices. Upstairs there's Orlando's Steak House for a full meal.

PET CARE

ESTES PARK PET LODGE
1260 Manford Avenue
(970) 586-6898
www.estesparkpetlodge.com
Don't leave your furry friend in the hot car (a no-no with Colorado's intense sun). Instead check out the Pet Lodge, where they'll receive some TLC while you play in Estes Park. Doggie day care and pet boarding is available at this facility seven days a week. They also offer 24-hour veterinary care.

REAL ESTATE

Estes Park is becoming a more year-round community. While it has always drawn retirees, lately there's a new demographic in town—computer commuters. As the Front Range booms, industries needing highly skilled workers move closer to Estes Park, increasing its draw as a bedroom community to Boulder. All this means Estes Park is getting younger, drawing families and a wider range of business skills.

In the good old days, you could find a rental when everyone left for the summer, but people aren't leaving so often anymore. For a summer rental, start checking six months in advance. For a long-term rental, get your name in six months early, then check monthly. Homes to purchase are more available than homes for rent. The average price of a home in 2007 was $285,591. The pop of air-gun hammers is more common around town these days and condominiums are springing up all around Estes Park. Though the valley is still a long way from reaching what is said to be its capacity, builders are booked a year in advance. Investors are holding their income properties, and just a few time-share opportunities are available. All of this information is not meant to discourage you, but rather remind you to start looking.

RESTAURANTS

Estes Park has a large number of restaurants and casual cafes to choose from, ranging from doughnut shops and pizzerias to fine French restaurants and gourmet Italian inns. Italian and Mexican food seem to predominate, but steaks, burgers, and trout are ubiquitous as well. Watch out for "Rocky Mountain Oysters." They're not seafood; in fact they come from a part of the bull that you might not want to consume. Fans say they taste a little like liver.

Even if you can't afford a meal at the historic Stanley Hotel, it's worth a visit for its landmark status, lovely setting, and the shiny green Stanley Steamer automobile parked in the lobby. Those on a budget can still enjoy coffee or afternoon tea at the Stanley on the front veranda or a snack from the bar menu.

Reservations are not required at most Estes Park restaurants but are accepted and recommended at some of the more popular spots, particularly for groups during the crowded summer season. Almost all restaurants of any size beyond a hole in the wall accept major credit cards.

Price-Code Key

The key below shows the price range for an average dinner for two excluding beverages, appetizers, desserts, or tip.

$ . . . . less than $25
$$ . . . . $26 to $50
$$$ . . . . $51 to $75
$$$$$ . . . . $76 and more

THE BALDPATE INN $-$$
4900 Highway 7 South, south of Estes Park
(970) 586-6151
www.baldpateinn.com
You'll get a lot more than lunch or dinner if you visit the Baldpate Inn. This classic mountain inn and historic local landmark was placed on the National Register of Historic Places in 1996. The inn, which is open Memorial Day until mid to late October, is 7 miles south of Estes Park at 9,000 feet altitude, across from the Rocky Mountain

National Park Visitor Center at Lily Lake. At lunch there's a unique salad bar set in an old claw-foot bathtub, plus delectable homemade soups, breads, and pastries. Dinner is equally charming and delicious; reservations are a must. Mae West, Jack Dempsey, and Rin Tin Tin stayed here, and you'll see their photos—along with those of opera singer Tetrazinni and world leaders—in the amazing collection in the dining room assembled by the two original owners. The inn has the world's largest key collection, which is open to the public. It serves lunch and dinner daily.

DONUT HAUS $
342 Moraine Avenue
(970) 586-2988
If it's just a doughnut you're craving, line up at the Donut Haus—there usually is a queue stretching out the door of this tiny doughnut bakery, which also has a large variety of other fresh-baked items. It's right beside the multicolored giant slides. It's closed on Wednesdays.

DUNRAVEN INN $-$$
2470 Highway 66
(970) 586-6409
www.dunraveninn.com
Probably not quite what Lord Dunraven had in mind, the Dunraven Inn calls itself the "Rome of the Rockies" and specializes in Italian food. (Lord Dunraven was the Irish nobleman who bought all of Estes Park in the 19th century to create his own private hunting reserve but was eventually ousted by locals.) The Dunraven Inn has long been a favorite stop for steak and Italian dishes, including shrimp scampi, lasagna, eggplant Parmesan, and chicken cacciatore, plus a large selection of Italian wines. Be sure to make reservations during the summer months, when the restaurant is packed. Dinner is served daily.

ED'S CANTINA AND GRILL $
362 East Elkhorn Avenue
(970) 586-2919
www.edscantina.com
In addition to all the Mexican favorites, plus

barbecued ribs and sandwiches for lunch and dinner, this comfortable South-of-the-Border spot serves the local microbrew from Estes Park Brewery. Ed's is open 7 a.m. to 10 p.m. seven days a week.

GRUBSTEAK RESTAURANT $
134 West Elkhorn Avenue
(970) 586-8838
This place has something for everyone, from beef and wild-game burgers to steaks to pastas and fish. Or maybe you're in the mood for a salad or sandwich? It's a great place to get takeout lunches for your hike, and they also offer a good breakfast during the summer months.

LA CHAUMIERE $$–$$$
US 36, Pinewood Springs
(303) 823-6521
www.lachaumiere-restaurant.com
Those with sophisticated palates who savor sautéed sweetbreads say La Chaumiere offers the best around. Another popular item is the duck liver paté. Classic French dining in a serene setting, complete with its own deer park, has drawn its faithful patrons to La Chaumiere for years. Though it's a bit out of the way (12 miles southeast of Estes Park), French food lovers don't mind the extra drive for the diverse, changing menu, including specialty game meats, lamb, beef, and seafood. The restaurant has its own smokehouse and organic garden and makes its own ice cream.

LAZY B RANCH CHUCK WAGON $–$$
1915 Dry Gulch Road
(970) 586-5371
For a family night out and a taste of the Old West, sidle up to the chuckwagon where wranglers are dishing out barbecued beef, baked potatoes, beans, and biscuits with coffee or lemonade (no alcohol allowed on the trail, partner). After dinner, there's a live stage show with Western music, stories, and jokes. Souvenir and gift shops are open before dinner and after the show. The Lazy B is open summers only; the schedule varies, so be sure to call ahead.

LOCAL'S GRILL $–$$
153 E. Elkhorn Avenue
(970) 586-6900
www.localsgrillestespark.com
Located in the heart of downtown Estes Park, this is a great family place with reasonably priced meals. The menu has just about everything from soups to burgers to steak and fish.

MAMA ROSE'S $
Barlow Plaza, 338 East Elkhorn Avenue
(970) 586-3330
www.mamarosesrestaurant.com
This tidy Italian restaurant in a pretty reproduction of an old Victorian home has a large selection of dishes. It offers a very pleasant veranda overlooking the river for dining. Choose from chicken Parmesan in wine sauce, seafood fettuccine, fresh basil pesto, baked pasta, and other Italian dishes.

THE MOUNTAINEER $
540 South St. Vrain Road
(970) 586-9001
Fast and friendly service is the hallmark of this unpretentious little cafe, with lots of granny-type knickknacks and corny paintings on the wall. But it's quite cozy and out of the hustle-bustle of downtown Estes Park. It's about a half-mile south on Highway 7, across the street from the Diamond Shamrock gas station and Estes Park Rehabilitation Center. Open daily for an early breakfast (at 6 a.m.), the restaurant features lots of morning food choices, including homemade biscuits and gravy and cinnamon rolls, and is quite inexpensive. Local climbers and mountaineers (and tourists) like to stop here for a tasty and inexpensive breakfast, lunch, or dinner.

MOUNTAIN HOME CAFE $
Stanley Village, intersection of
US 34 and US 36
(970) 586-6624
www.mountainhomecafe.com
Formerly known as Johnson's and right in the shopping center, this little cafe isn't glamorous.

But the food is quite good, especially the Swedish potato pancakes with sour cream and applesauce and the baked Alaska oatmeal. It's a favorite of area residents for the breakfasts served all day. You can also get lunch here Monday through Saturday, and the cafe is open Sunday for breakfast from 8 a.m. until 1 p.m. (closed afterward). Dinners are now served on Friday and Saturday nights during the summer.

NICKY'S STEAKHOUSE $$–$$$
1350 Fall River Road
(970) 586-5376
www.nickysestespark.com
Serving Estes Park for 36 years, Nicky's claim to fame is the delicious prime rib roasted in rock salt. Out a few miles on Fall River Road (a pleasant drive), this large, attractive restaurant has a huge menu with lots of variety, including Italian and Greek specialties, steaks, and a salad bar. It's open year-round, for breakfast, lunch, and dinner daily from June to September, and for lunch and dinner, with breakfasts on weekends only, the rest of the year.

NOTCHTOP BAKED GOODS AND NATURAL FOODS CAFE AND PUB $
Upper Stanley Village, intersection of US 34 and US 36
(970) 586-9272
This local favorite has a pub with its own microbrew—Notchtop, of course. Stop here for delicious pastries or an inexpensive lunch. Very casual, with newspapers and magazines to read (such as *Mother Earth News*), the little cafe is a nice break from the tourist scene and serves nutritious food and natural beverages, plus great locally roasted Silver Canyon coffees. The cafe is open daily from breakfast through dinner.

THE OTHER SIDE $$
900 Moraine Avenue
(970) 586-2171
www.theothersideofestes.com
Specializing in an "all-American" menu, this restaurant at the entrance to Rocky Mountain National Park at Mary's Lake Road has a pleasant view of a little duck pond. The menu offers seafood, steaks, prime rib, burgers, and a Sunday champagne brunch. Lunch and dinner are served daily, while breakfast is served Friday through Monday.

POPPY'S PIZZA AND GRILL $
342 East Elkhorn Avenue
(970) 586-8282
www.poppyspizzaandgrill.com
In the spiffy Barlow Plaza, this pleasant pizzeria has all types of pizza—pesto, Polynesian, Mexican, to name a few—for reasonable prices. There are also homemade soups, salads, desserts, and sandwiches. When the weather cooperates, you can sit outside on the nice patio overlooking the river. Poppy's is open for lunch and dinner year-round but closes for a time during January.

SAFEWAY $
Stanley Village, north of the intersection of US 34 and US 36, Estes Park
(970) 586-4447
For picnic or camping supplies on the way to Rocky Mountain National Park, look for the big Safeway supermarket up on the hill above the downtown area. There's also a salad bar and deli in the store.

THE STANLEY HOTEL $$–$$$
333 Wonderview Avenue
(970) 586-3371, (800) 976-1377
www.stanleyhotel.com
For a special treat, try the Stanley's Sunday champagne brunch, served year-round from 10 a.m. to 2 p.m. in the hotel's MacGregor ballroom. Unlimited champagne or mimosas accompany an unbelievable spread—every pastry you can imagine, and every breakfast dish, plus seafood, prime rib, and much, much, more. An eclectic mix of live music adds to the atmosphere (get dressed up if you want to, but casual is fine, too). For those with time and a hearty appetite, it's a real bargain for the $21.95-per-person price. Dinners at the Stanley are served in the Dunraven Grille. Choices include teriyaki ahi, chorizo-

smoked chile rellenos, prime rib, and elk with such side dishes as ahi or duck salad and spicy red bean or beer-cheese soup. The Stanley serves breakfast, lunch, and dinner daily year-round. The Dunraven Grille also offers a bar menu from 11:30 a.m. until 3 p.m. Monday through Saturday. During summer there's usually a long waiting list for tables on the hotel's lovely front veranda, which has a spectacular mountain view, and where breakfast, lunch, and dinner are also served.

WILD ROSE FOOD AND SPIRIT CO. $$
157 West Elkhorn Avenue
(970) 586-2806
www.wildroserestaurant.com

With a nice variety of items from delicious sandwiches to steaks and seafood, this is a great place for lunch or dinner. They have a good selection of wines as well. A children's menu is available, and don't leave without sampling the Wild Rose peach cobbler. Lunch is served 11 a.m. to 5 p.m. Dinner begins at 5 p.m. Online reservations are available.

RETIREMENT

Some locals estimate that more than half the full-time residents of Estes Valley are retired. That doesn't mean nonworking or seniors—many people have jobs because they enjoy keeping busy, and many others have taken early retirement from big companies. Whatever age they are and whatever "work" residents do, it's true that many people look all over the nation then choose to retire in Estes Valley. If you're among them, visit the Estes Park Senior Center.

A note regarding transportation: One local senior warns that you shouldn't come up here without your own, since there is no public bus system.

ESTES PARK SENIOR CENTER
220 Fourth Street
(970) 586-2996
www.estesnet.com/SeniorCenter

The center is open from 9 a.m. to 4 p.m. Monday through Friday. The Senior Center serves meals five days a week. About 25 meals a day are transported to seniors' homes. There's a blood-pressure clinic once a month. Exercise classes happen three times a week. The senior center is also a good place to connect with town activities, including book groups, lectures, art classes, and pinochle and bridge clubs. It hosts card games twice a week and a weekly oil-painting class.

SHOPPING

Estes Park's shopping area is an attractive but bewildering stretch of gingerbread glitz with a theme and style somewhere between Switzerland and Coney Island. Saltwater taffy in the Rocky Mountains? Unfortunately, some of the clothing, jewelry, knickknacks, "art," and other items found in the shops have nothing to do with Estes Park, Colorado, or the Rocky Mountains. Other offerings are more Southwestern and related to Native American tribes nowhere near the area.

Despite this, a really nice feature of the Estes Park shopping area is the riverside walkway called Confluence Park behind the main street of shops and right on the Big Thompson River. Lots of little wooden bridges provide access across the river to free parking lots all around. Almost all of the shops along the south side of Elkhorn Avenue go through to this very pleasant and relaxing walkway beside the tumbling river, with shade trees, flowers, and lots of benches to rest on.

i Take advantage of the free shopper shuttle provided by the Estes Park Convention & Visitors Bureau. The continuous loop shuttle runs from July 1 through Labor Day and takes riders through the core of downtown. Riders can catch the shuttle at seven different locations. Get route maps at the visitor center at 500 Big Thompson Avenue.

CANYONLANDS INDIAN ARTS
146 West Elkhorn Avenue
(970) 577-0479

This shop features top-quality Indian and Southwest jewelry, authentic pottery, kachinas, carvings, and Navajo rugs.

COLORADO CANDELABRA
157 W. Elkhorn Ave.
(970) 586-0091
www.coloradocandelabra
The smell is enough to bring you in the front door of this little shop, which sells just about every type of candle imaginable.

CRAFTSMEN IN LEATHER
135 West Elkhorn Avenue
(970) 586-2691
www.cileather.com
"Come in and smell the leather," invites this store. You can take a self-guided tour of the shop, try on some of the hats in the huge inventory—which includes everything from fur felt and suede to wool and straw—and learn how to care for leather goods. The store also sells belts and buckles, handbags and luggage, wallets, moccasins, and jewelry.

GLASS BLOWERS
126 East Elkhorn Avenue
(970) 586-5963
Those who would like a blown-glass hummingbird can find one of the best selections in the area at this shop. Most of the blown glass is made at the shop's other studio in Manitou Springs, Colorado. You'll find hummingbirds in every color of the rainbow here, from red and green ruby throats to copper rufous hummers. All types of other miniature figures are represented in glass as well.

HIGH COUNTRY AMISH QUILTS
870 Moraine Avenue
(970) 577-1557
www.highcountryamishquilts.com
In addition to offering Colorado's largest selection of Amish and Mennonite quilts and wall hangings, High Country now includes a fabric shop with quilt patterns, fabric, and embellishments. Not only do the quilts make distinctive gifts, they also are spectacular pieces of handcrafted art.

THE HIKING HUT
110 East Elkhorn Avenue
(970) 586-0708
This shop offers a nice selection of backpacks, jackets, sunglasses, and other accessories for hiking and camping in the mountains. They also rent snowshoes in the winter.

MACDONALD BOOK SHOP
152 East Elkhorn Avenue
(970) 586-3450
www.macdonaldbookshop.com
Established in 1928, this large bookstore in an old log cabin was originally the home of turn-of-the-20th-century residents. The owners have had the bookstore for four generations. The *New York Times* is available, along with a wide selection of hardcovers, paperbacks, children's books, books on cassette, magazines, and calendars. Be sure to read the history plaque out front explaining how the first bookstore on the site was opened in the owners' living room. Colorful Scottish plaid carpet and exposed log beams set the interior mood.

MOSES STREET PHOTOGRAPHY
157 West Elkhorn
(970) 586-7221
www.mosesstreet.com
Okay, it's not exactly shopping, but we thought you might want to know about this service. Moses Street specializes in portraits, but we're not talking about a stool in front of a fake bookcase. In addition to glamour portraits and family reunions captured on film, Moses will actually capture your image at the top of a mountain or canoeing across a crystal lake, if that's where you want to go. "We travel anywhere in the world to do any type of people photography," Moses promises.

THE OLD CHURCH SHOPS
157 West Elkhorn Avenue
www.churchshops.com
There are several distinctive shops and dining available at The Old Church Shops. The structure used to be the Community Church of the Rockies, and the southeast portion of the current building

goes all the way back to 1909. Each shop in the complex offers unique merchandise, not your usual chain-style stores.

OUTDOOR WORLD
156 East Elkhorn Avenue
(970) 586-2114
www.rmconnection.com
Outdoor World is Estes Park's largest outfitter. Shop here for a great selection of high-quality boots, backpacks, jackets, water bottles, and everything you need for the outdoors.

PARK THEATRE
Moraine Avenue and Rockwell Street
(970) 586-8904
Several small shops are nestled around the historic Park Theatre, which was built in 1913. The theater's impressive white tower—Estes Park's tallest structure—was added to the building by a former owner as a monument to a woman who left him at the altar. The Park Theatre's cafe and snack shops—open from 8 a.m. until 9 p.m. daily—are a good place to stop in summer.

ROCKY MOUNTAIN KNIFE COMPANY
125 Moraine Avenue
(970) 586-8419
This tiny shop bills itself as "the Biggest Little Knife Store West of the Mississippi." It's not just knives, though. The walls and shelves are covered with everything from kitchen cutlery to crossbows, swords and battle axes, tomahawks, blow guns and sling shots, water balloons, and martial arts supplies. They sharpen knives, too.

STANLEY VILLAGE
Intersection of US 34 and US 36
(970) 586-6114
This shopping center is located directly below the imposing, white Stanley Hotel, which is perched on a hillside above town—you can't miss it. Slightly to the east are a Safeway and a shopping area that offers visitors lots of necessary services. To the east of Safeway is a Coast to Coast Hardware store (970-586-3496), for those little gadgets you always end up needing on a trip. There's also

the Notchtop Baked Goods and Natural Foods Cafe and Pub, and Mountain Home Cafe (see the previous "Restaurants" section of this chapter for details on each) as well as many other shops and a movie theater.

THE TALKING TEDDY
521 Lone Pine Drive
(970) 586-6483
www.estesark.com
Visit this fun shop for a mind-boggling assortment of teddy bears in all sizes and styles, teddy bear–related items such as Smokey Bear hats, teddy bear–decorated T-shirts, and individual bears made by various "teddy bear artists." The shop also sells various other plush animals and collectibles.

SPORTS

Most people visit Estes Park to see Rocky Mountain National Park and go camping, hiking, or fishing. Yet in addition to these activities, you can participate in everything from sailboarding on Lake Estes to golf and tennis in Estes Park. Horseback riding is a popular activity in the area, with trails leading into the park or the surrounding national forest. Several rafting companies take thrill seekers to such frothy rivers outside the immediate area as the Poudre and Arkansas. The following are some of the town's many options.

Bicycling
COLORADO BICYCLING ADVENTURES
184 East Elkhorn Avenue
(970) 586-6548, (866) 303-6548
www.coloradobicycling.net
To rent a bike, or to get information about where to bicycle, stop here. It's a full-service bike shop offering sales and shipping. This shop not only rents brand-new mountain bikes in different models but also offers several different guided bicycle tours, including a downhill ride from the top of Trail Ridge Road in Rocky Mountain National Park. Cost is $75 per person and includes bike, helmet, and souvenir water bottle plus a continental breakfast. It's about a four-hour trip

from Estes Park and back again. No riders under age 10 allowed.

There's also a downhill tour in the North Fork Canyon ($55 per person) suited to riders of all ages—they've taken bicyclists ages 4 to 90. Another tour favorite is the Grand Tour, a seven-to eight-hour ride that includes lunch at the Grand Lake Lodge ($155 per person).

The shop also rents bikes and all types of bike accessories, including trailers to pull children, locks, packs, and car racks. It sells a guidebook of all off-road areas in Roosevelt National Forest and has free maps that show cyclists where to ride right from the store on their own.

i For a change of pace, why not take a bicycle tour of the area? Colorado Bicycling Adventures in Estes Park (970-586-6548, www.coloradobicycling.net) offers tours for all levels and abilities. See details under "Bicycling" in this chapter.

Camping

Two campgrounds are run by the Estes Valley Recreation and Park District: Mary's Lake Campground and Estes Park Campground. There are also a number of privately owned campgrounds in the area. (See the Rocky Mountain National Park chapter for information on camping in the national park.)

ELKHORN LODGE WILDERNESS CAMPING
600 West Elkhorn Avenue
(970) 586-4416
www.elkhornlodge.org
A 10-minute hike from the Elkhorn Lodge is the opportunity to experience Indian and Old West camping in your own tent or a rented tepee. Transportation to the campground, water, and a portable toilet are provided. There are no other amenities, but you live surrounded by wildlife and rugged trails leading through wilderness. If you decide to wimp out, there's a restaurant, saloon, swimming pool, and bathing facilities available at the lodge.

ELK MEADOW LODGE & RV RESORT
Highway 66, adjacent to the south entrance to Rocky Mountain National Park
(970) 586-5342
www.estespark.us
This is one of Estes Park's largest RV park and campground. With 170 sites, Elk Meadow offers history along with its views and amenities such as a country store, laundry, playgrounds, and nondenominational church services. The 30-acre site was originally a camping ground for Arapaho and Ute living in the area. In the 1960s, historical buildings were hauled to the site to create a "frontier town" for moviemakers. Still remaining, and in use, are the original Bear Lake Lodge, built in 1919 and later removed from the park, and a Central City brothel, now used as the camp's recreation hall. All sites are full hookup.

ESTES PARK CAMPGROUND
Highway 66 (Tunnel Road), a mile past the Estes Park Center/YMCA of the Rockies
(970) 586-4188
www.estesparkcampground.com
Peaceful and secluded, this campground has 70 sites, 26 with water and electricity. Head west on US 36 and then turn left onto Highway 66 (which becomes Tunnel Road). Continue for 3 miles; the campground is a mile past the Estes Park Center/YMCA of the Rockies, at the end of a paved road and adjacent to the national park. It is open mid-May through September. Costs range from $26 to $38, depending on date and utilities; amenities include showers and restrooms, a playground, a public phone, and firewood and ice for sale. Fishing, with a Colorado license, is available at a neighboring pond. Pets are permitted on a leash.

YOGI BEAR'S JELLYSTONE PARK
5495 US 36
(970) 586-4230, (800) 722-2928
www.jellystoneofestes.com
In addition to tent, camper, and RV sites, there are housekeeping and camping cabins at this park, which is 5 miles southeast of Estes Park on US 36.

The wooded sites are pleasant and quiet. It's open May through September and charges from $19 to $62 per night. Children and pets are welcome.

KOA CAMPGROUND
US 34, 1 mile east of Estes Park
(970) 586-2888
www.koa.com
Try out a rented tepee or set up your own tent or RV at this campground with showers, a grocery and gift store, fishing equipment, a game room, mini-golf, and laundry facilities. Call for rates.

MARY'S LAKE CAMPGROUND & RV PARK
Mary's Lake Road (directions below)
(970) 586-4411
www.maryslakecampground.com
Though not exactly remote or secluded, Mary's Lake has great views by a pleasant lake plus a heated swimming pool, hot showers, electrical service, a playground and basketball court, a store, and laundry facilities. Drive south of town US 36 and turn left onto Mary's Lake Road. The campground is 3 miles from town and the national park, and is open mid-May through September. Prices in 2008 ranged from $27 for tent camping to $36 or $41 per night for RVs, depending upon services chosen.

NATIONAL PARK RESORT CAMPGROUND
2501 Fall River Road
(970) 586-4563
www.nationalparkretreats.com
Right at the national park's beautiful Fall River entrance, this campground has hot showers, hookups, cable TV, a livery, and secluded, terraced sites. The 96-site campground is open year-round.

PARADISE RV & TRAVEL PARK
1836 Highway 66
(970) 586-5513
www.paradiservcolorado.com
Near the YMCA along the Big Thompson River, this park offers 30 sites with RV hookups, cable, bathrooms, fishing, and a laundry. Call for rates.

[i] Those who would like to rub shoulders with the daring rock jocks who climb the "Diamond" face of Longs Peak (a world-renowned climb) should try an early breakfast at either The Mountaineer or Molly B's. Climbers reputedly have their pre-climb breakfasts at these cafes.

Climbing

COLORADO MOUNTAIN SCHOOL
(970) 586-5758
(800) 444-0730 (outside Colorado)
www.totalclimbing.com
Learn rock climbing or mountaineering at this highly regarded school, ranked one of the top eight in the world by the *Ultimate Adventure Sourcebook*. One-day introductory classes prepare people to begin climbing with guides. The school offers guided hikes, climbs (including technical routes of Longs Peak), and equipment rentals. The school is open year-round, and reservations are requested. Lodging and excursions to other great climbing around the world are also available.

ESTES PARK MOUNTAIN SHOP
2050 Big Thompson Ave.
(970) 586-6548
www.estesparkmountainshop.com
This shop can handle all your mountaineering needs from skiing to biking to fly fishing to climbing. They offer climbing instruction and guiding both indoors and out. Learn to climb on the 3,000-square-foot indoor rock-climbing wall and practice these skills on half-day lessons in the field and full-day guided climbs.

TRAILRIDGE OUTFITTERS & INDOOR CLIMBING GYM
358 E. Elkhorn Ave.
(970) 586-4595
www.trailridgeoutfitters.com
In addition to being able to outfit you for just about any outdoor adventure, TrailRidge has a great climbing gym.

Cross-Country Skiing

See the Rocky Mountain National Park chapter for information on ski trails in the national park. Rental equipment is available in the following outdoor shops in Estes Park.

ESTES PARK MOUNTAIN SHOP
(see above entry)

TRAILRIDGE OUTFITTERS
(see above entry)

ESTES PARK SKI SHOP
161 Virginia Drive
(970) 586-2303
This shop carries downhill skis, snowboards, snowshoes, sleds, and tubes.

Fishing

Some local spots include the Big Thompson River, Lake Estes, and Mary's Lake. The best spot on the Big Thompson River is said to be the stretch 8 miles downstream from Lake Estes called Grandpa's Retreat (flies and lures only), where the Colorado Division of Wildlife and the USDA Forest Service have created several deep holes. The Big Thompson runs along US 34; there are small parking areas along the shoulder. You'll also find several wheelchair-accessible fishing ramps along this stretch.

Lake Estes, on the east side of town between US 34 and US 36, is stocked by the Colorado Division of Wildlife with rainbow trout and also has a few German brown trout. Mary's Lake inlet is another good spot to try. Follow US 36 to the east end of town to Mary's Lake Road at the traffic light, turn left, and drive 1.5 miles.

You can fish in Colorado without a license only on the first full weekend in June. Otherwise, you must have a license. Fishing licenses are available at several locations.

ESTES PARK MOUNTAIN SHOP
358 East Elkhorn Avenue
(970) 586-6548, (800) 504-6642
www.estesparkmountainshop.com

In addition to a complete fly shop and outdoor equipment and clothing, this shop offers rental equipment and instruction and guided trips in and around Rocky Mountain National Park.

KIRKS MOUNTAIN ADVENTURES
230 East Elkhorn Avenue
(970) 577-0790
www.kirksflyshop.com
Kirks offers guided fly-fishing trips to Rocky Mountain National Park and the Big Thompson River. Their shop carries quality outdoor gear and rental equipment and offers guided hikes, backpacking trips, and llama pack trips as well.

ROCKY MOUNTAIN ADVENTURES
(800) 858-6808 in Fort Collins
www.ShopRMA.com
This company offers year-round guided fly-fishing day trips on Big Thompson River a few miles from Estes Park, and overnights on the Poudre, Upper Colorado, and North Platte Rivers. The company is permitted by the forest service in those locations and licensed by the state of Colorado. The main office in Fort Collins is open year-round. The Estes Park office is open Memorial Day to Labor Day.

SCOT'S SPORTING GOODS
2325 Spruce Avenue
(970) 586-2877
www.scotssportinggoods.com
Stop by and ask owner Scot Richie—the local fishing authority and a third-generation Rocky Mountain fisherman—where to catch the big ones. He can also recommend and sell the best things to catch them with, including a selection of flies tied by local anglers who know what Estes Park fish like best. The shop also offers fly-fishing lessons and guided trips on the Big Thompson River and rents fishing equipment.

Golf

ESTES PARK GOLF COURSE
1080 South St. Vrain Road
(970) 586-8146
www.estesvalleyrecreation.com

This 18-hole course is one of the oldest golf courses in the state, dating from 1912. In early fall, elk wander onto the course—watch out for their divots. Check their Web site or call for updated greens fees.

LAKE ESTES EXECUTIVE COURSE
690 Big Thompson Avenue
(970) 586-8176
www.estesvalleyrecreation.com
This nine-hole course along the banks of the Big Thompson River provides a good game and a view to go with it. Check their Web site or call for updated greens fees.

Miniature Golf

Miniature golf may be little, but in Estes it's big. Courses are all mini amusement parks, where it's easy to spend money on silly activities. The cost is usually fairly reasonable. During the summer, these places often stay open from early morning until 10 at night.

ESTES PARK RIDE-A-KART
2250 Big Thompson Avenue
(970) 586-6495
www.rideakart.com
This mini amusement park has 36 holes of miniature golf, go-karts, bumper boats, a miniature train, and lots more.

FUN CITY
455 Prospect Village Drive
(970) 586-2828
www.funcityofestes.com
Kids will enjoy the miniature golf courses, bumper cars, video arcade, and the slide at Fun City, which is open every day in the summer, and on weekends only in the spring and fall.

TINY TOWN MINIATURE GOLF
840 Moraine Avenue
(970) 586-6333
Tiny Town features a 19-hole miniature golf course in a lovely garden setting, with lots of challenging and entertaining features. The course has

been in the same family for nearly 50 years, and the friendly owner is a great source of information about other fun things to do in the area.

Hiking and Backpacking

Most hikers head to Rocky Mountain National Park, but the nearby Roosevelt National Forest also offers excellent backcountry trails. Contact the Estes Park Office of Roosevelt National Forest for maps and information about hiking trails: 161 Second Street, (970) 586-3440. See "Hiking" in our Rocky Mountain National Park chapter for other hiking opportunities. You can also stroll along the Big Thompson River corridor from Lake Estes all the way to the YMCA Camp, or get sidetracked by the shop windows downtown and call it a hike. Or follow Highway 7 on a pleasant separate trail.

i Leave the driving to someone else! Catch the free hiker shuttle to Rocky Mountain National Park at the Estes Park Visitor Center, 500 Big Thompson Avenue. The shuttle is free but a park pass is required. Passes can be purchased at the visitor center.

CROSIER MOUNTAIN TRAIL
Devil's Gulch Road
www.coloradoparks.net
A moderately difficult 8-mile round-trip that climbs to the top of Crosier Mountain (elevation 9,250 feet), this trail runs through lush meadows and aspen groves past ruins of old homesteads. You'll have superb views from the summit. The trailhead is about 8 miles northeast of Estes Park on Devil's Gulch Road, a mile past Glen Haven. Look for a large gravel lot on the south side of the road to the right.

FISH CREEK TRAIL
US 36, Lake Estes
www.coloradoparks.net
This unpaved 6-mile (one-way) hike starts out easy but becomes moderately difficult when you reach the final 2 miles. It follows Fish Creek from

its mouth at Lake Estes to its intersection with Highway 7 south of Mary's Lake.

LILY MOUNTAIN TRAIL
Highway 7
www.coloradoparks.net
An easy 1.5-mile hike, this trail begins near Estes Park and climbs to 8,800 feet, with fantastic summit views of Estes Park, Longs Peak to the south, and the Continental Divide to the west. The trailhead is 6 miles south of Estes Park on Highway 7. Just before the 6-mile marker look for a small turnoff on the right, where there's a parking area and trailhead sign.

LION GULCH
US 36
www.coloradoparks.net
Another pleasant trail of moderate difficulty, Lion Gulch leads to an area of old homesteads and is about 3 miles one way. The trailhead is at mile marker 8 from Estes Park on US 36.

Horseback Riding

Estes Park has numerous stables and outfitters offering everything from kids' pony rides to trail rides and pack trips into the mountains. Most rides head into Rocky Mountain National Park. Virtually all the stables have the same rates—$20 for a one-hour ride and $35 for two hours.

ASPEN LODGE AT ESTES PARK
6120 Highway 7
(970) 586-8133, (800) 332-6867
www.aspenlodge.net
A 3,000-acre ranch resort, Aspen Lodge offers rides into both Rocky Mountain National Park and Roosevelt National Forest. It's south of Estes Park on Highway 7. There are meadow rides, cowboy supper rides, and half-day rides at Elk Park Ranch.

ELKHORN STABLES
600 West Elkhorn Avenue
(970) 586-5225
www.elkhornlodge.org
This stable offers breakfast rides; rides ending

with a steak dinner, country music, and dancing; hourly rides; and ponies for children. Open year-round, it guides trips into the national park. Take time to tour the 120-year-old lodge and stables.

SOMBRERO RANCH
US 34 East
(970) 586-4577, (303) 442-0258
www.sombrero.com
Sombrero offers rides into the national forest (not the national park). There's a breakfast ride, a steak-fry evening ride, and an overnight pack trip. In fact, at Sombrero Ranch you can ride all year long. Fishing trips are offered, too.

Rafting

There are numerous outfitters that will take you on full- or half-day trips on the Poudre or Arkansas Rivers and rather far afield to the Dolores and Colorado Rivers.

ESTES PARK MOUNTAIN SHOP
358 East Elkhorn Avenue
(970) 586-6548, (866) 303-6548
www.estesparkmountainshop.com
Inquire here about a variety of raft trips on different Colorado rivers; full- and half-day adventures are offered.

MOUNTAIN WHITEWATER DESCENTS
2050 Big Thompson Ave.
(888) 855-8874
www.raftmwd.com
Take a thrilling ride on the Cache La Poudre River near Estes. This company also offers kayak lessons and special packages.

RAPID TRANSIT RAFTING LTD.
161 Virginia Drive
(800) 367-8523
www.rapidtransitrafting.com
White-water adventures include full-day trips on the Colorado River and half-day trips on the Poudre River leaving from Estes Park. There's a variety of rafting, from exciting deep canyon rapids to relaxing float water stretches. Trips are suitable

for beginners as well as experienced rafters. All the necessary rafting gear, experienced licensed guides, and lunch or snacks are provided. Reservations are recommended.

ROCKY MOUNTAIN ADVENTURES
(800) 858-6808 in Fort Collins
www.ShopRMA.com
Half- and full-day and overnight trips are offered for white-water rafting from beginner to advanced levels. Trips are on the Big Thompson, Poudre, and North Platte Rivers. All the necessary equipment, plus lunch and snacks are provided, along with licensed guides. The company also provides kayak instruction and lake touring in sea kayaks on Lake Estes. The Fort Collins office is open year-round, and the Estes Park location is open Memorial Day through Labor Day.

Swimming
ESTES PARK AQUATIC CENTER
660 Community Drive
(970) 586-2340
www.estesvalleyrecreation.com
Just south of Lake Estes, the center has an indoor/outdoor pool. There are separate times for lap swimming, a ladies' night, lessons for first-time swimmers and mothers and babies, and a wading pool for toddlers.

LAKE ESTES MARINA
1770 Big Thompson Avenue
(970) 586-2011
www.estesvalleyrecreation.com
The waters of Lake Estes are too chilly for swimming unless you like wearing a wet suit, which can be rented here, along with sailboarding equipment and other small craft. The marina, which has beaches and picnic areas, is east of town on US 34.

Tennis
STANLEY PARK
380 Community Drive
(970) 586-8191
www.estesvalleyrecreation.com

Just south of Lake Estes and operated by the Estes Valley Recreation and Park District, Stanley Park has six courts, which are free.

Other Sports Spots
LAKE ESTES MARINA
1770 Big Thompson Avenue
(970) 586-2011
www.estesvalleyrecreation.com
This public facility offers fishing access, picnic areas, a hike and bike trail, bike rentals, and rental boats of all kinds—fishing, sport, pontoon, canoes, and paddleboats. There's also a marina store that sells fishing licenses, bait and tackle, snacks, and clothing.

ROCKY MOUNTAIN ATHLETIC CLUB
1230 Big Thomson Road
(970) 577-1900
www.rockymountainhealthclub.com
With all of the sports and fitness options in the surrounding outdoors, you might not think there's anything to be added by an indoor facility. Well, how about racquetball, handball, and squash court; free weights and resistance equipment with a view of the mountains; aerobics classes; therapeutic massage; and whirlpools and saunas? The Athletic Club offers all that, plus a treadwall that gives a taste of rock climbing and an aerobic workout at the same time. There's also a reaction-time workout station—wield a staff at randomly flashing targets a la Luke Skywalker. The guest fee is $10 per visit.

STANLEY PARK
380 Community Drive
(970) 586-8189
www.estesvalleyrecreation.com
Run by the Estes Valley Recreation and Park District, Stanley Park has a playground; basketball, volleyball, and tennis courts; baseball/softball and soccer fields; shelters; and a picnic area.

SUMMER CAMPS

Many lodging places around Estes Park offer special programs for children. Check the previous

"Accommodations" section in this chapter for possibilities. Summer camps around Estes Park are also organized by church groups, so check the "Worship" section of this chapter for some phone numbers you can call for more information. For instance, Covenant Heights (970-586-2900) is a conference center with facilities for up to 200 people that is used for a number of children's programs. The programs must be church-related, educational, or nonprofit.

CHELEY CAMP
(In winter) (800) 226-7386
(In summer) (970) 586-4244
www.cheley.com
Cheley's summer camp program has been featured in national magazines such as *Country Living*. It's probably the largest privately owned camp west of the Mississippi and has been around since 1921. Nearly 500 kids enjoy the fun, in camps of 60 each, grouped by age and sex. The camp sessions are four weeks or eight weeks. Mountaineering, with fabulous vistas everywhere, and horseback riding on nearly 150 camp-owned horses are especially popular activities. And with hiking right out the back door, the children get to know the Rocky Mountains. Cheley starts filling up by January, so apply early.

ESTES PARK CENTER/YMCA OF THE ROCKIES
2515 Tunnel Road
(970) 586-3341
www.ymcarockies.org
The YMCA has a summer day-camp program for kids with programs that are grouped according to age. The older kids can participate in leadership programs and adventure hikes. The youngest kids are more likely to stay close by. Pre-registration is required.

TOURS

AERIAL TRAMWAY
420 East Riverside Drive
(970) 586-3675
www.estestram.com

Right in Estes Park, this three- to five-minute ride overlooks the town with great views of Longs Peak and the Continental Divide. The tram takes you to the summit of Prospect Mountain, where you can take your time hiking, picnicking, and photographing the spectacular vista from the observation platform.

AMERICAN WILDERNESS TOURS
875 Moraine Avenue
(970) 586-1626
www.americanwildernesstours.com
Six-wheeled vehicles take you off the beaten path and into the backcountry. Some tours include steak dinners and sing-alongs. Tours for private groups are available. Call for prices.

ESTES PARK SHUTTLE AND TOURS
429 West Elkhorn Avenue
(970) 586-5151
www.estesparkshuttle.com
This company offers custom summertime scenic tours over Trail Ridge Road, a Grand Lake Tour, horseback riding trips in the park, Bear Lake hikes and Fall Foliage/Elk Bugling tours, as well as year-round shuttle service from Denver International Airport. Call for current rates.

WORSHIP

Estes Park has more than a dozen churches. Many offer Bible School, evening programs, and summer camps. Every Friday, the local newspaper, the *Trail Gazette,* lists services and church news. The Estes Park Center/YMCA of the Rockies (970-586-3341), has a full-time pastor on staff, plus facilities for church-related (and secular) events. See listing under "Accommodations" in this chapter.

Estes Park is less than an hour's trip to Boulder as the angel flies. Some Boulder County churches actually are closer to Estes Park than to the city of Boulder. So you can broaden your choices by also checking the Worship chapter.

INDEX

S
Sacred Heart of Jesus
  School, 266
safety, 296
Safeway, 317
sailboarding, 229
sailing, 229
Salberg Shelter, 204
Salsa Mountain Cantina, 184
Salvaggio's Italian Deli,
  58, 110
Sand Creek Massacre, 25
Santa's Workshop, 163
Sawaddee Thai, 46
Scandinavian Midsummer
  Festival, 308
School of Natural Cookery,
  The, 270
School of Natural
  Medicine, 270
schools, 263
Science Discovery Summer
  Camp, 148
Scot's Sporting Goods, 323
Scott Carpenter Park, 128,
  142, 204
Scott Carpenter Pool, 146
Scuba Joe Dive and
  Travel, 112
senior centers, 254
September School, 266
Service Exchange of Boulder
  County, The, 258
Shed, The, 178
Shepherd Valley Waldorf
  School, 266
Sherpa's, 55
Shining Mountain Waldorf
  School, 267
Shining, The, 298, 301,
  305, 311
Shuttles, Spindles and
  Skeins, 94
Siamese Plate & Sumida's
  Sushi Bar, 46
Silver Hawk, 169
Silverthorne, 187
Sink, The, 42, 70
16th Street Mall, The, 155

Skatepark, 204
skiing, 144, 175, 180, 229,
  295, 323
Ski Tip Lodge, 185
Ski Train, The, 175
Sleeper, 7, 33
sleigh rides, 180
Smith-Klein Gallery, 94, 202
Snake River Saloon, The, 187
snowboarding, 232
snowcat tours, 176
snowmobiling, 180
Snow Mountain Ranch, 176
snowshoeing, 232, 295, 296
Sobo American Bistro, 42
soccer, 235
Sombrero Ranch, 176, 325
Sommers-Bausch
  Observatory, 131
Souper Bowlder
  Promotion, 122
Sourdough Trail, 213
South Boulder Recreation
  Center, 208
Southern Sun Pub and
  Brewery, 64
Special Transit, 257
specialty-food shops, 109
sporting goods shops, 110
sports, 147
Sports Authority, 113
Spruce Confections, 95
Spruce Pool, 146, 204
Stanley Estes Park
  Fairground, 313
Stanley Ghost Stories, 311
Stanley Hotel, The, 301, 302,
  305, 313, 314, 317
Stanley Park, 326
Stanley Village, 320
Starbucks, 50
Starr's Clothing and Shoe
  Co., 100
state parks, 206
Stazio Ballfields, 129
St. Bernard Inn, The, 182
Stir It Up Cooking, 140
St. James Methodist
  Church, 173

St. Julien Hotel & Spa, 40,
  82, 84
Stone Cup Café and Gallery,
  The, 95
St. Patrick's Day Parade, 115
Strawberry Festival Antiques
  Show, 116
Streamside on Fall River, 301
summer camps, 147, 326
SummerFest at Boulder
  History Museum, 118
Summit County, 187
Summit County Chamber of
  Commerce, 186
Summit County Historical
  Society, 181
Sundown Saloon, 71
Sunflower Natural Fine
  Dining, 62
Sunnyside Knoll Resort, 302
Sunset Golf Course, 221
Super 8 Motel, 179
Superior, 247
Superior Liquor, 104
SushiTora, 47
Sushi Zanmai, 47
swimming, 145, 232, 326
Switzerland Trail, 127, 214
Sylvan Learning Center, 267

T
Table Mesa, 239
Table Mesa Shopping
  Center, 88
Tabor Center, The, 155, 159
Tahona Tequila Bistro, 61, 71
Taj, The, 55
Talbot's, 101
Talking Teddy, The, 320
Tandoori Grill, 55
Taste of Louisville, 118
Tattered Cover Book
  Store, 159
team sports, 147
Teddy Bear Picnic, 308
television stations, 279
Teller House and
  Museum, 171
tennis, 233, 326

Z
Zephyr Express, 176
Zephyr Mountain Lodge, 179
Z Gallerie, 106
Zolo Grill, 44, 72

ABOUT THE AUTHOR

Ann Alexander Leggett is a freelance writer, publication/web designer, artist and owner of OceanGirl Design. She is the coauthor of several books including: *Haunted Boulder, Ghostly Tales from the Foot of the Flatirons; Haunted Boulder 2, Ghostly Tales from Boulder and Beyond; Finding Hidden Valley;* and the 7th, 8th and 9th editions of the *Insiders' Guide to Boulder.* Her work has also appeared online, in national magazines, and in a variety of local publications. She lives in Erie, Colorado.